W9-CTI-189

EXORCIZING EVIL

The Bishop Henry McNeal Turner/Sojourner Truth Series in Black Religion

Previously published in the Turner Series:
1. *For My People* by James H. Cone
2. *Black and African Theologies* by Josiah U. Young
3. *Troubling Biblical Waters* by Cain Hope Felder
4. *Black Theology USA and South Africa* by Dwight N. Hopkins
5. *Empower the People* by Theodore Walker, Jr.
6. *A Common Journey* by George C.L. Cummings
7. *Dark Symbols, Obscure Signs* by Riggins R. Earl, Jr.
8. *A Troubling in My Soul* edited by Emilie M. Townes
9. *The Black Christ* by Kelly Brown Douglas

In the Turner/Truth Series:
10. *Christianity on Trial* by Mark L. Chapman
11. *Were You There?* by David Emmanuel Goatley
12. *My Sister, My Brother* by Karen Baker-Fletcher and Garth (Kasimu) Baker-Fletcher
13. *Embracing the Spirit* edited by Emilie M. Townes

Editor: Dwight N. Hopkins
The University of Chicago, The Divinity School

Associate Editors:
James H. Cone, Union Theological Seminary, New York
Katie G. Cannon, Temple University
Cain Hope Felder, Howard University, School of Divinity
Jacquelyn Grant, The Interdenominational Theological Center
Delores S. Williams, Union Theological Seminary, New York

The purpose of this series is to encourage the development of biblical, historical, theological, ethical, and pastoral works that analyze the role of the churches and other religious movements in the liberation struggles of black women and men in the United States, particularly the poor, and their relationship to struggles in the Third World.

Named after Bishop Henry McNeal Turner (1843-1915) and Sojourner Truth (1797?-1883), the series reflects the spirit of these two visionaries and witnesses for the black struggle for liberation. Bishop Turner was a churchman, a political figure, a missionary, and a pan-Africanist. Sojourner Truth was an illiterate former slave who championed black emancipation, women's rights, and the liberating spirit of the gospel.

**The Bishop Henry McNeal Turner/Sojourner Truth Series
in Black Religion, Volume XIV**

230.0904
K634

EXORCIZING EVIL

A Womanist Perspective on the Spirituals

Cheryl A. Kirk-Duggan

LIBRARY ST. MARY'S COLLEGE

ORBIS ✪ BOOKS

Maryknoll, New York 10545

The Catholic Foreign Mission Society of America (Maryknoll) recruits and trains people for overseas missionary service. Through Orbis Books, Maryknoll aims to foster the international dialogue that is essential to mission. The books published, however, reflect the opinions of their authors and are not meant to represent the official position of the society.

Copyright © 1997 by Cheryl Kirk-Duggan

All rights reserved. No part of this publication may be reproduced or transmitted in any form or by any means, electronic or mechanical, including photocopying, recording or any information storage or retrieval system, without prior permission in writing from the publishers.

Queries regarding rights and permissions should be addressed to: Orbis Books, P.O. Box 308, Maryknoll, NY 10545-0308.

Published by Orbis Books, Maryknoll, NY 10545-0308

Manufactured in the United States of America

Library of Congress Cataloging-in-Publication Data

Kirk-Duggan, Cheryl A.
    Exorcizing evil : a womanist perspective on the spirituals / Cheryl Kirk-Duggan.
      p.   cm.—(The Bishop Henry McNeal Turner/Sojourner Truth series in Black religion ; v. 14)
    Includes bibliographical references and discography.
    ISBN 1-57075-146-3 (alk. paper)
    1. Spirituals (Songs)—History and criticism. 2. Afro-Americans—Music—History and criticism. 3. Womanist theology. 4. Afro-Americans—Religion. I. Title. II. Series.
ML3556.K57   1997
782.25'3—dc21
                                          97-18357
                                           CIP
                                         MN

Dedicated to the Unnamed slave woman,
my great-great-grandmother,
who was taken from Tennessee
with two of her five children,
Cezor and Jack, my great-grandfather,
and brought to the red hills of North Louisiana

Contents

Acknowledgments   xi

Preface: Genesis of a Pilgrimage   xiii

Part I
Insight: Introduction and Background

1. **Meaning and Knowing**   3

2. **Context: The Social and Historical Setting**   16
   Slavery: A Peculiar Problem of Evil   16
   Racism: The Arrogance and Pathos of Power   27

3. **Theodicy in White and Black**   38
   Overview: Theodicy in White (Classical)   38
   Theodicy and Black Theology   47

Part II
Innovation: Inside the Spirituals

4. **Story: R-e-v-o-l-u-t-i-o-n**   57
   Roots, Wisdom, and Storytelling   58
   Music in the Diaspora: The Spirituals, the Psalms, the Bible   61
   Theodicy in Story   70

5. **Creative Spirit**   78
   Toward a Black Aesthetic   79
   Artistic Influences on the 1960s Civil Rights Era   87
   Musical Terminology and Concepts   90
   Musical Style, God, and Culture   97
   Hearing and Interpreting Performed, Living Texts   102
   Singing the Spirituals: Slavery and Beyond   103
   Music and Theodicy in the Spirituals   108

6. Faith and Thought   112

   Goal-Oriented Visions to Synergistic Harmonies: Africa
     and the Diaspora   112

   Unmasking Contemporary Sin: Theodicy and the 1960s
     Civil Rights Struggle   124

   Racism and Slavery: Theodicy in Dialogue   132

Part III
Intent: Womanist Design

7. Womanist Thought   137

   Womanist Sensibilities: "A Balm in Gilead"   138

   Reality Check: Oppression and God-Talk   139

   Servanthood Language: Skewed Presence
     or Divine Status?   141

   Ministerial Grace: Black Women and Dr. Jesus   142

   An Ebony Aesthete: Celebrating Black Women,
     without Exception   145

   Black Diamonds: Morality-Based Resistance   147

   Unmasking a Triple Threat   150

   Truth-Telling Time   151

   Anger, Social Witness, and Bible Time   152

   Sisterhood: Empowered Womanist Reality   155

8. Womanist Musings   158

   Divine Care, Divine Love (*Agape*)   159

   Affirming Identity   160

   Call to Conversion, Call to Praise   161

   The Search for Empowerment   162

   Honoring Empowerment and Community Building   164

   Community Solidarity   165

   Abolition Activists   168

   Evocative Expressionists   172

   Champions of Women's Rights   175

   Political Firebrands   180

   Catalysts for Human Uplift   183

   Talented, Transformative Teachers   191

   Social Strategists   194

   Witnessing Wordsmiths   197

   Womanist Creative Singing   200

   Womanist Creative Arranging   204

Part IV
Illustriousness: The Wellsprings of Our Texts

9. Mass Meeting   209
 "Oh, Freedom"   209
         Context   210
         Story   213
         Creative Spirit   217
         Faith and Thought   222
 "This Little Light of Mine"   238
         Context   238
         Story   242
         Creative Spirit   245
         Faith and Thought   248
 "Go Tell It on the Mountain"   250
         Context   250
         Story   254
         Creative Spirit   256
         Faith and Thought   257

10. Ensembles   260
 "We Shall Not Be Moved"   261
         Context   261
         Story   265
         Creative Spirit   271
         Faith and Thought   277
 "Ain't Gonna Let Nobody Turn Me 'Round"   280
         Context   281
         Story   284
         Creative Spirit   286
         Faith and Thought   288
 "Certainly, Lord"   289
         Context   289
         Story   291
         Creative Spirit   292
         Faith and Thought   293

11. Song Leaders   296
 "I've Been in the Storm"   297
         Context   297
         Story   303
         Creative Spirit   307
         Faith and Thought   310

"Walk with Me, Lord"   313
    Context   314
    Story   317
    Creative Spirit   318
    Faith and Thought   320

Part V
Inference: Our Living Texts

12. Womanist, Transforming Musings   325

Notes   337

Bibliography   381
    Books   381
    Articles   391
    Other Sources   399
    Theses and Dissertations   401
    A Selective Discography   402

Acknowledgments

This book has benefited from experiences, conversations, counsel, and support from numerous "midwives": *Parturiunt montes, nascetur labor amore.* To these helpmates I remain eternally grateful as my pilgrimage comes to fruition. I am indebted to Dr. Bernice Johnson Reagon for her courage and scholarship, which provided many primary and essential resources to this research. The Fund for Theological Education provided encouragement, financial support, and a network of scholars who shared my dreams during my doctoral studies. Their support made possible trips to national libraries, conferences, and meetings relating to justice, religion, and violence. I am grateful to Dr. Katherine Clark for pointing me toward my initial database. My thanks to Dr. Mikeal Parsons, the Westar Institute, and the Colloquium on Violence and Religion for introducing me to the thought of René Girard. Judy Moore, senior consultant with Eyes on the Prize, a PBS documentary project, graciously shared her own experience of music and the Movement. Prof. Doris McGinty offered helpful comments on Black music in general, and on the late Prof. John Lovell in particular. Thanks also go to Dr. Diana Culbertson and the Rev. Dr. Brendonly Cunningham for reading all or part of the final manuscript and offering valuable comments.

Baylor University graciously supported me financially and spiritually during my early endeavors. Many thanks to Meredith College, especially the Department of Religion and Philosophy and the Faculty Development Committee, which have provided support for performance and travel to related conferences. My deepest gratitude to my colleagues at the Graduate Theological Union, especially the Center for Women and Religion, for their tremendous support and excitement about my research and my performance projects. Assistance from numerous research and reference librarians at the following institutions was essential and outstanding: Baylor University; Austin Presbyterian Theological Seminary; the University of Texas at Austin (Perry Casteñada Library, Fine Arts Library, Barker History Collection); the Archives Center, National Museum of American History (of the Smithsonian Institution); the Library of Congress; Carlyle Campbell Library, Meredith College; the Fine Arts Library, North Carolina Central University; and the Moorland-Spingarn Research Center, Howard University.

Thanks to my collegial, biological, and extended families in Louisiana,

Texas, New York, North Carolina, and California, who have never tired of hearing me perform or of listening to my conversations about the Spirituals, reminding me about the importance of God and balance. My thanks to Drs. James Cone, the late James Washington, Donald H. Matthews, and Robin Hough for insightful questions and a zealous spirit to press forward with my project. I am indebted to Womanist scholars Alice Walker, the late Audre Lorde, and Drs. Jacqueline Grant, Katie Cannon, Cheryl Townsend Gilkes, Delores Williams, Cheryl Sanders, Emilie Townes, and Kelly Brown Douglas for blazing a much needed trail that makes a way for scholarship that recognizes those who suffer because of race/sex/class discrimination. Dr. Prescott Williams, Jr. has been a prophetic voice in the wilderness. Blessings and sincere thanks to the following Durham, North Carolina, pastors and congregations: Holy Cross Roman Catholic Church and the Rev. Bruce Bavinger, S.J.; and Russell Memorial Christian Methodist Episcopal Church and the Rev. Willie J. Sturgess, Sr. My deepest gratitude and admiration to the bards of the African diaspora who first created these collective songs of exorcism; and to the countless 1960s activists who championed these songs of liturgical reformation to awaken and confront the consciousness of a nation claiming to be "the land of the free and the home of the brave."

I thank my parents, the late Rudolph Valentino Kirk and the late Naomi Ruth Kirk for their loving support and for the opportunities they created to allow me to pursue excellence. Gratitude and my hat go to Dr. Dwight Hopkins, my editor, Robert Ellsberg, and my project editor, Sue Perry, for being willing to bring the power of theological and cultural exorcism to light. And a special thanks to my husband and partner, Michael, for being a gentle spirit, editorial pragmatist, enthusiastic cheerleader, stimulating conversation partner, and sine qua non.

Preface

Genesis of a Pilgrimage

I started
On a journey,
Unpacking Spirituals:
Musings of
Long dead martyrs,
Evoking God; Decrying injustice;
Girded up their heavy souls;
For pilgrimages of overcoming.*

The Spirituals have been part of me since childhood, ever since the dawn of my earthly pilgrimage. I sang my first Spiritual solo at four and began piano lessons at age five. Music in general, the Spirituals in particular, and God's presence were integral in the ministry at church and in my lifestyle at home. My family leaned and depended on God through the mornings of new life, the evenings of death, and the mountains and valleys of daily existence. This spiritual nurturing shaped our personal and public lives. God was the head of our household via parental partnership. My parents bolstered my self-esteem, loved me well, and encouraged me to think for myself. Both parents nurtured my musical abilities and encouraged my performing. My mother always played music, from classical to the Spirituals to jazz. My father sang the songs of justice. With a powerful bass voice, he always noted, "God provides." His theology was significant because he worked for the cause of justice as the first African-American deputy sheriff in the state of Louisiana since Reconstruction, and never had to fire his revolver in the line of duty. At age eleven, I became church pianist on the condition that my artistry was a gift of service, not salary! My professional musical pilgrimage continued with the church as pianist, then organist. I completed two music degrees (and have continued to perform to the present day). Years later, a seminary study tour to Central

---

*All the poems in this volume are the author's original work, composed in response to, and out of experiencing, living, and praying, the Spirituals.

America intensified my sense of urgency about the role of social justice, as my colleagues and I witnessed the undying, hopeful religious faith of the campesinos despite the ravages of war, greed, and dehumanization. The campesinos sang at the base Christian community meetings.

Music is the arena where I wrestle with good and evil, suffering and pain. I identify with both ancient and modern voices grappling with social and oppressive evil. I see the potential of evil and the eternal arduousness of good.

The evils of antebellum oppression, suffering, and sin became apparent when I studied the slave narratives of African-American history. The oral antebellum Spirituals are slave narratives, since they tell a story via song. While reading, I became angry at the evil and degradation perpetrated against my slave ancestors. My pain was intense. Initially, I could not read these narratives during the day, because I did not want to unleash my anger about largely nineteenth-century evil on my twentieth-century American surroundings. History and contemporary reflection made me reckon with the present-day remnants of slavery and of ongoing racism. As my friend, theologian, and literary scholar Diana Culbertson noted, "I had to name the evil, the violence, before I could see certain possibilities for transformation and forgiveness." Documentaries based on the 1960s Civil Rights Movement and my own distant memories placed me at the Woolworth counter in Albany, Georgia, the bloody campaign in Selma, Alabama, and the bombing of the Sixteenth Street Baptist Church, Birmingham, where four little girls—Denise McNair, Addie Mae Collins, Carol Robinson, and Cynthia Wesley—died. I felt the water hoses and the blood of the streets of Selma, Alabama, smelled the fear and suffering, claimed the dignity and tenacity of grassroots freedom fighters. I knew hope and anxiety, courage and fear, solidarity and divisiveness. I heard freedom fighters, via "live" recordings, sing those selfsame Spirituals that I have sung all my life, and I heard them with new meaning. Much of this journey crystallized during my doctoral studies.

During my pilgrimage through higher education, I studied that music which relates to justice, suffering, and evil. Dr. Jean Boyd suggested the Spirituals as examples of applied theodicy (the theology that questions the apparent contradictions of a loving God midst evil and suffering). My studies showed that the Spirituals are a unique tool for investigating the social, historical, cultural, educational, psychological, and political realities of the suffering experienced by African Americans. Traditional Spirituals express a theodicy that explores the presence of a just God within a society that is responsible for flagrant injustices. Clarifying the activity of God and humanity in the texts of these Spirituals leads to an interpretation of a theory and praxis of theodicy that has effected Christian transformation. The fact that African-American creativity birthed the Spirituals midst the evils of slavery and racism is ironic. How to analyze these songs is an interpretation issue. I visited the Underground Railroad Station in the

Harriet Tubman Memorial Room of the Second Baptist Church in Detroit, Michigan. There I sat in a sacred space where many Blacks, long dead, sang the Spirituals as they waited to "make a connection" that advanced their pilgrimage to freedom by crossing the Detroit River to Windsor, Canada. This experience set my heart on fire for this project.

My pilgrimage of spirituality and social activism has resulted in this book, *Exorcizing Evil,* a sacramental worship experience wherein I have met the theodicy immersed in many of the Spirituals common to the antebellum and 1960s civil rights eras. These Spirituals reflect a theodicy derived out of the life experiences of African Americans during the antebellum and 1960s eras. I examined certain Spirituals from (1) recorded field performances of civil rights activists, which comprise three performance styles: mass meeting, ensemble, and song leader; (2) live and studio-recorded concert arrangements of the Spirituals; (3) personal recollections of singing, teaching, and listening to live and recorded performances of the Spirituals; and (4) various manuscripts of the Spirituals.

These rousing, contemplative songs "spoke" to me and taught me how to listen and how to feel the meaning. This experience required that I be a signifier, teacher, preacher, singer, and writer who "needed to get the word out" about these living, performed oral testimonies, confessions, prayers, queries, and reflections. I sought to lay out the pieces and to observe and recreate the pattern. Why? First, I want to express and share with others the beauty, power, and meaning that come out of an oral history whose creators were severely oppressed but refused to give up—a key ingredient in working with persons who may chose to wallow in their victimhood, may deny the oppression, or may name the oppressor but not see that their lives can be any different. They may always expect a handout, to the point that they do not do things to help themselves. I continue to wrestle with the present-day reality that Black folk experience difficulty rallying as a collective, as extended families, to help each other and to accomplish tasks. Can the Spirituals help shift inordinate Black consumerism to Black self-help, cooperatives, investment clubs, and political strategies? Second, after Reconstruction and before the modern Civil Rights Movement (hereinafter referred to as the Movement), many churched African Americans frowned on singing the Spirituals, both because of their links to blues and jazz (which, for some, were crude and vulgar songs) and because they were illiterate songs that could thwart assimilation, part of an era that, in some Black folks' eyes, was better forgotten.

The Spirituals, songs created by African-American slaves, affirm God and cope with oppression, anchor my soul, awaken history for me, and reflect a significant portion of my life. The Spirituals are "that Balm in Gilead" that celebrate healing and wholeness; they allow human beingness and doingness. They allow for the magnificence God created in Black life, all life, that soars in a spirit of overcoming when we meet the challenges of life and transcend them. These dynamic melodies mirror God-infused experiences, critical thinking, music, and justice. Problematically, when we fail to study and know history, when we fail to celebrate the genius of folk culture, we often repeat our mistakes; we do not realize what has changed versus what has remained the same; and we do not appreciate our own legacies and the beautiful souls of humanity, especially the souls of Black folk. The Spirituals have much to say, and they make us look at a time period that markedly shapes today.

With these realizations, the Spirituals moved me toward four ways or tracks of interpretation that help reveal the power and message of the Spirituals (the combined words and music) and how they express theodicy: (1) actual historical contexts; (2) multilayered story; (3) creative, musical spirit; and (4) divine relations and faithful thought. Each of these four ideas became a process of discovery that led to paradoxes or contradictions as I simultaneously sensed good and bad, pleasure and pain. The Spirituals revealed the many sides of Black life, often as a response to Blacks' total environment, siphoned through the complex human mind. The reality of evil (slavery, oppression) and paradox means the slave mind had to wrestle with the contradiction of coexisting differences (White versus Black) and similarities (humanness) as the slave addressed questions of identity: "Who am I?" and "I am who?" Daily life filled with lynching, rape, and dehumanization meant that every person on the plantation—slave, overseer, master, and mistress—lived close to tension, guilt, conscious and unconscious manipulation of power, and amid life-and-death issues,[1] especially the basic paradox of good with evil, particularly in the treatment of human beings like brood mares and stud bulls. The Spirituals expose the coexistent presence of contradictory elements and frameworks.

The musical and poetic texts of the Spirituals, shaped by cultural forces and ideas, express the links between communities, persons, and texts framed by social, cultural, and historical diversity.[2] These musical stories or narratives communicate a history or living story of human life, and involve the political—the denial of power to some and the manipulation of power by others—that initiates remembrance or history.[3] Such musical poetry touches and unleashes the communal and individual stories of the heart and soul that provide insights into how an oppressed people coped and retained a hopeful imagination toward human transformation. Critical assessment of the Spirituals studies the slaves' life story (about the individual, the Black and White communities, and God), sets out theories, and offers ethical alternatives. I treat the evils of slavery and racism and their supporting myths, cultural stories, or themes that shape one's worldview and rituals and that prescribe ceremonial acts via African-American Spirituals. Prior studies focused on collecting and documenting the Spirituals or on giving a social, historical, cultural, and/or theological analysis of the literary texts alone, but ignored in-depth musical analysis.[4] My study analyzes taped live musical performances of the Spirituals, especially during the Movement, when the Spirituals spoke universally to the African-American community and promoted nonviolent protest. My investigation uses the Spirituals as a resource for doing narrative theology, specifically theodicy.

Part I, "Insight," defines the Spirituals; surveys the meaning and knowing in African-American traditions; places the Spirituals in their social, historical settings (slavery and the 1960s Movement); and reviews how Eurocentric and Black (male) scholars have dealt with theodicy, and how the Spirituals have informed some of them.

Part II, "Innovation," explores four ways that the Spirituals themselves show they need to be explored: (1) context; (2) story; (3) creative spirit; and (4) divine relation behind and within the Spirituals.

Part III, "Intent," defines terms, issues, and concepts of Womanist thought; explores the impact of Womanist thought on understanding the message of the Spirituals; and gives a Womanist reading on Black women living, using, singing, and arranging the Spirituals, highlighting persons from Harriet Tubman to Leontyne Price, Bernice Johnson Reagon, and Jessye Norman.

Part IV, "Illustriousness," analyzes the Spirituals as collective exorcisms, highlighting but not limited to live recorded performances.

Part V, "Inference," summarizes the contribution an African-American theodicy of the Spirituals makes to traditional or classical theodicy, and raises questions that lead to a viable theory and praxis of a contemporary usage of the Spirituals to effect justice, healing, and health.

History yields the vehicle; the Spirituals ordain the manner of interpretation. My analysis involves various dynamics and ways of talking about God, music, Afrosensitive thought, and Christian doctrine, and takes seriously the African and the African-American experience, as well as Eurocentric thinking, in working through questions about justice toward effecting liberation and transformation. This involves the critical and corrective task of advancing rigorous criticism against the negations and unsubstantiated insinuations of White studies of African Americans, society, and the world.[5]

The Spirituals tell us how the social and intellectual environment of African Americans survived in the United States, despite their being objectified. These songs also help us challenge Eurocentric ways of knowing and assessing meaning, and help us argue that human actions cannot be understood apart from related human attitudes, emotions, and cultural definitions. The Spirituals champion social freedom rooted in the reality of democracy and individuality, as freedom becomes the ultimate salvation of humanity from human history and human nature. In sum, studying the Spirituals from an Afrosensitive viewpoint forces us to look at the slavery question in an American society where liberal Democrats, stalwart Republicans, and some free Blacks owned slaves, coupled with the massive domestic breeding of slaves that fueled the economy.

The Spirituals sing America, giving voice to many who otherwise were silenced. These songs are not simply revisions of hymns. Their time frame embraces life on "both sides of Jordan," now and after death. My research, by definition and design, integrates both Afrosensitive and Eurocentric paradigms: I am an African-American woman trained in European-based universities, and I use both experiences to analyze the African-American living documents that are the Spirituals. Their vitality springs from the urgency for wholeness and justice. The hermeneutics of communication that creates this sense of justice includes the practice of musicking.

Musicking means to engage in the activity of creating music, or musical performance.[6] Oral and written dialogue and musicking practices show that Afrocentric communities experience life as an interrelated whole, not separately categorized. The trend in the West claims and senses that music is exclusively for those with the right talent and training. In African culture, being a musician is not an occupation. Music is the celebration of life; making "a joyful noise" is part of life's "ritual honoring life, honoring your parents, honoring the community. Every human being has the potential to be musical."[7] The Spirituals celebrate the communal and the interrelationships between music and life via the religious and the theological.[8] Because of these interrelationships, the Spirituals are worthy of study and historically contingent, and they exorcize evil by juxtaposing faith and humor/comedy.

The redacted or edited 1960s Spirituals are those Spirituals that were reshaped by persons in the Movement to make them even more relevant to the cause, because specific persons, events, and actions involved in and around a particular protest meeting or march were named within the song. These Spirituals function as "liturgical songs of reformation" that exorcize—expose and expel, and thus free one from—the collective sins of slavery and racism. These songs expose evils, which makes them tools for uncovering theodicy. Philosophers and theologians argue the question of theodicy by exploring the contradiction that both an all-good, all-loving, all-powerful, and all-knowing God and the exact opposite or absence of good—evil—exist. Many scholars ask the question, "Does God exist, given the historically identifiable reality of evil?" However, the theodicy of Christian thought expressed in the Spirituals presumes the existence of God; finds convincing that one may not ever know the answer to some questions; and analyzes the nature of relationship and responsibility between God and humanity within society. Racist evil is the product of misused freedom. The Spirituals challenge evil with a belief in the ultimate present that anticipates imminent salvation as liberation for all. Freedom and right relations are the essential elements necessary for a sound theodicy and place the oppressed at the center of the discussion. In this context, theodicy requires and refers to divine and human work for justice that overcomes the societal evils of slavery and racism. The Spirituals are an opportunity to discover whether music offers hope and mercy and whether it comments on the ongoing evils of racism, sexism, and classism.

Womanist, derived by Alice Walker from the term *Womanish*,[9] refers to Black women who are audacious, outrageous, in charge, and responsible; in other words, to Black feminists. Womanist theory focuses on oppression because of race, gender, or class, and on a use of power in American society midst personal and societal dualism. My study explores the history and meaning of the Spirituals, the cultural forces and ideas that shaped them, and their power for transformation, using the language of Womanist theory. Womanist thought makes visible Black women's experience, addressing those made invisible because of race, sex, and class oppression. A Womanist cares about "the least of these." She loves and combats all oppression due to labels and categories used to displace and control. Womanist theory, steeped in a faith-based curiosity, studies and honors Black women toward transformation. A Black woman can not avoid oppression. Society tells her that she is a servile robot or a sexual, erotic thing, the objectified "other," because she is not *really* made in God's image. This otherness, shared by all Blacks, makes Black women invisible.[10] The Womanist pilgrimage is a call to make the hidden visible, identify relevant issues and resources, uncover discrepancies, and right the wrongs of injustice. Through a liberating, biblical Womanist vision, people know God as a personal, powerful, compassionate liberator who has masculine and feminine qualities and is a "mother to the motherless and father to the fatherless."[11] Such a relationship lets one transcend and celebrate creation's gifts. As Walker says, Womanists are serious and commit to the survival and wholeness of all people.[12]

There is an inspiring, healing power resonant in the many pilgrimages that birthed the Spirituals, and in the Spirituals themselves. Yet this energy lies dormant when Spirituals are not taught, sung, studied, shared, and lived. Womanist theory provides some meaningful techniques for excavating and communicating the awesome, sacred stories of the Spirituals and the life forces that birthed them. I am a storyteller, a pilgrim who has faith in the Christian story. Telling that story involves theology (identity, sacrality, spirituality); the Bible and narratives (authority, community, history); ethics (visibility, integrity); context (culture, aesthetics, community); and the socio-cultural and historical analysis of music from a theologically informed perspective that illuminates the models of God-talk and religious/spiritual belief systems within the secular and the sacred.

As you read, you sing; as you sing, you experience the vibrancy and vitality, the heritage and the legacy deeded to all of us by the millions of pilgrims who died during middle passage and by the thousands who defied all odds, did what they needed to do, and survived. As you read and sing, you experience the creative spirit of hope and survival, the humor that fosters faith; expose the lies of racism, sexism, classism, and all "isms"; and feel how these songs, as ritual, affect a "collective exorcism" toward societal healing in the past, present, and future.

Pilgrimages
Then and now,
Begin and continue
Vast, small, in between:
An impact.

My heart aches and sings
Pondering
Pilgrimages
Of long-ago bards
Who sang:
"Let freedom ring!"

PART I

INSIGHT

Introduction and Background

1

Meaning and Knowing

Souls died:
During middle passage,
In slavery, the Civil War, WW I & II,
Korea, Vietnam,
In the 1960s on the Streets,
South, North, East, West,
High-tech lynching:
WARS
Souls died.
Many souls died.
Why?
Choice, Covetousness
Curse, Circumstance?
Did anyone sing for them?

Many non-Africans came to the United States seeking freedom from European despotism, seeking a new life. African Americans did not voluntarily come to these shores as willing immigrants, bondservants, or as convicted criminals.[1] From the seventeenth through the nineteenth century, African Americans were subjected to the moral and legal oxymoron of legalized slavery endorsed by church and state.[2] Both institutions validated this human bondage. Prior to the 1960s, many African Americans were subject to institutional racism supported and approved of by the nation's rulers, customs, and laws. One response by the enslaved Africans of the North American diaspora and by modern African Americans was the cultural artifact historically known as "the Spirituals." Using the phonodisc *Voices of the Civil Rights Movement: Black American Freedom Songs, 1960-1966*[3] as my primary database, in this chapter I set out a working definition of the Spirituals and question the ways African Americans handle meaning, knowing, and understanding.

"The harmonies and intensities of naked voices . . . all sounds, from the soaring gospel descants of the soprano soloists to the thunderous hand-

3

clapping of the congregation, were created by human flesh. The sounds harked back to the moods of the slavery."[4] African-American Spirituals mirror Black people's cultural, religious, and political experience in the United States. They document human existence and usage of power in American society. These folk harmonies that originated spontaneously exude life itself, foster pride, and conserve traditions and memories of life in bondage. These songs uniquely combine rhythm, melody, text, and harmony in a powerful sense of the religious and of rhythm. The mystery, beauty, and wonder of these melodies sound forth both a cry that ponders heavenly blessings now and the ongoing riddle of slavery midst the themes of prophecy, penitence, praise, fellowship, faith, aspiration, and advice. Slaves "smuggled" their valuable cargo, the treasure of their God-centered musical heritage,[5] aboard slave ships. The antebellum Spirituals were both a secret means of communication and a means to reaffirm the displaced African's status as *imago Dei*, as created in the image of God.

To be created *imago Dei* means all God's creations stand equal before God and have the possibility of being in active, loving relationships with God and with other human beings. Within the 1960s Civil Rights Movement, the Spirituals helped unify disparate groups to attack legalized racism via moral, nonviolent resistance, and organized protest. Thirty years before the language of multiculturalism surfaced, civil rights activists of all colors and creeds united, as they celebrated their mutual experiences of *imago Dei*, toward freedom and justice for all. That celebration largely included singing the Spirituals. These cultural chants enabled both generations to exorcize the collective racist evil in their North American "Egypt's land." This racist evil was a historical paradox: a country founded on the belief that all humans have inherent natural rights given them by their Creator, denied, by its practices and laws, these moral and legal rights to persons of color. This denial signifies and discloses the contradictions within American law, cultural mores, and practice. Historically, the signers of the Declaration of Independence posited that "all men are created equal," and it was understood that "men" referred to White (Anglo-Saxon) male, non-Catholic land-owners. Equality was not for African Americans, women, non-Christians, non-Whites, or White men who did not own property. Despite these paradoxes and inequities of the sociopolitical environment, the Spirituals embodied the African Americans' sense of themselves, their sense of God, and their relationship with God. The Spirituals incubated and delivered the souls of Black folk from total despair in both the antebellum and 1960s eras: "The spirit of the songs could sweep up the crowd, and the young leaders realized that through song they could induce humble people to say and feel things that otherwise were beyond them. . . . People who had inched tentatively into the church take up the verse in full voice, setting themselves against feared authority."[6] Faith overruled timidity and took fear hostage.

The faith, value, simplicity, and hope of Bible-inspired stories fuel the traditional Spirituals. These inspired tunes speak of suffering and sorrow, but they also speak of joy, Christian hope, and freedom in the year of Jubilee. The civil rights protest songs include redacted Spirituals and 1960s freedom songs that focus on "Freedom Now!" These updated versions of traditional Spirituals had a heightened relevancy to the 1960s because they include names of contemporary people, places, events, and singing styles. Freedom songs include secular songs, traditional Black gospel or hymnody, and other protest movement songs. Spirituals, spontaneously created songs by slaves, are in the family of Black music but are a different genre from the gospels and the blues. The gospels, the youngest of these song forms, are composed rather than being spontaneously created or "found." The blues, composed chiefly after slavery, focus on secular matters and, like the gospels, are authored by an individual or group of individuals. Both gospels and blues are *composed*; the Spirituals developed spontaneously in a setting and were later *arranged* for solo or choral performance. These Movement songs, remembrances, survivals, and expressions of identity and community, are a key to deciphering the riddle of the African-American experience.[7] The Spirituals, the "grandmother" of later freedom songs within the plantation environment, combined poetry and music to help those in bondage deal with all of their existence.

Often slaves made up new verses or blended several Spirituals to create a new Spiritual as they performed the ring shout. The shouters formed a circle and then went round and round in a slow march or processional, all facing one direction. With their hands in front and their palms together, the singers' bodies swayed at the hips, and they dipped as their knees bent; with each shuffle, each step, they advanced their bodies only slightly. Not all Spirituals used the shout, and even when they did, it took different forms: rocking, heel-toe movement, advance, and retreat—all as part of worshipping God.[8]

The variety of ring shouts mirrored the variety in the style and the particular collections of Spirituals throughout the South. The Spirituals from the Carolina low country calmed and encouraged boatmen rowing, broke the monotony of the repetitive physical activity of laboring in the fields and doing household tasks, and accompanied dancing. The Gullah Blacks of South Carolina, without European influence, sang the Spirituals with many variations and apocalyptic imagery as they spoke of their stresses, their anxieties, and their experiences, joys, and sorrows. In the Spirituals from Avery Island, Louisiana, there were eighty songs which did not appear elsewhere, and many of these songs had distinctive references to the weather, especially rainstorms. These Spirituals also celebrated themes common to other Spirituals: humor and biblical imagery, especially conversion or redemption, deliverance, freedom, life, and death. French Blacks of Louisiana sang *cantiques*, or Spirituals derived from songs taught to them by Catholic priests, songs which roughly correspond to the Spirituals sung by Protestants. In recent history, proponents of Black Judaism (which began in the South, moved to the North, and, in one instance, relocated to Israel) also sing the Spirituals. Members of the Black Hebrew Israelite Nation see the Spirituals as songs that are real for them, now. The Black Hebrews believe they now live the true meaning of Black religious music, and they contend that the Spirituals they sang while growing up in the South led them to Israel. They replace "Jesus" with words like "Our Lord" or "Rabbey" for their leader. For the Black Hebrews, music helps them maintain their group commitment and verifies the reality of a Black Jesus, a Black Moses, and a Black homeland in Israel.[9]

The Spirituals, which represent history in motion and a call to justice, provide a wealth of information about the impact of oppression on the actual relationships between God and humanity within American society. Because they assume the freedom of God and human beings, Spirituals tell us how people gain knowledge and give meaning to life. Spirituals have seen Black folk through being stolen from Africa and through being labeled, both in the larger culture and sometimes internally to the community: African, Negro, Negra, Nigger, Black, African American, Pan-African, American. Spirituals communicate ethnic identity—the changing process of stories, meanings, ancestry, and traditions that shape and affect Blacks in the tensions of being African, American, and African American, of being and knowing. One phrase that older African Americans exclaim when discussing knowing, meaning, and understanding (epistemology) says it best: "A heap see and a few know," by sharing information.

Black folk share information through storytelling. For example, one does not say simply, "I went to the store." One sets the scene, describes what happened prior to going to the store, the nature of the traffic, what friends were at the store, the bargains or outrageous prices, the items purchased, and the general "feel" of the store. If an item needed for a meal or an upcoming event was the cause of the store visit, one also talks about the menu, about who's coming to dinner, and/or about the event itself, particularly if a lesson can be taught or some wisdom can be shared. Parents and other adult relatives also relay information through anecdotes, by signifying or playing word games, and in community assemblies like church meetings, social or protest groups, and extended family gatherings.

Family gatherings are times when adults often tell children how much they resemble or act like an older relative, living or dead. Through short proverbs or stories of their own childhood escapades, they often pass on the "common sense" needed to accept reality, keep hope, and survive in life and in an oppressive environment. Traditionally, these lessons are shared at home, church, and school. For example, when money is limited and only certain foods are prepared, a child might ask, "What's for dessert?" A grandmother might answer, "Air sauce and wind pudding," or "Dessert yourself from the table." When people make comparisons, one might hear the phrase "Pot can't call kettle Black, and pepper can't call okra long mouth." If a person, especially a child continues to misbehave or get into trouble, someone might say: "A hard head makes a soft behind." These sayings, passed from generation to generation through oral retelling, relay Black folk thought. In intimate and larger social settings, children are often taught information through storytelling and action. Children get to tell stories themselves by making presentations at school and church. They learn self-esteem and public etiquette, and gain community support and nurture as they recite and perform stories. The development of such oral history over time evolves into an entire system of thought.

Many older sayings rely on images of the home, of planting, or of family to express an idea. These were key spheres of activity and child rearing during slavery and before World War II. These sayings also highlight much of what Blacks value in life and emphasize what they envision in terms of what it means to be human: the desire for freedom, equality, self-respect, creativity, and hard work so they can provide something better for their children. Common sense and "book learning" are both prized, although when an "educated fool" comes along, one can sometimes detect a spirit of anti-intellectualism. Rooted in the extended family tradition of Africa, family remains central to what it means to be an African-American human.

The record numbers of African-American family reunions and genealogy searches inaugurated since the first television broadcasts of Alex Haley's *Roots* and *Roots: The Second Generation* celebrate the importance of family. These productions gave modern Blacks the hope that they could find out about their ancestors despite the fact that families transported from Africa were intentionally split up. Black children and infants were often taken from their parents and sold. Black marriages were forbidden and not recognized as having legal status, even in "free" jurisdictions. Thus, the African-American experience of learning and knowing had to factor in the impact of slavery and racism and the way Black individuals and communities have had to be creative and secretive to survive.

Adults passed on survival strategies while teaching a child about family heritage, skills that involved everything from cooking, cleaning, and sewing to house and appliance repairs. Adults also passed on advice about life changes, adulthood, acquiring a trade, and marriage and family, while overtly or subtly passing on the "dos and don'ts" of being around White people. All African-American children growing up in the South knew the "gospel according to Jim Crow" for coping with White folk.

Some parents went to great lengths to spare children some of the grief of racism, but they could not totally shield their children from this evil. For example, where possible, many Black folk purchased big Buicks and Oldsmobiles, even if their houses appeared to be shacks. This purchase was not a frivolous or silly act. A Black person traveling in the South prior to the Civil Rights Movement needed a car with a large gas tank so that he or she could get from home to the destination. There was never a guarantee that one could always find a gas station; and if one found a station, there was no guarantee that the gas attendant would pump the gas or allow a Black person to pump his or her own gas. If a Black family's car broke down and they were near a White-owned hotel, they could not get overnight accommodations. Lyndon Johnson's Black chauffeur had to sleep in the limousine during the 1960 presidential campaign. Until the passage of the 1964-65 civil rights bills, public accommodation and transportation could be and were legally denied a Black person. In 1994, four Black Secret Service agents accompanying the vice president were refused service at a Maryland Denny's restaurant. Many Black children never knew that their families always carried fried chicken, sandwiches, pie, and drinks (soda, Kool-Aid, etc.) in their car whenever they traveled long distances because White-owned restaurants and drive-ins on highways did not serve Black people. A little metal "chamber pot" usually was carried on car trips, because there was no place to take Black children to use restroom facilities unless one happened to stop in a town with accommodations owned by African Americans. Often, these facilities were not on main highways. If Black organizations had regional or national meetings prior to the 1960s, chambers of commerce, major hotels, and motels did not greet them with smiles, a welcome, or keys to the city. On these occasions, Black people in the communities opened up their homes and "let out" rooms for the duration of the conferences. Thus the spiritual "Plenty Good Room" celebrates making a way and making room for others to become part of the whole. While forces conspired to limit the "room" for those deemed "other," especially African Americans, they continued to survive by using tactics which included the etiquette of vision and space.

In the most racist communities, Black folk learned to never look a White person in the eye; to step off the sidewalk if a White person approached; to drink only from the "colored" water fountain; and always to enter White business establishments from the rear. The innocent disregard for these unwritten but real subtle social mores cost Emmett Till his life in Money, Mississippi.[10] African-American athletes and other entertainers at particular arenas and hotels could not sleep or eat in the same places where they performed. Segregation did not, however, prohibit many Blacks from having their own businesses to cater to the African-American community. Segregationist behavior and attitudes also did not stop Whites from often patronizing Black-owned businesses, from slavery through the twentieth century, particularly given that during slavery and early Reconstruction most southern artisans were Black.

Segregation, a vibrant, powerful force in the worlds of business and the political, was equally harsh in the educational and community spheres. Many teachers in segregated schools, with substandard materials, made sure Black children learned. The idea of any child graduating without basic skills was not acceptable; rarely did Black athletes graduate without meeting the academic requirements. What Black teachers in segregated schools lacked in supplies and moneys they made up for with creativity, compassion, and commitment. These educators and other leaders were about the creation and development of a community of survival and over-coming. The Black community recognized two significant factors in ways of knowing, meaning, and survival within American social structure that have been in existence since antebellum times. First, Black children have always come in contact with Whites at an early age, unless they live in a totally Black community like Grambling, Louisiana, or Mount Bound, Mississippi. Yet many White children growing up in America, then and now, have had no contact with African Americans. This is unfortunate, since the lack of relationship often feeds and exacerbates fear and ignorance, which in turn feed racism. Second, although many Black domestics have nurtured and cared for White children from the crib to adulthood and the maid's children often played with the children of her employer until grade school, after that point the maid's children could no longer play with the White children. Under no circumstances would Black children be allowed to attend the same school or to socialize with or date the children of their mother's employer. These customs were and are critical to Black survival and therefore constitute the foundation of the many ideas and the many ways Black folk and White folk envision their realities and quests for survival. Although large populations of other non-White persons populate these United States, dealing with their various ways of knowing and with their oppression goes beyond the present work. One issue critical to their survival, and to that of Black folk, however, involves a politics of identity.

The politics of identity concerns how individuals and communities deal with issues of race, ethnicity, sexuality, and national and local identities; how those identities intersect; and the impact these various differences have on people's physical, social, and spiritual, emotional selves.[11] For Black Americans, the reality of being Black in America shapes personal and community existence. Neither personal accomplishments, contributions to the larger community, nor the promises of the constitutional amendments guarantee Black citizens equality and justice. During slavery and prior to the 1960s, political revolution and legal and social lines were legally impenetrable. While the 1960s made a legal difference in rights and opportunities, the poorest Whites and Blacks remained unaffected. With the shift in economic opportunities in the 1970s and 1980s and the technological explosion of the 1990s, the gulf grows wider between the haves and have-nots of all ethnic groups as the American class system becomes more and more rigid. Notions of class separation also relate to the focus, meaning, and stereotypes about the place and function of sexuality.

In the racist, sexist eyes of some, Black women are either bossy matriarchs or exotic, sensual beings who can show a man a good time in bed. In the racist, sexist eyes of some, Black men are deviant criminals or studs who chase anything in skirts, and, as the Rev. Good Doctor in Spike Lee's *Jungle Fever* says, especially the skirts of White women. These erroneous myths infiltrated antebellum, 1960s, and 1990s American culture. Print and visual media sensationalize Black-on-White crime, sexual indiscretions, and drug usage. This is not to romanticize, excuse, apologize for, or ignore the real problems in Black communities, for all communities have similar kinds of problems. The point is to expose some of the issues that affect how people know and ascribe meaning, positive or negative. Today, the fact that these stereotypes exist and the impact of the circumstances and the sensationalism surrounding the Clarence Thomas appointment, the Mike Tyson case, and the O. J. Simpson criminal and civil murder trials mean Black men, in particular, will be held suspect. I reiterate: this statement in no way denies the heinousness of sexual harassment and sexual abuse that lead to death. This ongoing suspicion about Black men in general has a profound effect on how Black women and men assign meaning and knowing. The growing class division and the wholesale assignment of sexual and moral traits to all because of the acts of a few (which affects one's experience of liberty and justice for all) push toward one of the questions to be addressed in the summary of this study: "Can the Spirituals speak to the oppressed of the next millennium, and if so, what is the message?" I think they can, because of their grounding in a theology of making do, going against the odds, building self by building community, and believing in a "way-out-of-no-way" God.

Many African Americans come from a heritage of Black folk who, while creating the Spirituals, appropriated English and Western ideals by "making do" and by serving a "way-out-of-no-way" God. They quilted rags to create bed coverings, an act of sharing and learning and giving meaning through ritual. They improvised with food scraps, like ham hocks and greens, and cracklin' corn bread made with bits of fried fatback, among other food combinations, to create soul food, "gourmet" fare from remnants and leftovers. The fat and salt in their diets enabled the slaves to work long days in cotton, sugarcane, tobacco, and rice fields midst intense heat. (Ironically, the "make do" diet that sustained Blacks in the heat of the day and amid a different "heat," the heat of "Uncle Tomming" and the compromise of bodily integrity in the house, is the diet that aggravates physical conditions that precipitate elevated mortality rates due to illnesses like high blood pressure and diabetes.)

In the midst of these and other innovations and improvisations, African Americans continued to develop loyalties, shape belief systems and values, deal with feelings, and maintain integrity.[12] They nurtured a sense of loyalty to God and family. Those allegiances shaped their core belief systems and governed what was important, how they went about accomplishing the tasks of life, the sense of responsibility accompanying those tasks, and the sense of what was right and wrong, and helped them determine whether to choose accommodation or protest. With accommodation or protest, the choices meant going along with business as usual or bucking the system. The Black disenfranchised symbolically and artistically responded to these life situations as they celebrated their identity, and they practiced and nurtured virtue while they grappled with the feelings, attitudes, desires, rules, aesthetics, and loyalties within Black life on the plantation dominated by a Eurocentric worldview. The development of these loyalties, values, systems, and attitudes during slavery, Reconstruction, and the great migrations to the West, North, East, and Midwest provided a culture and theology of overcoming and somebodiness. Thus, despite earlier physical restraint and oppression and later legal, social, and cultural oppression, Black folk have a heritage of resistance that affords acquiring knowledge and ascribing meaning toward self-actualization and transcendence midst difficult odds.

Because of who they are and what they look like, Black women have additional insight on knowing and meaning. Black feminist and scholar Patricia Hill Collins explores the ways African American women know, serve as agents of knowledge, define themselves, and empower themselves and others.[13] She builds on the everyday encounters of Black women who share their experiences of how they acquire knowledge rooted in an Afrocentric feminist epistemology. Her concept of how Black women know and determine meaning has four levels. First, a concrete experience of meaning (either knowledge or wisdom) creates practical symbols and images. These practical images help foster a sisterhood, along with a sense of connectedness. These images of connectedness are as diverse as persons (the stalwartness of Sojourner Truth or the wisdom and strength of "Miz Susie" or "Aunt Mary," neighborhood women who become extended family members as they share the fruits and wisdom of their life experiences) and concepts (traits learned and shared, from honesty, caring, helping others, and being a good listener to having good posture that connotes self-esteem). In relationships, friends bond and avoid pettiness and gossip, while they share a sense of community and determination.

Second, Black women use dialogue, conversation, to evaluate knowledge as they experience a connectedness, interaction, and encounter that reaps a holistic life concept, harmony, and community. These women actively participate in rhythmic, animated talking as they call and respond, listen and relate. Black women gather over coffee or tea, visit each other's homes, meet at restaurants, organize a bridge game or a hand of gin rummy or spades (in larger church settings, cooking large meals or playing bingo), and use the telephone to talk out issues and to be supportive of each other.

Third, Black women share knowledge and empower each other using an ethic of caring. Caring celebrates individual uniqueness as Black women praise each other when they do well, send special token gifts or cards to show encouragement, make phone calls to uplift, do what they do with a sense of excellence, and do unexpected goodwill for a friend. Caring occurs through personal and communal acts and reactions with the appropriate emotional response. A group of close friends use each other as a sounding board, but they will not take advantage of or abuse the friendship. Distance is not a factor when it comes to maintaining friendships. Caring emerges as empathy and compassion as Black women share a similar experience, want to make a person feel better, offer words of hope, and use or suggest biblical and other inspirational readings as a source of nurture and support.

Fourth, Collins sees an ethic of personal accountability wherein Black women value ethics and character. In some instances, women confront each other when a friend falls short or misbehaves. Sometimes, depending upon the comfort level and the nature of the relationship, if a Black female friend sees the other person is not ready, she may have to sit by and watch her friend make mistakes, love her anyway, and be there to pick up the pieces.

The experience of quilting together uses concrete pieces of fabric to create a bed covering, a process that creates a bond of sisterhood and involves telling stories related to the quilting scraps that once served as parts of clothing or are the remnants that remained after completing a garment. Sharing these stories and memories evokes wisdom and love. Conversations over tea or coffee while shucking corn or while planning events engage the passing of traditions and sharing of mother wit, or common sense. Being there, providing a shoulder to cry on, being godmothers and play sisters, knowing when to say no, are the nuts and bolts of an ethic of caring. Knowing that "the sermon I live speaks louder than the one I preach" is the lived reality of personal accountability, of being responsible. In the four categories about determining meaning mentioned above, reason, ethics, and emotions together provide the resources to help one unpack the African-American woman's experience of truth. Experiencing truth, one of the benefits of singing the Spirituals, supports the African-American woman's ability to identity her own self and to be accountable to others, to experience the self of Black people, rooted in freedom.[14]

That sense of freedom nurtures a wealth of human behavior or ethics and morality. Womanist ethicist Katie Cannon talks about these attributes of self-respect and self-critique as invisible dignity, quiet grace, and unstated courage. Invisible dignity is the hidden elegance often shattered by the oppression of race, gender, and class. That dignity enabled Black women to work as domestics, to give superb care to somebody else's White child, and to love her own child well after coming home bone tired. That dignity has emerged in the proud walk and elegance of older Black women who have paid their dues without becoming bitter, like the thousands of unnamed Rosa Parkses and countless Delaney sisters. Quiet grace is the hidden moral character that emerges in one's search for truth. Quiet grace is part of the core substance of grandparents who had to drop out of school before eighth grade but made sure all their children received educations, often advanced degrees. Quiet grace rises out of the strategies Black parents, depicted by the Miss Jane Pittmans of the world, used to buffer the nasty, acrid boundaries of racism and segregation from their children, young and old alike. Unstated or unshouted courage is the hidden "stick-to-it-edness" wherein one holds on with the tenacity of superglue, ultimately overcoming fear and effecting transformation. That courage undergirds the actions of the civil rights protesters when they knew each day, each moment might be their last.[15] Overt and hidden acts of dignity, grace, and courage occur daily in the lives of Black women and men in their spiritual ways of knowing, and in the totality of Black culture and communication.

Culture and communication are complex and have many different dimensions. Culture, which involves an exchange of information, enables Black folk to identify with each other and involves thinking or developing ideas and ways to express those ideas. Communication in Black communities and in the Spirituals deals with root questions and key arguments about life. Communication and meaning are critical to understanding what it means to be human, to be Black in America, and to develop relationships and organizational strategies wherein difference can exist without a sense of superiority or inferiority.[16] The common patterns shared by African Americans involve social organization, ethnicity, and race. These kinds of identity involve many shared traditions. Black communication involves the social and historical location of African Americans in the United States and how they have helped to create and maintain their culture. This process helps develop identity and diverse cultural experiences and behaviors. What do people need to know to be a part of, or to identify with, the Black folk?[17]

Core symbols or expressions of beliefs (e.g., the colors of the liberation flag of red, black, and green; natural hair styles; Kwanzaa; and extended family celebrations and traditions) help Blacks understand their social reality (who they are, what they believe and why, and how they act and react). Many "dos and don'ts" help African Americans determine appropriate personal and community behavior and ethics and how to relate to self, each other, and the world. Knowing and abiding by antebellum Black codes and twentieth-century Jim Crow laws, including contemporary unwritten but understood barriers of gender, race, and class, signified by "gated communities," has meant survival for those deemed "other." Despite these realities, those deemed other in many sectors continue to work and continue to hope, lessons explicit in the Spirituals. The Spirituals rehearse the abuse, humiliation, and oppression that often penalize Blackness, and they offer a liberating alternative. Often tediousness and predicaments involved in communication blur the possibilities for liberation and transformation in these songs, since all people differ in the way they understand, interact and make choices, and in what they "bring to the table." The beauty of Spirituals, of music, is that this experience includes and transcends difference and fosters togetherness. At the same time, the Spirituals have a way of communicating that bonds, protects, and empowers singers and activists amid friend or foe.

The Spirituals often use words that could have double meaning, a code that helps order, guide, and coordinate Black participation in the world. Singing "Trouble don't last always" is a way to say that you're OK, even if you're being beaten down, and that you can survive. Spirituals are conversations, patterns, ritual expressions of life. Every Spiritual is a dialogue, a message for the singer(s) and for the community, an experience of bonding, of commonality, of shared membership based on identity and place. The early Spiritual "I've Been 'Buked" said the same thing that the popular folk adage says in the '90s: "Been there, done that."

As communicative tools, then, the Spirituals mediated the ways slaves understood life and expressed their desires for freedom, salvation, and redemption in this world. The slaves expressed their feelings and interpretations of life by changing their tones, pitches, texts, and body language. Their sense of God with them and the divine within life itself shaped the way those in bondage used the Spirituals to get freedom, to affirm their human dignity and hope for change, to protest, to communicate multiple meanings, to praise God, to pass on traditions, and to survive. Skillfully, the slave bards used metonymy, the technique of using a name of one thing for that of another associated with it or suggested by it, to encode communication. Thus, "home" meant Africa or the location of known family; "bondage" meant slavery; "Satan" meant slave master; "Israelites" meant enslaved African Americans; "Egyptians" meant slave owners; "Jordan" meant the initial step toward freedom; and "King Jesus" meant one who helped slaves.[18]

The encoding process was part of the African Americans' way of perceiving their reality, their consciousness. Blacks tended to relate and think in terms of sounds, pictures, emotions, motions, and rhythms, rather than in the abstract notions of Western culture. Their experiences embraced four factors prominent in the Spirituals: the affective, or feelings ("Sometimes I *feel* like a motherless child"); the kinesthetic, or touching ("When I get to heaven gonna put on my shoes, / Gonna *walk* all over God's heaven"); the auditory, or listening ("My Lord, he calls me, he calls me by the thunder, / The trumpet *sounds* within a ma soul"); and the visual, or seeing ("I *looked* over Jordan, and what did I *see*").[19] The disenfranchised sang these songs—products of their actions in response to the action of others—to teach, affirm, and survive. They extended their imaginations beyond their immediate present to embrace a biblical worldview that proclaimed freedom. These songs embody the notion that freedom itself exorcizes evil.

In singing about freedom, there was a sense that the thirst for and awareness of freedom—of deliverance, salvation, emancipation, liberation, ease, and relief—began the process of lessening, of removing, of exorcizing, of cutting out the power of evil that the oppressor had over the oppressed. Singing about freedom was a way to begin to know that freedom, particularly in the coded words of the Spirituals when the outside, dominant group really had no clue as to what the slaves and later freedom fighters were singing about. The oppressed used their verbal skills both to salvage communal solidarity and values and to overcome and transcend their painful, restrictive, oppressive environment, to begin to experience liberation and the privilege of emancipation.

When circumstances made speech impossible, touching, feeling, hear-

ing, and seeing gave the slaves access to each other. Spontaneously singing the Spirituals, using improvisation to create communal consciousness,
also made coded communication possible. This kind of communication
bolstered self-esteem, hope, personal worth, and ultimate justice in a sacred world, a world filled with the divine. Uplifted voices gave meaning to
life as they imagined their own release, just as the Hebrew children marched
through the Red Sea, or as they saw themselves as overcomers, like David
overpowered Goliath. These visions made sense because the slaves'
chosenness, like that of their cosuffering Hebrew Bible compatriots, meant
they had a special relationship with a God who was just and merciful and
who cared.[20] And when slaves could not sing or laugh openly, they could
go to the brush arbor to pray and sing, or to the laughing barrel to experience humor, a tool of survival and healing. The laughing barrel tradition
parallels the custom of putting a wash kettle upside down in the middle of
the floor during a prayer meeting so the praying and singing sounds would
not reach the plantation. To laugh and survive, the slave went to the imaginary laughing barrel so that his or her mirth would not reach the big house.

Laughing and storytelling were ways slaves coped creatively and successfully. They had their own codes and mores, ways of knowing and sharing meaning. Under oppression, Black folk developed the Spirituals as another mode of self-expression. That creativity left us a rich collection of
songs and humorous stories that allow us to feel, think, sense, speak, and
cry for freedom and justice for us, for them, for everybody. Though the
earliest creators of these chants that expose and rebuke evil are long dead,
the songs are alive with their stories.

2

Context: The Social and Historical Setting

> Bound in constant pain
> A malaise:
> Sticky, miry clay
> When cleaned
> Traces remain.

The Spirituals exorcized and negated the evil powers of slavery and racism. These songs affirmed African-American personhood, freedom, and God "with them," and negated bondage, despotism, and institutional degradation in response to the life-and-death problems of evil, suffering, and injustice. Like the psalmist who knew the Lord would assure deliverance for those in the miry clay (40:1-2), troubled Black psalmists put the same stock in many of the Spirituals. The troubles indicated by the Spirituals evolved during the social history of pre-1860s legalized institutional slavery and the 1960s civil rights era. The Spirituals developed during both periods and served as internal bolsters and external weapons of moral wisdom and hope. In unearthing these gems of wisdom, prudence, and shrewdness we revisit the Spirituals and the history of slavery, racism, and civil rights.

Slavery: A Peculiar Problem of Evil

Slavery is evil. The systematic, legal practice of making people chattel, breeding them, punishing them with tar and feathers, lynching them, and cutting off their hands and breaking their legs as punishment because they tried to read, write, and run away was immoral, depraved, and base. This dehumanizing, vile institution in America was based on economics and greed, and used prejudicial, biblical, scientific, political, and psychological myths—collections of cultural stories or themes—to shape the United States' view of the "peculiar institution."[1] Slavery, which was old when Moses was young, existed in Plato's Athens, Caesar's Rome, Christian Europe's Middle Ages, and ancient Africa as the rules of war justified his-

16

torical slavery minus the race issue.[2] Slavery is old, but its practice in North America was different. North American slavery evolved from a moneymaking proposition for the intentional inhumane treatment of persons based on their skin color. The first Blacks who came to these shores (Isabella and Anthony, who fell in love and gave birth to William Tucker and seventeen other Africans) were *not* slaves. Although the first slaves on North American shores in 1619 were white European indentured servants and captive Native Americans, slavery was made official and Africanized in the Western Hemisphere with the beginning of slave laws in 1640.[3] Within the strictures of slave laws and southern "genteel culture," masters/slave owners and slaves were speaking different languages and living in different worlds regulated by evil.

The slave was caught between feeling spiritually free and being bodily enslaved; being human and being treated as an animal; being simultaneously feared and desired. How could the master say, "Love thy neighbor" yet treat some "neighbors" as property; despise Blackness but lust after female Black bodies; need slave labor but fear and despise the worker? Both Black and White were signaling, "Imitate me, but *don't* imitate me." Many Whites (masters) desired the perceived biological or sexual prowess, physical stamina, earthy resilience, and exotic coloring of Blacks (slaves). Blacks desired the perceived freedom, justice, and pursuit of happiness of Whites. Perception and desire led to ambiguity and created chaos. By pitting Black chaos or turmoil against White "holiness" or "virtue," racism was the culmination of sectional, class, gender, and ethnic conflicts.[4] In Spike Lee's *Jungle Fever*, the pain, dehumanization, schizophrenia, and double messages of such insanity penetrate the monologue of the Good Reverend Doctor as he reads the riot act to his married son, Flipper Purify, and Flipper's White girlfriend, Angie, in the presence of the Good Reverend Doctor's wife:

> You think I don't understand about the white woman committing Black adultery. But I do. . . . You see there were a lot of lynchings down in Willacoochee, Georgia, down where I come from. . . .White man say to his woman: "Baby, you are the flower of white Southern womanhood: too holy and pure to be touched by any man, including me. I'm gonna put you upon a pedestal for the whole world to fall down and worship you. And if any nigger so much as look at you I'll lynch his ass."

> . . . She [the White woman] believed him; thought she really was holy and pure like the Virgin Mary. She let him put her upon that pedestal. Meanwhile, the husband was soon somewhat down—down to the slave quarters, grabbing up every piece of Black poontang he could lay his hand on and running to the gin mill to brag about it. And that's how our blood got mingled: Black whores, quadroon, octoroons.

I'm sure that most of those high and mighty white ladies felt abandoned, but they were so proud to be white, and therefore superior; they kept their mouths shut and their legs locked tight. But in the midnight hour, then, alone, on the hot bed of lust, I'm sure they must of thought what it would be like to have one of them big Black bucks their husbands were so desperately afraid of. And I feel sorry for you. Here it is the nineties and you're still trying to make up for what you missed out on. But I don't blame you. As for the Black man, like my own son, who ought to know better, got a loving wife and daughter, still got to fish in the white man's cesspool; I have nothing but contempt. Excuse me, I don't eat with whoremongers.[5]

While these conflicts and mixed feelings existed during and after slavery, up to the present day, the almighty dollar was the god that ruled and that made slavery tenable and legal. The need for cheap labor, skewed biblical testimony, and the compromises found within the U.S. Constitution reinforced unjust slavery as a legal institution. Constitutionally, slaves were held as three-fifths of a person for the purpose of national elections and direct taxes.[6] This insured disproportional representation for the slaveholding states: slaves and women counted toward representation in Congress, but only White men could vote. American slavery created racial injustice. Given that "demoting other people from the ranks of humanity on the grounds of race or ethnicity is a horrendous sin,"[7] slavery was a moral, theological, ethical, and political issue. Notwithstanding the moral issues, the courts changed Blacks from humans to property through Chief Justice Roger B. Taney's twisted logic in the infamous Dred Scott test case.[8] Greed, "Christopher Columbus and sugar made the slave trade big business" in America.[9]

Slavery was big business in America, Europe, and Africa: it was a saga of marketing and merchandising people that involved millions of deaths, along with lies, thefts, and murder. The slavery involved slave trade. Slave trade was monstrous, involving everything from free Black Africans imported to America with bruises and brands on their chest, to mothers committing infanticide to avoid their children's having to live in slavery, to bishops baptizing slaves on their way to slave ships, to kings raiding their own villages to get slaves to buy liquor, to slave captains holding prayer services on a slave ship and later writing hymns. Bishop Bartolomé de Las Casas lived to regret that he suggested Spaniards enslave Africans when the bondage of Native Americans proved unsuccessful. Enslaving Whites failed, because they could get monarchical protection and could blend in with the crowd. Native Americans either escaped, given their familiarity with the land, or they got sick and died. Blacks were inexpensive, were strong, could not blend in, and had no protection from a sovereign government: so Black slavery it was. European countries raced to commandeer the slave trade once Portugal opened the doors. Though Spain was prohibited from African slave commerce by a papal ruling that gave it the New World, the African trade went from Portugal through Holland, France, and then to England. Spain, however, gave other countries a contract, the *Asiento*, to supply the colonies with human chattel. Once England had the *Asiento* in the eighteenth century, the foundation of European commerce, the reasons for most of England's wars, and the aim of politicians were to control the slave trade, known as "Black diamonds" and "Black gold." The level of degradation or civility surrounding the plight of slaves depended on the religious and ethnic sensibilities of their captors: Black captives crossed the sea surrounded by the carcasses of the dead as sharks followed the ships, and America enslaved millions of transplanted Africans as the mother continent looked in angst to God.[10]

As early as the 1640s in the United States, only Blacks and their progeny and captive Native Americans were made slaves for life. Discriminatory practices defined Blacks as different, and slavery was legal in regard to most Blacks by the 1660s.[11] Slavery for Native Americans ended with the need for Indian allies by both sides in the pre-Revolutionary French and Indian Wars. Slavery and racism may have equally initiated oppression as cause and effect, but many view slavery and racism as child and parent. Both guided Blacks toward total degradation.[12] The bodily vulnerability of Blacks to bondage, the world's ambiguity toward slavery, and the need for a cheap workforce may account for the bent toward slavery without fierce White racial bias.

Several factors fixed institutionalized slavery during the eighteenth and nineteenth centuries. First, a growing slave population stimulated White fears, leading to increased restrictions and severe slave codes. Unlike free Blacks in Brazilian plantation systems, southern free Blacks did not contribute to the security and growth of the plantation system. Second, the Enlightenment's view of the human as a natural, physical being instead of a child of God in creation led to the first orderly classification of the races and to scientifically documented differences. Third, a public racist philosophy developed along with the need to defend slavery against nineteenth-century humanitarianism. Fourth, Northerners could oppose slavery without commitment to racial equality, which explains why the Civil War produced emancipation but did not dissolve caste discrimination and the scourges of racism in the United States.[13] Fear, humanism, anti-humanitarianism, and blindness to the relationship between slavery and racial equality gave obeisance to the Black-chattel-generated dollars and cents.

The moneys from tobacco, sugar, cotton, and related industries that assured America's place in international markets came from the work, wombs, and weariness of dehumanizing slave labor. Some might raise the question, "Why raise all the fuss, since Africa itself had slavery?" African slavery had little affinity with the American institution. African slaves could gain wealth, manumission, and position, and were not bound by a hereditary or chattel system. While a few African chiefs sold their own subjects, most slaves were prisoners of war or were kidnapped from neighboring tribes. African slaves, particularly in West Africa, did have strong liabilities, but they also had rights of marriage, ownership of property, a day of rest to work for themselves, social mobility, and ultimately freedom. African slavery changed when Arab invaders increased external slave trade beginning in the twelfth century, but the Arabs honored the Qur'an in their kind treatment of slaves. That decent treatment waned with the second invaders, the Europeans, who made slave raids, kidnapping, and war a daily experience on the African continent. The European market tactics shaped slavery in America. This "made-in-America" slavery largely determined race relations, brought African heritage into a distinctive Black culture in the Americas, and exposed America's lie about liberty and justice for all.[14]

Slavery in America was a lifetime of servitude for nonfree Blacks and a lifetime of chattel service and labor for an initial payment and low upkeep for slaveholding Whites. Even children were commodities for sale to the highest bidder. For the slave owner, slaves did not have feelings, desires, or needs that were worthy of concern. Family relations were irrelevant, because slaves were considered property. When male slave owners sired children by their Black slave women, these children were considered property and followed the lineage of their mother. Without slavery, the United States, particularly the South, could not have prospered or maintained itself, particularly based on an agricultural economic system. With the American Revolution, the status of slavery shifted slightly in the North. As Blacks fought brilliantly on land and sea, and as the "Rights of Man" movement took hold, slavery began to die in the North, but it remained firm in the South with the push toward big business through the invention of the cotton gin. Nevertheless, by the end of the eighteenth century, the screw of hardness and oppression turned again, for along with the cotton gin came the Haitian revolution, an increase in the free Black population, and several slave insurrections, especially the Gabriel conspiracy in Virginia. Intentionally, the "Cotton Curtain" came down, and the fear, hate, guilt, and greed meant the total depersonalization of Blacks, as the big business of plantation and degradation reigned supreme. Within American capitalism, profit was key. That the business of slavery lasted almost 250 years meant slavery was profitable and created the bedrock of American prosperity before the Civil War.[15]

Then slavery had to justify itself to cohere with American Puritan ethics. A renewed slave institution, built upon the savage ways persons were stolen and shipped to this country like sardines, evolved as large-scale views of White supremacist imagery made acute, constant contrasts between "the good Negro" in his or her place and the vicious Black who rebelled. The desire for White dominance created these social and ideological stereotypes, that often served southern nationalism and secessionism.[16] Black savagery posed a threat against White society.[17] Stereotypes—exaggerated beliefs about "others," about Black folk—reflected the colonial

southern slavery culture and mind-set. White supremacist prejudicial attitudes justified "White over Black" and fostered active and overt hostility
toward perceived Black resistance and "uppityness."[18] While both Black
self-images and distorted stereotypes on the plantation often portrayed
either a happy slave or a dangerous savage, a truer picture of slave life
involved the nurturing roles of the slave family and the Black church, as
both institutions assisted Black life and survival. [19]

In the slave quarters, the African-American family in exile shaped the
true African-American personality. The slaves' personality, or psychological profile,[20] helped them cope and survive without submission by singing
their songs with their extended families.[21] Slaves related to each other in a
family setting free of the symbolism or coded language needed in the plantation community. Family helped to lift their spirits, and slaves foiled family separations by running away or by committing suicide, homicide, or
infanticide.[22] When they could escape, slaves often fled back "home," to a
former plantation, where they could experience strong family ties of their
immediate and extended family, the bastion of African religious unity and
sacred traditions.[23] Family unity created stability, transmitted culture, and
provided compassion and respect. In traditional African culture, the family included the unborn, the living, and the dead, biological and extended.
In the slave family, most slave women enjoyed companionship and love,
courtship and motherhood,[24] yet sexism for Black and White women in
antebellum America was real.

Sexism and racism determined class in antebellum America. Though
race overshadowed class as a factor of difference, slave women's situation
profoundly reflected the common experienced reality of most women in
America. In the case of slave children, most slave girls believed boys and
girls were equal. These children lived in age-segregated situations and had
little contact with teenage and adult slaves who worked in the fields. Girls
and boys played and worked together, gender was not the basis of differentiation, and the myth of the absent slave family and slave promiscuity
has been refuted.[25] In reality, the individual and community were one corporate personality, which participated in all events where singing and dancing were the norm, in all rites of passage.[26] If every Spiritual ever created
still existed, the stories of reciprocity and the recounting of many life events,
including texts on justice and suffering affecting the enslaved, would be
complete.[27]

From the 1830s, fear of slave insurrections spreading from the West Indies
was the social basis for coercive laws and inhumane punishment. Despite
these laws, some slave owners provided their slaves sustenance and religious study. Antiabolitionists declared slavery innocent because Mosaic
laws sanctioned slavery and because the New Testament did not view slavery or the ownership of persons as sinful. Society used the Bible and cultural differences between Blacks and Whites to justify the use and ownership of Blacks. Since God sanctioned Hebraic enslavement, some would

argue that God did, and continues to, approve or permit slavery as an institution.[28] Manipulating texts, economics, ignorance, and fear sustained the American mutilation of African human beings. Just as Plato and Aristotle associated slavery with an idea of intelligent and virtuous superior authority ruling the world, many Western scholars used biological, biblical, religious, and philosophical doctrine to justify American slavery.[29] Conversely, abolitionists, opponents of social systems that allowed slavery to exist, condemned slavery as evil and began the nation's first major moral awakening.[30]

Abolitionist groups organized around the immediate uprooting of slavery or around raising funds to send the enslaved back to Africa and to reimburse slave owners. Some antislavery crusades also strongly supported the struggle for women's rights.[31] Abolitionists argued for manumission. They believed slavery was opposed to the biblical commands to "love thy neighbor as thyself," and that slavery was an oppressive, cruel act. Slavery was evil because one could not justly define or use a human being as property. Such oppression denied the sacred gifts of God inseparable from human nature, and was idolatry since it worshipped a false image of God.[32] Many African Americans embraced the language of abolition, freedom, and equality before and during the American Revolution. Slave insurrectionists led their crusades and regarded Christian slaveholders as an oxymoron. This fervor paved the way for the 1833 founding of the American Antislavery Society by William Lloyd Garrison and others. Frederick Douglass, an agent of this society, damned slavery as morally wrong and called for its end through moral persuasion.[33]

Southern racism evolved in a distinctive social order that included numerous symbols, from social ideals and economic interests to climate and crops, with its moral interests and views. The evolving social order was tightly identifiable and aligned with Southern ideals and White self-affirmation. Slavery evolved from being an incidental component to the focal point that brought permanency to the ties between White affirmation, reaction, action, spontaneous living, and slavery. Southern apologists admired, honored, and failed to question the presuppositions of slavery. This pattern of southern life saw White supremacy as a given, because slavery, and later racism, was critical to their expectations for social stability, not because of overt economic forces. Ultimately, whether racism resulted from a need for social stability or from a notion of power, a need to control and enforce oppression,[34] both power and social expectations explain the reality of slavery, white supremacy, and racism. The issues of idolatry, meaning, status consciousness, social stability, and dominance as power, as well as economic forces, shaped the southern and, to a lesser extent, northern attitudes toward slavery. The Spirituals rose in response to these issues of theodicy, of evil and suffering.

The irony is that this blatant moral wrong was well entrenched in southern and northern Christianity. The paradox is that the slaves adapted the same religion used to control and oppress, to liberate in the truest sense. Initially, Christianity made little progress among American slaves. The earliest African arrivals practiced their rituals and lived a holistic, intimate religious life. Hesitant slaveholders and a shortage of missionaries hampered the propagation of the faith. Meanwhile, many slaveholders deterred Africans from Christianity, because justice as individual freedom was intrinsic to Christian theology, and institutionalized slavery would be at risk if slaves learned to read, write, and develop ideas of political and social freedom. Some argued that theologically, once a slave was baptized as a Christian, the slave became a free person both civilly and religiously. Individual states passed laws contrary to this belief, and the Society for the Propagation of the Gospel in Foreign Parts, chartered in 1701, tried to Christianize African slaves in America.[35] Many of the imported Africans knew the Bible and knew about Christianity in Africa.[36] Despite the tension of whether or not to convert slaves to Christianity, the Great Awakening helped spread Christianity among African Americans in North America during the eighteenth and early nineteenth centuries. Further, the invention of the cotton gin and the use of spinning and weaving machines required skilled workers amenable to the literacy requirements required for Bible-based Christianity. The battle between liberty and slavery became a domestic and a global issue between 1810 and 1860.

While most northern industrial states were embarking on or had completed abolition, the American Colonization Society reneged on its promise to reimburse slave owners whose property was to be freed and returned to Africa. The process reversed in the 1830s with Garrison's northern abolitionist campaign and with southern slave insurrections. New southern nationalism touted slavery as an economic necessity, while the French and British empires peacefully abolished slavery by reimbursing slave owners for the economic loss of their property by 1848. With the 1838 abolition of slavery in the British West Indies, planters were compensated for releasing their slaves.[37] Conversely, the preindustrial United States was unable and unwilling to reimburse slave owners for the total economic costs connected with the proposed abolition of slaves as property. For many small farmers in the South (the majority of slave owners), ownership of two or three slave field-workers (worth approximately $1,500 each) represented 90 percent of their capital investment, with land and buildings being of secondary importance. The political tensions within the splintered American Antislavery Society and within the country as a whole anticipated the ensuing schism and conflict of institutional churches within ecclesiastical denominationalism. While rumblings over slavery came in the late 1830s, the Methodists split in 1845, and the Presbyterians in 1857, into northern and southern divisions. A congregational polity allowed Baptists to avoid confronting slavery until the issue caused a Baptist regional separation in 1845. Slavery also divided local, autonomous Disciples of Christ congregations. American Judaism largely avoided the issue because it lacked a constituency in both regions. Lutherans, Episcopalians, and Roman Catholics remained undivided until secession created two sovereign nations. Meanwhile, slavery and the schisms had an impact on the formation of the African-American preacher and the Black church.[38]

The Black preacher played a significant role in African-American life. The minister was a leader, politician, intriguer, idealist, boss, and the conductor of praise and prayer, and was not unanimously submissive. Called by the spirit, some of these uneducated clergy promoted science, literature, and the arts. Some served in the military and the legislature.[39] From sonorous delivery to full-blown song, musically expressive Black preaching affirmed the will and power of God first and then offered protest against the world.[40] The preacher was leader and nurturer of the church, the most important Black institution after the family:

Armed only with the grace of God and the unique qualities of blackness, this spiritual paladin spawned a theology which enabled the woebegone black masses to transcend the vicissitudes of life. . . . When hope unborn had died, it was the Black preacher who saved souls and sanity . . . [who] gave realism and substance to things hoped for and a taste of things not seen . . . [who] took down the mutilated bodies of black men after the mobs had done their worst . . . [who] represented black people to a hostile white community . . . [who] did this, not for pay, not for glory, but only to serve. . . . In the tradition of the past these modern paladins are found wherever wrong reaches for justice; wherever the poor seek jobs and food, and wherever oppressed people cry out their heart. They are there confronting a denuded society with the burning truth, relentless love, and righteous judgment of Jesus Christ the Liberator.[41]

The invisible slave church folk left their masters' White-dominated Christianity. The apocalyptic and prophetic ideals of the slave revolts had convinced the slaves that they were vehicles of divine justice and inspired them to nurture the "invisible institution," the slave church. Slave churches, emerging out of the hush or bush arbors (secret, well-hidden areas amid bushes and undergrowth where slaves secretly worshipped), took shape around prayer and worship. Rhythmic, chanted sermons and the Spirituals nurtured the early African-American communities as they "created their own ritual to express the essential."[42] Black churches fostered economic cooperation, served as agencies of social control, and became surrogates for national identity and catalysts for sustaining racial solidarity among African Americans. But there is no single identifiable, empirical entity called the Black church.

The Black church is a multiform, diverse institution called such because the leadership and membership are now and have always been predominantly Black.[43] Historically, the Black church has been both a reactionary and a radical Black institution, since its focus has been the sociopolitical and cultural advocacy for its flock. This proud, independent, and divisive collective serves the needs of people and embraces cooperative groups that share similar history and doctrines, including Black subgroups within White denominations and non-Christian bodies. Three types of churches coexisted during the slavery era: (1) White churches with Blacks as restricted members of the congregation; (2) separate Black churches under White leadership and supervision (independent after the Revolutionary War); and (3) separate Black churches with Black leadership.[44]

The invisible antebellum institution became the chief visible institution of freed Blacks. After breaking with St. George Methodist Episcopal Church in Philadelphia and forming the Free African Society in April 1787, Richard Allen organized Bethel Church in 1793 and founded Bethel African Methodist Episcopal Church (AME) in Philadelphia in 1816; Absalom Jones and Peter Williams, Sr. founded the Zion Church in 1801, which became the African Methodist Episcopal Zion Church (AMEZ) in 1816 and held its first annual conference in 1821. Allen and Jones, Black theologians, also initiated the discussion of Blacks in the Bible during the 1790s. The Black membership that stayed in the Methodist Episcopal Church, South, after the Civil War organized a separate body, the Colored Methodist Church (CME) in 1870 (changing "Colored" to "Christian" in 1954). The Colored Primitive Baptists organized in 1866, and the Baptists formed the National Baptist Convention in 1895. The Cumberland Presbyterian Church divided in 1869. A fifth of the members left to form an autonomous Black church of the same name, officially founded in 1874. With the vitality of the now visible church, a semi-independent religious slave life evolved, strongly defined by revivalistic Protestant Christianity. Black religion provided the slaves a refuge and a mode of endurance, helped preserve their African past, and told them to seek liberation in Jesus.[45] Many of the Spirituals, in the process of being created, embraced the slaves' African past, responded to their American recent past and immediate present, and addressed their pleas for help to "the one who stilled the waters, the one who calmed the sea."

The Spirituals echo the victimization of exiled Africans on the slave-death ships, producing "the sincere and passionate belief that somewhere between [humanity] and cattle, God created a tertium quid [an intermediate person or thing], and called it a Negro."[46] Politics (e.g., police brutality and societal complacency rooted in the emancipation and the White southern police system), economics, housing demographics, and public opinion nurtured that tertium quid image. This was not the mythological South immortalized in *Gone with the Wind*, but a time of totalitarian, patriarchally regimented King Cotton. Children, scantily clad, were driven into forced labor during slavery and later during sharecropping. Intentional classism, by playing house slaves (the elite) against field slaves, was daily fare. Punishment was frequent and was sometimes given for no reason. Within the slave community, however, the slaves maintained deep respect for older male and female slaves.[47] Injustice and control were the tunes of the day, but the slaves sang about freedom, life, and hope, and would counter and deal with brutality and fear through song. Meanwhile, tensions within the police and private southern sector, along with misdemeanors by African Americans, forged the basis for Black and White injustice: a shift in political tensions from crime to color and to compromising freedom.[48] The rebellion against the continued compromising of African-American physical and spiritual freedom, set in the language and music of the Spirituals, was a resistance that used the language and sentiments of Africa, southern slavocracy, and Christianity, particularly the language of freedom.

Many Spirituals feature the idea of freedom as a God-given right, a gift for full humanity and life without fear.[49] Slave bards created coded "freedom" Spirituals that immortalized and disguised their strategies and subversive acts. Despite the blood sacrifice endemic to struggles against structural evil, African Americans during the pre–Civil War and the "Freedom Now" eras sang, engaged in insurrections, and were sustained by African traditional religious practices as they confronted racial injustice. The new religion of exilic Africans in America, rooted in West African religious traditions, preserved the continuity between the human and the divine. Possession by a God meant full integration of the self with the divine. The African tribal high God was a present, nonintervening truth. Other intermediary gods could bring new order into ordinary life to ban slavery. Ancestors, turned into gods, served as guardians of mores and law, and as intercessors between gods and mere mortals.[50] The gods transformed the devotee: they sanctioned the blending of the sacred and the irreligious worlds, the present and next, and used magic to empower the ordinary world. The West African cosmos embraced the extraordinary or religious via the ordinary to give a sacred, imaginative hue to daily events. West African traditions, slavery, and transplanted European Christianity helped forge the new Christian religion of the African diaspora.[51] Within this new Black religion, the Black church grew as an agency of social control and justice; the Black preacher was a catalyst for change; Jesus was a refuge and means of liberation; and song held them all together.

Messages through music have been a part of Black creativity, living, and coping since long before the first Africans set foot in this country. Music has always been a venue of empowerment, release, and response. The Spirituals during the antebellum era and the 1960s Movement delivered messages to the oppressed ("Freedom, your God-given right, is possible") and to the oppressor ("God says, 'Let my people go!' "). And the Spirituals proved to be dynamic vehicles of protest during both time periods. The 1960s antiracist, proequality, and projustice battles originated in slave narratives. These battles also grew out of early protest literature and sermons of persons like Jarena Lee and Sojourner Truth; the intellectual thought of Booker T. Washington, W. E. B. Du Bois, and Anna Julia Cooper; in the antilynching journalism of Ida Wells-Barnett; the pan-Africanist work of Marcus Garvey; and the social protest and organization of A. Philip Randolph.[52] The 1954 Supreme Court decision in *Brown v. Board of Education of Topeka*[53] hurled the United States into a modern sociohistorical revolution, struck the death knell to legalized Jim Crow, and led to an exorcism of institutional racism.[54] Clearly, the music was not an isolated, nonrelated event nor the source of sheer entertainment. The music is one way we can go back in time, just as we did with slavery, to reflect on the mid- to late twentieth century and see and expose racism for the evil it is.

Racism: The Arrogance and Pathos of Power

Racism is a use of power wherein the "haves" dominate the "others" and, thus, the oppressed, the oppressor, and society are denied the gift of wholeness. Such disruption, resulting in tension and dialectic, is evil and distorts divinely created goodness and relationships. Some view racism as a problem of the distribution of power; others view racism as a function or system of belief. Racism is evil, a form of historical, idolatrous faith institutionalized as slavery.[55] Racism, like other sins, is idolatry because it questions God's creation and offers a substitute god of biology or nature as the one to be honored and worshipped. This faith system establishes a set of beliefs, meaning, and values. Racism devalues life according to what it deems superior and inferior in its hierarchy of what is good. This evil illumines the insidious and pervasive attitude that shapes both personal theology, or sense of God, and personal ethics, the belief about how one ought to behave and the related actions or morals based on one's sense of what is good within secular and sacred society. To base faith and behavior on the alleged inferiority of other individuals because their skin color and related culture are different is evil, presumptuous, and blasphemous. Dominance, based on a personal theology and ethics, becomes the source of energy and the ultimate concern, and it reduces the import of humanity amid creation.[56] We have maintained and continue to maintain racism in the United States because we have the sustaining and teaching forces of myths (the way we talk about and experience reality in related stories) and rituals (daily patterns of behavior that are accepted as the norm, the etiquette).

Racism is an empowered state of consciousness wherein one group rationalizes its domination of another based on real or alleged genetic and/ or ancestral trait differences. Informal and formal social systems legislate policies that interpret these traits, ideologies, or mental postures, and attitudes. These social systems also shape dominance as they assert notions of purity in terms of its internal logic, and intensity in terms of the consciousness of being dominant.[57] Racism and dominance take a toll upon both Black and White communities. Racism, as a concrete result of historical attempts by Whites to critically answer how individual and societal existence can be saved in the light of what they discern as a threat to meaning, becomes a demonic attack that destroys human dignity. Ironically, racism claims to save essential life and speaks of wholeness, release, and healing, but overlooks distortion, possession, and disease.[58] Further, the irony for the Black community and the White South is that through a frightening and impressive network of cultural, social, economic, political, and educational patterns and policies, "the black person has traditionally been 'made into a nigger.' Then having accomplished the desired goal, the product is judged as having been this way all along and innately so. The black person 'as a nigger' then becomes essential to the white world."[59]

Stories about symbols and the way a racist society does things influence the way the people in that society think and interpret their reality. Rituals give a sense of purpose and honor and teach all of us to observe differences between groups and to set groups apart. These stories (some fact, some folkloric that people nonetheless give credence to) give meaning and shape to the world, and the related rituals or social practices make these belief systems sacred.[60] Under the Jim Crow system, the myths said Blacks were inferior to Whites in every way. The rituals of Blacks stepping off the sidewalk to allow Whites to pass and never looking White persons in the eye when speaking to them instilled in Blacks and Whites, and thus made true, the idea of Black subservience and inferiority. This ritual was sacred for American civil religion, as Blacks dared not disobey under threat of penalty for their "sin." These White supremacist myths helped Black and White participants and spectators manipulate their realities, particularly what became acceptable protocol, and the rituals reinforced these lessons.[61] These stories were not passed off as insignificant, but many of them created reverberations felt today; case in point, *Birth of a Nation*.

Older racist myths, like the infamous Thomas Dixon book *The Clansman* and the D. W. Griffith movie *Birth of a Nation*, which spawned the resurgence of the Ku Klux Klan in the early 1900s, and present myths about African Americans, like those touted in the offensive, pseudoscientific *Bell Curve*,[62] use science and religion to claim that Blacks have genetic inferiority and limited capacity for intellectual development; abnormal personalities from heredity or cultural disadvantage; lower moral standards; disproportionate criminal tendencies; greater likelihood for disease; and odd personality traits.[63] Racist stories and legends that claim Blacks are satisfied with their "inferior" status and that they have distorted natures and temperament have often been sanctioned scientifically, based on observed racial, anatomical, and physiological differences. Scientific and scriptural authority endorsed segregation as God-given and as best for controlling Blacks. Rituals and ceremonies like racially induced lynchings, Jim Crow, and legal segregation commemorated these racist, exclusionary practices and rehearsed stories of Black inferiority. Other racist practices included the separate but (un)equal doctrine promulgated by state legislatures and the Supreme Court in *Plessy v. Ferguson*[64] and customs that denied human dignity. These rituals took on a life, then a "truth," of their own, and ultimately maintained the status quo and excessive control of the dominant White population and the minority status of Blacks. Such control causes resentment and prejudice. Bare prejudice often emerges from a broad-based fear that the minority threatens or will threaten the advantaged place of the dominant group. Many dominant group members ideologically champion racism, hoping to shield personal prejudice, which is perceived as immoral, from scrutiny by means of a pseudo-objectivity.[65] Many leaders of Afrosensitive groups work to debunk stereotypes and recorded history and to reflect the true, the real. They seek to persuade the dominant class that African Americans deserve equal treatment with dignity. The debunking process confronts the arrogance and pathos of racism head-on. Others, like Richard Herrnstein, Charles Murray, and Dinesh D'Souza, seek to debunk the debunking process.

Racism has not been debunked and is alive and well in the 1990s. Racism is not a plague or an incurable genetic anomaly, but a social, historical product involving the interaction of politics, culture, and class. People are not born feeling threatened or espousing negativity, hate, or dominance; they must be taught. During slavery and today, White and Black children play together until schooling commences. The teaching and implementation of racism have allowed racism to outlive its child, slavery, and to grow stronger and take on a life of its own. In many areas, racism is so ingrained that the dismantling of it would require a complete overhaul of institutions, businesses, and practices. Racism, with its cultural, psychological, and intellectual roots of prejudice, is a complex phenomenon, formed, fixed, and fed by power—power exacted through force and intimidation; power fueled by a vision of slaves allegedly too barbaric and degraded to be freed.[66] Northern and southern racism thrive on a base of social power. Social power directs individual and communal life; involves choice, status, privilege, and hierarchy; and ranges from pseudo to coercive power that creates, sustains, or prevents observable social change. Power dynamics vary according to the health of the perceiver and may prevent or determine change.[67] Power steeped in illusion, manipulation, and conflict supports arrogance.

Antebellum racial arrogance endorsed antislavery but avoided abolition, and regarded interracial marriages with horror but ignored coerced intercourse of female slaves and slave owners. The offspring of these matings inherited the slave status of the female, not the master status of the slave owner. Racial arrogance saw colonialization (i.e., returning slaves to Africa) as the only solution to the race problem. Contemporary arrogance denies that American racism currently exists, despite the oppression in our "slaveless" republic. Racism, a preoccupation of the American mind, has so distorted Whites' vision that many cannot relate to Blacks as responsible humans.[68] A Gale Sayers can be a running back but is not qualified to lead the team as quarterback. A Willie Mays can play for the Brooklyn Dodgers but cannot manage the Los Angeles Dodgers. Countless Blacks who excel in everyday life and extraordinarily in the sciences, politics, business, and arts are seen as the exception instead of the norm. Racism, normative in contemporary U.S. society, is an old issue, one that evolved over time from a lifestyle to a strong belief system involving social, historical, and psychological forces and ideas. The arrogance of White racism against Black humanity resulted primarily from greed, selfishness, and the quest for privilege. Slavery ceased because the growth of racial slavery became incompatible with the push toward a unified nation-state shaped by a liberal, republican base. Racism and racist arrogance continued, along with their opposite, pathos.

Pathos, an experience that evokes pity, compassion, or sorrow, in the context of racism is a reaction to gross injustice and victimization. Racism, a pathological will to power,[69] distorts personality and impairs the psychological effectiveness of people who have been persistently rejected. Such bigotry warps the ego of both victim and victimizer, especially when human beings with power are unwilling to share that power. The conflicts between power, on the one hand, and love, kindness, and reason, on the other hand, show the sheer pathos of power and betray the dilemma of dealing with one's self.[70] The pathos of the ego finds that no amount of power can disguise one's essential inner powerlessness. Human pathos voices the 1960s anguished cries of Black power extremists and the racial cruelties and extremism of White supremacists as both groups attempted to fill or obscure the void within. The mysterious power and forces which come together in human consciousness dictate that being human means more than the incredible, finite mystery of life. People must affirm both humanity and the purpose and sacredness of human life in spite of human evil and injustice. This is the dynamic and saving pathos of power.[71]

One example of the destruction caused by human absurdity that provoked a pathos of racist power was Jim Crow. The Jim Crow era was a social and historical period of legalized segregation from about 1877 to 1954.[72] This institutionalized racism began with the withdrawal of federal troops from the occupied South and the abandonment of Blacks to racist southern Democrats. The nation left the adjudication of the visible problem of racism among segregated churches, public schools, and military services to the southern Democrats. This gave the Republicans the Presidency in 1876 despite a minority of the votes. Then too, the country was tired of paying for the military occupation of the southern states, especially in the face of a hostile Supreme Court. The South returned to extreme racism after three philosophies of race relations failed near the end of the nineteenth century: northern liberalism, southern conservatism, and southern radicalism. Ultimately, the segregation and discrimination that became custom and law led to Jim Crow laws that paralleled the massive papering of the South with "Colored" or "White Only" signs.[73]

Blacks have tended to respond to White racism in five types of African-American race-consciousness or social metaphysics.[74] The conventional integrationist claims, if you want to join them, be like them. The power-seeking nationalist is reactionary (if you cannot join them, vanquish them) and pragmatic (if you cannot join them, protect and depend on yourself). The Spiritual separatist believes, if you cannot join (or be like) them, join (or be like) your own group. The militant says, if you cannot defeat them, destroy their world. The ambivalent appeaser takes the attitude that if you can't join either group, keep it to yourself.[75] Some would argue that the primary goal of an African American is to love self, appreciate personal magnificence and communal Black heritage, and celebrate different cultures. Despite racial tensions, ideally one can relate interracially by relying on the many psychological attitudes and exploring the many phases of self without having to "be like them," "destroy them," or isolate oneself. Yet the punitive reality of racism in society often exacts a price because of those in society who see Blacks as the undesirable other, except concerning the issue of economic gain (e.g., superstar athletes and entertainers). Thus, dealing with racism involves the arrogance and pathos of the internal and external "Black" and "White" self. In addressing the arrogance and transcending the pathos of racism, African Americans have responded by using the Spirituals as documents of power. These songs were needed to help Blacks deal with two deadly, pervasive, destructive layers of American racism: the blatant southern version and the subtle northern variety.

The White southern view of social symbols and meanings and of Black people's ontology has not altered significantly. Racism is not dead but alive and thriving. Many factors within the southern socioeconomic and psychological demeanor nurtured the retention of old southern values, even while the southern system experienced disruption during the post–Civil War Reconstruction era in the form of defeat and fear, limited resources, a sense of threatened lifestyle, confusion about the immediate course of action, and the northern retreat from interest in the reconstruction.[76] At a time when the nation's attitude about racism could have shifted, too many factors stood in the way. The post-Reconstruction, Jim Crow, strict segregation of the races was not simply an expanded version of the antebellum system.[77] Although segregation was based upon old proslavery arguments, segregation could not have existed during slavery. Circumstances leading to segregation did not exist, because slavery required lives shared between the races. The adoption of extreme racism occurred because the forces that opposed legalized slavery were gone. The same "fear, jealousy, proscription, hatred, and fanaticism that had long been present" became dominant because of a "general weakening and discrediting of the numerous forces that had hitherto kept them in check"; these included "Northern liberal opinion in the press, the courts, and the government," and the "internal checks imposed by the prestige and influence of the Southern conservatives, as well as by the idealism and zeal of the Southern radicals."[78]

All the conflicts and sociopolitical movements, from the emancipation and Reconstruction to conflicting White attitudes and the need to keep

African Americans out of the White world, together forged the world of Jim Crow. Unfortunately, Populism, which could have galvanized poorer and lower-middle-class Whites with Blacks in the South, did not stand a chance. Intense "Negrophobia" and extreme racism existed in the class of Whites interested in Populism.[79] Racism was too imbedded. Like a cancer, this malignancy grew and spread, and was particularly potent at the beginning of the 1960s Civil Rights Movement.

The birth and then resurgence of the Ku Klux Klan meant a reign of terror of White mob violence, of lynchings that sometimes ended with Blacks being burned at the stake, and of gross efforts of intimidation and discrimination that were heightened and intensified, especially after war efforts when Black soldiers had warm receptions overseas. In White eyes, those kinds of affirmations would make Blacks in America think that they had a right to liberty and the pursuit of happiness to the east of the Pacific and the west of the Atlantic. With the election of President Rutherford B. Hayes in 1876, Republicans agreed to end Reconstruction in the South in return for twenty-two disputed southern electoral votes. While the Republican party, especially the radical Republican wing, was nominally dedicated to the continued emancipation of Blacks, Democrats were more interested in restoring home rule to the southern states and getting rid of rule by scalawags and carpetbaggers. The reduction of troops in the South after the Civil War left Blacks to their own resources, which were virtually nil, and was an opportunity for more oppression. In addition, Black voters were largely disenfranchised and driven from political activity in the South once Reconstruction ended. A major setback occurred when the Supreme Court invalidated the 1875 Civil Rights Act in 1883. There the court ruled that segregated public accommodations were constitutional by saying that a statute barring discrimination in transportation was unconstitutional. The southern-dominated Supreme Court continued to be the enemy of African Americans with these rulings and continued with the infamous *Plessy v. Ferguson,* which alleged separate but equal. President Woodrow Wilson, close friends with Thomas Dixon, author of *The Clansman* and other racist, propagandistic books, in 1914 resegregated a federal civil service that had been integrated. Racial stereotypes that denigrated Blacks became intricately woven into American culture because of the fallout from the *Birth of a Nation* motion picture, released with President Wilson's personal endorsement; and mimicry and negativity developed from minstrelsy and caricatures used in advertising. Communications media in the North and the South justified southern oppression and caricatured Blacks as inferior and morally depraved. What media—from magazines and newspapers to artistic advertisements and cartoons—did not accomplish, playwrights, scientists (through social Darwinism), and other writers did. Thus, American racism, particularly in the South, evolved toward the southern vision of sanity and permanency which held certain marks of the demonic: "fanatical assertiveness and an attempt to encompass the whole of reality in its dogma, thereby excluding other voices which challenged, or even appeared to challenge, its ultimacy."[80] Slavery, an institutionalized, legalized, and legitimatized racism, is a historical pathology. This pathology, based on past, present, and future events from a historical consciousness, teaches that evils like racism and national debasement spring from the lethargy and ambition of the rich, the wise, and the strong—not the poor.[81] The racism of the 1960s showed that America was not a good history student.

Racism emerges amid idolatry, the quest for dominance and power, social circumstances, and expressed fears of economic competition. White supremacist activists used these fears to sustain political power by appealing to the unhappiness and hopelessness of blue-collar and lower-middle-class Whites. Within systemic racism, people have little regard for the well-being of the human spirit and do not want to change or live in a transformed society. The reality that prejudice is a sin and racism is social oppression does not alter the stance of those anchored on the side of racist neuroses. Ultimately, racism, like other cultural pathologies, destroys the entire body politic, despite some personal and systemic changes.[82] This kind of destruction that surrounds racism and ethnic consciousness is inundated with issues of power.

Ethnic-racial consciousness, the awareness and attitudes that shape human behavior and social relationships, involves dominance and self-esteem, which wear the faces of denied and mutilated freedom.[83] The fight for freedom interlaces the moral, judicial, and legal fabric of America. The struggle for internal freedom, the other side of racism, is a personal dilemma of self-esteem. Many Black civil rights activists pursue political, social, and economic freedom; others evade the duties of personal freedom and rationalize their fears of increased social and political freedom.[84]

Notions of freedom shape one's notion of race. The social import of racial identity derives from personal judgment, not from natural laws; natural laws give human beings racial identity, not survival tactics. Most racial attitudes and behaviors reflect the idolatrous aspects of institutionalized American civil religion,[85] aspects that combine malevolence and racist injustices with supporting racist sacramental faith and rituals. American civil religion is constituted by those American religious, nationalist, cultural experiences and institutions that people prescribe as religious entities, and exists concurrently with other established religious bodies in the United States. These entities have their gods, prophets, martyrs, sacred events and places, myths, rituals, and symbols, and they regulate power through the gods of the presidency, political parties, and the Supreme Court; the prophets of sociocultural, journalistic, and economic forecasters; the martyrs for justice and of global wars; the sacred events of oaths to office and legislative sessions; the sacred places of national monuments, libraries, museums; sociocultural, historical, and frontier myths, patriotic rituals, and symbols; and local, state, and federal laws and governing bodies. American civil religion includes racist and nonracist persons, places, and events.

From the 1940s through the 1960s, Senator Strom Thurmond of South Carolina, Governor Orval Faubus of Arkansas, Governor George Wallace of Alabama, and Governor Ross Barnett of Mississippi served as false gods. Martin Luther King, Jr., Malcolm X, and John Doar, head of the Civil Rights Division of the Justice Department, were prophetic voices. Viola Liuzzo, Emmett Till, Andrew Goodman, James Chaney, Michael Schwerner, Medgar Evers, and the four little girls who died in the 1964 bombing of the Sixteenth Street Baptist Church in Birmingham—Denise McNair, Addie Mae Collins, Carol Robinson, and Cynthia Wesley—were the martyrs. The sacred events included the Little Rock High School integration, the Montgomery bus boycott, the march from Selma to Montgomery, the March on Washington, and the passage of the 1960, 1964, and 1965 civil rights legislation. The Lincoln Memorial, the Sixteenth Street Baptist Church in Birmingham, and the countless unnamed churches that housed civil rights mass meetings were the sacred places. Two contradictory myths permeated this civil religion: (1) integration promised freedom for Black folk and threatened freedom for White folk; and (2) separate but equal was fair and just for both races. The rituals included defiance at the school doors of Little Rock and the University of Mississippi, broad-based voter registration, and the first sit-in at the Woolworth in Greensboro, North Carolina. Two symbols of the civil religious experience of the 1960s involved respect, or the lack thereof, for the American flag, and a voter registration card. Consequently, American civil religion espouses a faith, has philosophical tenets, and inherently claims that American society is in accord with God's will—a society to be held up as a paradigmatic people to all nations, led by "divinely anointed leaders."[86]

Before the Civil War, slavery apologists rejected the tenets of the Declaration of Independence, Jeffersonian democracy, and Reformation religion as they envisioned a South governed by divine right combined with medieval chivalry.[87] By extending their Christian religious heritage to the secular, they cloaked the malevolent interests and ugly passions of slavery and racism in ethical decadence. Thus, the American "nation under God" is a peculiar rapprochement or reconciliation between church and society that burdens both church and society and leads to "Spiritual and cultural schizophrenia."[88] America is the only nation founded on a creed (the Declaration of Independence) that deals with justice issues and condemns anarchism, and that, by inference, is hostile to atheism. Ironically, a country that claims separation and barriers between church and state, which in many instances do occur, is a religious entity fraught with a paranoid schizophrenia that creates racist laws and mores. American civil religion espouses and sees racism as one transcendent ritual of societal strength and unity.

During the 1960s, American civil religion produced a mind-set in many Americans that America was the elect, with a universal destiny to use power for virtuous service;[89] some also subscribed to a meaning and destiny of racist behaviors that demanded loyal approval. Racism fostered inferiority, then justified liturgical exclusion, mistreatment, and genocide, deeming the Black segment of society less than human. Eliminating these subhuman stains upon normal society became a beneficial value as the Ku Klux Klan and other clandestine, racist individuals and groups persecuted or murdered countless Blacks with a sense of righteousness. As a vessel of redemption and manifest destiny, America has coupled religious activity with a civil nation. This liberal, racist commonwealth has produced a riddle which "mocks our cultural pretensions, enervates our national purpose and challenges the moral commitments implicit in our claim to be a nation under God."[90] American civil religion and racism reflect the complex, paradoxical juxtaposition of Whites and non-Whites within American society. These tensions infuse the language of the Spirituals.

The call for freedom now frees the oppressed and the oppressor from a paranoid schizophrenic existence and allows for an appreciation, rather than a fear, of differences. Both Black and White Americans have paid for the corruption of and devastation to human dignity resulting from racist civil religion. The ban on interracial marriages, the assessment of poll taxes, and the historically segregated churches in many states made Blackness a malady and Whiteness a gift. Society has romanticized these racist rituals and myths of American civil religion in art and literature, sanctified them by convention, and justified them by the doctrine of White peoples' responsibility for Black uplift.[91]

American religious culture appears to be the bastard child of the union of the Enlightenment and evangelical Protestantism, for slavery snuffed out the Enlightenment before it really took root, and America never recovered.[92] Slavery coexisted with the Christian religious revival among African Americans, and the confused, historical shifts in both civil and sacred religious practices informed the birth of and inherent messages about evil, suffering, and hope within the Spirituals. Throughout the evolution of American civil and sacred religions, exiled Africans saw the faith story of Spirituals as a mode of protest and praise. Spirituals, opposed to racist mythology, create another level of reality.

African Americans use the Spirituals to praise God, to protest in faith, and to seek civil freedom from structural malevolence. Singing the Spirituals allows Blacks to express a sense of community and to demand respect, justice, human freedom, and dignity. The blurred lines between church and state, and the friction between applied federal and states rights frame the sacred and the secular within the Spirituals. The Spirituals are one within the sacred and the secular without contradiction across the church-state dichotomy, amid the God of the Hebrew Bible (Old Testament) and the New Testament, the gods of other religious faiths, and the American secular gods of intelligence, science, and technology.[93] The 1960s Spirituals called for action within a sacred and secular union.

In confronting evil, 1960s freedom fighters rebelled and survived. They used spirituals to confront the complexities they experienced, and sang these songs hoping to inspire society to transcend color toward a universal experience of mutuality. The creative and sometimes deadly tensions present in society and in the Spirituals show that appearances may skew reality by either protecting or exposing evil and by engaging victimization and the quest for truth. The Spirituals were simultaneously religious and secular coping tools aimed toward social and political well-being and legal equality. The freedom fighters lived with the daily societal evil of racism under God, enduring suffering while calling for freedom, justice, and equality. The freedom fighters had neither time nor the inclination for philosophical abstractions about theodicy. Their experience of evil and suffering related to believing that God was on their side, that God cared; and they embraced justice for all, specifically the experience of "Freedom now!" The quest or experience of freedom permeated the redacted or edited Spirituals even though the constitutional compact "We the people" did not include persons of African descent.[94] Singing the Spirituals as freedom songs, moved to void the theory and reality that the White man in the United States would always know that he was superior to people of color, whose "servitude" mirrored the whiteness, freedom, and limitless options that were accessible to White men.[95]

Uniting African-American history with a modern freedom struggle, the freedom songs connected parts of the Black community when other communication forms failed. The traditional and redacted Spirituals inspired many people to fight injustice. Spirituals embodied persuasive ideological elements that celebrated humanity, and created a framework wherein the oppressed and the oppressor could begin to support each other's total human actualization. In calling for actualization, or the fulfillment of human potential and equality, Spirituals exposed past injustices and foreshadowed modern racism. People sang Spirituals during the events of 1954-55: *Brown v. Board of Education*, the Montgomery bus boycott, and the murder of Emmett Till. Singing of the Spirituals served as a badge of honor and a flag of defiance when the 101st Airborne troops monitored the halls at Central High for the safety of the Little Rock Nine. From Albany to Birmingham, Greensboro, and Raleigh, freedom fighters sang freedom songs during the sit-ins and boycotts, the passing of civil rights legislation and the Interstate Commerce Commission desegregation rulings (1957-62). During the March on Washington (1963), thousands of witnesses to the great proclamations for peace, justice, and freedom sang. During the Mississippi Freedom Summer led by members of the Mississippi Freedom Democratic Party, even on the floor of the Democratic Convention at Atlantic City people sang the Spirituals (1964).[96]

Spirituals buoyed these freedom fighters amid horror and degradation. Countless named and nameless persons sang and died for freedom before and after the brutal deaths of Till, Goodman, Schwerner, and Chaney. Unnamed persons sang, praising God. They sang, asking, "How long must we suffer?" They sang to protest, they sang to cope; they sang as a way to heal. In response to institutionalized racism and its idolatrous faith of the seventeenth through the nineteenth centuries, Black slaves begat the Spirituals. In response to twentieth-century racism, their descendants sang as they recounted their experiences, moving others to be sympathetic to their oppression and to all oppression in narrative or musical texts and in society.[97] Singing these freedom songs exposed the paradox of a racist society in a quasi-civil theocracy (a state or government ruled by or subject to religious authority). By using these "chants of collective exorcism," these Spirituals enabled the 1960s civil rights campaigns to move forward. They adopted the Spirituals as psychological and spiritual mechanisms to combat the illegitimate child of slavery: institutional and societal racism.

Spirituals attest the facts of God's benevolent justice, the African-American oppressed, the European oppressor, and the use of power in the United States. In the Spirituals, God is central to the African-American experience and thus inherent to an inquiry into slavery and racism that identifies the polarities of power: the pathological power that annihilates and the ambiguous power of the victim to survive and transcend. An Afrosensitive view of the Spirituals affirms an oratory or rhetoric of resistance that asserts power from the underside and places the African American at the center of his or her existence, functioning as a flight to sanity.[98] The slave experience embraces Afrocentricity to explain how Black human chattel endured and avenged their oppression and scapegoating, and how they knew empowerment through song.[99] Freedom fighters used the Spirituals as freedom songs to spark inspiration, hope, free speech, and affirmation. The more they sang, the more social reality changed. Even the jailers' physical threats could not stop the singing. James Farmer noted, "What they're trying to do is take your soul away. . . . [They] took the mattresses away and people sang as they had never sung before. We thought we were winning the battle, they [the victimizers] were on the run" from their own evil acts.[100] Spirituals so infiltrated the atmosphere in 1964 that Lyndon Johnson, a southern president, ended his personal appearance before Congress seeking successful passage of omnibus civil rights legislation with the triumphant words of "We Shall Overcome." Much was overcome, and much remains the same. Yet the haunting melodies and the powerful words of the freedom songs made it an undeniable fact that the United States had a bad heart condition, a condition of racism, at the very core of the Union's being. The songs enabled the protesters to be persecuted but to never turn back. The songs reminded America that pretending racism did not exist would not make it go away. On the six o'clock news all across America, the drama of singing freedom songs and protesting, over against the judicial resistance of heavy-duty fire hoses and police dogs attacking children, women, and men, left indelible marks of truth telling: "Whether White, Black, Brown, Red, or Yellow, racism is wrong, and we are not going to turn back, or let this country live the lie any longer."

3

Theodicy in White and Black

Are you listening?
Folks pryin';
Others lyin'
Too many dyin'!

Pain catapulted
Beyond belief.
No relief.
Too much deceit.

Church? State?
You? Me?
What's up?
Freedom, where are you?

Overview: Theodicy in White (Classical)

Theodicy is an issue for those believers who accept the existence of God and who must reconcile the existence of a benevolent, unlimited, powerful God (and therefore justice) with the co-existence of evil. Questions of evil and suffering for the nonbeliever are a matter of reality, life cycle, indeterminate chaos or destiny. In the Spirituals, theodicy exposes injustice, calls for accountability, relies on hope, and frequently poses one outcome of theodicy, freedom, a cherished concept for Black folk. Theodicy and the Spirituals go hand in hand because of the origins of the Spirituals, the number of enslaved persons, the number of persons who are victims of racism, sexism, and classism, and the amount of violence that exists in our society today. By the time the rationale for selecting Blacks as the best material for slavery was an issue of race, and the laws that stripped Blacks of all rights were in full swing, the Black population had grown from 20 in 1619 to 4 million in 1860. By 1960, the African-American population was 18,871,831 (10 percent).[1] In the 1990s, the Black population is 12 percent. We need the hope embodied in the Spirituals, because of the suffering and evil that have occurred and continue to occur among all people. Along with the war casualties across the years, we have daily wars in the streets and homes of America. According to recent statistics recorded by the Children's Defense Fund, for all U.S. children, every day in America: 1 mother dies in childbirth; 3 people under 25 die from HIV; 6 children and youths commit suicide; 16 children and youths are killed by firearms; 37 children and youths die from accidents; 92 babies die; 342 children are arrested for violent crimes; 2,444 babies are born to mothers who are not high school graduates; 6,042 children are arrested; 10,829 babies are born; every school day: 3,356 high school students drop out; 13,076 public school students are suspended.[2] All this pain, suffering, injustice: where will it end? How can we address and change this abomination? Scottish philosopher and historian David Hume expressed the question accordingly: "Is God willing to prevent evil, but not able? Then God is impotent. Is God able to prevent evil, but not willing? Then God is malevolent. Is God both willing and able to prevent evil? Then why is there any evil in the world?"[3]

This chapter surveys classical theodicy concepts employed by selected Eurocentric and Afrocentric theologians who wrestle with questions about relationships between God, good and evil, humanity, and creation. Traditionally, scholars discuss the contradiction posed by the coexistence of evil and justice by questioning God's existence using theories of nonbeing, despotism, dualism, and moral theory, both rational and mysterious.[4] A theory of nonbeing suggests that only one principle of ultimate being or power exits; therefore, the universe is a harmonious unity, and evil is only possible or imaginary and cannot exist. Despotism theory, the rule by an absolute, tyrannical power, distances God, claims evil does not exist, and, like the nonbeing theory, sees evil as a theological mystery. Dualism makes evil coequal with a benevolent God. Moral theory places human limitations upon God's power and places "God in a box" by restricting God's power to the smallness of human imagination. Nonbeing, dualism, and despotism negate the historical problem of evil, are contrary to Judaism and Christianity, claim that God is powerless, or discount God's freedom and God's power.

The logical argument explores the consistency of claims about the divine and about evil. The question concerning evidence deals with the amount and/or kinds of evil, claiming God could not exist if this much evil does, and making God's reality unlikely. The cognitive theocentrism argument assumes the existence of God and makes evil abstract, a theory. Ironically, many philosophers ponder the question of evil without seeing the contradiction involved in using race and reason to defend racial inferiority and to deprive African Americans of their humanity.[5] The "unanswered question" argument develops when believers need sound reason or logic to be able to justify why God allows evil to exist; they abandon the question "why" while believing God has a morally, sufficiently good reason for permitting evil.

Ironically, most theologians and religious scholars who ponder the question of evil fail to accommodate the problem presented by the historical conundrum that "the teachings of a Palestinian pacifist, Jesus, turned into a religion supportive of white supremacy and racial discrimination."[6] Despite this paradox, some theologians use thought and faith language to construct theodicies in three categories: remembering (retrospective), future (prospective), and revolutionary (disruptive). These theories, which deal with creative powers and future time, are mind games that fail miserably in the face of pain and suffering. Modern scientific data and innocent suffering require a sounder theodicy. Theodicy must express hope and confidence that in spite of human resistance and cosmic disruption, goodness and righteousness will overcome embittered life. Among other issues, the theodicist seeks to create a positive explanation for reconciling God and evil. In attempting such a reconciliation, it seems that most Anglo-American analytic philosophers tend to build a theodicy based on either Irenaeus's progressive human perfection theory or Augustine's free will defense.[7]

Irenaeus (c. 130-c. 200), Bishop of Lyon, builds his theodicy by highlighting the difference between the "image" and the "likeness" of God in human beings, and the Trinity, which expresses the gradual spiritual growth or progression of humanity, of soul making. He argues that God is an involved Creator, and Jesus is both fully divine and fully human in the Incarnation, which is the ultimate connection of God's activity with humanity in Jesus Christ. The *imago* represents the human being as a thinking, physical creature with the ability to fellowship with his or her Creator. The likeness of God in humanity represents the ultimate perfecting (moving toward holiness, wholeness, completion) of humanity by the Holy Spirit.[8] The Holy Spirit perfects and makes one in the "image" and "likeness" of God. Without perfection, one has the *imago* (moral freedom and responsibility) of God, but not the likeness (reflecting the Creator's essence). People are born immature and unsuited for receiving the highest divine gifts; thus, even if God had created human beings with perfection, they could not have received, contained, or retained that perfection. God can do all things, but people (the created order) must be inferior to God, because that order was created by God. God was not created, God has always existed. Irenaeus views God as compassionate and sees Adam and Eve's childlike act or sin as a result of their imperfections, their vulnerability, and their frailty. Yet God's revelation in history and the need for human response in faith assure human freedom. In works and faith, God places the will and control of human freedom with human beings. God's Son, Jesus Christ, experiences childhood so that humanity may receive the Son.[9] God the Father plans everything, the Son creates, the Spirit nourishes and increases created order, and people progress daily toward perfection, toward the Creator. With growth come strength, abundance, recovery from sin, and glorification with a beatific vision, or seeing the Lord. The growth process involves knowing and valuing the contrast between good and evil. In order to know what evil is (and its opposite, good), evil must exist in the world. Irenaeus states that if one cannot know both, one is stripped of one's human element.[10] Irenaeus argues for soul making and the spiritual and moral development of immature creatures shaped by divinely appointed good and evil toward God's perfection and good purpose.

Augustine of Hippo (354-430), an African bishop, follower of Plato, and fourth-century church leader, insisted that human freedom exists entrapped in sin, and answers theodicy based on a flawed free will. He developed a system of faith which views God's sovereign activity through the lenses of election and predestination, two Christian doctrines that claim God foreknows and ordains, from all eternity, who will and therefore who will not be saved. The saved and the damned coexist with the mystery of God's will. Augustine claims that God is good and sovereign and that everything God created is good. Evil, as pain and suffering, exists as a result of the Fall (Genesis 3). Augustine claims God must have permitted evil for some good reason, and justifies this idea with the notion of predestination. He defines evil as the lack, loss, or deprivation of good, which tends toward a void or an emptiness. The existence of the world requires general and specific forms of imperfect existence. In the long run, evil or particular imperfections will exist in a dependent, created universe. The whole universe includes contrasting good (light or beauty) and evil (dark or ugly) together, which may work together for the beauty of the whole. Augustine claims that although God knows everything before it happens, God's knowledge does not hinder human freedom. The right movement of human will requires the power of grace. God is innocent because God created everything good; thus, the nature of evil is the direct or indirect wrong choice made by free beings as they turn from the greatest good, God, to any lesser good. To turn from God is evil, is sin. The origin or source of sin is in the mystery of finite freedom.[11] Augustine's theory, a free will argument based on a Fall doctrine with a corrupted humanity, has many problems, including the obstacle of an impersonal God and logical and systematic problems too numerous to approach here.

Some scholars have tried to avoid the apparent contradiction between the existence of freedom and the need for grace by speaking of God's foreknowledge as outside of time and, therefore, unlike human foreknowledge, based on studied cause and effect. Scholars like Aquinas have used the Augustinian argument to posit another theodicy.

Thomas Aquinas (1225-1274), a Dominican and a medieval theologian, who championed and popularized Aristotle, wrestles with theodicy between the poles of good and evil. Aristotle claimed that all truth comes from God and asserted that humans can know God only via analogy. Aquinas views theodicy, via creation, as being balanced between good and evil in the context of grace and redemption. He argues that one cannot desire evil, the absence of good, because all desire must be directed toward the good. In short, evil can result only in good.[12] Problematically, his theory makes God responsible for the eternal evil of those who were created lacking the good, and has little to say to the perpetrator or the victim of evil and suffering.

Also following Augustine, John Calvin (1509-1564), a French Protestant reformation theologian, developed his doctrinal system about God's providence, salvation, scripture, the church, and Christ in the context of a theocratic state. In other words, Calvin designed the government of Geneva based on early church governmental form. Calvinist theodicy grows out of his doctrines of the Fall and predestination. God created human beings as immortal, righteous, obedient souls. But the Fall shifted humanity from perfection to deprivation and disgrace, even though God decides, prior to birth, whether a person will have eternal damnation or eternal life. Nevertheless, Calvin says that having a will, even a predetermined will, is having free, responsible will. His predestination doctrine, developed to show the wonder of divine grace, skews the place of an omni-God and reduces God's "infinite and irrevocable love" for all human beings to an elect in-group.[13]

From a different perspective, the Irenaean type of deferred theodicy emerges in the work of Friedrich Schleiermacher (1768-1834). Schleiermacher talks about theodicy in terms of Christian piety or an individual's religious consciousness, one's absolute dependence upon God. He suggests that all human experience can become aware of God and that finite people can become God's children and have eternal life. God's plan could be carried out and human beings could respond to God and share in the fulfilling of divine purpose. Sin occurs when people retard or diminish their God-consciousness, as a part of redemption, and relates to an awareness of guilt.[14] While sin is not inevitable, there is a curious alliance of individual responsibility and original sin. Through birth, each new person, apart from personal choice, becomes part of the common sinfulness and corruption that comes out of the endless wrong wills of individuals.[15] The guilt that arises from the corporate nature of sin requires universal redemption. Schleiermacher contends that evil—the distortions of sinful fear, anxiety, and sinful behavior—is an environmental affliction of humanity that obstructs human life. God does not inflict suffering upon humanity. Yet God is ultimately responsible for sin and suffering, since no difference exists between God causing evil and God permitting evil. However, Schleiermacher contends that humanity's creation distances humans from God and that sin occurs prior to receiving grace. With gradual perfection, sin is a measure of human development prior to full redemption. The first Adam had the potential for total God-consciousness; only the second Adam, Christ, has perfect God-consciousness. Christ's redeeming work draws all people into a community of God-consciousness with himself and creates a doctrine of the universal salvation of humanity, in contrast to the Augustinian and Calvinist doctrines of eternal damnation.[16]

In another light, Karl Barth (1886-1968) talks about theodicy in terms of *das Nichtige*, the reality and activity of evil, which mirrors the brokenness between Creator and creature.[17] Barth, a Swiss theologian and major sponsor of neo-orthodoxy—a new emphasis on "right teaching" of past Protestant reformers that critiqued religious liberalism and championed theology which explores the word of God—alludes to theodicy with the language of *das Nichtige*. *Das Nichtige*, often translated as nothingness, the null, the negative, and the nonexistent, embodies a hostile resistance to God and created order. This resistance can be abolished and overcome by the Cross. *Das Nichtige* is profound evil, "the shadowside," but is different from a negative aspect of the universe. The shadowside is irreconcilable spiritual evil, finitude, and imperfection.[18] Yet Jesus Christ reveals, discerns, and overcomes this evil. God's decision to make a good universe brought into existence one form of this evil: human sin, the enemy of God. Only the return of Jesus Christ will reveal the ultimate triumph over evil.[19] Barth's theodicy is problematic because he uses abstract philosophical language, requires that evil is part of the divine creation of the universe, and defers the triumph of good over evil to the end times, the final judgment. Yet Barth actually leaves the reader suspended. While he appears to say evil was a part of a good creation, he also denies both that evil was part of the divine will and that evil began as an independent need of created order. Barth warns that because evil ruptures created order, it cannot be understood as a creation of God, nor can it be reconciled with theory.[20]

Contemporary philosophers Alvin Plantinga and Eleanor Stump have also used the Augustinian perspective as a basis for doing theodicy. Alvin Plantinga (1932-) presents a free will defense, not a free will theodicy.[21] He claims that the omni-God's existence is true but not logically inconsistent with the evil in the world. God probably permits evil for some morally sufficient reason. Logically, God cannot create free creatures and guarantee that they will never do evil. God did a good thing in creating free creatures as morally responsible agents, not robots or androids, without assuring that they will not do evil. Human beings were created with the ability to choose to act for good or for evil. Plantinga's free will defense agrees with those lines of Christianity which believe that human response to God is not determined by God, but it is incompatible with those who hold God's power as absolute, such as Augustine, Aquinas, Luther, and Calvin.[22] Eleanor Stump (1947-) explores theodicy as she restates the idea of human beings having free will to claim that having and exercising free will are necessary for union with God and are critical for humans' salvation from their own evil. Thus, exercising free will outweighs all worldly evil. She uses her idea of free will and the "Fall doctrine" as the basis for a Christian solution to the problem of evil.[23] She says that the problem of evil requires repairing the defective human free will; that the value of a flawed will produces union with God, the ultimate good, and justifies God permitting such necessary, valuable evils; and that moral and natural evils are the keys to recognizing inner, personal evil and cause one to turn to God in repentance and salvation, toward union with God. She claims that doing the ultimate good, which is available only through suffering, justifies suffering and the evil which hastens that suffering. She argues that although evil is not the only means of obtaining ultimate good, evil may be the best and most effective tool. But this contradicts her own sense of necessary evil. Though Stump admits her theory is an oxymoron and not provable, she still uses it to demonstrate that the good always outweighs evil without telling the victim that God permits suffering for a basic abstract good.[24] Problematically, no amount of evil can assure that an individual will seek God's generous aid. Her argument that repentance and salvation require evil is morally bankrupt, especially her claim that every evil produces the sufferer's salvation. Stump implies that the bad things that persons experience actually result in their personal salvation! She builds her theodicy on free will theory, but it more closely resembles the Irenaean "soul-making" theory.

Contemporary philosopher John Hick (1922-) also chooses the Irenaean path of theodicy. Hick uses a Christian awareness of God in Christ, Christian stories about the Christ, and Christian theology as a well-organized presentation about a Christian experience of God to explore theodicy. Hick's soul-making theodicy puts evil at the center, where God shapes souls that grow into perfect relationship with God. Human beings are created gradually in God's image. Created spiritually and morally immature, human beings are granted the possibility of personal relationship, character development, and divine fellowship, whereby they eventually assume God's likeness as they move toward perfection toward eternal life, under the Holy Spirit. That God wants to move people toward being like Christ justifies the tough soul-making process and means that evil is necessary for the development of the traits required for soul making: fortitude, compassion, and courage. Hick's theodicy expects the results of and the answers to the mystery of evil in the future, which depend on seeing moral evil and suffering in relation to God's will, revealed in Christ Jesus.[25] Moral evil or human sin is ego or self-centeredness, deep-seated disorientation, and broken, destructive relationships, the opposite of God-centeredness. Sin is due to human freedom. The ultimate right relationship with God is in Jesus Christ. Broken relationships happen with an initial separation and independence from God (epistemic distance). God is hidden yet knowable in a way that invites God's presence, human response, and freedom. People manage their lives apart from God and remain free to accept God's grace and to come to God in love and faith.[26] God and the demonic exist but are not equal. In a society with moral beings and moral laws, people are responsible, but God is accountable for creation and for humanity living responsibly within the world. Hick realizes the randomness and senselessness of pain, misery, and suffering but does not explain them, and he values mystery as a vital aspect of soul making.[27]

Some scholars find soul making absurd, claiming that the theory is inadequate, wastes time, and makes a mistake by showing a God who is unworthy of love. For some, Hick's theory is about human responsibility, not divine responsibility for justice. Those who support Hick's theory agree with his view of divine and human responsibility, his eschatology, and his view of God's omnipotence, but they question the amount of evil and the evolution of spiritual consciousness and universal salvation, claiming that he actually develops an unlikely free will theodicy.[28] Hick claims his soul-making theodicy is successful and morally sound and justifies God permitting evil. But his work implies that the soul-making process is irresistible, and, by deferring the good, he questions divine and human Christian duty within a religion concerned with love, communal living, and freedom.

Kenneth Surin (1948-), a philosopher and theologian, criticizes the traditional way most scholars go about studying and analyzing evil and suffering. Surin argues that theodicists are unclear about their primary agenda and says no scholar should impose one standard, a "timeless reality," upon something that happens at a particular social, cultural, and historically conditioned time. Doing so frustrates any attempt to come up with a solid Christian reply to the problem of evil. To lump all the problems of evil in one category shows that people do not know what God is, but humans can talk about God in a sensible grammar in teaching salvation.[29] For example, before the Enlightenment, people did not see that the contradiction between an omni-God and existing evil was a basis for discarding their faith. During Augustine's time, Christianity became the Roman state religion, martyrdom ceased, and Augustine argued that conversion of the material world to the "City of God" would divinely transform human will and hence solve the problem of evil. During Irenaeus's lifetime, the early church tried to teach an apostolic faith despite the Gnostics, so Irenaeus claimed that the Incarnation solved the problem of evil caused by humans' arrogance, which distances them from God.[30] Surin respects past thinkers, but he appreciates historical and cultural contingencies. Because evil and suffering baffle the human mind, dealing with the problem of evil requires a mental dilemma, a crisis, that occurs when trauma makes one question earlier social and religious meanings. Such crises occur in the Christian's life when life stories of pain, failure, anguish, and oppression collide with the gathered Christian stories of a redemptive, triune God.[31] Surin reviews several theoretical approaches and objects to simplistic arguments. He challenges Hick's theodicy,[32] and he argues that no contrite belief or disbelief in an omni-God solves the problem of evil or answers Ivan Karamazov's challenge, in *The Brothers Karamazov*, about innocent suffering. Evil requires human response to sufferers, as humans live with the memory of suffering with inarticulate, heartfelt speech which opens itself to God's mystery.[33] Hearing in silence admits knowing that someone hurts so badly that that pain reflects the absence of healing and of the divine. One hears by siding with those who suffer through practice.

Surin probes a practical approach to theodicy which presents a saving God who crushes evil in its theology of the cross. Basically, the practical approach claims that the saving God is the historically incarnated God in creation.[34] While agreeing that everyone is at once victim, executioner, and spectator, Surin says solidarity with the victim will not overcome or change evil and oppression. He objects to linking the inner working of the Trinity with innocent suffering, and to a deferred transformation of human suffering, for the cross outweighs all human evil. The practical approach assumes the atonement of the Cross, and stands on the principle that God the Savior is God the Incarnate in divine creation. Surin argues that the solution to the problem of evil lies in taking suffering seriously in terms of an incarnated salvation. He says that the Christian who supports atonement does not need a theodicy, for God is available without being understandable. He stresses that the Christian answer to the problem of evil is in voicing the uncertain utterances of the reconciling action of the Christ event to speech. The theoretical approach asks, "Why, in general, does evil exist?" The practical approach asks, "Why is this distinct evil happening to me/us, by you/them, right here and now?"[35] Surin says there are times, like Auschwitz, when the "Why?" question can prompt only penance and conversion: for Auschwitz, theodicy has no answer. This dilemma requires a shift from salvation to a messianic praxis to relate to the space occupied by victims.

The answer can come only from within the circle of incarnational faith, *not* from universal evil; the ultimate bond of humanity with God via Jesus Christ yields the related atonement which probes the depth of human wickedness and the work of Christ. Only when people face their capacity for evil at the cross can the process of transformation toward salvific healing occur. First comes the experience of evil, then comes the theodicy, the discussion afterward. Therefore, Surin argues, the discussion cannot address the universal problem of evil in a way which provides us the means to justify God: not all stories include language that can or should be communicated (as in the primitive, incoherent sounds of Auschwitz).[36] Yes, society needs both the practical life stories and the scholar's theory to analyze and edit the stories. Praxis sustained by Christian faith commitments and theory can serve as a corrective. Unfortunately, Surin does not clearly articulate the process and particulars of his messianic praxis. In that sense, he fails, like those he critiques. In another vein, we need to form coalitions of messianic or another kind of trust that can never forget the reality of the most heinous suffering and our part in the malevolent affair.

We cannot speak rationally before the unspeakable. A Christian theodicy based on the truth of the Christ event, spoken by the Word of God, and given of the Holy Scripture either in silence or in a grammar of the cross and surrounded by an incarnational faith, are likely responses to objections raised by the protest atheist. Since Auschwitz, the words about how God interrupts human evil must include a hope that involves the conduct and practices of all who suffer, but must also remember the lie of those who pretend it did not happen and is not happening now. Both a sense of failure and the mystery of God and evil remind us that we live in and therefore must share in the word games that justify the acts and motives of sinners.

Theodicy and Black Theology

Much of Auschwitz, Rwanda, Burundi, and Bosnia-Herzegovina has been unspeakable. Many have stood by, sometimes with justification, other times with utter hopelessness, asking "What can I do?" in a way that says, "People have been killing each other for years; nothing will change," particularly in the many instances "when hope unborn ha[s] died."[37] These are practical evils for which, often, no songs of liberation have been sung. Such barbarism and inhumanity have only been met with silence. Conversely, the praxis of slavery and racism was often met with the utterances of song, of the Spirituals. As instruments of praxis, these "chants of collective exorcism" were sung by those trapped in the bowels of slavery and racism, as they voiced their existential pain. Those who sang knew a God who cared. Black folk had a lived theology and theodicy long before they were legally allowed to read, write, and attend school. Since the mid-twentieth century, Afrocentric theologians have looked to their experience of God, scripture, and life to help them articulate the lived theodicy of the people. Slavery and racism provided a practical experience of oppression. Many people have suffered throughout history, but the three-hundred-year history of suffering due to racism has had to be central to any U.S. writer talking about God and humanity. While some have ignored racism as if this problem were nonexistent or irrelevant, Black theologians have had to come to grips with this reality if they intended to write with integrity, rather than follow a more abstract, ideological model. They have needed to deal with the existential pain they, too, have experienced during their lives as Black folk, being the "wrong" color all the time, the color that sometimes sounded louder than any "joyful noise" could ever overcome. Accordingly, Black theologians, notably Howard Thurman, Martin Luther King, Jr., and James Cone, have explored thematic biblical liberation and community-based studies that include the Spirituals.

Howard Thurman (1900-1981), mystic, theologian, pastor, and ecumenist, proposed the idea of community, "the search for common ground," as a goal for all life, the basis for ethical reflection, and the essence of his theodicy: redemptive suffering.[38] True community concerns harmony, wholeness, and integration shaped by the individual, God, and the world. Creating community requires people being free internally and being responsible in life and to God. Freedom or liberty is an external privilege, option, or grant that society offers to an individual. For Thurman, an immanent and personal God creates all existence. God lives in everything, is over all human history and creation, and can only be understood as Presence. In God's love, life becomes an ordered system that creates harmony, wholeness, and integration. Thurman declares that evil obstructs his system of spiritual disciplines, especially prayer and suffering, which are necessary for achieving a common ground. Suffering concerns the personalized problem of evil and hostile activity toward God.[39] Evil, a positive and destructive principle, denies the good, is a part of personal experience, and represses community. Evil is part of life's cause and effect. In that sense, evil is present in the form of suffering, pain, or frustration; and natural, punitive, and moral evils are central to life and are a part of God's context. Thurman claims that all evil is redemptive, including the suffering of the innocent.[40] He argues that redemptive suffering, shaped by love, removes barriers like evil, while innocent suffering illumines the power and miracle of love for creating community. However, when you treat people as objects or as a means to accomplish an end, that act is evil. Racism, an example of sin against community, is social sin. Thurman sees theodicy as a question to help you determine what to do when something affects you privately for good or bad, and how to stop evil from destroying all meaning in human lives. In answer, Thurman states that you can do everything within your power to stop evil and to replace the evil with something good. You can replace evil with good by internalizing love and truth and then by working to perfect love and truth in society. One says "No!" to evil because the community's work is the Work of God.[41]

Thurman combines spirituality with the quest for justice, freedom, and a holistic, healthy life based on community interaction. Because he sees evil both as the cause of suffering and as always beneficial, Thurman assumes that when the opportunity arises, people will do something good to overcome evil. He sees suffering as a spiritual discipline that always brings one closer to God. His assumptions are puzzling when one looks at the evils perpetrated by individual humans such as the Hitlers, Stalins, and Eichmanns, the Jim Joneses, and the David Koreshes. The issues raised by the presence of evil humans within the good human community are critical, given Thurman's focus on community as an area where evil can be overcome. Both Thurman and Martin Luther King, Jr. focus on community as key to overcoming evil.

Martin Luther King, Jr. (1929-1968), minister, civil rights activist, apostle of nonviolence, and Nobel Peace Prize winner, begins his theological and ethical discussion, and thus his theodicy, with a search for "the beloved community," redemptive love and Black suffering at the cross. King saw nonviolent, direct action as the way to overcome racism, militarism, and poverty—the barriers to community on a domestic and an international level.[42] The beloved community, a Christian social and eschatological ideal, is a mutual, cooperative, and voluntary experience. King contends that the beloved community affirms solidarity and embraces relationships among people, God, and the world, for all people are ultimately good, created in God's image. Being created *imago Dei* makes all human beings free. Such freedom enables a person to weigh options, make decisions, and be responsible—the foundations for moral choice.[43] King saw the quest for the recognition of all human freedom and the sacredness of human personality, or self-respect, as the core of the 1960s Movement. Then, and in all situations of injustice, King claims that, morally, we must disobey unjust human rules, because oppressive forms like segregation break cosmic laws and violate democratic principles. The daily struggle of living a balanced life as spiritual beings, where the means of life do not surpass the ends, produces the likelihood of sin. Inclusive community, where being a neighbor overcomes religious, national, and racial boundaries, is the goal of life.[44] God, the rational, loving One who orchestrates purpose in history, sustains and creates life as a just God.

For King, one must pursue community in unity with God despite the barriers of sin and evil. One display of God's love and justice within society was the Movement, which challenged segregation.[45] Integration helps to fulfill the pluralistic and international scope of human society and requires moral commitment, but integration cannot be legislated. Desegregation affects only legal regulations of behavior in a state, a social and economic entity, that supports human society. How can integration best occur? King argues that God makes divine purposes known through the Christ event, and people acting as free, self-directed, and self-conscious participants cooperate intimately with God to create an integrated, pluralistic community.

The model and source for the beloved (integrated) community is Christ, and the cross symbolizes God's redemptive love. Human beings cannot create salvation because of sin and evil, but good ultimately triumphs over evil. King sees theodicy as God's limiting divine power to allow for human responsibility and freedom.[46] God does not cause evil, but permits evil to protect human freedom. Cooperation with God against evil is the way to overcome evil. King understood Black suffering under the cross as a model of redemptive suffering which brings new meaning into the history of civilization. People approach suffering by reacting in bitterness, by withdrawing, or by trying to transform suffering into creative energies. King not only claimed that human suffering could be redemptive, but also argued that since the most effective expression of Black redemptive suffering is nonviolence, the responsibility of African Americans is to love, forgive, and move to reconcile with other races.[47] Barriers to forming a beloved community are human sin (the struggle between human finitude and freedom) and internal ignorance, fear, and hate. People sin out of the need for recognition and attention. They want but cannot gain righteousness.

King focuses on the social expressions of sin, but an individual must also deal with the sin of acting against his or her personally chosen moral ideals. Moral sin produces economic injustice, racism, and war. Overcoming barriers of moral ignorance leads to inner harmony and world change. Ignorance or material sin is a sin against God's purposes and will, but commitment to the power of God helps one overcome internal barriers that create war, racism, and poverty.[48] Personal and social sin work hand in hand to cause injustice, oppression, and destruction. The key to overcoming these barriers requires the combined efforts of God and human beings through the actualization of love. King's beloved community is the model for life in all areas, from civil rights to world peace. *Agape*, ultimate love, allows one to be a good neighbor and to engage in forgiveness and reconciliation. The beloved community includes a loving, just God and a balanced life rooted in the love of one's neighbor, in self-respect, and in the power to choose, and signals possibility for transformation. Yet, where integration becomes the panacea for a just, equal society, King's theory implies that segregation by choice is always inadequate. King's Christ-centered view of the beloved community would make it difficult to create the beloved community in the United States because of the many non-Christians who desire the good but who could not in good faith subscribe to a theory based solely on Jesus Christ. Those who believe in an omni-God might also develop an idea of a limiting God.

While King focuses on a beloved community, Cone champions Black power. James Cone (1938-), systematic and Black liberationist theologian,[49] was the first scholar to present a broad, organized theological interpretation of what Black power means to Black religious people, as he declares that Black power, as liberation, is Christ's central message, the message of theodicy, to twentieth-century America. Black power means the absolute freedom and release of Black people from White oppression by any means African Americans find necessary, from selective buying and boycotting to marching or rebellion. Black power means freedom now, Black self-determination, and choosing to die standing up rather than to live while kneeling.[50] Cone distinguishes between Black hatred and Black power. Black hatred is the African American's disgust with, and dislike of, Eurocentric society. Rather than accepting integration (i.e., a limited number of Blacks harmonized into White institutions on White terms), African Americans need a sense of self-worth about Blackness. Black power means hope and freedom for African Americans. The hope and affirmation of one's existence as a Black person with the ability to choose,[51] along with his idea of God's righteousness, the Holy Spirit, the gospel of Jesus Christ, and freedom, forge Cone's theodicy.

Cone's model for theodicy is liberation. Jesus, the center of Christianity, is a burden bearer, a liberator whose message is the message of Black power. Jesus, within the gospel of the oppressed, makes Christianity compatible with Black power. Both Christianity and Black power preach a message of freedom. Freedom occurs when a person sees the fulfillment of his or her being and can help make that vision a reality. Freedom in Christ and Black power imply that the oppressed direct Christ's liberating work toward themselves. In the process, Christ liberates the oppressed and the oppressor. This freedom comes with a price. Mature freedom creates burdens and risks, which Black power can help shoulder to help people live freely. With God's righteousness, God creates freedom, does justice, vindicates the poor, and loves and acts on behalf of humanity, but does not condone evil. God's love affirms Black people and moves them to confront the White neighbor. Justice tempers love to make human relationships meaningful and reconciles Black power with the loving gospel of Jesus Christ. Black power seeks to meet the needs of the oppressed in love as the work of the Holy Spirit, of God's spirit. Thus, Cone sees Black power as God's new activity in the United States. The task of Black theology moves toward creating a new comprehension of Black dignity among Black people and providing the necessary soul in Black people to dissolve White racism. This type of transformation assures that Black theology ultimately address Black suffering as a social, political, theological, functional, "this-worldly," living reality.[52]

Cone's theodicy of meaningful relationships with God and humanity, wherein both oppressed and oppressor experience transformation, empowerment, and true liberation, states that God does not condone evil. Unfortunately, he fails to name who is responsible for evil, though he seems to imply that those who oppress are responsible. Cone draws distinctions between Black hatred and Black power, and maintains that the alleged existence of racism by Blacks is merely a justification of oppression developed by Whites. One must recognize, however, that racism exists within the Black community and is directed toward those "more Black" in physical appearance, as well as toward Asians, Hispanics, and poor Whites. There are also those who argue that one cannot be racist without a power base. However, antagonisms spawned by perceived racial differences fuel racism, a topic beyond the realm of this book.

Other Black theologians build their theodicies by using models other than community or power and do not rely on the Spirituals. Joseph R. Washington builds his theodicy on the suffering servant in a context of religious mystical teaching about perfection and spiritual peace with a transcendent God, wherein African-American suffering occurs as an option for God to save the whole world, to heal all people, to set everyone free. His answer to the question of theodicy is that God did not create the scenario where Blacks are abused, but God chose to use it as a means to salvation for Blacks; thus, God's responsibility does not lie in the situation, but in the limitations of the situation.[53] In response, William Jones contends that Washington does not allow for God's sovereignty and freedom, which makes human beings codetermining actors of power.[54] Willie Wright concurs with Jones but suggests that because human beings do not know the mind of God, the question of why Blacks suffer is ultimately a mystery as yet unsolved.[55]

Thus, Washington gives a reason for Black suffering and, like Thurman, places suffering in a spiritual, mystical realm. At the same time, Washington seems to glorify suffering. Is suffering a requirement for healing? Does such a focus on suffering hint of masochism? What is the difference between responsibility in the situation versus responsibility in the limitations of the situation? Major Jones builds his theodicy on a reconciliation motif that relates to his idea of suffering with God via Black culture. He views God as inseparable, deep-rooted, natural, inward, and heavenly, otherworldly, and superior. People share in God's suffering in a godless world, and God inspires and empowers Blacks to overcome suffering with Christ as the model for resisting evil. Yet God cannot help relieve those who suffer because of a ruthless enemy;[56] Blacks have to face their oppressors with God's love. People are basically good and are to work together toward communal well-being; therefore, while bad choices cause suffering, the ability to choose can become separated from one's freedom. For Jones, freedom to choose is a product of God's grace when one follows Christ toward reconciliation. One answers the question of theodicy by becoming reconciled to God, which includes being reconciled to the world. Jones argues that God is responsible for people, but not for what people do. Racist evil produces suffering as a product of wrong decisions by Whites. With God as a persuasive, noncoercive force, Blacks and Whites have an opportunity to work the issues amid God's vast possibilities.[57]

Jones builds a theodicy that champions human freedom, especially the gift of choice that involves an opportunity for community building and working together on causing change and transformation. Yet his idea that God in Christ did not change society causes one to question the relevancy of Jesus' earthly ministry and thus of Christianity. In addition, what is the extent of God's power, and should one worship a God whose love cannot help overcome evil? These theodicies based on suffering servants and reconciliation amid the freedom to choose are as problematic as Thurman's and King's redemptive suffering and Cone's quest for liberation without naming the seat of oppression. Do the Spirituals enhance or clarify how Thurman, King, and Cone treat theodicy?

The Spirituals embody a sense of life enhancement and overcoming that reflects the African-American religious life experience like the existential plays of Samuel Beckett.[58] From the stance of theodicy, they also assume that God exists but ask whether God cares. In asking whether God cares, Thurman, King, and Cone look specifically to the Spirituals for answers.[59]

Howard Thurman's search for the common ground asked how people handle issues affecting themselves privately, and how they stop evil from destroying all meaning in human life. In answer, people do everything within their power to arrest the process and the results of evil and to replace evil with something good. For Thurman, the Spirituals chronicle the slaves' experience of suffering and their identity with Jesus, proposing a universal gift of liberation. Martin Luther King, Jr.'s search for the beloved community led him toward the question of theodicy as he claimed that God limits divine power to allow human freedom and human responsibility, and God permits evil to support human freedom. The Spirituals are metaphors for King's own vision and faith and allow him to view the dialectics of good and evil, optimism and pessimism, hope and apathy, and affirmation and pain. James Cone's critique of Black power supports a theodicy that champions immediate freedom, Black self-determination, and the right to choose. The Spirituals are confessional statements, tools of resistance, and theological stories that address human suffering, self-affirmation, and freedom. Cone argues that the Spirituals do not raise questions about God's existence or matters of theodicy. Unlike Cone, I find that the notions of power and freedom within the Spirituals inherently address the question of theodicy.

The Spirituals record Jesus' suffering and gift of liberation for Thurman; provide symbols of personal vision, faith, and the dialectical nature of the spiritual, physical, and ethical life for King; and provide documents of confession, resistance, and theology to address human salvation as power for Cone. *In practice*, these three theologians used the Spirituals to do theodic reflection. They studied the places of God, the oppressed, and the oppressor regarding societal responsibility for evil and suffering, toward complete liberation. Their use of the Spirituals and their messages of theodicy parallel the theodicy uncovered in the 1960s redacted Spirituals. As profound as their analyses were, Black male theologians (Thurman, King, Cone, Washington, and Jones) failed to listen to the voices of Black females. The Black woman's voice, activities, thoughts, and feelings about the evils of racism and slavery and about God had been omitted in contemporary theological and general scholarly reflection until the emergence of Womanist scholarship.[60] Kelly Delaine Brown Douglas, theologian and Episcopal priest, states that many Black female writers and scholars recognized that although male-centered Black theology laid the groundwork for new theologies, the limits of this male-centered Black theology meant it could not help Black women articulate and think through Black women and Black men's labors to "make do and do better."[61]

One possibility for dialog and for transcending, while appreciating maleness and femaleness and differences, lies in the Spirituals. As Martin Luther King, Jr. and Malcolm X eloquently voiced the African-American plight and desires in a nonviolent and violent dialogue,[62] African Americans, grassroots leaders, and communal groups sang: "They were on fire for freedom. There was a spirit there that no one could capture again . . . it was so powerful."[63]

> Cryin' in the wilderness
> Injustice, poverty, and hunger,
> Neglect midst rich and poor,
> Rapes, murders, thefts;
> Lies, deceits, scams.
> No self-esteem, dreams
> No hopes, death
> Cryin' in the wilderness
> Brings life.

PART II

INNOVATION

Inside the Spirituals

4

Story: R-e-v-o-l-u-t-i-o-n

Righteous indignation
Forged the Movement!
The Revolution!
Empowerment
Of the shunned:
Poor, female, male
Black, red, white,
yellow, and brown:
God created them,
The Spirituals,
The Revolution!

The slave narratives[1] and parallel stories[2] of the 1960s civil rights era show that African Americans individually and collectively have never accepted enforced societal subjugation. They always desired freedom, a just verdict upon their betrayers' behavior, and a strategy for gaining equality in the future, as soon as possible. The desire for freedom and the desire for justice are the fundamental themes underlying almost all Spirituals and Black intellectual thought. These desires and the themes of social, political, and religious activism provided a catalyst for nonviolent protest and illustrate theodicy as they deliberate about justice, evil, and suffering. Even though free from legally sanctioned slavery since 1865, up to the 1950s, Blacks were disenfranchised and remained legally excluded from public accommodations, equal education, skilled employment, and decent housing. For example, the success of the Legal Defense Committee (LDC) of the National Association for the Advancement of Colored People (NAACP) in *Brown v. Board of Education of Topeka* (1954) destroyed the "separate but equal" fiction for public schooling.[3] That triumph heightened Black self-esteem but illumined the contrast, again, between the facilities for Blacks and those for Whites. Massive resistance led to new outlooks on the traditional White-only public accommodations, culminating in the 1960s student sit-ins and the "civil rights revolution." During these acts of civil disobedience, freedom fighters used the Spirituals. This chapter explores the complex nature of the story within and behind the Spirituals. This story unearths a lifeline between the antebellum slave insurrections and the 1960s Civil Rights Movement that embraced this revolution and provides the basis for the emerging themes that form a theodicy, themes rooted in the storytelling in the Spirituals in the mother continent of Africa.

Roots, Wisdom, and Storytelling

African religious and musical traditions accompanied the slaves who were exported to the American colonies. An oppressed people recited their existence in the Spirituals and other African-American stories. This is central to African communication, particularly as these parables and anecdotes provide an inseparable encounter of the sacred and profane, "the sacred story, the mundane stories, and the temporal form of experience itself" in the beauty of song.[4] The Spirituals champion life and worship—empowering experiences for peoples exiled in North America as they lived out a theodicy, a life that sought to experience justice and right relations with God and neighbor, told and retold by sages in Africa, and later on these shores.

Sages, or wise folk, raised their voices in speech or song to call society to account for present actions by recalling past behaviors and events. The African griots (public singers, oral folk-historians, and village storytellers) presented collected remembrances and history as they recited events or stories, making the later Spirituals oral storytelling. With dramatic, dynamic performance style, the fluid narrative action comes alive as the speaker/singer reacts and adjusts to an audience and a setting.[5] The Spirituals merge, describe, and explain human experiences, including the human and the sacred story of meeting with God. These sacred stories orchestrate a sense of world and personal order.[6] The sages tell of an ordering within some religious narratives that are overflowing with double meanings or ambiguity. How does this ambiguity work? Is the story the means, the form, or the end, the actual event of human, religious encounter that tells us about the sacred?[7]

Stories, both means and ends, help us identify individual and communal voices. The narrative or story line of the Spirituals becomes the means and the end. The means help us know someone else's life experience. The end brings us to the moment and event of encounter. The Spirituals as narratives mirror the other's experiences in moments of hope and misery as liturgical expressions of "patristic" story: we come to know worshipful expressions created by the early fathers and mothers who gave birth to the Spirituals. These songs become liturgical in their ritualistic expressions of a religious and cultural experience. The stories in and surrounding the Spirituals help us identify them within the Christian tradition in an African-

American cultural setting, allowing us the gift of reflecting on the personal with the human and divine encounter from a perspective of social, cultural responsibility.[8]

Such story theology requires that we use reason, objectivity, and human ways of knowing, including attitudes, emotions, and cultural design, to examine the stories in both the words and music of the Spirituals. The combined communal languages, first of faith, then of theology,[9] provide insights as to personal confession and objective social analysis shaped by an understanding of who God is in the Spirituals. Such a broader mental posture that looks at the personal and social helps us to uncover the many layers of interpretation within the Spirituals. Within these living documents, we can identify the social dynamics and the cultural reality, and can take seriously the people, the places, and the nature of existence in the cultures that produced the Spirituals. This narrative-theological approach that analyzes the stories and the stories behind the stories invites cultural reconstruction toward human change[10] and embraces an African sacramental worldview. The dynamics of act and being through characters, motive, and plot become apparent, save logical argument without sacrificing inclusivity, and involve those who do not share an Afrocentric worldview in securing meaning. Combining Western scholarship with Afrosensitive sensibilities, attitudes, emotions, and cultural design of the Spirituals enhances overall understanding about theodicy. The Spirituals authenticate Black life and make valid Black personhood and culture; they help define Black people in the United States by bringing self-definition. These Spirituals know literary independence as they stand on their own as a particular cultural form, especially as they exude Black distinctiveness. These narratives also reflect the music and religion, the dynamics of survival and overcoming, that permeate all African life.[11]

Narratives or stories order, empower, teach, celebrate, and destroy by affirming or demeaning the human psyche through retelling stories of religious traditions in which people get a glimpse of the divine as they relate to God and others. These momentary glances help us to create our own identities and learn how to live together in community. We teach each other and mimic each other through hearing stories and repeating actions we have heard come alive in those stories. Sometimes in telling stories, the pathological story and the actual traumatic events stand in creative tension, and sometimes they repeat themselves. Whole cultures engage in repetitive, terrible plots of stories, based on distorted psychological and religious stories, that include anti-Semitism, sexism, classism, and racism.[12] The Spirituals challenge the repetitive, terrible plot of racism by first telling the story and then suggesting a new vision of the story.

The narrative or story is a text which unfolds and touches us through language. In the Spirituals, the language tells about the evil and suffering, describes the relationships between divine and human characters; questions or describes the related action/reaction; and champions the just and decries the unjust. The hearers/participants and the performers come to the text of the story with a prior history or preunderstanding that allows them to pose questions. To be meaningful, the text must somehow relate to the world of the hearer, so that he or she can understand or be empowered to know and experience, and then to interpret, the text. As a historical language event, as verbal action in time, the story in the Spirituals reveals the world, understanding, and interpreting of human beings together experiencing this music.[13] Both the creator and the reader/hearer of texts are aware of the historical events surrounding the musical event, come with their own past and present experiences, and will be singing and/or listening for their own particular reasons. As they participate in the singing of the Spirituals, the given text, then, reveals yet conceals through language and raises its own historical questions. The meaning, intentions, symbols, and inflections of the sung word, together with how the reader/listener "hears the text," have much to do with how each person sings, hears, and is moved by the words and music of the Spirituals.

African-American Spirituals are stories formed and rendered in song. They are chants of collective exorcism, aural, oral stories or narratives that recite and expose communal subjugation and hope for change. These chants celebrate the remembrance that everyone has a right to live, a gift of life, and, therefore, a light to shine and a story to tell, indicative in "This Little Light of Mine":

> *This little light of mine, I'm gonna let it shine*
> *This little light of mine, I'm gonna let it shine*
> *This little light of mine, I'm gonna let it shine*
> *Let it shine, let it shine, let it shine.*
>
> *Everywhere I go, I'm gonna let it shine*
> *All through the night, I'm gonna let it shine.*

Exploring the dialectic in the narrative, the tensions in the Spirituals' texts uncover these stories of coded communication, of theodicy, from an actual oppressed American social and historical context. "This Little Light of Mine" sends the messages "I have a light to shine, ordained by God," "You cannot diminish my light, no matter what you do to me," and "I will let my light shine, regardless" as the persons singing this song affirm their beingness, their own importance, without ever using words of self-esteem or personal pride, and without talking about the revolutionary power of one light amid vast darkness. Exploring the various inner textual tensions defines the African-American experience as a twoness of being, a picture that is both visible and hidden at the same time, expressed by W. E. B. Du Bois's metaphor of the veil.[14] The veil symbolizes an interpretative horizon where the twoness exists in tension, and reminds us to fight against the barriers and the paradox of the racial line that violate personhood. This paradox induced the makers of the Spirituals to mask the authentic message symbolically and metaphorically:

> We wear the mask that grins and lies
> It hides our cheeks and shades our eyes,—
> This debt we pay to human guile;
> With torn and bleeding hearts we smile,
> And mouth with myriad subtleties.
>
> Why should the world be overwise,
> In counting all our tears and sighs?
> Nay, let them only see us, while
> We wear the mask.
>
> We smile, but, O great Christ, our cries
> To thee from tortured souls arise.
> We sing, but oh, the clay is vile
> Beneath our feet, and long the mile;
> But let the world dream otherwise,
> We wear the mask.[15]

The mask symbolizes the inherent contradictions or paradoxes within a racist society. Evoking the mask in general, and the tragedy-comedy mask in particular, represents the apparent and the hidden, the tension vital to theodicy: a vitality wherein both a good God and evil exist, without a sense of dual, equal powers. Such a dialectic recounts the degradation of slavery, the subsequent disillusionment over the limited gains of the 1960s Movement, and frustration over global unrest,[16] particularly when many of the perpetrators of this chaos claim to be religious. The specifics of this twoness reflect the working together of written and oral stories and criticize societal violence or chaos. The stories let us observe the diminished self-esteem, the self-loathing, and an overwhelming desire to be (like) the other, to be assimilated, sometimes to Black children's denial of characteristics of their Black selves, nurtured by the alleged separate and equal educational systems during the 1960s. That same pathology recurs today, in 1990s settings, through "tracking" and sometimes in magnet schools. This dual system, on many levels, exists when people are displaced, stolen, or placed in exile in a foreign land, under duress. Such was the plight of the Hebrew children in Babylon, such was the plight of Africans in America; both groups God's children, both groups looking for deliverance.

Music in the Diaspora: The Spirituals, the Psalms, the Bible

In ancient Babylonian and in more recent North American exiles, music and religion were key as both periods flourished with oral and written creative activity. Like African griots who told stories and relayed religious messages, Hebrew prophets told stories and cried out for justice in Yahweh's name. Many of these prophets left written works, calling Israel to relationship with God, defying the status quo, and preaching of doom, preaching of hope, in prose and poetic form. For the slaves who became bards and psalmists, the Bible, the world, and personal experience provided the material for crafting songs. These songs serve as a living documentary on slave existence and ontology, on acting and being.[17] The Bible was God's Word, a source of comfort, and the slaves' authority. They took many liberties with its basic theological ideas and adapted these ideas to express their religious worldview and passion for freedom.[18] The singers talked "face-to-face" with Hebrew Bible or Old Testament heroes and heroines and their New Testament, co-suffering Jesus. The beautiful cadences of the King James Version of the Bible provided assurance, vivid imagery, thematic material, and, coupled with the slaves' personal life, the interpretative process that shaped the Spirituals' core message.[19] The vocabulary of themes in these messages was vast and powerful.

The spirituals addressed daily life along with the slaves' experiences of cultic or worship practice. In the African traditional religions, religion and relationship with God were not "Sunday-only" affairs but were germane to the acts of breathing and being. Closely tied to life was the ever-present possibility of death. Death included the cessation of life and the possibility yet improbability of immediate change, closely related to the invigoration or denial of freedom and hope: "Befo' I'd be a slave, I'll be buried in my grave." Even the ultimate destination of death did not mean life was morbid or hopeless. Part of the slave community's agenda was celebration of, or agony over, protest and change. As they agonized over what to do, slaves championed Black solidarity and Black heroes. These valiant persons reminded those in bondage that just as God delivered the Hebrew children, there was an exodus in store for them; that they would escape and know deliverance. Deliverance was not only the responsibility of the slave community, but was also related to their praise of God, to communion, and to their relationship with King Jesus, the mighty One, their conquering monarch. Their understanding of the divine and of their ethics and moral responsibility pushed them to explore and talk about judgment, heaven, and hell. A possible escape from their "hell on earth," of oppressive and brutal life as slaves, pressed them to reflect on the hope for manumission and African colonization, one option circulated by some as an alternative to Blacks living in America. The talk of getting to freedom land, to Canaan (which sometimes referred to Canada), included themes about the Civil War and about those determined to see that they remain in bondage, the slave patrols.[20] A mutual religious concern of survival, the hopes of exiled peoples, and the final triumph of spiritual forces over earthly events lived in the Spirituals and in certain Psalms, a collection of confessional poems, songs, and prayers performed by communities and individuals of ancient

Israel, fully expressing human emotions in dialogue with God.

In the Psalms, the focus is on the exile, not the slavery itself. The exiled peoples were more like transplanted villagers, and there is little evidence about the life of slavery in the Babylonian exile. For example, Psalm 137 is a psalm from the exile (after 587 B.C.E.) that talks about the needs of the relocated who remember and hope to return home, as they long to see Jerusalem. Psalm 137 reflects the sense that things will not be just immediately, and maintains hope over despair despite knowing that the exilic situation is long-term. The song holds to ultimate return and "homecoming to peace, justice, and freedom. . . . Such a hope must necessarily be visceral and unapologetic."[21]

Both the Psalms and the Spirituals are poetic pilgrimage songs of faith, of homecomings, of life-giving vitality. They express the religious creativity of exiled peoples, the stories of their suffering and of their longing for freedom and justice. Both canons, the bodies of the psalms and the Spirituals, evolved pseudonymously over time and share psychologies that related individuals, the community, and their God. The Hebraic concepts of God, corporate personality, language, and the wholeness of life are similar to traditional African thought. The Psalms, particularly hymns, usually begin and end with a community call to joyful worship. They celebrate and motivate others to praise God based upon God's great deeds in creation and history as they are remembered and reenacted liturgically, centered upon life and joy. Laments or supplications have a strong prophetic influence, where Israel realizes that suffering, even that provoked by sin, can positively help people return to God. While hymns and laments are either communal or individual songs, the voice of a singular sufferer expresses the faith and prayer of the community with confidence and thanksgiving. Israel only responds to what Yahweh does. Wisdom or didactic Psalms, of nonliturgical origin, mirror the piety of sophisticated scribes and counter with retribution for virtue and sin. Like the Psalms, Spirituals express a large spectrum of emotions and concern all phases of human life, individually and collectively: times of great blessing, times of duress, times of grave angst, times of peace, times of intimacy with God, times of incredible loneliness. The African-American "pilgrims of faith" have struggled through decades and generations of subjugation and prejudice.[22] They have prayed by identifying with a biblical vocabulary while wrestling with their own reality and pondering how to talk about God. The Spirituals parallel the Psalms as "pilgrimage songs of faith and poetic compositions."[23] In particular, some Spirituals resemble individual and community Psalms of lament.

Born in a crisis, the redacted and traditional Spirituals often have the same types of categories (typology) as lament Psalms: invocation, complaint, petition, and conclusion. In the Spirituals, the speaker addresses a prayer to God and describes the crisis that prompted the lament. He or she pleads for help and concludes with an expression of certainty that God hears prayer: "Jesus Is on the Main Line, Tell Him What You Want":

Jesus is on the main line, tell him what you want;
Jesus is on the main line, tell him what you want;
Jesus is on the main line, tell him what you want;
Call him up, call him up, tell him what you want.

If you need a little more love, just tell him what you want . . .
If you need a little more grace, just tell him what you want . . .
Traditional

Songs listed here as traditional are in the Black oral-aural tradition. These Spirituals are passed from generation to generation through musical singing and sharing in the church, the community, and the home. Sometimes the Spiritual closes with a word of trust that God will answer prayer, or with an act of praise and a related sense of overcoming through that praise: "I'm Gonna Sit at the Welcome Table"; "Lord, Hold My Hand While I Run This Race."

"I'm Gonna Sit at the Welcome Table"

I'm gonna sit at the welcome table,
I'm gonna sit at the welcome table one of these days, hallelujah,
I'm gonna sit at the welcome table,
Gonna sit at the welcome table one of these days.
I'm gonna walk the streets of glory . . .
I'm gonna tell God how you treat me . . .

I'm gonna get my civil rights . . .
I'm gonna sit at Woolworth's lunch counter. . .
Adapted by members of SNCC[24]

"Lord, Hold My Hand, While I Run This Race"

Lord, hold my hand, while I run this race;
Lord, hold my hand, while I run this race.
Lord, hold my hand, while I run this race,
'Cause I don't want to run this race in vain.
Lord, speak to me, while I run this race . . .
Lord, search my heart, while I run this race . . .
Traditional

Specifically, the Spirituals resembling the Psalms of lament often share the subtype of setting, like those concerning prayers of the physically or spiritually sick: "Balm in Gilead"; "Walk with Me, Lord":

"Balm in Gilead"

There is a balm in Gilead, to make the wounded whole,
There is a balm in Gilead, to heal the sin-sick soul.

Sometimes I feel discouraged, and think my work's in vain,
But then the Holy Spirit revives my soul again.

Don't ever feel discouraged, for Jesus is your friend,
And if you look for knowledge, he'll ne'er refuse to lend.
If you cannot preach like Peter, if you cannot pray like Paul,
You can tell the love of Jesus, and say he died for all.

Traditional

"Walk with Me, Lord"

Walk with me, Lord, now walk with me,
Walk with me, Lord, now walk with me,
While I'm on this tedious journey,
Lord, I want Jesus to walk with me.
You walked with my mother, now walk with me . . .
Hold my hand now, Lord, hold my hand . . .
Be my friend now, Lord, be my friend . . .
Guide my feet, O Lord, guide my feet . . .

Traditional

Other prayers include those of the innocent ("This Little Light of Mine"), pleas for peace or asylum ("Get on Board, Little Children"), and prayers of the oppressed to be delivered from injustice ("Go Tell It"):

"This Little Light of Mine"

This little light of mine, I'm gonna let it shine.
Oh, this little light of mine, I'm gonna let it shine.
This little light of mine, I'm gonna let it shine.
Let it shine, let it shine, let it shine.

We've got the light of freedom, we're gonna let it shine . . .
Deep down in the South, we're gonna let it shine . . .
Tell Chief Pritchett, we're gonna let it shine . . .
All in the jailhouse, we're gonna let it shine.

Redacted[25]

"Get on Board, Little Children"

Get on board, little children,
Get on board, little children,
Get on board, little children,
Dere's room for many a more.

De Gospel train's a comin',
I hear it jus' at han',
I hear de car wheels rumblin',
An rollin' thro' de lan'.

De fare is cheap and all can go,
De rich and poor are dere,
No second class aboard dis train,
No diff'rence in de fare.

Traditional

"Get on Board, Little Children"

Get on board, little children,
Get on board, little children,
Get on board, little children,
Let's fight for human rights.

I hear those mobs a howling
and coming 'round the square,
Hollerin', Catch those freedom fighters,
But we're gonna meet them there.

As fighters we're not running
for we are here to stay
Forget about Ross Barnett
the Lord will make a way.

As fighters we go hungry,
sometimes don't sleep or eat
We're gonna keep on fighting for freedom,
in the end we will be free.

Redacted[26]

"Go Tell It on the Mountain"

Go tell it on the mountain,
Over the hills and everywhere,

Go tell it on the mountain,
To let my people go.

Paul and Silas bound in jail,
Let my people go;
Had nobody for to go thy bail,
Let my people go [LMPG].

Paul and Silas began to shout, [LMPG]
Jail door opened and they walked out, [LMPG].

Who's that yonder dressed in red, [LMPG]
Must be the children Moses led, [LMPG].

Who's that yonder dressed in black, [LMPG]
Must be the hypocrites a turnin' back, [LMPG].

I had a little book he gave to me, [LMPG]
And every page fell spell victory, [LMPG].
Redacted[27]

Some prayers addressed persecution of racism ("I Been in the Storm"), and other general laments highlight concerns of life: "Ain't Gonna Let Nobody Turn Me 'Round" and "We Shall Not Be Moved." These songs either implicitly or explicitly focus on the enemies:

"I Been in the Storm"

I been in the storm, so long
I been in the storm, so long children
I been in the storm, so long
Lord, give a little time to pray.
Traditional

"Ain't Gonna Let Nobody Turn Me 'Round"

Ain't gonna let nobody, Lordy, turn me 'round
turn me 'round, turn me 'round,
Ain't gonna let nobody, Lordy, turn me 'round
Keep on a-walkin', Lord,
Keep on a-talkin', Lord,
marching up to freedom land.
Ain't gonna let Nervous Nelly turn me 'round . . .
Ain't gonna let Chief Pritchett . . .
Ain't gonna let segregation . . .
Redacted[28]

"We Shall Not Be Moved"

We shall not, we shall not be moved
We shall not, we shall not be moved
Just like a tree that's planted by the water,
We shall not be moved.

Traditional

As shaped by the community, these Spirituals, like the Psalms, usually speak of a hopeful future, freedom, self-determination, hope, and fulfillment. How a group shapes or uses and interprets a particular story has a lot to do with their ongoing life setting and their needs, hopes, desires.

Along with songs of certainty, concern, asylum, and injustice, other Spirituals relate to praise. With music "more ancient than the words, . . . the voice of exile,"[29] Spirituals engage in praise of God that testifies to God's gift of deliverance: "Done Made My Vow":

Done made my vow to the Lord, and I never will turn back,
I will go, I shall go, to see what the end will be.
Done opened my mouth to the Lord and I never will turn back,
I will go, I shall go, to see what the end will be.

Traditional

Spirituals describe God as worthy of praise. They begin with praise, tell a story about a crisis, and conclude with praise: "Sing Till the Power of the Lord Comes Down"; "We Are Climbin' Jacob's Ladder":

"Sing Till the Power of the Lord Comes Down"

I'm gonna sing till the power of the Lord comes down,
I'm gonna sing till the power of the Lord comes down,
Lift up your head, don't be afraid
I'm gonna sing till the power of the Lord comes down.

Traditional

"We Are Climbin' Jacob's Ladder"

We are climbin' Jacob's ladder,
We are climbin' Jacob's ladder,
We are climbin' Jacob's ladder,
Soldiers of the cross.
Ev'ry round goes higher, higher . . .
Soldiers of the cross.

Traditional

Other Spirituals relate to wisdom Psalms because they instruct. These Spirituals concern themes of blessing, warning, respect of God, and daily life, and they imply a contrast between the righteous and the wicked: "I've Been 'Buked"; "I Want Jesus to Walk with Me":

"I've Been 'Buked"

I've been 'buked and I've been scorned,
I've been 'buked and I've been scorned, children.
I've been 'buked and I've been scorned,
I've been talked about sho's you born.
Dere is trouble all over dis worl' . . .
Ain't gwine lay my 'ligion down . . . .

Traditional

"I Want Jesus to Walk with Me"

I want Jesus to walk with me;
I want Jesus to walk with me;
All along my pilgrim journey,
Lord, I want Jesus to walk with me;
In my trials, Lord, walk with me . . .
When I'm in trouble, Lord, walk with me . . .

Traditional

The Hebraic worldview provided immediacy between creators of Spirituals and creators of biblical texts, sowing intimacy between song and singer. Though the differences between Spirituals and Psalms concern cultural development, historical background, and modes of retaliation,[30] these Hebraic and African chanted narratives recreate and confront myths and rituals to give meaning to the singers' worlds and to understand and communicate differences in those worlds.

The telling and retelling of these stories occur in such a way "that it constitutes help in itself."[31] This storytelling helps a society recognize key themes and motifs that allow it to interpret its own symbols and actions. Telling stories or narratives brings us back in time so we can remember and recognize what has already happened, which then gives us a clue to help explain what is going on in the present. The Psalms and biblical stories helped and continue to help the enslaved experience their reality and engage issues of respect, justice, suffering, evil, hope, and possibility. The slave-chanted narratives or Spirituals helped the 1960s freedom fighters see their modern reality and inspired new ways of being.

The Spirituals, songs of revolution, are filled with symbolic and mystical elements of faith. The Spirituals embody the past and make it come alive in the present, with many levels of meaning for the creators'/singers' sense of themselves and history. Through the interrelation of history, language, and being, one experiences interpretation–the process of getting behind the text through critical analysis. By getting back to the historical consciousness of a Spiritual's composer, the past and the present form a tension to enable the text to reveal its sense of truth, through memory and imagination.[32] Memory helps one recall prior experience through association, while imagination helps one foresee something that does not yet exist. Memory and imagination together, coursing through the Spirituals as living texts, affect how listeners receive their stories of tradition and the credibility about their oppression, how these Spirituals functioned to sustain and uplift, and other day-to-day life issues. This process—the power of conflict between appearance and reality, and the idea of reality within conflict and contradiction—is within the Spirituals. How, then, do we go about pulling together the themes and dynamics of contradiction and conflict that make up theodicy within the Spirituals?

Theodicy in Story

We begin by understanding that these tensions exist in oral or written texts, and we listen for the cultural voices of the Black community. These voices do not need to be superimposed, but recognized for the fact that the stories coming out of the community expose structural features that afford the survival of oppression and encode meaning within form or style. As the cultural styles influence and shape the individual and social lives of their communities,[33] cultural forms like the Spirituals reflect back that which has meaning for the individual or community. Once we have laid the groundwork for seeing the larger picture of cultural and religious issues, we then look for the distinctive themes and structures (the forms, meanings, and metaphors) in African-American culture and religion. We look for the ideas or events that complement or clash with each other, particularly where habits, mores, and values of Black folk differ from those of the dominant oppressors. Part of this foundation work is to acknowledge the presence of African cultural heritage, not as a curious historical artifact but as a meaningful resource that shaped and continues to influence African-American religion.[34] This larger religious and cultural setting is absolutely essential in a society of dominant/subordinate groups, to reconstruct how people in bondage were able to use language and music to survive using apparent and hidden meanings under God. The Spirituals are able to do this: they express the desires of the victim and the distortions caused by the victimizer within a world created by God. Seeing the dialectical tensions within Black religion exposes the interaction between the oppressor and oppressed while acknowledging the idea that meaning can be found within cultural structures.[35] After creating the basis for analysis within the social, cultural, historical, and religious realms, the next move toward building the theodicy involves confronting the pain and suffering of racism and what happens to both the individual and society.

The pain and suffering that result from racism for Black self-conscious personhood are a pilgrimage that must combat the cost, the schizophrenia, of becoming victim of being a divided self—"two souls [or consciences], two thoughts, two unreconciled strivings."[36] How did slaves deal with White contempt yet survive within a White society? How did the freedom fighters confront the bombardment of African harmony with racist disharmony? What was the cost, given that slavery and racism dictate that African Americans have to deal with the projection of what a dominant culture says about them based on race? This is often an experience of being suspended between the Black and White races—it appears harmless, but its fabric is an impregnable wall, the cradle of misery.[37]

Being Black in a White world plays out in many ways. Some know and disavow their mixed racial heritage. Some are deemed Black if at least 1/32 African blood courses through their veins. Many are despised because of their Blackness, a reality often felt like a tragic cornerstone of living contradiction. That contradiction rejects, differentiates, and shuts off African Americans from their world.[38] During slavery and at the dawn of the twentieth century, Blacks were often murdered and starved, which gave them a sense of urgency, steeped in music, oral dialogue, to express their predicament in a Black aesthetic, in word and song.[39] But there was and remains semipermeable layers of difference between Black and White America. A theodicy from the Spirituals must deal with the relationships between the darker and the lighter races, with embracing the difference, and with the impact of different shadings of color within races (e.g., African Americans range in hues from blue-black to light brown to high yellow to milky white). Sometimes historically, and regrettably, even in the 1990s, lighter-skinned Blacks have fared better within and outside the Black race, while darker-skinned Blacks have often experienced discrimination from the inside.[40] Dealing with color is a question of freedom in the quest for justice; part of the cost of racism; and how individuals and groups deal with differences within society, and with their relationships with God. Those relationships of differences between divine and human involve the nature of power, relationships, and human identity. The desired theodicy will push us to name the racist-driven pain and then to observe the healing responses, the "I am-ness" of humanity, within the Spirituals—a challenge for everyone to listen well to appearances and reality. Reality includes recognizing victimization by "physical oppression, social ostracism, economic exclusion and personal hatred on the part of the White proletariat,"[41] conflict, and the quest for truth, both curse and gift. The societally-imposed curse is a boundary of bondage and an obstacle, a somewhat depressed personality and a moral hesitancy that destroy self-confidence and tear the soul apart. The tales of many Blacks, of many souls decimated by compounded racism, are stories particularly rife with pain and often not optimistic—stories of wasted lives, of silent hatred and distrust of any- and everything White, the tears, the anguish, the bitterness which wonders, "Why did God make me an outcast and a stranger in mine own house? The shades of the prison-house closed round about us all: . . . unscalable to the sons of night."[42] Timeless, yet limited by language and time, the Spirituals remain critical today. Their message of hope is necessary for Blacks who are often those last hired and first fired; those who make up a disproportionate number of the prison population; and those who become the statistics of homicides, both as perpetrators and as victims. Moving from the individual to the collective, to the contradictions in worldwide political economics that evolved into the evils of collective and class oppression, and to those in domestic racism, classism, and sexism, ironically marks the somewhat penetrable boundary between Blacks and Whites, the cultural distinctiveness of African Americans[43] that may also bring about a gift of life—part of this theodicy project.

The gift of life enables the celebration and transcendence of the differences between Black and White, a vision of reality, and the choice of protest over accommodation. The gift is the gift of story and song, of toil and the spirit.[44] The gift enables Blacks to derive beauty from their own culture. African Americans can be both Black and American and maintain racial integrity while freely associating with all Americans, participating broadly in American culture, and contributing to American freedom.[45] The price of the juxtaposition of Black and White, of racism, where Blackness must remain hidden, is the absence of power, not a weakness but a contradiction. A theodicy of the Spirituals must expose the cost of prolonged, institutionalized racism that negates Blackness as gift, marginalizes the Black community, and forces the African-American experience to remain hidden. Part of that hidden Black reality, captured in stories spoken, in those perceived by the ear, and in those committed to paper, encompasses the human struggle germane to a living theodicy: liberation and affirmation. Nevertheless, the sad truth is that the African American's attempt to "gain self-consciousness in a racist society will always be impaired by the fact that any reflected image that he or she seeks in the gaze of white Americans is refracted through the dark veil-mirror of existence."[46]

Blackness as gift champions spirituality and fights to transcend human rupture: discord, breakdown, trauma, and misunderstanding. While the reality of race defines relationships in areas from communication and demographics to intellectual dialogue and religious and ethical concerns, Blackness as gift is an opportunity for hope. Conversely, racist greed and hate mean skin tone hinders both Black and White and thwarts reconciliation. As part of the basis for building a theodicy, the gift of Blackness means we note how American industrial imperialism denied African and Native Americans democracy and American freedom through racism, fear, deceit, and ignorance through the antebellum era and the 1960s, causing a sick rupture and malignant pathology. At the same time, it is an opportunity to celebrate the potential for the communion and friendship of all persons and a special belief in African Americans, in race pride, and in total liberty.[47] Viewing Blackness as gift moves us toward truth telling about justice issues, about the treatment of persons, that inform the context and content of the Spirituals.

Truth telling about justice asks questions of mutuality and respect. Do the texts indicate that African Americans were treated as humans, or were they treated as objects, which violated the religious and intellectual heritage of Africans and Europeans? The questions of justice and mutuality require that we ask about African contributions to Western civilization and vocalize the issues of African personhood and culture silenced during slavery and beyond. What difference does it make that Blacks created a new dialectical religion—African-American Christianity—by adopting the words and ways, but not necessarily the theological interpretations, of their captors?[48] How did this hybrid Christianity, a product of many contradictory forces that provided openings for an emerging African-American rhetoric, become the bedrock of the powerful, eloquent usage of speech found in the Spirituals? How did this hybrid Christianity fuel the quest for African freedom that held African and Christian elements in creative tension?

The quest for justice and freedom asks questions about cultural bigotry within the African-American community, as projected back through the White community and against prevailing myth and stereotypes. Questions arise concerning the chaos that results from racism and the move to obliterate "the courage and faith and deeds of ten thousand thousand people."[49] Institutional racism covers up societal violence or chaos, the ambiguity, the positive and negative of this hidden life. The complex tensions, symbolized by the context and stories of the Spirituals, are a mystery and a paradox that involve the contradiction of coexisting distinction and identity.[50] "Who am I?" addresses being excluded because of being different and being included through participation, acting as both object and subject at the same time.[51] Asking questions about justice and about a call for mutuality and respect requires that we identify, name, unmask, and engage the contradiction, dichotomy, ambivalence, and mystery.[52] The contradictions and multilevels of the stories parallel the tensions and complex dimensions of theodicy (ranging from causality to chaos theory, which remain beyond the scope of this study),[53] realizing this exercise seeks to make visible that which the larger society has wanted to remain hidden, and wondering what is the cost:

I am an invisible man . . . a man of substance. . . . I am invisible, understand, simply because people refuse to see me. . . . It is as though I have been surrounded by mirrors of hard, distorting glass. When they approach me they see . . . everything and anything except me. . . .

That invisibility to which I refer occurs because of a peculiar disposition of the eyes of those with whom I come in contact. . . . You often doubt if you really exist. . . . You ache with the need to convince yourself that you do exist in the real world. . . . You curse and you swear to make them recognize you. And, alas, it's seldom successful.[54]

After exploring the culture, the many stories (including biblical referents, questions of difference, and questions of meaning, identity, form, and mystery), the pain of racism, the gift of Blackness, and the quest for justice and mutuality, we can then glimpse visions of theodicy. The Spirituals, as narrative representations of three gifts exiled Africans brought to this country—gifts of story and song, of sweat and brawn, and of the spirit[55]—are stories which echo hope as faith in ultimate justice. Race is an artificial barrier created by human beings because of the visible difference between the darker and lighter skins. Color is real, and cultural differences are real, but these facts do not imply that biological differences between the races either give credence to or support the myths, stereotypes, or any theory of inherent superiority of one race over another.

Sometimes even the Spirituals cannot relay the personal or societal cost or grace and triumph of being Black. During the 1920s and 1930s, to hedge this cost, many African Americans became card-carrying members of the American Communist Party, because the party was the only group speaking up for complete social and political equality. Yet if one can transcend the divided self, then personhood is no longer a dream historically deferred: such transcendence empowers an African American to be both African and American, as gift, without overwhelming contradiction. That gift also can produce morbidity and wrench the soul or spawn hypocrisy, revolt, or radicalism. Is the theodicy of slavery the same as that of the 1960s in the Spirituals? Yes and no.

The Spirituals, from a perspective of theodicy, are always about naming evil and suffering, being hopeful for transformation, and doing what one can to effect that change, working in concert with a God who cares. The antebellum Spirituals involve songs for daily life about religion, food, kinships, work, transformation, empowerment, being responsible, and hoping for a new day. The Spirituals, whether sung in a traditional manner or redacted or edited during the 1960s, were intentionally about attaining civil rights, about securing the rights to vote and to have access to public accommodations and integrated facilities, from education through employment. The freedom singers intentionally named the evil and the evildoers; they named the places of suffering; they named their goals and how they intended to effect change. In this way, the theodicy in the 1960s stories is more blatant. In both instances, in both eras, the Spirituals are rich and must be experienced as performed living documents to really hear the message of theodicy. The hearing of and the living with these texts, embodying the pain and the victory surrounding these texts, moves us toward a cultural reconstruction of human transformation.[56] Only by experiencing the lived reality can we hope to glimpse how slaves and civil rights activists dealt with the evils of institutionalized racism, freedom, and God in the Spirituals. Only by experiencing these songs as living documents can we hope to know the power of Black southern cultural traditions and the tenacity of men and women like Sojourner Truth, who would rather shoot slaves than have them go back and reveal the Underground Railroad; can we begin to know these "songs as the language that focused the energy of the people who filled the streets and roads of the South" during the Civil Rights Movement;[57] and can we know what it means to be willing to die for freedom and justice measured not in dollars and cents or fame and fortune, but in the dignity of being human and being duly accorded such respect: a curious revolution, indeed.

To tap into these revolutionary issues, the following questions will serve as guideposts for working with the richness and complexities of the Spirituals. Freedom fighters sang hundreds of songs of actualization and protest during the 1960s Movement. The Spirituals embodied a self-expression and communication that indelibly marked the world. The analyses of representative Spirituals from the Civil War and civil rights eras reveal elements of this self-expression. My analysis names, unmasks, and engages the various elements of context, story, creative spirit, and faith and thought. This analysis recreates the generative context of the Spirituals, cultural artifacts containing theodicy, that relate to naming, unmasking, and engaging.[58] *Naming* (N) focuses on identification. *Unmasking* (U) relates to revelation. *Engaging* (E) deals with exploration and fusion toward transformation, ultimately a theomusicological statement about theodicy. These songs, taken from live recordings, make distinct statements about theodicy, as diverse performance styles enhance literary texts.

Context. This analysis asks questions concerning the usages of power and historical consciousness, along with myths and rituals:

(N) What is the thesis or main idea of the song?

(N) What event prompts or shapes the singing of each song, and what are the particular words of the song?

(N) What critical events occurred that specific year in the Movement?

(N) What issues of slavery and racism provide context for the song?

(N) What issues involve state versus federal government (i.e., American Civil Religion)?

(U) What is the interplay of the arrogance and pathos of power?

(U) What is the significance of viewing this history via Afrosensitivity?

(E) What are the issues of desire and tension?

(E) How were the Spirituals redacted to answer these questions?

Story. The ideas of Blackness amid dominant Whiteness, the color line, facilitate an examination of the slavery and racism which undergird the Spirituals, viewing the tensions or dialectic within the text:

(N) Given meaning and context, what is the message of the story?

(N) How do the meaning and structure of the text stand together?

(N) How does the oral tradition around the text frame African-American individual and social identity?

(U) How does the biblical story inform the dialectic?

(U) What is the spirit of Blackness in the specific setting?

(U) What are the issues of projection from the dominant Eurocentric society?

(U) What are the specifics of ambiguity?

(E) What are the means of transformation? How does the narrative order, empower, celebrate, or destroy the freedom quest of the 1960s Movement?

(E) When trying to achieve true self-consciousness, does the African American want to be the other or be like the other, and in what ways?

Creative Spirit. This analysis addresses style and performance techniques from an Afrosensitive perspective. The ensuing questions help unveil that experience for the music and lyrics for each song:

(N) What are the intent, basic opinions and the performance goals?

(N) What are the key literary, musical, and rhetorical factors?

(N) What is the embedded dream?

(U) What is the process of signifying and the import of intertextuality?

(U) What are the significant aspects of musicking in each song? How do the integrated lyrical and musical texts work together? How was the song used in the movement?

(E) What relationships lie within the many layers of meaning in the text?

(E) What rhetorical-musical questions do the combined texts raise?

The responses gained from this analysis provide insight that moves toward understanding the key faith-based thoughts of the Spirituals. This component builds on the other positions and moves toward making a statement about theodicy within Christian thought.

Faith and Thought. This process relies on normative, descriptive, and redactive queries:

(N) How does the song view the Godhead and humanity?

(N) What are the philosophical and historical concerns?

(N) What injustices does the song address? What version of justice undergirds the song?

(N) How does the song relate to freedom?

(N) What is the distinctive Afrosensitive theological perspective? What are the ethical issues?

(N) Is the concept of Blackness a physical (ontological) state of being or a metaphysical image?

(U) How does the traditional African heritage mold the song?

(U) What issue/device reflects evil or theodicy in the text and music?

(U) Do freedom songs remain liturgical?

(U) What are the similarities and dissimilarities between the traditional and redacted song versions?

(E) Does the music become therapy and thus soften the cost of racist, psychological abuse?

(E) Can this song teach anything about racism?

(E) What is the nature of a black theodicy in the Spirituals?

(E) What powers are named, unmasked, and engaged?

(E) Because Black women (Womanist) writers emphasize life within the community and Black men writers tend to focus on the conflict with outside forces across the veil, how does a Womanist critique temper double consciousness?

5

Creative Spirit

Feel the Fire:
The Spirit's Fire,
Holy Ghost, Life-giving Power,
Signifying reality,
Signifying tough,
Signifying bad!
Joyful noises,
Soulful melodies,
Blackness personified.

The Spirituals celebrate the lifeforce and power of African-American creativity, spirituality, and sacred overcoming. The pulses of the music replicate the heartbeats of the oppressed. The songs relay a connection between God Almighty and the souls of Black folk. Such musical power, using individual and communal participation, allowed an exiled people to survive, subvert, and in many ways surpass a patriarchal, racist system. Living and examining the music forged by that outrageous spirit to live when reality said to die, reveal the personal and communal truths and the contexts of combined sound and silence. The words and sounds, the effective and persuasive use of language and melody in the Spirituals, evoke a strong response, because music has a much richer vocabulary than words alone for conveying emotions.[1] Understanding this folk vocabulary, the creator (performer) and hearers (audience) become one voice. This oneness occurred with the antebellum community-based singing of the Spirituals and with the 1960s Civil Rights Movement singing in traditional Black American congregational or choral song style. The singing styles of both eras occurred without distance between performer and audience. Once a song leader initiated a song, the others joined in and helped "grow" the song towards its full potential.[2]

This chapter analyzes the words and the music of the Spirituals by (1) exploring the impact of their underlying Black aesthetic; the musical style and form of the Spirituals, from their African origins through the Black

Renaissance and Civil Rights eras; theomusicology, ethnomusicology, and musicking (the act of creating music which includes the elements of music, dimensions of musical form, instrumentation, and performance techniques) as tools that help us unpack the musical aspect of the Spirituals; and literary patterns and devices, like signifying, and the audience's/participants'/hearers' responses;[3] and (2) by then applying these tactics to the Spirituals sung during slavery and the 1960s, as we make clear the role of the Spirituals in the singers' work for justice.

Toward a Black Aesthetic

Black aesthetic analysis uses strands from folk and formal life experiences to define and identify ideal motivational aspects—freedom and literacy—of a politically based African-American life, based on Black spirituality and aesthetics.[4] Long before the 1960s cry of "Black is beautiful," the Spirituals embodied this beauty, for those folk who were otherwise silenced, objectified, or deemed ugly. Singing the Spirituals is a celebration of African social and cultural richness preserved within living, beautiful, artistic stories. Spirituals, as chants of collective exorcism, convey ancient music and utterances of exile, then and now. They are chants or music that includes dirges, invocations, hymns, praise songs, and psalms. They are collective, for these songs originated from mass or group singing. They exorcize, because they name and unmask the evil; the singing drives out the power of the oppression to harm one's soul. And the process of communal singing creates a bondedness and frees one from the total control of the dominant oppressor. Spirituals blend African, American, and African-American musics and elements as they name and expose the dilemma of the presence of good and evil in a less-than-perfect world to then create a new music, to effect healing. The activity of societal racist evil between Blacks and Whites under God in the struggle for freedom, the essence of the Spiritual, is a function of divine and human justice. In the Spirituals, justice is profound, beautiful. Music as art involves beauty, has depth, and makes a lasting impact. The Spirituals, as life giving art and music, are beautiful, soulful, and therapeutic, not merely entertaining.

The Spirituals are not music as entertainment, but embody a collective Black folk aesthetic, with Black traditions dating from about 1800, and White elements, that together utter a visceral word to spiritual, mental, emotional pleas and praises. Entertainment involves the aesthetic and the immediate but is less in-depth and less lasting than art. Since the Spirituals are a reinterpretation of American ideals through the prism of Black American experience,[5] Black slaves used the Spirituals to imitate life, to remake reality, and to know art as life.[6] This experience of true soul theology or self-consciousness, often cloaked in silence for the sake of survival, comes alive in the Spirituals as functional, useful art affording glimpses of true humanity. Slave bards produced more than six thousand still extant Spirituals despite the prohibition of slave education.[7] So many exist because there was so much to say, to share, in codes that those beyond the community were not privy to understand.

By using an active imagination and disrupting preconceived judgments, we can begin to discover the many levels of meaning within the Spirituals.[8] Such a Black aesthetic means we must shake loose faulty, preconceived ideas to unearth the "archaeology of knowledge," the questions that already exist, within the texts themselves.[9] Shaking loose the old helps us hear the new. Much of the information about the Spirituals occurs in dialogue when we listen well. An archaeology of knowledge within Black history helps us discover certain governing statements related to theological justice within the Spirituals,[10] which may include slogans, like "Freedom," "Eyes on the prize," "We shall overcome," and "Black power" of the 1960s Civil Rights Movement because they voice key sentiments that supported and shaped the Movement.

The quest for African-American freedom, democracy, and transformation depicts stories of justice and liberation that embody those governing statements. In pro-democracy and protest activities like the 1960s Movement, people sang liberation songs of hope and determination across time and space, decades and continents.[11] "Freedom" refers to justice and equality, an ability to make conscious choices and to act on those choices without coercive restraint. "Eyes on the prize" concerns an immediate eschatology—communal and personal intent to gain freedom now. "We shall overcome" ritualizes the struggle and victory of the Movement. "Black power" graphically evokes unity, community, and social and political sovereignty and esteem. These governing statements are categories of discovery—ways people find out about themselves and their community, particularly during crises grounded in historical reality.[12] These themes or statements describe some of the creative spirit which produced and color the Spirituals.

This creative spirit resonates in the beauty of justice, which includes human communion with God and God's creation, as well as divinely ordained human creativity and survival. The historical setting of slavery produced these chanted narratives from a substantial mythology, remembered story and belief systems, that encompasses patriarchy, economic paternalism, southern aristocracy, and northern ambivalence. These myths reflect the reciprocal influences of other institutions shared by language.[13] Language itself is a social institution. In the Spirituals, language, especially certain figures of speech, includes divine names and other major characters, metaphors, stimulus-response language, synonyms, and repetition. Blackness as an inner, organizing principle and a force of folk life, values, and beliefs shaped a Black urban vernacular or Black form of English language during the 1960s. Awareness of a Black aesthetic gives a broader perspective for analyzing the Movement's Spirituals whereby we can look for the meaning of America (and of dreams deferred); the concept and boundaries of race; the failure of Black power; and the relatedness of culture, consciousness, and society.[14] Part of the Black aesthetic, this integral beauty within the Spirituals involves playing with words, from repeating and revising words to using words in a humorous manner.

In the Spirituals, signifying means to repeat, revise, echo, mirror, or respond to words in many ways.[15] Signifying, part of the social and musical infrastructure of Black language systems, gets transmitted in the social rituals which surround family gatherings, barbershops or beauty parlors, and other gathering places as Blacks talk about talking. These word games are both distinctive and communal. Hearing the Spirituals requires an awareness of these word games, because people under oppression talk about life differently than those who are not, especially about the concern for freedom, justice, and the distribution of power, coded in the Spirituals: "I'm Gonna Sit at the Welcome Table":[16]

> *I'm gonna sit at the welcome table,*
> *I'm gonna sit at the welcome table one of these days, hallelujah,*
> *I'm gonna sit at the welcome table,*
> *I'm gonna sit at the welcome table, one of these days.*

> *I'm gonna be a registered voter,*
> *I'm gonna be a registered voter one of these days, hallelujah,*
> *I'm gonna be a registered voter,*
> *I'm gonna be a registered voter, one of these days.*

> *I'm gonna tell God on ol' Massey,*
> *I'm gonna tell God on ol' Massey one of these days, hallelujah,*
> *I'm gonna tell God on ol' Massey,*
> *I'm gonna tell God on ol' Massey, one of these days.*
> Traditional

To sing "I'm Gonna Sit at the Welcome Table" revises reality, because Black folk were not welcomed where Whites dominated in the racist society of the 1960s. Thus, the singers would make themselves welcome whether someone extended an invitation or not. "I'm Gonna Sit at the Welcome Table" mirrors what the singers want to happen; therefore, the ability to "sit at the welcome table" implies that they were telling the public, without telling them, that the singers would use public accommodations, would register to vote, and would tell God about anyone who had been abusing them. By singing a particular person's name, they told the world about that person's business. In other words, they put that person's business out in the street, just like Luther nailing his ninety-five theses on the door at Wittenberg, saying, "You are a racist! And we are not afraid of or intimidated by you. You may control our jobs, our housing, our ability to get loans from the bank, but you do not control our hearts, souls, and minds." By signifying in this matter, the singers empowered themselves and others to do what they said they would do.

Sometimes the texts of songs involve revisions, repetitions, shared elements and differences within a particular text, and they may or may not draw upon other texts. Black composers and writers hear, read, repeat, imitate, and revise each other's texts. This way of listening and imitating occurs in both the traditional and redacted Spirituals: "Free of the White person's gaze, Black people created their own unique vernacular structures and relished in the double play that these forms bear to White forms. Repetition and revision are fundamental to Black artistic forms."[17] For example, "This Little Light of Mine" has multiple meanings of signification.

John Lovell, Jr. claims that slaves believed that any bit of light can penetrate a great deal of darkness. Slaves would not let their lights "go out, die down, or be hidden. . . . If [they] had no other creative concept, this one alone would admit [them] to the ranks of respected poets."[18] Light refers to the soul as one aspires to do good. Light represents the life that God gives; as God's gift, light represents freedom. Shining one's light means breaking the shackles of any prejudicial and demeaning constraints of life, and represents a call to self-esteem and communal solidarity. Light answers the theodicy question with empowerment, taking responsibility for actualizing justice. The quandary of achieving justice in society demands attaining freedom while surviving injustice. Light overpowers evil imbedded in institutions, systems, and people. In this Spiritual, light has numerous functions: light glorifies the *imago Dei* within all humanity and commands a faith that scandalizes the disbelief of racism. Light effects healing midst humor, is courageous, champions mutuality, and shuns dysfunctionality. Light cancels the disruption of life by chaos and violence. Just as this Spiritual signifies about light, other Spirituals have particular themes or ideas that involve storytelling.

In the Spirituals, storytelling relays information that includes communication with God that is not exclusively on or about God. The Spirituals portray God as immanent and caring, not distant. Signifying makes clear that God is on the side of the oppressed, and encodes and names Black independence. The slaves spontaneously and communally composed, sang the stories related to God, and uttered sounds to apparently unmeaningful jargon that was actually full of meaning. Therefore, the Spirituals can imply a call for freedom and justice without using those exact words, as they surreptitiously call for right relations within society and with God amid evil and suffering, as they encode their self-preservation.[19] Signifying is part of that self-preservation.

Signifying is a process of revising stories, poems, songs, and figurative language as shared knowledge: the speaker or singer and hearers recognize that word play is going on, ignore the dictionary meanings of words, and sense a second, encoded, silent meaning.[20] The signifying and encoding in the Spirituals mask or hide the elements of justice, often to produce a humorous effect: "Truth . . . begot Common Sense. Common Sense begot Wit who married . . . Gaiety, by whom he had a son: Humour. Humour . . . derived a great deal from his mother, and whatever his state of soul, he never failed to make people laugh."[21] Humor and laughter critically generate anguish and constructively generate balance, victory, and relaxation. The intellectual phase is irony.[22] Irony opens the way to a religious view of humanity, which justifies and saves. "Humor bursts open the cocoon in the direction of life, of progress, of risk."[23]

> The Negroes, through their songs, were able to develop a vocabulary and means of expression that was entirely their own. This was done by sprinkling their melodies with symbols, images, and concepts borrowed from their African past and completely unknown to the whites. By developing this symbolism as a universal language among themselves, they were able to harbor and express thoughts that were not understandable to others. Their masters never realized this; instead they poked fun at the Negroes for using a jargon which apparently made little sense. The Negroes gladly endured this ridicule, knowing that by doing so they helped preserve a degree of intellectual freedom. Little did the whites realize, as they ridiculed the slaves for their "ignorance," that those slaves were enjoying the satisfaction which goes with a sense of superiority. Here, indeed, is a lesson in tolerance.[24]

Comedy or humor applied with faith among the victimized is therapeutic. Therapeutic humor portrays one type of African-American survival in an unjust environment. This attitude strengthens a holistic life, helps people defy their lot with passion and spirit, and ultimately helps one see any event, even parts of a painful reality, as light drama. Humor involves relationships and transcendence, creates respect between persons, symbolizes God's presence within humanity, and blooms amid love.[25]

Spirituals draw out humor in several ways. For example, humor is apparent in "He's Got the Whole World in His Hands," for this song ridicules the idea that "he," a white slave owner, is in control; God, not white slave owners, has ultimate power:

> *He's got the whole world in his hands,*
> *He's got the whole wide world in his hands,*
> *He's got the whole world in his hands,*
> *He's got the whole world in his hands.*

> *He's got the birds and the bees right in his hands,*
> *He's got the birds and the bees right in his hands,*
> *He's got the beast of the field right in his hands,*
> *He's got the whole world in his hands.*

He's got the woods and the waters in his hands,
He's got the woods and the waters in his hands,
He's got the sun and the moon right in his hands,
He's got the whole world in his hands.

He's got you and me right in his hands,
He's got you and me right in his hands,
He's got everybody in his hands.
He's got the whole world in his hands,
He's got the whole world in his hands.

Traditional

"Ezekiel Saw the Wheel" extends other distinct meanings to the wheel, which relates to the divine freedom to empower by grace, the human movement toward freedom, and the cost of human responsibility:

Ezekiel saw the wheel,
way up in the middle of the air;
Ezekiel saw the wheel,
way in the middle of the air;
The big wheel runs by faith,
the little wheel runs by the grace of God,
A wheel in a wheel,
Way in the middle of the air.

Better mind, my sister, how you talk on the cross,
way in the middle of the air,
Yo' foot might slip and your soul be lost,
way in the middle of the air.

Let me tell you, brother, what a hypocrite will do,
way in the middle of the air,
He'll low-rate you and he'll low-rate me,
way in the middle of the air.

Ol' Satan wears a clubfoot shoe,
way in the middle of the air,
If you don't mind, he'll slip it on you,
way in the middle of the air.

Traditional

In "Ride On, King Jesus," Jesus exposes the failings of a racist society to ultimately "hinder me"; no one can hinder me because Jesus rides on a stately horse and crosses the River Jordan:

Ride on, King Jesus, no one can a hinder me,
Ride on, King Jesus, ride on, no one can a hinder me.
For he is King of kings,
He is Lord of lords,
Jesus Christ, the first and last,
No one works like him.

King Jesus rides on a stately horse,
No one works like him;
The river of Jordan he did cross,
No one works like him.

For he is King of kings,
He is Lord of lords;
Jesus Christ, the first and last,
No one works like him.

King Jesus rides in the middle of the air, oh
He calls his saints from everywhere, oh

Ride on, King Jesus, no one can a hinder me,
Ride on, King Jesus, ride on, no one can a hinder me.
For he is King of kings;
He is Lord of lords;
Jesus Christ, the first and last,
No one works like him.
Redacted version by author

The music and text integrated with comedy/humor and faith foster survival. Humor sensitizes religious persons to holiness, mystery, suffering, and joy. Graced with humor, the slaves' holistic faith tolerated ambiguities and contradictions but affirmed that these tensions were not the last word. Their use of humor sustained their survival and helped them, the subjugated, transcend the mundane. Using humor tempered their lives and helped sustained their faith, a way of being in the world, so that in that faithful context, humor had therapeutic effects. The humor helped them to challenge their destiny with enthusiasm when possible, with resignation when needed, and often with festivity.

Therapeutic humor helped nurture and preserve Blacks' well-being and sanity, and therefore inwardly freed them to be creative and loving.[26] Humor and comedy supported their religious experiences and moved them toward a rock-steady faith. The Spirituals represent songs created in and shaped by humor within a religious sensibility. In African-American religion and music making, the Spirituals thwart the barbaric, by relying on comedy/humor. Faith knows laughter and shapes our concept of finitude. In the Spirituals and in life itself, humor and comedy therapeutically re-shape the human condition and help sustain hope when reality causes futility. Alongside the incongruity or disparity in the Spirituals is tragedy; yet tragedy often occurs alongside transformation,[27] resonant in "We Shall Not Be Moved."

When the 1960s protesters sang "We Shall Not Be Moved," they would not be moved from an antiracist stance even though the "system" tried to move them by imprisoning, beating, or killing them. In the process of choosing "not to be moved," the protesters affirmed self and grew closer as community, experiencing affirmation, actualization, and ultimately transformation—acceptance, fulfillment, conversion, change. The irony is clear, since the song "We Shall Not Be Moved" inspired the freedom fighters and thus moved the U.S. Congress to pass the first Civil Rights Acts since 1876: on August 29, 1957, and August 6, 1965, to protect Black voting rights, and on July 2, 1964, to ban discrimination in jobs and public accommodations. Three realities then and now are irreconcilable: the refusal of the signifying freedom fighters to stand for injustice; the relationships of the oppressed toward American racist traditions; and the Movement's protest against White supremacy. The activists experienced incongruity when they suffered in the wake of the presumed "liberty and justice for all" and as they fought for inner and external wellness and battled their oppressors. They confronted adversaries through song without explicitly informing the hearers. Many times singers used ironic parody to twist the intent and to transmit an opposite meaning, and they identified strongly with biblical characters such as Noah, Job, David, Joseph, Mary and Martha, and Paul and Silas, who became their heroes and evoked a sense of a harmonious society. The justifications for racism became comic as racists applied faulty, wicked logic to the wrong problems and the wrong persons. A sense of comedy allowed the oppressed to discover life on a larger scale, to make God's attitude their own without setting themselves up to be God.[28]

Often, real-life situations reflected in texts and stories are so absurd and so life-denying that the unbearable, total hopelessness pushes the oppressed to humor/comedy in order to exist.[29] Bernice Reagon claims that many times the slaves' singing, "I got shoes, you got shoes, all God's chillun got shoes," involves many levels of experience, especially when viewed politically:

> *I got shoes, you got shoes*
> *All God's chillun got shoes*
> *When I get to heaven, gonna put on ma shoes*
> *Gonna shout all over God's heaven, heaven*
> *Everybody talkin' 'bout heaven ain't goin' there, heaven, heaven*
> *Gonna shout all over God's heaven.*
> Traditional

Reagon feels that Black folks were acting like they were going to get to heaven and take over, and that everybody who talked about having shoes did not own a pair of shoes but knew that someday their offspring would. There are practical and sharp edges to this song. If African Americans were not going to go crazy, it was necessary to have a hundred lessons that said in the same spoonful: you can take the bitter with the sweet; where you hurt, you can laugh. People in the 1960s Civil Rights Movement felt safest when singing the songs that challenged them as they experienced the fears and the glory. They used ambiguity, irony, and caricature. They preferred life over death and affirmed the existence of a just created order. The inherent humor helped them re-echo these older stories in the Spirituals within each hearer, an art mastered by Jesus in his parables.[30] The Spirituals are parables of fiery rhetoric that scorched the surface of America's conscience as the freedom fighters sang and were hosed and pistol-whipped; and these parables soothe, as a "balm in Gilead." The power innate to both extremes is the beauty of the Black aesthetic.

> Feel the Fire
> Motivating you and me
> Motivating justice;
> Stirring in your heart,
> Feel the blood
> Coursing through your veins.
> Feel the Fire!!

Artistic Influences on the 1960s Civil Rights Era

The fire of the Black aesthetic, of Black beauty, undergirds the artistic influences on the 1960s Movement that helped mold the Spirituals: the Black Renaissance, the Old and New Left, and the People's Songs movement. These activities, rooted in justice, galvanized people toward desiring and effecting change, change that would create the right kind of relations between diverse human beings, and between them and God.

The Black Renaissance was a rich fertilization of creative energies in African-American cinema, dance, graphic arts, literature, and music during the post–World War II Black freedom movement. Liberating artistry inspired liberation politics. Poets and musicians, as "prophetic Black Artists of New Creation," attended gatherings formed to debate issues and plan strategies. These "Cantors of people's agony, vision and hope" made public the price of democracy. Their poems and songs permeated the fabric of the nation's thinking. These modern-day griots revealed the spiritual and religious roots of all human art and showed the importance of creativity in a democratic, compassionate society.[31] The songs and poems moved people to think, to get conscious about the depths to which America was not a melting pot, and to be aware of the extent to which the bells of freedom were not ringing for everyone. With respect and insight, these guardian-philosophers helped to move society toward acknowledging the pain-ridden crises and toward seeking a cure, effecting healing by being conscious of the conflict between society and societal ideals:

> The call for healing . . . is ultimately an invitation to the . . . final bonding connections between the poets and the musicians who were redefining the world from the ground of their Blackness (from the underground where they had been driven). . . . For what we may see as we peer over the barricades of our hearts is the astonishing possibility that songs resurrect, that poetry makes alive, that dancing revives the dead, that Gabriel blows a tenor sax, that people who had been physically buried in the American earth were once again shaken into revival by the Freedom Songs, all the heroes marching, all the martyrs' blood rising from the South.[32]

Along with the Black Renaissance, the Old and New Left shaped the music of the 1960s. Those of the Old Left were New Dealers, Communists, Trotskyites, and socialists; those of the New Left were opposed to the Vietnam War. The Old and New Left intersected in their commitment to civil rights. The People's Songs movement located the climate of protest in the 1950s and 1960s. At hootenannies, sit-ins, coffeehouses, and college campuses during civil rights and antiwar demonstrations, folk songs expressed solidarity and discontent, and called for just treatment and equality. The hootenanny was a singing party that grew out of a long tradition of songfests used to unify social movements throughout American history.[33]

People's Songs was an organization founded to write, endorse, and distribute songs about American people and labor. It relied on significant global protest traditions, "because they represent areas of human experience, aspiration, and achievement which the dominant culture neglects, undervalues, opposes, represses, or even cannot recognize."[34] People's Songs produced films, song sheets, records, and a songbook to foster political action through music. This singing social, political force and the Movement were grassroots networks that used songs to empower people and help them form community. People's Songs focused on recovering traditions, generating and distributing commentary on current politics, and offering options for the future. The founders of People's Songs were young, had musical talent or interest, and were committed to folk music. Some members had leanings toward Communism. During its heyday, People's Songs had upwards of three thousand members, under the auspices of scholars and performers, and its board of sponsors included Leonard Bernstein, Aaron Copeland, Paul Robeson, and Oscar Hammerstein II. In 1946, People's Songs elected a national board of directors that included Alan Lomax, Pete Seeger, Woody Guthrie, Bess Hawes, and others.[35]

People's Songs created songs, participated in spreading the democratic message, and encouraged others to write songs. Southern labor schools, especially the Highlander Folk School in Monteagle, Tennessee, collected and disseminated folk music and folk-based songs. Highlander used an educational process for effectively organizing unions that made singing and dramatization paramount. People's Songs and the labor schools dedicated themselves to promoting song as a weapon. Many of the freedom songs were shaped and reworked, either at Highlander or later by Highlander students.

Highlander provided the ethos and space for much of the protest song development. Highlander, founded by Myles Horton as a planning and retreat center for community activism, involved adult education and student development in discussions of race and politics, did not follow segregationist mores and laws, and was an ideal place for Septima Clark, who, having been fired because she refused to relinquish her NAACP membership, then became the director of workshops. Highlanders students talked; they sang; they focused on creating the tools and the environment for social and political change. Highlander created workshops that built on local cultural traditions to bring together Blacks and Whites, college students and rural citizens. Highlander helped forge a sound and a sense of movement that produced leaders who could sing with power and with understanding of the power, and who knew the importance of singing freedom songs.[36] Many of the voices at Highlander, from Alabama, Georgia, Mississippi, Tennessee, and North Carolina, were voices of grassroots women and women leaders, particularly Ella Baker, Fannie Lou Hamer, Septima Clark, Bernice Johnson Reagon, Joanne Robinson, and Coretta Scott King. Rosa Parks, who greatly admired Clark, met her at one of the workshops. After the state of Tennessee had successfully closed Highlander School and sold off its property without giving Horton any compensation, SCLC took over sponsorship of the citizenship programs, as arranged by Horton with Martin Luther King, Jr.

The citizenship workshops taught about basic constitutional rights, the American political system, and how to organize for change. The workshops had films or lecturers, ranging from Eleanor Roosevelt and local university professors to ministers like King, who put their social problems in a theological perspective. Attendees also sang songs familiar to southern folk— Spirituals, ballads, and gospel hymns—often fitting new words to old tunes.[37] Music appealed where speech was ineffectual or less powerful, for music making gave the oppressed access to creative activity. Their songs moved people and perhaps permanently changed people's consciousness toward conversion, new thinking, and new actions about justice and life. People's Songs initially enjoyed positive media response. The intensification of the Cold War and the lack of popularity of American Communism, however, lessened their influence.[38] People's Songs both influenced and shared several experiences with the Movement.

People's Songs continued to support racial equality despite media and governmental attacks by focusing on the performance by Black artists and Black music based on freedom of songs about African roots, antislavery, and anti–Jim Crow.[39] If we could go back in time, we could monitor society's reactions to these songs, note the audience makeup, see and hear the meanings attached to the songs, observe how those meanings shaped the social and political organizing/performing group, and analyze specific word choices and the multiple meanings behind those words. People's Songs popularized folk music. As it used song to educate people about current events, People's Songs' artistry and music helped shape the 1960s cultural experience and provided a sense of continuity and history.[40] People's Songs sang various types of protest music and music of the folk, particularly Black folk song.

Black folk songs communicate by using a complex, distinct language that uses oral shorthand, values, symbols, accents, sound, and silence, mixed with mysticism, symbolism, and irony, to speak and interpret their exploited beings. Mysticism in Black folk music embodies mystery, revelation, faith, and the human transcendent soul in communion with God. The symbolism expresses affection, hope, grief, loneliness, regret, toil, struggle, faith, and death. Together, the mystery and revelation, the emotions and capacity for endurance shape the storytelling in the Spirituals and the way in which the story unfolds.[41] Pathos and humor blend to frame the words and the music. In traditional and redacted Spirituals, most songs have two to six verses with chorus; similarly, improvisatory music frames each verse. This kind of Black folk communication vocalizes the injustice of victimage. The creative energies of the artistic community exposed the injustices as the singers voiced their concerns about justice, human rights, suffering, racist evils, and freedom in poem and song, or theodicy. Their messages are the language of African-American biblical Christian stories framed by music. Along with a Black aesthetic and the cultural forces shaping the setting, the words, and the experience of the Spirituals are the musical dynamics and components.

Musical Terminology and Concepts

Spirituals are as faith-engendering and life-affirming for us in our time as they were for the community of believers that originally created, shaped, and preserved them. Old songs can be sung with new meaning, and new songs can be created so that the burdens that weigh us down can be made lighter—as . . . slaves who actually experienced freedom from their chains while singing praise [to the Lord].[42]

Black American choral singing is a unique experience that calls the music to serve the human community in its internal and external relationships with members of the society. While conveying emotion within a complex blend of melody, harmony, time, and timbre to provide unforgettable musical experiences—experiences that engage the entire being of the singer and the listener[43]—Black American choral singing builds on European musical forms, the environment, and slavery.

Born amid radical change, the freedom songs induced courage, exalted liberation, and preserved the dignity and spirit of the people and the Spirituals. In the African-American choral singing tradition, singers participated in large choruses with doubling of parts, improvisation, harmony, and counterpoint. Swaying bodies marked the basic metrical framework of the Spirituals, while head movements punctuated the smaller rhythmic fragments.[44] This creative, complex musicking activity soared before and during the Civil War and 1960s Civil Rights eras. Musicking is a living process that involves creating and recreating music toward praise and protest, followed by change and healing. The music was a living, inspiring, intense, spontaneous entity:

> The whole group swung to and fro and from side to side with the rhythm of the song. . . . [They] snapped their fingers . . . [there was] spirited singing . . . [and] the inspirational quality of the group-feeling made this music seem a lambent, living thing, a bit of "divine fire" that descended upon these black people like the gift of tongues . . . extemporaneous part-singing . . . the music as a whole so completely possessed by them all (or so utterly possessing them!).[45]

The antebellum Spirituals permeated the fabric of the South, in the fields, in religious meetings, and at chores, where many could hear them, but those outside the immediate culture did not necessarily understand their meaning:

> Singing Spirituals involved long minutes of strange intensity. . . . The creative thrill dart[ed] through people like an electric vibration, that same half-audible hum arose . . . in musical cadence . . . another voice improvised . . . other voices joined in the answer, shaping it into a musical phrase; and so before our ears, . . . a new song was smithied out, . . . by no one in particular and by everyone in general.[46]

The 1960s freedom ballads penetrated the public arena so that all people heard the songs. The singing was a communicative and eucharistic tool: hearers and singers experienced the visual message as they saw the singers' transformed faces and bodies. They had a verbal, theodic experience when hearing the specific words. All heard the combined music and literary texts vocally expressed in the choral singing of mixed ages, sexes, races, and sociocultural and economic worldviews. And, the singing embodied rituals of renewal and rites of passage from oppression to freedom. Their singing told a story. These songs of exorcism enabled those of goodwill to overcome their apathy, and live out a sense of accountability:[47]

"Ella's Song"

We who believe in freedom cannot rest;
We who believe in freedom cannot rest until it comes.
We who believe in freedom cannot rest;
We who believe in freedom cannot rest until it comes.
Until the killing of black men, black mothers' sons—
Is as important as the killing of white men, white mothers' sons—
We who believe in freedom cannot rest;
We who believe in freedom cannot rest until it comes.

. . . .

Struggling myself don't mean a whole lot
I've come to realize,
That teaching others to stand and fight
Is the only way our struggle'll survive.
We who believe in freedom cannot rest;
We who believe in freedom cannot rest until it comes.
I'm a woman who speaks in a voice
and I must be heard.
At times I can be quite difficult
I'll bow to no man's words.[48]

Spiritual, historical, political, and ethical concerns underlie the analytical musical issues. The live recordings of the Spirituals in the Black congregational singing tradition is a close approximation to how the Spirituals sounded 350 years ago. Although we have no extant recordings of slaves singing the Spirituals, some early field recordings of children of ex-slaves exist, as well as recordings from the Georgia Sea Islands, where there is a greater retention of Africanisms because of the Islands' long-term isolation from the mainland United States. I selected live recordings of the Spirituals that come out of the 1960s Movement for analysis, because of the integrity of the performance; the commitment of the singers; and the integral nature of these performances to a liberation movement which echoes the freedom quest during slavery. From a technical standpoint, my musical analysis uses Western theory shaped by those social and cultural dynamics which I introduce here as a way to invite persons who have not had the privilege of learning music theory an opportunity to participate with me in this discussion.

This voiced/heard music involves a cultural performance event that concerns human behavior. An awareness of the behavior, social interaction, and dynamics of the performance setting for each song opens up the context and meaning of the communication and reveals the theoretical and practical implications of nonmusical elements that influenced musicking during Movement meetings.[49] My analysis concerns the impact and religious message of the music, given that certain aspects of the performance cannot be transcribed.[50] Two related, indispensable elements for analyzing the Spirituals concern the musical vocabulary and how one assigns meaning to music. The musical vocabulary relates to terms that denote musical dynamics and organization. The musical terms essential to an analysis of the Spirituals are those respecting duration and intensity (*rhythm*, especially *meter, pulse, syncopation, accent*, and *tempo*), and expression (*form, improvisation, call-and-response, tonality, harmony, consonance, dissonance, timbre, texture, vocality*, and *affect*).

Rhythm, essential to all African-American music, gives music its ordered process of weak and strong impulses produced by durational differences. Rhythm, unaccented beats in relation to accented beats or pulses, is the feeling or sense of movement in time, while motion is movement in space. The rhythmic energy of a musical work involves complex movement and vibrant events that divide time into units called beats or pulses, intervals of time as sound or silence. African-American music incorporates uneven or syncopated rhythms with regularity, with preexisting patterns as the basis for the changing mixed meters of duple and triple time. *Meter* involves sensing the regularity of accented and unaccented beats. Time signatures, which resemble fractions, represent the meters: the top number notes how many beats are in each measure; the bottom number indicates which note gets one beat. For example, the 4/4 time signature is a standard pattern with specific measures of four distinct accented and unaccented beats.[51] *Pulse* perception embraces a "metronomic" or mechanically regulated action sense of recurring accented beats.

Syncopation, where accents do not occur on the upbeat or downbeat (normally beats one and three in European music), is a second key trait of African-American music. *Accent* refers to experiencing the basic beat or impulse. *Tempo* is the rate of speed of a musical work or excerpt.[52] These musical terms of duration and intensity are the ABCs of an "occurring in time," or temporal perspective. Creative, stylistic utterances enhance the temporal, as the mutually enriching temporal and stylistic moments evoke a message and tell a story through musical and lyrical texts. Music and text also include the concepts of form, improvisation, call-and-response, tonality, harmony, consonance, dissonance, timbre, texture, vocality, and affect.

Form is the extension of temporal tonal design, which engages sameness (unity) or difference (variety) or juxtaposes the two (repetition after contrast).[53] *Improvisation* is a form type wherein musicians spontaneously embroider variations of lyrics and melodies in the moment. In African-American improvisation, "each voice or instrument frequently performs simultaneous variations on the same melodic line."[54] Improvisation is especially important where the call-and-response operates. *Call-and-response* is an antiphonal process. "Singing in alternating choruses,"[55] the second part answers the first. The first and second voices may overlap. Antiphonal or two-part singing occurs frequently in Black music, patterned as leader and group, solo answering solo, or group answering group, which can affect how the listener hears the song's tonality.

Tonality refers to the tonal center, a preference for the first tone (tonic). A song's themes revolve around and react to the tonic, which has roots in West African music, and incorporates partially flatted notes and the octave performed in multiple ways, fully exploring the full capabilities of the human voice. Performers skillfully employ these distinctive tones along with pentatonic or five-toned scales. These techniques do not occur by chance or conform to the tempered scale. African-based tonality differs from but is not inferior to or dependent upon European tonal systems.[56] Tonality, or tones based on a twelve-tone scale, is the basic material of music, comprising the building blocks that make up the themes, melodies, and motifs. Tonality interwoven with movement is the question of pitch-motion. Up/down movement creates a rising and falling emotional sense. Away/back connects with the beginning and continuing activity. Out/in includes the other two. Falling notes exude a gravitational pull toward the tonic, and rising notes assert against that pull. The various expressions of tonality and pitch-motion are particularly visible in vocal music. Tonality situates the harmony.

Harmony refers to chordal (three or more notes sounded simultaneously) structures, functions, and relationships. A harmonic field refers essentially to any notes sounded simultaneously and how they influence melodic rhythms. In African-American music, the call-and-response polyphony may produce harmony. Simultaneous rhythm and tonality make up the normative performance and composing technique of polyphonic Black music.[57] Bringing many voices together involves the consonance and dissonance created by vocal and tonal coloring of the music. *Consonance* relates to the harmonious; *dissonance* pertains to disharmony or discord. Consonance and dissonance coexist, paradoxically, as part of the musical relationship passed down through oral tradition. This musical relationship allows for differences of degree, not kind, that create an arena for aesthetic creativity that conveys emotion.[58]

Emotion, human feelings or psychic, physical reactions, colors the tone. Tone color, or timbre, enables one to distinguish a specific sound from others of the same volume and pitch, and to identify its cause or source.[59] *Musical texture*, another type of identity, consists of horizontal or successive sounds which form melodies and vertical or simultaneous sounds which form harmony. The most remarkable of all musical instruments, human vocality, has an expansive variety of timbres, texture, and expressive effects. The nature of the human voice depends on physiological factors, sociocultural influences, demographics, and musical traditions.[60] The variety of voice types parallels the variety of vocal or instrumental timbres used in Black music: falsetto; humming, moaning, and groaning; portamento—gliding or sliding from one tone to another; and foggy, rough, or raucous vocal singing. As in all folk music, the predominant element in African-American folk music is the voice.

The Black human *voice* joins with the percussive activity of hands and feet to exercise complex rhythmic patterns, to create intense vocal color, and to engage in total communal and personal self-expression and celebration. Physicality, musical duration, intensity, dynamics, and organization combine to create an *affect*, a mood. Performed Spirituals create the moods that declare joy, sorrow, hope, protest, and praise.[61]

How do we assess meaning? Religious and artistic meanings involve the functions of signs and symbols, and the relationships between music and society.[62] Music has meaning because it relates to someone or something else as art within human purpose and culture. The human environment provides the arena for the reality of music as an aesthetic product born of human knowledge and creative skills, and as a form that expresses, represents, and transforms existence in a prophetic manner. That prophetic or revelatory manner engages the body, mind, and heart to affect the entire self or soul of the individual and the individual's religious community. Music has the most religious significance where music discerns what institutionalized or personal religious forms need most to see.[63]

Music expresses the deepest and sometimes most elusive unconscious self. Music, an activity that can motivate the human spirit, involves human emotions. Music replicates self and society and becomes a forum for social formations. Using the sociology of music and musical aesthetics,[64] we come to experience musical meaning as subject of social and philosophical aesthetics, which examines what music does, how to talk about what music does, and what music did specifically as it moved 1960s civil rights participants toward harmonious communal and personal existence.

Music strengthens and intensifies experiences, the mood or emotion performers and listeners express at any given time. Music causes revelation, insight, empathy, and sensitivity to the divine, the other, the self, and it creates social cohesiveness. Music stimulates healing and affects the conscious and the unconscious mind. The nature of music produces its expressiveness. Music not only has the capacity to symbolize a vast emotional vocabulary, but is an intentional human act geared toward communication. Experiencing a musical moment "is the center both of a vital dimension of emotional experience and of music's link to the bedrock of ethical and spiritual life,"[65] and is unique. People know this experience through the language of music.

Musical language involves the many dimensions of pitch, time, and volume as they are colored by texture, tone color, and characterizing agents:

Pitch-tensions . . . [are] tonal tensions (what the actual notes of the scale are) and . . . intervallic tensions (in what direction and at what distance the notes are from one another). . . . Time functions in a greater variety of ways. . . . *Rhythmic accent*—by which one note can be made more important than another . . . [has] a sub-category here— that of *syncopation*: the accent is removed from a strong to a weak beat. . . . *Duration*—notes may be longer or shorter than one another . . . functions in three ways: as *tempo* (slow-fast), *movement* (even-jerky), and *phrasing* (staccato-legato).[66]

While most musical theorists and philosophers know that particular music has an impact and arouses specific emotions, the fact that we cannot explain how certain music specifically arouses explicit emotions does not deny the observed phenomenon that music can and does result in particular emotional responses in many people. We do say that the experience of music, including the performers, aesthetic shaping of rituals, audience participants, and the lyrical and musical texts together, create a kind of participation in the total institution of musicking that brings people together, has an impact, causes powerful cohesion, has a socializing power,[67] and touches the heartstrings of all participants. One's musical imagination, living musical tradition, and use and power of language reproduce the corresponding tone of the emotion expressed in the songs.[68]

The voice serves the human spirit in two languages: the intellect and purpose; and the sentiment and transcendental urge.[69] The enslaved and the freedom fighter used both languages to articulate the Spirituals. Filled with nobility, pathos, and a devotional fervor, the voices of the enslaved burst forth in spontaneity.[70] The passionate magnificence of the African-American communal singing experience surpasses Eurocentric concepts of song delivery toward transcendence beyond the music itself. This earnest music of ancient and recent freedom fighters came out of a world of diversity and contradictions, of peace and war, of tears and laughter, that involved every possible living circumstance as the singers protested and anticipated their transformation, as they "celebrated their existence in sound."[71] This music, as offering to God and message to humanity, is a creative process that calls for a higher quality of life, for justice, with a prophetic voice. This music is liturgical, is worship, as it elevates God's beauty, ethical and moral beauty that is beautiful in the *way* it is said and is about truth in *what* it says. The Spirituals honor God and the image of God in humanity, in supporting excellence within human community and in celebrating authenticity via the desire for true liberation of all people. The Spirituals analyzed here have both authenticity and integrity, because it is in the process of performance that they are complete, vital, and grace-filled.[72] While we use the term *freedom* often, many questions arise when we listen to and sing about freedom: What does one gain freedom from and freedom to do? Can one be both illiterate and free? Is it necessary to bury that which threatens? When does slavery end and freedom begin?

Musical Style, God, and Culture

In exploring the Spirituals from a musical perspective, we analyze the combined textures of sound and silence and performance methods to glean the message of combined lyrics and music. Song and related patterns of musical behavior comprise musical style, which includes all elements of musical production: relationships between audience and musicians, use of the physical body, vocal dynamics, social function, psychological content, distribution, and formal elements. Musical style, from its vocal technique and group participation to emotional and physical tension, places the functions, moods, textures, and the communal or individual nature of music in a particular historical framework. The songs identify and reinforce cultural dynamics—the way people participate in society—and the various institutions relate to religious and social behavior. Such structures help shape and qualify the performance, production, form, environment, theory, and value of the Spirituals. We can uncover cultural patterns, values, and human experiences. For example, by identifying distinctive musical patterns in oral traditions, we see that the music implies a human social response. When the singers of Spirituals sing and use call-and-response without boundaries between leaders and audience, they set up a pattern of community where people value unity as they work to experience solidarity and justice. Their musical style becomes a diagnostic and predictive tool.[73] When we explore the musical style of the Spirituals by asking questions specifically related to the divine, we move into the realm of theomusicology. Theomusicology is a discipline, a way of using music to talk about the sacred, pertaining to religious or churched people; the secular, those who believe in God but do not participate in organized religion; and the profane, those who believe there is no God and have no religious tendencies. This music functions therapeutically. Theomusicology involves cultural, social, mental, soulful, and philosophical elements, with a particular interest in how music affects the human psyche.[74]

Studying the Spirituals in this manner includes decoding the sacred and popular beliefs that stand in tension. The lines between the sacred and the secular in the Spirituals are obscured, blurred, because the exiled Africans had a holistic view of life. The Spirituals, as instruments that empower and heal, function as therapy in the church and community. Theomusicotherapy fuses God-talk, or theology, and music to stimulate healing, and reveals the many layers of meaning within the secular and the sacred. Racism demanded that the singers hide a great deal of real poetry and meaning beneath conventional theology. Given that the search for meaning is a theological concern, seeing a secular and a sacred spirituality within the Spirituals helped society (the singer, researcher, reader, and others) recognize the broad spectrums of the sacred, the disclosure of God through ordinary and extraordinary life events. God speaks through people, nature, art, music, and poetry, and through people and leaders of the institutional church; and God reveals, God "self-communicat[es] as She manifests Herself in the wonders and the graces and the renewals of hope in secular life," where the ultimate of life itself lives in other living beings.[75] In hearing and listening critically to the Spirituals, we experience the ordinary and extraordinary, the conflicts and contradictions experienced by the peoples of society, the oppressed and, perhaps, the oppressor.

Hearing music in this way lets us see the ongoing practices of oppressive evil, and criticizes the church and society for failing to respond seriously to these social denials and dissonances, or the "hidden cracks beneath the social surface."[76] Prior to the 1960s, both church and society accepted the "hidden cracks" of racism, sexism, and classism as the status quo. Both church and society usually ignored the ramifications of these "cracks" as they denied the humanity of the oppressed and turned blind eyes and deaf ears to the legal violence against many minorities. These cracks occur alongside the desire for change and the move toward hope. A musical study of how God communicates within the sacred and the secular gives us a mutual understanding that helps clear up distorted vision and creates a harmonious conversion: "And be not conformed to this world, but be transformed by the renewing of your mind that you may prove what is the good and pleasing and perfect will of God" (Rom 12:2; author's translation). Many studies show that slaves never conformed to the belief of the larger society that they actually were slaves. Slaves knew they might be hidden cracks to society, but they were free and visible in the Lord.

Theomusicology, like theology, aims to stay in touch with the visible and invisible quest for freedom and justice and with reality, labor, suffering, worship, and prayer through prayerful thought and life. Theomusicology describes music creators and hearers; compares these creators and hearers with church doctrine; and predicts where popular priests and leaders are leading society and how theomusicology can effect healing.[77] Studying music through the lens of the sacred aims to "abort" intellectual arrogance and invites the academy, church, and society to a communal ethics of accountability. We learn, through detailed analysis of the sacred, secular, and profane in music, how people discover the universal mysteries that surround their mortal existence and how the ethics, theologies, and myths they condone shape their worlds and the universe.[78] Through music, singers/participants may begin to identify the problem; and only when societal problems belong to all do they become important enough to treat.

In creating a theomusicological treatment of the Spirituals, the African experience is at the center of analysis and practice. The process does not simply replace European theology with African theology, exchanging one ideology for another. The Afrosensitive perspective involves theological interpretation and understanding of Black religion, which sustains and overshadows all African-American experience.[79] As part of a whole, an Afrosensitive view celebrates the African concept of *nommo* or word power, in singing, preaching, rapping, and signifying. *Nommo* helped freedom fighters rebel and resist. *Nommo,* the vital life force, unites the spiritual and the physical, names, hears, and calls as it gives, embraces, penetrates, and causes all life.[80] The communal consciousness of the Spirituals' melodies as the preached Word represents one spirit and one body. That consciousness allows for an intense union of God and community in daily prayer and praise through songs in motion.[81] Spirituals express *nommo*. With *nommo,* the Spirituals communicate from person to person, from soul to soul, and exude a life philosophy, for they share a common culture. Group members either consciously or spontaneously react to and share the words, events, or situations as a group, and then relate to the performance or accomplishments through debate, discussion, dance, song, or questions and answers.[82] Theomusicology synthesizes and integrates these elements and elevates a God-consciousness, a sense of the sacred in the Spirituals, while ethnomusicology reflects scholarly interest in folk music—music as culture.

Ethnomusicology, the study of living musics and musical cultures and histories, past or present, analyzes the shared cultural meanings of musical sounds, views musical practices in their widest manner, addresses oral tradition first, and then tries to locate music in its social and cultural context. This discipline pays attention to a culture's thinking, activity, and systems; notes the mutual influences of one on another; and compares groups within a culture and with several groups that are similar or different from a cultural and technical standpoint.[83] Ethnomusicology, concerned with living oral music, studies the culture and music of nonliterate people, orally transmitted music from Asian and African high cultures, and folk music. The key question concerns how music and song texts function in a culture as a culture distinguishes its various types of discourse.[84] Yet there remains ambiguity about the meaning of this discipline.

Ethnomusicology asks anthropological questions that historical musicology (the study of music history) does not ask. How does a scholar grasp the nuances observable at a live performance when using a fixed recording? How does a scholar determine scope, technique, or method, and integrate non-Western personal biases with those of Western musical scholarship? If music style is the result of patterned behavior, how does one determine which elements to include and exclude and which disciplines are integral or marginal? What are the goals of written transcriptions, and how can one grasp the participants' attitude to the style and use of music? Further, how does a scholar deal with historical change in analyzing living musical performances? What are the relevant ethical considerations of bias relating to field research in studying one's own culture?[85] Beyond these issues, there are important topics that ethnomusicology does not address, such as theodicy.

Tools from ethnomusicology can be used to focus on the cultural phase of the Spirituals, but ethnomusicology has no specific agenda to handle questions of the sacred and healing. Theomusicology claims that human beings exist in present time, shaped by the past and perceived future, and in the religious, holy time of Black ritual, where time stands still. Theomusicology investigates music from a theological perspective.[86] Black theomusicology, which has the task of interpreting and theologically understanding Black music, identifies the errors attached to Black cultural analysis; uses theomusicology's sacred and academic conversations to create a rhetoric of resistance in confronting systematic oppression; and searches for a way to do analysis of African cultures that helps create a harmonious life with self, neighbor, and nature.[87] Black theomusicology warns against making its subjects the object of Eurocentric analysis (implying a "superiority" to European ideology), which seeks to use scholarship to control, predict, and confine. The theomusicological interpretation consciously empowers the Black participant and the Movement by placing the story in the mouths of those who tell the stories which rule society. The goal of theomusicology is to gain a voice and therefore to coparticipate in social and self-government. Using theomusicological analysis, we study the story of the Civil Rights Movement with particular attention to realizing that the mobilization of national resources, not irrational collective behavior, initiated the Movement and thus informed the freedom fighters' perception and use of the freedom and protest songs (e.g., the Movement used the tradition of Black Spiritual resources as tools to support more physical and organizational resources); and that theomusicology must not repeat the mistakes of liberation theology, by claiming that God liberates the oppressed without accounting for the fact that liberation does not exist at all levels and seems not to be key to our national agenda.[88] Though a youthful discipline, theomusicology does not limit itself to the study of Christian or African-American cultures. Its focus on the sacred, secular, and profane in music helps us gain literary and aesthetic insight into the justice intent and the transforming powers of performed text and music: musicking.

African musicking, the parent of all Black music, is the social activity of creating and recreating music. Musicking, central to the Black experience, has long been a vehicle of praise and protest toward change and healing. Black musical behavior is "movement with" existence, a cultural link and a religious ethic that refer to an African's devoted sense of being and behaving musically. Musicking is musically informed communication. In musicking, "feelings of acceptance occur through effective Reacting, Perceiving and Producing that constitute the core of selfhood."[89] Musicking expresses the bitterness known by Blacks of the post–World War II period. That bitterness sprang from the living death of remaining hope, a loss of respect for the system, and a debunking of the American dream. Having put racial grievances on hold to support the World War II effort, Blacks experienced double-sided morale, social, cultural, theological, and ethical paradoxes. Black morale was low regarding the war effort but high regarding race consciousness. Failure by Blacks to realize American democracy, along with continued lynchings, riots, and intensified discrimination, made African Americans aware that (1) this country still viewed Black men who were fighting the Japanese and dying for the "red, white, and blue," as second-class citizens; and (2) affirmation and solidarity would have to be self-generated. A move toward greater solidarity meant a move toward race consciousness. The democratic ideals of the war forced a reevaluation of the color line and heightened the sense of militancy. In these circumstances, God-centered hope and cynicism coexisted in the Black mind after Pearl Harbor: the pot on the back burner that held the ingredients for a stew of discontent, indignation, and protest was about to boil over.

Agitation for mass pressure had grown since the failure of a group of Negro leaders to gain any major concessions from President Franklin D. Roosevelt in September 1940. . . . Various organizations . . . held mass protest meetings around the country in late 1940 and early 1941. . . . [A. Philip Randolph] consolidated this protest. . . . To focus the weight of the Black masses, he suggested that 10,000 Negroes march on Washington, D.C. . . . The MOWM [March on Washington Movement] clearly foreshadowed "the goals, tactics, and strategy of the mid-twentieth century civil rights movement." . . . Only Roosevelt's agreement to issue an executive order establishing a President's Committee on Fair Employment Practices led to a cancellation of the march.[90]

America and its African-American citizens were ready for change. The seeds of freedom planted during the W. E. B. Du Bois and Booker T. Washington era of 1880s Black intellectual protest, the post–World War I years, the post–World War II unrest, the *Brown* decision, and the readiness of grassroots social and political groups to protest flourished from 1954 to 1965. One of the catalysts for the profusion of activity was the power of song.

The zenith of the 1960s freedom struggle parallels the apex of singing as a weapon and viable catalyst for inducing hope and social change. Music as sound reverberated in local protest as freedom fighters evangelized and proclaimed the gospel of freedom and equality. The combined sound and silence of the Spirituals helped mobilize masses who dramatized injustices and symbolized liberation. Music as "silent dissonance" paralleled the emergence of Black power over nonviolent direct action.[91] Music is and was one way of perceiving the world. Silence, the moments of rest or pause, metaphorically refers to instances when African Americans were voiceless, disenfranchised, and powerless; and to the diminished use (silence) of music, because Black power activists did not use singing as a tool. Black music combines sound and silence to represent the essentials of the Black experience in the United States and communicates a universal access to the human condition.

Black music, marked by distinctive patterns, cadences, timbres, nuances, inflections, and devices, recites the struggle-fulfillment scenario of the human condition from an African-American perspective. This music communicates meaningfully and empathetically. Listeners can perceive, appreciate, and personally appropriate those traits peculiar to the music of Black people in the United States. The power of these chants lies in the heritage of the traditional Spirituals. While slaves had no rights, they had a life through musicking that remained unchained, unexpressed human thought given wings via song.[92]

Hearing and Interpreting Performed, Living Texts

In the Black protest music of the 1960s, four types of songs emerged: (1) redacted or edited traditional Spirituals, (2) original songs by freedom fighters, (3) popular tunes with new freedom texts, and (4) a group composed of traditional gospel songs and Protestant revival-type hymns.[93] The Spirituals and freedom songs, songs about justice, equality, and empowerment, embody signification and musicking. These songs fall into three performance categories: mass meetings, ensembles, and song leader. A detailed analysis of these Spirituals allows us to discover their power and message, especially certain aspects of theodicy, by analyzing the performance practices within a cultural setting.

Theomusicology, ethnomusicology, and musicking help us hear the Spirituals in a profound way. We experience the performed songs as intricately woven psalms that integrate techniques like improvisation, call-and-response, dance, vocal textures, a variety of intervals and scales,[94] and musical textures like tempo and many simultaneous rhythmic patterns. These African qualities sustained the midwifery processes that united the spontaneous composition and performance of text and melody. The African traditions in song and poetry, and of institutionalized slavery influenced by the gift of song, created a scenario where "for generations hammers, and the songs, 'kept-a-ringing'!"[95] Rhythmic colors, mixed pulses—sometimes stressing two pulses, other times three, or multiples of both—and rhythms support percussive playing and singing. The antiphonal (answering) phrases and structures exist on different levels. Contrasting sounds tend to exist within a high density of musical events set within a short musical sequence. Physical body motion often accompanies these sounds as a key factor of musicking,[96] of how the rhythm, melody, and culture relate to the human and divine energies and freedom.

When the singers perform, we note the variations in vocal expression and style, which indicate approval or disapproval, defiance, sorrow, joy, fear, and unity. Verbal and body language merge with musical improvisation to show emotions and coded messages of spirit and hope. Artistically and interpretatively, the Spirituals celebrate life in a unified, musical recital of history. Their unity and integrity protect self-esteem and promote a hopeful community. The songs focus on freedom, afford mental release, and reaffirm faith.[97] These are the avenues that theomusicology, ethnomusicology, and musicking awaken for us in analyzing the Spirituals during the antebellum and 1960s periods.

Singing the Spirituals: Slavery and Beyond

During slavery, the exiled African kept certain variables from the mother continent which provided a unique tool for the birth of the Spirituals. These gifts included natural voices nurtured through daily out-of-doors singing, and a functional musical sense that planted the dramatic in word and music. The Africans also knew and embodied rhythm. Dispersed throughout America, Africans discovered additional musical scales and a musical structure with a sense of timing and a way of phrasing songs from Christian traditional songs learned from church meetings, revivals, and other folk songs. They developed beautiful tones by using harmony, melody, and the unifying psychological benefits of good choral group singing.[98]

The singing of traditional African-American college choirs like Fisk's and Hampton's, starting during the 1860s and 1870s, preserved and popularized the Spirituals and increased the technique of choral or part singing. Their success led other Black colleges and academies in programming the Spirituals for tours, leaving two indelible marks. First, the tradition of touring choirs, quartets, and glee clubs emblazoned the Spirituals on the minds of the American public and produced a unifying and spirited effect.[99] Second, their style of singing and the "standard" repertoire of selected traditional Spirituals inspired the performance style and canon, or accepted body of Spirituals, adapted during the 1960s civil rights protests by the freedom fighters. The freedom fighters followed several traditions and styles of Spiritual singing: the American beginnings, pre–Civil War, congregational, Black college choir, civil rights protest, and contemporary solo recital programming. Solo recital programming involves entire concerts of Spirituals by trained African-American operatic singers. How these songs "move" people springs from the psychology or expressiveness of the music itself.

The Spirituals express the experience of life amid injustice through human speech and human passion. The essence of music is a "play upon feeling with feeling . . . the nature of esthetic experience, and . . . the 'creative feeling' as it operates in the composer."[100] This dialogue involves emotions, images, ideas, thoughts, and ideals set in sound, gains coherence and creates a pattern.[101] The Spirituals, then and now, engage the melody framed, determined, and characterized by the text. The Spirituals as dialogue are performed artifacts shared by the composer and the listener that the composer shapes melodically and harmonically. Similar to other songmakers, the freedom fighters used specific tunes to express an emotion or mood out of historical events and used musical tempo or time to express feelings about those events.[102] In short, they wrote a particular song in a particular manner at a specific moment in historical time. The range of musical pictures and experiences includes the nonhearing senses, expressive and structural musical properties, and cultural settings. The performance of music outwardly projects or inwardly evokes an aesthetic sense that calls to mind certain feelings and activities. Music either expresses emotions that one would feel if one were experiencing that particular thing face to face, or expresses the emotions that those things express, or both.[103] As the protesters sang "If You Miss Me from the Back of the Bus," they stated their defiance of segregated mass transportation in the 1960s United States:

> *If you miss me from the back of the bus*
> *And you can't find me nowhere,*
> *Come on up to the front of the bus,*
> *I'll be waiting up there.*
>
> Redacted

> *If you miss me from praying down here*
> *And you can't find me nowhere,*
> *Come on up to bright glory,*
> *I'll be praying over (up) there.*
>
> Traditional

Fannie Lou Hamer, Mississippi freedom fighter, sang "Go Down, Moses," a call to oppose a racist legal system, in the vein of Harriet "Moses" Tubman, to let her people (all African Americans embroiled in a segregationist system) go (be released from segregationist practices).[104] Hamer combined words and music from two traditional Spirituals, noted in the following choruses of (1) "Go Tell It on the Mountain," and (2) "Go Down, Moses," to create her version of (3) "Go Tell It on the Mountain":

> *(1) Go tell it on the mountain,*
> *over the hills and everywhere*
> *Go tell it on the mountain,*
> *that Jesus Christ is born.*

> *(2) Go down, Moses*
> *way down in Egypt's land*

Tell ol' Pharaoh
To let my people go.

(3) Go tell it on the mountain,
over the hills and everywhere
Go tell it on the mountain,
To let my people go.

The Spirituals, as narratives, represent a body of work that has "a depth of sophistication in 'literary' and 'psychological' matters, a preference for the 'inner' over the 'state of nature,' multiple levels over single ones, double meanings over literal ones, allegory over simple story line, . . . a story told in words and illustrated in music."[105] The experience of music making involves the telling of stories within complex levels of social groupings, represented economically, aesthetically, and legally. Black music making involves improvisation, a technique that represents one way the dynamics of music making are disrupted and explored.[106] The musicking of the Spirituals involves these various techniques and shapes them in such a manner that they enabled willing hearts to transcend much of what separated people, and brought them together during the 1960s. The Spirituals provided profound opportunities for people to share their feelings and express themselves. The poetry intensified the message of the music, and the music intensified the meaning of the words. The lyrics revealed specific human feelings and thoughts, and gave the music a keen expressiveness that pure instrumental music lacks.[107] (As poetry interprets music, the question remains as to whether or not strophic and folk music in and of themselves have a singular expressive character when the same music accompanies many different verses of a poem.)[108] With early musical cultural studies through phonophotography, we see a distinctive use of melody that allows an inherent melodic expressiveness in the Spirituals. Black singers take license using sweeping attacks, shortened notes, vital falsetto, rich voices, and vibrato in the attack and release of the tone. Music, a powerful stimulus, affects human beings, especially during protest, as music arouses thoughtful and affective comprehension.[109]

This poetic and musical license taken by African-American singers with the Spirituals, through liberal ornamentation, soaring rhythmic movements, and sharp syncopation, is one triumph of their resourcefulness. Embellished or decorated notes and rhythm allow a beauty that differs from, but ranks with, the vibrato which is typical of concert-art-song singing. A vibrato, a fluctuation in frequency that affects musical tones and thus how the voice sounds to the ear, relates to how one "places" the voice, which shapes vocal color and resonation, and to how far a person's voice projects without using amplification. The singers express intense feelings with transition tones. The Black bard freely improvises, gliding up and down between notes, conveying deep feeling to the listener in a beautiful outpouring of soul that cannot be formalized, offering both pleas and demands for the cause of justice. The singers also repeat vocal patterns and use dialect to accommodate the text, which represents a natural movement toward the musical vowels; that is, singers spread vowels and omit final consonants.[110] This type of singing, which characterizes much of the Movement singing, is Black American choral (congregational) style:

> Most Civil Rights Movement singing was congregational: songs sung unrehearsed in the tradition of Black American choral song style. This style has its own set of aesthetics and principles governing the birthing and execution of a song, its own parameters defining the range and use of the vocal instrument, its own rules setting out roles for all singers within the group. . . . The qualities of a good song leader are both musical and organizational. . . .The song leader is the galvanizer, the maker of the group. . . . The vocal qualities of the Black American traditional singers are distinct and, in some instances, run counter to Euro-American music traditions. There is a strong appreciation for the use of the vibrato, producing an expansive and warm tone; vocal textures and colorings must cover a wide range, from smooth and clear tones to those with a gravel-like feel. The strong Black American song leader must be able to sing on the edge of the voice with tones uncovered, often intentionally producing a break in the voice to heighten the tension. Aspirations for the covered, carefully modulated tone have little place in the Black American traditional music setting. The agility of the singer, the ability to "worry the line" (sing several notes on one syllable), to scoop and glide, to issue strategically sustained and textured calls: these are some of the qualities which establish musical grades within the Black American community.[111]

How these songs move performer and listening participants is the function of a particular note in a particular phrase in a particular song performed in a particular place. Music moves one through its poignancy, its implied and embodied beauty, in ways that most people do not understand but leave to a notion of divine mystery.[112] Yet hearing voices throughout the world singing "We Shall Overcome," in a quest for peace and democracy moves one to an aesthetic appreciation of the consummate human spirit. The Spirituals honor that beauty, that aesthetic, as freedom.

History and southern Black communities' creativity produced the freedom songs, slow Spirituals and hymns, rhythmic Jubilee Spirituals, and bright gospel songs which proclaimed hope and determination, protested vigorously, and celebrated ultimate victory.[113] The singing Civil Rights Movement evolved over time. During its infancy, freedom songs had not yet come of age. The music held in common was church music, but not all church music fit the young Civil Rights Movement geared for change. The music evolution occurred within interracial gathering places of the Movement, like the Highlander School in Monteagle, Tennessee. During the labor movement, Highlander learned that group singing is a potent unifying force in times of struggle. The most effective songs were the most common ones, especially southern religious and gospel songs with repetitive stanzas. These songs were easily adapted with new words to address the immediate situation. In 1945, Pete Seeger shared his music at Highlander, where he began to popularize the labor-organizing version of "We Shall Overcome," coined by striking Food and Tobacco Union workers in Charleston, South Carolina. Soon the practice of adapting folk and gospel songs and the Spirituals to deal with the problems of the day became a matter of practice.[114]

The songs adapted for the Civil Rights Movement came out of the African-American oral-aural tradition. The freedom songs used at mass meetings, sit-ins, and conferences and in jails championed the old and the new. The activists' songs and prayers provided armor and identity. Student activists led the local Movement's song repertoire that shaped the Movement culture, the Southern Black oral tradition, in communities like Greensboro, North Carolina, Albany, Georgia, and Hattiesburg, Mississippi. The Civil Rights Movement accelerated throughout the South when student activists and grassroots citizens could "no longer tolerate the abuses of racism. . . . [They began] to try to register to vote, to apply for a job, or to use a public facility previously reserved for whites."[115] The Civil Rights Movement merged the power sources of traditional oral-aural utterances with day-to-day Movement experiences.

African-American congregational, improvisational choral singing style gave the Spirituals power. That power helped maintain communal unity over against severe hostility and physical threat. While the earliest sit-ins occurred in silence, the freedom chants grew with the evolution of workshops, rallies, and mass meetings. The mass meetings reflected the role of the church as a source of tradition and a forum for experiencing new communal activism. From the Montgomery bus boycott to the 1968 Poor People's Campaign, congregational singing based on church music was the fulcrum of mass meetings. Guest solos and freedom songs from the street supplemented the repertoire. With the organization of the Student Nonviolent Coordinating Committee (SNCC) and the Southern Christian Leadership Conference (SCLC) in southern cities, many Civil Rights Movement preachers adapted church songs as Movement songs.

Community leaders directed the mass singing. The church hosted the meeting and the keynote address, but the songs did not always come from the traditional Spiritual leader or minister. Sometimes a lone voice would "raise up" a song from the congregation, and others would join in. The song swelled, the congregation's energy level soared, and a rich shower of "Amens" accompanied the ending of the song. They reshaped Spirituals into local statements by editing the standard verses. Any competent song leader had to know stock (have an ample repertoire of traditional Spirituals) in order to function capably in a mass meeting:

> Tight, clear harmony could not be discerned because every sound and texture space between the strongly identified chord and harmony lines seemed worked over for variant lines by the congregation. Volume levels were also not at all matched; one heard the soft subtle voices as distinctly as the loud powerful ones. . . . One can experience the congregational learning process in operation as the singers discovered something new being added and made the adjustment to the new lyric line.[116]

The traditional Spirituals, reshaped as "new music for a changed time," became the redacted Spirituals or freedom songs: "[L]yrics were transformed, traditional melodies were adapted, . . . old forms were blended with new forms . . . expressing the force and intent of the movement."[117] Freedom songs soared during the freedom rides of 1961. As members of the Congress on Racial Equality (CORE) joined the freedom rides, many freedom fighters spent large amounts of time in jail. While incarcerated, they created or adapted songs and strategies as they planned future protests. They used gospel, rhythm and blues, and hymn-singing styles and tunes. Their extended protests required added verses that could express their complex complaints and expose oppression. One common textual change in the redacted Spirituals involved the shift from first-person singular to first-person plural. "*We* Shall Overcome" was originally "*I* Shall Overcome."[118] Singing escalated, and the Movement activity of the music workshops, the Newport Folk Festivals of 1963 and 1964, and the SNCC freedom singers set the tone for the Civil Rights Movement.[119]

Music and Theodicy in the Spirituals

Singing tempered reality. Singing diffused the oppressor's hostility and quieted the oppressed's emotions: "it was a defensive weapon of mitigation as well as an offensive banner of courageous self-assertion."[120] The performances, techniques, and contexts of the Spirituals reflect a word play and a musical style that embody African-American sensitivities. These sensitivities embraced the oral-aural tradition of the spoken word, crucial in Black cultures, to expose the lie on injustice and to elevate and empower those lied to, the oppressed Black folk. The slaves' ideas and the freedom fighters' dreams of life and justice, often impenetrable to outsiders, are accessible through the Spirituals.

The Spirituals, like other folk songs, tell a people's history that is vivid, alive, and rife with color, truth, and the political, "a living, talking chronicle resonant with the past."[121] By definition, the poetic justice-related texts, enhanced by and integrated with the music, express theodicy. The communal concern for justice expressed in the Spirituals infuses the music's performance and structural design, which are aimed at humanity and God via the text and the communal singing style that color performance. How do these diverse elements, as they come together to expose theodicy, issue from the distinctive African-American cultural self during the antebellum and 1960s eras?

These time periods have many similarities and dissimilarities for the people of God who suffered and protested in different ways, with and without song. During slavery, "freedom now" was hoped for, was implied, but the language was more guarded, in a period when it was illegal for Blacks to read or write. The Spirituals included songs of freedom, work songs and songs of salvation, judgment, creation—songs, about all of life and about the slaves' relationship with God. These songs were tied to daily life experience, and all life experience on some level recognized that slaves were in physical bondage. The slaves recognized that reality, while hoping for a change in the near future. That the majority of the Spirituals have a "pie-in-the-sky" eschatology, that is, "I'll suffer here, but know when I die and go to heaven I'll get my justice," is erroneous. As long as the slave trade continued from Africa, many knew freedom before getting to these shores. When international slave trade ceased and most slaves were bred here, they heard stories about freedom and possibly knew free people of color. Even without these references, the differences in the way slaves and Whites were dealt with was evident, and those in bondage did not desire the grievous treatment they received. They wanted their freedom despite their legal status of being three-fifths of a human being and often being considered heathens. While slaves were physically enslaved, their minds and souls were free to contemplate, to imagine, to dream, to hope. They sang their hopes and dreams in the Spirituals, either a capella or with the accompaniment of clapping hands and tapping feet. They sang in congregational form, where all joined in together to sing about the desire for freedom, just like the children of Israel. They knew that God was on their side and that their suffering was wrong. They were not sure when freedom would come, but they knew that it would come one day; if not for their generation, then for those generations yet to come. They sang about Jesus being their liberator, the one who made them invincible. They sang about the rewards of justice. Some of the Spirituals focused on the event of freedom; others celebrated the desire for freedom and justice. Some Spirituals focused on human responsibility to God and community in effecting justice; others assumed a community and concentrated primarily on who the liberator, the redeemer, is: God, Moses, Jesus, or a composite of two or three. Some were songs of defiance that claimed such a powerful relationship with God that they did not have time to die:

Lord, I keep so busy praising my Jesus,
Keep so busy praising my Jesus,
Keep so busy praising my Jesus,
Ain't got time to die.

I keep all of my time to praise my Master,
all of my time to praise my Lord;
If I don't praise him the rocks gonna cry out,
Glory and honor, glory and honor,
Ain't got time to die.

Traditional

The focus on Jesus in no way mitigates the reality of bondage. The slaves' African religious heritage so entwined daily life with the religious that part of attaining a just life included the proper adoration and worship of God. The slaves did not think God had abandoned them, but that cruel White slave owners were the culprits. After Black college choirs like Fisk and Hampton popularized arrangements of Spirituals in four-part harmony, Spirituals were sung throughout the world. During the early twentieth century, many newly freed slaves and their descendants did not want to sing the Spirituals. They felt that singing those songs would bring up the past, and this was a case of letting the dead bury the dead. When people resurrected these songs for the 1960s reformation protest, then, the songs address a much later generation that unfortunately was dealing with an old problem: the evils, hate, attitudes, and ignorance that create racism.

Why were two-hundred-year-old songs so integral to a twentieth-century crisis? Most of the mass meetings to strategize for the Movement were held in churches, and the music included songs people were familiar with. Many college students involved in the protest had learned some Spirituals in their choral groups as well as in the church. Moreover, the Spirituals had a relevant message to announce, and that message touched the heartstrings of those who were allegedly free on the law books, but in practice were in bondage. The separate and unequal facilities, the constant humiliation of having to step off the sidewalk to let Whites pass by or having to enter any establishment from the rear, the requirement to drink from water fountains marked "colored," the poll taxes, the banning from total access to public accommodations, the peonage called sharecropping, and a culture and legal system that attested to alleged Black inferiority spelled bondage.

Many of the strongest song leaders sang when they needed hope and needed to encourage others, Fannie Lou Hamer and Bernice Reagon being two cases in point. Music brought the protesters together in a way that no spoken word could. These freedom fighters sang Spirituals that again made clear the fact that God was on their side. Racism, injustice, segregation, hate, and the related violence was caused by human beings, not God. Racism was not a deserved punishment, because Black folks were Aunt Hagar's children (Gn 16, 21, 25) or the offspring of Ham (Gn 9). Like their ancestors, these protesters did not use philosophical language or deal with evil as if it were abstract. They knew too many people who had been murdered, brutalized, intimidated, and dehumanized because of racism. They sang the songs not as entertainment or as escapism. The 1960s freedom warriors sang to strengthen and encourage themselves. They sang these songs to give a clear message that enough was enough! These songs were not work songs nor particularly about only judgment, salvation, or the religious life. These pilgrims for justice sang about freedom, about a salvation rooted in their experience and desire for liberation not from personal sin, but from the sins of injustice and racism. They understood that they wanted a piece of the pie now, not by and by.

Singing the revised Spirituals or freedom songs abated tendencies to give in to fear and fostered the onset of radical change.[122] People sang about theodicy, about freedom, suffering, and justice, while the Movement lauded civil disobedience. They sang and marched and sang and went to jail for the cause of freedom. They sang of theodicy as they named the evildoers and the suffering that institutionalized racism and its racist followers caused. The source of evil was no mystery but resulted from the belief systems and actions of White supremacists. When the freedom fighters sang, they were echoing the prayers, complaints, laments, praise, thanksgivings, and assurances of those who sang the traditional Spirituals centuries before. This time the singers were not chattel or in chains and leg irons, but the exclusionary practices of law and custom prohibited African Americans from having full access to certain public accommodations and to the rights allegedly granted to all American citizens. The freedom songs named the ways the protesters would overcome the evils and sins of racism and would experience freedom and equality. Singing helped propel the Movement and the protesters toward the "American dream." The spirit of freedom was in the air, in the hearts of many persons who fought for change during the 1960s. The spirit erupted the conscience of the nation and of the world as the fire of freedom burned fiercely.

> Fire burns,
> Within a ma soul!
> Hot coals
> Black, hewn power
> From the bowels of Africa
> Black beautiful
> Red hot coals
> Justice smolders
> When oppressed.
> Feel the fire!

6

Faith and Thought

Sing a story of freedom:
The wounded, the hurt,
Some know joy;
Some build community.
God cares, God heals.

The Spirituals, liturgical songs of reformation, united the communities
of slaves and the 1960s freedom fighters in adoration of God and the democratic promises of America. The social, historical, economic, cultural, political, and philosophical conditions demanded reformation. The schizophrenic Union of 1788-1861 and the tumult of the 1960s reeked of decadence
that sprang from the abusive penances and indulgences of racism. The
Spirituals ritualized God in song and called for reform, for change, for liberation.[1] They registered discontent with racist beliefs and practices of
both pre–Civil War and the post–World War II America by calling for change
in the thoughts and lived faith of American civil religion. The Spirituals,
antebellum cries of emancipation and modern cries of liberation, equality,
and freedom, were the theses nailed to the doors of the American collective consciousness. This chapter delves into the collective conscience of
the Black bards via the faith, theology, and reasoning that emerge within
the Spirituals, from their African roots and American exile to the volcanic
overflow of the 1960s.

Goal-Oriented Visions to Synergistic Harmonies:
Africa and the Diaspora

A goal-oriented ultimate vision or Black eschatology in the Spirituals
helped the oppressed see their lives transcend present historical limits.
Singing the Spirituals momentarily denied the psychological restraints and
the temporal harshness of slavery and placed the future in the present.
The slaves' Christian life was activity, growth, and faith amid blessedness

112

and peace, and ended with holiness. God was freely present with slaves, and they knew the experience of heaven:

> To interpret Black eschatology [means] to take seriously the culture and thought of a people seeking expression amidst the dehumanization of slavery. . . . The gospel message is not dependent on its pre-scientific world-picture. Is it not possible that the same analogy is true in regard to the heaven theme in the Spirituals? . . . The Spirituals are primarily "historical documents." They tell us about the Black movement for historical liberation, the attempt of Black people to define their present history in the light of their promised future, not according to their past miseries. . . . For early Black slaves [heaven] referred not only to a transcendent reality beyond time and space; it designated the earthly places that Blacks regarded as lands of freedom. Heaven referred to Africa, Canada, and the states north of the Mason-Dixon line. . . .
>
> Not all Black slaves could hope to make it to Africa, Canada, or even to the northern section of the United States. Black slaves began to realize that their historical freedom could not be assured as long as white racists controlled the governmental process of America. And so, they found it necessary to develop a style of freedom that included but did not depend upon historical possibilities. What could freedom mean for Black slaves[?] . . . Must they continue to define freedom in terms of the possibility of escape and insurrection as if their humanity depended upon their willingness to commit suicide? . . . [It was in] response to this situation that the concept of heaven developed. . . . Heaven meant that the eternal God had made decision about their humanity that could not be destroyed by white slave masters. . . . [that] God had chosen Black slaves as God's own and that this election bestowed upon them a freedom to be, which could not be measured by what oppressors did to their physical body. [Heaven meant] ways for Black people to affirm their humanity when other people were attempting to define them as nonpersons. It enabled them to say "yes" to their right to be free by affirming God's eschatological freedom to be for the oppressed.[2]

But these bonded folk did not simply dream up their concepts of theodicy and heaven, central to the applied theology in the Spirituals, from their American experience. Their religious leanings had deep roots in Africa.

The thought and experiences of most African people involve a mental attitude, understanding, perception, and logic that frame the way African persons think, speak, and act. Because no distinction exists in African-based thought between the sacred and the secular, the African philosophical and religious material and the Spirituals coexist in synergistic harmony. African spirituality concerns African-combined powers of existence as model, image, and a key part of how traditional Africans think about their world and their lives. The African self embodies the unity and identity of self and ancestry, with a concern for self and surrounding environment. Africans exist communally, as part of religion. For the African, life without religion equals being personally absent from total societal life. The African individual embodies and therefore carries his or her religion wherever he or she goes. For Africans, people are religious beings, and religion is within their entire cosmos of being.[3]

The traditional African religious worldview is a dynamic one that consists of a Creator God, ruling powers, spirits, and human beings. Africans see the world as a forum for activity, and life as a practical reality, not a time for abstract thought.[4] Africans know God through ritual and usually do not concern themselves with clear-cut philosophical or theological distinctions. They believe that by conforming to a universal order, they are close to God. Proverbs, prayers, brief statements, songs, names, myths, religious rituals, and stories express African knowledge of God. African peoples' religious beliefs vary in their number and nature.[5] The Ibos, for example, link the metaphysical, nonphysical sphere to tangible, physical experience. Both spheres are part of reality, and the passage between the two is natural. In Fanti thought, one knows God innately; children are born knowing who God is.[6] In Bantu thought, where language classification affects words and not grammar, there are four categories of African thought: *muntu* (human being), *kintu* (thing); *hantu* (time and place), and *kuntu* (modality). All reality comes in these categories as forces, for the *ntu* is Being itself, where Being (the Divine) and being (the created) meet. *Ntu* is the point of convergence where opposites are no longer thought contradictory. Understanding the category of *muntu* may shed light on another reason why it was relatively easy for the enslaved to identify with Jesus Christ, and why Jesus as liberator appears in so many Spirituals.

Muntu, which involves the living, the dead, and various holy persons, is an intelligent force which can control *nommo*, the word force of the living and the ancestors. God is often known as the great *Muntu*, the great, powerful Life Force. The great *Muntu* is not an engineer who designs, but one who begets the ancestors. Begetting means the world is flesh. Thus, *muntu* means human and divine: both *muntu*, life force, and *nommo*, word power, together create life. Given the Christian term for Jesus—*Logos*, or Word—and the Incarnation—the divine-human quality present in Jesus and in *muntu*—the association is easy to make by the displaced African. The relation becomes clearer since, technically, *muntu* has a visible body, but that body is not itself *Muntu*. And, when a human being dies, the *Nommo* that forms the personality and the *muntu* remains.[7] The knowledge and relationship with God is paradoxical: "God confronts [human beings] as the mysterious and incomprehensible, as indescribable and beyond human vocabulary."[8]

The more inaccessible God seems, the greater the traditional African's

need of God becomes. Traditional Africans approached God with an attitude of humbleness. While aspiring to unite with God, the traditional African favored the earth as the place for a beatific vision. African spirituality
affirms the individual's power, allowing one to give of the self, always toward personal and communal empowerment. As the African's thought and
religious views support the ethical, self-knowledge leads to self-mastery.
Africans' social consciousness and value of others allow them to dominate
their own emotions, behavior, passions, and acts. Self-esteem is the crux
of the African religious architecture that leads to personal dignity and the
value of humanity. Africans have a religious, social way of expressing themselves in human culture.[9]

Many slave narratives, including Spirituals, show that slaves knew that
with God comes mutual dependence and freedom. One needs God in order
to be; God needs one for the very meaning of life. John Mbiti claims that
most African peoples see God as final guardian and source of moral values,
and humans or other spiritual beings as the arbiters of evil. In traditional
African religions, "something is [found to be] evil because it is punished: it
is not punished because it is evil."[10] A kind of dualism exists between good
and evil. In some settings one cannot offend or feel guilty toward God, but
can offend the living, the dead, and the spirits, the mediators between God
and humanity. Community members cause moral or natural evil by virtue
of class status and by who does evil to whom. Here evil means trespass on
and harm to the neighbor; denying the personhood of the other; oppression and subjugation. Moral evil is evil against another where relationships
are hurt or damaged. In traditional African religions, natural evil is harm to
a being that involves experiences such as disease, suffering, calamity, and
pain. Nothing happens by accident or chance. Something causes the evil.
Natural evil often occurs because immoral agents exist. If God does evil in
a given setting, that evil is viewed as punishment in this life. Each community has legal and moral forms of punishment or restitution.[11] Thus, justice
administered as a curse happens if a person is guilty; if the person is innocent, the curse will not function. The enslaved Africans of the diaspora
embraced tenets of traditional African life in their communal sense of being, in daily life, and in song.

In deference to intimacy with God and to the path of being more God-
like, as in African religions and Eastern Christianity, Western religions, especially those following the thought of Augustine, Luther, and Calvin, tended
to focus on the innate depravity of the human condition: evil and sin.[12]
African religion focused on a holistic view of life in which religion infused
all human existence and sustained the unity and sacredness of life. This
statement is not an attempt to deny the harsh realities of the problems of
slavery and other shared human frailties on the African continent. The
point remains that for traditional Africans, the religious realm and that of
human life and nature are intimately related. Africans devoted their intelligence to learning how to *live in* the world, not how to *master* the world;

and they fully celebrated life within society as family, through communal singing and dancing.[13] The imposed religious behaviors of Christianity, Islam, and indigenous African religions merged with the slaves' Reformation-based redemptive devotion. The Bible was the starting point, the source for sermons and song that framed historical revelation as the community met God in their quest for freedom.[14] Slaves knew a Creator God, an afterlife, and a final judgment, and they had related belief systems. The U.S. Constitution categorized a slave as only three-fifths of a person, and society regarded slaves as heathens who could not and should not be converted to any form of White Christianity. Ironically, many of these "non citizens" who lacked an orthodox Western religious experience had inherited a rich African religious tradition of native, Christian, and Islamic beliefs. Many slaves shunned organized worship, because White American religion was no religion at all: its practitioners were evil, amoral.

Slaves prayed with Jesus and adopted Christian symbols, but not the self-righteous practices of Christian religiosity. Slaves trumpeted elemental, compassionate justice. Without this triumph as an experience of God's love and their own related sense of community, slaves might have rejected Christianity outright.[15] In the Spirituals, as in the Sermon on the Mount, God champions the downtrodden. Spirituals reveal love and praise for God, the slaves' source of unity and mercy.[16] God in Christ embraces all hopes and relates to all problems and to all persons. Incarnate love, as compassion, empowers a person or community to resist subjugation and violence. The pre–Civil War abolitionist movement and the freedom fighters' Civil Rights Movement confronted and resisted the cruelty of American apartheid.[17] In the heart of confrontation and protest, African religious and musical traditions of exported slaves merged with American colonial Christian beliefs. White religious leaders and slave owners fed slaves Paul's injunctions of obedience to defeat any empowerment that a religious African American might attain. This religion for profit sanctioned slavery and created scapegoats of the victimized by violating their personhood. This hypocrisy did not daunt the slaves' belief in the freedom struggle, because Jesus Christ was the Liberator. Their ability to relate to Christ was related to their regard for life as sacred.

An African sense of being or ontology regards all life as sacred or "saturated with being."[18] In African religions, the four concepts of "vitality, humanism, wholeness, and continuity meet in a fifth, health."[19] Vitality is the life power which makes being possible. Africans, in contrast to secular humanists, who have a pseudoreligion which speculates on individualistic humanity instead of on nature or God, have a communal, nonindividualistic humanism. Wholeness includes the physical environment and transcendent time that makes present time continuous with the past and the future, and refers to the unveiling of the sacred through unity, for the whole is holy. Central to this wholeness is communal and individual health. Health relates to healing, to the restoration or preservation of human vitality within the whole community.[20] Enslaved Africans, dispersed across the Atlantic, expressed their being and their sense of wholeness with a biblical and Christ-centered agenda.

Arriving on the shores in shackles and separated from family and all that was familiar, as aliens in a strange land, these bondsmen and -women relied on *nommo* and *muntu* and on the music that so penetrated their very personhood, to help make sense out of a senseless reality. The merging of their African and American experiences fostered the Spirituals. The Spirituals dared the American conscience to reexamine the places of God, humanity, evil, and freedom. The slave bards affirmed freedom in linguistic passion, rhythm, and motion. Their musical works advocated the consistency of Black liberation with divine revelation, of communal encounter where grace heals brokenness.[21] Brokenness was the catalyst of reformation, while singing fueled change.

Slaves consciously distinguished between historically contingent, applied, and universal justice. Universal or eternal justice was the only hope for society. The slaves did not think abstractly about theodicy, they lived it. The premises of theodicy indicted slavery and the scholarship, thought, and religious practices that nurtured and justified racist thought and customs. Yet when thinking about theodicy, we must think about authority and power. History is most helpful in analyzing issues like power and authority[22] and links social and historical processes, political practice, and cultural and philosophical enlightenment by means of an ethical perspective. This reading of the Spirituals helps us to see the truth within the Eurocentric and African religious traditions as they contributed to or suffered through the experience of slavery. This reading of the Spirituals takes seriously the human dimensions of ultimacy, intimacy, and sociality, and involves a prophetic Christian tradition that speaks with power and insight to the multiple nature and historical modes of human experience.[23] In hearing the Spirituals, we see how close slaves felt to the divine, as well as the role of society in the aberrant forms of Christianity that supported slavery but also gave the slaves additional vocabulary, which they incorporated into the Spirituals, particularly from biblical passages.

Slaves found power in religious experience as deliverance. They sang about ultimate and immediate power based on passages from Revelation, Matthew, John, Genesis, Exodus, and Isaiah.[24] Pharaoh was *the* symbol of earthly, human power. Jesus symbolized power now and in the future. The language of divine justice in the Spirituals parallels the biblical language of Job and Habakkuk. Job claims that the suffering of innocents does not negate an omni-God, for divine and social justice are inseparable.[25] Slaves suffered physical bondage in union with God, and slave owners suffered spiritual bondage while alienated from God. Yet love combats and transcends historical and systematic social injustice. Habakkuk protests that God neither hears nor acts, and thus he negates law and justice even as he recalls God's saving acts. Neither Habakkuk nor Job questions God's power amid God-permitted injustice and suffering. Accordingly, a believer can endure pain without losing faith, through divine self-revelation. Habakkuk's struggle with redemption and righteousness amid evil is the victim's struggle. Job and Habakkuk expose many areas of human thought, desires, and deeds as individuals experience suffering and oppression in their faith journey toward perfection in God. Both Job and Habakkuk know that God explains divine righteousness in history as encounter (meeting God) or that God reveals, discloses, Godself. Neither Job nor Habakkuk offers a philosophical resolution to the problems of theodicy. Thus, not only does faith endure suffering and transform it as an act of redemption, but encounter is the ultimate answer to the faith question.[26]

Conversely, racists have used biblical faith to promote the racial myth of the inferiority of African Americans and to claim that Blacks were enslaved because of "the curse of Ham," despite the fact that Noah curses Canaan, not Ham, in Genesis 9:18-27. Based on Philemon 8-20, racist Christians sanctioned prejudice and bigotry, because Paul approves of restoring Onesimus to his master as a slave, though Paul implies that Philemon ought to treat Onesimus as a brother. What Paul states and the many ways this scripture can be heard result in ambiguity, instead of condemnation of slavery, sin, and oppression. Biased scholars, hiding behind scriptural authority, defended slavery.[27] They asserted that Black people did not descend from Adam and therefore are a genetically inferior race with abnormal personalities due to heredity or cultural disadvantage. The genealogy of racism in the modern West parallels the appearance of the term *race* for classifying natural history data to indicate skin color. Certain biological and social scientists built a rationale for scientific racism based upon their assumptions of racial differences within genetics, anatomy, and physiology. They used White supremacist ideology, expanded with the idolatry of the Greek ideal based on research and on the rise of anthropology (the study of culture), phrenology (the study of the skull to determine mental abilities and character), and physiognomy (the study of outward appearance to discover temperament and character). These scholars supposedly promoted African-American well-being by supporting integration, assimilation, and intermarriage. The respective ends of uplift, civilization, and dilution of future negroid features led to an ugly view of darker color. That view of color framed the indictment that granted Whites the duty of denying the freedom of many.[28] Some schools of biblical interpretation and theological language favored enslavement and prejudicial behavior. In practice today, many still do. The language of noble servitude justified the master-servant dynamic while images of God's absolute authority, power, and knowledge fashioned apartheid ideology.

A biblical reading of life requires that we loosen the "stammering tongues" of the world's victims, and a Christ-centered reading requires that we view the world in terms of the scandalousness of the cross. For many, the cross illumines our relative victimizing and victimization[29] and shows that the dominant power usually overrides or misinterprets the victims' voices. Womanist theologian Delores Williams argues that the traditional way of viewing redemption causes critical questions when one considers Black women's experience of surrogacy and the many forces that worked to erase African-American women's power to resist and transcend obstacles, symbolized by the biblical character Hagar. Williams uses revelatory and revolutionary ideas of survival within African-American biblical appropriation, as well as the concept of the wilderness experience in her analysis of Hagar's plight, as she talks about the liberation of African-American women amid their risk-taking faith.

In the context of wilderness, Williams presses questions about the cross, asking how can a God who sends Jesus to be a surrogate for human sin save Black women? Does such an image lead to greater exploitation? What does such an image teach about Redemption? Instead of returning to traditional theories of atonement (ways of achieving right relationship with God),[30] Williams suggests that the life of Jesus teaches another model. God's spirit in Jesus as a revelation of redemption is a perfect *ministerial* vision. Jesus' teachings and ministry of working with women and men, of healings, and of feedings bring abundant life where the victory of atonement is about right relationships, not about a bloody cross. Can't one remember the cross without glorifying it? Why not? Because what happens to Jesus Christ on the cross is a mockery of Jesus' ministerial vision, person, dignity, and integrity and makes the cross a symbol of defilement, of depravity, of evil. Jesus does not conquer sin on the cross, but overcomes the sin of temptation in the wilderness, in life, not in death.[31] For many, Williams's interpretation of the cross is scandalous, even heretical: How could one not believe that the only way to atone for—to ask forgiveness or pardon for sin—in the Hebrew Bible is through blood sacrifice? Isn't Jesus the worthy, sacrificial, slain lamb of Isaiah 53 and Revelation 5? Countless church hymns, anthems, Spirituals, and gospel songs celebrate the cleansing grace of blood that washes away sin, washes one "white as snow."[32] For others, this idea may free African women from a doormat-victim-persecution mentality. But how can a Black person washed "white as snow" separate the whiteness that symbolizes purification, from the Whiteness of Eurocentric culture, without somehow negating part of the divine within his or her Blackness? If following a ministerial vision uplifts one, yet being like Jesus means always to experience persecution, how can one still see the possibility for change or that doing anything can make a difference? Williams's thoughts on this issue bear serious consideration.

The question of a ministerial vision in the Spirituals would ask, do they glorify Jesus, the cross, both, or neither? How does Hagar, a Black slave woman, fare? How did the Hagars fare during slavery? How does the slaves' reading of Jesus and the cross influence their primary theme of freedom and liberation from sin? While an in-depth focus on the specifics of how the slaves dealt with atonement and the cross is beyond the scope of this book, the Spirituals do tell us who African Americans are and whose they are, the actual children of a liberating, compassionate, deliverer God.

These songs of reformation talk about "the children of Israel" as cosufferers of evil. With God's compassion as a sustaining power, slave bards could withstand their misery. That compassion meant that God and human beings together could make choices that would transform culture toward justice and would redeem the brokenness resulting from racist evil. God's compassion, a loving, noncoercive power, could change the self-absorbed racists and move them toward caring. The Spirituals sensed the tragedy wherein divine love sees social suffering caused by divinely created beings, without a sense of total abandonment. Slaves did not give up, despite their suffering, and they addressed many theological topics in the Spirituals, from God's attributes, kinship with Jesus, the quest for liberation, the loneliness and hurt and humor and hypocrisy of the human predicament, and life, death, and the afterlife, to eschatological hope. They sang and lived a "theology of experience, a theology of imagination, a theology of grace, and a theology of survival."[33] They knew that in the midst of God's immanent compassion stands the evil ordained by finitude. Evil exists, but the power of love transcends evil, overcomes sin. Love shared between God and creation joins with the loving power of redemptive love, divinely empowered, active love, love in the form of Christ.

Christ's resurrection was the slaves' hope for progress, renewal, and the liberation of all those enslaved by powers and principalities, though the question of atonement remains problematic for many twenty-first-century minds and spirits. Slaves ignored the debate over the question of Jesus' divinity and humanity, claiming that Christ's divinity defines his supernatural power and atoning work and that his humanity mirrors his empathy for suffering slaves. In the slaves' worldview, Jesus symbolized and taught a common message—total freedom—and so did heaven. Heaven is the "New Jerusalem," God's throne, a place of endless Sundays, in present and future spatial time. Heaven is the free land with the Prince of Peace and Justice. The slaves' view of God, not Christian teaching and preaching, defined the slaves' view of divine justice and human freedom.[34] They relied on an immanent, loving God, not an abstract, deist being—so much so that some Spirituals view God and Jesus synonymously; in others, Jesus becomes a composite of Christ and Moses. In still others, Jesus and the Holy Spirit are identical. Scholars debate an implicit or nonexistent Trinity because of the omission of the term "Holy Spirit" in many of the Spirituals.[35] Essentially, the Spirituals celebrate the totality of God as giver of freedom:

Moses the human liberator; Christ the holy Spirit; Jesus, comforter and redeemer of sin; and the transcendent God revealing God's real person in situations of liberation: God the Creator-Revelator (Maker), God the Freedom-Fighter (Christ Moses), God the Redeemer-Comforter (Holy Spirit Jesus)—God the Revelator, Freedom-Fighter, Liberator . . . the godhead are one.[36]

The homage to the vastness of God and the unusual omission of devotions to the Virgin Mary[37] may show that the Spirituals recognized the feminine aspect of Jesus, whereas traditional Roman Catholic dogma and much Protestant thought until the 1960s feminist movement regarded Jesus as wholly masculine. A few of the early Spirituals do celebrate explicitly Jesus' nativity. Primarily, however, the Spirituals celebrate an adult Jesus—God become poor—who liberates the poor from religious hypocrisy, political injustice, and racism as ethnic injustice.[38] The slaves remembered these possibilities, just like their earlier Hebrew brothers and sisters had done.

Just as the quest for righteousness and the justice of solidarity trigger remembering,[39] the Spirituals as remembrances make ritual crucial and show the critical proximity of the sacred to daily life. Remembrances such as the Eucharist empower through right relation or justice, as in "Let Us Break Bread Together":

> *Let us break bread together, on our knees*
> *Let us break bread together, on our knees*
> *When I fall on my knees, with my face to the rising sun,*
> *Oh, Lord, have mercy on me.*
> *Let us drink wine together, on our knees . . .*
> *Let us praise God together, on our knees . . .*
> Traditional

The practice of remembering in the Spirituals is worship, a part of Black ritual life. The Spirituals as liturgy become "the work of the people," for liturgy "provides the context of meaning."[40] Singing "This Little Light of Mine " celebrates the light of God in the freedom fighters, which empowered them to work for freedom. Singing this song was a time for remembering the reasons why and the persons who worked in the past and present for justice. These liturgical songs affirmed that Christ the King enabled African Americans to transcend slavery and racism. While White instruction avoided political liberation, the slaves required a vital, timeless God-image, a mature Christ. The oppressed remembered and appealed to the crucified and resurrected Christ when facing a crisis. This intimacy with Christ empowered their efforts toward right relation or justice.[41] This Christ judges and liberates humanity from the duel with power, fear, and sin. Many Spirituals commemorate the eschatological healing, saving power of Christ in the Eucharist, a meal of sharing and reconciliation. A review of the common meal tradition offers an additional paradigm for talking about justice, which is important, particularly given the place of food in Black culture.

The common meal tradition, an ancient and complex social institution, combines patterns of social relations. This is a ritual and a time of bonding, obligation, stratification, and equality. This meal probably resulted from many origins central to communal self-identity and identity related to its innate meaning within a particular culture. The communal meal both defined boundaries and bonded community. This tradition serves as a model whereby worship can address personal and social issues, like racism. In the African-American community, people come together to share a meal to show love and concern. During lean times, the fare may have been greens, pot liquor, corn bread, "hoppin' John," and a few sweet potatoes. The joy and camaraderie and nurturing elevated the feast to caviar.[42] The power of the common meal urges the consideration of a broad-based liberation or a messianic motif that includes the exodus, the wilderness, the cross, and the Eucharist, with an implicit Pentecost. The common meal celebrates reconciliation and blessed relationship. When visiting Black folks had not had anything but corn bread and milk, the common meal tradition was activated, and they would always be made welcome. Neither individuals nor families let the ugliness of slavery impede the beauty of hospitality.

Being hospitable, however, in no way meant that the slaves did not see the sin and evil among them. They knew the reality of the sin of slavery, but they did not deal with that sin as a theoretical problem about the existence of evil per se in the Spirituals. Slaves knew that God was not punishing them and that slave masters were the arbiters, the go-betweens, the coaches and performers of racist evil. Slaves wrestled with the existing world, not with what could or should have been. Evil was not an explicit theme in and of itself, but the slaves held evil in a context with God's freedom and justice, liberation and salvation, and the slaves' freedom to be.

With freedom came an empowerment that sustained an understanding about the beginnings of ultimate life issues, an inaugurated eschatology or goal-oriented vision, which maintains the tension between the *now* and the *not yet*. Although God's righteous and ultimate or eschatological judgment overwhelmed victim and victimizer alike, a Christian eschatological life meant the defeat of slavery. Christian slaves could modify their masters' claims, confront tyranny with love, and call for obedience only to God. The slaves' destruction lay in slavery; their deliverance came through Christ Jesus. The Spirituals portrayed heaven on earth before physical death, as well as heaven as the home after death. Life-and-death issues significant to eschatology are present in the Spiritual "I Am a Poor Pilgrim of Sorrow." Eschatology means more than soul salvation, personal rescue, and personal comfort from an evil world and a tormented conscience: eschatology means the reality of an ultimate, not an immediate, hope of justice, the humanizing and socializing of humanity, world peace,[43] and a sense that a person has some responsibility in his or her own life:

I am a poor pilgrim of sorrow
I'm tossed in this wide world alone
No hope have I for tomorrow
I've started to make heaven my home.

Sometimes I'm both tossed and driven, Lord
Sometimes I have nowhere to roam
I've heard of a city called heaven
I've started to make it my home.

Traditional

In the Spirituals, the slaves know responsibility along with that despair and suffering which set their life's agenda. God's goodness and justice, however, are not a problem. Central to the slave's existence is the community's faith: "The sadness and pain of the world [may] cause the community to lose heart and thus fall prey to the ways of evil. . . . The slave focuses on present realities of despair and loneliness that [will] disrupt the community of faith."[44] Their belief system relies on life-giving affirmations of a strong oral tradition. This system of "soul theology" empowers and gives healing to psychic and spiritual survival. Soul theology distills the core theological and cultural beliefs of African Americans and declares the grace, goodness, providence, justice, majesty, ultimate power, and knowledge of God, along with the goodness of creation and the equality, uniqueness, mutuality, perseverance, and communal nature of persons. In this system, the justice of God espouses a biblical assertion that people "reap what they sow." Divine justice limits exploitation and helps one to make sense out of a powerless existence. The subsequent equality of persons proclaims "no big I's and little you's," but "us," where God's justice is the rhetoric of impartiality.[45]

In the midst of impartiality, God's word of freedom defies slavery. God freely creates humans as moral agents able to choose good or evil. The evil or sinful act of slavery distorts this relationship with God and with one's neighbor. Spirituals affirm that Christ redeems from sin, and require a radical conversion of all relationships not already aligned with the love of God and neighbor. They demand a faith set in time, and they communicate value. A sense of Christ's imminent return and the brutality of slavery intensified the desire for imminent and eternal freedom. Slaves saw true time as eternal,[46] viewed the Christian life eschatologically, as goal-oriented, and believed that a loving Jesus meant freedom and justice in the *noumena*: something that can exist but may not be experienced. The focus on Jesus was a focus on God, and the image of God in others was the relational world of the eternal, neither in space nor in time.

Relation occurs in nature, in life with humanity, and in life with spiritual beings. In life, while encountering others, we encounter God as All.[47] When one steps before the full countenance of God, the paradox of existence as human and spirit ceases, because there is only True Being. Slaves explored their existential concerns about total personhood, freedom, and life and death via the Spirituals. While death combines a state of resignation with fear and dread, Spirituals profess a Christ who defeated death, suffering, and nothingness. Christ assures the faithful of an eternal life in a state of goodness. Death never conquers life. Life in Christ conquers living and actual death, both the deathlike state that comes of oppression, depression, evil, and no hope, and the death that comes with that last breath. Life is a pilgrimage, a mysterious given. This mystery frames the complex relationships that cause the oppressed to seek double liberation: from physical, racist oppression and from sin and guilt.[48] Dual liberation with dual salvation effects transformation: "God's work of salvation in Jesus Christ is human liberation."[49] The Spirituals understand the theological concept of biblical salvation as integral to social and political liberation. True emancipation and salvation are reciprocal, immanent, and transcendent components of freedom. The faithful endure and transform suffering into redemption as they experience God.[50] Conversion is the move from an enslaved self to a self free from being enslaved and free from needing to enslave others. The transformed slave and the transformed slave owner move from brokenness, including sin, to wholeness.

Slave owners used Christianity to control slaves. Since slavery allowed only an inner vision of freedom and harmony, the slaves used the framework of Christianity to express their sense of being. According to several former slaves, slaves converted God to themselves. God gave them a sense of balance and demanded only unqualified faith. These slaves met God and had vivid conversion experiences. Having known heaven and hell, they continued to live with Christ in a new fellowship, not rebirth. The slaves willed self-expression: sins would take care of themselves. One account claimed that the most significant sin was to doubt God's existence and God's goodness.[51] God gave the gift of salvation and opened one to experience life. According to the testimony of many slaves, the conversion experiences left an indelible mark on them as they experienced the beginning of freedom by knowing the love of God.[52] The slaves' experiences foreshadowed the religious hypocrisy that gripped the United States during the 1950s and 1960s Civil Rights Movement. An important part of dealing with the hypocrisy, the slavery, and the racism is to name, unmask or expose, and engage or deal with the evil—to exorcize evil.

Unmasking Contemporary Sin: Theodicy and the 1960s Civil Rights Struggle

Singing fueled the 1960s Civil Rights Movement and American civil religious reform, because songs aroused support and left an indelible mark, and they embodied the language of power and survival that celebrated African Americans as *imago Dei*. As *imago Dei*, each Black soul is an authentic human being who can be and act amid grace. Singing by Black and White souls left an impact on humanity that was not possible via the spoken word. Every singer became a potential participant in the American dream as Blacks developed a philosophy and theology of protest, the thought and faith of self and of communal completion as "one nation under God, indivisible, with liberty and justice for all." Singing the redacted or edited 1960s Spirituals celebrated inclusive liberty and justice for all under God. Singing created an authenticity that enabled the protesters to resist the schizophrenia caused by being Black in a White world, and moved them toward wholeness beyond survival to liberation, a celebration of mutual respect. The Spirituals champion that reality—a reality of right relation, of justice. They offer a universal challenge to all people, to a life of faith, comedy, humor, and transformation, of survival and power.

The realm of "powers and principalities" allows a critique of actual, individual, and communal evil. "Powers and principalities are a generic category referring to the determining forces of physical, psychic, and social existence."[53] These "powers" describe an outer or visible display, such as customs, laws, or officials, and an inner or invisible spirituality enveloping all existence that legitimates the outer visible entities. These visible and invisible powers may occur individually, in pairs, in clusters, or in a series. The manifestation of these powers involves those beings and their behaviors that are commonly identified as good and evil.[54] "Naming" involves acknowledging racism as an evil power. "Unmasking" unveils the manifestation of power as racism, freedom, and deliverance, and expresses the empowerment of the Black soul as *imago Dei*. "Engaging" sets out a synthesis of concerns that evolves from the "naming" and "unmasking." Hence, racism and slavery, as powers, effect the production of the Spirituals and provide additional tools for seeing and hearing the voices of divine and human relationships, faith, and thought in the Spirituals.

The faith and thought behind the Spirituals name and unmask racism as human sin, the evil that negates the vision of a totally just society, although justice is possible. Limited human language reconciles God's revelation about justice and recites human awareness of divine revelation, particularly about the place and power of justice in society. In the Spirituals, a vision of justice builds on a kind of prophetic Christian heritage that sees and opposes ongoing anguish, oppression, and oppressive acts and thoughts. This view that engages power and survival seeks to illumine the idea of theodicy and reminds us that we can never forget the many injustices, occurring in the midst of the paradox of the coexistence of evil and suffering with a good God.[55] We must first acknowledge the sins and injustices of racism before we can hope to resolve them.

Racist myths and rituals reinforce societal racist acts. Prejudice may be a universal human sin, but racism is "America's original sin" amid a system of social and economic oppression. Racism is America's original sin because subjugation and genocide perpetrated on African and Native Americans occurred prior to the Revolutionary War and the formation of the United States as a nation.[56] Racism is a philosophy which theologically has cultural, psychological, sexual, religious, and political racist roots and products. Racism, a distortion of power and a practice of idolatry, evolves as a theoretical justification for creating political and economic power.[57] Racism has cultural, social, political, and economic features that claim others are somehow different and inferior; relegate people to perpetual servitude; and permit and encourage violence. Race becomes the standard for assessing value to the point of idolatry, since racism allows the human factor to surpass God as ultimate.[58] Racism feeds on warped myths and disrupts Afrocentric harmony and sensibilities. Racist religion and scholarship bastardize the God-given gift of creation, of freedom, the absence of Machiavellian human power, constraint, or coercion. Racist thought categorizes all Blacks as inferior to any White, and the related stereotypes are the linguistic idols of this sickness.[59] Within American civil religion—the faith and thought of an ethically based life—racism is the disease, the parasite, which destroys the health of the entire body politic.[60] As a reservoir of pain and idolatry, racism is an outgrowth of human sin found in most, if not all, cultures.

What, then, is justice? For Aristotle, who held that women lacked souls, justice relates to distribution. For Plato, justice concerns a personal dimension within issues of ethics and one's well-being. Both reveal European-centered, dominant, liberal biases and operate on an individualistic understanding of human nature. Both philosophies ignore class analysis and the resulting conflicting elements. The literature shows that there is no single satisfactory theory or definition of justice. In working with the Spirituals, we find helpful a working theory of justice which takes a social distributive approach that concerns the appropriation of opportunities, goods, and powers: Who gets to make decisions, and how? What is the nature of basic respect between people? What is the basic configuration of society? Distributive justice in an inclusive sense asks who shares, what and how much they share, and who determines the matter.[61]

Ideas of communal and social justice call society to reckon with how it denies privileges to some but grants the right to exercise freedom to others. Private, self-creative interests are unbalanced with the public, social quest for human solidarity and justice. The vocabulary of justice is public, shared, and dialectical. A society accomplishes solidarity and asserts individual freedom by extending the societal sense of "we" to people that society has previously thought of as "they."[62] To move a racist society toward greater "we-ness" requires the transformation of thought and of sociopolitical structures.

A sense of justice that champions "we-ness" looks for a holistic remedy concerning those "philosophies" that include genuine repentance, conversion, changed behavior, and reparation. Racism concerns the power to dominate and enforce oppression. In America, that power is in Eurocentric hands. Within the Spirituals, the distribution of power concerns the characterization of God and Jesus. Most slave singers assumed God's loving righteousness, justice, and goodness of relationship, not human manipulation and dominance. Jesus gave them relief in confidence and joy. Evil was not eternal but was God's problem. Slaves set their questions to God in prayers, dialogue, or addresses. The challenge to God can be heard in the songs the slaves called "seculars," the blues. The traditional Spirituals honor God's love as a benevolent power of creativity, wisdom, and compassion that encounters suffering.

Compassion embraces suffering as love, as the power that stands forever against evil; unmasks deceit and pain; brings justice and restoration to those twisted by brutality; frees creatures from self-preoccupation; and stimulates one toward artistry, care, and joy. Paradoxically, compassion is a power that does not coerce. In a theology of divine love, evil occurs because of finite existence, while fragileness and conflict coexist within creation. The power of redemption complements the power of creation's love (eros) and providence's love (love that addresses suffering). God empowers a mutual, interactive love and acknowledges freedom not as a form of paternalistic charity but as a radical love that offers liberating power. God's compassionate, empowering presence offers the holy power of mercy, comfort, justice, and redemption.[63]

Compassion fueled the desire to transcend brokenness, in a language of power and survival, toward "Freedom now!" and moved the Black community to act. When men and women of goodwill can sustain a moral life by building new forms of community, both morality and civility may survive present and future moral and social decay. Efforts like the 1960s Civil Rights Movement included in their goals a call for new forms of community that could champion the best of the past and civilize the present toward the good life.[64] New forms of community could help sustain the moral and therefore just life, by recalling past history to learn from its mistakes and by working from a savage state to civilize the present. Society may hold in tension the quest for individual freedom and common purpose while developing new forms, through a creative use of language in bricolage, taking some phrases, leaving out others, and arranging them to end up with a moral language one proposes to use.[65] These new communal forms stress new configurations of justice and equality that censure racism.

A desire for new forms of justice and equality empowered freedom fighters to sing, "Get on board, children, children. . . . Let's fight for human rights," with the assurance that society would change to accommodate the rights and freedom of African Americans. They also sang, "I'm on my way to freedom land, Great God, I'm on my way." They redacted "I'm so glad trouble don't last always" to become "I'm so glad I'm fighting to be free."[66] Freedom for Blacks meant freedom for all. Compassionate love embraced mutual, interactive love. This empowered love was the love of a liberating God. Many 1960s freedom songs or redacted Spirituals implicitly hold to God as Liberator. Traditional Spirituals glorify the God who offers liberation to the oppressed, who declares "I am the Lord your God," and invites acts of protest. For both audiences, Christ is God breaking into and transforming the historical present, commemorated by the celebration of the Eucharist.

Even the Eucharist, which represents and ritualizes the giving of Christ and the free, democratic spirit of the common meal, remains problematic. The altar is a depository for differences, a place for a common meal and a context of healing. For many, the problem is that the seat of the Eucharist is the institutional church, and the institutional church is perceived as racist. The growth and changes within the American institutional church since the Civil War and 1960s Civil Rights eras do not alter the fact that the most segregated times of the week in America are still those when organized worship services occur, especially the traditional Sunday eleven o'clock worship hour. A segregated church with separatist, supremacist leanings is by definition racist and is also likely to be sexist and classist. The power and justice of God, together with those church members who desire the good, mean the institutional church can act justly if the church makes that choice. The American church embodies an American Biblical Christian cultural story, a story specific to the affirmations of persons who participate or live in the United States, where many people in the sacred and secular realms relate to the Bible, claiming either to be Christian or to be governed by ideas and rules that imply Christian principles. Many members of local American churches still nurture the injustice of racism that Spirituals fought and transcended during the 1960s. 1960s activists believed that "God is on our side." This God acts out of mercy, loving-kindness, and justice, and gives the privilege of knowledge to the oppressed and to those engaged in a hands-on struggle for justice.

In the Spirituals, the reconciliation symbolized by the Eucharist affirms a living, personal and community experience. This communal experience, the combination of relations between the divine and humanity, ultimately concerns whether we treat others as if they embody the divine or as if they are subjugated property, an "it." To treat a person or group of persons as an "it" smacks of detachment, of injustice. Recognizing the image of God in another is the ultimate in relationships of integrity and in mutual encounters of grace, of respected presence. "It," however, spells a manipulated thing. Ultimate relationships evoke relation from the beginning. Treating someone as an "it" speaks separation. Some experience being *imago Dei*, being in intimate relationship with God and with other human beings, as the model of total personhood in Jesus Christ, or of some other experience of God. The question of respecting or using someone naturally flows to a practical issue of power that fuels evil and suffering and to African-American response via the Spirituals.

Evil occurs when a particular power (political structure, social system, institution) "becomes idolatrous, placing itself above God's purposes for the good of the whole."[67] Evil negates true relationship.[68] True relationship occurs when mutual respect and dignity exist between two beings. Evil occurs when one being totally bends and gives up in relationship with another. Evil occurs when people give up who they are, their power and essence—their true selves. The evil person is one who bows to cause and effect and who lacks love. Evil is not inherent in those who perpetuate racism. Evil is a choice.[69] True relationship suggests deepest meaning; subjugating others allows personal bias. The world of true relationship is the world of freedom. True humanity occurs only in relation to God, love, and the daily world of relationship with others.

God's love molds God's covenant of righteousness amid historical consciousness and biblical remembrance. That covenant embodies the just Word to human brokenness. Justice as a corrective restoration, in the Spirituals, often incorporates the exodus image of liberation, the Jubilee image of new beginnings, and the christological image of identification with the poor and the oppressed.[70] The Eucharist may be an opportunity to confess injustice and to celebrate justice. The Bible, as a living cultural story and memory of a people, provides stories that critique injustice and illumine justice within the Spirituals. Spirituals affirm God's love, compassion, and justice as empowerment when "they" become "we."

This kind of justice begins with a correction of injustices. Injustice, as the point of departure for developing justice theory, moves from analysis toward change and just order. Injustices feed each other. The web of political, economic, verbal, ethnic, and sexual injustices ensnares and destroys those within, resulting in human ruin. Justice is grounded in a relationship between God and human community. God's justice embraces a mystery that transcends human capacities. God's silence or reticence signals a mutual sense of justice whereby God and humans together struggle against injustice. Justice resides in an encounter based on relationships: in responsibilities, not rights. Faithfulness to the demands of relationship is the root of justice.[71] Determining the elements of such a theory of justice can help qualify the allocation and access of goods, opportunities, and powers with a sense of immediacy. Born of distorted relationships, the Spirituals offer the possibility of providing a vision of a constructive theodicy or theology of justice that unveils the evil or sin, effects transformation, and makes healing irresistible. Hence, the Spirituals reflect a faith with "the capacity to circumvent obstacles and to find fresh avenues for its expression," but Spirituals do not withhold the pursuit of worldly pleasure before heavenly joy:[72] such as "Ain't Gonna Let Nobody Turn Me 'Round" and "We Shall Overcome"

> *Ain't gonna let nobody turn me 'round,*
> *turn me 'round, turn me 'round,*

Ain't gonna let nobody turn me 'round,
Keep on walkin', keep on talkin',
Marchin' up the king's highway.
Traditional

We (I) shall overcome, we shall overcome
We shall overcome, someday (today)
Oh, deep in my heart, I do believe
We shall overcome, someday (today).
Traditional

This eschatological view of justice, germane to the inner workings of the Spirituals, concerns transcendence and divine freedom, and makes clear that, ultimately, the question of racial-ethnic consciousness is that of internal and external power: self-esteem contrasted with social acknowledgment. The question of internal power probes the integration of the self toward wholeness as *agape*. The traditional question of external power asks why an omni-God knowingly makes creatures who can choose evil and who permits their evil choices. The Spirituals qualify the questions and provide a context for discerning how historically suffering persons deal with evil.

The Spirituals actualize the essence of a constructive theodicy. In the Spirituals, a constructive theodicy accepts the defeat of death on the cross and the gift of life through the Resurrection. This theodicy celebrates the invitation to the victim and victimizer for reconciliation toward healing offered at the Eucharist—affording both new choices. A constructive theodicy theorizes, creates, and recreates from the Spirituals themselves. These chants of collective exorcism celebrate an omni-God, critique evil and sin, and champion freedom and justice—being engaged in empowered, right, just relationships. They hold human choice responsible for personal and institutional evil. The slaves and 1960s freedom fighters focused on their communal faithfulness, not on debating God's justice and goodness in the presence of evil.[73] Nevertheless, the Spirituals allow reflection on past and present victimization toward a transforming vision and related accountability. Most scholars agree that the creators of the Spirituals assume retributive justice, that ultimately, their masters or contemporary oppressors will have to compensate for their wrongdoing; however, revenge *by the slaves* is not a governing motif.[74] 1960s freedom fighters were not focused on revenge but wanted immediate reformation.

Spirituals avoid a speculative theodicy that would rationalize the suffering of innocent people. They hold that the law and desire of God command the good, which sinning slave owners or racists disobey. We must be aware that we live with the ambiguous and the dialectical, that the oppressions of then and now do not make sense. The good news is that, ultimately, true liberation becomes salvation. Salvation affirms God's benevolence.

Liberation probes divine and human responsibilities in the particular social setting. We all have questioned God's goodness when cruelties against persons occur that erase human sensibilities. In addressing an ancient problem, however, most people still see evil from a safe distance. Yet, evil forces its victims to cope with "the ugly graffiti it has scribbled on the walls of their psyche."[75] History and the Spirituals themselves remind us that everyone is both a potential perpetrator and a victim of the internal or external exercise of evil.

In assessing the exercise of evil, Black theologian William Jones argues that if Christ actually lived, died, and was resurrected, then divine hatred is a necessary conclusion. Jones abandons other theodicy options and instead suggests a human-centered idea about God, humanocentric theism, a constructive Black theodicy which supports creating a theology of justice from a Black perspective.[76] Jones's theory champions human freedom and duty, reshapes divine powers, negates divine approval of human (ethnic) suffering, avoids escapism, and makes human activity the deciding factor for one's salvation or liberation. Major Jones claims that William Jones posits a limited God. William Jones claims that belief in an unlimited God has moral and logical contradictions: either God is not an omni-God, or God is a racist. While the limited God view attempts to remove the total responsibility of evil from God and enhances the import of human beings, victimized persons need the assurance of final victory in divine good. In Black theology, God can be viewed as weak-armed but never "weak in the knees."[77]

The Spirituals pronounce a theology of justice which indicts American slavery and racism: theodicy questions the systemic evil and suffering perpetrated by some of God's children on their siblings of different racial and ethnic origins for reasons ranging from the economical and philosophical, to the psychological and political. These reasons require a Black living, goal-oriented theodicy, because White American religion sustained the dehumanization of African Americans. Some slaves made no distinction between true Christianity and that practiced by slave owners. Others were ambivalent. Many slaves believed in a just God; others were confused. Human revenge was not allowed to figure into Old Testament or Hebrew Bible thinking about justice: only God does justice and can be trusted with vindication. The English phrase " 'Revenge is mine', saith the Lord" is a crude mistranslation. The Hebrew term translated erroneously as revenge actually refers to Yahweh's deliverance or rescue. The normal Greek translation, the language of the New Testament, refers to "deliver" or "vindicate."[78] Self-help forms of vengeance were socially unacceptable even before the Hebrews settled in Palestine. Therefore, when a call within the Spirituals asks for some form of punitive action, the aim of the call is relief, redress, deliverance, and comfort to the long-suffering as an experience of justice. Such a call does not refer to vengeance or revenge, either divine or human.

Racism and Slavery: Theodicy in Dialogue

The slaves and African Americans in the 1960s lived within a society that used power structures within various systems to victimize or limit the *power* of individuals. Slavery and racism are evil, sinful, offensive acts toward God and humanity. These evils abuse the God-given power of freedom. The presence of these evils defies justice. Made effective through human beings or institutions, power reforms and elevates or ruins and erases. With an ability to heal or destroy, the dynamics of power penetrate all existence, including language. In the traditional Spirituals, certain powers depict the slaves' personification of hostile power; certain powers reflect the liberation of God. In the redacted Spirituals, singers use metaphors and name the particular oppressive, evil powers or events. In naming the particular powers, we begin the process of unmasking them.

The unmasking process examines the "powers" known as Satan and the demonic. Satan symbolizes (1) culture withdrawn from God, (2) the image of unredeemed humanity's collective life, and (3) knowledge that people live in a world where evil, that is, some irreducible power, cannot be humanized, integrated, or cured.[79] In the language of the "powers," Satan is more than abstract, supernatural evil, "represent[ing] the concrete presence of evil in human society. . . . Satan controls the kingdom of hell and seeks to convince people to follow him and not Jesus Christ."[80] The demonic, the malignant, refers to the surrender of persons to oppressive power structures and to the results of breakdowns in personal development. Racism and slavery, as collective possessions, occur where the demonic becomes a mass psychosis or insanity. The treatment for collective possession is a collective exorcism. The nineteenth-century abolition movement and the twentieth-century Civil Rights Movement represent collective exorcisms, large-scale expulsions of evil. The Spirituals, ritual components of a collective exorcism, enabled slaves and 1960s activists to fight evil with the power constructs of freedom and justice through song. Unmasking certain dynamics of racism provides keys to unlocking how this evil affects the function of the Spirituals as response in the antebellum and 1960s Civil Rights movements. Naming and exposing racism and the potential for justice and freedom are central to seeing the dynamics of the "powers," especially the more visible forms of institutionalized powers, as we shift to engaging the powers.

The critical power manipulated by the oppressors and championed by the oppressed has been freedom. Freedom is an essential component of divine and human justice. Slaves sang about freedom as freedom to be, to live with mutual respect, to experience the rights of humanity, to be free from spiritual sin, and to experience salvation. The activists called for "freedom now," freedom from the sins of injustice and the daily onslaught of racist, segregationist, White supremacist practices. The 1960s activists sang

Spirituals as part of their freedom song repertoire. Similarly, the slaves expressed their desire for freedom in the Spirituals a century earlier. Slaves resisted bondage and prayed for the emancipation resounding in Israel's exodus and Jesus' Resurrection. Internally, most Blacks never saw themselves as true slaves.[81] In singing the Spiritual "Oh, Freedom," the bards claimed that "before [they would] be a slave, [they would] be buried in [their] grave." For slaves, God's rule meant an ideal earthly life of freedom, of living, eschatological reality in historical settings where, ideally, everyone acts with vision and integrity, especially when given an invitation to life in Christ. Christian slaves were an eschatological people who created eschatological music of hope.

Choosing freedom over slavery and oppression means championing hope over fear. The enslaved put these emotions, reflecting the hardships of daily bondage, into coded lyrical expression. They sang of their real existence, not of a romanticized plantation life. While many abolitionists and White churches advocated treating slaves in a romanticized, paternal fashion according to the Golden Rule, the Black church remained the center of slave culture, nurture, and protest.[82] Slaves fully participated within an ambiguous yet defiant Black religious experience. Spirituals dramatized Black religious themes that spanned slavery, rebellion, resistance, and death.[83] The Black church gave impetus to economic cooperation among African Americans and was a safe refuge from a hostile world during the antebellum and 1960s eras. While there is no such single entity as the "Black church," religious institutions identified as such serve as a surrogate for nationality, a vital means of preserving racial solidarity. The Black Church is the radical, independent, yet sometimes divisive body imbued with Afrocentric and Eurocentric cultural stories and values collected in the Black community. Black churches were the sites of most of the mass meetings and planning sessions for the 1960s protests. The concerns of those earlier slave bards in the antebellum Spirituals sustained the Black protest of the 1960s civil rights era, a protest grounded in biblical imagery.

The Spirituals tell the African-American liberation story through the exodus as they wear the mask of authentic, audacious confrontation, conflict, and revelation. The liberating dimensions of the Hebrew Bible, linked with real, communal experiences of African Americans, shape many Spirituals and freedom songs. In these chants of collective exorcism, all meet Jesus face to face and in each other. These combined forces involve the voice of suspicion that opposes the evangelical veto of the Hebrew Bible's communal salvation; the voice of remembrance, which connects the prophetic God with modern suffering; the voice of grace, which names the lie of evil and offers hope and reconciliation; and the voice of creative actualization that engages the listeners. These voices celebrate the essence of a powerful, able God who is "a mother to the motherless and a father to the fatherless." Together the voices of suspicion and remembrance set a comprehensive reading of powerlessness over against a language of power and survival.[84] The language of power and survival combats the mythologies of Black inferiority, divinely mandated enslavement, and distorted descriptions of the divine will that slave apologists used to legitimize their hermeneutics of oppression.[85] For the slaves then, and for twentieth-century African Americans now, freedom must include freedom of soul, body, spirit, and mind and liberation from racism, especially racist language; for language socially and politically restrains.[86] The Spirituals call for naming and unmasking all evils and sins, particularly those that oppress because of difference; they pronounce the language of survival and empowerment to the least of these; and they engage us in the life pronounced and ushered in, in Genesis: that humanity, everything created of God, is good. That goodness is an invitation for our thought and faith to be imbued in a freedom that gives us permission to celebrate, not destroy, difference.

> Freedom from anguish
> Freedom from nothingness
> Freedom to be,
> Freedom to do;
> Tell them a Story of Freedom,
> God cares, God heals.

PART III

INTENT

Womanist Design

7

Womanist Thought

I am Black and Woman;
A Black rainbow priestess!
Do I frighten you?
I am ebony and sepia,
Goldenrod, crimson-tan,
Mahogany, blue-Black,
Almond, white, and paler:
Do you complain?
I am in love with me;
I love my people,
I sing my people well.
I love God.
God loves me, loves us.

An African-American study that takes seriously the cultural, religious, social, and historical experience found in the Spirituals is incomplete without a Womanist reading and hearing. Womanist theory, which exposes the oppressions of race, gender, and class, embodies reformation. Such reformation confronts the many complex problems of evil, suffering, oppression, and injustice to reflect a vision of theodicy that champions immediacy and inclusivity. The 1960s Movement relied on women to do much of the footwork but failed to acknowledge women as equals or to deal with sexual oppression. Similarly, the class question, the plight of the poor, remained unaddressed, unanswered. Womanist vision searches for a way to champion the freedom, dignity, and justice of all people. My Womanist, Afrosensitive reading examines the Spirituals via narrative theological conversations as a way to analyze an oppressive racist, sexist, and classist society from a historical, eschatological, and creative viewpoint. This and the next chapter use Womanist insights to illuminate the theodicy found within the Spirituals and to champion a freedom shaped by ethical and social concerns.

Womanist Sensibilities: "A Balm in Gilead"

There is a balm in Gilead,
To make the wounded whole,
There is a balm in Gilead,
To heal the sin-sick soul.
Sometimes I feel discouraged,
And think my work's in vain,
but then the Holy Spirit,
Revives my soul again. . . .

Traditional

"There is a balm . . . [that] revives my soul again" pronounces and affirms the attitude of Womanist scholars as they study, teach, preach, write, and live the tridimensional race/sex/class oppressive experience of Black women. The reality of the balm is the impetus that causes change for the better when confronting systemic and personal evil. Alice Walker coined the term *Womanist* and claims that a Womanist is courageous and in charge, and loves and commits to the wholeness and survival of all people.[1] Jacquelyn Grant, an ordained minister in the African Methodist Episcopal Church and a Womanist theologian, defines a Womanist as

> a strong Black woman who has sometimes been mislabeled as a domineering castrating matriarch . . . one who has developed survival strategies in spite of the oppression of her race and sex in order to save her family and her people . . . the active struggle of Black women that makes them who they are. For some Black women that may involve being feminine as traditionally defined, and for others it involves being masculine as stereotypically defined. In either case, Womanist just means being and acting out who you are.[2]

Many strong Black women do not know the term *Womanist* and have not identified themselves as such. In a recent conversation, Womanist ethicist and Presbyterian minister Katie Cannon stated that *Womanist* is a confessional term; that is, some Black women do not make this claim or support all the components of the Womanist definition. Nevertheless, many Black women are Womanist by virtue of the experience of oppression and the desire for liberation, which serves as a catalyst for developing the aforementioned attributes.

The term *Womanist* arises from the use of the term *womanish* in African-American communities and refers to a Black feminist who takes seriously the experience and oppression related to gender as well as race and class. Womanist theory arises out of a "least-of-these" theology, a call to love, be concerned for, and provide uplift for Black women and for all people experiencing oppression and marginalization because of labels and categories used to separate and control those who are different. While the "whys" behind the distaste for difference are beyond this book, often people who are different prove to be psychologically unsettled, and their personal confidence in their worldview is undermined. Then one engages in a series of behaviors, from conversion to destruction, that serve to reduce one's anxiety, perhaps to the point that denies the right of the other to exist.[3] Womanist theory, midst a faith-based curiosity, seeks to observe, analyze, and celebrate the lives and gifts of Black women toward the transformation of themselves, of other African Americans, and of society: it fosters empowerment instead of denial and destruction.

This chapter explores the related vocabulary, issues, and techniques of Womanist theory and practice based on Black women's experience of racism, classism, and sexism in the United States. Out of this oppressive context, a Womanist stance involves theology (identity, sacrality), the Bible (authority, community), ethics (visibility, integrity), and community. Particular scholars and their thoughts on Womanist theory are noted as part of the tradition of women who have lived and continue to live out the justice called for in the Spirituals.

Reality Check: Oppression and God-Talk

Regardless of her social location or life context, a Black woman cannot avoid oppression. Some people practice a "theology of otherness": since God obviously made Whites superior, an African-American woman, because she is Black, *must* be inferior. Society tells an African-American woman that, because she is not *really* made in God's image, she is either a servile or a sexual thing, either a scrubber of floors or an object of erotic fantasy. Many people choose to see her Blackness, her gender, and her class as carte blanche to control her. Clearly, Black women live with the reality of tridimensional oppression. This oppression employs violence to subjugate Black women as the "other," the object to be controlled and used.[4]

The oppression shared by all African Americans combines to form the African-American female experience. Sex and race oppression, coupled with classism, often made African-American women invisible.[5] Black women were rarely selected to hold national leadership positions in the 1960s social and political protest organizations.[6] The Womanist perspective seeks to make the invisible visible through a theology of empowerment. Womanist thought is part of the fight for the rights of all women, of all people, and is sensitive to oppression in narrative and in society. The Spirituals, as narratives, exposed this oppression in covert ways and empowered the oppressed, making them a natural for Womanist studies. Theologically, from narratives and from life itself, Womanists seek to identify relevant issues and resources, to uncover discrepancies, to right the wrongs of gender, class, and race oppression, and to make Black women visible.

Womanist theology champions Black women's struggle for freedom. A spirited and enlightened Womanist theology deals with the oppression in society and in the church—the mandate for silence and submission[7]—by unfolding an African-American vision of freedom and justice that springs from the feminist aspects of the Black religious folk expression of mothers to their children. Womanist insight and critique create a way of seeing that is eschatological or goal-oriented and concerns the holistic or total health and liberation of individual and communal mind/soul, spirit, and body. Womanist theory focuses on the relational and historical Black experience by examining real feelings, experiences, and actions, and simultaneously presses for a transformational, life-changing process that enhances everyone. Through an Afro-Christian, liberating, biblical Womanist vision, identification and healing in communion with a living God intensify. Thus, people know "who God is."

God is a personal, powerful, compassionate, liberating God who encompasses masculine and feminine qualities and cares about individuals and communities. This God of Black folk combines a "making a way out of no-way God" with a God who is a "mother to the motherless and father to the fatherless."[8] Relationship with this God allows one to accept the gifts of creativity and substance, to survive and transcend, and to celebrate the gifts grounded in that creation. The Womanist view of God celebrates a relationship with persons that produces intimacy, mercy, love, compassion, and solidarity. This God is real and present. Persons created by this God are created in *imago Dei*, created in a life experience of diversity, mutuality, and wholeness. A Womanist theology calls for an inclusiveness which invites us to be concerned about the "least of these,"[9] according identity and respect for all life. An awareness of the historical and current ramifications of such a theology calls for an in-depth archaeological excavation of past faith and thought within narratives, to learn where we came from, to see how we are doing today, and to learn how we can hope for the future.

Historically, Black women in America have experienced abuse, exploitation, separation, incompletion, and suffering; yet thousands of African-American women did not despair, give up, or acquiesce. This history shaped and inspired the Spirituals. Many slave women, who professed belief in a "mighty God," practiced a theology of suspicion, resistance, redemption, remembrance, and retelling. Womanist Catholic theologian M. Shawn Copeland uses the stories of slave women to note that a Black woman often experienced savage beatings, mutilations, seduction, rape, and sexual abuse from her arrogant male slave master, and jealousy, rage, hatred, and harassment from her ambivalent slave mistress.[10] Despite this horrid reality, many slave women used their resources of Christianity, biblical imagery, the Spirituals, African traditions, "mother wit," and language to survive, develop self-esteem, protect themselves, bolster their spiritual, psychological, and emotional health, and speak the truth. In the midst of their suffering, these women used their suspicion to explore situations and to be leery of naive idealism that did not support their realities and values. They honored themselves and their ancestors through remembrance and retelling as they celebrated God's redemptive nature and believed that God would deliver them out of bondage. Black slave women resisted their incarceration and developed their own sense of Christianity and communal life which contrasted sharply with the hypocritical use of Christianity by their slave owners. The language of retelling and remembering serves as a powerful language of empowerment and survival in slave narratives, the Spirituals, and slave sermons.

Sermon texts, in the church and in the literary writings of Black women, deal with oppression, human conduct, their relationships with a loving God, and the nature of meaningfulness in the lives of Black folk. These sermons rely heavily on a poetic, dramatic delivery and a text full of biblical imagery and symbols that name the oppressions and present possibilities for overcoming daily life struggles. Katie Cannon suggests that sermons in literature authored by Black women explore the reality of suffering, particularly as they name and unmask the uses of negative female images and sexist models, echoed in too many weekly sermons uttered from pulpits across the nation.[11] One question Womanists ask when analyzing these sermons is, "How has the rhetoric of the pulpit contributed to the empowerment or the abuse of Black women?" The use of dramatic, biblical language and its transmission process, so rooted in Black culture, can be liberating or oppressive. One of the ways sermons can be oppressive concerns the use of "servanthood language."

Servanthood Language: Skewed Presence or Divine Status?

Many have used the excuse that since the Bible recognized and did not outlaw slavery, then slavery, whether found as antebellum chattel systems or as 1990s sweatshops, is permissible. Too often, "church leaders" use biblical texts to brainwash women into believing that women ought not preach, that women have no business in the pulpit, and that any woman is subservient to all men. However, since God has the audacity to call some of us women, some of us women have the audacity and joy to step out on faith and find an arena where we are nurtured and where we do express our ministerial gifts. While many of the men and women protesting the place of women's ordination claim to love and respect God, they seem to twist that respect and attempt to deny God's freedom to call women to the pulpit! This smacks of gross hypocrisy and idolatry. Others have ministered and "made a way out of no-way" for their families by working as domestic servants. Domestics and servants "wait" on others and sometimes bear the physical and sexual "weight" of those others. In the eyes of some, their occupation makes them subservient, inferior to those who employ them or who dominate culture. Others invoke the language of the "suffering servant" in Isaiah to claim that God intended Black folk to suffer. How is it that certain folk insist that they have the inside scoop on what God knows, wants, and does? Where is the sense of human responsibility for what some human beings put on others and expect them to bear? Jacquelyn Grant addresses the problematic nature of servant language and affirms that a Black woman's Jesus is a cosufferer, an empowerer and that one who empowers is a friend.[12] In the Spirituals, Jesus is a friend, and servants are empowered, not exploited. Certainly, true friends do not abuse, do not identify an individual with the job she or he performs, and definitely do not label one who serves as servile, slavish, beggarly, groveling, submissive, or low.

Servant language becomes problematic because many Black women domestic service workers have been in a subordinate/dominant relationship with White women. Service, for many African Americans, has not been an avenue to liberation and empowerment but an alley to exploitation. Grant contends that the tridimensional experience of Black women pushes society to unmask and expose, not to cover up harsh realities with pretty, conciliatory language. Admitting these ongoing oppressions also demands that society not categorize people and not devalue people's lives because of who they are. She argues for a reworking of the language of inclusive discipleship, an experience of partnership, justice, mutuality, and liberation.[13] Womanist analysis desires to bring about freedom and to transform the results of sin for all people, especially Black women. Along with handling "servanthood" language, part of achieving liberation is the task of reexamining and refashioning a faith language. Faith language breaks the silence and isolation of any type of abuse, gives voice to Black women, and deals with the language of sin and surrogacy.

Ministerial Grace: Black Women and Dr. Jesus

Delores Williams, a layperson, Presbyterian, and constructive, Womanist theologian, explores the Black religious experience midst a crucible of faith—a faith that lets her embrace African-American folk culture, Black literary and intellectual protest thought, and Black women's experience. Her Womanist God-talk grows out of a prayerful Womanist faith journey of teaching testimony within an experience that includes a wilderness, survival, reproductive, ministerial motif. That experience teaches the sacred, spiritual, and secular moments of Black women's everyday lives. Those lives gain strength by reading the Bible through the lens of a survivalist and a quality-of-life tradition. The biblical voice of Hagar spans time and lets sisters of ancestral glory resonate with sisters of today. A complex fugue, a counterpoint of themes from biblical and extrabiblical materials, is revealed in faith, hope, and struggle. These themes include survival, one's quality of life and experience with God, rape, homelessness, surrogacy, the wilderness experience, and social, economic, and sexual oppression, including forced "motherhood." The concept of forced motherhood, with

Black women as mothers and nurturers, involves the forced exploitation of Black women by White men, White women, and Black men. Motherhood envelops the development of stereotypes, authority shifts, and the celebration of Black women's spirituality and contributions to social change.[14] Acts that assault motherhood and exploit Black women's personhood devalue God's children, thwart right relationship, and produce sin.

Sin involves social and personal or individual iniquity. In her study of the Spirituals and autobiographical slave narratives, Williams found that selected Spirituals view sin as trouble and as a heavy psychological state, with Jesus as the one who conquers sin. Sin also concerns White oppression, stumbling blocks to community development, and certain undesirable personal activities, like playing cards. Sin involves wrongdoing for the sake of survival, and collective social wrongdoing or evil, two kinds of immoral acts. For Williams, Womanist sin doctrine does not discount these understandings of sin but focuses on the total well-being of Black women. Consequently, sin, from a Womanist perspective, concerns physical abuse and the detriment of one's sexual being, and the devaluation of the *imago Dei*, the image of God, present in Black women's sexual beings. Sin involves anything which creates a sense of unworthiness or a lack of self-esteem in Black women, and anything that defiles or violates Black women and nature.[15] Overcoming sin is a shift toward atonement, toward being at-one with God and with others.

The crucible of atonement in the ministerial vision of Jesus teaches, loves, and empathizes but does not subjugate, belittle, take advantage of, a surrogate of, or defile creation. Surrogacy, a structure of domination, names Black women's oppression.[16] Along with surrogacy, Williams names the abuse and devaluation meted out against the darkest ebony-skinned African Americans. This abuse includes oppression by lighter-hued Blacks, along with the pathological White racial arrogance and narcissism of American national consciousness and the social and political symbolism that affects Black women's survival and resistance in the wilderness. The "wilderness experience" symbolizes the place where Hagar and Black women and their children encounter and are cared for by God. In Black culture, "Hagar-in-the-wilderness" embraces both the decisive Black slave religious experience of meeting God in an isolated place and the postbellum experience of "pioneering" in a world opposed to African-American social and economic advancement. "Wilderness" symbolizes the place of "risk-taking faith" exercised in a crisis when a woman meets and receives individual direction from God. Williams quilts these themes into a creative hermeneutic of risk-taking faith, suspicion, reality, liturgy, and audacious being in the world.[17] For many Black women, that risk-taking faith involves their commitment to and intimacy with the one who is their rock, sword, shield, friend, and defender; the doctor who never lost a case; the one who always answers because "Central is never busy": Dr. Jesus.

Because many Womanists see Jesus Christ as central for Black women, the concern about sexism means differentiating between Jesus' maleness and his being the Christ. As savior of all, his humanity, not his particular sex is crucial.[18] If to be Christian means to be Christlike, then Womanists contend that on a daily basis we are to respect other humans and other living things. Kelly Brown Douglas calls for Womanists to claim a holistic, life-giving, relational God as we relate via reciprocity, equality, and respect toward the survival and wholeness of extended, communal family.[19] This life-giving God is incarnated in a Black Christ. A Black Christ calls the community and the church toward wholeness, allowing Black folk—young, old, middle-aged, female, male—to see Christ in them and them in Christ, in the "lived sermons" of their ancestors.[20]

The image of a Black Christ is a wake-up call to Jesus' message of empowerment and freedom. The call is a prophetic cry from Womanist scholars to the church and the world that asks, "How can we be our sister's and our brother's keeper in a manner that benefits all and marginalizes or dehumanizes none?" This vision of Christ has no room for oppression due to race, gender, or class. This call is an invitation to reexamine how we appropriate Christian language:[21] "How do we deal with the signs, symbols, interpretations, and communications from the church and from American civil religion in a society where the impact of drugs, education, mobility, economics, and politics seems to be pulling us further apart?" One way is to begin to revise our use of language, our thinking, and ultimately our actions toward ourselves and each other as neighbor, by revisiting Genesis and considering the essential created nature of people as good.

The call to view language in the context of the initial Genesis notion of humanity as good is critical, because everyone has the option of using body, sign, or verbal language to empower or to exterminate. The Womanist call to wholeness is an invitation to be honorable and responsible in our use of language as we talk to and about people and God. In the first creation story, God spoke, what God spoke about came into existence, and God pronounced that existence good. This faith statement signals a hopeful context for dialogue and ministry toward conversion and holistic health.

Patricia Hunter, Womanist and ordained American Baptist clergywoman, echoes my sentiments about image-of-God language. Hunter sees image-of-God language as a viable way to affirm women, but she questions how we can do this if all God language is limited to masculine and father images, given the many realities in human relationships. First, absent or abusive father experiences cannot be positive, in concert with the fact that masculine language has been used to control and dominate women, as well as to keep them out of leadership positions, especially that of pastor. Second, some women undermine other women, because they have been taught not to trust women. Third, often women and men sabotage even the possibility of female pastoral leadership because of a fear of erotic power emanating from the pulpit. Many women have heaped attention and gifts on male ministers, the idealized sons and husbands that they wish they had.[22]

Often the desire for one in the pulpit who is supposedly unattainable creates a sense of heightened sexual appeal, like an aphrodisiac. Womanists, therefore, must take note of reality and the use of power, the responsibility of the church to do right by all women, and the notions of Black female beauty versus Madison Avenue beauty norms as we move toward holistic lifestyles and empowerment. "Doing right" by Black women is the move toward sacrality, seeing the sacredness of all who are created in God's image. Celebrating that sacredness moves a warped society toward a balanced worldview. A sense of balance helps enhance one's God-given inner and outer beauty, one's self-esteem and love for community, without having to be ashamed or having to recreate the self.

An Ebony Aesthete: Celebrating Black Women, without Exception

Cheryl Gilkes, religion sociologist and ordained Baptist minister, also focuses on Black women's image midst the *imago Dei* shaped by a healthy resistance to Madison Avenue. Gilkes notes that Madison Avenue beauty norms so inhibit the self-esteem of many African Americans that it becomes difficult for them or their community to experience a vision of freedom. The problem is especially critical for many Black women as they deal with their bodies. Thus, cultural humiliation due to beauty norms, a major kind of racial oppression, skews the vision of many Black women. When they see themselves in their mirrors, they do not identify themselves as being created in God's image if their image of God is an old White man or an anorexic White fashion model. Gilkes celebrates the diverse colors and experiences of Black women and calls our attention to the assumptions of Black and White society about darkness, lightness, full-featuredness, and thinness. Gilkes calls for a liturgy of rehumanization that builds on Alice Walker's Womanist ideal of loving self, life, food, and roundness over against the cruelty, destruction, exploitation, dehumanization, and violence perpetuated by an "idolatry of Whiteness" that creates a ministry and ethics of self-hatred at the altar of racism, sexism, and classism.[23] Walker's kind of love gives voice and ultimate freedom to all people. This loving does not deny the need for balance, for proper diet and exercise; but this loving is mindful of genetics, of inner and outer beauty, of the richness that looking, talking and acting different brings to culture, and of celebrating the many images of God on the planet which do not, cannot, and need not conform to Ken and Barbie. The a cappella female inspirational and protest singing group Sweet Honey in the Rock says it best in a quintessential liturgical statement about beauty, the Spiritual "No Mirrors in Nana's House":

> *There were no mirrors in my Nana's house*
> *No mirrors in my Nana's house;*
> *There were no mirrors in my Nana's house*
> *No mirrors in my Nana's house;*

And the beauty that I saw in everything
The beauty in everything
Was in her eyes.

I never knew that my skin was too Black
And I never knew that my nose was too flat
And I never knew that my clothes didn't fit
And I never knew there were things that I missed;
'Cause the beauty in everything
Was in her eyes.

I was intrigued by the cracks in the wall
The dust in the sun looked like snow that would fall
The noise in the hallway was music to me
The trash in the rubbish would cushion my feet
And the beauty in everything
Was in her eyes.

The world outside was a magical place
I only knew love
And I didn't know hate
And the beauty in everything
Was in her eyes.[24]

Giving and receiving love as ways to resist oppression are also ways to creatively grow and help bring about transformation. The celebration of the beauty of humanity created in God's image causes us to restructure our use of all language and to tap into hidden and well-known sources of power. Those who control and fix the "norms" and language of beauty control and cripple those denied power due to race, sex, and class. Those without power cease to be a threat and lose the opportunity to love. Womanist theory suggests that the qualities that make people easy targets of oppression do not necessarily make these people victims. The same set of circumstances which remove power are opportunities to create new bases of power or to creatively work within an oppressive system. Slaves operated out of a theology of ingenuity whereby they "took what they had to make what they wanted." Black theologian Will Coleman recalls that our ancestors are always with us.[25] Their ability to take common words and create uncommon power constructs, and then to put them to song as Spirituals, is always with us, if we so choose. A Womanist theology of survival and resistance relies not only on "book knowledge," but also on personal and community experiences, along with the remembrances and the ever present spirits of the "ancestral cloud of witnesses." These resources provide a "rock steadiness" that allows us, if we choose, to create and develop our own power, from the center or, more than likely, from the periphery.

I am Black and Woman
When we walk together, children,
We hear the voice of God saying:
Children, I'm on your side.
I made you, I know you, I love you
Resist with Joy, with integrity
Love mightily,
Know my grace.
Do unto others, as I do for you.
Be of good cheer, not dismayed
Feel not betrayed.
Rise: Stake your claim
You are Black, and Woman, of God!

Black Diamonds: Morality-Based Resistance

Rosita Mathews, Womanist theologian, ordained American Baptist clergywoman, and chaplain, lauds an applied theology of empowered survival from the periphery. Mathews gives a call to resistance, but not from a theology of "an eye for an eye" or from an ethics of "I got mine, you get yours the best you can." She calls for an ethics of morality-based resistance that requires us to think and evaluate before we act. Since Mathews has "been there, done that" in corporate, ecclesial, and political offices of leadership, her theory comes out of lived experience. The choice of resistance is the choice to be both powerful and impotent, safe and in danger, prophet and target. Despite these paradoxes, Mathews creates a language of survival whereby one can create a power base without harming others and without losing oneself. Dealing with systemic evil requires a prescription for loving and health, where the guidelines are a faith statement for professional activity. Personal integrity must come before personal or professional advantageousness, and places dignity before getting ahead. Mathews advocates that one becomes a part of and responsive to community, and that makes commitments and values a priority.[26] No accomplishment or position can ever justify the selling of one's soul, one's health. If any system proves too detrimental for one to work from the periphery, then the community has to create new systems and new opportunities. To create these new systems requires the development of a way to think about these issues. Delores Williams clarifies the following components of Womanist theory that expose oppression and that do not condone the destruction of ourselves or of the environment that sustains us: the dialogical, liturgical, confessional, ecumenical, and pedagogical.[27]

The *dialogical* affords honest conversation and ethically based research to expose evils and empower conclusions beyond the tediousness of bias, greed, and power. Fruitful talk requires being grounded in an ethics of accountability and in sensible praxis. The question remains as to whether scholars help people address difficult issues and help develop possible solutions that benefit the "least of these." The Spirituals embody dialogue in that their construction emerged out of singing conversations among one another during the forum of oppression called slavery, and were edited in the forum called institutional racism. One type of situationally based dialogue inherent to the Spirituals is worship, the liturgical.

The *liturgical* calls for a celebration of life: for appreciating every day of life as a gift and for being responsible enough to care, to make a difference, to help people learn to fish and to not be so ready to give them a fish when to do so lowers self-esteem and feeds dysfunctioning systems. In addition, the liturgical calls for designing worship services that inspire and do not always find fault. The Black church needs a more critical ear to the words of our music, to pay close attention to words that perpetuate racism, sexism, and classism. The liturgical calls for an aesthetic appreciation that causes us to think about salvation as a factor concerned with all basic human needs—needs of self-actualization, from the physiological and safety-oriented to the aesthetic[28]—toward a harmonious environment. Traditional African thought and God-talk see no separation between life and death, between the inanimate and the animate, with the High God as head and all reality having some of that divine within. The liturgical factor calls for an attitude that celebrates life and that practices a divinely inspired sense of gratitude, which makes it unacceptable to violate ourselves, other persons, or our universe. The liturgical sets the framework for the confessional.

The *confessional* invites us to revisit the garden, to not be ashamed of our bodies, our wants, and our needs. The confessional challenges us to see and give witness to the *imago Dei* within all humanity, which makes us avoid destructive acts to ourselves and our world. The confessional requires that we claim and identify who we are and act accordingly. If we are children of God, then we ought to care about what we confess with our words and our deeds. Many of us would never touch an assault weapon and have been conscientious objectors. But the language we use to denigrate ourselves and others destroys as much in human potential, self-esteem, and wellness as did the bomb at Hiroshima and the Scud missiles in Iraq. The confessional calls us not to take our lives or our talents for granted. The confessional reminds us to not take more than we give back; to avoid always measuring progress in dollars and clout; and to avoid worshipping a God who does not love us.[29] The confessional encourages us to enjoy an eschatological, goal-oriented life of holistic dimensions and to create a grassroots-to-global awareness of the ripple effect generated by human words and actions. This form of sacrament also invites us to plant a tree when someone is cruel to us or our loved ones.[30] The Spirituals are confessional as they challenge us to be real, to empower, to celebrate life as gift, to live a goal-oriented life, and to have a global awareness. A solid confessional base makes it easy to build bridges across ecumenical lines.

The *ecumenical* invites us to affirm stewardship (being responsible and accountable as we hold our lives and blessings in trust) as part of our religious life. The ecumenical reminds us of the tensions between religions, the frequent ecclesial, systemic control of women, and the divisiveness of denominational religious practices that blight and pollute our spiritual environment. The communion and community generated by the ecumenical perspective remind us that change cannot occur without modeling or teaching, the role and function of the pedagogical.

The *pedagogical* calls us to teach, preach, write, and live in an exemplary manner, cognizant of who we are and why we are here, and to see our lives and our universe as gift. The gift of life and the universe is to be respected, not idolized, not violated. The Spirituals are both ecumenical and pedagogical, as they have brought together people throughout the world, from various walks of life and from diverse faiths, creeds, and races, to teach about justice and freedom, about God and empowerment. The theological first presents a blue-print for action; that action becomes lived in the realm of ethics.

Womanist thought deals with ethics, the study and application of holistic core values and beliefs that help people deal with life issues and conflicts of interests concerning human behavior toward the benefit of personal and societal well-being. The awareness needed to benefit individuals and societies requires the exploration of present and past realities in addressing liberation from an eschatological awareness or goal-oriented historical consciousness. The oral and written traditions of a Womanist perspective critically document "the 'living space' carved out of the intricate web of racism, sexism and poverty . . . [that] parallels Black history. It conveys the assumed values in the Black oral tradition."[31] Womanists, with ingenuity, create their own values and master the negative dictates of the dominant society with coping devices steeped in the traditional Black communal religious culture. They realize that those Black women who have known oppression have outlined symbols for a new womanhood.[32]

Christian Womanist educator Evelyn Parker develops the impact of a Womanist ethics as religious-moral value theory through life stories of African-American adolescents, using values determined through studying the lives of four paradigmatic transformative Black women: Sojourner Truth, Anna Julia Cooper, Fannie Lou Hamer, and Bernice Johnson Reagon. Parker seeks to facilitate faith formation and the transformation which helps all members of a community of faith be critical thinkers and agents of individual and corporate change. That facilitation also involves modeling instruction as co-learning, and developing pedagogical ways to develop and nurture people to wholeness. The resulting values champion self-worth, love, and justice which empowers, just as therapy creates healing, enables one to respond well, and ultimately produces unity, reconciliation, and liberation.[33]

As Womanists engage in multiple dialogues, liturgy, teaching, and using female imagery and metaphorical language, several underlying values emerge: (1) *confronting oppressive authority*, wherein one responds to a perceived injustice or unfairness during conflict with an authority figure; (2) *uncompromising commitment to the liberation of African-American people*, wherein one makes an unwavering commitment to help Black people address any form of oppression; and (3) *hope for human emancipation*, wherein one expects a good future that facilitates individuals and communities fulfilling their God-given human potential. Reagon, one of Parker's models who "grew up" via the Civil Rights Movement, reveals the import of the Spirituals and demonstrates the possibilities for current and future use of the Spirituals for ethical, theological, therapeutic, and spiritual empowerment within the individual and community. Reagon exemplifies uncompromising commitment through her earlier participation in SNCC; her work for the Smithsonian Institute in the Black Culture program, notably her recent documentary *Wade in the Water*; and her more than twenty years of work and performance with the all-female a cappella group Sweet Honey in the Rock, which she formed.[34]

All of these Womanist values emerge in the Spirituals. Reagon sang them during the Movement, was transformed by them, and saw others, both the oppressed and the oppressor, transformed by them. That is the power of singing. Given the historical and eternal vitality of Spirituals, songs that lived during the antebellum era and continue to live today, I suggest that the Spirituals are prime resources for doing in-depth, conscious psychological and spiritual therapy to address many ills apparent in our present world. The fact that the Spiritual "We Shall Overcome" has been heard from Selma to Tiananmen Square makes the same statement. Using a Womanist model and Parker's values toward a liberation struggle, new possibilities emerge to achieve the health and wholeness of all people.

Unmasking a Triple Threat

In nurturing and challenging this new womanhood, Katie Cannon suggests that we remember that the tridimensional oppression of African-American women shapes the moral counsel that comes out of their need for coping mechanisms to survive their cultural plight. The impact of such oppression on Black women theologically, ethically, ontologically, and existentially—in doing and applying God-talk, in being, in existing—makes them Womanist. African-American women continue to be the last hired and first fired on jobs which Whites and dark-skinned men will not do, at salaries others refuse to accept. For most Black people, suffering is the norm. For Cannon, as long as White men continue to set the ethical norm, African Americans and others will endure certain oppression as Whites define and orchestrate Black lives. A White-controlled capitalist sociopolitical economy within a patriarchal climate has caused Black women to continue to experience great oppression. Black women survive a triple oppression as part of their daily moral life.[35]

Womanist ethics makes the invisible visible by applying what we learn about the theological focus of identifying and making sacred the plight of Black women. Ethics examines human behavior, identifies the norms of behavior toward maintaining and supporting the good for society, and then puts into practice activity that supports that good as moral action. Womanist ethics seeks to empower and provide models that give individuals authority over their own destiny. Cannon speaks of "quiet grace": a power of moral character as truth that moves within, connects with other spirit beings, and builds community.[36] The process of building community gives women their voice. Womanist ethics "hits a straight lick with a crooked stick" in the process of transcending the dilemmas of socially and historically conditioned obstacles, power relationships, and value judgments.[37] This ethics champions Black women's experiences, contributions, and activities as moral agents. Womanist ethics quilts the Black woman's life as quiet grace, an elegance that transcends negativity and subjugation, and places Black women at the center of their own reality.

One of the first jobs of a Womanist ethicist is to explore the moral situation and to engage all available means to revise the response to Black women as other with nobody-ness, to important with somebody-ness. This new reading of Black women's reality requires having a moral vision for a transformed reality that assumes the authority to make a difference and that makes a difference through individual commitment and social witness.

Truth-Telling Time

Marcia Riggs, Womanist ethicist, sets out a platform of assessment, damage control, and accountability based on a call to a new moral vision in dealing with the relational, social, and psychological experiences of the diverse Black communities in America today. Blacks mete out rage and envy against each other, part of the embodiment of the fallout from race, sex, and class oppression.[38] Riggs avoids the comfort zone of only recognizing the oppressive tendencies from outside the African-American life experience by challenging us to unmask internal oppression, the evil some Black folks do to other Black folks. Such evil can be as benign as the Black middle class ignoring the Black underclass. Generally, the notion of classism within the Black community is not a topic of discussion. Yet we must talk about Black class divisions and look for remedies. The changes brought about by the 1960s Civil Rights Movement hardly made a difference to the Black underclass, the inner-city dwellers, and those who lived beyond "the wrong side of the track," in more urban and rural areas: "po' Black folk." Yet, class divisions are not a recent development. Social stratification (divided layers), a class-caste, race-class, competitive system based on race, property ownership, occupation, and income among Whites, free Blacks, and slaves developed during slavery.

Riggs prescribes a Womanist liberationist ethic modeled after the nineteenth-century Black women's club movement as a way to approach our ongoing problems due to racism, sexism, and classism.[39] Black women's clubs, seeing the problems due to racism, sexism, and classism, came together on behalf of Black women and for the good of all society, by using an ethical, social, and religious agenda grounded in a view of divine justice and of God's decree for justice for African Americans. By taking on the attitude of Black club women that allowed them to transcend the barriers that divide us, we can develop an ethics of empowerment when we can renounce privilege (give up that which keeps us apart) and build coalitions with the church and other groups toward social and communal uplift and liberation. Womanist liberation ethics, like the ethics that undergirds the Spirituals, calls for an agenda whereby we embrace and live with the resulting tensions within ourselves and our community when we build on common ground and renounce what separates us; appreciate and include those who are different; and become individually, socially, and religiously responsible. To mediate or apply a moral vision requires power. The successful use of that power means that, first, we must recognize that with exposing the blatant and subtle ramifications of racism, sexism, and classism, there must be a focus on the creative use of anger.

Anger, Social Witness, and Bible Time

The late poet and author Audre Lorde teaches us that anger does not destroy, but hatred does. Hatred may seek to destroy us when we foster actual change and do not rhapsodize with mere academic, theoretical speech. Hatred is the energy whose object is death and destruction. Anger is a community-based, distorted grief that desires change. Though society often teaches us to see any difference beyond sex as a reason for destruction, dark-skinned women have matured amid anger, forced silence, and neglect, knowing their survival happens in spite of those who judge them less than human, fit only for servitude. Black women know a "symphony of anger," not discord or chaos, because they must orchestrate their anger in a way that does not cause them to self-destruct. Black women are not interested in espousing hate or guilt, because guilt is a response to personal actions or lack of action, not to anger.[40]

Womanists channel their anger toward analysis, protest, survival, and justice. Anger concerns justice because we can use anger to destroy self and others by choosing evil, or we can use anger to empower ourselves and others by choosing good. Anger as transformed energy can bring growth and healing—the use of anger for good. Womanists thus articulate the formerly invisible, using disciplines in the traditional arts and sciences, to empower and to tell the truth about African-American women's roles throughout American history. The Spirituals embody this creative anger as power toward the good. The effective use of that power requires authority.

Emilie Townes, Womanist ethicist, explores authority that rejects suffering as the mode of existence for Black women, and authority as a vehicle for developing shared power as partnership. Like Riggs, Townes wants us to admit to a reality that often gets lost in the subterfuge of trying to make sense out of pain: suffering is *not* God's will. Suffering is sinful, for it thwarts God's gift of wholeness, and Womanist ethics moves to change this way of being.[41] Shared authority equips a community to cooperate and respect each other in the quest for justice. Rooted in the risen Christ, such justice generates accountability, mutuality, conversation, responsibility, critical evaluation, healthy relationships, intimate knowledge of God, and a prayerful, active personal and social witness of togetherness, out of the church and into the world. Authority to be a liberated being amid those most often oppressed requires teachers, witnesses, and griots to live and recite new possibilities of empowerment. Social witness engages in the struggle for human salvation or liberation in all aspects of life. The Spirituals have been the reformation hymns of social witness that have called for freedom from poverty, wrong-doing, poor self-esteem, narcissism, brokenness, and freedom to be in healthy relationships with self, God, and others.

Womanist social witness, grounded in spirituality, requires personal and communal love and justice. Such social witness must bring the concerns of the Black underclass to the table and must begin to address the complex social network of American society, rather than dismiss the Black underclass as being immoral or lazy. We must let the Spirituals remind us that all enslaved Black folk were part of America's underclass, and most of them are the ancestors of many of us, Black, White, and Brown alike. Womanist spirituality screams with outrage at the demeaning ways we view people because of what they look like, how much is in their pocketbook, and where they stand on the ladder of status and affluence. Womanist spirituality protests with indignance the lynching ropes of externally produced toxic waste, marginalization, and social and political control, along with internal self-destructive behavior, classism, skewed agendas, passivity, and blindness as to who we are. Womanist spirituality calls for an ethics of accountability and gift that shuns abstract thoughts and deals with lived reality. This spirituality knows history and recognizes the biases due to color prejudice within Black communities, and the detriment such oppression causes. Such an ethic looks at what has destroyed and continues to destroy Black extended families and the results of Black middle-class flight. Womanist spirituality has an apocalyptic (dramatic, crisis-oriented, symbolic, inclusive) vision that knows that to change the lived experiences of the underclass means we must build some new allegiances, and that the Black church must take a reality check in assessing, "Who is God, who is our neighbor, and how do we minister?"[42]

Ministering to churched Black women requires that we examine how they read biblical texts. Renita Weems, preacher, speaker, and Womanist biblical scholar, notes the importance of determining the impact, influence, and tremendous appeal the Bible has in African-American religious life despite the many instances of oppression in the biblical texts. These biblical texts certainly shape and form a large percentage of the vocabulary of the Spirituals, in the use of both biblical characters as metaphors and biblical themes as subject matter. Early on, because reading was illegal for slaves, they experienced the text as oral and fluid. First, the slaves were not wedded to a particular interpretation or authoritative reading of the text. Second, because the Bible tended to be the one, if not the only, book passed down from generation to generation, Black women were taught that this prized book is a vehicle for knowing the Christian God and is a guidebook for human behavior. Third, despite the general reading strategies offered to Blacks, African-American women have critically listened to the biblical text with their *total* health in mind, from the psychological and religious to the emotional and political. Fourth, since the Bible was not compiled with Black women in mind, they experience mixed messages when reading/hearing the text. Fifth, Black women remain intrigued with the biblical text because of the voices that speak against oppression: if God could and did deliver the Hebrew children out of bondage, God could and would deliver Black folk.[43]

While Weems teaches us about reading strategies, Womanist biblical scholar, Clarice Martin calls for relating the Bible to daily life practices. Martin invites us to an applied strategy: to remember people's spiritual journeys or autobiographies that protest evil and proclaim a faithful, sustaining, loving God. Often we think that the world has "gone to hell in a handbasket" and that we are a hopeless, unredemptive society where no one cares about his or her neighbor. During slavery, U.S. society, especially slave owners, perpetuated the lie that slaves were not really people, that they were worthless, had no morals, and had perverse living styles. The need to control those in bondage warped the slave masters, who ignored the contradiction that some of these same inferior, subhuman slaves cared for the slave master's children, cooked the master's food, and in some instances bore the master's children. Martin notes that several slave women's spiritual autobiographies refute the slave masters' argument. Some of their accounts of spiritual experiences inform and color the thousands of Spirituals coined by slave bards. These bold women focused their personal spiritual lives and those of the communities on their experience of God's grace through conversion. The conversion experience led to a regrouping that produced a new strength, independence, and freedom. That freedom allowed slave women to select liberating texts over oppressive ones and to know that the God who delivered out of Egypt (Exodus) and the God who triumphed over Babylon (Revelation) is the helping God on the side of the slaves. Martin invites us to remember, retell, and rehearse the stories of these slave women.[44] Our ancestors remembered, retold, and rehearsed that God cares, God helps, God rescues, God empowers; God is slow to anger, is just, is merciful. Remembering removes the lie of isolation that keeps us from having hope. Remembering teaches that they got over, and we can too. Remembering resurrects the ancient cloud of witnesses. Cheryl Sanders, Womanist ethicist, witnesses and reminds those who live the intersection of Blackness and femaleness that to interpret biblical texts means to employ bold strategies to resist evil, to affirm the ethics of values, loyalty, and identity, and to see empowerment as the product of divine and human activity in Black women's lives.[45]

Intersection in Womanist witness takes the analyses of theology, ethics, and biblical studies and applies them to building church and secular community. Womanists, in oral and written recital, stand for the wholeness and survival of their entire community. Black women and Womanist scholars, via their cultural and religious experiences, have generated alternative ideas, images, and encounters to societal oppression, a liberating, mutual theodicy of love and empowerment. Toinette Eugene, a Catholic Womanist and social ethicist, notes that Womanists have held to a just God and the reality of liberation based on a communal ethic and on their heritage of an antebellum religiosity.[46] Thus, a Womanist rhetorical reading of theodicy values differences and becomes a political and social activity. A Womanist reading, in discovering the tensions between texts and performers, aims at liberating the race, sex, and class victimage of African-American reality. Although Womanist theories are recent and therefore reflect back from the present, the activity and issues have existed since slavery. Womanists realize that when the tools of racist patriarchy examine the fruits of that patriarchy, only the most narrow parameters of change are possible and allowable.[47] Womanists have found their own strength and then contributed to the community through the power and nurturing traditions of African women's female bonding. In the church and society, that bonding embraces the language and experience of sisterhood as a way to overcome public and private suffering and injustice as well as a way to celebrate the private and public gifts of leadership, proclamation, and visibility.

Sisterhood: Empowered Womanist Reality

"Sisterhood" is the relationship of a female circle of friends, of mutuality and neighborliness. Sisterhood brings together women as colleagues, associates, protectors, collaborators, and helpers in a kinship of biological or extended family where women share common character, ancestry, allegiance, or purpose. These women foster empowerment and contribute to the well-being of others. Womanist sisterhood calls for the empowerment and health of all people.

Black feminist bell hooks examines history and calls for truth telling about sisterhood. hooks claims that most women have bought into the quest for the status quo of White male privilege and that White feminism has not fostered a sisterhood with poor women or women of color. Many slave women and antebellum White women accepted the oppressive racist, sexist, classist society as the ideal, and thus became party to the continued enslavement of all women. Yet nineteenth- and twentieth-century Black women have struggled to change the negative images which Whites have perpetuated about Blacks. Many twentieth-century Black women have thought feminism is a "White woman's thing." The White women's sisterhood itself has not dismantled the triple oppression experienced by Black women. Until women in the United States cease to base liberation on achieving what White men have, liberation and sisterhood will never occur. True sisterhood requires action and solidarity. Such sisterhood is yet to be accomplished, and hooks sees the possibility for sisterhood only if women work together to take apart the psychology of dominance throughout Western culture. Change happens when people take action. Nineteenth-century women acted, and we call twenty-first-century women to do the same and to not be afraid of change.[48]

Change requires that we break the silence about oppression by exposing the pathology, the disease, of suffering and that we hold persons in the church and the community accountable for their race, sex, and class injustice, including injustice perpetrated by Blacks against Blacks. Change requires that we recognize the God-talk, the vision, the preaching of nineteenth-, twentieth-, and twenty-first-century Black women, understanding that a "woman's place" is everywhere God calls her to speak, from pulpit to pew, as heads of state, in the boardroom, and at home. Change demands that we scream out against institutional, systemic violence. Change means that we work toward a vision of communal and collective justice, that we live as well as sing the Spirituals. A Womanist vision provides more depth to the reflection on the many civil rights protests from a social, historical, philosophical, and theological viewpoint. A Womanist theological vision of antebellum life, the Movement, and contemporary issues intentionally listens for and communicates with diverse communities, with a liturgical intent to take seriously the action, worship, and thought of Black churches; a didactic intent to be faithful to teaching theological reflection; and a pledge to use female imagery in theological reflection.[49] This vision helps us see the call for justice in the Spirituals and the magnificent contribution women have made and continue to make toward liberation.

While society often ignores the feminine way of acting and being in the world, we must use universal symbols like the Spirituals to help all people transcend race, gender, language, and religious differences.[50] Is the process of transcendence really inclusive? Since the 1980s, Womanists have sounded the alarm for the world to be inclusive. Black theologian James Cone, in the twentieth-anniversary edition of his original Black power text, admits that those oppressed by gender and class have been excluded in the work of Black theologians writing in the 1960s. Black theology and the 1960s Civil Rights Movement made a political statement by focusing on Black men but denied the contributions and needs of Black women. Although a male-consciousness motif pervaded society during the late 1960s (possibly due to the male revolt against postwar societal expectations), Black male chauvinists and Black women both remained a part of the Movement. African-American plays, movies, and novels of the 1970s tended to stress violence and male assertiveness and Black women's weakness and passiveness, and celebrated Black males' sexual exploits and the role of the pimp.[51] This representation of Black life upon the heels of the 1960s Civil Rights Movement indicates what went on before and during the Movement. Because Black and feminist theologians did not address sexism and classism, Womanist theology, the most significant recent advance in American Black theology[52] and one of the bright lights in twenty-first-century religious studies, came into being. The Womanist scholars involved in the conversation of this chapter have powerful stories to tell with tremendous social witness, for all that they speak of relates to the life cycle of the African-American oppressed and therefore is germane to the foundational concerns of the Spirituals.

Womanists love God and life, living from a perspective of sacrality. Womanist thought, embodied in the Spirituals, embraces identity, visibility, integrity, community, authority, and sacrality. Sexism, racism, and classism cause violence and subjugate. An in-depth exegesis of the Spirituals requires a Womanist reading—a reading that intentionally listens for the silenced voices. Such a reading requires that the reader become conscious of the pathology of oppression to illumine the experiences of the texts and to let the music and texts ask questions about our lives, and particularly about justice, that otherwise will not yield a response. Have global Black women learned to transcend the distorted relationships that inculcate ignorance, fear, and greed? Are there symbols in place to celebrate the awesome beauty of Blackness? "The Black Virgin . . . stands for the conjunction of the opposites which are generally embodied in different women: the dark, ugly and approachable, and the beautiful but inaccessible," which all come together in the Black Madonna.[53]

> We, and I are Black, and Woman!
> People of the world—
> Hear my love and passion
> Hear my joy.
> My sense of God
> My quiet elegance
> My loud pleasure
> My awesome strength
> See and celebrate my Blackness
> Believe part of me made you.
> I am Black and Woman;
> Come celebrate it with me.

8

Womanist Musings

Oh, Black, Beautiful Woman:
Old as time
Young as the day
Cherished by some;
Thrown aside by others;
Magnificently made;
Honored by God
Elegant heart beat
Sing the pulse of life.

Spirituals are songs of motivation that champion the possibility, the process, and the product of liberation and freedom. Slaves and freedom fighters identified with Paul and Silas as they walked out of jail. They knew they had stayed in the wilderness too long. Although the search sometimes seemed as elusive as the quest for the Holy Grail, these seekers of freedom never gave up, never questioned the rightness and the goal of the quest. Womanists look at the Spirituals and see the distant and recent past, the present, and the future. Each existential moment is one of cruelty yet one of hope, with opportunities for affirmation and liberation. With power and love, Womanists know that the wholeness of no person is complete until the African-American woman is no longer the victim of race, gender, and class bias and prejudice.[1] Womanists hear the plea of the Spirituals for freedom, justice, and personal and communal empowerment. In our search for unearthing the hidden and not-so-hidden priceless lessons in the Spirituals, this chapter thematically probes the impact of Womanist thought toward understanding the message of the Spirituals during slavery and the 1960s Movement, and involves a Womanist reading of Black women living, singing, and arranging the Spirituals.

African-American women have lived, sung, or arranged the Spirituals and have engaged in erasing oppression in various forms, and this chapter celebrates their contributions and the significance of their work. These women are African Americans whose lives and contributions echo the desires that undergird the Spirituals, that unmask the oppression of gender, race, and class. Thus, the Spirituals become a symbol of Womanist empowerment.

The Spirituals symbolize the quest for justice, empowerment, and liberation now, right now, and at the same time later. They are eschatological in that whatever goals not met in immediate time will ultimately be met. While the Spirituals certainly see suffering as unmerited and paradoxical, these songs do *not* see God as manipulating evil toward the Christian's advantage or toward some form of heaven or deferred well-being.[2] Spirituals tend not to ask for retribution, but they do not assume enslavement is a game wherein African Americans are pawns to be redeemed later. The Spirituals want justice, oneness with God or heaven *now*. Many slaves already had a concept of God and a concept of retributive justice (i.e., "you reap what you sow") before being stolen from Africa. Their intimate notions of God with their daily life would argue that those in bondage trusted that God would deliver them. They certainly knew they had done nothing to deserve what they experienced in slavery. Deferred deliverance is not the same thing as allowing an evil to exist for the sake of a religious or faith goal. Slave owners were the oppressors, not God. Further, many of the slaves, encouraged by the call for freedom and justice, used these songs as an impetus to take action themselves. Surely countless runaway slaves and those Blacks conducting the Underground Railroad did not sense a call to acquiesce or accommodate in the Spirituals. This broader reading/hearing of the Spirituals involves the theoretical and emphatically deals with the practical. Oppression is real.

Divine Care, Divine Love *(Agape)*

The Spiritual "He's [God/Jesus] Got the Whole World in His Hands" reflects a foundational concern for Womanists: God cares; and, as beings created in God's image, we care. Caring requires active courage. Since arriving on these shores, Black women have exercised strength and boldness in their daily acts of survival and overcoming. A Womanist reading sees and experiences as a call to be bold and to take outrageous steps to care about all babies—the babies of national political leaders, the babies of mothers on Aid to Dependent Children (ADC), the babies that die from violence, those that die a living death due to neglect; and the babies in all of us that somehow never mature. A Womanist reading looks for the many infant ideas in the Spirituals yet to be unearthed and considers these songs, born in response to evil and sin, as a potential antibiotic, depressant, or stimulant. Since the Spirituals can be vehicles for healing in a way as yet not fully developed, working with them from a Womanist perspective insures the caring of others as this experience triggers the act of love and the process of identity.

Womanists love all people in all kinds of ways. The Spirituals celebrate love as *agape*. *Agape* as love envisioned in the New Testament is a love that creates community and communion. This deep yet gentle transcendent feeling of affection and solicitude of lived, divine grace and charity embraces others, shares affection, and shares a meal. *Agape* love invites one to be a part of the larger body, as signified in the Spirituals, "I'm Gonna Sit at the Welcome Table" and "Let Us Break Bread Together."

To break bread or sit at the welcome table means one has the opportunity to avoid hunger, false imprisonment, ignorance, brutality, and injustice. Consequently, our children will not have to fight some of the same inane battles that their parents have had to fight. We can hope, can trust, and must participate in communal and self-actualization, for God cares, and "[We can] tell God how you treat me." Spirituals that sing of inclusiveness, of being welcomed, mean individuals and societies have choices about their activities. That inclusiveness symbolizes Martin L. King's dream of people being judged by the content of their character as opposed to the color of their skin, their political connections, or their pedigrees. These Spirituals announce the possibility of leveling the playing field toward equality and justice for all. Womanists remind us that, globally, many have yet to receive an invitation to the table. At best, some have received nothing, some have been served scraps, some have been denied even a drink of water; others have been ridiculed or totally dismissed. The welcome table stands before us as a reality check to both the oppressor and the oppressed and asks questions of identity and visibility: who are you, where are you, where are you going?

Affirming Identity

The Spirituals affirm the identity of Black folks—the interconnectedness of their individual and collective human experiences of body, spirit, mind, memory, personality, and patterns of conscious acts, needs, and desires. The Spirituals reflect this essence in bad times and good. "I've Been 'Buked" remembers the scorn and the troubles that most people experience during the course of life.

Nevertheless, the taunted ones vow that, no matter what, they will not "lay my 'ligion down!" They will not give up their faith in God or their hopes in new possibilities. These oppressed also realize that each individual must participate in his or her own empowerment, and consequently, they see the need for strong, faith-based community solidarity. Communal solidarity, as vital as it is, does not always protect community members from the impact of harm's way. "I've Been in the Storm" rehearses the long season of oppression and difficulty experienced by most African Americans. Even so, the devastation of the storm can be life-giving; and God's justice and mercy mean that "trouble [unwarranted, uncivilized suffering] won't last always." The singers know that they do not stand alone, and therefore they ask for prayer time:

I've been in the storm, so long
I've been in the storm, so long, children
I've been in the storm, so long
Lord, give a little time to pray.
Traditional

Prayer acknowledges the reality of God and gives the oppressed visibility. Often the move from invisibility and silence to visibility and speaking is the first step toward being all God created one to be. Self-actualization relates to the Womanist focus of survival and wholeness.

Throughout history, Black folks survived: across middle passage, in the bowels of slavery, and through the false promises of Reconstruction, the insanity of many wars, the hope of the Civil Rights Movement and the Great Society, the economic strain of Reaganomics, the conservative bent of the Bush era, and the promises and shortcomings of Clinton. This quest for survival affects all people, Black and non-Black, female and male. Since the Spirituals are an oral documentation of the antebellum and civil rights eras and still are sung to the present day, singing these songs celebrates the survival and wholeness of all people, along with the possibility of a relationship between the community and God. Like ancient Israelites, Black folk have traditionally trusted God. "My Good Lord's Done Been Here" honors a surviving people who know the reality of God:

My good Lord's done been here,
Blessed my soul, my soul and gone
My good Lord's done been here
Bless my soul and gone.

O, brothers, where were you?
O, sisters, where were you?
O, Christians, where were you?
O, mourners, where were you?
When my good Lord was here?
Traditional

God is not an abstract, absent being. God is present, and that presence provides blessing. This Spiritual also calls everyone, regardless of color, to experience conversion.

Call to Conversion, Call to Praise

Conversion, a prerequisite needed for injustice to cease and for justice to exist, occurs when one adopts a new religion, faith, or belief. The conversion or transformation of people and of social and political systems revives the *imago Dei* in humanity. Divine-human encounter occurs and elevates humanity to the level of the sacred. Not only does singing the song itself transform one's spirit, but meditation on the song helps reveal that there is another way to experience life other than the present one where the cries of wrongdoing drown out those of praise.

The praise of God acknowledges that humanity recognizes its fragileness, its inability to control everything, and its gratitude toward God for the blessings of life and possibilities. "Certainly, Lord" is a praise response about Spiritual health and well-being. The leader asks, "Have you got good religion?" And the chorus responds, "Certainly, Lord!"

> *Have you got good religion? Cert'nly Lord!*
> *Have you got good religion? Cert'nly Lord!*
> *Have you got good religion? Cert'nly Lord!*
> *Cert'nly, Cert'nly, Cert'nly Lord!*

This type of praise response is not about religiosity, hypocrisy, or window dressing, but values who people are and what the community can be. Participation in such praise response proclaims that "I Wanna Be Ready" to "walk in Jerusalem just like John":

> *I wanna be ready,*
> *I wanna be ready,*
> *I wanna be ready,*
> *To walk in Jerusalem just like John.*
> Traditional

To walk like John gives one a sense of authority, integrity, and visibility here on earth. African Americans were active in this country before it became a republic, which justifies a Womanist reading of the Spirituals because of the historical, liberating, transformational tenets and possibilities of looking at the past to learn where we must go for the future. The Spirituals, indeed, are metaphors for two key movements that altered the meaning of living in these United States: slavery and the 1960s Movement.

The Search for Empowerment

Many women and men sang freedom songs in the 1960s with the intent of empowerment and creatively used their anger to protest the ravages poured out on African Americans. Too often, however, the voices of women have been silenced. In honor of theological justice or theodicy, that voice is awakened here. Black women experienced and participated in the Movement; the insight of Black women as intracommunity oriented brings a focus on the participant as protagonist; and contemporary Black women's poetic abilities mirror the Spirituals and honor Womanists' moral judgments and ethical choices, in life and in literature.

The redacted Spirituals embrace the experience of the 1960s activists, especially the call for freedom now, for deliverance from all oppression. The Womanists who sang the Spirituals expressed a desire to fight for justice as they imitated their mothers, grandmothers, and great-grandmothers, singing the Spirituals as an act of storytelling, as a "habit of survival" in response to pain and suffering that lessens anger, gives a sense of self-control, and offers hope.[3] Through the Spirituals and other stories, Womanists address the dynamics of the gifts of freedom: self-empowerment and intracommunal development, with implications for intercommunal relations. Singing the Spirituals for a Womanist is an act of naming the violence, pain, and hope, unmasking the issues, and engaging each other and the system to create change.

A Womanist vision recalls the many times when movement was only internal for the Africans of the diaspora and celebrates the "quiet grace" reflected in the courage of those who faced death in the wake of demanding equal treatment. Womanist ideas help us to focus on issues internal to the community, to see the female and male characteristics of the Spirituals, and to call attention to one segment of society that symbolizes those oppressed by race, sex, and class, illuminating the complexity of justice praxis in American society:

> I think songs are both male and female. I think they are projectile. They can have a piercing, penile energy; and, they also absolutely can rock you in a womb-like way. But within the range of an African-American musical experience you would have both. 'Cause that "going forward thing" has a thrusting to it. And I think what you get is both forward motion, thrusting as well as nurturing, womb, healing, taking care.... I think you have both.
>
> Can we say that there is a sense in which the songs acted or songs could act to be a liberating force from that place of racism, sexism, or classism? . . . . I'm not conscious that there was a consciousness of those things in that way. I think reading back, you can talk about that, but I think it is stretching it. . . . My sense is that a song and singing in the Black tradition is an instrument that is shaped by the singer so that it could actually liberate if that is the point, but it is not. It does not operate or stand outside of the intent of the singer. . . . [Some] great Black singers [are] despots. . . . The singer is wonderful and is used in terrible ways. . . . So singing does not exist outside the intent of the singer.[4]

Spirituals have been sung by men and women with the intent of empowerment. Too often, however, the voices of women have been silenced. In honor of justice or theodicy, that voice is awakened here.

Womanists knew the tensions enmeshed within the Civil Rights Movement as part of one's life cycle. A Womanist grasp of "We Shall Not Be Moved" made one accountable for movement within the community and reminded others of their need to deal with their own movement or lack thereof. Two African-American women who opposed oppression, Rutha Harris and Bernice Johnson Reagon, together with two male singers, Cornell Hall Reagon and Charles Neblett, transcended the fear of death as they toured throughout the country as the Freedom Singers, singing for justice and righteousness. Womanists celebrate the authority to speak out and celebrate community, by all people, everywhere.

Honoring Empowerment and Community Building

The Spirituals, born in community, are a means to get behind history and glean insight about how extended families and communities helped Black people survive. The survival of all people depends largely on seeing all of humanity as human beings, not as "others" to be denied. A Womanist reading of the Spirituals celebrates the power that holds the community together—the God of mercy, love, and solidarity. With the work toward solidarity comes the effort of letting people be who they are and helping them to be whole and well without hurting others. One of the best ways to help transform a moment of anxiety and to help heal the hurt is to get someone to sing. Singing brings people together as a group and provides hope; singing requires that we breathe. People in the middle of an anxiety attack forget to breathe. A sense of wholeness understands the possibility of spiritual transformation that can occur through meditative deep breathing, a by-product of certain types of singing. Just as God "breathed breath" into clay and created a human being who became a living, sentient creature, singing and breathing can help bring a sense of new life into a hurting community.

Community singing can also bring meaningfulness to empty hearts. Most professional African-American entertainers, even today, got their start by performing in church. Performing helps to instill self-esteem, confidence, and a sense of belonging. The experience of belonging reinforces the ability to survive and to enjoy a supportive quality of life. The singing says "No!" to stereotypes and sinful acts and says "Yes!" to worthiness and well-being. The message of these Spirituals affirms a risk-taking faith that requires one to take a stand in the church and the world. The holistic, life-giving, and relational God of the Spirituals calls for us to be like-minded: to care and to be just and merciful. The prophetic voices which speak of this relational God reveal the prophetic voice of the Spirituals, as in "O Daniel" and "Didn't My Lord Deliver Daniel?":

You call yourself a church member,
You hold your head so high,
You praise God with your glitt'ring tongue,
But you leave all your heart behind.

Oh my Lord delivered Daniel
O Daniel, O Daniel
Oh my Lord delivered Daniel,
O why not deliver me too?
Traditional

Didn't my Lord deliver Daniel,
Deliver Daniel, deliver Daniel?
Didn't my Lord deliver Daniel?
Then why not every man?

He delivered Daniel from the lions' den,
And Jonah from the belly of the whale,
He delivered children from the fiery furnace,
And why not every man?

If you cannot sing like angels,
If you cannot preach like Paul,
You can tell the love of Jesus
and you can say He died for all.
Traditional

Prophets deliver God's message. This God-message says there is a Messiah and a God who delivers. Because God delivers, we are to share that message and help empower peoples to get out of situations that oppress them.

Community Solidarity

The communal sense inherent in the Spirituals signifies that it matters if our neighbors are in pain, are abused, or lack self-esteem. Singing the Spirituals presses one to use God language to help people fight for themselves, not acquiesce to dominating persons, and to avoid situations or persons that can sabotage their mental, moral, and/or spiritual health. The long-dead voices of earlier composers of the Spirituals faced daily destruction, exploitation, dehumanization, humiliation, and violence. Womanists help awaken these voices and help us hear them in a way that ministers to our own internal and existential brokenness. Often the first step toward healing is the recognition that the pain and brokenness exist. One can then help others, by assuring them that, despite their present state, they are worthy. The first step is an invitation to celebrate themselves and to celebrate life:

Dere's a little wheel a turnin' in my heart
Dere's a little wheel a turnin' in my heart

In my heart, in my heart,
Dere's a little wheel a turnin' in my heart.

O I feel so very happy in my heart,
O I feel so very happy in my heart,
In my heart, in my heart,
Dere's a little wheel a turnin' in my heart.

O I don't feel no ways tired in my heart,
O I don't feel no ways tired in my heart,
In my heart, in my heart.
O I don't feel no ways tired in my heart.

Traditional

Womanist theory calls us to be inclusive and to love each other well. Active love empowers and gives me an opportunity to know that because I am worthy, I am worth fighting for, and I can choose to stand up for myself or for some other worthy cause:

You got a right,
I got a right,
We all got a right
To the tree of life.

Traditional

When we stand up for ourselves, we affirm with the community:

Done made my vow to the Lord
And I never will turn back.
I will go, I shall go
To see what the end will be.

Traditional

Out of this lived experience, we can tell others:

Ain't gonna let nobody turn me 'round.
Turn me 'round, turn me 'round,
Turn me 'round.
Ain't gonna let nobody turn me 'round.
Keep on walkin', keep on talkin',
Marchin' to freedom's land.

Redacted civil rights version

These Spirituals afford us an ethics of resistance to all unhealthy experiences and move us to an ethics of aesthetics, a way of seeing and being in the world that brings out the best in us. The Spirituals embody a form of Einstein's $E = mc^2$ where the energy of equality equals the matter of music multiplied by the creative desire for reform squared to embrace both the oppressed and the oppressor. In celebrating this energy as new possibility using old songs that remain eternal, I turn now to examine the women, past and present, who have lived, sung, and arranged the Spirituals in a way that has and is having a major impact on American life and culture.

Black women signify as they wear and celebrate the garments of self-expression via living, singing, and arranging the Spirituals. The Spiritual "On My Journey" is a testament about the unwillingness of an individual to be downhearted, discouraged about, or deterred from his or her task or journey. No system or male human being could silence Black women's signifying—the revising and renaming—of their realities. In communicating, these women used coded language, gave old ideas new names, and edited their conversations, so that those listening who were not supposed to know the full reality of what was transpiring would not understand.

On ma journey now, Mount Zion [pronounced Zine],
Ma journey now, Mount Zion,
Well I wouldn't take nothin', Mount Zion
For my journey now, Mount Zion.
One day, one day,
I was walkin' along,
And de elements opened,
And the love come down, Mount Zion.

Well, I went to de valley,
And I didn't go to stay,
Well ma soul got happy,
An' I stayed all day, Mount Zion.

You can talk about me,
Just as much as you please
Well, I'll talk about you,
When I get on ma knees, Mount Zion.
Traditional

These magnificent creatures of ebony, chocolate, and cocoa butter gave utterances of exultation and excitement, pleasure and pain, love and life, anxiety and anger, relief and reverence for God. With the onset of slavery, sounds of Black women's daily life in the African motherland became mere echoes of the near yet distant past, as slave ships rocked midst the waves of the Atlantic during middle passage. Middle passage, the denigrating journey toward institutionalized slavery, brought African women to these shores. The stench of death and nausea, the near starvation and the angst of hopelessness dampened but did not kill their spirits. Not the intentional separation of peoples with similar language and culture, the dehumanization of bodies packed like sardines, the loss of home and country, nor the fear of what was to come could silence Black female signifiers.

From the beginning of civilization to the present day, these women have signified as I now signify about them. Black women's signifying, or play on language, is part of the social, musical infrastructure of Black language systems and embraces the rhythm of Black life itself. The beautiful and the brusque shape these women's creative utterances as they signify via word, song, dance, politics, education, and domestic and graphic art, in praise and in protest, about their existential life rhythms. In revisiting these women's lives, we celebrate the smorgasbord of Black women's signification in the areas of art, literature, music, education, social protest, and religion, by interweaving biographical commentary with the words, songs, and expressions of Black women throughout history, from the antebellum period through the 1990s—protesting, signifying, testifying women symbolized through living, singing, and arranging the Spirituals. History provides the categories; Black women's lives provide the material.

Abolition Activists

The first signifiers via the Spirituals are abolitionist activists Sojourner Truth, Maria Stewart, Harriet Ross Tubman, and Frances Watkins Harper. Sojourner Truth (c. 1799-1883) lived the Spirituals as abolitionist, feminist, and religious leader, for she fearlessly signified freedom, liberation, and truth. Truth wrote orally, not with a pen. Celebrated for her 1851 "Ain't I a Woman" speech, Truth took the position made into a hallmark by Womanist scholars: she dealt with issues of race, gender, and class. (Some recent scholars claim this speech did not occur; yet the story of her audacious statements has inspired many women.) She defied those who wanted to deny Black women the status of being female and the status of being Black. In 1858, Truth again defied sexism and slavery by publicly baring her breasts in answer to the claim by some men who argued that such a forceful speaker could not be a woman. Between 1826 and 1827, Truth gained freedom via emancipation by New York State law; she successfully sued for the freedom of her son, who had been illegally sold into slavery in Alabama; and she had a dramatic religious conversion experience and joined the Methodist Church. The Second Great Awakening, as well as the related piety and religiosity of Methodism, had a lasting impact on her, particularly when many unlettered itinerant preachers of both sexes, often in the Quaker and Methodist traditions, began to preach and evangelize. She began to preach during the 1830s and aligned with several millenarian groups who thought judgment was imminent. In 1843, she changed her name from Isabella to Sojourner Truth (itinerant preacher) and left her home to preach Jesus to all, as commanded by the Spirit, without telling her family. In the latter

1840s and the 1850s, Truth met with Frederick Douglass and William Lloyd Garrison. She lived for a while within a utopian community, the Northampton Association, which supported abolitionist activities and feminism. Sojourner Truth preached to audiences as an antislavery feminist, basing her authority on her slave experience. She published *The Narrative of Sojourner Truth*, in 1850, which allowed her to support herself and pay off her mortgage in Massachusetts (a second edition appeared in 1875). She worked against poverty and petitioned Congress to demand that land in the western frontier be set aside for freed African Americans. Though the petition failed, many Blacks began traveling toward Kansas. A feminist, Truth supported women being included in the drafting of the Fourteenth Amendment to the Constitution: in debates at an 1867 Equal Rights Convention, Truth argued that both Black men *and Black women* were disenfranchised. For Sojourner Truth, one must claim the Spiritual "I'm a Rollin' ":

I'm a rollin', I'm a rollin',
I'm a rollin' thro' an unfriendly world
I'm a rollin', I'm a rollin',
Thro' an unfriendly world.

O sister, won't you help me,
O sister, won't you help me to pray,
O, sister won't you help me,
Won't you help me in the service of the Lord?

O brothers, won't you help me,
O brothers, won't you help me to pray,
O brothers, won't you help me,
Won't you help me in the service of the Lord?
Traditional

Preacher, singer, and antislavery lecturer, Truth knew she was "a rollin'," knew she needed to hold on to the gospel plow, and as such, she was an evangelical spokesperson for the cause of justice and humanity.[5] Like Sojourner Truth, Maria Stewart also sang the cause of freedom.

Maria Stewart (1803-1879), an orphan nurtured in a parsonage via religious rhetoric and philosophical conviction for self-help and community service, lived the Spirituals as an advocate for abolition, freedom, and equality for African-American slaves. She was the first woman ever to give a public lecture series before both race- *and gender*-integrated audiences. Stewart's outspokenness about major contemporary issues, from colonization and racial unity to self-determination and race pride, remained part of her teaching philosophy when she taught in New York and Washington, D.C. Racism and sexism hindered nineteenth-century America from embracing Stewart's public political dialogues and her published pamphlets.

Because Stewart had a bold message she wanted to proclaim, the Spiritual "Peter, Go Ring Dem Bells" could announce her message, for she had "heard from heaven" and wanted all to hear her words:

> *Peter, go ring dem bells,*
> *Peter, go ring dem bells,*
> *Peter, go ring a dem bells,*
> *I heard from heaven today.*

> *Wonder where ma mother has gone,*
> *Wonder where ma mother has gone,*
> *Wonder where ma mother has gone,*
> *Heard from heaven today.*

> *Wonder where Sister Mary has gone . . .*
> *Wonder where Sister Martha has gone . . .*
> *It's good news, and I thank God . . .*
> *Wonder where brother Moses has gone . . .*
> *Wonder where brother Daniel's gone . . .*
> *Wonder where Elijah has gone . . .*
> Traditional

Abolitionist William Lloyd Garrison reported Stewart's four speeches in his abolitionist newspaper the *Liberator*.[6] Just as Stewart spoke and taught with vigor and tenacity, so did Harriet Tubman drive those in her trust through unspeakable hardships to freedom, to Canaan.

Harriet Ross Tubman (c. 1821-1913) lived the Spirituals as the "Moses of her people," the best-known Underground Railroad conductor. She was a feminist, Union spy, social reformer, and provider for African-American aged and indigent. Born into slavery in Maryland, Tubman escaped to Philadelphia and worked to garner contacts and resources to rescue her sister and her sister's children out of slavery. This started Tubman's mission to help runaway slaves with shelter, clothes, money, disguises, or transportation, and this earned her the epithet "Moses." The Spiritual that signifies Tubman best then, is

> *Go down, Moses,*
> *Way down in Egypt's land* [the South].
> *Tell ole Pharaoh* [slave owners; racists]
> *To let my people* [the oppressed] *go*
> Traditional

Tubman feared no one. Formally uneducated, she knew nature, the Bible, music, and southern contemporary folklore. She used these assets to communicate safety or danger to her hidden, waiting passengers going north. She disguised herself, used various routes, and kept a gun to discourage any runaways from leaving the freedom train; she kept paregoric to quiet any crying babies. Tubman was so successful that Maryland slave owners offered a $40,000 reward for her capture. She worked with a network of Black and White abolitionists, with all people, regardless of race, gender, or socioeconomic status, including Frederick Douglass, William Lloyd Garrison, John Brown, Susan B. Anthony, and Ralph Waldo Emerson, as she testified about the horrors of slavery and continued to move runaway slaves north. Tubman operated out of Canada for a while because of the Fugitive Slave Law of 1850. This law threatened the Underground Railroad and all free northern Blacks, for now the federal government could be used to arrest and return escaped slaves anywhere in the country. Tubman continued to provide safe passage for slaves until late 1860. Black leaders including Tubman, Sojourner Truth, and Frederick Douglass were upset and irate about President Abraham Lincoln's denial that the war was to abolish slavery, and about the fact that Blacks were not welcome to participate in the Union Army. Lincoln did finally issue the Emancipation Proclamation announcing that slaves in rebellious states would be free on January 1, 1863, and that Blacks could enlist in the army in early 1863.

Tubman, as scout, nurse, and spy, distinguished herself as the only woman to plan and execute armed warfare against the enemy in American military history. She was present at the battle of Fort Wagner, where the Black Massachusetts Fifty-Fourth Regiment with Colonel Robert Gould Shaw (lionized in the recent novel and movie *Glory*) gave their lives for the Union cause. After the Civil War, Tubman did other humanitarian work. She participated in Reconstruction work, nursed the sick and wounded soldiers, and taught newly freed Blacks strategies for self-sufficiency. With assistance from the Massachusetts Antislavery Society, she bought a house for herself and her parents. Tubman purchased twenty-five adjoining acres, where, with some of the military pension she had to fight the government for thirty years to receive, she built the Harriet Tubman Home for Indigent Aged Negroes, which formally opened in 1908. With other women, Tubman helped provide social services and relief for the families of Black soldiers and for recently manumitted slaves.[7] Along with Tubman, other women, like Frances Harper, worked as abolitionists.

Frances Watkins Harper (1825-1911) lived the Spirituals as a member of the Underground Railroad, an abolitionist lecturer, one founder of the American Woman Suffrage Association, a member of the Women's Christian Temperance Union, an officer of the National Association of Colored Women, an officer of the Universal Peace Union, the director of the American Association of Educators of Colored Youth, a member of the National Colored Women's Congress, and a tireless worker in the African Methodist Episcopal Church. She was an internationally recognized poet, writer of essays and other fiction, and journalist who focused on women's rights, Black achievement, and temperance, among other topics. Some essays were response papers to contemporary writers like Charles Dickens and Harriet Beecher Stowe. Harper took controversial stands, not as a separatist nor an assimilationist, but she preferred education to violence. Harper clarified the record about slavery and Reconstruction and about the import of Christlike humanity, and she chastised White southern women who would not work with or see the common interests they shared with Black women.[8] Along with activism through writing, Harper empowered by teaching others about an ethical life through her dedication to social service, together with the place of beauty and the love of freedom. Born to free parents and orphaned at an early age, Harper lectured on equal rights and antislavery throughout New England and southern Canada. As Harper stood up and spoke out, she epitomized the Spiritual "I Shall Not Be Moved": "I shall not, I shall not be moved. . . . Just like a tree planted by the water, I shall not be moved." The abolitionist activist women signified through words and actions. Three other women joined their commitment to empowerment and liberation through aesthetics and art: Katherine Dunham, Faith Ringgold, and Toni Cade Bambara.

Evocative Expressionists

Katherine Dunham (1909-   ) lives the Spirituals through the music of dance and through her accomplishments in social activism, anthropology, and education. Her work in the Caribbean with Melville Herskovits enabled her to mine African ritual, dance, and musics of the African diaspora. She expresses her political awareness and social conscience through her art of dance. For example, she created a ballet, *Southland*, which dramatized lynching during the aftermath of the 1954 Emmett Till torture/murder in Mississippi. Dunham worked with the NAACP and the Urban League to fight segregationist practices in public accommodations. This international choreographer and winner of countless awards began the Katherine Dunham School of Arts and Research in New York, where students studied dance, literature, art, and world culture. The Katherine Dunham Troupe toured internationally from 1940 to 1963. After teaching and training dancers in Africa, Dunham returned to the United States and moved to East St. Louis to develop a performing arts and training center with a multicultural program that embraces culture and dance. Dunham's exuberance, energy, and impact on the world echo the sentiments of this Spiritual:

> *Oh, when the saints go marching in*
> *Oh, when the saints go marching in*
> *Oh, Lord, I want to be in that number*
> *When the saints go marching in.*
>   Traditional

Dunham wants everyone "to be in that number" of those who celebrate life and celebrate themselves. Dunham has also published many works, including her autobiographical *A Touch of Innocence* (1959). Her teaching and concerts use her acute understanding of people, culture, beauty, human psychology, social values, and commitment to justice and human well-being.[9] The protest and encouragement that Dunham expresses through dance, Faith Ringgold expounds with paints and cloth.

Faith Ringgold (1934-) lives the Spirituals in her artwork, beginning when she decided to train herself during the 1960s. Previously, her teachers did not know how to help her mix paints to capture black skin tones. While doing French impressionist styles, she was told that a Black woman was incapable of doing good Eurocentric art. After reading Amiri Baraka and James Baldwin and living through the shifting political scene from civil rights to Black revolution, Ringgold used her artistry to evoke the dignity and pride proclaimed in the words of Adam Clayton Powell Jr. and Stokely Carmichael. Her paintings of the early 1970s period, including *The Flag Is Bleeding, U.S. Postage Stamp Commemorating the Advent of Black Power,* and *Die*, contain imagery characteristic of African art. Ringgold empowered Black women by making portrait masks of Harlem women and painting a mural at the Women's House of Detention on Rikers Island, New York City, to show that women could do many different kinds of jobs. In this manner, she championed the possibility of rehabilitation. Though Whites found her work too political and too Afrocentric, and Black men found her work too Africanized and too soft, Ringgold continued to protest against sexism and racism in her work and in political and artistic arenas. With others, she protested the exclusion of Black artists from a 1970 Whitney Museum of American Art exhibition of artists from the 1930s. After much protest, the show was opened to minority artists and women. Ringgold joined the Ad Hoc Committee on Women Artists and Students for Black Liberation, which brought pressure on museums to show the work of women artists. In 1976, Ringgold focused more attention on performance art as a vehicle for political and artistic protest and expression. Her soft sculptures and masks recounted the African-American experience. She turned to quilting as a form that powerfully tells the stories and experiences of African-American women's lives.[10] Her social vision for change echoes the power of this Spiritual:

I'm a witness fo' ma Lawd
I'm a witness fo' ma Lawd
I'm a witness fo' ma Lawd
I'm an everyday witness fo' ma Lawd.
I'm a Monday witness fo' ma Lawd. . . .
I'm a Wednesday witness fo' ma Lawd. . . .
I'm a Sunday witness fo' ma Lawd. . . .
Traditional

What Ringgold has seen she has shared via act, paints, clay, and cloth. Ringgold paints and quilts; Toni Cade Bambara painted, wrote, and told stories.

Toni Cade Bambara (1939-1995), artist, writer, and activist, lived the Spirituals in her self-proclaimed ambassadorship to tell the truth and not be compromised by prevailing stereotypes. Her stories and edited anthologies champion this social, cultural, and political commitment to African-American well-being. Her work covers vast pockets of Black cultural experience and exposes divisiveness between various spiritual, psychological, and political forces within the Black community. Bambara studied and worked in Milan, Italy, took a master's degree, worked in many neighborhood programs, and taught in the New York City college system. She participated in the women's liberation and Black nationalist movements but realized neither activity fully dealt with Black women's issues. She responded to that abyss by editing *The Black Woman: An Anthology.* In her edited anthologies and collections, Bambara empowers Black women, encourages young readers to learn through living history and storytelling, and inspires them to write, read, and think critically. With her travel abroad and her work in community groups, Bambara uses art to communicate social and political messages about the well-being and wholeness of the African-American community.[11] Bambara's many collaborative efforts call to mind this Spiritual:

> *Plenty good room, plenty good room*
> *Plenty good room in my Father's kingdom*
> *Plenty good room, plenty good room*
> *Plenty good room, choose your seat an' sit down.*
>
> *I would not be a sinner*
> *I'll tell you the reason why—*
> *'Cause if my Lord should call on me*
> *I wouldn't be ready to die.*
>
> *I would not be a backslider*
> *I'll tell you the reason why—*
> *'Cause if my Lord should call on me*
> *I wouldn't be ready to die.*
> Traditional

Bambara wanted all to know that there's "plenty good room" to work together to spread the message of social and political justice. The social and political messages central to the life and work of Bambara often served as catalysts for the African-American women who live the Spirituals through their commitment to political activism on behalf of African Americans, especially as they champion the rights of women as Womanists, feminists of color. These women include Naomi Anderson, Mary Church Terrell, Nannie Burroughs, Daisy Lampkin, Pauli Murray, and Dorothy Height.

Champions of Women's Rights

Naomi Bowman Talbert Anderson (1843-   ) lived the Spirituals' quest for justice as she supported the Black women's club movement. Born of free Blacks, this nineteenth-century feminist participated in and encouraged westward migration, self-help, and feminism. Though she experienced numerous hardships with family deaths and illnesses, Anderson remained fearless and supported various feminist activities, including temperance and woman suffrage; protested against sexism and racism; and worked on behalf of housing and care for Black children. Her life was dedicated to the service of women and African Americans.[12] Anderson's focus on collective response underlies the Spiritual "Give Me Yo' Hand":

Give me yo' hand, give me yo' hand,
all I want is the love of God.
Give me yo' hand, give me yo' hand,
You must be loving at God's command.

You say you're aimin' for the skies,
Why don't you stop your tellin' lies! . . .
You say you're glad you been set free?
Why don't you let your neighbor be?
Traditional

Like Anderson, Mary Church Terrell worked on behalf of women's rights as an early precursor of the foundations of Womanist theory.

Mary Church Terrell (1863-1954) lived the Spirituals as an African-American female activist for more than sixty-six years. In 1890, Terrell voiced what Womanists today explore: White women have a handicap of sex; Black women have a dual handicap of sex and race. This handicap is not inherent to Black women but is the burden society imposes. Born into a family of African-American elite, Terrell did not experience classism and, initially, was also protected from racism. Terrell's growing awareness of discrimination and oppression led her to do well academically and helped her exemplify the strengths and abilities of Blacks, especially African-American women. In the United States, her intellectualism was dismissed, and she was under constraints to be an ideal Victorian woman and to stay in her place. When faced with oppression because of her race and gender in the United States, Terrell went to Europe. She returned after two years and started the National Association of Colored Women (NACW) to cultivate unity through self-help and to focus on the problem of oppression due to race and sex—one problem, not two. The NACW worked on improving Black living standards, set up supportive institutions (such as day care, kindergartens, and mothers' clubs), and focused on fund-raising for schools of domestic science and homes for the sick, the aged, and girls. Terrell began to concentrate on the accomplishments of African Americans despite oppression. Through her speeches, articles, and short stories, Terrell bolstered Black morale and exposed lynching, Black disenfranchisement, chain gangs, classism, and the passing of mulattos. She criticized anyone, Black or White, who did not have the best interests of humanity at heart. In the last twenty years of her life, Terrell became more militant. Her battle cry against oppression is the thrust of the Spiritual "Joshua Fit De Battle of Jericho," for the fate of these walls was her envisioned fate for racist evil:

> *Joshua fit de battle of Jericho*
> *Jericho, Jericho*
> *Joshua fit de battle of Jericho*
> *And de walls come a tumblin' down.*
>
> *You may talk about the kings of Gideon*
> *You may talk about the men of Saul*
> *But there's none like good ol' Joshua*
> *And de battle am in his hand.*
> Traditional

Terrell despaired the continued economic difficulties of Blacks and the irony of Black soldiers fighting for democracy overseas when they were denied that same democracy here. She realized that morality and interracial dialogue had not abolished and would not abolish racism. In response, she began to picket, boycott, and participate in sit-ins. She worked with others to successfully struggle against segregated eating establishments and lived to see the blow to segregated public education in 1954 with *Brown v. Board of Education*.[13] Terrell not only participated in the struggle, she nurtured and mentored others, like Nannie Burroughs, who would carry the mantle for justice.

Nannie Burroughs (1879-1961) lived the Spirituals as she made an outcry against sexism and led the struggle for women's rights, desegregation laws, industrial education for girls and women, and antilynching laws. Her passion for courageous change echoes the sentiments within this Spiritual:

> *Little David, play on your harp, Hallelu', Hallelu'*
> *Little David, play on your harp, Hallelu'.*
>
> *God told Moses, O Lord!*
> *Go down into Egypt, O Lord!*

Tell ole Pharo', O Lord!
Loose my people, O Lord!

Down in de valley, O Lord!
Didn't go t' stay, O Lord!
My soul got happy, O Lord!
I stayed all day, O Lord!

Come down angels, O Lord!
With ink an' pen, O Lord!
An' write salvation, O Lord!
To dyin' men, O Lord!

Traditional

Burroughs was a David who helped kill off bits of the Goliath of ignorance, helplessness, sexism, and racism. Burroughs took the helm of leadership in many arenas: religion, education, women's clubs, politics, and
civil rights. She was instrumental in forming the largest African-American
women's organization in the United States, the Woman's Convention Auxil-
iary of the National Baptist Convention. Mentored by Anna Julia Cooper
and Mary Church Terrell, Burroughs grew in her oratorical abilities and in
her commitment to empowering Black Baptist church women in the fight
against injustice. Burroughs initiated National Women's Day, a day celebrated in most Black Protestant churches to honor sisterhood and as a
means of fund-raising. She encouraged Black Baptist churches to support
women's suffrage and political empowerment as a way to overcome racism and sexism. Committed to overcoming the wholly impossible,
Burroughs worked to instill Black pride and racial self-help; stressed the
import of Black women being self-sufficient employees; founded the National Training School for Women and Girls (1909), renamed the Nannie
Helen Burroughs School for Elementary School Education (1964); fought
for justice and equality; and demanded that Blacks protest and fight injustice with dollars and ballots, and not beg Whites for mercy.[14] Burroughs
radiated the commitment to women and Blacks that was inherent to the
life and work of Daisy Lampkin.

Daisy Adams Lampkin (c. 1884-1965) lived the Spirituals through her
work with civil rights, the National Council of Negro Women (NCNW), and
the National Association of Colored Women (NACW). Lampkin worked for
the equality of women and Blacks. Her humanitarian activities were vast,
and she mentored numerous persons in their public careers. As the national field secretary for the NAACP, Lampkin was a fundraiser and fighter
for many civil rights organizations. She worked as president of the Negro
Women's Franchise League (1915), with the National Suffrage League, and
in the women's division of the Republican Party. Her work with the NAACP

and the *Pittsburgh Courier*, from 1912, helped Lampkin foster success, particularly in the victorious battle against the nomination of pro-segregationist Supreme Court nominee Judge John J. Parker. In an earlier gubernatorial campaign, Parker had argued that Blacks should be excluded from the political process, and in 1954 he wrote the narrow lower court decision in *Brown v. Board of Education,* which held that nongovernmental segregation was lawful. Lampkin, Roy Wilkins, and Walter White together formed a powerful triumvirate whose work laid the foundation for successes in civil rights throughout the nation. The Spiritual "Swing Low, Sweet Chariot" champions Lampkin's inclusive zeal to enlist and then to gather and carry all to empowerment:

> *Swing low, sweet chariot*
> *Coming for to carry me home [justice, freedom]*
> *Swing low, sweet chariot*
> *Coming for to carry me home.*

> *I looked over Jordan, and what did I see?*
> *Coming for to carry me home*
> *A band of angels coming after me*
> *Coming for to carry me home.*

> *If you get there before I do*
> *Coming for to carry me home*
> *Tell all my friends I'm coming, too*
> *Coming for to carry me home.*

> *I'm sometimes up, I'm sometimes down*
> *Coming for to carry me home*
> *But still my soul feels heavenly bound*
> *Coming for to carry me home.*
> Traditional

Lampkin had phenomenal success in boosting funds and membership for the NAACP along with being active in the NACW, NCNW, and Delta Sigma Theta, a service sorority. After giving up her post as field secretary for the NAACP due to extreme fatigue, Lampkin continued as a member of the board of directors. From 1930 to just months before her death, Lampkin continued to devote herself totally to "the cause" of justice and civil rights.[15] Lampkin's call to fight for justice was part of Pauli Murray's call to the law and the gospel.

Pauli Murray (1910-1985) lived the Spirituals as an advocate for women's rights, as lawyer, poet, teacher, and minister, and as a founding member of the National Organization for Women (NOW) in 1966. Murray tried unsuccessfully in 1938 to thwart racism by applying for graduate school admis-

sion at the University of North Carolina at Chapel Hill. Audacious, she gradu-
ated from Howard University Law School as first in her class, and the only
woman. Her 1965 doctoral dissertation from Yale University Law School
was: "Roots of the Racial Crisis: Prologue to Policy." Murray was an early
activist in civil rights from the New Deal through the 1980s. She participated in freedom rides and sit-ins, crusaded as a human rights attorney,
and kept the mantle for justice as a professor, a civil and women's rights
activist, a poet and writer (writing the first textbook in a series on African
law), and an Episcopalian priest. After receiving her call to ministry, Murray
completed a Master of Divinity and was ordained as the first Black female
priest of the Episcopal Church in 1977 at the National Cathedral in Washington, D.C. Murray's call to justice included an autobiography, *Song in a
Weary Throat: An American Pilgrimage* (1987), two other books, and many
articles and monographs.[16] Murray's evangelical propensities reflect the
impetus within the Spiritual "I Wanta Live So God Can Use Me":

> *I wanta live so God can use me*
> *Victorious in this lan'*
> *I wanta live so God can use me*
> *Victorious in this lan'.*
>
> *I wanta walk so God can use me . . .*
> *I wanta pray so God can use me . . .*
> *I wanta sing so God can use me . . .*
> *I wanta work so God can use me . . .*
> *I wanta preach so God can use me . . .*
> *Treat my sisters so God can use me . . .*
> *Treat my brothers so God can use me . . .*
> *Treat my children so God can use me . . .*
> *Treat my neighbors so God can use me . . .*
> Traditional

Murray worked tirelessly to see that "dis worl' is on fire" for truth and
justice. The journey for Murray had evangelical tenets, the tenets that filtered through women's club movements in the person of Dorothy Height.

Dorothy Height (1912-) lives the Spirituals via her activism and leadership toward rights and equality for all humanity. Height began her service career working against sexism and on behalf of women's rights with
the National Council of Negro Women, the Young Women's Christian Association, and Delta Sigma Theta. In the 1930s, Height dealt with the Harlem
riots, became one of the leaders of the National Youth Movement during
the New Deal, and joined Mary McLeod Bethune in the fight for full, equal
employment, equal pay, and educational opportunities. Height spearheaded
Delta's activism, volunteerism, social protest, and educational interests.
Her concerns for women's rights encompass international concerns. The

Spiritual that reflects Height's words of encouragement to countless women across the years is:

> *Oh, Mary, doncha weep, doncha moan*
> *Oh, Mary, doncha weep, doncha moan*
> *Pharaoh's army got drownded*
> *Oh, Mary, doncha weep.*
>   Traditional

Height taught that there is no reason to cry and fret, for, like Pharaoh's army, oppression and remnants of sexism and racism "got drownded." All the organizations she has led have been influenced by her focus on human and international relations. Her tremendous leadership has brought about justice and empowerment in numerous arenas: women's rights; child care, education, and development; food drives; housing projects; and positive Black family life, celebrated in the national Black Family Reunion Celebration that Height envisioned and created in 1986.[17] Often the lives of Black women working on behalf of African Americans and for African-American women support, influence, and overlap activists who are more focused in the political arena, for the moment one participates in relationships and in seeking justice, one has become political. The political activists include Shirley Chisholm, Mary Frances Berry, Marian Wright Edelman, and Elaine Brown.

Political Firebrands

Shirley Chisholm (1924-   ) lives the Spirituals as she seeks to empower African Americans and women, on a sure, independent platform stated autobiographically: *Unbought and Unbossed* (1970). Along with being the first African-American woman elected to the U.S. House of Representatives (1968-1982), Chisholm has worked for civil rights and women's liberation issues. She was the first Black person to run for U.S. President in the Democratic party. Disappointed by the cool response from Black male- and White female-led organizations, Chisholm retired from politics and spends her time on the educational lecture circuit.[18] The response to Chisholm's efforts in national politics reflects the essence of the Spiritual "I'm a Rolling":

> *I'm a rolling*
> *I'm a rolling*
> *I'm a rolling*
> *Thro' an unfriendly world.*
>
> *O brothers, won't you help me,*
> *O brothers, won't you help me to pray?*

O brothers, won't you help me,
Won't you help me in the service of the Lord?
O sisters, won't you help me . . .
O preachers, won't you help me . . .
Traditional

Chisholm's political savvy and eloquence parallel the scholastic excellence of Mary Berry.

Mary Frances Berry (1938–   ) lives the Spirituals through her academic distinction, political activism, and public service that authorize and ground her fight against immorality and impropriety of domestic and foreign racist policies. In addition to her many publications, Berry has excelled in educational administration and served as assistant secretary for education in the Department of Health, Education, and Welfare from 1977 to 1980. She has lived the Spirituals as a member of the U.S. Commission on Civil Rights; was arrested protesting South African apartheid; and was a cofounder of the national Free South Africa movement. Berry has worked in numerous grassroots organizations and in advocacy with other scholars in filing amicus curiae (friends of the court) briefs in defending the civil rights of African Americans.[19] Because of the choices that Berry has worked to make possible in America and Africa, a Spiritual that embodies where she is and what she asks is this:

Lord, I can't stay away,
I can't stay away.

I got to go to judgment to stand my trials,
I got to go to judgment to stand my trials.

They're coming from the east, coming from the west,
Coming from the north, coming from the south,
Coming on the rainbow, coming on the cloud.
Traditional

Both Berry and Marian Edelman have signified in the national government arena.

Marian Wright Edelman (1939–   ) has lived the Spirituals as a sit-in participant in Atlanta, a worker for voter registration, and an intern for the NAACP Legal Defense and Education Fund. Edelman has worked to use laws on behalf of the poor. She developed the Children's Defense Fund, begun as the Washington Research Project, to advocate for children and youth. Her work concerns teen pregnancy, child care and health, social service, youth employment, child welfare, and adoption. Edelman, an author and a 1985 MacArthur Foundation Fellow, is a skilled lobbyist on behalf of children and the poor.[20] Edelman's advocacy on behalf of children proclaims the message of this Spiritual:

> *Dere's a little wheel a turning in my heart,*
> *Dere's a little wheel a turning in my heart,*
> *In my heart, in my heart,*
> *Dere's a little wheel a turning in my heart.*

> *I feel so very happy in my heart . . .*
> *O I don't feel no ways tired in my heart . . .*
> *O I feel like shouting in my heart . . .*
> Traditional

Edelman's passion for the plight, care, and love of children echoes a similar concern for children and for student welfare held by Elaine Brown.

Elaine Brown (1943-), having grown up singing in church choirs in Philadelphia, first lived the Spirituals by teaching piano to children in Watts. This privilege of working with and empowering others led to her participation with the Black Panther Party (BPP) during the 1960s and 1970s. Brown was a member of several Black student political organizations. After moving up the ranks, she became chairperson of BPP and led it into being an important force in Oakland, California, especially concerning voter registration. Brown's work on behalf of others celebrates the Spiritual "We Are Climbin' Jacob's Ladder," the ladder of success:

> *We are climbin' Jacob's ladder,*
> *We are climbin' Jacob's ladder,*
> *We are climbin' Jacob's ladder,*
> *Soldiers of the cross.*

> *Every round goes higher, higher . . .*
> *Do you think I'd make a soldier . . .*
> Traditional

Brown has worked to establish social programs for the poor and for African Americans by forming coalitions between legal constituencies and the community. Brown released two albums that contained songs based on her BPP experience: *Until We're Free* and *Seize the Tie*.[21] Brown's work with voter registration and community uplift echoes the work of African-American women who have lived the Spirituals through their engagement in human uplift, especially with civil rights, including Ida Wells-Barnett, Septima Clark, Ella Baker, Rosa Parks, Fannie Lou Hamer, Daisy Bates, Constance Baker Motley, Unita Blackwell, Eleanor Norton, and Barbara Jordan.

Catalysts for Human Uplift

Ida B. Wells-Barnett (1862-1931) lived the Spirituals through upholding African-American civil rights, economic rights, and the rights of women. Wells-Barnett's gifts as an activist and journalist enabled her to expose race, gender, and economic oppression. Wells-Barnett did not let the threat of physical harm or social isolation dissuade her from exposing and confronting oppression through teaching, debating, and writing pamphlets and newspaper articles. Her articles appeared in local and national publications, including features in the *Memphis Free Speech and Headlight*, the newspaper in which she held part interest. Rosa Parks was not the first to not want to give up a seat. Wells-Barnett was physically removed from a train in 1884 for refusing to ride in the rear, segregated car. After three Black independently successful colleagues were jailed, shot, and lynched because they refused to acquiesce to a competing White grocer, Wells-Barnett began to question and investigate lynching. Most Americans assumed that Black men accused of rape were the persons who were lynched. Wells-Barnett determined that lynching was a racist tool for eradicating financially independent African Americans, designed to terrorize Blacks into accepting the labels of inferior, unequal, and subordinate. In fewer than twenty years, she documented more than 10,000 lynchings of unarmed and powerless Blacks. After she challenged local justice in Memphis and the notions of White female purity in an editorial, her newspaper office was destroyed and her life threatened. Wells-Barnett went to New York and continued to focus on lynching. After two tours to England, she became more controversial for exposing White so-called supporters of Black causes who remained silent on the problem of lynching. Wells-Barnett and others met with President McKinley to protest the horrid injustice of lynching. After her involvement with the 1893 Chicago World's Fair, Wells-Barnett stayed in Chicago, where she supported and founded organizations that supported reform and women. Her antilynching activities triggered her initial involvement in the NAACP, though she left the organization later because of its timid stances and predominantly White board. Wells-Barnett worked with and successfully integrated the United States suffragette movement, for she felt the vote was the key to Black empowerment and to social, political, and economic equality. For Wells, the Spiritual "The Crucifixion," also known as "They Crucified My Lord," is what happened to countless Blacks, as, ironically, their judges and executioners "never said a mumblin' word" of truth or justice about their victims:

> *They crucified my Lord,*
> *And he never said a mumbling word*
> *Not a word, not a word, not a word.*

> *They nailed him to the tree . . .*
> *They pierced him in the side . . .*
> *He bowed his head and died . . .*
> Traditional

Wells-Barnett's support of Marcus Garvey and her dislike of Booker T. Washington's accommodationism, together with her concerns about lynching, disenfranchisement, and unequal segregated public education, caused the U.S. Secret Service to dub her a dangerous individual and a radical. Valiantly, she continued to write about lynching, riots, and exploitation of African Americans in her many articles, speeches, and reports, and her autobiography, *Crusade for Justice: The Autobiography of Ida Wells* (edited by her daughter, Alfreda Duster), was published posthumously in 1970.[22] While Wells-Barnett engaged in civil rights activities as a protest journalist, Septima Clark used politics and education to make a difference.

Septima Poinsette Clark (1898-1987) lived the Spirituals as a civil rights leader, educational reformer, political activist, and champion of citizenship education. Clark embraced the assertiveness, dignity, gentleness, and nonviolent temperament and importance of education from her parents. She resolved to bring health and educational reform when she worked in the economically, hygienically, and socially horrendous circumstances on John's Island, South Carolina. Inspired by studies with W. E. B. Du Bois, Clark was an advocate for equality in educational facilities and teacher salaries in South Carolina. She saw the links between protest, education, and documentation. Her work with the NAACP in protest and litigation was a fight against injustice. After teaching for forty years, Clark lost her teaching job and retirement benefits, because her work helped overturn many segregationist laws and because she refused to stop working with the NAACP. At the invitation of Myles Horton, director of the Highlander Folk School in Tennessee, Clark helped this citizenship school mobilize to support local social protest programs. Clark had studied at Highlander and was impressed by its biracial, humanist approach to working on national problems, teaching civil disobedience, democratic empowerment, and literacy empowerment. Her zealous efforts in education and protest echo the temperament in the Spiritual "Sit Down, Servant":

> *Sit down, servant, I can't sit down*
> *Sit down, servant, I can't sit down*
> *Sit down, servant, I can't sit down*
> *My soul's so happy,*
> *That I can't sit down.*
> Traditional

Clark still had too much work to do to sit down. Her work with Highlander in training settings all over the South transformed southern political systems, and she did similar work with the Southern Christian Leadership Conference. Clark noted that along with the racist harassment, beatings, murders and oppression by the KKK and the White Citizen's Council, she and women like Ella Baker and Rosa Parks had to fight sexism and were often not recognized for their contributions to the Civil Rights Movement.[23]

Ella Josephine Baker (1903-1986) lived the Spirituals through her grassroots work and behind-the-scenes activity in Black politics from the 1930s to her death. She was a worker and an advocate in several arenas: on behalf of civil rights in Harlem; against poverty and hunger (1930s); as an NAACP field secretary and director of local branches (1940s); and in outreach, volunteer, and voter registration work for the SCLC (1950s). Baker helped found the Student Nonviolent Coordinating Committee (SNCC), a new, independent youth organization with militant tactics and an egalitarian structure, for she did not want the movement to fizzle out or to be coopted by more conservative and moderate African Americans. The SNCC, with Baker's leadership, helped start the grassroots Mississippi Freedom Democratic Party. Baker's legacy affected causes including the Students for a Democratic Society, the Black Panther Party, mainstream elections, and women's liberation activities (1970s). Baker built bridges between the civil rights activities of the 1950s and 1960s, and Black resistance through the 1980s. Affiliated with more than fifty coalitions and organizations, Baker used her upbringing in southern Black culture with the traditions of mutual cooperation, self-help, and extended family, which made for close-knit communities, to enrich her fight for democratic principles, cooperative leadership, inclusion of women, and grassroots participation. Personally and politically, Baker refused to accept a "woman's behavior and place."[24] Baker accomplished much because she could bring people together in the manner celebrated in the Spiritual "Four and Twenty Elders":

> *Dere are four and twenty elders on their knees*
> *Dere are four and twenty elders on their knees*
> *An' we'll all rise together,*
> *An' face the risin' sun,*
> *O Lord, have mercy if you please.*
>
> *Dey are bowin' 'round the altar on their knees . . .*
> *See Gideon's army bowin' on their knees . . .*
> *See Daniel 'mong the lions on their knees . . .*
> Traditional

Like Baker, one day Rosa Parks refused to accept the place society relegated to her—to sit in the "Colored" place, in the back of the bus.

Rosa McCauley Parks (1913-   ) lives the Spirituals through her civil rights activism as she has challenged and helped transform southern racist traditions and laws. With the support of the Montgomery Improvement Association, the Montgomery NAACP, and the Women's Political Council (led by Jo Ann Gibson Robinson), Parks sat down on the bus in Montgomery, Alabama, in December 1955. Her stance was a catalyst for the historic Montgomery bus boycott that ended when the Supreme Court decreed that city bus segregation was unconstitutional. The boycott helped to usher in the 1960s Civil Rights Movement, together with organized, massive nonviolent disobedience and the national leadership of Martin Luther King Jr. Both Parks and her husband, Raymond, were active in their local NAACP chapter. Parks also trained at the Highlander Folk School with others who were concerned about the struggle for justice and equality. Parks relocated to Detroit and received an appointment as staff assistant to Congressman John Conyers. In 1987, Parks was able to fulfill a long time goal by starting the Rosa and Raymond Parks Institute of Self-Development in Detroit, which focuses on career training for African-American youth and supports her commitment to human rights struggles.[25] Parks had learned that even if the progress of the Movement echoed the following Spiritual, she would persevere and could say, "There I'll take my stand":

> *Done made my vow to the Lord*
> *And I never will turn back.*
> *I will go, I shall go*
> *To see what the end will be.*

> *Goin' to serve my Lord while I have breath*
> *To see what the end will be.*
> *So I can serve Him after death.*
> *To see what the end will be.*

> *When I was a sinner, just like you . . .*
> *I prayed and prayed until I come through . . .*
> Traditional

While Parks was busy protesting in Alabama, Fannie Lou Hamer helped effect change in Mississippi.

Fannie Lou Hamer (1917-1977), who lived and sang the Spirituals in protest against injustice, was a symbol of the 1960s Civil Rights Movement. Hamer was a sharecropper who shaped the Movement as one committed to voter registration, as an orator, and as a political activist with two social activist bodies: as a field worker with the Student Nonviolent Coordinating Committee (SNCC) and as one of the founders of the Mississippi Freedom Democratic Party (MFDP). In the process of overcoming the racist literacy tests to become a registered voter and a member of SNCC, Hamer became the brunt of economic intimidation and physical violence. Her life and the lives of her family were constantly threatened. Hamer captured the nation's attention with her televised objection to racism at the 1964 Democratic Convention, where the MFDP challenged the seating of the all-White Democratic delegation from Mississippi. Though the MFDP's challenge failed, the resulting action was that the national Democratic Party pledged not to seat any delegations that excluded African Americans at the 1968 convention. Until her death, Hamer fought for human rights as she sang and lived "This Little Light of Mine" and "Go Tell It on the Mountain"[26]:

> *This little light of mine, I'm gonna let it shine*
> *This little light of mine, I'm gonna let it shine*
> *This little light of mine, I'm gonna let it shine*
> *Let it shine, let it shine, let it shine.*
>
> Traditional

> *Go tell it on the mountain,*
> *Over the hills and everywhere*
> *Go tell it on the mountain,*
> *To let my people go.*
>
> Hamer's redacted version

Hamer's perseverance on behalf of justice shifted the politics of Mississippi and the nation, just as the protest work of Daisy Bates helped transform politics and educational discrimination in Alabama.

Daisy Gatson Bates (1920-   ) has lived the Spirituals as a freedom fighter via journalism, as a civil rights participant, and as a catalyst for integrating the public schools of Little Rock, Arkansas. Bates and her husband, L. C., began a weekly newspaper, the *Arkansas State Press*, an independent voice that worked toward improving the economic and social lives of Blacks and that exposed brutality by the police. Bates was president of the Arkansas NAACP when the U.S. Supreme Court handed down the 1954 decision in *Brown v. Board of Education*, which overturned the legal standard for segregated public school education. In 1957, Bates, a thousand paratroopers, and the national NAACP leaders worked to get nine African-American students into Little Rock's Central High. This courageous charge for justice led Bates and her students through the scenario of this Spiritual:

> *We will walk through the valley in peace*
> *We will walk through the valley in peace*
> *If Jesus himself be our leader*
> *We will walk through the valley in peace.*

> *We will walk through the valley in peace . . .*
> *Behold I give myself away . . .*

We will walk through the valley in peace . . .
This track I'll see and I'll pursue . . .

There will be no sorrow there
There will be no sorrow there
If Jesus himself will be our leader
We will walk through the valley in peace.
                                        Traditional

Bates remains active in African-American community, social, and economic activities in Little Rock.[27] Bates worked as a citizen to effect change, while Constance Baker Motley has helped transform the reality of civil rights in America as a litigator and judge.

Constance Baker Motley (1921-   ) has lived the Spirituals by using the U.S. courtrooms to do battle for justice, for civil rights. An activist during high school, Motley worked for the National Youth Administration. She later attended college with the help of a benefactor and got her law degree from Columbia Law School in 1946. While working with the NAACP Legal Defense and Education Fund as assistant counsel, she faced racism and sexism in the public arena. In this capacity, she tried cases and wrote briefs for Supreme Court school desegregation cases against southern universities that dealt a blow to legal institutional racism. Motley won nine out of the ten cases she argued before the Supreme Court, served in the New York State Senate, and was elected as the president of the Borough of Manhattan for four years. All along, Motley's call for justice has been the call symbolized in the Spiritual "Honor, Honor":

King Jesus lit the candle by the watuh side,
To see the little children when dey truly baptize',
Honor, honor unto the dying lamb.

Oh run along, children, an' be baptize',
Mighty pretty meetin' by de watuh side,
Honor, honor unto the dying lamb.

I prayed all day; I prayed all night,
My head got sprinkled wid duh midnight dew.
                                        Traditional

After staunch sexist- and racist-based opposition to her nomination as a U.S. district judge, Motley was confirmed in August 1966. Motley continues to uphold the fight for justice as a senior district judge in New York.[28] While Motley sits on the bench, Unita Blackwell has pursued justice through civil rights protest, in state politics, and on the local level, in city government.

Unita Blackwell (1933-   ), a Mississippian, became the mayor of a town where she was once forbidden to vote. Blackwell lived the Spirituals during the 1960s Civil Rights Movement as a member of the Student Nonviolent Coordinating Committee. She participated in voter registration and civil nonviolent protest, and was arrested and jailed more than seventy times. A founding member of the Mississippi Freedom Democratic Party, she helped to bring suits challenging segregation. The many struggles Blackwell experienced meant that some days Blackwell would think the words of this Spiritual:

> *Nobody knows the trouble I've seen,*
> *Nobody knows but Jesus*
> *Nobody knows the trouble I've seen,*
> *Glory, hallelujah.*
>
> *Sometimes I'm up, sometimes I'm down,*
> *Oh, yes, Lawd,*
> *Sometimes I'm almost to de groun',*
> *Oh, yes, Lawd.*
>
> *Although you see me going long so . . .*
> *I have my trials here below . . .*
>
> *One day when I was walking along . . .*
> *De element opened, and de love came down. . .*
>
> *I never shall forget the day . . .*
> *When Jesus washed my sins away . . .*
>   Traditional

Blackwell's commitment to social action permeates her work involving rural development and housing, energy conservation, and support of low-income housing opportunities, as well as her work with women.[29] Like Blackwell, another Mississippian, Eleanor Norton, has also worked as activist, litigator, and educator in state government and for humanitarian rights.

Eleanor Holmes Norton (1937-   ) lives the Spirituals through her lifelong commitment to civil rights. Her journey has included her work with the Student Nonviolent Coordinating Committee, her participation with the Mississippi Freedom Democratic Party, and her tasks as a national staff member for the 1963 March on Washington. Norton has championed civil rights and civil liberties in her work with the American Civil Liberties Union in New York City, especially when she represented former Alabama governor George Wallace, who wanted to have a political rally at Shea Stadium. She has also worked for civil rights issues with the New York City Commission on Human Rights (1970-77); as chair of the Equal Employment Opportunity Commission; as a law professor at Georgetown University; as a congressional representative for the District of Columbia; and as legal scholar and coauthor of *Sex Discrimination and the Law: Causes and Remedies* (1975).[30] Her unceasing work on behalf of humanitarian rights indicates a sense of preparation undergirding this Spiritual:

> *I wanna be ready, I wanna be ready,*
> *I wanna be ready*
> *to walk in Jerusalem just like John.*
>
> *John said that Jerusalem was four-square . . .*
> *I hope, good Lord, I'll meet you there . . .*
> *When Peter was preaching at Pentecost . . .*
> *O he was filled with the Holy Ghost . . .*
>   Traditional

Like Eleanor Norton, Barbara Jordan's work blended a concern for civil rights with the law and education.

Barbara Jordan (1936-1995) lived the Spirituals in her legislative work as a state senator and U.S. congresswoman on behalf of the disadvantaged, the poor, and African Americans. She tolled the bell for justice with her activities during President Nixon's impeachment hearings. As a senator, she worked for the Workman's Compensation Act; as a congresswoman, she worked to expand the 1965 Voting Rights Act. The former increased the maximum amount of benefits an injured worker could be paid; the latter covered Mexican Americans in southwestern states and in other states where minorities had their voting rights restricted via unfair registration practices, or where they had been denied the right to vote. Hers was the voice of cool disdain in evaluating the impeachment of President Nixon. The thrust of Jordan's political agendas shows that she had her ear attuned to the public, implied in this Spiritual:

> *Listen to the lambs, all a cryin'*
> *Listen to the lambs, all a cryin'*
> *Listen to the lambs, all a cryin'*
> *All a cryin', all a cryin'.*
>
> *He shall feed his flock like a shepherd,*
> *And carry the young lambs in his bosom.*
>
> *Come on, sister, with you' ups an' downs,*
> *Listen to the lambs, all a cryin';*
> *Angels waiting for to give you a crown,*
> *Listen to the lambs, all a cryin'.*

Come on, sister, and a don't be ashamed . . .
Angels waiting for to write your name . . .

Mind out, brother, how you walk de cross . . .
Foot might slip, an' your soul get lost . . .
Traditional

After leaving pubic political office in 1978, Jordan served as a professor at the Lyndon B. Johnson School of Public Affairs at the University of Texas at Austin, where she taught the preaching she formerly practiced.[31] Jordan used the university podium to share the cause of justice and civil rights. The classroom podium has long been the arena for many African-American women, as they live the Spirituals through the ministry of education, including Sister Aloysius, Anna Julia Cooper, Mary McLeod Bethune, and Marva Collins.

Talented, Transformative Teachers

Anne Marie Becroft, or Sister Aloysius (1805-1833), lived the Spirituals as she gave Black females education and religion in a society where slavery, racism, and sexism were rampant. Her activities helped to shape Black U.S. Catholic history. Becroft, an excellent teacher, with the help of other nuns, ran an academy for students until 1831, when she left to join the Oblate Sisters of Providence in Baltimore and became Sister Aloysius. Sister Aloysius taught her students English, math, and embroidery but died just one year after taking her habit.[32] Her dedication to the ministry of education and of the church in thanksgiving parallels the focus of this Spiritual:

Oh, rise an' shine, an' give God de glory, glory
Rise an' shine, an' give God de glory
Rise an' shine, an' give God de glory
In de year of Jubilee [freedom].

We are climbing Jacob's ladder . . .
Every round goes higher and higher . . .
Rise and shine . . .

Sister Aloysius believed and lived that one could "rise and shine" to freedom from oppression, freedom to love, and freedom of knowledge. The enlightenment that Sister Aloysius accorded students in parochial schools was the goal of Anna Julia Cooper in public and private school education, in human rights activities, and in Black women's organizations.

Anna Julia Cooper (1858-1964) lived the Spirituals as an individual who, early on, committed to the empowerment and education of women. She exemplified this quest in her intellectual pursuits from St. Augustine's Normal School and Collegiate Institute in Raleigh, North Carolina, to the Sorbonne in Paris. In addition to being an educator, Cooper was a human rights advocate, scholar, essayist, author, lecturer, feminist, and vital participant in the Black women's club movement. Throughout her life, Cooper addressed the needs and situations of the oppressed, especially the indignities and unequal treatment experienced by Black women. Her evocation to Black women embraces the words of this Spiritual:

> *March on! March on!*
> *Way over in de Egyp' lan'*
> *You shall gain de victory*
> *You shall gain the day.*
>
> Traditional

After teaching at Wilberforce and St. Augustine, Cooper was invited to teach in the public school system of Washington, D.C. She was active with nineteenth-century Black intellectuals and was the only female member of the American Negro Academy. Cooper completed her dissertation at the Sorbonne at the age of sixty-six, which indicated her scholastic excellence and interest in pan-Africanism. It was titled "The Attitude of France toward Slavery during the Revolution." Cooper became the second president of Frelinghuysen University, a nontraditional group of schools founded to educate working African Americans in Washington, D.C. Though lack of funding caused the demise of this institution, Cooper's accomplishments were vast. This teacher, lecturer, poet, writer, feminist, and activist addressed many themes, gave of herself tirelessly, and did not retire until age eighty-four.[33] Cooper shares the ranks of the tireless worker in higher education with Bethune.

Mary McLeod Bethune (1875-1955) lived the Spirituals as a most extraordinary public figure—educator, politician, administrator, and diplomat. She championed the well-being of African Americans, especially women and youth. Her belief in God and in herself, along with her missionary spirit and tremendous teaching ability, moved Bethune to begin a training school for girls (1904) that later merged with Cookman Institute to become Bethune-Cookman College. Bethune cared for empowerment, economic and community development, and Black culture. She also trained her students to sing the Spirituals. Her political and social service activities included national leadership of the National Association of Colored Women's creative and leadership interests in the National Council of Negro Women, a national umbrella organization for existing national women's organizations; and work with public housing, army desegregation, and civil rights. Along with the federal Council on Negro Affairs with the New Deal in Washington, D.C. Bethune was instrumental in many avenues, and this power was supported by her close liaison with President Franklin Roosevelt, Eleanor Roosevelt, and President Harry S. Truman. Despite her sponsorship of democratic ideals and patriotism, Bethune was a victim of the House Congressional Committee on Un-American Activities. She still continued to work for justice and equality. The weight of her responsibilities and her missionary spirit probably came together prayerfully in a manner displayed by this Spiritual:

> *I want Jesus to walk with me*
> *I want Jesus to walk with me*
> *All along this tedious journey*
> *Lord, I want Jesus, to walk with me*
>
> *In my trials, Lord, walk with me . . .*
> *When I'm in trouble, Lord, walk with me . . .*
>   Traditional

Bethune was instrumental in the development of the National Youth Administration (NYA) and the Civilian Conservation Corps. She facilitated employment and equitable educational opportunities for Black Youth through the NYA. Through more than fifty years of service, Bethune championed both accommodationism (self-help, vocational skills, and appeals to philanthropic Whites) and, later, full citizenship rights, governmental assistance, and higher education.[34] Bethune's quest for expansive education for her students, including the best in the arts and sciences, was one of the major building blocks of the curriculum designed by Marva Collins.

Marva Collins (1936-   ) lives the Spirituals by standing up to the Chicago public school system, using creative and progressive concepts to educate previously neglected children on Chicago's West Side. Collins began Westside Preparatory School as an alternative educational institution. She wanted to establish the same kind of nurturing environment she grew up in for Chicago's African-American children. Collins used personal funds, dedication, confidence, a strong will, and love for young people to overcome racism, classism, low expectations, and low self-esteem that had kept many Chicago youth in bondage. Collins's success in creating excellence has been documented in two *60 Minutes* features, in invitations to be the U.S. Secretary of Education, and in the adaptation of her ideas and methods by school systems in Ohio and Oklahoma. The 1995 *60 Minutes* feature showed that twenty years later, all of the first class of Collins' Westside Preparatory were college students or graduates, and all were successful. None had succumbed to crime or failure.[35] Collins celebrates the success of her methodology with her students, as proclaimed in this Spiritual:

> *Glory, glory, hallelujah!*
> *Since I laid my burden* [the load of inept education] *down*

Glory, glory, hallelujah!
Since I laid my burden down.

Friends don't treat me like they used to,
Since I laid my burden down . . .

I'm goin' home to live with Jesus
Since I laid my burden down . . .
Traditional

Just as Black women have lived the Spirituals via education, others have chosen other avenues of expression. Three women who have signified via religion or social change include Jarena Lee, Josephine Allensworth, and Mother Hale.

Social Strategists

Jarena Lee (1783-) lived the Spirituals and signified despite the prejudice against a woman preacher, by proclaiming the Word of God. This antebellum feminist was the first woman to ask the African Methodist Episcopal Church for the authority to preach in 1809. Lee claimed authority to preach via an inner spiritual experience. Lee had wrestled with her conscience, and her relationship with God for many years. After several bouts with near suicide, Lee had a conversion experience. After experiencing sanctification, she knew a flush of ecstasy, of light and bliss, and received a call from God to preach the gospel. Against opposition, Lee asked why people should think it improper for a woman to preach, since the Savior died for women as well as men. Their denial did not stop Lee. After the death of her husband, Lee continued to have a commitment to preach the gospel while caring for two small children. Lee asked the then bishop Richard Allen, a second time, for the authority and freedom to hold prayer meetings and to preach in her own home. Lee made no apologies, for her life was contained in this Spiritual:

I know the Lord, I know the Lord,
I know the Lord has laid His hands on me.
I know the Lord, I know the Lord,
I know the Lord has laid His hands on me.

Did you ever see the like before?
Know the Lord has laid His hands on me.
King Jesus preaching to the poor,
Know the Lord has laid His hands on me.

Oh, wasn't that a mighty day . . .
When Jesus washed my sins away . . .
Traditional

After granting permission, Allen publicly acknowledged her ministerial and preaching gifts. Lee preached throughout the Northeast, and she likened herself to Paul of Tarsus as she traveled to deliver the Word of God. Lee recorded her experiences in two works: *Life and Religious Experience of Jarena Lee, a Colored Lady, Giving an Account of Her Call to Preach* (1836), and *Religious Experience and Journal of Mrs. Jarena Lee, Giving an Account of Her Call to Preach the Gospel* (1849). With only three months of schooling, Lee felt safe in, protected by, and led of the Lord. Just as Lee made strides for the call of women to ministry, Josephine Allensworth, the spouse of a minister, made great strides by working on behalf of Black veterans and by founding a town.

Josephine Leavell Allensworth (1855-1939), born in Kentucky, lived the Spirituals as one of the leaders in social change and as an emblem of racial advancement in the development of Allensworth, California, an all-Black colony (1908-1950s). She and her husband, Allen (a Civil War veteran, Baptist minister, and chaplain for the U.S. Army, 24th Infantry), founded this settlement to afford a home for Black soldiers, fair and equal treatment, and freedom from race restrictions. She worked with the school board, started a library, and worked with social and educational groups. Although the colony failed, Allensworth's activities provided housing, education, and political opportunities for many. The gift and beauty of the city to empower others is embodied in this Spiritual:

Oh what a beautiful City,
Oh what a beautiful City,
Oh what a beautiful City,
Twelve gates unto the city, a Hallelu'.

Three gates in uh de East,
Three gates in uh de West,
Three gates in uh de South,
Three gates in uh de North,
Makin' it twelve gates unto the city, a Hallelu'.

My Lawd built uh dat city,
And He said it was just a four-square,
And He said He wanted you sinners,
To meet Him in uh de air,
Makin' it twelve gates unto the city, a Hallelu'.
Traditional

The care Allensworth exhibited for the masses resembles the care and compassion exhibited by Mother Hale for Black babies.

Clara (Mother) McBride Hale (1904-1992) lived the Spirituals as a humanitarian, homemaker, and licensed foster mother who devoted her time and life to taking care of numerous drug-addicted and unwanted Black babies, when young mothers brought their babies to her. Mother Hale, so named by her charges, began Hale House in 1970. In more than twenty years, Mother Hale and her staff cared for more than eight hundred babies born either with AIDS or addicted to drugs.[36] The special, devoted attention Hale House provided for the unwanted and the displaced is the healing power of this Spiritual:

> *There is a balm in Gilead,*
> *To make the wounded whole,*
> *There is a balm in Gilead,*
> *To heal the sin-sick soul.*
>
> *Sometimes I feel discouraged,*
> *And think my work's in vain,*
> *But then the Holy Spirit*
> *Revives my soul again.*
>
> *Don't ever be discouraged,*
> *For Jesus is your friend,*
> *And if you lack for knowledge,*
> *He'll ne'er refuse to lend.*
>
> *If you cannot preach like Peter,*
> *If you cannot pray like Paul,*
> *You can tell the love of Jesus,*
> *And say He died for all.*
>
> Traditional

Mother Hale wrote love and care on the hearts of her wards; many other African-American women, such as Charlotte Grimké, Maya Angelou, Lorraine Hansberry, Sonia Sanchez, and Nikki Giovanni, have written words that have inspired, challenged, and entertained us.

> Singing coast to coast
> With words, with songs
> Across the sea
> In city, and in country
> 'Til the walls of injustice
> Came tumbling down.

Inspiring thousands
Joyful noises
Your moan incarnated
The silent prayer
Of folk in bondage:
Unjust laws
The nonessentials of life;
The hopelessness beyond pain.

Witnessing Wordsmiths

Charlotte L. Forten Grimké (1837-1914) lived the Spirituals in her anti-slavery crusades and her poetry. Many of her antislavery works appeared in antislavery print media such as the *Liberator*, the *National Anti-Slavery Standard*, and the *Anglo African* magazine. She empowered her students by teaching them about Black leaders and liberators. Grimké wrote about the life of the Sea Islands to show the northern reading public that Blacks wanted to work, learn, and be citizens. She continued to write and advocate for Black civil rights, repeating that Blacks wanted all the rights accorded all American citizens.[37] Grimké wanted her students to know the reminder in this Spiritual:

> *Somebody's knocking at your door*
> *Somebody's knocking at your door*
> *Oh, sinner, why don't you answer,*
> *Somebody's knocking at your door.*

> *Knocks like Jesus, Somebody's knocking at your door . . .*
> *Can't you hear him, Somebody's knocking at your door . . .*
> *Answer Jesus, Somebody's knocking at your door . . .*
> *Jesus calls you, Somebody's knocking at your door . . .*
> *Can't you trust him, Somebody's knocking at your door . . .*
> Traditional

Born more than a century after Grimké, Maya Angelou inspires all who listen to rise to the heights of human magnificence, through her words and support of protest.

Maya Angelou (1928-   ) lives the Spirituals through the majesty, protest, and empowerment of her poetry, prose, and song. She transcended early rape by her mother's boyfriend by choosing silence and by ultimately having a perpetual love affair with libraries and books. During the 1960s, Angelou, with Godfrey Cambridge, wrote a revue to help raise funds for the Southern Christian Leadership Conference. After living and working as a journalist, editor, and professor in Africa, Angelou returned to the United

States in 1966 and wrote the autobiographical *I Know Why the Caged Bird Sings* in 1970. Her autobiographical works, poetry, and other presentations are a lesson to all, celebrated in the Spiritual "We Shall Overcome":

> *We shall overcome, we shall overcome,*
> *We shall overcome, someday [today].*
> *Deep in my heart, I do believe,*
> *We shall overcome, someday.*
>
> *We'll walk hand in hand . . .*
> *The Lord will see us through . . .*
> Traditional

A professor at Wake Forest University, Angelou continues to inspire and call for the eradication of injustice and cruelty.[38] While Angelou evokes and proclaims in prose and poetry, Lorraine Hansberry electrified and inspired via drama, and she participated in fund-raising.

Lorraine Hansberry (1930-1965) lived the Spirituals in her dynamic writings, notably *A Raisin in the Sun*, which opened in New York in 1959. The play depicts the lives of working-class Black folk as they deal with overcrowded living conditions and racist, restricted housing covenants that mean that white homeowners will not sell their property to Blacks. (The staged and televised versions of this play contained Hansberry's revisions that reflect the growing militant mood of African Americans in the 1960s.) Hansberry knew racism, though she grew up in a middle-class family. She knew the plight of Black tenants who rented from her father. She supported the 1960s protests by raising funds to help support civil rights organizations and the southern freedom movement. Along with desire for social and political change, Hansberry helped transform American theater by shifting from characters rife with despair to characters that celebrated and affirmed life in spite of cruelty, destruction, and disappointment. Hansberry empowered Blacks and women before the 1970s feminist movement began.[39] Her dramatic messages reiterated the gifts of freedom in this Spiritual:

> *No more auction block for me,*
> *No more, no more,*
> *No more auction block for me,*
> *Many thousand gone.*
>
> *No more peck o' corn for me . . .*
> *No more driver's lash for me . . .*
> *No more pint o' salt for me . . .*
> *No more hundred lash for me . . .*
> *No more mistress call for me . . .*
> Traditional

The change effected by Hansberry's plays embraces some of the revolutionary voice of Sonia Sanchez.

Sonia Sanchez (1934–) lives the Spirituals in her commitment to civil rights and to improving the quality of African-American life through her writings. A 1960s activist, Sanchez spoke out against poverty and substandard educational opportunities. She helped to raise the consciousness of students at several major universities and continues to teach at Temple University. Sanchez uses colloquial conversation and street language to expose the oppression of Blacks, and she critiques racism, sexism, capitalism, child abuse, drug abuse, generational conflicts, initiation rituals for women, Black-on-Black crime, imperialism, womanizing and useless men, and the death and destruction of key Black leaders. Sanchez's poetry and poem plays remind African Americans not to fall prey to a valueless life trapped by materialism and the objectification of human life, and remind White America about the price of continuing Black oppression. She continues to speak nationally and internationally against violence and turmoil and against the oppressions of racism, sexism, and capitalism.[40] Her writing and speaking extol the message of the Spiritual "I Ain't Got Weary Yet":

> *I ain't got weary yet,*
> *I ain't got weary yet,*
> *I've been in the wilderness*
> *A mighty long time,*
> *An' I ain't got weary yet.*
>
> *I ain't got weary yet,*
> *I ain't got weary yet,*
> *I've been on my knees . . .*
>
> *I've been praying like Silas,*
> *I've been preaching like Paul,*
> *I've been serving my Lord . . .*
>
> *I've been walkin' with the Savior,*
> *I've been talkin' with the Lord,*
> *I've been in the wilderness . . .*
>   Traditional

As Sanchez issues warnings about being, but not getting stuck in, the wilderness, Nikki Giovanni unearths bad attitudes and aimlessness, and teaches about Black ancestry.

Nikki Giovanni (1943–) lives the Spirituals through her written, poetic, militant calls against American racism and injustice, and through her commitment to the Civil Rights Movement. Giovanni exposes African-American notions and attitudes of inferiority as she calls for a sense of personal direction and nonviolent protest. Her work reflects her personal evolution, independence, and courageous temperament. These sentiments are found in this Spiritual:

> *Good news! De Chariot's coming*
> *Good news! De Chariot's coming*
> *Good news! De Chariot's coming*
> *And I don't want her leave a me behind.*
>
> *Get up in de chariot, carry me home . . .*
> *Dar's a long white robe in de heaven, I know . . .*
> *Dar's a golden harp in de heaven, I know . . .*
>   Traditional

Giovanni celebrates and creates stories about the power of ancient Black civilizations and writes for adults and children. Her work often focuses on the connections between arts and culture, and she makes casual yet insightful comments on the political and social situation in America.[41] The symbolic living of the Spirituals has existed and continues to emerge in the powerful social, political, religious, educational, life-affirming signifying of many African-American women. Likewise, the realm of the aesthetic, often framed by the political, social, and religious, has been blessed and elevated by African-American women who sing the Spirituals, including Marian Anderson, Mahalia Jackson, Odetta, Leontyne Price, Jessye Norman, Kathleen Battle, Barbara Hendricks, Bernice Johnson Reagon and Sweet Honey in the Rock, and Sister Thea Bowman.

Womanist Creative Singing

Women who sing the Spirituals sing them because they are moved to do so. Marian Anderson (1902-1993) sang the Spirituals and brought them to the world in hundreds of recitals. First singing in the church choir, Anderson studied vocal technique in high school. Racism thwarted her path when the Daughters of the American Revolution refused to let Anderson perform at Constitution Hall in Washington, D.C. Eleanor Roosevelt helped secure her an invitation to sing at the Lincoln Memorial, where she sang before 75,000 people on Easter Sunday, April 9, 1939. Anderson served as a goodwill ambassador and as an ambassador to the United Nations. The programming of her more than fifty farewell concerts, culminating more than thirty years of performing, included the Spirituals.[42] While Anderson took thousands to the heights of majestic elegance on the operatic and concert stage, Mahalia Jackson moved thousands up a little higher singing the Spirituals and gospel songs.

Mahalia Jackson (1911-1972) sang and lived the Spirituals. She supported and encouraged civil rights protesters as she sang the Spiritual "We Shall

Overcome" and the gospel "If I Could Help Somebody." Though primarily a singer of gospels who bridged the distance between secular and sacred music, Jackson sang the Spirituals with a rich contralto voice, using a full range of emotions, vocal techniques, lyrical and rhythmic freedom, and an emotional power that often signified black preaching. Her singing "I Been 'Buked and I Been Scorned" at the 1963 March on Washington made Jackson a public symbol for the 1960s protest. Financially, she supported the movement and the educational opportunities of black youth. Her deep faith through song was one gift she gave internationally to millions.[43] Just as Jackson sermonized through religious songs, Odetta preaches to and about life and people through folk songs.

Odetta (1930-   ) has sung the Spirituals and other folk songs for more than forty years. She has lectured throughout the United States, has appeared in numerous plays and films, and celebrates and captures the folk idiom, which has endeared her to the folk and to the feminist movement. This citizen of the folk and of the world honors and gives praise to the ancestors, who have shown Odetta the import of "positive energy in vanquishing the negative forces that keep the struggle from advancing."[44] While the travels of Odetta have been extensive, Leontyne Price has also traveled worldwide and has brought the folk gold through her sound.

Leontyne Price (1937-   ), "La Diva" of opera, has sung the Spirituals all her life. Deciding to become a musician after hearing Marian Anderson, Price entered the Juilliard School with a commitment to excel. Price developed an international opera career that has taken her to all the major world opera houses. Price concluded her strenuous operatic career of more than thirty years with a performance of *Aïda* at the Met in 1985. She equally excelled in the Italian operas of Puccini and Verdi and in German, Slavic, Spanish, French, and American works, including her powerful rendering of the Spirituals. Price always celebrates her lush sound as dark and smoky, and as the gift of her Blackness, the pigmentation of her skin. Since retiring from the opera stage, Price has continued as a recitalist.[45] Price once told Marian Anderson, "Because you were, I am." Certainly because Anderson and Price were, Jessye Norman now is.

Jessye Norman (1945-   ) sings the Spirituals with the bravura and commitment of a consummate artist and of one who has lived them. Her mastery, musical commitment, understanding of history and texts, and impeccable scholarship make her music soar. Her vast range and bearing, apparent in her televised live recording of the Spirituals with Kathleen Battle, made these powerful songs come alive once again.[46]

Kathleen Battle (1948-   ), a native of Ohio and product of Cincinnati College-Conservatory, made her debut at Spoleto in 1972. Battle is an international opera singer, soloist, and recitalist. Her performances of the Spirituals can be intensely joyous, silvery brilliant, and filled with precious intimacy. The live recording *Spirituals in Concert,* with Battle and Jessye Norman at Carnegie Hall in March 1990, continues the recital tradition of concert artists singing arranged Spirituals. Her renditions are versatile, sacred and secular, and transforming.[47] Born the same year as Battle, Barbara Hendricks also brings a distinctive, inspiring singing style to the Spirituals.

Barbara Hendricks (1948-) sings the Spirituals from a context of celebrating her heritage, seeing Blackness as compassion for other Black folk. Hendricks has an international career as an opera singer and recording artist. Her singing empowers others, and she was appointed goodwill ambassador to the United Nations. Having grown up in a Methodist parsonage where her mother sang, early in life Hendricks focused on church and on praising God. Her understanding, interpretation, and being moved by her own memories of the Spirituals, merge to enrich her performances of the Spirituals. Though originally intent on group singing, Hendricks renders a solo performance with rich and powerful ambiance.[48] A testament to solo and communal singing of the Spirituals finds signification in Bernice Johnson Reagon and Sweet Honey in the Rock.

Bernice Johnson Reagon (1945-) signifies through weaving together her skills and experiences as a civil rights activist, singer, writer, historian, and social protester. Reagon, born in Albany, Georgia, started the Grammy-winning women's a cappella group Sweet Honey in the Rock (1973), is a former curator at the National Museum for American History at the Smithsonian Institution, and received a prestigious MacArthur fellowship. She has signified by editing the three-disk field recording collection *Voices of the Civil Rights Movement: Black American Freedom Songs, 1960-66*, a music history journal with an illustrated booklet. In 1994, Reagon helped to launch the series Wade in the Water: Black Sacred Music Tradition on National Public Radio.[49] Reagon and Sweet Honey in the Rock have performed at churches, concerts, and festivals throughout this country, and internationally they have performed in Ecuador, Mexico, Germany, Japan, England, Canada, Australia, Africa, and the Caribbean. Sweet Honey in the Rock sings the Spirituals and other songs of struggle. It builds on the Black congregational church-singing style and proclaims to listeners the need for all to fight for social justice and equality. The group sings West African chants, Spirituals, Black gospel, field hollers, reggae, rap, and urban blues. Sweet Honey in the Rock deals with human concerns including apartheid, AIDS, economic oppression, homelessness, self-esteem, community building, civil rights, political prisoners, and global human rights.[50] A testament of Reagon's commitment, and of those similarly committed, is a song that Sweet Honey in the Rock often sings:

> *We who believe in freedom cannot rest*
> *We who believe in freedom cannot rest until it comes.*
> *Until the killing of Black men,*
> *Black mothers' sons*

Is as important as the killing of White men,
White mothers' sons . . .[51]

Similarly, Sweet Honey in the Rock addresses the issues of women:

WOMEN!
Should be a priority, respected and upheld in society
Given all the proper notoriety
Never used or abused by authority figures
Like the media that trashes us
Play down the hype that constantly bashes our image . . .
Use women's bodies to create a sick sideshow
Too many times seen as a sex symbol
No real intelligence, just a brainless bimbo
Not taken seriously, for who she needs to be
A human being with the right to be free . . .[52]

The power, passion, and presence of Sweet Honey in the Rock is magnetic; the presence of Sister Thea was prophetic and dynamic.

Sister Thea Bowman (1937-1990) sang, taught, and lived the Spirituals as a prophet, evangelist, singer, dancer, liturgist, and educator. Bowman preached the good news and brought together people from various walks of life as a pilgrim on a journey. Sometimes she felt "like a motherless child," but she always knew she was God's special child, as all people are beautiful, special children of God. Sister Thea joined the order of the Franciscan Sisters of Perpetual Adoration in La Crosse, Wisconsin. After she completed her doctorate, Sister Thea's work included teaching English, including Black literature at all levels, and starting and directing the Hallelujah Singers, a choir that specialized in the Spirituals as sung in the African-American South. Sister Thea promoted multiculturalism before it was in vogue: she built community between Blacks, Whites, Native Americans, Hispanics, and Asian Americans. Sister Thea was living inspiration as she used the Spirituals to help people improve their quality of life and to know joy.[53] Like Sister Thea, Eva Jessye taught others and directed choirs which sing the Spirituals, and, like a few other musicians, she arranged the choir's music.

You affect sound
Teaching, arranging
Building on traditions
Of unsung poets of old;
Ancestors sharing the blood
Sharing the creativity
Of African soil
Mist American ethos;

As prelude and offering
For a new day;
The ritual of possibility
A clarion call for change
A prophetic word
Announcing:
Awake, Arise, Act.[54]

Womanist Creative Arranging

Eva Jessye (1895-1992) lived the Spirituals through her numerous contributions to music, her directorship of the Eva Jessye Choir, which sang a variety of works, including the Spirituals, and her work on American music and folklore. "I've got a song, you've got a song, all of God's children got a song" is the litany for choral directors and arrangers—there are always songs to sing, to shout "all over God's heav'n." For more than seventy-five years, Jessye was involved in acting, directing, and choral conducting. She was the musical director of *Hallelujah*, the first motion picture starring African-American actors. Jessye directed major choral performances on radio and was the unofficial protector of the *Porgy and Bess* score. George Gershwin, the composer, appointed Jessye as the choral conductor for *Porgy*, and she did much to sharpen the cultural flavor of the work and to maintain its integrity for more than thirty years. Her choir toured as ambassadors of goodwill, and Jessye worked on behalf of peace, the arts, and women's progress, as poet, actress, composer, inspirational lecturer, and choir director.[55] Other African-American arrangers of Spirituals include Margaret Bonds, Undine Moore, Rachel Eubanks, and Lena McLin.

Margaret Bonds (1913-1972) arranged the Spirituals as part of her prolific repertoire of compositions. Hailing from Illinois, Bonds received numerous awards, performed with many orchestras, and worked with the Cultural Center in Los Angeles. Bonds, influenced by jazz, blues, and her interest in social themes, composed music for many genres: ballet, orchestra, art songs, popular songs, piano pieces, and arranged Spirituals. Her music illumined her sense of ethnic identity. Her association with other African-American artists, poets, and musicians greatly influenced her work. Leontyne Price commissioned and recorded many of Bonds's arrangement of Spirituals. Some of her arrangements include "Didn't It Rain!" "Ezekiel Saw De Wheel," "Five Creek-Freedmen Spirituals," "Mary Had a Baby," and one frequently performed and recorded, "He's Got the Whole World in His Hands."[56] A composer-arranger of Spirituals who hails from Virginia is Undine Moore.

Undine Smith Moore (1905-   ) arranges and composes, and is an organist, pianist, and educator, especially in the states of North Carolina and Virginia. She was instrumental in cofounding and codirecting the Black Music Center and in developing the Black Man in American Music Program at Virginia State College. Moore's repertoire of Spirituals includes "Fare You Well," "Rise Up, Shepherd, and Follow," and "We Shall Walk through the Valley."[57]

Rachel Eubanks (1923-   ), educator, musician and composer, arranges Spirituals for solo and choral voices. Eubanks has headed music departments at Wilberforce University and Albany State College. She began the Eubanks Conservatory of Music in 1951. Concerned with the study of diverse kinds of music and music history, Eubanks also supports African-American musics and the work of women in music, and has been so honored for her participation and musical excellence. Some of the Spirituals Eubanks has arranged include "Deep River," "Jesus on the Waterside," and "Let Us Break Bread Together," all for solo voice; and the following Spirituals for choral ensemble: "Ezekiel Saw the Wheel," "I Want Jesus to Walk with Me," "It's a Me, O Lord," and "Let Us Break Bread Together."[58]

Lena Johnson McLin (1928-   ) is a composer of more than two thousand compositions that include cantatas, anthems, piano works, orchestral works, and arranged Spirituals. McLin is also a singer, conductor, and educator. She founded and directed the McLin Ensemble, a small opera company. The Spirituals McLin has arranged include "Cert'nly Lord," "Done Made My Vow to the Lord," "Glory, Glory Hallelujah," "Give Me That Old Time Religion," "Gonna Rise Up in the Kingdom," "I'm So Glad Trouble Don't Last Always," and "My God Is So High."[59] Other African-American female composer-arrangers of the Spirituals include Jacqueline Hariston, Betty Jackson King, Eurydice Osterman, Zenobia Powell Perry, Charlene Moore Cooper, Barbara Sherrill, Patsy Ford Simms, and Jean Taylor.[60]

"I am woman, hear me roar" pealed forth in the 1960s but was sounded more than a century earlier; as Black women like abolitionist Sojourner Truth said, Jesus came from "God and a woman—*man* had nothing to do with it." [61] Harriet Tubman, Union spy, freed slaves, established a home for the aged, and worked with Ida Wells-Barnett in the suffragette movement and the antilynching campaign which helped launch the modern Civil Rights Movement. Their politics and struggle presaged the lives of Fannie Lou Hamer, Ella Baker, Septima Clark, Rosa Parks, and the countless unnamed, outrageous Black women who lived and fought and sang for twentieth-century freedom. Male privilege denied these women national leadership positions, and most Black male theologians failed to address sexism. From the 1800s through the 1960s, African-American women reclaimed family ties after the Civil War, worked for suffrage, founded colleges, worked for educational reform, and formed women's clubs like the National Association of Colored Women (NACW), which predates the NAACP. Those women, with outrageous courage, fortitude, and brilliance, lived the Spirituals. Many have sung the Spirituals, transforming lives, launching careers, and spreading the gospel of freedom, justice, life. Others have arranged the Spirituals in ways that make them timeless and profound. Womanists live, sing, teach, and preach the Spirituals as they defend Black women against White male

sexual exploitation. Womanists liberate Black women from Black male subjugation and transform the minuscule way in which some Black women
see themselves. Womanists work for justice, and labor to overcome poverty. They give support to Black women individually and as a group, and
criticize negative Black male attitudes about Black women. They work for
health care and work to shatter the stereotypes about Black women.
Womanists inspire African-American women to celebrate, appreciate, and
love themselves.[62] The Spirituals are metaphors for holistic health, for spiritual transformation, for creating opportunities for justice. Women have
sung, marched, and conquered. Without the participation of women and
Womanists, many would have remained enslaved, much of the Civil Rights
Movement would not have happened, and there would be a lot less compassion in the world. Womanists call us to "be there" for the "least of these."

> Oh, Beautiful Blackness
> You sing with melodious voices
> Alto, contralto, soprano,
> Lyric, coloratura, gospel persuasion
> On stage, at church, in fields.
> You sing
> Only for the ears of God
> Other times before great halls of justice
> Broadcast before shuttering masses
> As deputized lynched mobs
> Lurked in the shadows.

PART IV

ILLUSTRIOUSNESS

The Wellsprings of Our Texts

9

Mass Meeting

So get on up, so today,
No babies need live enslaved
Get on board
The train of life
Get off
The road of strife.
Get on board
The train of love
Get off
The train of destruction, hate, greed
Do any of us pay heed
To the fact: time's running out;
Train's a coming:
Get on board!

Singing the Spirituals puts us on the Underground Railroad with the hundreds of slaves who stowed away, and stole away, north. They took the train toward salvation and liberation—the train that always has room for "many a more." During the 1960s, there was plenty of room for those who wanted to join the Movement for freedom and equal access. One experience of riding the train occurred via mass meetings at Black churches, urban and rural, where people prayed, planned, and trained to effect the change born in the hue and cry of freedom. This chapter carefully delves into three powerful spirituals sung at mass meetings—"Oh, Freedom," "This Little Light of Mine," and "Go Tell It on the Mountain"—using the tools developed thus far to unpack the theodicy radiating from the words and the music. These "chants of collective exorcism" come alive as we explore them by examining their context, story, creative spirit, faith, and thought via a Womanist reading to answer the question of theodicy.

"Oh, Freedom"

"Oh, Freedom" tells a story of theodicy where freedom exorcizes the racist evils of forced segregation and calls for peace and mutuality in mass meeting style. Freedom, key to human well-being, exists at home with the Lord God who creates everyone in freedom. With the majesty of a processional hymn set in the key of B major, the tonality, delivery, and fervor of the music and the words announce some dynamics of a theodicy. From the Montgomery bus boycotts (1955-56) through the 1960s jail-ins, pray-ins, public accommodation protests, freedom rides, voter education projects, and marches, people sang. From Louisiana to the Carolinas, Blacks, with a few White supporters, sang freedom songs, the lifeline of mass meetings. Mass meetings, usually held in churches, "became a major source of communication for the local Black community and provided necessary moral and spiritual support."[1]

Context

"Oh, Freedom" declares the inauguration of freedom and speaks death to the injustices explicit in segregation: intimidation tactics, shooting, and the resulting need for mourning. Freedom, the paradigm for life, is the life force that empowers the singers to demand an end to oppression. Personified, freedom takes on a life of its own. Such a demand was in the air in Mississippi in 1963.

Hollis Watkins, a Student Nonviolent Coordinating Committee (SNCC) field secretary from McComb, Mississippi, lined out the lyrics to "Oh, Freedom," at Jackson, Mississippi, during the fall and winter of 1963. The leader gave the words of each new verse to the congregation using the tradition of lining-out words, which became a shout.[2] The original, unredacted text grew out of more than one hundred slave revolts. African Americans met in secret, urged escape, and laid out northern escape routes. "Oh, Freedom" was a marching song of Black regiments during battle, a cry of victory after Emancipation, a chant during a race riot in downtown Atlanta, Georgia, in 1906, and a rallying song during the radical 1930s union activity.[3] During the 1960s, the song was a moving, powerful, hand-clapping, striking jubilee. The following verses comprise the original, pre–Civil Rights musical source:

Oh, freedom, oh, freedom,
Oh, freedom, oh, freedom over me;
And before I'll be a slave,
I'll be buried in my grave;
And go home to my Lord and be free.

No more moanin', no more moanin',
No more moanin' over me . . .
No mo' weepin' . . .
There'll be singin' . . .
There'll be shoutin' . . .
There'll be prayin' . . .[4]

"Oh, Freedom" has a strophic form, a verse form with five lines. The stanza's last three lines accompany each verse and serve as a refrain: "And before I'll be a slave, I'll be buried in my grave; / And go home to my Lord and be free." The textual structure for the entire stanza involves a mixed rhyme scheme, *abccb*, while the musical pattern of the verse and refrain complement each other. Verse and refrain echo an indicative mood with dramatic overtones that evoke a majestic, dramatic monologue or soliloquy. The sense of community embodies one lone voice. In a similar vein, the redacted texts include the refrain and new verses:

> Refrain: *And before I'll be a slave,*
> *I'll be buried in my grave;*
> *And go home to my Lord and be free.*

> *No segregation, no segregation* [pronounced: surgergation],
> *No segregation over me;*
> *And before I'll be a slave,*
> *I'll be buried in my grave;*
> *And go home to my Lord and be free.*

> *No more dogs, no more dogs,*
> *No more dogs biting me;* . . .
> *Nothin' but freedom, nothin' but freedom,* . . .
> *No more shooting, no more shooting,* . . .
> *No more mourning, no more mourning,* . . .

> *Oh, freedom, oh, freedom,*
> *Oh, freedom over me;*
> *And before I'll be a slave,*
> *I'll be buried in my grave;*
> *And go home to my Lord and be free.*

Additional lyrics used during the 1960s struggle included the following verses:

> *No burning churches* . . .
> *No more Jim Crow* . . .
> *No more Barnett* . . .
> *No more Pritchett* . . .[5]

During 1963, critical events shaped the direction of the Movement and involved dialectical American civil religion. The country commemorated the centennial of the Emancipation Proclamation amid the slaying of sacrificial lambs at the altar of democracy. High Priest Theophilus Eugene "Bull" Connor, Birmingham, Alabama's, public safety commissioner, and his flock obtained court orders forbidding the free speech of protests, sit-ins, and picketing. Local police, the attending acolytes, enforced Connor's proclamation by using dogs and nightsticks against the demonstrators and turned high pressure water hoses on a thousand schoolchildren. Like John at Patmos, Martin L. King Jr. penned his epistle from a Birmingham jail in April 1963. Archbishop George Wallace, governor of Alabama, proclaimed segregation and defied a federal court encyclical to integrate by blocking the doorway of the University of Alabama. Fearless freedom fighters in Birmingham worked with the Southern Christian Leadership Conference (SCLC) and with SNCC, raised funds, enrolled the support of children and adults, and withstood the Ku Klux Klan.

A High Mass solemnizing freedom and solidarity took place at the March on Washington on August 28, 1963. Eighteen days later, four little girls—Denise McNair, Addie Mae Collins, Carol Robinson, and Cynthia Wesley—died in the bombing of Birmingham's Sixteenth Street Baptist Church. The martyred Medgar Evers had lain dead since June. White Mississippi used the sacrificial offering of Evers to appease the god of institutionalized racism. Yet the Council of Federated Organizations, an umbrella group, launched its "Freedom Vote" project "to demonstrate to Mississippi whites and the federal government that, despite segregationist claims to the contrary, Blacks were indeed interested in voting, and to provide practice in casting the ballot to people denied that right all their lives."[6] The song leader, Hollis Watkins, a participant during an earlier 1960 sit-in at a McComb, Mississippi, White-only Woolworth lunch counter, continued to participate in the Movement at the great risks of personal ostracism, repercussions due to his protesting, lost education and employment opportunities, and jeopardy for his parents and his future progeny. Yet he worked with grassroots organizations in the Mississippi Freedom Summer in 1964.[7] The courage of Watkins and other grassroots participants moves one toward an experience of pathos and a disgust for racist arrogance.

> *No more dogs, no more dogs,*
> *No more dogs biting me; . . .*
> *Nothin' but freedom, nothin' but freedom, . . .*
> *No more shooting, no more shooting, . . .*
> *No more mourning, no more mourning, . . .*

The resounding "no more" dogs, shooting, or mourning evokes pathos toward Watkins, toward Black Mississippians, toward all those who daily experienced the physical violence of biting dogs, shooting guns, burning fires, and exclusion from public accommodations. This song indicates that some Whites had the audacity to deny, to segregate, to hate. The pretense of superiority that allows White supremacists to dominate and to think they have the privilege and authority to deny Blacks their God-given rights is the arrogant abomination to "liberty and justice for all." To confront this absurdity and champion this justice for all, especially for African Americans, requires a reading that reveals the lies which undergird the social, historical, cultural, aesthetic, psychological, and theological justifications for slavery and racism. These lies and manipulation of power helped forge the desire for power by Whites to dominate Blacks and the desire for Blacks to have freedom from oppression and freedom to have the same privileges exercised by Whites. The initial version of "Oh, Freedom" sets out a general philosophy that Blacks will no longer have to weep or groan but will be able to shout, pray, and sing in victory. The redacted "Oh, Freedom" addresses the specifics of overcoming oppression toward empowerment: the freedom fighters answer "No!" to segregation and intimidation via dogs, shooting, mourning, Jim Crow, and racist law officials. They sing "nothin' but freedom," which removes all options to be controlled, manipulated, or intimidated, even at the price of death. Singing "No!" empowers one to take a stand for self and community and to abandon the practice of idolatry which reveres Whiteness as the object of worship.

Story

The story of "Oh, Freedom," a freedom quest, juxtaposes the oppressed against a counterfeit democracy. The segregationist and hate tactics pervading McComb, Mississippi, mirrored the nation. These attitudes made it almost impossible for Blacks to experience freedom legally. Yet activists demanded freedom and opted for human dignity and integration. The call to end the "mourning" implied an end to racist-inspired suffering and death. During slavery and the 1960s, singers believed they were free despite systemic physical, legal, or psychological bondage. The first three verses of the McComb version of "Oh, Freedom" set out an accompaniment for an exorcism ritual to remove the cancer of subjugation. The latter three verses created a "balm in Gilead," a soothing salve to create wholeness and to affirm the healing message of "freedom now."

The demand for liberation placed "Oh, Freedom" amid the oral tradition and the social identities of African Americans, shaped by a veil of racism and undergirded by cultural mores because of America's historic impenetrable veil of freedom. Fear, ignorance, and greed shaped this veil. The veils of oppression and freedom hang in unequal access. In "Oh, Freedom," these complex veils are direct objects: "[We will endure] no more dogs, no more segregation," and so on. Those projecting the veil from a dominant stance saw no contradiction in the baseless pursuit of Black human beings by White human beings with attack dogs, which created a paradox of nonhuman human beings by acts of inhumanity. As power brokers, the dominant forces played God by usurping the God-given status of African-American humanness. This breaking of right relations is one theodicy issue undergirding "Oh, Freedom." The freedom fighters stood firmly committed that the biblical declaration of God to Pharaoh was a biblical mandate to American White supremacy: "I am who I am," "I am the God of Abraham, the God of Isaac, and the God of Jacob" who says, "Let my people go " (Ex 3:6, 14; 5:16). The biblical legal mandate of the Torah, the Law, had not yet overridden the ethos and legal statutes of American racism.

This "legal" veil disavowed full citizenship for African Americans. The legal dialectic of "separate but equal" and the poll tax laws forbade African Americans equal access to education, public accommodations, and voting rights. Blacks dreamed of transcending the veil of racism toward a life of mutuality and freedom. Civil rights activists made demands that would make the veil less impenetrable and would end legal and moral oppression. "Oh, Freedom" states that African Americans have never accepted enforced societal subjugation. Freedom meant a self-defining life of justice as dignity, respect, balance, and choice without unwarranted constraints. Many Whites were determined to fight equality, integration, and freedom, for they were committed segregationists, and many believed Blacks were unequal and were cursed, due to these Whites' misreading of Genesis 9:27, which implies that Ham, and not Canaan, was cursed because Ham saw his father naked. The misreading assumes that those of African descent descend from the cursed Ham and therefore ought to be denied freedom and equality. The story of "Oh, Freedom" says no to the myth that Blacks deserve to be cursed, deserve to be oppressed; unmasks the arrogance and pathos of racism; and demythologizes social power, stereotypes, and history to reflect the true and the real.

The civil rights activists used "Oh, Freedom" to confront the arrogance that demanded segregation and Jim Crow: the relentless antiphonal clapping physically symbolized defiance, as each ascending melodic phrase with a repetitive text intensified the move against a nation that condoned racial arrogance, a product of manipulative social power. America claimed that Blacks were inferior, yet America denied that racism existed. "Oh, Freedom" called for peaceful and mutual coexistence. Freedom fighters in Mississippi and elsewhere sang "Oh, Freedom" and other Spirituals in the midst of mob hysteria to sustain themselves and to express the spectrum from sadness to respect. The singing embodied pathos, for the firm rhythm had a sacred tone with peaceful legato tones that evoked compassion.[8] They confronted the enemy through song when Blacks and Whites protested together. Bob Zellner, a young White SNCC activist raised in Alabama, commented:

> I went to McComb for the purpose of attending a staff meeting. . . . I had no idea it was going to be my baptism by fire. . . . We were meeting . . . and we had the distinct feeling that the real action was somewhere else. . . . In the middle of the afternoon we heard singing. . . . Soon the stairs were filled with young people coming up, setting about the business of making picket signs.
>
> . . . I knew that if I went on the march I'd be the only white person.

They might put me in the newspaper. . . . I might provoke more violence than would occur otherwise. My parents would get in trouble. . . . All in a flash I said, I have to go. How can I not go? . . .

People just couldn't believe it when they saw me. They went into a level of hysteria. . . . I began to observe . . . the interaction between members of the mob and the police. . . . They would take a swing at me . . . they would look for the reaction of the cops. And the cops very clearly with their body language and everything else said, "Sure get that [SOB]." . . . I was also aware . . . [that] others, too, came to where I was and attempted to stand between me and these white people that were after me. And the first action of the police was to come over and get them and beat them with blackjacks. I remember the sound of the blackjacks as they hit [their] heads. . . .

[They had] baseball bats, pipes, wrenches. . . . The crowd started screaming in a high-pitched, shrill scream that sounded like grief to me. It was just unreal. . . . Then one of the guys got behind me. . . . He intended to gouge my eye out.[9]

With victim or victimizer, no power could disguise individual, essential inner powerlessness—the pathos of power. The inner powerlessness, the pathos of racism, betrayed the self and produced gross injustice, an injustice where the roots of White racist arrogance against Black humanity lay in greed and acquisition of power. This pathos of humanly induced evil and humanly experienced suffering permeated the air when the singing of "Oh, Freedom" accompanied the anguished voices of Black activists and White supremacists in McComb in 1963. "Oh, Freedom" supported the desire for justice and the quest for imminent freedom, and functioned paradigmatically to epitomize the power of Spirituals and to expose the inherent contradictions and ambiguity of racism.

One confronts ambiguity and absurdity within the dialectic of freedom and oppression. Freedom is an ambiguous force shrouded in the distribution of power. Within the story there are many rhetorical or hypothetical questions as answers—questions specific to the context of freedom movement, and those specific to the performed "Oh, Freedom." Both types of questions are pertinent to arriving at the connection between the theological message and how music serves as its agent. Questions that focus on the larger freedom issue ask: If African Americans really gain freedom, who will take their place as scapegoats? Does an American capitalistic economy need the "enslaved" to maintain its unbalanced balance of power? Being engaged in the performance of "Oh, Freedom" troubles our sensibilities and triggers the following: Can one simultaneously be free yet illiterate and disrespected? Can one be free in a patriarchal, ethnically conscious, and financially hierarchical society that sees color, gender, and class before character? Can society come to appreciate differences without celebrating them? What sense does it make that a Black maid could suckle and tend to a White child during his or her most formative years, yet that Black maid's child ought not go to school, befriend, live on the same block with, nor marry that White child?

These were some of the issues African Americans singing the Spirituals faced. Activist James Bevel, an SCLC organizer and veteran of the Nashville sit-ins, echoes these sentiments in his freedom song about his family and his White next-door neighbors. Both families had many children but forbade them to play together, because of race. Yet their dogs always played together:

"Dog, Dog"

Lead: *Dog, dog, dog, dog,*
All: *My dog a-love-a your dog*
and-a your dog a-love-a my dog
and-a my dog a-love-a your dog
and-a your dog a-love-a my dog . . .

. . . .

and then-a why can't we
sit under the apple tree . . .
You walk, a-walk with me,
Oh, you walk, a-talk with me,
well-a why don't a-you hold my hand,
tell me a-you understand,
now can't you see
that you and me
a-will-a be so-a happy,
sit under the apple tree . . .[10]

Having named and unmasked the evils of segregation, hate, and racism, the freedom fighters wanted to know why these systems needed to remain intact. Having determined that these southern traditions needed to be dismantled, the freedom fighters, students, and ministers studied nonviolent direct protest to arm themselves with the tools to confront segregation directly. They also learned that music was a viable tactic to empower and sustain them. The freedom demonstrators did not want to become White and did not want White citizens to lose their civil rights, but they wanted all persons to have access both to freedom and to first-class citizenship. Music supported their efforts:

Somehow this music—music I could use as an instrument to do things with, music that was mine to shape and change so that it made the statement I needed to make—released a kind of power and required a level of concentrated energy I did not know I had. . . . The Freedom Singers used the songs, interspersed with narrative, to convey the story of the Civil Rights Movement struggles. The songs were more powerful than conversation. They became a major way of making people who were not on the scene feel the intensity of what was happening in the south.[11]

Creative Spirit

The traditional setting of the text employs "freedom" as a governing statement based on an archaeology of knowledge that concerns the total liberation process. The process of signifying, the movement of inclusion, involves repetitive use of "Oh, freedom, oh, freedom," the opening line and thematic statement of the song, as an interjection which expresses strong, sudden feeling.

The essence and beauty of "Oh, Freedom" are the identity or "naming" issues of the rhetoric and music as creative spirit. "Oh, Freedom" is a call to order with an intent to persuade. This jubilant reformation song invites all to mutual participation, refuses to tolerate further subjugation, and affirms the singers' right to know freedom. It also puts all racists on notice of the singers' intent to gain freedom. The call for freedom, for change, involves the "enhancement of meaningful engagement with music," and the value and power of music to induce social cohesion and to develop or enhance the a priori sense of emotions the listener already experiences as the music begins.[12] While human response to music depended on style, performance setting, and personal identity with the audience, musical encounters allowed freedom fighters to share a moving experience with others.[13] In singing "Oh, Freedom," they met past futility and present hope. The emotions that surfaced during the performance pressed them to recall the frustration and degradation of Jim Crow. The singing of "Oh, Freedom" evoked the dialectic of jubilation tempered by fear from past memories. This chant commanded that the walls of segregation come tumbling down, and echoed the call of Dr. Martin Luther King, Jr. for nonviolent direct action, and the rhetoric of Malcolm X to self-actualize and stand for truth by any means necessary.[14] These reactions flowed from the fusion of the text and the music intoned by human voices.

Vocal performances present involved patterns that offer ideas for social organization and interaction. In musical performance, culturally learned expectations shape the musical presentation and the emotional response of all participants and hearers.[15] Some patterns present models built on coherent arrangements that involve ongoing processes. These models of improvisation, harmony, and counterpoint can offer

[a more] appealing resolution to our most serious social problems than the usual statistic-mongering, policymaking, and politicking. . . . Attention to musical experience can suggest a better central model for ethics than the moral dilemma. . . . Music reveals the possibility of

coherent and dynamic conceptions of our ethical situation as involving problems in transition and tensions that need not necessarily be considered problems. Music . . . is a better model for human life.[16]

"Oh, Freedom" offers a model of mutuality, as text and music together invite reform and participation. The opening refrain, "And before I'll be a slave . . .," ascends and then descends toward resolution. This musical line, with a B major tonal center, begins the protest statement that decries bondage. In "Oh, Freedom," the ascending lines connote dignity, and the major modality creates dynamic and positive expressions. Most intervals in the refrain that revolve around major seconds imply commitment and tenacity. Together the tonality and lyrics awaken a sense of desire and closure. The verses revolve around a tonality, and this expressive means connotes triumph at McComb. The lead singer's embellishments in triplet rhythm on the word "and" and the quasi-triplet sense with the word "grave" create moments of intense passion yet finality. These techniques help communicate the drive and determination of the activists. The syncopated duple rhythms over a pentatonic or five-tone scale create a rocking, comforting motion. The uses of these five tones undergirding the lyrics, in proximity of less than an octave mirror certainty and a growth potential as they evoke a sense of the familiar and of new possibilities. This scale provides the melody throughout the verse. The exception occurs with the soloist's ornamentation, using E on the word "me." The repetitions of tones also reflect certainty and solidarity. By their simplicity, the lines of music and lyrics represent the stark reality and thus the complexity of freedom, the theodic issue, the focus of the dream that had been deferred too many times. "Oh, Freedom" reflects the dream for ethical and legal equal treatment and the opportunity to exist without intimidation because of ancestry and ethnicity, using the mass meeting musical performance style.

This key communicating vehicle garnered the inherent intensity and fervor of hundreds of singing people jammed into small churches. Their soulful singing seemed to bombard the church walls; that their voices "blended so forcefully, vibrantly, joyfully, told the blending of their wills; the music spoke as one person formed of all the many people, saying that it was more than all of the many people combined."[17] The singing escalated across the South as people sang "Oh, Freedom." Their serious, peaceful, purposeful faces became transfixed as the singing moved them from desperation to glory. In the mass meetings, people sang song after song of freedom, starting as suddenly as they ceased—"the sudden quiet as full of meaning as the great hall of song. . . . Hushed decorum settled over all, . . . then the speaking began."[18]

As people sang together, they also shouted and sustained cries of joy, sound, and silence in the Black singing tradition. Amid communal interaction between the crowds and speakers, a social, psychological drama unfolded. The meetings inspired the activists and created a mystical, ecstatic, and reverent mood that shored up the participants.[19] The act of singing set in motion communion with God and the neighbor. The meetings reinforced participants' stamina and their relationships, as singers and audience became one. When singing "Oh, Freedom," they embraced their physicality, and their passion and commitment intensified as the percussive, antiphonal hand clapping, stamping feet, and nodding heads became more complex. A repetitive victory chant of "FREEDOM, FREEDOM, FREEDOM" provided accompaniment and helped unleash the joy, the fervor, of the meeting.[20] Most mass meetings had song leaders who inspired the liturgical gathering.

Hollis Watkins, a high baritone, led the song in a lined-out style as the voices of children and adults answered, producing a call-and-response. Groups of children and lower- and higher-pitched adult voices entered improvisationally, creating a three-part harmonic texture without a particular pattern. The singing integrated the human persona and brought harmony within the person and the community throughout the Movement:

> I saw people in church sing and pray until they shouted. I knew *that* music as a part of a cultural expression that was powerful enough to take people from their conscious selves to a place where the physical and intellectual being worked in harmony with the spirit. . . . The Civil Rights Movement changed my view of music. It was after my first march. I began to sing a song and in the course of singing changed the song so that it made sense for that particular moment. . . . This was one of my earliest experiences with how my music was supposed to *function*. This music was to be integrative of and consistent with everything I was doing at that time.[21]

The integrative function of the music touched the protesters' social and psychological well-being. Singing Spirituals like "Oh, Freedom" announced the African-American community's existence and served as the means and the ends of self-expression: what Blacks aimed toward, and the process of sound running through their bodies:

> You have to do this [fully self-express] if you're going to do congregational singing. . . . But the reason . . . is to go through this exercise and I am talking about a culture that thinks it is important to exercise this part of your being. The part of your being that is tampered with when you run this sound through your body is a part of you that our culture thinks should be developed and cultivated, that you should be familiar with, that you should be able to get to as often as possible and that if it's not developed, you are underdeveloped as a human being. If you go through your life and you don't meet this part of yourself, somehow the culture has failed you. . . . Once you start to put sound out on that level, you're out. There's no hiding place. You're exposed.[22]

The performance mood for "Oh, Freedom" was jubilation and anticipation. The song leader and other participants sensed that singing the Spirituals was "an act of creation—the moment at which religion informs art, and makes it greater than itself"; for words describe, and painting suggests, "but music alone enables the listener to participate, beyond conscious thought."[23] The technical perspectives of the music bolstered a sense of well-being, and the swinglike tempo was engaging and effervescent. The soloist used ornamentation like the portamento that beautifies and emphasizes words, especially in the phrase "over me; / And before." The singers also altered the words and music by lengthening and shortening notes and by modifying vowels and eliminating final consonants, e.g., "surgergation" and "before." Using modified language or dialect is neither ignorance nor a crude attempt to pronounce English words, but "an instinctive modification" of the harsh, guttural sounds within English to satisfy the African American's "natural preference for soft and euphonius vocables characteristic of [traditional] African speech."[24] That is, softened consonants and elongated vowels "sing easier." The use of dialect, rhythms, passionate melodies, and repetition gives the Spirituals beauty and vibrancy, creating a "hypnotic effect and spirit exaltation on both singers and listeners quite beyond the power of other music."[25] Musical beauty, value, and vibrancy mark the vitality related to the dynamics of theodicy basic to "Oh, Freedom," where musical performance empowers and builds right, just relationships.

The performance of "Oh, Freedom" was an outpouring of Afrosensitive, sacramental, narrative theology. The singers used texture,[26] rhythm, melody, tempo, text, ideas, and method of reception[27] to communicate about societal freedom, justice, and equality. The dynamics of act and being were fulfilled through characterizations, motive, and plot of the song. The "I" in "Oh, Freedom" is protagonist and victor, but not egoist, one who depends on security needs. One acts falsely to fulfill those needs, rather than logically and scientifically. Freedom, however, is the ability to achieve one's needs from nature without violating or being violated by people.[28] African-American congregational-style singing involves communal inclusiveness, the antithesis of violation and violence. Communal expression celebrates the differences in created order as the communion of divine and human freedom. Many "I" songs became "we" songs during an integrated 1960s protest:

> Changing songs [from "I"] to "we," . . . that's the presence of white people in collaboration with black people because in order to express community you have to go to the first person plural. And in the black community, when you want the communal expression, everybody says "I." So if there are five of us here and all of us say "I," then you know that there's a group. And a lot of times I've found when people say "we"

they're giving you a cover to not say whether they're going to be there or not.[29]

The mixed congregational voices also incorporate these modifications. The group includes sopranos, altos, tenors, and basses singing in a quasi-unison manner that evokes harmony. The mixed voices create viscerally secure, round, open tones. Soloist Watkins's warm, nasal sound projects to the audience and stirs the listener with his embellished "And before" triplets and his aggressive lining out: "No more shootin'!" or "No more mournin'!" Performing the diverse textual feet with patterned music involved musicking, the activity wherein spontaneous singing becomes the vehicle for expressing power and communal unity.

Womanists saw the ongoing contradictions and the possibilities for unity and change amid the various doubles created through imitation, consciousness, and signifying.[30] A womanist view of "Oh, Freedom" invites an inquiry into the place of freedom within the African-American community. Womanist theory, especially from a literary perspective, focuses on the intracommunity lifeline versus the intercommunal interests of Black male writers.

A query about the internal freedom implied in the refrain raises questions about the role of women during the 1963 struggle. What were women experiencing in McComb, in Birmingham, in Albany? They protested, sang, and portrayed the inherent empowerment of freedom: a unified front of Black support that demanded an end to subjugation. Women's voices reflect Womanists' participation in the Movement, the activity by Black women who experience race, sex, and class oppression. Although the term "Womanist" is confessional, many women who were not acknowledged by national media and national civil rights organizations during the 1960s responded to the Movement and to their communities with Womanists' sensibilities and concern. Many Black liberationist women led the Spirituals recorded at mass meetings. Betty Mae Fikes, Rutha Harris, Bernice Johnson Reagon, and Fannie Lou Hamer are some of the local workers, leaders, and soloists who are part of this discussion. These often invisible women were visible in their accomplishments as they lived out the visions of Harriet Tubman and Sojourner Truth, Anna Julia Cooper and Ida Wells-Barnett: they worked with the NAACP as attorneys and volunteers, and with political councils and groups of professional women; they boycotted, sat in, and integrated schools. Women like Ella Baker helped organize NAACP and SNCC chapters, traveled nationally, and braved violence to tell the story. The push within the ranks for male leadership, male-dominated media, and the sway of the patriarchal Black church tended to ignore local women activists. The story of freedom is a dialectic of an internal and external struggle.

Beyond describing freedom, how can society redistribute power to make freedom available to all? Together, music and words of "Oh, Freedom" fashion a thesis about freedom as power that demands personal, social, and ethical accountability. The emotional impact of the texts presses the listener to be cognizant of history and to recall the stories that convey the presence and absence of freedom. "Oh, Freedom" dares one to deny others access to freedom and presses for the ultimate guarantee of freedom, a concern for divine revelation and faithful contemplation.

Faith and Thought

The "naming" component that reveals and ponders in "Oh, Freedom" probes the notions of God, humanity, freedom, intent, and ethics within an eschatological life. "And go home to my Lord and be free" is the singular explicit statement about God, set within a simple yet majestic cadence-like phrase. This phrase resounds in the last line of each stanza. God is creator, protector, parent, liberator; God is far and near: God is the northern abolitionist, and God is in one's soul. African Americans look to "God in the soul," the God who comes "on wings of song."[31] This relationship with God is basic to experiences underlying a lived theodicy inherent in the Spirituals. God is not an alternative to freedom. Knowing God's presence is the beginning of freedom for many. Experiencing God, synonymous with the idea of home, is a metaphor for the place where freedom exists—where family lives. Family, as well as other human beings, are to live an ethical, eschatological life. An ethical, eschatological life of immediacy exemplifies a freedom that encourages and respects the other and desires community.

"Oh, Freedom" represents an experience of actual goal-oriented or existential, eschatological freedom critical to personal identity. The full-bodied, quasi-harmonic sound yokes personal identity with the self and the community. This Spiritual gave African Americans permission to be free "in the sense of being one" with themselves, a freedom shared by the Black church.[32] The spiritual nature of freedom is intentional, "symbolic of the steps which blacks take to remove themselves from disabling emotional distress and spiritual debilitation."[33] This empowerment lifts one from scapegoat to victor, toward wholeness, self-actualization, and an ethical life, as the Spirituals "represent the black knowledge of self, love for the black community, a well-directed sense of personhood, and most significantly, a direct artistic renunciation of the historical injustices that are the real America."[34]

The process of "naming" in "Oh, Freedom" testifies to the theodic imagery of the potential beauty and the memory of the despicable in the human spirit. Freedom, the key theodic ideal, names what it will and will not tolerate. Freedom, the antithesis of racism, is life-affirming and involves the relationships among God, the oppressed, and the oppressor: "The ultimate logic of racism is genocide, and genocide of the mind and spirit is more deadly than genocide of the body."[35]

The singing of "Oh, Freedom" penetrates the logic of racism and exposes an incongruity, a paradox, of racist brutality that could not fill or obscure the void within, nor could it squelch the mystery present in *all* human life. The singing of "Oh, Freedom" pressed Whites and Blacks to deal with their own internal freedom, a conflictual, personal, psychointellectual dilemma between one's values and the facts, against the discord of race relations. With each new verse of "Oh, Freedom," the leader lined out a "call" for a new encounter of freedom. The spirited melody underscored the differences in people while implying equal treatment of diverse others. The creating, recreating, and transforming powers of performed words and music from a theomusicological perspective, including communicative goals and performance practices of "Oh, Freedom," infer social being, communal desires for justice, equality and solidarity, and new possibilities. "Oh, Freedom" implies the value of self and communal actualization, rooted in elements of a theodicy that respects difference. "Oh Freedom" celebrates a justice, a theodicy, in which the gifts of Blackness and Whiteness triumph as reflective of who God is.

"Oh, Freedom" calls for this meditative theology of mutuality and passion that does not demonize skin color, gender, or economic status. "Oh, Freedom" answers the problem of evil by demanding release from bondage and by choosing life. This story defies personal and communal subjugation and offers transformation. This song that exorcizes or cuts out evil refutes the projections from a society that deems Black people inferior. This passionate coded chant says, "I will only be a slave in death; in death I am free"—a paradox. Death means the demise of existential, actual being, the "living dead," and death as the end of life.

Life and death are the polarities of a living eschatology—a goal-oriented life view. Eschatological immediacy stimulates the call for freedom that challenges and bolsters change from any acquiescence to the status quo, and from violence that followed the African-American presence in America. The desire for choice, life, and dignity in the 1960s represented the collected remembrances or history of earlier dispersed peoples. Singing redacted songs like "Oh, Freedom" "conveyed the message that the Black struggle had a long history."[36] The telling and retelling of these performed narratives became a communicative means or form whereby the singing of "Oh, Freedom" allowed the singers and the audience/participants to view each other's experience. Singing "Oh, Freedom" was an encounter of freedom that became the liturgical, religiocultural sharing of power and space: "Our image of ourselves was enlarged when the sounds of the freedom songs filled all the space in that church."[37] Singing "Oh, Freedom" created self-definition and autonomy and celebrated Black distinctiveness—ways and means of dealing with evil and suffering.

The activists wanted respect, dignity, and equal access to public accommodations, interstate commerce, and voting and educational opportunities: transformed tenets of an applied theodicy. Singing "Oh, Freedom" was a way of affirming these desires which made their daily life process bearable. The daily life survival process within the Movement rested on their quest for freedom. During the second reconstruction period of Black America, 1945-1990, African Americans held to a particular quest, a particular dream, a particular vision:

> Within this turbulent historical process, as the African-American people experienced war and segregation, death and disfranchisement, there has also existed a nearly unbridgeable gap between American democratic theory and political practice by the white majority. Yet against all reason and collective experience, millions of blacks harbored a deep vision, a dream of democratic social order with unfettered access to political, economic and social rights, regardless of race, gender and class. Black Americans have given this dream a name: freedom. It is this unyielding belief in human freedom, more than any other single factor, which has sustained and nourished the American identity of the African-American.[38]

This vision of freedom prevailed in African-American musicking: "The community is healthiest when it sings. Singing is the process of creating a communal voice."[39] This Afrosensitive community did not see suffering as a necessary component of their lives. Suffering was a product of White supremacist racism, the antithesis of "Oh, Freedom." The activists always sang "Oh, Freedom" as a reformation hymn *in protest*, as a tool of self-definition and empowerment that sustained an ethics of mutuality and respect:

> Freedom was very concrete. During the civil rights movement it was again very concrete. . . . Freedom really had to do with having the right to be in the world on your feet as tall as you are. 'Cause by the sixties we were living in a society which let us be, by and large—as long as we occupied the space carved by people who did not know or did not want us to stand as big as we were. And freedom had to do with just, you will not shape my space.
>
> And that's the way it felt. . . . That we were using a different kind of space, we were taking over a different kind of territory. That was freedom during the Civil Rights Movement. And I think, I *feel* in some way I've been free since then. That, there's a just taste . . . you get in your mouth when you know who you are.[40]

The "unmasking" phase of divine relation, faith and thought portrays evil, eschatological time, messages of freedom and a theodical comment on evil as the Spirituals combine the first-order communal faith language and the second-order discipline of theology to evaluate society. The experience precedes the analysis. Spirituals are discourses on life, suffering, and evil, on expectations for current salvific freedom. The singing of "Oh,

Freedom" blasted "the sickening spectacle of American racism, the reality
of white democracy," and the persecution of demonstrators with fire hoses,
dogs, clubs, tear gas, guns, and electric cattle prods during the 1960s.[41]
"Oh, Freedom" uttered an immediate eschatological hope for justice and
mutuality, making deferred freedom unacceptable. The singers confronted
particular evils of racism by singing, "No more mourning!" "No more dogs!"
and "No more shooting!" commandments reminiscent of eight of the
Decalogue's "Thou shalt nots." These sung commandments reflected personal confession and afforded objective social analysis shaped by an understanding of who God is. "Oh, Freedom" asserts the following theodic
message of American socio-cultural responsibility and mutual relations:

- No African-American self was created to be a slave.
- Enslavement, fashioned as racism, is unacceptable.
- Racist human beings perpetrate racism.
- African Americans know true freedom in that place called home
  where one dies to enslavement and lives in freedom with God.
- The experience of being with God is freedom.
- God did not create slavery and oppression.

The message of "Oh, Freedom" is that freedom is an ontological and
existential reality of the soul. We are free to choose when being and acting.
We are not in bondage to or controlled by another, even if our freedom to
choose results in our death. With freedom, people are clear about their
own identity, their own purpose, their own sense. Those who shy away
from freedom often do not want the responsibility that comes with the
gifts and rights of freedom:

> You have some way to know what you should be doing from the inside.
> . . . Freedom has to do with whether anybody can take your heart or
> your mind and own your integrity. And what I came through the
> movement understanding was that you had a way of never being
> owned by another person, if you held on to letting your insides tell you
> where you were supposed to be and who you were. And did not deny
> that. Somebody could kill your body but they could never enslave
> you. But the question from that point to this day is always whether I
> can find the courage to walk what I feel inside. It's a big thing because
> I see so many people denying the inner voice.[42]

To take a stand and create community was a key motive for singing "Oh,
Freedom." During mass meetings, singing freedom songs helped minimize
the differences, for "making a song required an expression that was common to us all. . . . This music was like an instrument, like holding a tool in
your hand."[43] The plot or story line was a theological tool that upheld boundaries and aspirations in human relationships. "Oh, Freedom" described

survival and the willingness to foster integrity, freedom, and soul knowing "that there were some things in life worse than death,"[44] and some things more important than life. In singing "Oh, Freedom," the participants chose life. They used song to be "visible and overt" about attaining freedom:

> The announcement was out, and song was the announcer! And, you know when you go to a mass meeting and you worry, you didn't ask your mama whether you could go or you didn't tell your husband you were going; or, you didn't know if you would get fired from your job the next day. The cameras were there. You would go in and almost the only way you could stay was through the singing. Because, the singing reaffirms why you were there and made you larger than yourself.[45]

The "unmasking" shows that traditional and redacted versions of "Oh, Freedom" share more similarities than dissimilarities. Both versions use the original text. The 1960s version qualifies the specific instances of racist evil targeted by the freedom fighters. The activists retained the basic musical line as a framework but continued to improvise, and shifted from a slow tempo to a jubilant, up-tempo swing. Changes in the music and lyrics of the freedom songs reflected the essence of racism, demands for reform, and issues that induced and precluded change during the years of "reform demand" (1954-1960) and of mass protest "toward overcoming"(1960-1965), summarized here:

- Desegregation moved slowly as African Americans experienced humiliation and exploitation in southern apartheid-type social relations; White police officers routinely picked up African-American female pedestrians and raped them at gunpoint.
- White supremacist hate groups reigned in terror over proponents of Black freedom.
- The contradiction between a call for freeing Africa and unfree African descendants in the United States became excruciatingly apparent.
- Racist trade union practices thwarted African-American efforts to attain work commensurate with their talents and training during the shift in the Black political economy.
- Blacks demanded that economic reforms be a central Movement concern.
- The struggle for Black equality concerned sociocultural assimilation into mainstream America but resisted the imposition of White capitalist order. Beyond that, the consensus for alternatives fell apart. Conversely, Black nationalists held antiracist and anti-integrationist stances and supported all-Black social, political, and economic institutions.
- The rise of the Nation of Islam was successful, due to its efforts to

minister to and transform the most oppressed African Americans (perennially unemployed, convicts, prostitutes, pimps, criminals, and addicts) and to the rhetorical gifts of Malcolm X.

- Student nonviolent, direct-action protests such as sit-ins, stand-ins, wade-ins, and pray-ins from 1960 on, at lunch counters, theaters, pools and beaches, and segregated churches, markedly speeded up the rate of social change, influencing the mode of protest strategy for the next five years.

- The White response to student nonviolent African-American protest varied. Some places offered little resistance to change; in others, Black protesters suffered cigar and cigarette burns on faces and arms; received blows and cuts with knives and razors; were spat on and kicked to the floor; and were locked up by police and placed by the thousands into unsanitary, cramped jails.

- Young people in SNCC and CORE, often led by Black ministers, chiefly conceived, planned, and administered the 1960s battles.

- African Americans could no longer wait for benevolent Whites to free them.

- Racist violence continued unabated; the movement by the Kennedy administration during 1963 was not a function of its discomfort with racial segregation but was due to cold geopolitical facts: pictures of battered and bloody Black children in American southern streets could only undermine the image of the United States in nonaligned countries.

- In the eyes of many moderates, the 1963 March on Washington was the greatest ritual experience of their lives; for many radicals, it was a "farce on Washington." Instead of being the mass protest of a nonviolent army, the occasion was more attuned with a ceremony to tout Kennedy's civil rights bill before Congress.[46]

Singing "Oh, Freedom" evoked an image of freedom and dynamics that effected freedom. With an Afrosensitive hearing, the ideal for many Blacks was the White experience, because Whites had freedom and justice. Freedom meant equal opportunity and access by integration and the ability to be. Justice meant no more "mournin'," "shootin'," or brutality. For many Whites, freedom for Blacks would threaten the status quo, particularly if Blacks could have social and economic power and control, and Whites would no longer be able to maintain a superiority complex effected by maintaining a subservient group. Blacks desired the apparent freedom, justice, and pursuit of happiness of Whites. Whites desired the perceived biological or sexual prowess and physical stamina of Blacks and needed to control Blacks' social, economic, and cultural mobility. "Oh, Freedom" announced that African Americans had been but were no longer willing to be the scapegoats. "Oh, Freedom" exposes paradoxes inherent to many facets of theodicy. The performed song conceptually acknowledges the Black-

White notions of what it means to be Black. Yet "Oh, Freedom" argues that the 1960s freedom fighters demonstrated in a real world that prescribed separate and "not equal" under the law. "Oh, Freedom" was a sword that rent the curtain of White supremacy, segregation, and Jim Crow by arguing against applied racism, and that inspired activists and their empathetic leaders, which led to new legislation and changed attitudes that achieved legal Black freedom. Despite that veil, African Americans had a sense of self and the community. They believed in their freedom under God, within themselves, and in their humanness. They believed in their right to equality and justice, to be free and to know love. Nurtured by community and the church, Blacks sang "Oh, Freedom" to overcome, and to solidify their community and their chances to attain political and legal freedom. Their singing echoed both hushed, ancestral voices and those that were native-born but relegated to second-class citizenship. Singing "Oh, Freedom" celebrated their true selves and their desires for a better life:

> I am brown and I have experienced life as a brown person. . . . Brownness was always compared to whiteness in terms that were ultimately degrading for brownness. . . . This message, however, was first and most transmitted by brown. . . . No matter how good, how pious the brown, they could not equal or reflect the ultimate good and right—white.
>
> . . . Brown is not The Oppressor but the victim. But part of our victimization is self-oppression. Our adaptations were creative, the end goal, survival. . . . Helplessness and powerlessness combined with the pride and hope that comes from surviving, mixed with the shame of surviving the humiliation of servitude, and the rage of being considered nonhuman. The system's apex is the reality that while adapting to white . . . [culture] we had not gained social acceptance. Further, while sacrificing, working, praying, singing, fighting, and dying for and with white, we had not gained equality, economic security, or freedom. What we had gained was an insidious, terrifying, self-negating desire—even need—to be white.[47]

When singing, African Americans spoke to these mixed messages with their whole being. They recalled the history of slavery and knew their disenfranchisement and segregation, but desired physical, mental, emotional, and spiritual freedom and wholeness, a freedom that led to salvific liberation, the freedom to be.

"Oh, Freedom," a challenge to have the same rights as those granted the dominant, White class, often juxtaposed the desire for integration with the quest for nationalism and self-reliance. The color line was the winding sheet and the cooling board for "Who or what died?"[48] Part of the human spirit died with each bombardment of racist evil. Part of the community's vitality died with each blow to justice. Singing "Oh, Freedom" in McComb called for the death of racist practices and the resurrection of the oppressed, accomplished by vacating the oppressor's old demonic subjugation practices. The freedom-to-be uncovers diverse meanings involving disclosure, masks, and symbols (i.e., signifying).[49] The multiple meanings and voicing of signification communicate the voices and acts of God, the oppressor, and the oppressed with key words: freedom, slave, dogs, shooting, mourning, and segregation. The singing activists saw the signifying and ascribed a second meaning to the text. Signification uncovered the original and the coded utterances of spiritual freedom within legal racism, which in turn produced mental, emotional, physical, social, and political bondage and oppression at best, and created the ambiguity of holding together a sanity daily tested and pushed toward schizophrenia at worst. In holding themselves and their communities together, freedom fighters during the antebellum and 1960s eras used particular musical elements or musical lines to color certain words as part of the signification process.

Many musical attributes contributed to the impact of the singing. The melodic line supports the lyric line by (1) not overwhelming the words; (2) emphasizing key words through sustained notes by dragging out the subject, like segregation, and through tonal and rhythmic inflection of the soloist as the soloist sings "over me, over me; / And before"; (3) using a moderate but steady walking tempo with percussive hand clapping, which evoked determination and a sense of redemptive hope; (4) doing clapping and foot tapping that have a quasi-staccato feeling that gives an impression of vitality and energy; and (5) punctuating individual and communal relationships by using added harmonies, which adds a cohesive feeling that embraces the singers and the audience.

Freedom implies choice, emancipation, absence of constraints, free will, discretion, and the mutual gifts of self to the community and of community to the self. "Slave" is the antithesis of freedom, yet a sense of mutuality in community remains constant. "Dogs" and "shooting" evoke images of violence and the destruction of personhood and property. "Mournin'" concerns sadness, regret, loss, and death. "Segregation" pertains to separateness, inequality, difference, annihilation, and dismissal. In Black vernacular, signification is culturally specific, though the process of signification may have a similar network of associations key to spoken communication in similar cultures. This process involves regional revisions and persuasive, indirect verbal or gestural language. In "Oh, Freedom," the shared history about freedom, dogs, shooting, mourning, and segregation suggests the dual spectrum of that Movement: humiliation, violence, and racist subjugation versus communal solidarity, faith, courage, and transformation. The ambiguity and tension that developed within such diverse realities become a contemplative, chronicled view of prophetic Jewish and Christian ethical ideas wherein relationships are critical in combating suffering, justice, sin, and evil.

In "Oh, Freedom," the dialectic of evil orchestrated by alleged Christians ideally reiterates the contradictions in how people relate to God and others in the context of justice. In the actual Movement, "Oh, Freedom" celebrated the social relationships of the common meal tradition: the call for mutuality, bonding, and equality that spans race, gender, and class. "Oh, Freedom" commemorated the ultimate, mutual encounter of grace and embraced relationships between God and humanity, between persons and persons, between persons and communities, and between communities and communities. "Oh, Freedom" pronounces "No!" to separation, subjugation, and racism, and "Yes!" to the ability to participate in the relational, reciprocal world of God.

"Oh, Freedom" provokes a commitment toward inclusivity and "we" intentions where "they" become "we." Such a reconciliation creates a new moral vision of community and relationships where society can exact a vision that includes a theology and an ethics of liberation. Ideally, "Oh, Freedom" posits that "all of God's children" are created as *imago Dei*. These reflections, blended with traditional African religionist ideas of vitality, wholeness, humanism, and continuity toward health, help others value difference, the difference celebrated in "Oh, Freedom," where finding value yields balanced relationships as true relational freedom, the hallmark of righteousness underpinning a healthy theodicy.

Difference can celebrate identity. Difference represents the many polarities within the individual and society where creativity illumines the dialectic and the raw and magnificent connection that provides personal power.[50] The performed "Oh, Freedom" champions these differences and the repetitions found in music and lyrics. The place of difference over against repetition and identity counters ambiguity against certainty. The many life stories of Movement participants reflected in "Oh, Freedom" provide a nondivisible encounter of the sacred and the profane in the aesthetics of song.

The aesthetics or beauty of song comes alive as we "engage" the texts, which leads to exploration and fusion toward transformation. One 1960s contextual "engaging" moment of "Oh, Freedom" occurred as a struggle being born in Mississippi during this period of American history. Singing "Oh, Freedom" was one cornerstone of the civil rights reformation that helped this country examine its potential and that enabled African Americans to create the space they needed to be themselves.[51] Like their ancestral counterparts, the freedom singers had an attitude of nonviolent militancy and freedom grounded in a religious and spiritual space. The singers protested despite violence and hate. Activist-singer Hollis Watkins recounted the terror and the struggle his community faced when night riders gave African-American landowners twenty-four hours or less to leave their homes. He knew the pain when his father had to leave because he "had words" with a White man over "words" that White man said to Watkins's grandmother. Watkins struggled with the conflict between the love and harmony preached in church and the injustice he saw daily. He recalled his mother's prayers and moans as she knelt down by his bed and said, "Leave it in the hands of the Lord." Watkins could sing "Oh, Freedom" because he knew if the Lord was in him and within other people, then he had to get involved in the Movement. These experiences situated Watkins at a mass meeting in McComb, Mississippi, in 1963.[52] Black congregational singing was the genre that successfully brought these components to bear in one setting.

Black congregational singing is an invasive tool that goes inside you and works the territory within, if you know how to sing a note and "spread" or treat that note with emotional feeling. The feeling "has to be internal to the pitch." The note must be a genuine moan, must be "cried through." The singers must participate with the intention of nurturing, of keeping sane, of helping the spiritual part of humanity through song.[53] This experience involves physiological and spiritual phenomena:

> These things were not an aural experience. I mean you could hear it, but it did a lot more to you than just deal with your ears. . . . It seeped inside of your being looking for something to stir up; and it almost felt like it knew what it was looking for. . . . There is some place in us this thing could go and work and stir up that nothing else could quite touch. And it might not be a place that you actually like to visit so much or even wanted to know you had it. So the hymns are invasive. . . .
>
> The emotional feeling has to be internal to the pitch, which means you can't sing the note and then as a good actress color the note with a feeling so that it will sound as if you're crying. . . . You have to cry . . . you have to moan when you sing; . . . if you go to those places with your singing voice, then the . . . melodies, the harmonies and then the vocal textures—actually gets to do its work in that congregation. In those places in your life, places in my life where I cry, places in my life where I am heavy.[54]

Music thus moved the Movement. Music embodied the 1960s struggle for liberty canonized in "Oh, Freedom." Thousands worked and sang and prayed and suffered; some died for the Movement. They looked within themselves and the Movement and used musical stories to galvanize the community with the courage and stamina present at mass meetings throughout the nation. The solidarity and community replicated itself in the Mississippi mass meetings during 1963 and in the voter registration drive of the Freedom Summer, 1964. Singing "Oh, Freedom" symbolized the liturgical exemplar of an intense desire for liberty and solidarity. The disenfranchised sharecroppers wanted freedom, and they sang until that desire somehow became their own. Fannie Lou Hamer, leader of the Mississippi Freedom Democratic Party, epitomized need transformed to intimacy, toward the actualized expressions of theodicy as harmonious relations, which allowed Hamer to know freedom. Hamer sang of freedom as she led the challenge to the Mississippi delegation and to the credentials committee at the 1964 Democratic Convention.[55]

Others met the challenge when inspired by stories. Eight years before Watkins led "Oh, Freedom," the image of Emmett Till's mutilated body stimulated the anger and interest of African Americans nationwide. Till and countless other "disappeareds" were part of the history of Mississippi from 1955 to 1965. The terrorization and murder of innocent Blacks were the norm.[56] Ironically, the process of transformation began in Mississippi, despite the unjust acquittal of Till's murderers: an African American stood in a courtroom and testified against White people. That courageous act triggered the next decade of repeated nonviolent direct action, lauded in word and music—especially the Spirituals. McComb epitomized Mississippi and the South.

SNCC and CORE workers bonded with southern youth and college students in their quest for freedom, they sang, marched, and sat in.[57] They embodied the communal "I," the key character developed in "Oh, Freedom." Essentially, the story line was the refrain, "before I'll be a slave. . . ." Midway in the narrative, the singers claimed, "Nothin' but freedom." Before and after, the characters sang the "No mores." The characters strongly affirmed their own free being, qualified their boundaries, and saw the curtains of racism without being deterred from seeking justice and equality. "Oh, Freedom" was an unofficial signature song: the singers' daily lives revolved around freedom. Their singing became therapy, as music became their holistic approach to reality.

The singing allowed people to make statements, to claim their own space and territory, and to experience healing. When renegade sheriffs tried to break up mass meetings through intimidation, someone would start singing. Other activists joined in, and the singing kept them in the room and filled up the space. The power generated by the singing forced the police officers to leave, and the activists overcame their fear. In singing, they transcended racism toward the life-affirming empowerment of the "good" factor of theodicy. When singing songs like "Oh, Freedom" or "Over My Head, I Hear Freedom in the Air," the singers faced past years of fear and the present fear of what was next:

> *Over my head, I hear freedom in the air*
> *Over my head, I hear freedom in the air*
> *Over my head, I hear freedom in the air*
> *There must be a God somewhere.*
> Redacted by Bernice Johnson Reagon

Singing kept activists in the moment, especially when they realized that being in a mass meeting tonight did not guarantee they would be alive to attend a mass meeting the next day: "That's another work; that's like living through the hours and living through the days. . . . At that moment, it is really very important, and the first line of work is the comfort it gives to you to be in that space with so much disapproval. . . . The next day the church is gone."[58]

Fear no longer held them captive when their daily acts of courage and commitment arrested international attention. Human lives often paid the price for the resulting changes, but the fear of death was rendered powerless. Biblical freedom grounded these beliefs and provided a religious sense, the root of "Oh, Freedom," to the Movement.

The Black church and its attendant religious experiences, built on biblical stories, has supported generations of Black freedom seekers. By giving the antebellum church confidence in the omni-God and a sense of being discontent with their hostage situation, Black religion called the enslaved to rebel for freedom.[59] The Black church sang "Oh, Freedom" to nurture and sustain; it gave its constituency all that society had stolen, assured communal confidence in God, and encouraged discontent with Jim Crow. The church was the hub for educational, civic, and cultural activities, from holding mass meetings and helping raise bail money to providing transportation, food, and funds to those with nowhere else to turn.[60] The same Scripture that bolstered the antebellum church fueled a late-twentieth-century Black church when read differently.

Black churches have long relied on a biblical vocabulary of freedom toward liberation for unliberated people in the themes of exodus, Jubilee, victory, survival, prophecy, and deliverance from evil. The church was central because institutionally it could claim, "The power is in this circle."[61] With the best interests of Black people at heart, the church went about "making a way in this world that would give us a chance to be different from the recipe that brought us here."[62] The centrality of the Bible was not disruptive, despite the ambiguities and many perspectives in the biblical text. The Hebrew Bible (Old Testament) shows both the cruel Egyptian oppression of ancient Hebrews (Ex 3:7-9; 5:10-21) and the slavery practiced by the Hebrews after their own liberation (Ex 21; Dt 15). Apparently in the Hebrew Bible, freedom is a religious or socio-political ideal as opposed to a practical daily actuality.[63] While the New Testament sanctions some slavery, most texts stress the import of freedom, especially that the household of faith be free of certain Jewish religious laws, free of assenting to standard values, and free of materialism. Jesus, the model for living freedom, exercises his *freedom from* assaults by the devil and his *freedom for* service on behalf of God.[64] Jesus Christ represents freedom as an agapic force that shapes theodicy as freedom to be, freedom to love, freedom from sin.

The Black church identified with the liberated Hebrew children and with the Liberator, Jesus, as they sang "Oh, Freedom," the experience of trying to be free in the middle of great trials.[65] The slaves had a creative bent in their exegesis and reinterpretation of Scripture through song. While no clear documentation exists, the refrain of "Oh, Freedom" appears to use remnants from Psalm 88, a Psalm of lament. Both songs use the ideas of freedom and the grave in concert. The confession of the psalmist and that of the slave bard create patterns in opposition.

> I am counted among those who go down to the pit;
>> I am like a [person] without strength.
> I am set apart with the dead,
>> like the slain who lie in the grave,
> whom you remember no more,
>> who are cut off from your care.
>
> Psalm 88: 4-5 (NIV)

> *And before I'll be a slave,*
> *I'll be buried in my grave;*
> *And go home to my Lord and be free.*
> Refrain, "Oh, Freedom"

Psalm 88 speaks with ancient Israel's voice to report Yahweh's absence. The lament proper (verses 1-2) intimately addresses God, depicts need, and expresses praise. Verse 5 is in the complaint proper (verses 3-5a). In anger, the psalmist tries to persuade God to answer, for the pit (grave) is not final judgment but stands beyond the range of communion with God, which is everything for the speaker. Thus, the isolation from community with God and humanity exists: "the dead" are in no sense alive. The speaker appeals again (verses 6-9a). Yahweh causes death. Verses 10-12 reveal a series of rhetorical questions about the speaker's situation juxtaposed to words characterizing Yahweh's usual activity: "dead," "shades," "grave," "abandons," "darkness," and "land of forgetfulness" versus "praise," "steadfast love," "faithfulness," "wonders," and "saving help."[66] This drama displays the incongruity between the speaker's milieu and what God does. This scene precedes a prayer without answer (verse 13). The third appeal (verses 14-18) confronts Yahweh's absence, reiterates the situation, and recalls a lifetime of troubles, of terrors from God's hand. In Psalm 88, "Faith faces life as it is. . . . Israel must deal with Yahweh in [Yahweh's] life-giving speech and answer . . . words that could comfort . . . words [that] assert . . . a tenuous link between the darkness and the Lord of life."[67] The creators of "Oh, Freedom" create another scenario.

"Oh, Freedom" implicitly celebrates these activities of God but finds solace in the grave. The grave stands within the veil of communion with God, as part of the Christ event—ultimate victory in the Resurrection. Being home with God in faith allows one to know victory and helps one become aware of the relationships between difference and victimization, justice and freedom, suffering and salvation—some dimensions of theodicy as praxis. With such an awareness, African Americans must deal with Yahweh by hearing words that comfort and words that create tension between the present evil and the Lord of Light. The freedom singers heard and recognized other tensions between the dictionary-syntactical meanings and the silent meanings of the phrases.

"Oh, Freedom" meant justice and equality and referred to personified freedom as an unfailing God, as a Jesus who liberates, as a place to truly call home, a place safe from dogs. "No more dogs" echoed actual attack dogs and symbolized all other intimidating persons, events, systems, and feelings—actual and metaphorical evil. The redacted "Oh, Freedom" added issues that confronted inter- and intracommunal violence in Black communities. Whites used violence to inhibit the exercise of freedom by Blacks. Using "shooting" and "mourning" called attention to the senseless deaths perpetrated by racism, nonbelief, and apathy. The triple repetition of key phrases for each verse and for the music is part of an adult ritual that uses language to share information, to support, and to hope for a better day today, for the present generation.

The combined literary, rhetorical, and musical factors in "Oh, Freedom" paint a detailed picture of the life and time of subjugated people who have chosen to protest, given the paradoxical nature of all life. The paradox embodies many gray areas when defining freedom and when redistributing power in a way that lifts but does not demean anyone. For example, the lyric or musical lines of "Oh, Freedom" exposed the 1960s social and historical representation, where singing the spirituals became a viable way to combat oppression. With increased and repetitive activity came stereotypical language and action: cities across the nation retaliated against integration and persecuted innocent people. These factors reflect the composite of oppression within a capitalist society through the negation of justice and mutuality. The factors combine to reveal a depth of creativity in difficult times. One method of coping with difficult times is notably the exercise of humor.

With "inside humor," one member of a group says something to another member of the group that is not obvious to nongroup members. Consider the inside theological humor of this paraphrase of John 1:5 (NIV): "The Light [of humor] shines in the darkness [of the uncomprehending "outsider"], but the darkness has not understood [overcome] it."[68] For example, with "*Massa's in the Cold, Cold Grave*," a slave-owning family would think, "How wonderful that the slaves feel so sorry for the massa and grieve his passing." However, the slaves took delight. They had no heating or warm clothing; their massa would now experience this lack of warmth. What he gave to them, he would now receive and could not avoid. Within the Spirituals, the same type of sardonic humor occurs, but with more subtlety. The submerged humor is apparent to those singing the song, who are "inside," but not to those who are "outside" this culture. The dialectic of humor moves between physical and aesthetic sensibilities. The balance between anguish and victory is the irony that moves toward a religious view of humanity. Therapeutic humor in "Oh, Freedom" implies divine desire

for humanity to be whole, to be well. "Oh, Freedom over me" is a personification of an entity who is in control, when the singers themselves become more powerful as they struggle to attain that which often appears to
be unattainable. The sardonic aspect was the inside message: the master
never realized he was the subject of ridicule by the slaves that he owned.
The slaves ridiculed him by saying in "Oh, Freedom" that they were not
slaves, they were the masters of their own fates: "And before I'll be a slave,
/ I'll be buried in my grave." In the redacted Spirituals, the same phrase,
"And before I'll be a slave / . . ." ridiculed racists for even daring to think
that they could enslave or dominate the civil rights activists. Oppressors
could enslave their bodies but not their souls. In "Oh, Freedom," humor as
hyperbole occurred when singers mocked institutionalized racism by talking about institutionalized slavery. However, if you have to explain the
humor to the "outsider," the one who does not get it, the laughter van-
ishes. When you analyze or explain the text of humor, the spirit of laughter
escapes. Such creativity within chaos gives birth to an experience of re-
formed American civil religion from the other side—the activity and ideology of Black religious experience.

"My Lord" is the explicit identity of God in "Oh, Freedom." "My" refers
to possession by me and us, just as the "I" refers to "I" and "we." "My Lord"
connotes a God of intimate and powerful dimensions, including a composite of a liberating Jesus and Moses. "My Lord" is the one who, even in this
quasi-secular Movement, "stills the water," "is a rock in a weary land," "is
the alpha and the omega," and is the one "who watches over me." "My
Lord" is an omni-God who loves, is just and merciful, holds the world, and
cannot be fragmented, for there is no discontinuity. There is the transcendence of pain and suffering where one can envision a world of less racism.
This new worldview reflects the probability of an answer to theodicy rather
than an eternal problem of blatant racist evil. "My Lord" is the God of African-American experience who affirms the unity of life, patriotism, and loyalty amid racism, and who has a critical awareness of the promises of un-
fulfilled legal justice and race pride or activism.[69]

Implicitly, God-talk frames Black rhetoric in the Spirituals, with a religious bent toward existence. In "Oh, Freedom," God is personal, powerful,
compassionate, and liberating, creating a space where the powerless become powerful.[70] Together with God and the church, African-American communities survived. The church remains a lifeline, an institutional defense
against the problems of theodicy, of evil and suffering:

In the beginning was the Black church, and the Black church was with
the Black community, and the Black church was the Black community.
The Black church was in the beginning with the Black people; all
things were made through the Black church and without the Black
church was not anything that was made. In the Black church was life,

and the life was the Light of the Black people. The Black church still shines in the darkness and the darkness has not overcome it.[71]

"Oh, Freedom" is a litany of appreciation for the authentic human magnificence exemplified in this quotation, for God declared all divine creation very good. African Americans celebrate this magnificence in the family, community, church, and humanity as *imago Dei*. *Imago Dei* declares the authenticity of each Black soul. Authentic humanity resists a schizophrenic lifestyle that forces one to deny the power of "Oh, Freedom" by becoming totally other at the expense of losing the self. Healthy children are not born hating. Hateful, abusive, angry, oppressive persons teach such behavior that exacts cruelty and annihilation. Singing "Oh, Freedom" acknowledges the dilemma and the hope framing theodicy, the reality of oppression and the prospect for transforming both victim and the oppressor.

This Spiritual outlines African-American life in the United States, from repression to a salvific, liberating freedom. Shaped by a stalwart, strophic melody, "Oh, Freedom" encourages daily liberation and growth. The salvific quality of "Oh, Freedom" presses for a holistic life that affirms freedom, justice, and equal treatment for all humanity,[72] and posits a word of transformation. This freedom reckons with oppression and calls for a distribution that makes everyone accountable for the well-being of the total society. "Oh, Freedom" calls for a theodicy of mutuality and a realized eschatology but never condones deferred liberation.

The quest for liberation set in "Oh, Freedom" theomusicologically celebrates the sacred and the secular in a reconciling act that embraces the other and thus appreciates difference. Ultimately, only when the oppressed knows freedom is the oppressor truly free. No oppression is acceptable, for oppression is the curse. The gift of "Oh, Freedom" recognizes the authentic self apart from the self projected by society, and celebrates the creativity of the human spirit and the power of language. Signifying has allowed African Americans to communicate safely at multiple levels through music in often threatening situations. "Oh, Freedom" calls for balanced relationships for equality and mutual, social freedom. That call for reform is an opportunity to rethink communal and civil rights versus communal and individual responsibilities. "Oh, Freedom," part of the liturgical music of the 1960s Movement, a movement based on rational resource mobilization,[73] indicts, convicts, and inspires toward a healthy actualization of theodicy as the freedom to choose. That freedom chooses unity, noting that under God, people are the same:

> The basis of our unity is that in the most important way we are all in the same boat all subjected to the violent pernicious ideas we have learned to hate that we must all struggle against them and exchange ways and means hints and how tos that only some of us are victims of

sexism only some of us are victims of racism of the directed arrows of oppression but all of us are sexist racist all of us [spacing of original text].[74]

"This Little Light of Mine"

Another mass meeting song that exclaims "no" to oppression, to the sins and evils of racism, sexism, and classism, but "yes" to liberation at all costs is "This Little Light of Mine." "This Little Light of Mine" declares that a person chooses to let his or her light shine in time and space wherever he or she goes. "I'm going to let it shine" symbolizes the individual as well as the imperial or collective "we." The freedom singers tell the listening audience about their intentions and advise the listeners to tell specific political figures that the protagonists will let their light(s) shine. With toe-tapping energy and a revivalist spirit, this song of Jubilee, set in the key of B-flat major, celebrates the vitality of life and the power of self-esteem within a communal self. The context of this Spiritual, like that of "Oh, Freedom," is the time of mass meetings in the South during struggle and turmoil, the rise of the Southern Christian Leadership Conference (SCLC) in Alabama after King penned the "Letter from Birmingham City Jail," and the March on Washington, but before Freedom Summer, 1964, and the passage of the 1964 Civil Rights Bill. Even though the Civil Rights Acts of 1957 and 1960 protected African Americans' right to vote, few Black citizens were registered, due to Jim Crow practices of White voter registrars.

Context

"This Little Light of Mine" speaks about the individual and communal ability to choose. Letting one's light shine signifies human choice about the nature of individual and human life in community. This Spiritual announces that one may be prohibited by social, political, sexual, or racial constraints from exercising that choice, but those constraints neither diminish the potential good nor are impenetrable to change. Black persons living in Selma, Alabama, were ready for change in 1963.

Betty Mae Fikes, director and soloist, led the Selma Youth Freedom Choir in performance with piano accompaniment and audience participation. The performance practices engaged everyone present and supported the community's shaping of the song. Fikes's gospel-singing style stirred the entire congregation into fervent singing as they all shaped the song. The traditional version of "This Little Light of Mine" involved the body and soul of the singers as they knew an inner transformation that happened when they recalled their African religious experiences and could know joy despite the circumstances. The singers could then share this joy with others. When all of the individual lights shine together, they become a resource for all acquiring freedom and transformation in the present.[75] The following traditional text formed the basis for the Selma adaptation of "This Little Light of Mine":

> *This little light of mine, I'm going to let it shine, oh,*
> *This little light of mine,*
> *I'm going to let it shine, hallelujah*
> *This little light of mine,*
> *I'm going to let it shine, oh,*
> *Let it shine, let it shine, let it shine.*
>
> *Everywhere I go, I'm going to let it shine, oh,*
> *Everywhere I go, I'm going to let it shine, hallelujah*
> *Everywhere I go, I'm going to let it shine, oh,*
> *Let it shine, let it shine, let it shine.*
>
> *All in my house, I'm going to let it shine . . .*
> *All through the night, I'm going to let it shine, hallelujah . . .*
> *I'm not going to make it shine, I'm going to let it shine . . .*
> *Out in the dark, I'm going to let it shine . . .*
> *Everywhere I go, I'm going to let it shine . . .*

"This Little Light of Mine" begins with the chorus and contains numerous verses; both verse and chorus use the same music and conclude with the refrain, "Let it shine, let it shine, let it shine." The textual structure involves three repeated lines of text followed by the refrain line: *aaar*. The verse and chorus both have recurring lines of text. The melodic structure corresponds with the syllabic melodies of the verse and chorus, depending upon the setting of the song. A strong vocal leader, Fikes led the following redacted version of "This Little Light of Mine" as the singers localized and particularized this Spiritual to convey who and what they were fighting:

> *This little light of mine, I'm going to let it shine*
> *This little light of mine, I'm going to let it shine*
> *This little light of mine, I'm going to let it shine*
> *Let it shine, let it shine, let it shine.*
>
> *Tell Governor Wallace, I'm going to let it shine . . .*
> *Tell Jim Clark, I'm going to let it shine . . .*
> *Tell Judge Boone, I'm going to let it shine . . .*
> *Everywhere I go, I'm going to let it shine . . .*
> *My God give it to me, I'm going to let it shine . . .*

In 1963, Selma, Alabama, had a population of about thirty thousand. Although African Americans made up about half the voting-age population, only 1 percent of them were registered to vote. SNCC workers held voting clinics, but, for various reasons, Selma's Black constituency was reticent about registering and voting. Some resisted because they could not read or write. Some thought Blacks had no business being concerned about voting; others feared retaliation and harassment from Whites. When SNCC held a Freedom Day in Selma on October 7, 1963, 250 African Americans waited to register outside the county courthouse. Sheriff Jim Clark, along with helmeted, armed deputies, blocked their entry to the building. The police harassed and arrested SNCC workers. Even if any Blacks could get into the courthouse to register, they faced additional troubles: these "citizens" had to fill out four pages of forms, and their photographs were taken and then published in the newspapers as a way to intimidate them by getting them fired.[76] While African Americans protested in Selma, Alabama, in Africa, citizens of Kenya won their independence on December 12, 1963. During the fall of 1963, Black Selmans protested and sang to combat racism and oppression.

In "This Little Light of Mine," the Black community made a localized social, political, and spiritual statement when they incorporated characters who gave rise to the Selma Movement through their racist and unjust practices. These descendants of slaves and free Blacks stood up for themselves. For the singers, light represented freedom, a gift from God. Governor Wallace, Sheriff Jim Clark, Judge Boone, and Mayor Hines were figures that personified oppressive power and malignant agency. The text affirms that in spite of these positions of power, the singers would not be intimidated. In spite of adversaries like Wallace and Clark, the singers demanded a life of freedom.

Through song, both leader and choral participants affirmed a willingness to live their lives in a way that reflected persons who demanded and claimed the full rights accorded them by created order, as well as their constitutional rights. The threat of suffering at the hands of the political power structure did not overwhelm, because any such threat could be overcome when they "let their lights shine." The continuous repetition of "let it shine" demonstrates a commitment on the part of the singers to let their lights shine. They choose life, because light represents self-actualization, and this concept of light permeates all verses and chorus. Yet some Blacks and most Whites had no desire to "let their lights shine."

High Priest Sheriff Jim Clark and his assistant priests or deputies did all they could to thwart any movement toward freedom and empowerment for Blacks. Their racist rituals, conducted in tandem with American civil religion, effectively caused much sacrifice and pushed forth an idolatrous agenda: the worship of White supremacist doctrine. When taking pictures or verbal harassment failed, the police sang the hymns and pronounced the litanies of economic retaliation. The state's civil religious activities were reinforced by a federal faux pas. Several early appointments of southern federal judges by President Kennedy were ardent segregationists—elders, presbyters, and deacons—who honored the Baals of racism. The tension between "religious" segregationist power brokers and the disenfranchised pitted the arrogance of racism against the pathos of power.

Despite the privilege, arrogance, and dominance of Whiteness, "This Little Light of Mine" specifically names the perpetrators of evil and injustice. Many White political high priests and bishops proclaimed "segregation now, segregation forever" from their pulpits anchored in the Confederacy and draped with a rebel flag. As these blasphemers and idolaters preached about separatism and hate, freedom fighters responded with prayers and songs of hope and reformation. The repetitive "I'm going to let it shine" summoned forth pathos toward the work of the local Dallas County (Alabama) Voters' League (DCVL), led by Amelia and Samuel Boynton. Amelia Boynton had invited SNCC to come to Selma to work for voter registration. Many thought that students could bring an energy and a force to the Movement and could create change, and the students felt they were obligated to go. Pathos and arrogance mixed in the tensions underpinning the first Black community mass rally in May 1963, which was met with resistance from Whites and some Blacks.[77] DCVL began in the 1920s, petered out because of lack of interest, then was resurrected in 1936. Some Blacks were afraid or complacent, or decided to please White folk rather than risk their lives. Those Blacks who did take a stand, like the Boyntons, faced the absurdity of racism as they worked for voting rights. By viewing the Selma story from an Afrosensitive stance, we see the history of hardships, of psychological and economic warfare from Whites, of acquiescence or snitching to the White political structure by some Blacks. The Boyntons would not be deterred. This husband-wife team taught people how to fill in the difficult questions on voter registration blanks and went with them to the clerk's office to register. After Samuel Boynton died in 1963, Amelia Boynton continued to support registration activities, despite the fact that few Blacks gained access to voting for the next eight years.[78] When Black Selmans felt SNCC's progress was too slow, Boynton got in touch with SCLC to request that SCLC come to Selma. SCLC arrived in Selma after working in Albany, Georgia, and Birmingham, Alabama. When SCLC members came and worked in Selma, they often used humor as well as song to sustain and press themselves forward.

In Selma, freedom fighters had to deal with the way authority figures like Sheriff Jim Clark perpetrated evil by making scapegoats of Blacks and Whites who supported integration. Clark became enraged when people defied his authority. Neither state nor local authorities wanted change. Freedom fighters would not take no for an answer, because they wanted freedom. The freedom fighters continued to meet, sit in, and protest. No hostility could dampen their lights and quests for justice. "This Little Light of Mine" answered this hostility with a loud "No!"

The themes and message about light question theodicy, question a system of injustice, and question who is responsible for actualizing justice.

Questioning access to justice involves the quest for freedom while the oppressed struggle to survive injustice. Daily, those desiring liberation had to deal with psychological adjustments and pathos experienced while living with the historical reality of an unjust society and coping with that evil and sin. Those who inhibit freedom cause evil and suffering. The singers do not assume that overcoming racism and injustice is impossible, because God gives the gift of life and freedom that in turn requires human responsibility. At the same time, because of the light, the oppressed cannot choose to acquiesce, despite the threat of pain and death. How they faced the tension which comes of living in such persecution unfolds under the rubric of story.

Story

In Selma, the story of "This Little Light of Mine" concerns how public officials assured that the color line was drawn clearly and plainly for all to see. Reading this Spiritual as story conveys the message that the faithful protesters knew the line was drawn, yet they believed that options existed for justice. They refused to allow circumstances to dampen their hope and fully control their lives. The hope and provision for earlier slaves and for freedom fighters were not the leaders of Selma, but God. By telling and living these truths, the antebellum slaves and the freedom fighters claimed that one can ultimately reduce suffering and injustice. They did not romanticize the suffering caused by racism but saw that suffering as a negative force that could be eliminated. The concept of this hope embodied in light permeates the entire song.

The Selma text incorporated three traditional stanzas with chorus and added four stanzas that use light to reflect local concerns. Each verse develops themes that delineate light as freedom, active grace, and communal and personal empowerment and esteem. Verse 1 affirms survival while demanding freedom, commits psychologically to endurance and community actualization, and narrates a life cycle of coping. Verses 1-3, which focus on particular political leaders, claim victory in freedom and daringly announce the boldness of the oppression. Light juxtaposed against the manipulation of power makes evil a human responsibility, protests racism, and seeks empowerment through justice. These political statements also concern multidimensional time (past, present, and future) and foster continuity through human relationships. Choosing to live in community with an attitude of benevolence is antithetical to a life forged by sinful racism. Letting one's light shine, the key repetitive motif, means breaking the shackles of any prejudicial and demeaning constraints against life. Such a move calls for change in persons (the oppressed, the oppressor, and the so-called indifferent), systems and rituals which keep oppression in place. The final verse, "My God give it to me . . .," views the human life cycle as sacramental and celebrates God as loving, just, and worthy of praise. As one of the

songs from the protest movements of the 1960s, "This Little Light" under-
went variations by at least eight leaders in the Albany, Georgia, movement
and SNCC. In addition to the new verses added to the Selma text, other
verses included the following:

> *Up and down this street, Lord, I'm going to let it shine* . . .
> *Every time I'm bleeding, I'm going to let it shine* . . .
> *Voting for my freedom, I'm going to let it shine* . . .[79]

Within these verses, slaves and later freedom fighters stood as Black
folks who cannot always voice their thoughts, because of the need to survive. While singing "This Little Light of Mine" to an unknowing public or to
Whites unaware of signifying, the singers would appear to be within the
status quo. The singers have not appeared to make a claim about equality,
justice, or freedom. The protesters appear to be singing some church ditty
about light. To the protesters, singing about light placed them within and
beyond the evils of racism. They could protest in coded language and, at
the same time, they were transcendent, for in singing "This Little Light of
Mine," the singers claimed the ultimate ability to go beyond and overcome
segregation and racist hate, and even the capacity for the most avowed
racists and racist institutions to change one day. Governor George Wallace
and the Universities of Alabama and Mississippi ("Ole Miss") are cases in
point.[80] Specifically, the Selma text names the bigots and tells a racist governor, sheriff, judge, and their constituents that no amount of intimidation
can quiet the call to freedom.

Everyone in Dallas County and beyond knew who the culprits were. Black
folks knew they were despised, yet in framing their own individual and
social identities, these freedom fighters refused to acquiesce. As the whole
country watched the racist events of 1961-1963, Blacks in Alabama knew
and recognized that Governor Wallace, the symbol for southern resistance,
touted what most believed: segregation now, tomorrow, and forever. The
grapevine called Birmingham "Bombingham" because of the number of
firebombs going off in the city. Though Black Selmans knew about White
resistance and knew the fight for freedom would not be an easy walk, they
continued to let their lights shine, on and off television screens. The national media broadcast this moving morality play as this nation, the United
States, formed around the celebrations of overcoming and the grief of defeat to racism.[81] The Selma resistance movement rooted the protesters'
commitment in the biblical texts that call for justice and the end to oppression. The parallels of the movement to the biblical texts occur not only in
sentiment but in the place and power of unmasking the dynamics of light
and the related dialectical tensions.

Several biblical references focus on the hiding and or the shining of
personal light. In Job 3:4, 9, and 20, Job curses the day of his birth and calls
for darkness, the darkness of infants who never see the light, though ironi-

cally, within this darkness a slave is free from his or her master. Job sees God as one who causes good and evil, while slaves see God as providential and do not equate evil with God. The evils of slavery occur because of wrong human choice. In the process of praying for healing, the psalmist signifies the power of light to strengthen and illumine, while lamenting that his or her strength and sense of vision has left (Ps 38:20). In celebrating the rule of God, the psalmist sees light as an expression of confidence in divine justice (Ps 97:11). Third Isaiah touts the time for Jerusalem's restoration—by implication, the time for the enslaved, the exiled, to be restored to *imago Dei*, reflecting the image and glory of God (Is 60:1). At Antioch, Paul rehearses his call to be a light to the gentiles (Acts 13:47), just as the slaves and freedom fighters brought the light of justice to oppressed and oppressor. Singing "This Little Light of Mine" claims that those sons and daughters of the light are spiritually enlightened as they transcend darkness or evil and as they fellowship with one another (1 Thes 5:5; 1 Jn 1:7). The Matthean text from the Sermon on the Mount particularly undergirds "This Little Light of Mine": not only are you the light, but as you let your light shine before people, they see your good deeds, and that activity glorifies God (Mt 5:14, 16). This text implies that light, which can reflect godliness, refers to the essential human being—the manifestation of the image of God in a person. Metaphorically, light means soul-spirit. That image defines a person as one who has the ability to do the good as part of a good created order. The crux of the problem, however, is that living in Selma was not an experience of good created order for African Americans.

Living in Selma meant being Black in a racist town that declared an African American a subservient being who should not have access to integrated public accommodations. Living in Selma meant living in Alabama, a place where the dominant Eurocentric cosmology of politicians and leaders had no problems with using fire hoses, with water pressure that equaled one thousand pounds per square inch, to stop children from demonstrating against racism. Just as in other segregated communities, Black folk could work for Whites, but their children could not go to the same schools. Black maids could cook Whites' food but could not sit down with them at the same lunch counter and eat. Singing "This Little Light of Mine" meant, "We will take our stand, even unto death. We understand who we are and who our God is, and that God is not Sheriff Pritchett or Governor Wallace." Just as lighting a match in the darkness brings light, singing "This Little Light of Mine" brought light to the darkness of slavery and the harshness of 1960s racism. Singing transformed the attitude of the singers from fear and hopelessness to strength and fortitude. The words helped the freedom fighters to order their lives toward a commitment to nonviolent direct action. Many courageous souls empowered by this song also ended up in jail, beaten, or dead. For many, being in the Movement was a coming of age. Holistically, that coming of age meant having access to freedom—not being other, being White, but having access to the privilege that society accorded those who were White. Those who did not know who they were often did not want the alleged privilege, the lifestyle, the persona of achieving a sense of light. For some, that meant actually being White. The problem with assuming a sense of light that equals White is that that assumption categorically denies one's Blackness. The denial of one being created in God's image as Black creates major problems that can result in schizophrenia and other pathologies. When Betty Fikes led the singing of "This Little Light of Mine" in Selma, the mass meeting participants celebrated their Blackness and their quest for freedom as themselves, not to be other but to be beautiful, free Black children, women, and men. Their quest for freedom fueled their creative, burning spirits.

Creative Spirit

The leader, Fikes, and the chorus sang in the call-and-response style of African-American preaching and singing, that includes textual and improvisatory phrases that vary in use, meaning, and voicing. The songs, the impetus for the continued protest, incorporated improvisation through vocal embellishments and phrases new to the received setting that localizes the song in Selma. Strikingly, the soloist's use of moans and yells colors the Selma version of "This Little Light of Mine." Influenced by Black gospel music, Fikes's unique yell issues the call for each new verse midway through the last line of the previous verse.[82] Fikes's "wells" or moans ("wailed, soulful prayers") introduced new verses to help line out the next phrase and to then call the group to a vocal response. The juxtaposition of the leader's "wells" in free-flowing rhythmic, recitativelike style over against the hand-clapping, steady pulse of the chorus set up an infectious polyrhythmic feeling that strengthened the solidarity of the group and spilled over into additional body movement. Vocal and body response became the catalyst for action that encouraged participants to work for social change. Fikes modified the text and set the larger tempo, volume, and emotional thrust of the performance atmosphere.

Many of the moans ("well-ell," "wu-oah") offer encouragement and embody non-linguistic commentary that gives declarative statements an imperative thrust. The moan "good Lord" expresses conviction in divine purpose and human solidarity. "Come on and tell" invites the listener to join in by carrying the message, bonding the entire body with each other and with the Movement for freedom. "Let me tell you" and "Come on and tell" communicate self-actualization, which enhances the strength of the individual and the community. Many of the moans tend to outline the multiple messages of light: a call to the self and the community, a call to self-esteem and communal solidarity. The musical framing of the moans keeps the message uncluttered but poignant. Fikes and the congregants sing out about their dream of not having to worry about when and where their lights shine. They champion the idea that sharing their light will one day lead to mutuality and equality for all.

As Fikes leads the Selma congregation with a gospel swing, her use of words and sounds signifies a solidarity that others adapt through their participation. Her signifying and use of revision rely on the traditional text of "This Little Light of Mine" and on the living text of the ongoing racist history of Selma. This new edited version enhances the earlier one without minimizing the message or power of the traditional version. The living texts of the ordinary citizen and the notorious political vanguard were exposed and challenged. They were challenged boldly, yet on one sense enigmatically, through music. After all, how could Black folk in Selma, with no apparent power, be powerful? Couldn't their singing about Governor Wallace and Sheriff Clark just be their way to get attention, to signal honor? To the insensitive ear, yes. To the ear aware of signifying, no! Had any African American made an outright statement and explained the magnitude of what singing "This Little Light of Mine" meant and what that singing did for the empowerment of Selma Blacks, that person might have been found dangling at the end of a rope. The magnitude of that message was shielded amid the setting and the texture of the music.

In a meeting at a Selma church, Fikes, as song leader, begins the first line of each verse or chorus and gives the new lyrics to the congregation, and they keep the momentum going. Fikes's version of "This Little Light of Mine" is close enough to the traditional song style that the congregation follows the words and the gospel style easily. The choir responds with clapping and cheers.[83] Like an emcee or evangelist who participates with, not against or ahead of, the audience, Fikes' skillfully engages the congregation in singing in the key of B-flat major, the key that the transposing instruments in orchestras tune to, and the key of military and festival marches and fanfares.[84] Many groups of mixed voices in Black congregational singing often locate around B-flat or C major, for both high and low voices can be pitched relatively easy, with a full, round sound. Their singing in 2/4, marchlike time fueled them to press on, to move forward in their fight against injustice. The key and march tempo served as unifying elements that created spiritual order amid racist, sexist, and classist disorder; balanced out the sense that it was time to change; and allowed for a space where the freedom fighters could help effect that change. The marchlike tempo simulated the consistency and necessity of the human heartbeat. Without a pulse, without the Movement, there would be no life. As the repetitive, rhythmic actions of sound and hand clapping brought order from oppressive chaos, the rhythmic consistency was rooted in the protesters' bodies like all other aspects of human physicality: breathing, walking, heartbeat, and sexual intercourse.[85] The vitality of the singing echoed the vitality of freedom that often remained repressed among Black folk. Singing "This Little Light of Mine" was a ritual of celebration where lyrical and musical texts flowed together to affirm and inspire the masses. Singing engaged everyone. The audience would imitate the singer, and together they created a desire to have the White privilege of freedom now! Singing allowed them to stand up for themselves, because the White power structure could not stop the singing; even the singing by those long dead was echoed in the voices of the living. And the living signified whenever they sang this song, being truly outrageous and audacious as they claimed a larger space than any of their White detractors could ever imagine: "There was this joy. . . . We had been too long out of the Light. It was our time. It still is."[86]

The specific rhetorical devices in this work that focus on light shining seem straightforward, but it is with simplicity that power takes on quiet, prayerful elegance. This song calls the divine God and primarily engages the metaphors of a little light along with dark, night, and house, to denote historical time and place. The protagonist(s) "I" lets the God-given light shine through the life he or she lives. In the redacted Selma version of "This Little Light," the most significant rhetorical devices concern the additional specific characters related to the social and political context of the local Civil Rights Movement and the repetition of "let it shine." John Lovell, Jr. suggests that "This Little Light" concerns the slaves' borrowing from the creative function of stars, the sole expression of shining. One reason for shining is because one worships a God who created light and who deals with light. Lovell sees the light of Genesis as sheer creative expression, the sentiments of the Spiritual poet. The Spiritual poet develops his or her own special attitude, short on theology but long on celebrating light. Lovell erroneously attributes his source (Mt 5:13, 16) to the Gospel of John.

But the poet develops his own special slant, with little or no theology in it. The poet is fully aware that his is a modest talent; nevertheless, he is going to put it forth with all the power he can. Though it is just a little light, any bit of light can penetrate a mighty lot of darkness. He is proud to be a light and to know that he has the gift of shining. No matter how much energy and trouble it takes, he is determined to be a beacon. He will never let his light go out, die down, or be hidden. If he had no other creative concept, this one alone would admit him to the ranks of respected poets.[87]

"This Little Light of Mine" was one among many Spirituals that referred to an "educational desire and determination which only the totally blind can miss."[88] Lovell argues that light relates to the desire of the folk community for increasing the power of education. This desire led to their enthusiastically creating Spirituals about reading and writing, about books, and about souls shining in a new environment where opportunities for personal expansion would exist. Slaves, like future generations of free African Americans, cherished skills, because slavery (of body, mind, soul, being) was proof of a distorted world that needed to change. The mythology of the Christian religion is a mythology of radical change, but the real change had to be a change in human beings. The best place to begin that change was within oneself.[89] For those of traditional African descent, to know oneself is to know God, to resonate with the divine and the faithful.

Faith and Thought

Within the theological and ethical themes and messages of "This Little Light of Mine" the faithful believe that options exist for justice, but they do not equate these options with redemptive suffering. In other words, Black folk have not been suffering just so that God could then miraculously liberate them. By telling and living the truth, one can ultimately reduce suffering. Suffering caused by racism is not romanticized but is seen as a negative force that can be eliminated.

"This Little Light of Mine" sees God as the CEO in the business of liberation. The singers express conviction in the divine purpose of emancipation and human solidarity, because God is the provider who instills the light of life within the participants. Consequently, the participants can bond together with a sense of mission. Lovell argues that the singer/poet has little concern for theology in the development of the song. If by "little concern," Lovell means the divine name occurs only once in most versions of the song, then he is correct. Lovell views God as the giver of life, of the ability to express light. If God is the giver of life, then the Spirituals are inherently theological. Building on such a theological base, the Selma movement was committed to making a stand in favor of justice.

The Selma protesters called into question those persons and institutions that perpetuated racial injustice through deed and word. The product of such racist dominance results in a warped historical system of power and authority, which determines that Blacks have no say-so and are not accorded the rights and resources of ultimacy, intimacy, and sociality. Facing and overcoming the abyss, the emptiness created because of such debasing behavior, becomes an urgent call for hearing the prophetic voices that both precede and accompany "letting one's light shine." From a theological and ethical perspective, singing "This Little Light of Mine" is an affront to conventional authority. Singing usurps dominant authority and can be as venomous to political sensibilities as when Jesus startled the money changers by overturning their tables and driving them out of the temple (Mt 21:12). Essentially, "This Little Light" calls for the overturning of oppression, the driving out of bigots, and the elevation of freedom, truth, and justice that appreciates and does not penalize difference. This overturning, however, comes with a price. As Jesus had upset an economic base of the temple and had ignored certain institutional authorities, he had to die. Once King attacked the evil of the Vietnam War, a blow to certain economic and political sensibilities, he had to die. Undergirding "This Little Light" is the question, "Are you willing to die?" Death may mean losing one's life literally. Death certainly means debunking all "isms" to afford one the freedom of expression, of action, of being. Is death too high a price?

Is death merely a door to life? From an Afrosensitive perspective, the theology that blazes forth from "This Little Light" may be one candle.

The candle's blaze is not the fire of Dante's *Inferno* or the purifying suffering of purgatory, but the flame of possibility. That flame has as much power as a laser. For the light of one human being is the light of God, a light that cannot be hidden. Such a light has the potential to liberate both the oppressed and the oppressor and can create a heightened awareness of God, the Spirit within. At moments of encounter, during the mass meetings in Alabama, North Carolina, Mississippi, and Georgia, like Hagar, one could meet God as the wilderness became an oasis, a metaphor for plenty, regarding new possibilities and numbers of participants. Black folk have known the power of one embodied in many. They have known the paradox of having the audacity to let Blackness produce light. Blackness connotes power, solidarity, strength, and infinity, and it embodies many colors. Light occurs in waves and particles and cannot be reflected from a perfectly black surface, yet the light of one match can permeate a vast darkness.

The notions of light and Blackness press one to qualify the concept of Blackness as physical, ontological (a state of being), or metaphysical (spiritual). The one who controls the images of a culture affects the experience of Blackness that results from those images. Images of Blackness, characterized and legitimized by early Greco-Roman and Christian thought, have evolved over time. Disdain for Blackness as skin color has permeated the West and the East, in the latter as early as 3000 B.C.E.[90] Light, often translated as Whiteness over against Blackness, involves tensions between the erotic and the carnal, sanctity and magic, evil and sin, the exotic and the sensual. Blackness has connoted inferiority, regardless of the theological call of Christian faith to tolerance and inclusivity. The phenomenon of Blackness (black complexion) includes the social stigma against Blackness within a Greco-Roman Black aesthetic; the Persian dualistic, cosmic struggle that concerns forces of dark and light; the demonizing of Satan, where blackness takes on the ideas of sin and evil; and the misreading of the alleged curse on Ham. Add to this mix the other political, theological, and mythical factors of the Middle Ages, and the result is a sense of Blackness as both evil and erotic before the Mayflower, before institutionalized U.S. slavery.[91]

The freedom singers sang out of a sense of Blackness that was beautiful, triumphant, good. Their traditional African heritage reminded them of their oneness with God, with music, with life. Their very singing about light meant death to the evils of darkness, ignorance, cowardice, greed, and subservience. Singing anointed their actions as a sacramental activity that engaged the divine and all humanity toward a wake-up call, a summons, a benediction of justice. As sacrament, the process of singing also became therapy, rehabilitation, a rebirthing of the singers' humanity and the humanity of all people. Singing about their own humanity taught the freedom fighters that oppression in any form causes those within that system to live a lie. Talking about theodicy, a theology of justice, had to begin with unmasking the lies and engaging everyone in some truth telling and truth living. Truth living became an opportunity to tap into the powers intrinsic to equal opportunity, respect, honesty, godliness, and love. The beauty of this sacramental revelation helped to open many doors previously closed. The ugliness of this pronouncement was that, previous to the 1970s and 1980s, most ethical thinking people saw the conundrum of racism but tended to ignore the offensiveness and repulsiveness of sexism, classism, and colorism from both inside and outside the Black community. Womanist critique says that singing "This Little Light of Mine" means that no one has the right to oppress, abuse, or confuse a child, woman, or man, because of that person's differences. All human lights are godly lights. The moment one human represses another because of differences previously defined, that person has ultimately been blasphemous and has sinned before God. Those women who lived the commitment of Womanist thought, like Fannie Lou Hamer, signified through grassroots movements, and often in the national arena, about this blasphemy through word and songs like "Go Tell It on the Mountain."

"Go Tell It on the Mountain"

"Go Tell It on the Mountain," a song that commands a theodicy of praxis, tells one to take immediate action. The messenger must go tell Pharaoh, the person or personification of oppression, to let God's people go. With a sense of immediacy, the messenger delivers this decree of liberation, and the seeds are planted that will result in shifting the worldview and power structure for both the oppressed and the oppressor. Just as God commissioned and then empowered Moses to lead the Israelite children out of Egypt, surely God had called or was in the process of calling some Black prophet to set God's African-American children free. This reformation hymn, set in the key of C major, is a redacted version of a traditional Christmas song that proclaimed the birth of Jesus Christ. Other traditional verses concern conversion and liberation from spiritual sin.[92] As a mass meeting liberation song, "Go Tell It on the Mountain" proclaims the rebirth of humanity and holistic salvation.

"Go Tell It on the Mountain" calls for action in the spirit of Genesis 1, where God speaks and that which is spoken comes into existence. Song leaders would intone this song, and others would join in. In congregational-style singing, there are no soloists, like in gospel music, but song leaders. Song leaders helped in organizing activities in Mississippi during the critical years of 1961-1963 and during the Mississippi Freedom Summer of 1964.

Context

"Go Tell It on the Mountain" does not coddle, ask, or plead, but demands. This imperative requires a prophetic voice to cry out from the wilderness and relay a message of liberation. People or institutions are in darkness, and the messenger brings a word of redress and hope, to be followed by action. For the Christmas hymn, God sees a troubled world and chooses to self-reveal via Jesus, the beloved Son. For the version with the bent toward conversion, the song conveys the process of knowing sin, looking for help, and becoming a participant, a messenger who looks out for others. The 1960s freedom cry weaves together Hebrew Bible and New Testament imagery and persons amid contemporary rhetorical, ethical questions and the chorus of the Spiritual "Go Down, Moses" to set the scene for the announcement, "Let my people go." Fannie Lou Hamer, a grassroots Mississippian, led this song in the fall of 1963 in Greenwood, Mississippi.

A coalition of local and national civil rights groups that banded together under the umbrella of the Council of Federated Organizations (COFO) in 1962 launched a voting project during the fall of 1963. They focused on showing White Mississippians that Blacks did want to vote, and they conducted training through a mock election. The civil rights coalition, along with sixty White students from Stanford and Yale Universities, campaigned and worked through Black neighborhoods, proselytizing about the practice election. There was some hesitation about having White students around, since most Black Mississippians were accustomed to an extremely segregated, closed society and had little cooperative contact with White people. However, several local leaders, including Fannie Lou Hamer, offered a resounding "Yes!" to the idea of having young, energetic, idealistic people to come help the cause of liberation in Mississippi. Hamer epitomized the vibrant, rich human Mississippian resources. She was a local, sharecropping, grassroots worker who had come into her own sense of power to lead and to help cause change, and she would not be intimidated. Despite coercion and harassment, 93,000 people voted in the mock election. This dry run was the precursor for Freedom Summer 1964.[93]

During the early 1960s, there were plenty of Pharaohs who were unwilling to let God's Black Mississippians go. The police, the Ku Klux Klan, the Citizens' Councils, and the Democratic Party state organization strongly resisted any notions of Black equality and liberation. In 1963, only about 5 percent of voting-age African-American Mississipians were allowed to vote. Medgar and Myrlie Evers, Amzie Moore, Bob Moses, Bob Zellner, John Doar, Fannie Lou Hamer, and Ella Baker were key organizers in Mississippi. In 1963, Medgar Evers was assassinated and Fannie Hamer was arrested and beaten half to death; in June, the March on Washington occurred; in August, the Sixteenth Street Baptist Church in Birmingham was bombed; and in September, churches were burned and college students and other protesters were shot, beaten, and murdered. On June 21, 1964, in the wake of the 1964 Civil Rights Act, which had limited immediate effect on Mississippi, Andrew Goodman, James Chaney, and Michael Schwerner disappeared. During the search, federal and state authorities found many bodies in the Mississippi River and bodies buried near roadsides—all forgotten

Black bodies. On August 4, via a paid informer, the FBI found the bodies of Goodman, Chaney, and Schwerner, riddled with bullets, in an earthen dam near Philadelphia, Mississippi. In August 1964, the Mississippi Freedom Democratic Party (MFDP) made an unsuccessful bid to be seated at the Democratic Convention in Atlantic City. Fannie Lou Hamer represented the MFDP, and her presence caused such a stir that President Johnson pre-empted her speech on national television.[94] Wherever Hamer went, she sang "Go Tell It on the Mountain."

The traditional words for the Christmas version of "Go Tell It on the Mountain" are as follows:

> *Go tell it on the mountain,*
> *Over the hills and everywhere,*
> *Go tell it on the mountain*
> *That Jesus Christ is born.*
>
> *While shepherds kept their watching,*
> *O'er silent flocks by night,*
> *Behold throughout the heavens,*
> *There shone a holy light.*
>
> *The shepherds feared and trembled,*
> *When lo! above the earth*
> *Rang out the angel chorus*
> *That hailed our Savior's birth.*
>
> *Down in a lowly manger,*
> *The humble Christ was born,*
> *And God sent us salvation*
> *That blessed Christmas morn.*

The words for the traditional version that concerned conversion and salvation were these:

> *Go tell it on the mountain,*
> *Over the hills and everywhere,*
> *Go tell it on the mountain*
> *That Jesus Christ is Lord.*
>
> *When I was a seeker,*
> *I sought both night and day;*
> *I asked my Lord to help me,*
> *And he taught me to pray.*
>
> *When I was a sinner,*
> *I prayed both night and day;*

I asked the Lord to help me,
And he showed me the way.

He made me a watchman,
Upon the city wall;
And if I am a Christian,
I am the least of all.

"Go Tell It on the Mountain" uses a four-line strophic chorus and verse pattern. The textual rhyme scheme and musical structure for both traditional versions of the chorus are the same: *abac*. The textual structure for the verses of the Christmas version is *abcb*, based on biblical pageantry of messianic beginnings. The textual structure for the conversion text is mixed, *abca* or *abcb*, in a testifying mode with a sense of urgency. The musical pattern for both verse and chorus involves hymnlike chordal progressions, where the descending chorus reflects a beacon, a pedantic call, beckoning one to act. The verse has ascending movement with a reflective tone that recalls some past event that has contemporary importance. The redacted Hamer version maintains the original textual pattern for the chorus, *abac*, and has a different verse pattern from either the Christmas or the conversion text, *abab*. The musical pattern for the chorus stays the same, while the pattern for the verse is more close-knit:

Go tell it on the mountain,
Over the hills and everywhere,
Go tell it on the mountain,
To let my people go.

Paul and Silas began to shout,
Let my people go.
Jail door opened and they walked out,
Let my people go.

Who's that yonder dressed in red?
Let my people go.
Must be the children that Moses led,
Let my people go.

Who's that yonder dressed in black?
Let my people go.
Must be the hypocrites a-turnin' back,
Let my people go.

I had a little book he gave to me,
Let my people go

And every page spelled victory,
Let my people go.

"Go Tell It on the Mountain" targets apathy and sins of oppression, and shares the gospel message that a Savior, and consequently a Liberator, is born. The judicial, executive, and legislative governing high priests and papal curia, including "Pope" Lyndon Johnson, on local, state, and federal levels had been reminded that Black Mississippians were not going to remain enslaved. American civil religion would have to adjust its dogma and faith claims and convert to a more inclusive creedal lifestyle. They knew that:

> Freedom has to do with whether anybody can take your heart or your mind and own your integrity. And what [we] came through the Movement understanding was that you had a way of never being owned by another person. If you held on to letting your insides tell you where you were supposed to be and who you were. And did not deny that. Somebody could kill your body, but they could never enslave you. But the question from that point to this day is always whether [we] can find the courage to walk what [we] feel inside.[95]

The freedom fighters felt they deserved to experience the constitutional privileges granted all citizens, and therefore they had to confront racist arrogance with a pathos for those in bondage. All "Pharaohs" of Mississippi had to be told to "Let my people go!" This prophetic call illumined the blatant inequities and the pain exacted by authoritative arrogance. Exposing the lies perpetuated since slavery about the ineptitude and ignorance of Blacks exposed the use of scapegoating. Scapegoating involved the desire to make Blacks responsible for a state's ills, and the tensions of simultaneously controlling people to build a state's resources, especially sharecropping; the act of denying those same people access to public privilege and public accommodations; and the anxieties that result when both oppressor and oppressed want something of the other, and the violence and confused messages of identity that can develop in the process. To these questions, "Go Tell It on the Mountain" cries, "No longer will we tolerate your plantation mentality. We recognize your hypocrisy; we call you on it, and we say, 'Let our people go!' "

Story

In Greenwood, Mississippi, the story is the "liberation" of Black persons in bondage to sharecropping, disenfranchisement, and starvation when the Leflore County Board of Supervisors in Greenwood voted to halt participation in a federal food distribution program that supplied surplus food to needy families.[96] The story of Greenwood, through the lens of "Go Tell It on the Mountain," is a command to cease the oppression of Black Mississippians. The dream of freedom has been deferred too long; now is the time for freedom. Fannie Lou Hamer and Carlton Reese redacted this song, and the redaction process created a song of inspiration, power, and reformation toward a new world order.[97]

The Greenwood text does not name specific local oppressors but presents the message to all who fit the category. The commentary on Paul and Silas claims that even if protesters are arrested, like their biblical counterparts, the freedom fighters will walk away from persecution. The other verses signify using specific colors or a book as metaphors for liberation behavior. Those dressed in red are symbolically full of passion, anger, love, and living blood, and are on their way to freedom, following Moses. Those dressed in black represent the solidarity and power of the Movement but also expose the hypocrites who stand in fear of the possibility of infinite power and of the results of this new surge of Black leadership and communal, human resources. The "little book" that spells victory ironically plays off the power of the biblical message of liberation, while it reminds us of the attempts of James Meredith to integrate the University of Mississippi, with the assistance of Justice Department officials. Governor Paul Johnson barred Meredith's entry, as Mississippi launched its last-ditch effort to play out the last chapter of the Civil War.[98] In the face of confronting these "residual rebels," the freedom fighters did variations on the theme:

> *Who's that yonder dressed in red? . . .*
> *It must be the children Bob Moses led . . .*
>
> *Who's that yonder dressed in black? . . .*
> *It must be the Uncle Toms turning back . . .*
>
> *Who's that yonder dressed in blue? . . .*
> *It must be the registrars coming through . . . .*[99]

During the troubling days of antebellum slavery and of the early 1960s in Mississippi, freedom singers seemed to focus on clothing colors and design, when the focus was actually calling out specific actors within the blossoming Movement, from the stalwart to the sordid. This song was one of many that served as poems, prayers, and hymns heralding freedom. The songs traveled from one mass meeting to another and were written down later. Often a song leader would improvise the words, based on the most recent events, to inspire individual courage and communal commitment. The human commitment echoes God's commitment to Israel and to disciples in Exodus and Acts.

Yahweh tells Moses and Aaron to tell Pharaoh to "Let my people go!" (Ex 3:10, 18; 4:22; 5:1; 6:11, 27; 9:1; 10:3). God wants Israel, the elect, the firstborn, the chosen, to be free of slavery. Consequently, God must want his African-American children to be free. In Acts 16:19-40, Paul and Silas are thrown in jail, but they do not let that situation deter them. They pray and sing; the doors of the jail open; ultimately, the magistrates order that they be let go, and go in peace. Paul and Silas refuse to go out secretly. After receiving an apology from the magistrates, they leave the prison and go to visit their friends, preach, then continue on their preaching ministry. Antebellum slaves and the freedom fighters have also prayed and sung. Many times they were jailed, but other times the jail doors were opened. The freedom fighters and slaves did not go secretly but existed in history and later, across the waves of international press and television, claimed their right to tell the Mississippi "Pharaohs" to let God's people go.

To the command of "Go Tell It on the Mountain," most White Mississippians wanted no part. They saw these "niggers" as good for nothing but sharecropping and did not want any idea of freedom to change their "gone-with-the-wind" myths of mint juleps, southern hospitality, southern belles, and strict segregation. The lines of ambiguity hinged around the distortions of "freedom and justice for all" when Blacks experienced violence and death. "Go Tell It on the Mountain" shouts a resounding "No!" to deceit and injustice, and drives home a message that when the oppressor lets go, the oppressed experience liberation. The song acknowledges victors and hypocrites, celebrates new possibilities, and fueled many an antebellum Underground Railroad transfer, and many 1960s meetings, sit-ins, and protest marches. Participation in these protests bolstered self-esteem and community building, whereby African Americans could know they had value and were not the "wretched of the earth." These magnificent, courageous, grassroots folk witnessed to the world a rehearing and reliving of the exodus story as creative, inspirited beings.

Creative Spirit

The intent of the traditional settings of "Go Tell It on the Mountain" is to tell the stories of incarnation and salvation. The redacted version proclaims the cause of freedom and embodies an evangelistic thread. The crusading, soulful spirit of the song pushes the question-answer as call-and-response, repetition, and vibrancy. The soloists name or inquire about the characters, and for each question, the lead singer answers, singing, "Let my people go." More a prophetic vision than a simple dream, this Spiritual wants to disrupt oppressive business as usual in a call for reordering racist institutional and communal structures. This song calls for an empowering dialogue, as a liberative moment for all parties. In signifying a holistic liberation, the Greenwood version of "Go Tell It on the Mountain" involves intertextuality through adaptation, by blending the sentiments and specific choruses of two texts, "Go Tell It on the Mountain" and "Go Down, Moses," to create one reformation hymn. The seamless textual revisions, the varied textured voicing, hand clapping, and use of repetition animate the musicking in the Greenwood text.

"Go Tell It on the Mountain," performed in the key of C major in 4/4 time, involves intergenerational, mixed choral singing. Fannie Lou Hamer calls the community together with her rich, alto voice with chesty resonance. Together, they sing a cappella, accompanied by foot stomping and hand clapping, both on and off the main beat. To Hamer's call comes a response by youthful voices singing, "Tell it, tell it," at the end of Hamer's phrase. A third layer to that mix is a lyrical, falsetto, adult tenor voice that sings an obbligato series of "oohs" that form a countermelody with Hamer. Their singing recalls the "generations of shared memory" where "great singing soldier[s]" sang and helped tear down the walls of injustice and evil, especially as they went out into the dark of night or the light of day into the danger that simmered beneath the boiling, not melting, pots of White supremacist hate.[100]

That hate, rooted in paranoia, fear, and the need to control, was the impetus for the ritualized violence that earlier slaves sought to avoid and freedom fighters wanted to halt. Since many Mississippi Whites thought Blacks were less than chattel, Blacks experienced the ritual lynchings, symbolically or literally, via rape, castration, emasculation, or a rope around the neck. Whites used rituals of exorcism to eliminate their perceived Black "beast" or evil, when Whites engaged in an evil that itself needed to be exorcized, including the hidden agendas of perceived sexual competition between Black men and White men, and the roles of White women.[101] At the same time, Black Mississippians knew they had to use furtive words when speaking out. They knew that the dominant society did not value their lives, and it was important to survive in the process of overcoming. The question of what, when, and how one can overcome and can effect liberation was the question during slavery and during the 1960s Movement, and it remains an operative question today. Who, when, and how one must tell the message of liberation often largely depended upon one's support system. For many, that support system was the community, in relation with God.

Faith and Thought

"Go Tell It on the Mountain" concerns a God on the side of the oppressed who calls out a decree to oppressors to let the Creator's children go free. This divine call dictates that neither the oppressed nor the oppressor ought to retain their roles. All are to be free. With the esteem that most readers of the Hebrew Bible give to the book of Exodus, it makes one wonder how some of those same folk can simultaneously abuse and persecute due to differences in race, class, or sex. This Liberator God is the God who acts on behalf of God's people. Slaves interpreted the exodus story to mean that God would liberate them too. From a prophetic historical and ethical view, the dialectical tension looks at the double relatedness within right relations. "Go Tell It on the Mountain" celebrates the power of communication and the need for a community not only to raise a child, but also to develop healthy outlooks and a healthy society. To "tell it . . . everywhere" implies that everyone needs to hear the news. The good news, or gospel, sets up an opportunity for a community to experience mutuality and love of the neighbor. Is it possible for a socioeconomic system based on capitalism to put loving the neighbor into practice and not need to have a group that can be seen as other, to do the less desirable activities needed to run a social system?

"Go Tell It on the Mountain" exposes any oppressive activity and notes that a relationship of mutuality does not involve a situation where one group has dominance or claims superiority over another person or group. No group has a right to subjugate another group by making them objects. In associations of mutuality, certain behaviors cannot be tolerated. Uncle Toms are called on their accommodationist tactics that undermine the entire group; Governor Wallace is told that death may come knocking on his door if he does not curtail his White supremacist activity; hypocrites are told that their jig is up; and voter registrars are told that the time for Jim Crow poll tax laws is short. This reformation song looks for hope and strength beyond the singers' immediate lived reality, for they sense that God is aware of their difficulties. Christ, as the God of suffering and compassion, a liberator and peacemaker, brings freedom now, already, and at some time in the near future, through a rupture in history and time.[102] "Go Tell It on the Mountain" calls for the distribution of justice (citizens' rights and privileges) and freedom to both Black and White Mississippians. This Spiritual calls for an examination of slavery and recent racism as both moral and business issues that concern capitalism, paternalism, exploitation, and dominance.[103] Such analysis calls one to an ethics of accountability, community, and freedom. The freedom from oppression in the Southern Egypt of the Mississippi Delta is freedom to experience Blackness as a celebration of one's physicality, culture, and state of being. The Black experience was one bond of extended community, a concept retained from traditional African practices that allowed young and old, Black and White, women and men to fight, march, and die together for freedom. The heartfelt call of the chorus "Let my people go" and the repetitive "Tell it, tell it" reflect the signified constraint of the rights and fairness of one group by another. This call for liberation remains liturgical, as a ritual that involves the American civil religious practice of segregation via "Baal gods," and as the oppressed offer a wake-up chorus before Almighty God. Thus, dialectical tensions exist between divine persons, the relationship between the gods and human beings, and the restraint or release of freedoms.

These multiple tensions, the right and wrongs within community structures signified in "Go Tell It on the Mountain," exist in both the conversion and liberation versions, which differ from the Christmas version. The Christmas version focuses more on the birth of the incarnated Christ, who comes to bring salvation. The other versions imply a Liberator, a salvific, adult Christ-God. The three versions imply the activity of salvation in all arenas of life, as communal therapy that seeks to bolster the morale of participants and to give them a hope for change. Their hoped-for change names the social ills of oppression, unmasks the possibility for transformation, and engages the singers in nonviolent protest. "Go Tell It on the Mountain" tells the reality of Black suffering, the creativity of Black survival, and the transformative resilience of Black community. A Womanist reading of "Go Tell It on the Mountain" evokes a consciousness of the oppression present in all communities, across genders, and amid classes. Addressing oppression on all levels leads to the possibility of awakening the consciousness of both oppressor and oppressed, reduces hypocrisy, and heightens the chance for mutuality, freedom, and balance in the Greenwoods of the world.

10

Ensembles

Glad, I'm so glad,
I only need live for today.
Yesterday is gone,
Oppressions of today
Make yesterdays of slavery
Seem way too real.

The move toward and participation in change was the theme of 1960s protests and their antebellum counterparts. Protesters sang Spirituals of gospel joy as an opportunity to make a difference. Many small ensemble singing groups went about the nation teaching and preaching the efficacy of the Movement and pronounced a message of holistic salvation, redemption, and change. Ensembles involve organized and rehearsed groups of singers, usually trios and quartets. Many members of ensembles were also solo leaders in their own right. Many of the ensembles were sponsored by or attached to a particular civil rights group or from a particular region. The original SNCC Freedom Singers—Rutha Harris, Bernice Johnson, Charles Neblett, and Cordell Reagon—grew out of the Movement in Albany, Georgia. The second group of SNCC Freedom Singers was an all-male quartet—Matthew Jones, Marshall Jones, Emory Harris, and Charles Neblett. The third of the Freedom Singers SNCC ensemble was a trio—James Peacock, Bill Harris, and Cordell Reagon. The Nashville Quartet, aka the American Baptist Theological Seminary Quartet, was born at that seminary in Nashville, Tennessee. Montgomery, Alabama, produced the Montgomery Gospel Trio, and the Alabama Christian Movement Choir formed in Birmingham. The CORE Singers evolved within CORE meetings.[1] These groups rehearsed and honed their "sound" and their particular repertoires. In mass meeting singing the music is fluid, spontaneous, and heavily improvisatory, although the person in charge of the music may predetermine which songs he or she will use. Ensembles were organized as performing units that used Black congregational-style singing as a foundation, interweaving musics of arranged Spirituals, gospel, and rhythm and blues (R&B). They worked together consistently and developed sounds that melded together with joyous power. By their consistency and commitment, the ensembles were able to spread the gospel of the Movement.

"We Shall Not Be Moved"

"We Shall Not Be Moved," sung by an ensemble, reflects those aspects of a theodicy where movement equals choice. The quartet's music, in F major, has a rocking, ballad style that evokes imagery of human growth and of boats moving on water. The alto, tenor, and bass responses to the soprano's embellishments highlight the tension and thus the text's theodic nature: moving melody reveals words that reject coerced movement. The movement of this work resembles close-knit ensemble work, yet the vocal color and accented stress on the lyrics move with sustained vowels and evoke motion, the absence of coerced movement. Movement discloses a freedom of justice, true being, and wholeness: a God of justice and mercy allows people to choose or reject movement.

Context

"We Shall Not Be Moved" pronounces the refusal to acquiesce, for no external thing or spirit can force movement when the subject refuses to move. To deny externally forced movement is to affirm internally chosen movement toward justice and victory. Nonmovement in tension with movement is a paradox—the juxtaposition of justice against evil, action against stagnation—that shapes right relations. The dynamics of movement join the element of choice to create a physics of life-giving energy and to sustain human dignity.

"We Shall Not Be Moved" has a strophic form of four lines, where the last two lines of the stanza are part of each verse and act as a refrain: "*Just like a tree that's planted by the water— / We shall not be moved.*" The edited version has four verses, with verse 4 repeating verse 1, and a repetitive rhyme scheme, *aaba*. The melodic structure follows the text but alters the pattern to *aabc*. Each stanza, composed as a call-and-response, uses an indicative mood with undertones of the imperative. The song commands that one listen and be clear that coerced movement is unacceptable. An implied militant tone signifies that the choice for self-appointed movement is nonnegotiable, a key conviction for the SNCC Freedom Singers.

The original SNCC Freedom Singers, Neblett, Johnson, Reagon, and Harris, with Harris as soloist, led "We Shall Not Be Moved" at a meeting in Los Angeles in August 1963. Harris lined out the phrase and the members of the ensemble joined in. This Spiritual was part of the standard Black sacred song and labor union repertoires used "to organize Black laborers during the 1930s and 1940s."[2] The original musical source includes the following verses:

I shall not, I shall not be moved.
I shall not, I shall not be moved,
Just like a tree that's planted by the water—
I shall not be moved.

Jesus is my captain, I shall not be moved. . . .
On my way to glory . . .
I'm climbing Jacob's ladder . . .
Old Satan tried to stop me . . .[3]

The traditional setting of the text employs a governing statement based on freedom of choice as the archaeology of knowledge. The signification involves repetitious, biblical, and religious language set in the past and future tenses. "We shall not be moved" is an independent clause, a declaration which expresses choice. In choosing not to be moved, the singers chose to move themselves. The nature of movement from oppression to equality involved a process using the dualities surrounding movement that penetrates the veil. The redacted texts involve the following lyrics:

We shall not, we shall not be moved;
We shall not, we shall not be moved
Just like a tree that's planted by the water—
We shall not be, we shall not be moved.

Oh, we're on our way to victory, we shall not be moved;
We're on our way to victory, we shall not be moved
Just like a tree that's planted by the water—
We shall not be, (you know that) we shall not be moved.

Segregation is our enemy, it must be removed;
Segregation is our enemy, it must be removed
Just like a pail of garbage in the alley, oh—
It must be removed.

Additional texts used during the 1960s Movement include those listed below:

We are fighting for our freedom, we shall not be moved . . .
We are Black and White together, we shall not be moved . . .
We will stand and fight together, we shall not be moved . . .
Our parks are integrating, we shall not be moved . . .
We're sunning on the beaches, we shall not be moved.[4]

The redacted version of "We Shall Not Be Moved" shared the national environment and recording year of "Oh Freedom," but its story began in

1961 in Albany, Georgia, when field representatives from SNCC arrived to organize the Black community against segregation. The student-led SNCC helped to cultivate long-lasting solidarity and natural leaders in Albany, while SCLC worked with Black professionals as leaders. The tension that existed between the SCLC, NAACP, and SNCC led to the formation of "the Albany Movement, an umbrella organization that would attempt to coordinate the activists."[5] Albany's first mass meeting occurred three days after SNCC and NAACP formed a temporary truce in November 1961, following the arrests of many protesters. Albany's strong folklore, Black cultural ties, and indigenous power unleashed a true singing movement.[6] The people of Albany protested through 1965, sustained by music that transformed the singers and the Movement.

African-American natives of Albany and journalist Robert Shelton, on assignment for the *New York Times*, reported that music was the bedrock of Albany, a deeply spiritual community: "Recordings and Northern concerts . . . could not 'catch' the power of the music with their cameras and microphones. . . . The thousand voices seem so big one can scarcely believe the surging power they create."[7] Reflecting years later, Bernice Johnson Reagon corroborated this sentiment:

> Songs were the bed of everything, and I'd never seen or felt songs do that [before]. I'd had songs in college and high school and church; but in the movement, all the words sounded different. . . . We varied the verses. . . . The voice I have now I got the first time I sang in a movement meeting, after I got out of jail. I did the song, "Over My Head I See Freedom in the Air," but I had never *heard* that voice before. I had never *been* that me before. And once I *became* that me, I have never let that me go. . . . A transformation took place inside of the people. The singing was just the echo of that.
>
> They could not stop our sound. They would have to kill us to stop us from singing. Sometimes the police would plead and say, "Please stop singing." And you would just know that your word was being heard, and you felt joy. There is a way in which those songs kept us from being touched by people who would want us not to be who we were becoming. . . . The only way you survive the singing is to open up and let go and be moved by it to another place [emphasis added].[8]

The SNCC Freedom Singers traveled throughout the United States telling the civil rights story, bringing inspiration, and raising funds for the Movement. As these beacons of light traveled, many Whites in Albany chose to deny the message and maintained the hold of southern, oppressive American civil religion.

Police Chief Laurie Pritchett and Mayor Asa Kelly presided as high priests at Albany's altar of White supremacy. The liturgical practices included harassment and the enforcement of city and state ordinances, segregationist and Jim Crow laws, and federal injunctions. High Priest Pritchett took his scriptural authority from the adage, "It's just a matter of mind over matter: I don't mind, and you don't matter."[9] Albany's main eucharistic sacrament (a communion and/or act of sharing a common faith and discipline) was steeped in the racism of the executive session of the City Council. The council resolved that no common ground could exist between the church of White Albany and the civil rights activists. The council could dictate when, how, and if Albany's African Americans would be moved. The congregation was the eyes of the world, for every major world newspaper and all major television networks came to Albany. The leaders of the Movement knew that the only way to garner enough pressure to evoke change in Albany and throughout the Movement would be "for the media to call to the attention of those outside people what was happening."[10]

Undaunted by racism or media exposure, Rutha Harris lined out songs for the Freedom Singers. As she traveled with the freedom quartet, Harris vowed in her songs that nothing and no one could stop her work for freedom. The Freedom Singers were the oral journal, the "Black paper," that carried the news when the print media failed to do so.[11] That the media failed to do so involves the unmasking of the pathos and arrogance of racism, a response to the functions of movement and inertia, especially in semirural Dougherty County, Georgia. "We Shall Not Be Moved" challenged the arrogance that assumed that dominant, White voices were the ideal and Black voices were inept. This Spiritual became an axiom that renounced prior theories about race relations, especially southern paternalism. "We Shall Not Be Moved" called for reassessment by Blacks and Whites, and acknowledged the power of communal solidarity to cause change. People sang "We Shall Not Be Moved" to thwart the racial arrogance of the Pritchetts and Kellys of their world. Albany's Black constituency turned that arrogance on its head as they made mistakes, regrouped, and affirmed their commitment: "Some people talk about failure. Where's the failure? . . . Did we stop at any time? What stopped us? . . . Did any black man stop us? Nothing stopped us in Albany, Georgia. We showed the world."[12]

Ideally, in "We Shall Not Be Moved," the pathos of racism involved the personal inability to recognize an inner choice to move or to make the first step toward becoming powerful. The fear of movement stymied an ability to choose, resulting in a pathological state of being a paralyzed or "dis-eased" self. "We Shall Not Be Moved" offered a method for treating this societal illness. The song prescribed freedom of choice, the freedom to refuse to step aside, to say no to coercion, to say yes to life. Risking to choose created an identity change that enhanced the self, whereby an individual became whatever he or she had to become, and believed that he or she was "entitled to the rights as well as the responsibilities of the new identity."[13] Grasping new identity altered human relationships. That change affected the realm of applied justice—a justice of respect and the equitable distribution of rights. "We Shall Not Be Moved" helps us both to empathize with the critical dynamics of blatant oppression in Albany and to canonize the untiring efforts of the Albany community to create change.

The "engaging" analysis explores the social and geographical context of Albany as "a living text" that used the Spirituals (oral living narratives) to give voices to the voiceless. This thrust affected the performance and had an impact of national and global proportions. The SNCC Freedom Singers put their collegiate careers aside to work with rural and urban communities for equality and justice as they changed traditional Black sacred songs into freedom songs. Singing "We Shall Not Be Moved" fortified the Movement and the movers with an intensity and a vigor that were antithetical to lethal racist-induced inertia. The quartets toured the country to stir the social and political "living dead" toward an immediate eschatological encounter with God and justice, in line with their ancestors. Slave testimony claims:

> Their encounter with the Spirit of the Lord enabled them to evolve a critique of racism and racists, dream a grand vision of freedom, nurture communal relationships, fight for freedom, defend each other, affirm their humanity, and hear the melody of the future with such clarity that they literally, in faith, were prepared at great cost to dance to the melody of the future by acting in the present to create it.[14]

The various ensembles recreated freedom songs just as Africans of the diaspora had conceived Spirituals two hundred years before. Both groups of singers spontaneously created these chants of collective exorcism through divine revelation. Fashioning spirituals like "We Shall Not Be Moved" was the mark of prodigious spirits and a testament of commitment to justice, righteousness, and benevolence.[15] Singing "We Shall Not Be Moved" with sophisticated artistry, the Freedom Singers represented the civil rights message of self-movement to people whose lifestyles greatly distanced them from the struggle.[16] Their solidarity and hopeful imagination enhanced the musical dissemination of the theodic message. The imitative freedom songs were the DNA/RNA molecular basis that allowed Movement musicians to protest nonviolently and to rise above the "pressures and needs involved in maintaining group unity on the community level, while working under conditions of intense hostility and physical threat."[17] Within a performing ensemble format, the SNCC Freedom Singers did a cultural exegesis of living texts, especially the Spirituals, where they helped forge transformation and fix a sense of relatedness in those knowing their sound.

Story

The "naming" of the story in "We Shall Not Be Moved" identifies messages and the Womanist concerns about intracommunal relations by focusing on the community's commitment and on the performance method of close-knit ensembles, rather than by defining the conflicts between Black and White community. The dynamics of movement versus inertia and coerced movement versus chosen movement within "We Shall Not Be Moved" recall other polarities that permeated the Movement: sound versus silence, power versus powerlessness, and appearances versus actualities. Singing "We Shall Not Be Moved" became an exercise in what could and could not be moved by communal decision. As overcomers, Albany's African-American populace would no longer stand aside for racism or be scapegoats. They chose to move themselves, and that movement relates to power.

Albany's social, historical, and cultural practices in the 1960s had a power base with two sets of rules for the two races, exemplified in a folk rhyme song that claimed, "If you're White, you're right; if you're Black, step back; if you're Brown, stick around."[18] Society orchestrated the racial symphony by fixing high-fidelity sound for White folks and relegating Black folks to silence. The tunes of decision making and pervasive authority secured power for Whites. Dominant Whites relegated insignificant accompanying choruses to powerless Blacks, making them inconsequential to daily life performances. The displacement of power gave the appearance of a healthy White society. In reality, White oppressors lacked a certain wholeness experienced by oppressed Blacks. Albany's African Americans largely did not depend upon Whites to validate their true sense of personhood. The choice to move against racism and not be moved from taking a stand attests to that reality. Black Albany knew that movement within a good creation signified the unmoved "tree that's planted by the water."

That anchoring, by itself, seemed out of step with the tension that hung between and penetrated both Black and White cultures. The anchoring of the "tree that's planted by the water," the key metaphor to all verses, helped stabilize the freedom fighters as they claimed their victory before their victory was in hand. This victory announced the freedom resonating from their visions of integration and equal treatment. Old obstacles became new opportunities. With the dismantling of the enemy, the "garbage pail of segregation," new opportunities developed. Personified segregation became the metaphor for the enemy who had robbed African Americans of their heritage, legal rights, and dignity. Singing "We Shall Not Be Moved" put on notice all who denied personhood to the Black community. Bernice Johnson Reagon explained how the singing Black body refused to be moved,

> because in the songs you could just name the people who were trying to use this [incarceration] against you. . . . This behavior is new behavior for black people in the United States of America. You would every once in a while have a crazy black person going up against some white person and they would hang him. But this time [in Albany], with

a song, there was nothing they could do to block what we were saying. Not only did you call their names and say what you wanted to say, but they could not stop your sound. . . . No matter what they do, they would have to kill me to stop me from singing. . . . Your word is being heard. There was . . . clearly empowerment, and it was just like saying, "Put me in jail, that's not an issue of power. My freedom has nothing to do with putting me in jail." And so there was this joy. . . . We had been too long out of the light. It was our time. It still is.[19]

Freedom fighters challenged segregation, and they wanted segregation's power base—the garbage, filth, decay, and waste—eliminated. Yet garbage converted into compost begets new and invigorated life. Black people of Albany did not have to leave Albany to get freedom. Freedom could be brought to Albany. How could the Black citizenry move White Albany to share their environment with equity? The ensemble sang about nonmovement, but the rhythmic integrity of the song helped move the song that moved the entire Civil Rights Movement. The music in Albany attracted national attention and was the life force of the Movement.[20] Without the music, the Albany Movement could not have happened: "We could not have communicated with the masses of people without music and they could not have communicated with us."[21] The movement of the people and the movement in the songs was "an inspiring fire." Rutha Harris's full, rich-textured sound cut through the ensemble's accompanying embellishments and responses, as "We Shall Not Be Moved" penetrated people's souls.

"We Shall Not Be Moved" pressed one to be accountable for the Civil Rights Movement, for movement within the community, and for personal movement or lack thereof. The Freedom Singers transcended the fear of death as they sang. In the 1960s, students at all-Black Albany State resisted systemic bigotry by protesting through the NAACP's Youth Council. These students and others in the Black Albany community used the Interstate Commerce Commission's ruling banning segregation in Albany's interstate train and bus stations, even when the resulting discord tore Albany apart. The students' move to be responsible and stalwart reflected a life of moral wisdom amid the tensions of socialized evils eloquently portrayed in Zora Neale Hurston's metaphor of "quiet grace."[22] "We Shall Not Be Moved," sung with "quiet grace," offers a note of steadfastness. In "quiet grace," this Black community maintained the status quo in public, yet transcended reality among each other. Part of dealing with the veil of Blackness was to partake in storytelling and song-singing traditions. Bernice Johnson Reagon, founder of Sweet Honey in the Rock and a native of Albany, told stories as a child through a cappella music, using her hands and her feet, at church and at school. Since the church where her father pastored did not possess a piano until she was eleven, Reagon, then and now, is only comfortable with a cappella music.[23] This oral singing tradition shaped the powerful singing experiences of African-American individuals and the Albany community and, in turn, moved the Movement.

The "unmasking" of the story of "We Shall Not Be Moved" implies an adamant faith that envisions an integrated, balanced Albany. Such songs have tremendous drive and hand-clapped accompaniment. Singing these songs changed the human condition—people's hearts beat faster, they experienced exaltation, and the intense energy around the singing proved cathartic as singing became theomusicotherapy:

> There were people who were in the movement who wouldn't go anywhere without these [songs]. So if they were going to be there, the hymns were going to be there. . . . Those songs created a powerful energy. . . . And you always had to dig down and work the territory of whatever was deep and inside. You never [just] worked the part of you that went forward, and didn't work the part of you that was inside and unseen, sometimes even by yourself. And the songs really worked with those two parts of yourself. Really worked those parts.
>
> So you're both being stretched and healed [simultaneously]. . . . Have to. And I always think of a going—the slow ones like a going inside and lifting something up like if you have a rock or something stuck, and you gotta get it out. And the song just gets under it and just lifts it up. This will not hide here, you will know. Yes, you will go forward, but you will go forward understanding what the load is to some extent.[24]

The inner and external working or forward movement of the self propelled the telling and retelling of the "living Albany text" as both means and end. Singing "We Shall Not Be Moved" inspired those gathered to unite and support communal movement toward freedom, even though the jails bulged from the protesters' repeated, prolonged incarcerations. Singing "We Shall Not Be Moved" produced a cultural fortress that assured that no forces could ever move the singers from their commitment to liberation and equality. As means and end, the "living Albany text" merged with the living text of "We Shall Not Be Moved" to initiate a communion ritual: the created, symbolic transformation allowed the singers to respond, influencing others, to biblical themes.[25]

"Unmasking" the impact of biblical story, themes and characters involves an intertextual link between "We Shall Not Be Moved" and the first line of the refrain, "Just like a tree that's planted by the water." The selected texts are Psalm 1:3 and Jeremiah 17:8:

> He is like a tree planted by streams of water,
>   which yields fruit in season
> and whose leaf does not wither.
>   Whatever [he] does prospers. (Ps 1:3, NIV)

> "He will be like a tree planted by the water
> that sends out its roots by the stream.
> It does not fear when heat comes;
> its leaves are always green.
> It has no worries in a year of drought
> and never fails to bear fruit." (Jer 17:8, NIV)[26]

A comparison of Psalm 1:3 with "We Shall Not Be Moved" demonstrates a kinship among the psalmist, the antebellum bard of the diaspora, and the 1960s poet. The creative forces arise from a religious context. Hebrew Bible scholarship classifies Psalm 1 as a wisdom psalm, based on its style and content. *Wisdom* has many definitions. Broadly stated, *wisdom* refers to a capacity to know, to comprehend, in a way that lets one discern patterns, qualities, and relationships of God and creation, involving materials naturally observed and technical data that require ample scholarship.[27] Psalm 1 pits the righteous against the sinful dialectic of life. The righteous person resembles a tree moved to the water's edge, an experience of productivity, durability, freshness, stability. This fertile setting represents a level of existence where the leaders of God's people must help the community of faith endure difficulty, confident of a successful completion. Evil and immoral conduct ultimately ends in death.[28]

A midrashic application, or commentary, of Psalm 1 to "We Shall Not Be Moved" and to civil rights protest builds on wisdom. The wisdom of God and that of social and political realities allowed Movement leaders to see patterns, qualities, and relationships with God and society. Biblical wisdom pertains to a modern term about writing that flourished in ancient Israel and throughout ancient Near East that embodies some basic truth about life, a way of understanding the world. Wisdom claims that underlying all the apparent confusion, injustice, and disorder of life is a basic pattern, an ordering by which all such phenomena can ultimately be understood. Movement leaders grew up observing injustices and spent a lot of time and research planning strategies to uplift oppressed people and to disturb the world's conscience. "We Shall Not Be Moved" presents the dialectic of movement by choice (righteousness as liberation and equality) and coerced movement (sinful life). The freedom fighters (righteous persons) chose not to be moved, yet chose their own movement that would be a fruitful experience on the water's edge. Choosing not to be moved was part of the strategy for moving the country to change the legal system so that it would open the doors of productivity, durability, freshness, and stability to African Americans. They wanted a new level of socio-cultural order where civil rights leaders would continue to help God's people, the community of faith, to endure difficulty. With the redaction, those singing this Spiritual refused to be moved or hoped not to be moved, rather than being moved. The activists and the communities they served were sure of a future of justice and the successful completion of a long struggle to overturn racist evil that otherwise would ultimately lead to society's death.

Psalm 1 contains four rhetorical characteristics that distinguish wisdom literature: an address to a human audience; an 'ashre or blessing formula; a simile or simple comparison, as between grain and chaff; and a distinctive poetic vocabulary. "We Shall Not Be Moved" addressed a human audience. God's blessing provided the strength to defy dominant culture through this song. The simple comparison concerned free versus forced movement, and the poetic vocabulary relied on metaphors and personifications in the Spiritual. Thematically, Psalm 1 embraces five leitmotifs: (1) the implied fear of Yahweh; (2) a focus on the Torah; (3) the practice of daily ethics; (4) the contrasting of righteous and wicked lifestyles; and (5) the nonambiguous function of retribution.[29] Most people singing "We Shall Not Be Moved" had deep religious faith and a fear of, or respect for, Yahweh. Antebellum slaves and modern African Americans posited a theology based on their structural cosmology of "God, Jesus, and human action that sustained them."[30] Both of these generations of African Americans used the Bible as the basis for their religious life and to inform their wisdom anecdotes, moral language, creative expressions, and practical daily ethics. The living kingdoms of God (justice and righteousness as liberation and equality) and of Satan (the demonic reflected in slavery and racism) mirrored the contrasts between a righteous and a wicked lifestyle. Many of the Spirituals had an implicit "reap-what-you-sow" theory of retributive justice, where justice is meted out according to personal acts. These leitmotifs indicate a political theology, involving questions of characterization, time, and cultural resistance, where serving God is different and is unlike serving any earthly master.[31]

The protagonists of "We Shall Not Be Moved" were the disenfranchised of Albany and their supporters. Ideally, the collective "we" and the dynamics of movement reflected the true self. The relational, social, collective self included processes of self-affirmation and self-awareness. The advent of the Movement began a new order that could reshape African Americans' way of thinking, of ascribing meaning, of setting values that could fuel mass nonviolent resistance.[32] This reconstitution of a sleeping mind-set waiting to happen (immediate freedom) embraced a countermovement that moved to "transcend the immediate conditions of an undesirable relationship."[33] Albany's oppressed sang "We Shall Not Be Moved" as they moved away from imposed racist practices and cultural mores.

The time framing "We Shall Not Be Moved" embraced the spread through time (diachronic) and the parallel or limited time (synchronic) elements. African Americans and their supporters had fought for freedom since the colonial period. The 1960s Movement had its origins in Black intellectual thought beginning around the turn of the twentieth century. The 1960s protest escalated the sequence of change as pockets of civil rights activity occurred at once throughout the South. Marches, sit-ins, freedom rides, and voter registration campaigns were immediate concerns. With urgency, these activities engaged the legal system and became cultural resistance.

African Americans living under racist American civil religion adopted a culture of resistance. "We Shall Not Be Moved" reflected at least two elements of this cultural ethic: a duality of survival and a discourse of solidarity. The duality of survival referred to the conscious decision by slaves to wear a mask before the master and to be an authentic self in the presence of other African Americans, a sober assessment of reality as opposed to wearing the face of fear. The slave-self would not tell on runaway slaves nor betray fugitives.[34] For the slave-self, "We Shall Not Be Moved" portrayed a desire to choose not to be moved, to reveal the true self and not betray the community. 1960s Black freedom fighters wore the masks of hope and possibility out of self-defense against racist social politics. Singing "We Shall Not Be Moved" affirmed the continuing need to survive and to remain a part of a community, which meant an ongoing therapeutic process that affirmed unity and saw the need to present different faces. Many of these different faces signify different voices who used "We Shall Not Be Moved" to remove any notions of ambiguity about the targets of rebellion and protest.

The "engaging" activity of the "story" of "We Shall Not Be Moved" reverberated from the mouths and pens of countless artists who harnessed emotions from desperation and rage to incredulity and hope, and then channeled that energy into commentary, indictment, or sermon during the 1960s. The spirit of "We Shall Not Be Moved" produced conscious, intentional movement. Coercion was inappropriate and ultimately had no power over the essential self. The singers claimed the right not to be moved despite the threats to life, and they claimed the right to move themselves. The downtrodden challenged racist evils from an inspired music power base as they sang about the death of bigotry and inequality. In keeping their focus, those in the Albany Movement shifted from an applied theodicy of the problematic living as Jim Crow's victim to an overcoming lifestyle that demanded equal treatment and personal choice. The act of choosing allowed African Americans to celebrate their Blackness and allowed non-Blacks to choose to support, retaliate against, or be indifferent to the cause. Much of the impetus for recognizing and selecting the option to choose arose through music, through their creative spirits.

Creative Spirit

The images of "naming" as creative spirit in "We Shall Not Be Moved" ask, what did "movement" mean for the 23,000 Blacks living among 33,000 Whites in rural southwestern Georgia, where peanuts, corn, and pecans had usurped King Cotton?[35] What were the rhythmic sensibilities when Blacks heard freedom in the air but felt billy clubs on their backs? The freedom fighters marched to a cadence of nonviolent protest, determined to succeed and not to accommodate. Albany's Blacks had heard about the national Movement and wanted the Movement active in their hometown. They moved beyond the false innuendos of SNCC's alleged Communist ties, the tensions among civil rights groups, mass arrests, and Police Chief Pritchett's strategy of meeting the protesters' nonviolence with his own nonviolence (Jim Crow laws). Albany's freedom fighters moved by launching a bus boycott and allowed no racist authority to move them.

The singing Albany Movement chose to move themselves and society: "The civil rights movement gave [them] the power to challenge any line that [limited them]. . . . [The] movement said that if something puts you down, you have to fight against it."[36] The singing Albany Movement, a moral victory and an educational event, changed participants' attitudes despite the fight against integration, continued segregated schools, and closed parks. The singing helped reshape people's understanding of theodicy, of their gift of right relationship and self-chosen movement. However, national media coverage and public support were not guarantees for resolving confrontations for the federal government defense of civil rights. From then on, people remembered Albany.[37] Remembering and dreaming, facets of musical aesthetics, respect the differences in personal tastes, expressions, and habits that dictate the types of music that individuals favor.[38]

"We Shall Not Be Moved" was part of the freedom song repertoire from Albany's religious musical experience before Cordell Reagon, the Nashville Student Movement song leader, came to help shape the music in the Albany campaign. Reagon and fellow SNCC worker Charles Sherrod focused on singing, voter registration, and nonviolence workshops.[39] The music helped SNCC workers communicate data and transcend the differences of tastes and habits within the Albany community. The small groups of three or four made a powerful impact. They sang "We Shall Not Be Moved" to create a litany of intention. The physical and emotional responses to the performance allowed the group to engage in a "dialogue of solidarity,"[40] which placed the Albany community within the text as the community became a mediator of meaning. This relationship between the text and the context of the hearers, in creative fidelity, changed Albany into a "living text," a text woven deep into the melody and words of Spirituals like "We Shall Not Be Moved."

Performances of the combined text and music of "We Shall Not Be Moved" served as catalysts that prompted both individual and community to make ethical, healthy choices about this movement, and gave participants permission to create the boundaries necessary to challenge behaviors by the oppressor that deny the oppressed respect and humanity. This song stands between a triumphant processional and a cheerleading yell. The minimal movement of intervals within each stanza denotes stability, certainty, and unshakable commitment.

The initial fanfare of "We shall not [soloist only], we shall not be moved [soloist with full ensemble]" weaves a pattern that connotes a tapestry of togetherness. The second line begins tonalities that evoke feelings of brightness and hope throughout the song. The soloist provides the basic melody, while the accompanying voices harmonize. The harmonies and vocal textures color the words with desire, joy, and integrity. In the last phrase, the accompanying voices sustain the solidarity as they sing repetitively "We-ee, we-ee, we-ee, we-ee shall not be moved." These pulsating phrases between tones resemble heartbeats. The tight harmonies and limited vertical movements depict the solidarity produced when one takes a stand. This solidarity and life-affirming unity bespeaks a theodicy in which the oppressed move toward empowerment and demand the oppressors' respect. The oppressed exist "like a tree," immovable but life-producing. The triumphal, processional feeling in duple meter creates an air of expectancy, bravery, and unity. A cheerleader style, coupled with the intimacy of a quartet, resembles the vigor exercised at championship athletic events. These drum majors and cheerleaders for justice "moved" themselves and their listener/participants toward a united, harmonious way of being-in-the-world that offered people choice: "Any given way of being is a 'choice' . . . in the sense that there are always alternative ways of being and that a person can accept some responsibility for the way he or she lives."[41] The combined texts about movement signified that other options exist for both oppressed and oppressor where balance and freedom of choice become central to interracial communal existence. A balanced being-in-the-world meant that some dreams could no longer be put on hold and that the time for freedom was immediate. While the sentiment of immediacy was stated clearly in words alone, the singing of these words made such an impact that when the singing stopped and the meetings were over, the spirit of movement lay heavy in the air.

One of the forces that sustained the power of movement in "We Shall Not Be Moved" was the "ensemble" performance style. The group of musicians performed as a unit to create superb balance, compatibility among the voices, and outstanding sound production. Their level of musicianship and artistry gave them a great deal of creativity and involved musical, personal, group, political, and social growth and movement. The singers (movers) embodied the music and the activity (movement). SNCC's first singing ensemble provided strong educational and economic support to the Movement.

The CORE Freedom Singers, the Montgomery Trio, and the Nashville Quartet had already made music a key Movement tool. The SNCC Freedom Singers strengthened and expanded the use and potency of music and song. Singers Reagon, Neblett, Harris, and Johnson began traveling across the country in the winter of 1962 to teach about the Movement and to build moral and monetary support.[42] The Freedom Singers sang of the marches, the jails, and the rallies. This ensemble moved the local audiences as they blended traditional Black idioms with modern gospel, rhythm and blues, and Spirituals. The singers who made up this quartet were living witnesses and prophetic voices throughout the nation, telling the story of oppression of those who had lived through Jim Crow. The 1960s national resurgence of folk music boosted the Freedom Singers to national acclaim because of their arresting singing, honed by the intentional crafting of their harmonies, rhythms, solos, and vocal placement in the Southern a cappella tradition, and because of the urgency of their message. Reagon reflected on their group, saying, "The Freedom Singers are the ablest performing group to come out of what is perhaps the most spontaneous and widespread singing movement in the world today."[43]

The Freedom Singers' creative solidarity let them improvise while bringing a message of hope and solidarity. "We Shall Not Be Moved," recorded in 1963, is a testament to the creative imagination of the quartet. They had a magnificent rapport: their voices were individual yet one when stretching the melodic, rhythmic, and harmonic fields of the song. Their performances inspired and satisfied the expressive needs—the feelings, the emotions, the wants—of the Movement and within themselves. "We Shall Not Be Moved" was a descant or aural discourse of themes regarding the act and being of freedom fighting in Albany. The poets formed a trust; they stood by their philosophy of resistance. Any decision to move would seek new, free goals.[44] The vocal colors of Harris's soprano, Johnson's contralto, Neblett's "walking" baritone, and Reagon's tenor enveloped the audience and heralded Albany's new goals. Harris announced the good news. Johnson, Neblett, and Reagon responded as a lush, innovative "A-men corner." Their singing was immediate and transcendent of all associations—of history, thought, and culture—as they matched text, melody, and body to tell the story. In many meetings, despite the intimacy of the four singers, "before the first phrase was completed, the entire congregation joined in."[45]

In "We Shall Not Be Moved," the SNCC Freedom Singers harmonically accented or rhythmically emphasized particular words in particular moments of repetition or rise and fall of pitch to tell a message.[46] Sometimes the soloist held notes for a long time over against the other voices. This response of the soloist to the other singers depicts the cooperative spirit of communal movement. In stanzas 2, 3, and 4, the solo line (Harris) does a variation on the initial rhythmic scheme with melodic improvisation. Harris's lyrical tone propels the force of the text as she sets out the dare, implying, "You may want to move us or think you can move us, but we shall not be moved." She also stresses the "we" by sustained notation; suspends "not" within an extended interpolation; emphasizes "tree" and "planted" through syncopation; and highlights "water" by using a fast tone attached to a sustained note, followed with a sense of three against two in the accompanying voices. Harris employs a sense of suspended syncopation in each of the verses: twice as verbs, "shall not"; and twice as direct objects, "victory" and "enemy." Although her phrasing is similar to the other voices, her poignant, provocative singing leaves a new, indelible mark on the listener's conscience with each stanza. The nuances and textures of her voice so affect the listener that the message of theodicy surfaces: the choice for movement shapes relationships with God and society toward the good, toward freedom and justice, and away from the evil, from racism. The three accompanying voices also use rhythm to make a point. For example, their use of rhythm and volume with "ma Lordy" affirmed divine presence and compelled others to receive the message. Under much of the soprano's improvisatory ornamentation, the alto, tenor, and bass provide a solid chordal-type accompaniment. In the final phrase for verse 1, however, the alto shifts to a syncopated variation on "We shall not be moved," then rejoins the tenor and bass in a final hymnlike phrase beneath the soprano's melodic line. In different ways, they stress the communal "we," "shall not," and "be." After each verse, the soprano announces the next expectation of the freedom fighters, which the other singers confirm with "ma Lordy" and then join in with the verse. The singers employ enough vocal diversity to depict individual choices, yet their blending connotes unity, symbolizing the need to include society. Thus, with choice comes responsibility—a prerequisite for harmony and empowerment. "Song leaders emerged spontaneously and came together to form core song leading units" on a mission, just as Jehoshaphat's appointed singers sang to the Lord as they went before the army (2 Chr 20:21-22).[47] In moments of silence, they listened; then, as they made sound, they knew healing.[48] The diversity of rhythm indicates the inner complexity of the simple lines of text and provides the framework for the musicking process.

The primary musicking elements in "We Shall Not Be Moved"—ensemble-style singing and communicative goals—inform the artistry of performance, as they merged the multiple singing traditions, the natural beauty and power of the four voices and their expressive demeanor using varying dynamics, coloring, and percussive use of words, their blending sound as four yet one, and the exercise of spontaneous improvisation. The diverse musical styles, forms, and performance techniques of the Freedom Singers from across American society[49] enhanced the freedom songs. The quartet demonstrated a wide range of creativity, including spontaneous improvisation, "the experience of making music for well-being."[50] Music grasped the audience's attention and moved that audience toward solidarity and wholeness.

The "engaging" of the creative spirit in "We Shall Not Be Moved" helps us observe the processes of intertextuality and textual revision, repetition, or response. The singers heard both the dictionary-syntactical meanings and the silent meanings of "We Shall Not Be Moved." Freedom of movement served as a metaphor for appearing inert while moving, and appearing to move while inert. This motif permeated the text and technique employed by the SNCC Freedom Singers. Their singing "moved" the audience to cultural resistance. The performance embodied movement set in a tight harmonic and tonal scheme. Maya Angelou's poem "Our Grandmothers" chronicles some varied dynamics of the Womanist movement that crossed social, historical lines and penetrated the sacred and the secular. "Our

Grandmothers" epitomizes communal and personal resistance, echoed in the refrain "I shall not be moved":

"Our Grandmothers"

She lay, skin down on the moist dirt,
the canebrake rustling
with the whispers of leaves, and
loud longing of hounds and
the ransack of hunters crackling the near branches.

She muttered, lifting her head a nod toward freedom,
I shall not, I shall not be moved.
. . . .
You have tried to destroy me
and though I perish daily,
I shall not be moved.
. . . .
I have a certain way of being in this world,
and I shall not, I shall not be moved.
. . . .
In the choir loft,
holding God in her throat.
. . . .
In the classroom, loving the
children to understanding.
. . . .
However I am perceived and deceived,
however my ignorance and conceits,
lay aside your fears that I will be undone,
for I shall not be moved.[51]

The revision or redaction of "We Shall Not Be Moved" added sentiments that indicted racism and acclaimed change. Segregation killed societies. The eradication of segregation appeared to be a solution for altering the mores of separatist inequality. Segregation as "enemy" and "garbage in the alley" defined the system as fatal. What each phrase meant and how the repetition affected the singer or listener depended upon who did the evaluation. Many repeated phrases involved repeated improvisations. The full-bodied sounds emblazoned the waiting ears with adamant resistance. The activists hoped for freedom. Singing "We Shall Not Be Moved" encouraged them to ask: "Who are we? Will we allow ourselves to be moved? If yes, what do we lose or gain? If so, do we sign our death warrant? Can we afford not to be ready to die?" "Immersed in a dialectic of despair and hope, they were led to hope and work for freedom . . . their expectations of hope and justice [were] to be found in the promissory character of God's eschatological presence in their community."[52]

Faith and Thought

The "naming" of faith and thought focuses on how civil rights participants relied on a God of justice and mercy and on Christian precepts during the inception of the modern Movement.[53] This liberator God created Blacks and Whites and made the trees and the waters. This creator God looked out for all of nature, including humanity. God, as shepherd and nurse, was on the side of Albany's protesters. While it could be said that "God is on our side," there was also a theological discussion arguing that maybe one should say, "We are on God's side": "God was lucky to have us in Albany doing what we were doing. . . . What better case would [God] have? So it was really like God would be very, very happy to be on my side."[54]

"We Shall Not Be Moved" implied that God empowered the protesters to claim their space. This Spiritual depicted the theme of perseverance born in the lay testimony and prayer traditions of the Black church. A functional faith and a sense of a good creation (Gn 1:26-31) relied on God's transforming grace and challenged persons to exercise free will and self-expression. Using traditional African belief systems, many African Americans gave little assent to the Calvinistic notion of total human depravity. The tenacity and endurance of the Freedom Singers and of Albany's "soul community" helped them tie their identity and faith to affirming God and themselves. The commitment to persevere nurtured character, human need and will, and ethical praxis amid joy. Joy celebrated the blessedness born of certainty about personal identity and self-expression. Perseverance embodied "the continuation of one's highest quest, regardless of opposition, in the faith and hope that one is providentially guided, cared for, and guaranteed fulfillment, here or hereafter."[55] Theologically, to have the freedom to choose healthily and to live according to those choices that harm neither another nor the self is an experience of wholeness and justice. The "naming" process in "We Shall Not Be Moved" tells a story of triumphal splendor indicative of a personal understanding of theodicy that sustains the option to choose. "Movement" can be a decision to let appearances dictate that racism precludes change, or it can make us focus on the possibility for change. The option to persevere celebrates a community as a "living text" which remembers and dreams toward engaging a life and an ethics of mutuality with God and society. The communal life—God's grace grounded in community health—is an experience of quintessential Blackness, of metaphysical, spiritual, and physical celebratory humanity that moves toward righteousness. Righteousness also forms the basis for some reasons not to move.

"Unmasking" in "We Shall Not Be Moved" implies that there are some places from which persons did not want to be moved. The sounds of freedom encouraged protesting Albany to no longer accept freedom as a "dream deferred." People of Albany knew that movement would not create a panacea, but an option to choose would make deep inroads against local institutionalized racist evil. As the SNCC Freedom Singers evoked response by singing and organizing, they sensed the fearful attitudes of many Black residents who shunned risking White reprisals by attempting to register to vote. Many student demonstrators from Albany State faced reprisals from their own college.[56] The evils of racism and blatant, crippling accommodationism were attempts at controlling persons who chose to move from acquiescence to disruption. Singing "We Shall Not Be Moved" allowed those who were tired of racist Albany to retaliate with nonviolence, passion, and creative defiance.[57] Whether in jail or at protest meetings, their singing became liturgical, like the prayers of psalmists and the oracles of prophets assured of a certainty that God heard them, as they called out to the nation, "Enough! Repent, restore and be a good neighbor: the day of the Lord, the day of our freedom is at hand."

The traditional and the redacted Albany versions of "We Shall Not Be Moved" share this kind of liturgical, profound conviction, with differences of setting and language. The 1960s social and cultural milieu catapulted these redacted versions into being. The original texts had an explicitly religious tone: "I" as subject, "Jesus" as liberator-captain, "glory" as the goal, "Jacob's ladder" as facilitator, and "Old Satan" as deterrent. With urgency, the 1960s text reinforced the civil rights agenda in its focus on victory and its naming of segregation as garbage, as inertia. Movement becomes the metaphor for the internal growth of individuals and communities first, and interracial and cosmological growth second. The object is not to romanticize cultural expressions and their power to transform, but to pay attention to the intent of the people who are creating the expression, with a leverage of inclusivity tempered by critical social and cultural explanation or exegesis.[58]

An exegesis of the cultural milieu and of the song itself focuses on the unmasking of faith and thought within "We Shall Not Be Moved." Dominant White supremacists desired that Blacks stagnate—move backward or move away. Blacks desired freedom to vote, to integrate, and to experience first-class citizenship, metaphorically symbolized by a lack of movement. Blacks wanted to imitate the ability of Whites to move on diverse levels without undue restraint, while a stance against coerced movement transformed the self and created movement. The nonviolent resistance of African Americans contradicted the Eurocentric wish to deny equal access to movement and claimed space for Blacks in Albany, Georgia, within this resistance against segregation and garbage. "We" represents the oppressed, the scapegoats. The "tree" alludes to strength, rootedness, and the state of being anchored against an onslaught of difference. From a christocentric perspective, a tree can represent the cruelty of crucifixion and death as well as an immediate vision of heaven or upwardly moving life. The well-being of the tree depends on the use of water, which leads to victory. Water images have multiple, contrasting meanings. Flowing water symbolizes life, the roaring sea portrays turbulence, and baptism indicates new life. Deep rivers suggest inner spiritual grounding or in-depth turmoil and soul searching. Deep rivers also symbolize the dividing line between present enslavement (calling for immediate liberation) and eternal freedom.[59] Victory embodies the end of blatant racism and the beginning of full citizenship privileges with the phrases "Segregation is our enemy" and "Just like a pail of garbage in the alley." Segregation signifies all systemic evil, the theodic problem. The language of this reformation hymn looks toward the efficacy of transformed human intention, which secures right relationships.

Right relations challenge people to claim their own space, their personal territory, without bending to reductionism, acquiescence, or greed. "We Shall Not Be Moved" signifies the difference in relationships among God, societal oppressors, the oppressed, and the movement rooted in creation theology. Balanced relationship of humanity within the movement of Genesis can be a query of ethics or epistemology, the issue of human behavior or of how humans learn. Is personal and communal movement based on a decision of value or an issue of knowing? Movement is ultimately salvific: it frees the human mind, body, and soul.

In the original version of "We Shall Not Be Moved," the "engaging" elements explicitly deal with the program and person of Jesus and the realm of the Godhead as glory. Albany's redacted version builds on an implicit presence of God. And a silent God is not an absent God. Psalm 1 implies a God of creation who creates out of love, a God whose quiet presence can move mountains. A silent God resounds in the actions of people. God is free, just, righteous, and sovereign; is on the side of the oppressed; is revealed love; is manifested as the Spirit; and is Jesus. And Jesus is the crucified people.[60] Thus, God stands relationally to humanity in *agape* and wholeness over against a problem of evil or a pathological sense of theodicy. God grieves, marches, and groans with Albany. God's overcoming power and nurturing love move Albany to act.

In Albany, the SNCC Freedom Singers, other civil rights groups, and their followers became singing units for justice. Even the close-knit structure of the ensemble symbolized the one and the many. Sometimes it was difficult to discern vocal parts, although the many layers of rich harmony involved four distinctive lines. Similarly, human communities operated as the one and the many. Through faith and hard work, the oppressed community worked toward an inclusive worldview.

The repetition of the communal, oppressed "we" as a force against the powerful "they" of the police became humorous. The repetition of "we" created a "we" that had more actual power than the establishment with its armed, physical, and political power. The sung "we" generated a power so great that unarmed Blacks intimidated armed White police, and the police had to leave. The performance of this song occurred in meetings when racist police stood as an irresistible force. "We Shall Not Be Moved" called for change in confronting the immovable object of a segregated society, with the police as social barometers. The rigid, "immovable" racist, segregated society had to move. With humor, the "we-ness" destroyed the illusion of the power of the dominant group at the point of inducing or stifling change. Another facet of humor occurred when activists marched (moved) in protest while singing that they would not be moved, as their "we-ness" depicted community.

"We-ness" verbally liberated those previously silenced. "We-ness" challenged the use of time in engaging choice and in opting for change. "We-ness" supported individuals and communities claiming their space, and opted for a balance of power and redistribution. "We-ness" did not reverse the roles between the oppressed and the oppressor, but sought equality and the enhancement of all life in American society. "We-ness" made an ethical statement based on solidarity, which produced agapic treatment with relations between God and the neighbor toward a living theology of justice, whereby the singers knew that God created all human beings to experience freedom. "We-ness" entered the sacred and the secular through music to inspire, to teach, to heal, and to musically represent God.

Born of the tradition of music about the salvation of life experience, "We Shall Not Be Moved" encourages healthy self-actualization throughout a society where time and cultural resistance were both gift and curse. As curse, the time needed to effect change was and continues to be too long. The curse of cultural resistance existed when "we-ness" meant the flaunted, abusive exercise of superiority. People experienced blessing as they took the time to make a difference. Cultural resistance stood up for equality and for the celebration of cultural distinctiveness. The gift and curse of time and cultural resistance were part of signifying, which allowed the oppressed to use language and song as transcendent communication and as a morale booster. On many occasions, singing "We Shall Not Be Moved" allowed the protesters to stay in a meeting, in jail, or with the Movement. Staying with people under the threat of death was a relational act. True relationships, critical to Albany's public health, celebrated the existence of "we-ness," the reality of salvific power related to a salvific theodicy where "we-ness" molded relationships and initiated the beginnings of a more inclusive society. When cruel treatment of a person because of race, sex, or class ceased, bonds were broken and freedom spoken. This release from bondage is a growth process from victimization to victory with God, self, and others as shared freedom. That freedom offers empowerment for those with the courage to choose the direction of their movement.

"Ain't Gonna Let Nobody Turn Me 'Round"

"Ain't Gonna Let Nobody Turn Me 'Round," sung in ensemble style, tells a story of theodicy that claims that no person, power, or entity can stop us from assuming the rights and privileges of being created in the image of God or of being a United States citizen. Neither antebellum slaves nor 1960s freedom fighters allowed oppression to thwart their quest for justice. Since God was on the side of the protesters, all other obstacles could and would ultimately be overcome. Part of the civil rights strategy was to carry the message to local audiences as effectively as possible. Toward that end, many strong Movement song leaders forged small ensembles, units of collective or communal singing. The various ensembles, especially three groups of SNCC singers, took the message of liberation on tours throughout the nation and intensified the role of grassroots quests for freedom.[61]

Context

"Ain't Gonna Let Nobody Turn Me 'Round," the message of steadfast commitment to a cause, expresses the cause of truly being the self God created one to be, and motivated communal action toward victorious empowerment. This Spiritual signifies a life process of moving from one place to another, a goal-oriented or eschatological life in the present. The idea of needing to say, "I will let nobody turn me 'round" implies that an individual or community is probably on its way to a life-changing goal or event. Amid civil rights activity in Albany, Georgia, in the summer of 1962, Cordell Reagon led the SNCC Freedom Singers in rendering "Ain't Gonna Let Nobody Turn Me 'Round" as a response when Judge Tuttle, of the Fifth Circuit Federal Court, issued an injunction to ban all demonstrations. During that same summer, the Reverend Ralph Abernathy taught this Spiritual to persons gathered at the Mount Zion Baptist Church for a mass meeting. CBS filmed the Freedom Singers being arrested and carted off to police paddy wagons, singing this song:[62]

> *Ain't gonna let nobody turn me 'round,*
> *Turn me 'round, turn me 'round;*
> *Ain't gonna let nobody turn me 'round*
> *Gonna keep on walkin',*
> *Keep on talkin',*
> *Walkin' up the king's highway.*
>
> *Ain't gonna let my mother turn me 'round . . .*
>
> *Ain't gonna let my brother turn me 'round . . .*
>
> *Ain't gonna let the devil turn me 'round . . .*

One Mississippi version from the oral tradition, courtesy of choral director Mary Lue Chavis Jones and Gladys McKnight of Louisiana, had only four lines:

Ain't gonna let nobody turn me 'round,
Turn me 'round, turn me 'round
Ain't gonna let nobody turn me 'round,
I'm gonna wait till my change comes.

Don't let nobody turn you 'round,
Turn you 'round, turn you 'round;
Don't let nobody turn you 'round,
Wait until your change comes.

I say that I'm gonna hold out,
Hold out, hold out;
I say that I'm gonna hold out,
Until my change comes.

I promised the Lord that I would hold out,
Hold out, hold out;
I promised the Lord that I would hold out,
Wait until my change comes.

"Ain't Gonna Let Nobody Turn Me 'Round," a strophic form with six lines, evokes the imagery of people on the move. Protesters marched and sang, sang at sit-ins, and went to jail and sang, because they were not "gonna let nobody turn [them] 'round." The recurring triple repetition of "turn me 'round" or "hold out" creates imagery of survival and persistence. The verses have a textual structure of *aaabbc* or *aaab*. This Spiritual, with overtones of a dance tune or work song, has a sense of expectancy and vigorous determination, particularly as the song evolved during the 1960s Albany protest:

Ain't gonna let nobody turn me 'round,
Turn me 'round turn me 'round;
Ain't gonna let nobody turn me 'round
Gonna keep on walkin', Lordy,
Keep on talkin',
Marchin' up to freedom land.

Ain't gonna let Chief Pritchett turn me 'round . . .
Ain't gonna let no city commissioner turn me 'round . . .
Ain't gonna let segregation, Lawd, turn me 'round . . .

Other verses include:

Ain't gonna let no jailhouse turn me 'round . . .
Ain't gonna let no police dogs turn me 'round . . .

Ain't gonna let no sheriff deputies turn me 'round . . .
Ain't gonna let Nervous Nelly turn me 'round . . .
Ain't gonna let Mayor Kelly turn me 'round . . .
Ain't gonna let no injunction turn me 'round . . . [63]

Verses learned in the Mississippi oral tradition from Evelyn Parker include:

Ain't gonna let White folks turn me 'round . . .
Ain't gonna let Uncle Toms turn me 'round . . .

"Ain't Gonna Let Nobody Turn Me 'Round," a song of defiance, says "No!" to extensive caution that says one must wait until everything is safe before rallying for change. The protesters had to sing this Spiritual, because they were in the middle of life-changing and life-ending crisis. As the protesters sang, they stood together, relying on the best possibilities and life potentials from their various religious traditions, to create vital empowering, interfaith meetings that offered encouragement, hope, and assurance. In an ocean of powerful spiritual waves of religious ecstasy in the various communities in mass meetings, often led by ensembles, Black folk "had to sing songs taken from the deep reservoirs of their forebears' religious genius and then respond with their own revised versions of majestic hope. . . . They had to sing everything they could sing," as they used "the great resources of their religious heritage."[64]

Their religious heritage confronted the heritage of American civil religious idolatry that worshipped the gods of oppression and practiced the rituals of supremacy. Demigods like Bull Connor and Laurie Pritchett tried to use hate tactics and to develop strategies or rituals counter to that of nonviolent direct action. While these racist overseers captured and locked up bodies, they could not capture those Black and White souls and singing voices of protest. The power of their holy sounds was expressed with their holy voices, from one of the many cavities of the human body that rely on powerful holy breath—the breath of life, the breath of God—to utter holy sounds, sounds they had to sing of life itself.[65]

That very engaging of breath, of godliness, was an affront to the arrogance, the presumption, of being right that was professed by White supremacists. That same breath fueled the pathos, the passion, of the antebellum slaves and the 1960s freedom fighters, toward their commitment that they "[wouldn't] let nobody turn [them] 'round." The interplay between the arrogance of racists and the pathos of liberationists often led to numerous protests, arrests, and deaths, but it also led to heightened national and global awareness, greater commitment by many Blacks and Whites, and changes in state and federal laws. To see this history is to see both trepidation and triumph; to recognize the fear and trauma; and to see the sense of invincibility that rose above the fear because the protesters knew a higher sense of authority and believed that that divine authority was on their side. When a civil authority like Judge Tuttle issued an injunction against demonstrations, the protesters regrouped and were willing to go to jail in defiance of that order. So, the Black protesters had to sing "Ain't Gonna Let Nobody Turn Me 'Round" because the law *said* one thing, but the country *lived* another.

The First Amendment protects the right of citizens to assemble peaceably. The Thirteenth Amendment (1865) banned slavery and involuntary servitude except for criminal punishment; the Fourteenth Amendment (1868) said that all persons born or naturalized in the United States were citizens; the Fifteenth Amendment (1870) said that not race, color, nor previous condition of servitude could deny a person the right to vote; and the Nineteenth Amendment (1920) stated that no citizen could be denied the right to vote because of sex. The law did give African Americans the right to assemble to protest peaceably. The law did give African Americans the right to vote. While the law on the books stated that Black men and women were citizens, could assemble, and could vote, Black and poor White citizens did not fully obtain the right to vote until the passage of the Twenty-fourth Amendment (1964), which forbids the federal and state governments from denying or abridging the right of United States citizens to vote due to failure of paying a poll tax (an assessment levied mostly against African Americans and poor Whites to keep them from voting). The redacted version of "Ain't Gonna Let Nobody Turn Me 'Round" proclaimed and confessed that no civil or political authority, no injunctions, and no Nervous Nellies (i.e., segregationists) would stop the Movement's commitment to unseating injustice. This commitment further unfolds in viewing this Spiritual as story, veiled vision, or dialectic.

Story

From Albany, Georgia, to Los Angeles, SNCC Freedom Singers sang "Ain't Gonna Let Nobody Turn Me 'Round," a striking confession and promise of immediacy. They sang out of a conviction that freedom was accessible, not a phantom or fantasy. African Americans, together with other like-minded persons (e.g., the Quakers and abolitionists), had fought for justice and equality, with varying degrees of progress. The protesters revealed their intent and pledged their resources, including their lives, toward the fight for freedom, now!

The Albany text had five verses, with an additional six verses often incorporated into the singing. Each verse said "No!" to a person, institution, or other entity that symbolized injustice and oppression. Some of those persons indicted were central cogs in the social and political wheels of Albany. Some of the structures and institutions involved national racist practices and means of control. The repetitive phrases "Ain't gonna let" and "Gonna keep on walkin', / Keep on talkin', / Marchin' up to freedom land" insure the unconditional nature of the profession of faith: under no circumstances shall injustice and oppression be tolerated any longer. For years, throughout the more blatant segregationist South and the more subtly racist North, African Americans tried to work within the system and moved at a pace that would not cause them to be the brunt of more vehement retaliation. But the lynchings went on, and Jim Crow reigned supreme. A new fervor came with the 1960s, a fervor that pushed African Americans to transcend hints that they were inferior and deserved second-class treatment, to a passionate outcry of Black power. The beginnings of verbalizing what many had felt but had been afraid to utter grew out of the powerful singing of the Movement. The sentiments of the singing were infectious. Singing "Ain't Gonna Let Nobody Turn Me 'Round" meant that the Black folk who thirsted for liberation would never settle for such debased treatment again. They sang this Spiritual as police officers picked them up two by two and loaded them into the paddy wagons. The powers that be could lock their bodies up but not their spirits, not their souls. Their singing involved a strong oral tradition that helped to solidify their identity as a viable community with empowered individuals. Naming one's identity involved a shared message, a message passed from generation to generation about the quest for justice, and the determination to participate in acquiring that justice was rooted in the biblical text.

Three scriptures are relevant to the traditional text of "Ain't Gonna Let Nobody Turn Me 'Round": Numbers 21:22, Genesis 19:17b, and Jeremiah 4:28b. In two biblical traditions of the Israelites attempting but failing to enter Canaan from the north, the Israelites shift to march north from Kadesh. In the process, Israel sends a message to the Amorite king that says, "Let us pass through your land. We will not turn aside, we will not drink your well water. We will take the king's highway." Though the king resists, Israel is victorious and comes to dwell in former Amorite land (Nm 20:1-21:31). Antebellum singers identified with the absolute steadfastness of the Israelites to not be turned around. The Israelites were eschatological in that their goal of forward movement toward claiming the land was forthright, just as the freedom fighters were clear that their end result was freedom. The Lot story in Genesis 19:17b echoes the "not turning" in Numbers with "not looking back or stopping anywhere" en route lest the Israelites be consumed. The freedom fighters and the slaves before them knew the cost of segregation and did not want to be further consumed by oppressive actions. In a conversation about judgment, exile, idolatry, repentance, and a foe from the north (Jer 3:6-4:31), Jeremiah acknowledges God's judgment on Judah and Jerusalem, as well as the terrible results of God's irrevocable judgment, when the divine voice says, "I have spoken, I have a purpose, and I will not turn back or give in" (4:28b). African Americans saw examples of the divine and of other human beings who would not turn or look back lest they be impeded. By the time of the 1960s protests, the freedom fighters were most familiar with being Black individuals and communities, when others saw this Blackness as the reason to always turn back, to not even start, to not hope, to acquiesce to injustice and bigotry.

To be true to themselves meant finessing multiple realities and heading off racial schizophrenia and misplaced identity. They also faced those White supremacists who thought nothing of lynching a Black person for walking on the sidewalk instead of stepping off so a White person could pass. Freedom fighters faced a world barely cognizant of Vietnam and of the number of Blacks who died for the USA on those eastern soils. So, fighting someone dubbed "other" was in the air. The protesters also faced the ambiguities of naming and claiming this conviction of not turning around while also facing the difficulty of transcending racist persons and institutions like laws and rules that had enforcers: the sheriffs, mayors, and city commissioners. But that was the power of song.

Ain't Gonna Let Nobody Turn Me 'Round" provided a sense of urgency and a possibility of fulfillment. The protesters saw that a changed and hopeful mind would allow the space for changed action. Singing this spiritual allowed them the room to confront their oppressors and, for some, their worst nightmare: that when it counted, they would not be able to fight for freedom. This Spiritual celebrates the joy of self-actualization and a community stance against being manipulated or forced into acting in a demeaning manner. As the "me" stands for the single and collective, singing this Spiritual presented an arena where one could be Black and beautiful.

Creative Spirit

"Ain't Gonna Let Nobody Turn Me 'Round" has a gospel quartet feel; the ensemble has a unified sound with high energy and fortitude. This Spiritual begins with a semi–call-and-response as the leader, Cordell Reagon, lines out "Ain't gonna let nobody" and the other three voices of the SNCC Freedom Singers join him on "turn me 'round, turn me 'round." The ensemble style here provides a sense of "staying power" for themselves and the larger audience; for song was always the life force that freedom fighters used so that they could stay in the room. It was the force that filled up the space, that empowered, that helped them overcome terror and fear of the present, and of what would happen soon. Song helped the protesters press on and form community wherever they gathered to meet and strategize.[66] The ensemble of tenor lead, soprano, alto, and baritone served as an impetus for "taking care of business," as they sang a cappella in the key of G minor.

The quartet used syncopated rhythms with quarter-note triplets, which, in addition to the cut-time signature, gave the sense of three within a feel of two. Using a good mix of sound and silence in their singing, the ensemble used repetition to solidify and reinforce their message of an unconditional "No!" to being distracted from their journey. Based on a five-tone scale, this Spiritual calls for reform and liberation. That reform involves the embedded dream that not turning around will make a difference and that grassroots participation is significant, for those who want democracy must participate in creating that democracy. The call to reform engaged the process of signifying, as the singers implied to their oppressors: "Do you dare try to stop us?" and "Are you willing to take a risk by impeding our movement?" The Spirituals, as crisis texts, question and revise and restate. Thus, the traditional versions focus on moving toward perfection and waiting for one's change to come. While many read these lines as signifying about the death of sin in life, the texts clearly have implications for total salvation of mind, spirit, and body. The 1960s redacted version speaks of a liberation that comes through participatory action, and a blatant denial that outside forces can stop the process. The traditional version addresses the change that the redacted version implies.

The ensemble, grounded in a responding baritone line, highlights the nuances of participation and denial and uses answering, extemporaneous soprano and alto lines with tenor lead. Their four-part harmony has a feel that is more improvisational but not the strict chordal barbershop-quartet style, despite the fact that the singers tend to harmonize in standard chords of thirds. They skillfully use rests or silences, which both embody syncopation and represent the heartbeat or pulse of a protesting community. Their sound is vital and soulful, and blends the richness of Pentecostal gospel and evocative R & B (rhythm and blues). Their presentation reminds one of church testimonials and the traditional "call to discipleship" in many Protestant worship services, when "the doors of the church are opened," the "right hand of fellowship" may be extended, and one is invited to become a member of that particular church body. The Freedom Singers invite all listeners to participate in the Movement. The influence of work songs in this arrangement is also apparent, as one can envision slaves simultaneously rowing large boats or working on railroad chain gangs. There is no ambiguity about where the rowers, chain gangs, or freedom fighters are headed, as they geographically locate liberation in freedom's land. The singers end prayerfully, as they lower the dynamic level and portray an even more soulful, poignant sound.

Within these rich sounds, the freedom fighters will not imitate a past of separatism and segregation, nor do they wish to continue the role of scapegoat. They want the right to hold the offices of police chief, city commissioner, and mayor. This desire pushes them to experience the power of having an elected political position. No longer will African Americans have to apologize for their own existence; to apologize by drinking at "colored only" water fountains, riding in the back of the bus, stepping off the sidewalk to let a White person pass by, paying poll taxes to vote; or to be denied access to public accommodations. The singers boldly signify and call out the names of oppressive institutions and persons. Having made these courageous and daring pronouncements, what happens if "they" continue to attempt to turn "us" around? What price do the freedom fighters pay if they continue to protest? Would the cost have been greater if they had acquiesced? When the singers use "Lawdy" or "Lord" as part of their response, is this a theological statement, or a standard response mechanism?

Faith and Thought

"Ain't Gonna Let Nobody Turn Me 'Round," in the traditional version, depicts God as providential, concerned with transformation, and both hidden and somewhat recognized as a facilitator toward getting to freedom land. Human beings are actors in the drama of liberation: they are the oppressors, who can change their vindictive behavior; and the oppressed, who are not victims because they can participate in their own liberation. The Spiritual does not blame the oppressors per se, but "Ain't Gonna Let Nobody Turn Me 'Round" does shame them by naming them. Given the circumstances in Albany and the world during 1962, where are the prophetic voices? What are the goals when the freedom fighters get to freedom land? Where is freedom land? What happens when leadership changes? How do they reformulate themselves as a new community with particular rights?

The rights espoused in "Ain't Gonna Let Nobody Turn Me 'Round" highlight issues of social and economic justice that involve good stewardship of social and material resources concerning legal and institutional arrangements and the place where humanity's being created in God's image can be realized. Justice is an opportunity to transcend the human tendency, both in community and as individuals, to focus on special self-interests. Economic justice, a subset of social justice, concerns the material part of social activities and social relationships that deals with the production, distribution, and consumption of goods and services.[67] "Ain't Gonna Let Nobody Turn Me 'Round" says "Yes" to right relations between various communities and with God. The metaphor of "walkin' and talkin' " symbolizes one of the key ingredients of justice—freedom to choose, freedom to be, and freedom to change and foster mutuality. Theologically and ethically, change involves a community where being created in the image of God governs how people think about God and about themselves, and how that thought plays itself out in human behavior as responsible stewardship. Theologically, we must ask how culture, ethnicity, gender, and class influence the reality and activities of justice. Justice as applied equity for African Americans concerns how they experience their Blackness. During the 1960s and 1970s, the change in ethnicity designation from colored to Negro to Black indicates a heightened awareness of Blackness from being the despised to being the admired and the beautiful, encompassing the physical state of being and the spiritual realms. The new sense of worth taught through song and other rhetoric occurs through the powerful sense of oral discourse in African traditions. Oral speech told everyone who the enemies were. The enemies in "Ain't Gonna Let Nobody Turn Me 'Round" signify embodied evil, which is presented through closely woven intervals.

These close musical movements help the Spiritual remain liturgical by implication. Since nobody and nothing stands in the way or can coerce an individual, then he or she does not acquiesce to idolatry. Instead, one experiences a sense of mutuality and balance. When some are empowered and are open for "others" to likewise be empowered, relations become mutual. As "Ain't Gonna Let Nobody Turn Me 'Round" teaches oppressors that they do not have to wound and manipulate and teaches the oppressed that their plight can change and that they have choice, the singing creates a therapeutic environment and shifts the impact of racist abuse. This Spiritual implies that racism does not have to exist but is a choice about the use of power and the regard for human dignity.

The place of human dignity, as a central component of social justice, is the essence of theodicy. Such a theology of justice builds on the ethic of "Love thy neighbor as thyself, and love the Lord your God" as the context for social, economic, and political justice. This song reflects the shared distribution of power in these three realms which supports responsible stewardship, community solidarity, and individual esteem. In working toward communal and individual enrichment and change, Womanist scholars see "Ain't Gonna Let Nobody Turn Me 'Round" as an affirmation that all oppressions are interrelated and involve entangled evils that come from and have a domino effect on every aspect of human life. Consequently, true liberation—true choice about when and how to turn and about the ability to move forward—involves the elimination of all forms of oppression.[68]

"Certainly, Lord"

"Certainly, Lord," the last ensemble-style song, depicts a theodicy that focuses on the individual's commitment and allegiance to the practice of salvation, which takes a christocentric reading of Micah 6:8, which tells what the Lord requires of us: to do justice, to love kindness, and to walk humbly with God. The redacted version of the song focuses on an applied theodicy that tests the commitment of persons to the work of liberation, of nonviolent protest, and of spreading the word. The CORE Freedom Singers sang this Spiritual in a revivalist, questioning manner with gospel-type accompaniment of piano and Hammond organ (the organ of choice for many gospel piano and organ players). With a call-and-response format, the baritone asks the question, and the other singers respond in mixed choral style with the message of liberation. The CORE Freedom Singers sang this arranged Spiritual in their travels throughout the United States, especially during 1963.[69]

Context

"Certainly, Lord" involves a series of questions and answers about individual and communal participation in the experience of salvation and in the quest for liberation. "Certainly" is the affirmative answer to all the questions. The Spiritual, like a prophetic oracle, involves the questioning divine voice and the human acknowledgment of both the divine presence and the human participation in the event. From the first sit-in in Greensboro, North Carolina, by four North Carolina Agricultural and Technical College students beginning on February 1, 1960, sit-ins spread throughout the South, SNCC evolved, the freedom rides garnered support for CORE, and the Movement went to newer levels: increased development and use of nonviolent tactics; intergenerational conflicts between parents, students, and organizations; and increased participation by young White activists.[70] The traditional version of "Certainly, Lord" questions one's experiences of rituals and life changes that come with salvation:

> *Have you got good religion? Certainly, Lord!*
> *Have you got good religion? Certainly, Lord!*
> *Have you got good religion? Certainly, Lord!*
> *Certainly, certainly, certainly, Lord!*
>
> *Have you been redeemed? Certainly, Lord! . . .*
> *Have you been to the water? Certainly, Lord! . . .*
> *Have you been baptized? Certainly, Lord!. . .*

"Certainly, Lord" has several stanzas with the main repetitive refrain of "Certainly, Lord." The textual structure involves three repeated lines of text and has a refrain line: *aaar*. The melodic structure for the response is closely knit and higher pitched than the response, which falls about a third lower. A strong (unnamed) baritone leads the CORE Freedom Singers as the redacted version of the song asks whether one has experienced various components and experiences of racism:

> *Well, have you been to the jail? Certainly, Lord!*
> *Well, have you been to the jail? Certainly, Lord!*
> *Well, have you been to the jail? Certainly, Lord!*
> *Certainly, certainly, certainly, Lord!*
>
> *Well, did you give thirty days? Certainly, Lord! . . .*
> *Well, did you serve your time? Certainly, Lord! . . .*
> *Well, will you go back again? Certainly, Lord! . . .*
> *Well, will you fight for freedom? Certainly, Lord! . . .*
> *Well, will you tell it to the world? Certainly, Lord! . . .*
> *Well, will you tell it to the judge? Certainly, Lord! . . .*

The singers expressed their feelings and communicated the message of possibility and the importance of standing up and fighting for freedom. The ritual practices of White supremacy and racism had made segregation and oppression the law of the land. As Blacks and Whites, Jews and gentiles marched, sat in, and rallied at the altar of freedom, they sought to expose the idolatry of racism and the arrogance and dominance of hate. The impassioned and confessional "Certainly, Lord" evokes a pathos for the work of the nonviolent protesters and for the plight of all poor people. Seeing this paradox of poor people suffering and dying for their purported constitutional rights exposes democratic hypocrisy. Seeing this situation from the realm of protest perspective calls us to be mindful of the hundreds of unsung grassroots persons who inspired slave insurrections, who protested via intellectual thought, who participated in early suffragette movements, who were wounded in the various wars for this country but still could not command respect and get a job upon return to these shores, and who have protested on behalf of justice and human rights during the 1960s and today.

The call to protest asks, Why risk one's life for a cause? If people risk their lives in protest, will that change the "other" status of the protesters to that of "one of us"? What changes their status from that of scapegoat? What do protesters want from society? What does society want from them? What is the interrelationship between all of these questions? "Certainly, Lord" implies that liberation comes only with a price and a responsibility through giving of self in a manner that makes a difference. "Certainly, Lord" adds a sense of immediacy to the freedom quest. In talking about specific places, time served, level of commitment, and the taking of the message both to a judge and to the world, this Spiritual notes that freedom is worthy of desire and asks about the levels, costs, and participatory nature of desire and liberation.

Story

The story of "Certainly, Lord" relates to how slaves and freedom fighters dealt with their own ability to participate in the ongoing course of their lives. Viewing this Spiritual as a story invites an appreciation for a group forced primarily to react, moving to a proactive stance on their own behalf. Traditionally, one could not be saved if one did not have church membership or "good religion." One was not a full participant in the Civil Rights Movement if one had not gone to jail, done time, or stood in front of a judge regarding Movement activities. In both song accounts, the individual and the related community have a key participatory function in their salvation or liberation. The traditional version has four call-response stanzas that reflect on the practice of Christian faith. The Movement version has seven call-and-response stanzas that embody both the pride and the cost of protest. The ability to exclaim, "Certainly, Lord," both the title and the key repetitive motif, means that through God's caring, as well as human effort and human willingness to change and be changed, oppression can end. Because not everyone wanted to change the traditions of racism, there were no guarantees about the protesters' success rate. These freedom fighters had a vision of the United States in line with Martin Luther King, Jr.'s dream, that people would be judged by the content of their character as opposed to the color of their skin. Long before Jesse Jackson's rhetoric of "I am somebody," Black extended families instilled those words in their children. The griots of the diaspora passed on gems of mother wit that bolstered self-esteem and community unity. In the Spiritual "Certainly, Lord," the oral tradition makes the individual important enough to be both recipient and contributor: one can receive the baptism of salvation or liberation by water or by jail experience, and can participate by walking and talking as a saved or liberated person.

Many slaves and freedom fighters identified with Christianity in terms of salvation, or freedom from sin. Various scriptures inform the traditional version, which questions one's choice and practice of right or pure religion (Jas 1:26-27) and of being redeemed (Dt 15:15; Ps 107:2; Gal 3:13), with numerous texts that talk about water and its relationship to baptism (including Mt 3:11, 13-17 and Mk 1:8). The slaves understood life as an experience of vitality that daily included the praise of God, the importance of rituals, and the gifts of salvation. In singing "Certainly, Lord," the singers confirmed their beliefs and praxis. The redacted version elevated the experiences of nonviolent direct protest to that of ritual and salvation. That awareness added the spaces between experiencing Blackness as ordained by God, and the negative image projected back on the freedom fighters by racists, along with the experience of blending the sacred and the secular (which were always interconnected in Black culture) at the level of local and state government. While these categories often overlap and the specific type of oppression may blur, "Certainly, Lord" is a song of reformation that erases ambiguity and shouts with clarity the requirements for communion in liberation.

Such a feast of freedom begins the process of transformation. "Certainly, Lord" empowered freedom fighters with a sense of direction and celebration through ritual. In the process of going through the rituals of mass meetings, sit-ins, prayer vigils, and other steps taken toward integrating the United States, these rituals became a part of seeing the real self and knowing pride in that realization. To know oneself was also to know a bit of the spirit of God.

Creative Spirit

Empowered by divine spirit, the singers knew that praise involved both a worship of God and an inner strengthening of self. The ensemble rendering of "Certainly, Lord" is more like a small choral group than a quartet; the leader calls out, and the other members harmoniously respond. The gospel-style piano and organ accompaniment provides both joyous, spirited introductory bars and an instrumental interlude. The "boogie" gospel playing provides a sturdy backdrop for the vocal call-and-response. As the soloist issues the call, he sounds like a preacher; those responding sound like the "A-men corner." This worshipful moment involves a series of testimonials and confessions. The words evoke the various rituals of liberation, and the music lets one "make a joyful noise unto God!" (cf. Ps 66:1).

The joyful noise involves a jubilant line of repetitive notes in the key of B major. With the focus on the last word of the question, the first time "to the jail" moves down and then up; the second time the interval moves up, then down; the third time the phrase is tighter, with a slight move down. These differences in spacing between the notes, as well as whether the note ascends or descends, reinforces the intensity of the question. The way the phrases move up and down symbolizes clarity and resolution. The resolution involves the dream that one can ultimately experience liberation and can have the strength to be relentless in pursuing this goal.

With "Certainly, Lord," signifying only once involves the naming or renaming of a particular person, a judge. The other stanzas focus on sequences of time, movement, and place, as the specific texts flow in a logical fashion. For example, one gets a jail sentence before finding out the length of the time to be served; a freedom fighter cannot go back again if he or she has not already been to jail. The close-knit, straightforward melody lends itself to this series of questions. The repetitive answer and simple melody do not bore the singers and audience participants; rather, the familiarity of that sameness strengthens and provides assurance to a troubled people who desire human fulfillment and social justice. By singing "Certainly, Lord," the freedom fighters became able to meet the task as the possibility for actually experiencing justice became more real, more tangible. "Certainly, Lord" highlights the desire for justice juxtaposed against the desire to repress, and the aura of oppression amid the hope of enlightened respect and mutuality; and signifies the voices of liberation from spiritual, physical, and psychological bondage. For those wedded to bondage, "Certainly, Lord" asks: If you are not protesting, what are you doing? If you need to oppress, what is your fear? If you do not believe you can participate in change, where is your faith and hope?

Faith and Thought

"Certainly, Lord" answers the questions of faith and hope in the context of God and community. The protesters believe that God is on their side and that as a community they can stand up against intolerance, hatred, and fear in ways that a lone individual cannot. The Movement was not an "I" activity, but a "we" and an "us" relational situation. While there could be differences of opinion, as a body the protesters maintained a rhythm of celebrating life and fostering unity. They focused on affirming personal and communal intent and action toward the cause, which follows the adage "God helps those who help themselves." The point is not to claim that God could not or would not help people who did not participate, yet some got on a revivalist bent and implied, "God has no hands but our hands, no eyes but our eyes." God empowers, and human beings certainly can participate. Yet because of the continued oppression, what are the dimensions of certainty? Do freedom fighters view their God as the Hebrew children saw their God? How long will the protesters have to sing and believe "Certainly, Lord" before a credible change occurs? As long as the change does not occur, injustice exists. "Certainly, Lord" unmasks the injustices of a biased judicial and political system, of silenced voices and unspeakable evils. In so doing, "Certainly, Lord" articulates justice as faithfulness to the particulars of relationship.[71]

Given that the dynamics of relationships are critical to the experience of freedom, "Certainly, Lord" pointedly asks, "Will you fight for freedom?" Freedom is a significant component of wholeness and justice. When any sector of a society does not experience freedom, ultimately the entire society is not free. "Certainly, Lord" proclaims that Black folk, all folk, as children of God, are to experience freedom, respect, and the rights accorded any United States citizen. Previously, African Americans have been denied these rights and privileges, due to the perception of their Blackness by those in power. Underlying "Certainly, Lord" is a concept of Blackness that identifies the diversity and beauty of physical Blackness, the rich mysteriousness of ontological Blackness, and the ethereal power of metaphysical or spiritual Blackness. Taken together, these multiple experiences of Blackness infuse the traditional African heritage (e.g., call-and-response, lush vocal sound, and import of rhythm) in "Certainly, Lord" that gives this Spiritual a hopeful, positive message—a message antithetical to the evils of oppression.

In "Certainly, Lord," the first half of each question (e.g., "Well, will you") sets up a sense of the conditional, and the second half of the question (e.g., "go back again?") focuses on the object of time or movement that indicates an oppressive reality. Musically, the initial part of the question has eighth or running notes, and the object in the second part has sustained and slurred notes. Lyrical and musical texts work together to signify the issue of evil or theodicy. As one of the crusade songs, "Certainly, Lord" remains liturgical, given the implications for reform within the text. The call for reform is a call to balanced association where intimate relationships exist between God and humanity and within the realm of global humanity. "Certainly, Lord" is the reminder that in the context of creation theology, the possibilities for such mutuality already exist. The traditional and redacted versions of "Certainly, Lord" both hint at a unity with God and a purpose and context for human life. While the traditional version calls for salvation and living a redeemed life, it focuses less overtly on a holistic life experience. The redacted version focuses on the experiences of nonviolent protest during the Movement, with an ultimate vision of a holistic, healthy life experience. In the experience of creating this wholeness, "Certainly, Lord" becomes an experience of therapy and helps protesters finesse the ravages that result from the daily onslaught of racist, oppressive activities. "Certainly, Lord" says that people are not helpless concerning their own reality. God has the power and can effect change, but people need to do the footwork. Liberationist footwork or praxis and commitment for change have overcome pockets of racism.

What does "Certainly, Lord" teach us about dealing with racism? This Spiritual supports the notion that racism is not a good, that racism is idolatry. That idolatry perverts the potential for justice and thus creates a theodicy of distortion wherein relationships involve manipulation, control, oppression, even death. "Certainly, Lord" says "No" to distorted boundaries and "Yes" to empowerment, self-actualization, and community growth. "Certainly, Lord" names the powers of integrity, participation, and communication; unmasks the powers of hatred, manipulation, and injustice; and engages the powers of hope, potentiality, and new insights. For Womanists, true liberation requires new, more inclusive insights in "Certainly, Lord" that announce people that must no longer assume that Black women can support all of Black and White society. Black women, the ones who most often feel the brunt of racism, sexism, and classism, are often those who are forced into specific roles of maid, mother, and wife. "Certainly, Lord" calls for a Womanist ethics of justice that confronts silent oppression, knows and celebrates global histories and cultures, and must concern all segments of society toward the perpetuation of social well-being. The goal of communal wholeness requires a critical analysis of racism, sexism, and classism, along with a self-critical analysis of Womanist ethics, all of which ultimately enable the building of a liberation community.[72] "Have we got good religion?" Only if the evidence of our daily lives depicts a health, an inclusivity, and a love for all—although not necessarily a like—that actively allows us to claim the other as neighbor. Only then can we answer, "Certainly, Lord!"

> Glad for those who stood, stand,
> Will stand up
> Against injustices, from every realm.
> Glad today is another chance
> To know
> "Trouble don't last always."

11

Song Leaders

Come, oh let the people come!
Raise their voices and their hearts,
To the cause of justice,
For freedom, for life,
For La Chayim!
For life, of love and hope,
No need for life of hate.
Let the people come together,
Led by you, led by me
Praise God.

Almost forty years after the 1960s Movement, more than twenty-five Black churches in the South, from Texas to North Carolina, have been burned in 1995 and 1996. Synagogues and Jewish cemeteries were desecrated. Muslim shrines have been defaced. Babies are having babies, and kids are killing kids. Song leaders helped bring about transformation then; we need them to sing today for the changes they sang about in the 1960s. Song leaders have always been important in Black music, especially Black church music. The individual soloist would often line out or sing the words and give the tune first, especially where no keyboard instruments were available, hymnbooks were scarce, some of the music was only in the oral tradition, and many in the congregation could not read. The preacher sometimes doubled as the song leader, or sometimes the song leader and the preacher together would carry the service.

Song leaders can make or break a service, just as they helped rejuvenate meetings and workshops during the Movement. Song leaders were both female and male, young and old. They sang a cappella and were accompanied either by instruments or by the foot tapping, hand clapping, "A-mens," and moans of a waiting congregation. Sometimes members of the congregation would join in, even with the soloists. Song leaders could inspire and heighten the intensity and passion of a crowd, or they could bring calm to a waiting, agitated audience. A singer with a powerful sense of witness, who is open for the Spirit to use him or her, could move people to tears, could inspire people who have never even seen hills to leap mountains. The song leaders prepared the crowd and set them up to be in one accord and to hear the message of the civil rights leaders, who were often ministers. Sometimes that message would mean putting their lives on the line the next day. The powerful vocal and personal style of song leaders was like a gumbo or goulash, a tremendous mix of different styles, influences, and cultural resources. Sometimes song leaders led songs at mass meetings; sometimes they sang at various citizenship and nonviolent, direct action training workshops. Their activity was pedagogical and ministerial. The songs were teaching empowerment and proclaiming the message of justice and freedom. Some song leaders hailed from the rural and urban South, the hotbeds of blatant Jim Crow racism; some song leaders and songwriters were from more metropolitan, northern cities and brought with them songs of a more topical and folk song revival tradition. The song leaders taught and shared their new material with the protesters as they "focused on the role and importance of freedom song culture to the work of the Movement."[1] We still need God to come by here; there is still much work to be done. Song leaders still need to sing about freedom, hoped-for change, the reality of chaos, and being in a storm.

"I've Been in the Storm"

"I've Been in the Storm," led by Bernice Johnson (Reagon), describes the tensions of a theodicy where one can endure suffering. The rich, intense quality of Johnson's singing in the key of D minor, with rich, haunting tones, enhances her ability to paint stark images of ongoing pain and suffering with her contralto voice. Using her inner strengths and divine grace, she finds hope despite ongoing societal evil. She, as the protagonist, represents that all of the oppressed have endured and will continue to endure until change comes. Hope amid evil portrays one reaction to the problem of evil. In "I've Been in the Storm," the singer communicates with God, the being who helps us endure pain and chaos, through prayer, assured that the divine and the human together can cause liberation.

Context

The "naming" factors of "I've Been in the Storm" describe time and space and imply that I, meaning the one or the many, have existed prior to this moment and now am a real being, free in spirit, though I exist in real time caught between disruption, violence, turmoil, and chaos. Despite the length of suffering she has experienced, the singer asks God for time to pray, because no storms can make her forget prayer time. Despite physical and emotional pain, hope and prayer remain constant and provide the one assurance that chaos, suffering, and storms do end.

Soloist Bernice Johnson Reagon, an original SNCC Freedom Singer from Albany, Georgia, sang "I've Been in the Storm" at a song leader's workshop in Atlanta in 1964. A series of song leader workshops brought together major singers from local community struggles, as well as more seasoned African-American singers. Song leaders were central to the performance styles of mass meetings and for ensemble singing. Johnson Reagon sang "I've Been in the Storm" as a song leader during a strategic training session.[2] The original musical source included the following text:

I been in de storm so long,
I been in the storm so long, chillun,
I been in de storm so long,
Oh, gimme little time to pray.

Oh, let me tell you, Mother,
How I come 'long,
Oh, gimme little time to pray,
With a hung-down head and a achin' heart,
Oh gimme little time to pray.

Now when I get to Heaven,
I'll take my seat,
Oh, gimme little time to pray,
An-a cast my crown at my Jesus' feet,
Oh, gimme little time to pray.[3]

Another source of the original text, with chorus and six verses, broadens the scope of the story. The verse has four lines, and the sequence of repetition varies. This version reverses lines 3 and 4 of the chorus:

I've been in the storm so long,
You know I've been in the storm so long,
Oh Lord, give me more time to pray.
I've been in the storm so long.

I am a motherless child,
Singin' I am a motherless child,
Singin' oh Lord, give me more time to pray,
I've been in the storm so long.

Lord, I need you now,
Lord, I need you now,
Singin' oh Lord, give me more time to pray,
I've been in the storm so long.

My neighbors need you now,
My neighbors need you now,
Singin' oh Lord, give me more time to pray,
I've been in the storm so long.

My children need you now,
My children need you now,
Singin' oh Lord, give me more time to pray,
I've been in the storm so long.

Just look what-a shape I'm in,
Just look what-a shape I'm in,
Singin' oh Lord, give me more time to pray,
I've been in the storm so long.[4]

"I've Been in the Storm" has a strophic form with a four-lined chorus and two five-lined verses. "(Oh) Lord, give me a little time to pray" recurs throughout. The chorus's textual structure has the same rhyme scheme and melodic shape: the chorus is *aaab*, and the schematic for the verse is *abcb*. The performance scheme sets out the chorus as a "call" and the verse as the "response": chorus, chorus, verse, chorus, verse, and chorus. The prayerful confession of chorus and verse offers a rhetorical statement that signifies for others what they have been unable to say for themselves. The redacted text incorporated the following lyrics:

I've been in de storm so long,
I've been in de storm so long, children,
I've been in de storm so long,
Lord, give me a little time to pray.

Oh, let me tell you, Mother,
just how I come along,
Oh, give me a little time to pray,
With a hung-down head and an aching heart,
Oh give me a little time to pray.

Oh let me tell you, Elder,
just how I come along,
Lord, give me a little time to pray,
With a hung-down head and an aching heart,
Oh give me a little time to pray.

The redaction of "I've Been in the Storm" is implicit. The intent of Johnson Reagon makes it possible to bring personal experience to the song leaders' conference. The text has minor changes and includes stock phrases (i.e., phrases that appear in numerous Spirituals), such as additional lyrics included in "I've Been in the Storm" during the 1960s:

> *This is a needy time . . .*
> *Look what shape I'm in . . .*
> *Mend all my wicked ways . . .*
> *I am a motherless child . . .*
> *Lord, I need you now . . .*[5]

Johnson Reagon stood within a religious tradition that spoke almost three hundred years ago and that spoke again thirty years ago during the Movement, as she sang. The daughter of a minister who pastored in Worth County, Georgia, she also had a faithful, supportive mother. God has always been a part of her life, just like the breath that she breathes. Her breathing and singing brought her to the Albany Movement, as her songs gave life, transformed, made one feel good, and instilled an ability to fight. Aware of lynchings, boycotts, sit-ins, and school desegregations throughout the South, she joined the youth division of the NAACP, marched, sat in, and sang songs as mass meeting singing moved the Movement. After losing her job and being expelled from school, Johnson Reagon and the other forty-seven suspended students were offered enrollment in schools in Atlanta. Songs helped people keep sane in jail, helped people transcend class differences, and helped define leadership.[6] The protesters changed the songs so that the songs would speak for them. Singing gave them more space in a jail cell that had no space. Like others, Johnson Reagon, living in a Eurocentric culture as an African American, used her individualism as a Black poet "to pass all—religion, poetry, language, music—through the crucible of [her] perceptual consciousness, whence emerged a product bearing the unmistakable marks of the Negro genius in the way of form, rhythm, sound and imagery, fused with Western melody, language and religious content."[7] Johnson Reagon sang "I've Been in the Storm" as one of the 1960s reformation hymns.

Nineteen sixty-four was both a banner and a catastrophic year for the Movement and for American civil religion. The Council of Federated Organizations (COFO) in Mississippi, an umbrella organization of SNCC, CORE, NAACP, and SCLC, constituted an Ecumenical Council in 1962. Reacting to racist oppression, the council withstood the "storms" and resolved both to show that Blacks wanted to vote and to set up voting practice sessions for disenfranchised Blacks. In the wake of Vatican II (1962-1965), COFO called for *aggiornamento,* for a new wind to blow, and launched Freedom Summer 1964. COFO galvanized forces for implementing its goals to increase Black voter registration; organize freedom schools to teach Mississippi children basic education; set up community centers to assist indigent Blacks legally and medically; and found a legally constituted Freedom Democratic Party to challenge the segregated traditional Mississippi Democratic Party.[8]

A "counterreformation" challenged the activity of the COFO. Three civil rights workers turned up missing less than twenty-four hours after the first northern college recruits came to Mississippi to begin the summer project on June 21, 1964. Through an informant, search teams found the bodies of Michael Schwerner, James Chaney, and Andrew Goodman on August 4, 1964, a few miles from Philadelphia, Mississippi. Although local police made arrests in December and subsequently dropped the murder charges, six of the twenty-one suspects finally went to jail in 1967 for violating federal civil rights laws. The violence that exploded in that hot Mississippi summer exploded in a different form at the secular "ecumenical council," the National Democratic Convention, in Atlantic City in August 1964.[9]

Blacks and Whites together established the Mississippi Freedom Democratic Party (MFDP), with a membership of 80,000 by late August 1964. With renewed hope and pride, the MFDP expanded and prepared to attend the national convention and demand to be seated. Fannie Lou Hamer, the epitome of grassroots leadership, had weathered many storms in moving from sharecropper to lobbyist. Hamer testified to the credentials committee on national television and subsequently asked, "If the Freedom Democratic Party is not seated now, I question America. . . . Is this America? The land of the free and the home of the brave?"[10] Infuriated with these televised proceedings, President Lyndon Johnson held a press conference to preempt the live coverage. Johnson successfully used political ploys to control the convention and to halt the seating of the MFDP. Hamer, herself a song leader, never quit. She led the delegation in singing freedom songs on the convention floor, with a sense of purpose and a clear vision for change, for transforming justice:

> One reporter asked Hamer if she was seeking equality with the white man. "No," she said. "What would I look like fighting for equality with the white man? I don't want to go down that low. I want the true democracy that'll raise me and that white man up . . . raise America up."
>
> [We] learned the hard way that even though we had all the law and all the righteousness on our side, that white man is not going to give up his power to us. . . . We had to build our own power.[11]

In 1964, Muhammad Ali became the world heavyweight champion in February. Malcolm X returned from a hajj, a pilgrimage to Mecca, in April. Lyndon Johnson signed a civil rights bill on July 2. Riots occurred that summer in Chicago, New Jersey, New York, and Philadelphia. Martin Luther King, Jr. received the Nobel Prize on December 10. These stormy events heightened African-American visibility, permeated the very souls of the song leaders, colored their tones, and intensified their fervor. They shook loose the cobwebs of feigned democracy to reveal closets of hegemonic racism and patriarchy, and set the stage for the 1964 Atlanta workshop.

Song leader Johnson Reagon led freedom songs throughout the country.[12] Having grown up singing songs of love and resistance, she knew that people could announce and transform their existence by singing. Freedom songs captured the practical, everyday African-American cosmology and gave the singers time to tell their story. The songs were part of a cultural experience that became sacred in the moment. The culture "empowers you as a unity in the universe and places you and makes you know you are a child of the universe."[13]

In unmasking the context, "I've Been in the Storm" moves the individual and the community and helps them to appreciate their own magnificence. Despite the reprehensible duress experienced by people of a different race, sex, and class orientation, people survive and people change. In a storm, a fragile spirit diminishes; a personal, communal, God-centered spirit survives with dignity and can speak peace to other sufferers. The fragile spirit emerges as the person paralyzed—the oppressed or the oppressor. In "I've Been in the Storm," pathos celebrates differences between oppressed and oppressors; opens them both to healing, offers to the oppressed the ability to forgive the oppressors, and to the oppressors, the ability to forgive themselves; and creates an environment where the disruption presses both to employ a "hermeneutic of otherness and engagement."[14] In bicultural societies, the "other" (the less socially and culturally powerful) cannot escape the paradoxical alienation that comes of being in both worlds and being in neither.[15] Racial arrogance allows Whites with societal dominance to exaggerate their own worth and to put stereotypes and xenophobia or exaggerated fear into a praxis which denies Blacks respect. "I've Been in the Storm" is a critique of such individual or communal narcissism and recognizes the "we-ness," the similarities of human existence "in the storm," as an opportunity to overcome racial arrogance. In African-American culture, "I" refers to the individual and the community, the "we." Blacks understand that all African Americans have experienced some facet of racism. Hearing "I've Been in the Storm" from a context of "engaging" is an opportunity to know the "other" Black or White self, in humility and empathy, to know and see the other, and to hear new stories and old stories in new ways.

Johnson Reagon sang "I've Been in the Storm" during the 1964 Atlanta National Song Leaders' Workshop as she stated the great cost of the struggle, for the storms of racism rained down massive oppression, death, and injustice. "I've Been in the Storm" rehearsed the cruelties of domination and served as a prelude for change, for new opportunities for oppressed and oppressor "to act justly and to love mercy and to walk humbly with [their] God" (Mi 6:8b, NIV). This was an opportunity to cause change, transcending bad with good, and uplifting desire. In 1964, the Movement included members across the boundaries of race, gender, and class, although much of the social, historical, and cultural scholarship did not adequately address this participation or the ramifications of oppression beyond race. The Movement seeded future movements against injustices known by other oppressed peoples. "I've Been in the Storm" codified that common bond.

This Spiritual embraced and addressed all listeners as children, honored prior liberation seekers as mother, and acknowledged governmental and religious powers as elder. Johnson Reagon, as soloist, brings a poignancy and a passion to this song that do not often occur with group singing. Her singing as one, however, represented the collective experience. When she sang, "With a hung-down head and an aching heart," she exposed and symbolized the pains of oppression and change. "A little time to pray" evoked special, nurturing conversations with God with the hope that those who had been through storms would not be in jeopardy always and that they could make a difference. Justice, peace, and equality were the premier desires for all those singing "I've Been in the Storm." The confluence of the Movement and the antiwar protests, of the many song leaders and justice seekers, created a fusion of optimism for a better world.

Story

When Johnson Reagon sings the story of "I've Been in the Storm," the energy created is like a great agitation, shuddering with spasms of the crisis and violence spawned by the racism that has shaped social and cultural history in the United States. The storm embodied rage and multilevel assaults on African-American personhood. Storms are natural phenomena that have beginnings and endings. Racism, as assault, began at some point, given that no one is born racist. The physical properties of circular motion and completed cycles implied that the storms of racism could recur, lessen in intensity, or end. Thus, protest, legal changes, and familiarity could help end racism. In the social, cultural, and performance context of "I've Been in the Storm," storms involved the daily rain of Jim Crow, the lightning of burning crosses and lynchings, the thunderous noises that claimed that equality could not happen, and the motion where Blacks progressed too fast. These elements paralleled the combative forces of denial and subjugation used to manipulate people. Conversely, a lone singer, with passion and fortitude, could become a tornado that could help wipe out cancerous, crippling racism. And the rainbows that follow storms signify the ongoing ray of hope. Hope and despair have been a familiar dialectical companion to the African-American experience.

The actual performance of "I've Been in the Storm" by Johnson Reagon, one who embodies the courage and commitment to empowerment indicative of Womanist thought, was moving. Using her powerful voice, Johnson Reagon's performance invited the audience to dare to dream of self-actualization and to participate with her in an earthy, robust, magnetic fashion. She argues that singing is important in doing justice because:

the community is healthiest when it sings. Singing is the process of creating a communal voice. And from the day I was born, I knew we had come together when there was singing. There were not always social justice campaigns when that happened. African-American culture uses singing to express unity. . . . I sing in mixed company—where everybody is not African American—to get people to try and experience that announcement that we are all in the same place. . . . I think I make people feel that if they don't sing they are going to die. They don't feel there's a choice. I build a space that makes people feel very bad if they decide they don't want to sing.[16]

"I've Been in the Storm" embodied the opportunity to envision change, to create new spaces, to experience metamorphosed life. Lighthouses pointed the way within the turbulence toward the need for conversion. Conversion helped one face the ambiguity of the calm before the storm, survive the storm's inherent chaos, and have a willingness to change, having "considered suicide when the rainbow is enuf,"[17] thus celebrating life despite experiencing injustice. Weathering the storm meant combating the hopelessness or nihilism that closed the human organism and prohibited one from experiencing the joy often found in Black religious communal traditions. Overcoming nihilism involves personal, political, and religious conversion. Personal conversion means experiencing the love of another who is strong enough to persuade one to move from a nihilistic to a meaningful mode. Political conversion engages a cause or ideology that supports the shift to meaningfulness. Religious conversion involves any faith that persuades one to avoid nihilistic traps, including destructive habits, for there are strong reasons to live and serve.[18] When Johnson Reagon sings "I've Been in the Storm," conversions happen.

For Johnson Reagon, the Movement was a conversion experience. She had "been in the storm." Her voice changed and became more powerful as she sang to protest. The Movement and her "participation in it [were] the most dramatic internal and external change in [her] life."[19] Her engagement in this spiritual, physical, emotional, and intellectual conversion process allowed Reagon to know the dialectic of freedom and oppression, and that of despair and hope, which permeated the "storms of life." Singing moved the Movement; singing moved her. Her singing echoed the curse of the storm's tempest and the blessing or gift of the hope of being transformed, admitting the past without becoming bitter or entrapped. "I've Been in the Storm" reminds us of what happens when we become stagnant or make ourselves into gods. Within an African-American oral tradition, one learns that only God can be a god; when the self becomes a god, destruction soon follows. "I've Been in the Storm," in sound, shows the fury of destruction but the possibility and the implications of changing weather that help us move toward an optimistic attitude that empowers.

"I've Been in the Storm" celebrates the survivor who knows that "weeping may remain for a night, / but rejoicing comes in the morning" (Ps 30:5b, NIV). Sharing the story of being in the world as victim of the storm creates solidarity and faith that the storm will not continue forever. "I've Been in the Storm" does not rely on direct biblical witness, but several passages share a similar scenario that includes key elements of storm or excessive waters, in some instances the point of contact with God, and a focus on prayer. The following passages could not help but color Johnson Reagon's singing of this Spiritual: Genesis 6-9; Job 38:1; Psalm 32:6-7; 46:1-4, 6; 107:29; and Mark 4:37-40.

Genesis 6-9 recites the story of Noah's salvation that portrays God's redemption for God's children, set in the midst of a flood. At the end of the ordeal, God sets a rainbow in the heavens as a sign of a covenant with Noah and humankind. The interest in Noah's flood story focuses not so much on the destruction as on the covenantal rainbow that occurs after the storm. Job 38:1 is a theophany, God's first discourse with Job, set within a storm. Psalm 32, a wisdom psalm, addresses God as a confession and is intended for the ears of the worshipping community. Here the mighty waters portray threatening circumstances or forces. Psalm 46, a Zion psalm, also relates to raging waters that intimate a storm, while using language concerned with political and social upheaval. This victory hymn focuses on many of the same themes as "I've Been in the Storm": a people's firm trust in God, asserting God's protection, and ascribing ultimate victory to God. Psalm 107, a community thanksgiving psalm, exhorts one to praise God, and includes how God delivers from the problems of the sea. In Mark 4, Jesus calms the storm at sea and questions his disciples concerning their faith.

These passages qualify various aspects of a storm. Storms are historical and sometimes end with good news and/or positive results. Storms also portray an event where God communicates deliverance, a time of prayer. At other times, storms destroy. Destruction may cause ambiguity or death. For the Israelites, God accompanied and provided for them through natural events; or God could choose to punish them through natural events, because God wanted to bring them back into right relationship, back into covenant, after they had strayed so far away. For the slaves and for the freedom fighters, for Johnson Reagon, God spoke to the storm, calling for peace. "I've Been in the Storm" was the life of protesters, of song leaders, of the Movement.

As the Movement spread, Highlander and other organizations and individuals set up programs and workshops to educate and inform through music. During the 1960s, both the Movement and the nuclear disarmament/antiwar groups used music to record feelings and to inspire citizens to protest.[20] The civil rights struggle embraced a congregational style, and the antiwar effort employed a highly individualistic, performance-oriented style.[21] Johnson Reagon also sang "I've Been in the Storm" at the Sing for Freedom Workshop in Atlanta, sponsored by SNCC, SCLC, and Highlander. Organizers extended invitations to singers from the many powerful singing movements,[22] some older traditional southern artists, and a small conclave of northern singer-songwriters.[23] "I've Been in the Storm" celebrated the solidarity evinced at such workshops and the efforts of empowerment on the local level; the song is an experience of theodicy that takes strength from God and finds God in others, which establishes relationships out of love and responsibility.

"I've Been in the Storm" told the story of societal relationships and pressed the civil rights community to grow and stay with the Movement. Protesters stayed in touch with the magnitude of current events and maintained hope without succumbing to self-pity. Singing "I've Been in the Storm" challenged them to keep their "eyes on the prize":

> *"Keep Your Eyes on the Prize"*
>
> *Paul and Silas, bound in jail,*
> *Had no money for to go their bail.*
> *Keep your eyes on the prize, hold on, hold on.*
> *Hold on, hold on,*
> *Keep your eyes on the prize,*
> *Hold on, hold on.*
>
> *Freedom's name is mighty sweet,*
> *Soon one day we're gonna meet. . . .*
> *Got my hand on the gospel plow,*
> *I wouldn't take nothing for my journey now. . . .*
>
> *The only chain that a man can stand,*
> *Is that chain of hand in hand. . . .*
> *The only thing we did wrong,*
> *Stayed in the wilderness a day too long. . . .*
>
> *But the one thing we did right,*
> *Was the day we started to fight. . . .*
> *We're gonna board that big Greyhound,*
> *Carryin' love from town to town. . . .*
>
> *We're gonna ride for civil rights,*
> *We're gonna ride both Black and White. . . .*
> *We've met jail and violence too,*
> *But God's love has seen us through. . . .*
> *Haven't been to heaven but I've been told,*
> *Streets up there are paved with gold. . . .[24]*

The motif "eyes on the prize" is a governing statement about thematic developments that works as a beacon during the storm. People "hold on" and strive for "sweet" freedom within the tempest, symbolized in "Keep Your Eyes on the Prize" as journey, chains, wilderness, Greyhound (interstate commerce), jail, and heaven. Such language gestures help create a vital, living text. Singing "I've Been in the Storm" recreates a living text that has universal and regional meaning. This freedom song caused one to reflect and had a cathartic effect.

Johnson Reagon's performance of "I've Been in the Storm" was an opportunity for personal and communal assessment and growth, to "press on to take hold of that for which Christ Jesus took hold of [them]" (Phil 3:12, NIV). "I've Been in the Storm" reminded all of the gravity of the events of the 1960s—the potential for change and the horror if things remained the same. American civil religion, underlying the American public mind, had not yet sanctioned the civil rights given by the Thirteenth, Fourteenth, and Fifteenth Amendments. As a national song leader, Johnson Reagon sang of a movement under God; she knew that Blacks must begin to tell their own story, write their own lectures, paint their own pictures, chisel their own busts, and acknowledge and love their own peculiarities.[25]

Creative Spirit

The "naming" phase of creative spirit in freedom songs such as "I've Been in the Storm" highlights the fight against racial injustice because of the singers' grounding "in the fertile and fructifying musical traditions" of African-American culture.[26] This song informed and inspired people, telling them that they had choice and could withstand storms, though storms were more intense when people permitted circumstances to make them victims. "I've Been in the Storm" implied the awesome beauty and malevolence in nature, and that the eye of the hurricane is calm, albeit outside this eye chaos reigns. Being in the storm was a moment to claim space, to discover unknown strengths as one related to God. Prayer time with God created a hopeful imagination, a conduit for change. Rains brought new life; raging elements paralleled the fury within humanity. The activists recognized the inappropriateness of racism, saw the rage, found an appropriate release, and could move toward health and wholeness. The storm symbolized the interaction between text and music, as they both relentlessly focused on "give me more time to pray" and "I've been in the storm so long." Intimate concerns connected with trusting God and hoping for a better life emerged within time and existence, as the soul force encapsulated underneath "I've Been in the Storm" relayed personal needs and a desire for relationship.[27] Two melodies available from the sacred repertoire for this song have different styles but equally support the sentiment of the words in different ways. The redacted version has a ballad like schematic, sung poignantly with full, contralto-alto voice. The optional tune is hymnlike, sung slowly in a quasi-lined-out sense with embellishments and many intricate rhythmic patterns.[28]

The tempo, improvisation, repetition, vocality, and use of the D minor in "I've Been in the Storm" create an arresting mood. Johnson Reagon employs a slow, passionate tempo that emphasizes the key words "storm," "long," "children," "pray," "mother," "elder," and "heart." Johnson Reagon sustains and/or embellishes particular notes to communicate her angst and her trust that "a new day is coming." The tempo creates the aura of a prayerful lullaby that offers comfort. Her improvisations incorporate grace notes and blue notes, extended slurred phrases, and rubato, where she arbitrarily lengthens or shortens a note, "inviting" one to recall similar experiences and to establish relationships. Her fluctuation of speed within a musical phrase and her sustaining a note beyond its full value enable her to give additional emphasis to the pain and suffering of racism. She "works with" and sculpts each note. Musical and lyrical texts complement each other by her use of repetition.

The repetition hammers out the dynamics of the storm: the threats to life, the opportunity for choice, and the hope for change. The storm also personifies the issue of theodicy, the meeting of divine benevolence and human suffering. The first three lines of chorus that repeat "I've been in the storm so long" begin with ascending leaps that denote straightforwardness; and lines 1 and 4 of the verse begin with another leap that registers a sense of clarity and immediacy. Lines 2 and 5 of the verses are the same: "Oh (Lord), give me a little time to pray." The rest of the musical line expresses a sense of intimacy, contemplation, and anticipation. The intimacy that Johnson Reagon, as a song leader, creates echoes the proximity of and contingency between organisms and forces within nature. She articulates the improvisation and the repetition with elegant, burning artistry.

That artistry comes out of shared pain, the power in her voice, and the power in the song amid reflection and inspiration, the point where one can probe the performance style. The song leader musical style of "I've Been in the Storm" symbolized the singing Movement, where the leaders used Spirituals and other freedom songs as products of a national culture, to inspire and educate.[29] Song leading was a communicative tool. Performing music was not about self-aggrandizement and acclaim. Soloists became song leaders to strengthen and intensify the listener's mood or emotion, to focus on contemporary freedom culture, to reclaim the African-American past, to sponsor local folk festivals, and to explore the use of older cultural traditions in modern struggles.[30] The workshops tapped into the psychic energies of the Black music tradition to promote the survival of oppressed people and the definition and survival of their music.[31] A respect for tradition and the welcome gifts of new voices were a function of a creative, spirited worldview. "I've Been in the Storm" breathed life and hope into social discourse when much tragedy filled the air. The song leading workshops affirmed mutuality and a balanced social sense of being with an inclusive spirit. The penetrating, cellolike rendition by Johnson Reagon was a liturgical witness to the possibility of personal and social conversion and a tribute to those martyred for justice and solidarity.

The liturgical witness sprang forth from the concept of a storm's accompanying rain, thunder, lightning, hail, and winds. Johnson Reagon's interpretation of the vast nature of storms suggests that life is not fair. After all, God "causes [the] sun to rise on the evil and the good, and sends rain on the righteous and the unrighteous" (Mt 5:45b, NIV). These options for growth and decay invite an ethical, eschatological vision of immediacy, a vision that fixes a vocabulary based on a hermeneutics of curiosity and adventure. Johnson Reagon sings to let us hear the voices of new encounters that require an interest in history and a willingness to hear new voices, augmenting our ability to hear our own expanding voice. Black musicians learned that vocal and instrumental artistry made them powerful and allowed them to communicate, to signify. Black music, a product of creativity and improvisation, exhibited rhythmic and tonal examples of structured freedom. By signifying, Johnson Reagon embraced the dynamic and explosive powers of Black music that moved people toward spiritual liberation.[32] Part of that liberation, a sense of classical humor, occurs in "I've Been in the Storm" as absurdity: the activists sing about being in a storm (racism) in meetings about combating the storms of racism (for freedom and equality), yet their own protests (nonviolent direct action) place them in the eye of life-threatening storms. They get out of one storm by creating a second storm. In George Gershwin's opera *Porgy and Bess*, a climatic motif is provided by the hurricane that symbolizes humanity's powerlessness.

The key repeated terms of "I" (subject), "been" (verb), "storm" (object), "to pray" (infinitive), and "so long" or "along" (adverb) create a scenario that talks about oppression. As Reagon sings, her "I" becomes "we," because the music breaks down everyday barriers and invites people in. Through her passion and artistry, Reagon enlivens the text, and the words take on a life of their own. In the human voice, some of the lowest tones evoke a restless urgency pregnant with ideas waiting to be born. The middle register has a mellow, calm sense of comfort. Higher tones create suspense, drama, or awareness as these notes above the tonic want to resolve down to the tonic. Johnson Reagon's performance has a mellow, haunting, and dramatic character of urgency as she recreates her experience for others.

Movement activists identify with the length of the storm and recall sit-ins, freedom rides, and marches where the storms of verbal abuse and physical assault threatened life. The storms often brought rains of death. Each time one sang "I've Been in the Storm," a revision of the living text occurred— the storm incarnated the most recent collective and personal events of act and being. The response to these storms lay amid the literary texts, shaped by the musical texts, that raised questions about life and vision.

The music of "I've Been in the Storm" reiterates the tempestuousness of the storms of life and racism, impresses the memory of historical events, and triggers questions about freedom and oppression: What kinds of meteorological as well as metaphorical storms has the reader/listener experienced? Was the encounter destructive? Did the storm occur at a critical moment in the listener's life? How did the people listening to "I've Been in the Storm" react? Was the performed song a source of comfort or a stimulus? What is the nature of storms that makes them a helpful resource for thinking about freedom? Do the properties of storms tend to generate a fatalistic view of life? How does singing/hearing "I've Been in the Storm" empower? How a person approaches and answers these questions affects the dynamics of theodicy and relates to how we view faith and thought.

Faith and Thought

Questioning thought and faith in Spirituals like "I've Been in the Storm" calls for one to embrace the prayers and yearnings of slave bards.[33] The songsters' concerns with freedom and life framed their makeup as religious and God-fearing people. The African-American eschatology operated out of "a rhythm and vision of life" where "life itself is pervaded with religion and religion is infused with music." [34] According to cultural observers, even those African Americans who had no particular ties to the institutional church had a sense that "God is on our side" and thus tied their liberation struggle to an idea of God. "I've Been in the Storm" relies on the idea of a religious conviction to withstand and transcend the storms of life in a gospel song by Charles Albert Tindley (1851-1933):

"Stand by Me"

When the storms of life are raging, stand by me;
When the storms of life are raging, stand by me;
When the world is tossing me,
Like a ship upon the sea;
Thou who rulest wind and water, stand by me.[35]

"I've Been in the Storm" identifies the human as one who suffers yet who resists suffering as the sole agent for shaping his or her spirit. The one who suffers does not suffer alone. When Johnson Reagon sings "I've Been in the Storm," a chanted prayer for the people, she calls for a word of assurance by asking for "time to pray." By addressing the children, the mother, and the elder, she reminds us of the freedom to go through the storm, since we all have been through storms before. The storm is a time of assessment and planning. A concern for communication with God and for being a responsible member of the community and the church (implied by addressing an elder) underlies the formation of an ethic that nurtures

survival and coexistence, and a theodic vision that comes after the storm—
the rainbow.

The rainbow signifies change and symbolizes conversion and transformation. "I've Been in the Storm" implies that conversion experiences helped
to expose evil and appropriate rage, for the transformed eye differentiates
good and evil and becomes sensitive to injustice. Singing "I've Been in the
Storm" and other freedom songs in the 1960s Movement was a process of
searching for truth and community through traditional and contemporary
songs.[36] These songs provided a creative channel for the rage commensurate with years of oppression, and afforded an opportunity to discover a
larger unity and an inclusive experience of social order within a creative,
cultural art form. As Johnson Reagon sang, the creative phase first embraced the moment of origin, then the communication of artistry, across
the space between her and the receptive public mind.[37] Music, apropos for
communicating the experience of human "storms," nourishes internal life,
ministers aesthetically, and has a spiritual, almost baptismal effect, symbolizing healing and renewal.[38]

This healing effect permeated both the traditional and redacted versions of "I've Been in the Storm" in the desire to understand and then transcend some of the unnecessary pains of life. Both versions claimed relationships among the protagonist(s), society, and God. Both versions share
the pains of living in the storm, which causes one to have "a hung-down
head," "an aching heart," and a desire that the Lord "give me a little time to
pray." The lack of specific persons, places, or events relevant to the Movement in the redacted text does not lessen the impact of "I've Been in the
Storm." The "storm" can serve as a metaphor for experiencing personal
and social limits. These limits, coupled with an exercise in faith and hope,
open up new fields for transformation in and beyond time. The activists
were a part of, but were not the storm itself. They saw the dualities of the
present as an opportunity for empowerment instead of victimization.

Revealing or unmasking the dynamics of power and empowerment in
"I've Been in the Storm" takes us back to the 1964 Atlanta Song Leading
Workshop that invigorated and inspired people to continue to protest lo-
cally and nationally through 1965. The ideas about faith and thought in
"I've Been in the Storm" cause one to recall that the 1964-65 Selma protest
required that the United States Army escort the marchers on the Selma-to-
Montgomery, Alabama, march. Nonviolent direct action was still the heart
of the Movement's strategy and song, even though riots and rebellion raged
in Watts. Some activists wrote songs to reflect the discontent that led to
the angst of Detroit, Chicago, and Watts.[39] "I've Been in the Storm" recognized the anxiety and the nonviolent protest that exploded across the nation, and anticipated the upcoming Black power movement.

In the wake of disruption, people continued to sing "I've Been in the
Storm," reflecting the restless climate. While the storms of life raged, the
liberating Lord was with the oppressed. The Lord who could "give me a

little time to pray" was the Lord Black people knew as a friend and sustainer in the middle of the storm. The redaction did not lessen the power and beauty of the Spiritual. Such longevity is a testament to African Americans' spiritual and religious basis. A balanced view of the strengths and weaknesses of the storm is an invitation to appreciate the struggles that human beings face. In "I've Been in the Storm," an individual can be the subject "I"; implicitly, when pathologically anxious, one becomes the storm. A Christian reading provides the ability to march and protest with diverse others and an ability to love, to become "the neighbor" (see Lv 19:18; Mt 19:19; Gal 5:14). Being the neighbor set in music is theomusicological dialogue, which concerns the power dynamic between those involved in relationships.

The differences of people within relationships are part of the storm ultimately signified by the rainbow. "I've Been in the Storm" celebrates being a part of and acting ethically and consciously within the rainbow. The "storm" implies that many world events and forces are larger than one human being's experiences. Yet, the magnitude of the storm does not discount the value of every human being. Souls lost in the storm matter. "I've Been in the Storm" acknowledges the difficulty of being "I" amid the winds of change in the storm. Being "I" was to be responsible, to act, amid the spectrums of survival and fear, triumph and certainty, ambiguity and mystery. Johnson Reagon knew that all these storms were part of everyone's world and knew these storms herself while protesting in Albany, on the streets, and behind jail doors. Did "storms" leave an imprint for change on community in the 1960s?

A divine word and human cooperation offer a possibility for change and renewal. Again, the communication of double entendres in the texts and the perspective of a singer/hearer affected one's interpretation. The slave bards knew they could not openly state their desires. Many times they rationalized their plight and then sang and prayed for the opposite of what they really wanted to be or do.[40] Sometimes slaves used coded language and inference to share their outlook, just as "storm" in the Spiritual usually pertains to rough life situations. Racists set the boundaries in the lives of the oppressed and shaped, to a large extent, how and where Blacks lived, worked, and played. Did the "storms" effect change? In retrospect, some answer "No!"; others answer "Yes, but not enough!":

> For the consciousness to make a difference, it has to exist in song. Songs carry so much of historical, analytical, philosophical perspectives of African-American legacy. There is so much we know about the nineteenth century because of the songs that were passed from one generation to the next. If you take a song like "I got shoes, you got shoes, all God's children got shoes; when I get to heaven gonna put on my shoes, gonna walk all over God's heaven"—you take a political

analysis of this present, [and] everybody talk about heaven ain't going to heaven. . . . just what that song conveys to you. . . . Sometimes I'm singing that song and sometimes I think about the fact of life that people who sang the song didn't have no shoes, right? And it has taken my survival to make that true for them. . . . They knew that what you got I got. We are not talking about a difference here. And even if I ain't got it right now, I got it. There is a leveling. That song is one that I think of when I try to think of concepts of justice that really stretch you because you have to go on more than immediate evidence to understand what is being said.[41]

Womanists argue that when viewing, guarding against, and fighting "storms," these storms pertain to race, gender, and class issues, issues that segregate, denigrate, humiliate, and make someone(s) other. For us to sing a Spiritual about storms asks: When did we open our doors on a stormy night to one in need? When did we take a stand in the middle of a storm to call a halt to oppression? When have we broached a storm where we insisted on being a neighbor to someone deemed other in our own culture? Have we said "No!" to the lie of oppression when people punish, humiliate, or denigrate because of alleged or apparent differences? To sing a Spiritual about shoes calls us to ponder: When did we walk in someone else's shoes? When did we buy shoes for someone else who needed a pair? Have we walked in our shoes in a way that would invite someone else to one day walk in our shoes? For Womanist scholars, no matter which Spiritual we sing or live, we must follow the adage of Sweet Honey in the Rock, who sing, "We who believe in freedom cannot rest." Johnson Reagon preaches and teaches and lives her pedagogy and ministry of social justice, the call for Womanists. In her travels, Johnson Reagon sang with Fannie Lou Hamer many times, and built up years of experience of community empowerment.[42] The Movement helped her challenge any limiting boundaries, and she evolved into an awesome spirit, activist, researcher, curator, writer, historian, musician—a majestic personality with a strong social, political, and economic consciousness, who works to provide new spaces for people to live and act in new ways.[43]

"Walk with Me, Lord"

"Walk with Me, Lord," sung by song leader Fannie Lou Hamer, proclaims a theodicy where people closely associate personal and communal well-being in their walk with Jesus. Hamer sings this prayerful confession a cappella, in G or A minor, as members of the congregation intermittently join in. The straightforward presentation symbolizes the clarity of their mission, to gain freedom. Things can change when Lord Jesus walks with me and befriends me (meaning us) on this tedious journey.

Context

"Walk with Me, Lord," both lullaby and call to action, says that "I am in the process of participating in my own liberation!" Hamer's comforting, unhurried ease soothes the anxiety that accompanies oppression and takes seriously the feelings of those often deemed other. As a call to action, "Walk with Me, Lord" strikes a sobering note, that regardless of my great ideas, I cannot do it alone. But when many "I's" become "we" and when we look to spiritual empowerment, we can make a difference. Neither I nor we are victims; we are pilgrims on a journey.

"Walk with Me, Lord" has a chorus and three strophic verses of four lines. In the verse, the first line repeats, followed by a conditional clause ("When") with the last line of resolution that restates, "I want Jesus to walk with me," the first two lines of the chorus. Stylistically and musically, the verse and chorus are the same. The textual structure of the verse and chorus involves the repetitive rhyme scheme *aaba*. The melodic structure supports the text with a slight modification: *aa'bb'*. Hamer sang this version of "Walk with Me, Lord" in Hattiesburg, Mississippi, in February 1964. This song was sung often at mass meetings. The traditional musical source includes the following verses:

> *I want Jesus to walk with me,*
> *I want Jesus to walk with me,*
> *All along my pilgrim journey*
> *I want Jesus to walk with me.*

> *In my trials, Lord, walk with me, walk with me, [2x]*
> *When the shades of life are falling,*
> *Lord, I want Jesus to walk with me.*

> *In my sorrows, walk with me, walk with me, [2x]*
> *When my heart is almost breaking [or] within is aching,*
> *Lord, I want Jesus to walk with me.*

> *In my troubles, walk with me, [2x]*
> *When my life becomes a burden,*
> *Lord, I want Jesus to walk with me.*

The traditional setting hinges on the power that comes when a friend, especially a supernatural, walks with someone. The repetitive use of "walk with me" assures that the singer conveys the message, "I want Jesus to walk with, be with, and befriend me as I go through life knowing joy, sorrow, pain, suffering, trouble, aging, and burdens." The ability to ask someone to walk with you establishes the presence of self-worth, self-esteem, and community unity. The text arranged and sung by Hamer included the following words:

> *Walk with me now, Lord, walk with me*
> *While I'm on this tedious journey*
> *I want Jesus to walk with me.*

> *Be my friend now, Lord, be my friend*
> *Be my friend now, Lord, be my friend*
> *While I'm on this tedious journey*
> *I want Jesus to walk with me.*

> *Make a way for me now, Lord, make a way for me*
> *Make a way for me now, Lord, make a way for me*
> *While I'm on this tedious journey*
> *I want Jesus to walk with me.*

The redacted version of "Walk with Me, Lord" pushed the freedom fighters to keep going, to commit to the struggle, and to befriend others who were like-minded. Hamer and others sang this song throughout the South and across the nation as they engaged in nonviolent direct protest, voter registration, and school desegregation rallies. The 1960s were a time of change, a time of epiphany, a time of waiting and then moving on to experience the advent of a new day.

Hamer, a civil rights activist and sharecropper, wanted a new day because she was "sick and tired of being sick and tired," her epitaph echoing the exhaustion, weariness, and frustrations of Black Mississippians in their justice quest. She believed that everyone should work until all people could live in America, and she became active in the Movement in 1963. In 1964, Hamer and other Black Mississippians ran for the U.S. Congress, a first since reconstruction. She extolled, "Is this America?" that year before the Democratic Party credentials committee. She challenged America to deal with its ongoing hatred, hypocrisy, bigotry, intolerance, and racism. Despite persecution, death threats, the arrest and job loss of her husband and daughter, and brutal beatings for three days that left her with permanent damage, Hamer kept on protesting and inspiring people with her voice.[44] Despite the finagling and compromising maneuver by President Johnson, Walter Mondale, and Hubert Humphrey, the MFDP rejected the compromise which would have seated only two MFDP members. Hamer led the MFDP delegation in singing freedom songs on the convention floor.[45] Even King was a behind-the-scenes culprit, seeking to placate MFDP members. Though disillusioned, this invincible woman showed the country that knowledge, wisdom, and organization skills did not come with academic degrees. As Hamer stated, "Whether you have a Ph.D., D.D., or no D., we're in this bag together."[46]

The new day stood in contrast with the past and the present. For slaves and for freedom fighters, the past and the present meant subjugation, repression, dismissal. African Americans knew the experience of being objectified, restricted, and ignored. Hamer knew these restrictions and instead sang "Walk with Me, Lord" to affirm the spoken and the unspoken. In oppressive situations, Hamer, symbolizing all Black folk, knew what it was like to have tedious journeys in all walks of life, to be betrayed, and to have stumbling blocks put in the way. And she knew that Jesus, as Liberator, could offer possibilities of companionship and eternal friendship; that Jesus could make a way out of no way; and that other believers could band together so that many people, Blacks and Whites, old and young, could walk together to help relieve the world of so much oppression. The oppression had become so ritualized within American civil religious practices of obeisance to Whiteness and negligence to Blackness as a part of daily life, that many did not, could not, see the blatant injustice. "Walk with Me, Lord" was one of Hamer's songs that offered a wake-up call to such idolatry and disregard while confronting the pathos and arrogance of oppression.

Hamer sang "Walk with Me, Lord" as a challenge to the White arrogance of making other Black folks invisible, of forgetting, of thinking only about issues related to those who thought, looked, or acted like them. This Spiritual also challenges the arrogance of Black or White self-doubt as well as egoism, of extreme individualism, and of being too self-sacrificing. "Walk with Me, Lord" reveals and debunks a pathos that thinks that "everyone else is better than me" and that "I don't deserve" to walk, to know respect, to have access to complete U.S. citizenship. Hearing the history of Hattiesburg and of the United States in "Walk with Me, Lord" exposes the arrogance and pathos of racism, sexism, classism, and all "isms" that destroy the health and well-being of the body politic, and allows one to move toward a transformed life for self and the community. In "Walk with Me, Lord," the oppressed desire both a walk with the Lord and all the rights and privileges that that walk symbolizes: the freedom to move, to accomplish, to be, to express, and to be in relationship. The oppressor already has these options, and the tension arises in determining how these experiences can be made available to those held inferior without actually or perceptually threatening the status of the oppressor, the problem of some affirmative action programs. Hamer knew this, and she wanted all America to know the same. Given that often the oppressor still wanted to scapegoat the oppressed, Hamer's singing implied another underlying question: Can mutuality and equality exist in a capitalistic economy, where apparently the system depends on a hierarchy of haves and have-nots? "Walk with Me, Lord" reflects the ongoing pressures of attaining equality and balance in the statement "While I'm on this tedious journey." The last word, however, is not the tedium but the invitation to Jesus to "walk with me."

Story

The story impressions of the redacted or edited "Walk with Me, Lord" set out an expectation of change in the present and the immediate future. Using the imperative verb form, the singers command that the Lord walk with, befriend, or make a way for them (me) *now,* and in the future, which effects change now and later. Hamer wanted change in the present, not when she got older or when she died. Making a command assumes authority and a relationship that can and will bear out that authority. In the traditional version of "Walk with Me, Lord," an emotional context ("In my sorrows") and a desire for support ("Lord, walk with me") precede the command ("Walk with me"), and a fleshing out of the emotional context ("When my heart is almost breaking") follows. The verse closes with a repeat of the desire ("Lord, walk with me"). In some versions, the command ("Walk with me") immediately follows the emotional context ("In my sorrows"). Each phrase begins three musical steps higher; thus, as each line ascends, the intensity of the command, desire, or context increases. Within the ebbs and flows of intensity, the main character appears to be talking singularly about a walk with Jesus and affirms self and the community while making plans to transform everyone. The repetition of "walk with me" signals the practice of speaking and singing through the oral Black tradition of signifying, particularly through the biblical story.

While the slave bards did not rely on any specific texts in toto for "Walk with Me, Lord," several texts that speak about God or Jesus walking pertain here. In the story about humanity making wrong choices, where the created try to become the Creator, God is heard "walking in the garden," after which both the man and the woman attempt to hide from God (Gn 3:8). In a description of what God requires of humanity (Dt 10:12) and in a sermon about justice (Dt 19:9), Moses tells the Hebrew children to walk in the ways of the Lord their God. Jesus walks along the Sea of Galilee at the start of his ministry (Mt 4:18) and walks on the sea (Mt 14:25; Mk 6:48; Jn 6:19).[47] Thus, if God walks in the garden and God's people are to walk in the way of their God, then God walks with all humanity, and they can walk with God. If Jesus walked during his ministry and on the sea, then slaves and freedom fighters surely can walk through and over the sea of injustice toward the land of freedom, of liberation. The metaphor of walking embodies certain movement toward a goal of transforming liberation within an ocean of uncertainty about the exact when and where of change and how the dominant society will act. The certainty of Jesus assuages the anxiety that comes with uncertainty. The past and present certainty of the oppression of dominant Eurocentric society requires a certainty of faith. While the specifics of timing, personnel, and immediate impact remain ambiguous in "Walk with Me, Lord," that change will happen is clear.

"Walk with Me, Lord" celebrated the dignity of all peoples brought about inherently through birth and made sacred by the struggle for change and liberation. Hamer knew intimately her modest beginnings, but she also stood stalwart and backed down to no one in the face of death. Beyond the point of tolerating the despicable, African Americans fighting for freedom and justice could stand beyond the pettiness and absurdity of racism then, and along with sexism and classism now, because this campaign for freedom had divine intent. "Walk with Me, Lord" implied, "accept me as I am; whether I am Black, White, Red, Brown, or Yellow, all are precious in Jesus' sight. I can celebrate my Blackness, and I can celebrate your own reality. I need not change my way of being or acting, because the Lord walks with me."

Creative Spirit

"Walk with Me, Lord" opens with a chorus about a personal and communal relationship of intimacy: "walk with me." The repetitive nature of this particular expression clarifies the beneficiary of any action. With the traditional version, the journey is a pilgrim journey. Though Hamer's version omits the word *pilgrim*, the intent remains. A pilgrim for freedom embarks on a crusade and travels as an evangelist and proselytizer on the campaign for liberation. This is a commitment to confess the story and to tell the story everywhere, that Jesus walks with me and that I am entitled to be free, to experience total salvation.

Hamer sings about this notion of salvation with a sense of humble joy. Hamer, a paradigm of grassroots organizing, of quiet, unpretentious, elegant power, reflects the commitment of countless unnamed others. She sings plaintively, powerfully. Her interpolations, turns, and sustained tones on particular words (e.g., "me-e-e-e," "te-e-e-tchius" [tedious], "Je-e-e-su-uh-us," "wa-a-ay") tell all who hear that this command is not a conditional, fainthearted proposition. The silences that indicate a pause or focus point are brief. Hamer has so much to say, and with such an urgency, that little "time" remains for listener or for the country. The time is now. Like Sojourner Truth before them, both male and female song leaders, as well as other Movement leaders, knew that now was not the time for hesitancy. That sensibility emerges out of Hamer's singing. She sings the dream of a new order, of a Mississippi that no longer turns a blind eye to lynchings and no longer treats its Black citizens like chattel, but of a time and a place where the mighty Mississippi River roars and the magnolias bloom to the tune of peace and justice for all Mississippians.

Hamer's Mississippi version of "Walk with Me, Lord" involves a blending or intertextual use of hymns and stock phrases in the African-American religious oral tradition. The hymn "What a Friend We Have in Jesus," so popular in many Protestant churches, along with the theology of Jesus/God as a way maker and friend to the friendless, and the gospel song "Just a Closer Walk with Thee," would be part of Hamer's belief system and in her repertoire:

"What a Friend We Have in Jesus"

What a friend we have in Jesus,
All our sins and griefs to bear!
What a privilege to carry
Ev'rything to God in prayer!
O what peace we often forfeit,
O what needless pain we bear,
All because we do not carry
Ev'rything to God in prayer.[48]

"Just a Closer Walk with Thee"

Just a closer walk with Thee,
Grant it, Jesus, if you please,
Daily walking close with Thee,
Let it be, dear Lord, let it be.

I am weak but Thou art strong,
Jesus, keep me from all wrong,
I'll be satisfied as long,
as I walk, let me walk close with Thee.

Through this world of toils and snares,
If I falter, Lord, who cares?
Who with me my burdens shares?
None but Thee, dear Lord, none but Thee.

When my feeble life is o'er,
Time for me won't be no more,
Guide me gently, safely o'er,
To Thy kingdom's shore, to Thy shore.[49]

"Walk with Me, Lord," sung in 4/4 time at a moderate tempo, exudes faith and confidence. As members of the congregation sporadically join in with the soloist, they do so with ease, like an accompaniment. The 4/4 time echoes the easy pace of one walking along with Jesus, a prime motivation. Hamer's powerful presence puts everyone in the right frame of mind to receive the inspiration, then to go out and work for the cause. "Walk with Me, Lord" is not a song about being victim or about being resigned to suffering. The words and music of this Spiritual focus on "me," which simultaneously refers to the self and the community, being in partnership with Jesus, the one who cares, to end hate, discrimination, and segregation. Set in a minor key, "Walk with Me, Lord" does not have the brightness or jubilation of praise; nor is this Spiritual about being sad, depressed, and hopeless. The tonality of this Spiritual connotes prayer, lament, and contemplation, forged by hope, about the life-threatening realities of oppression.

The oppression, one catalyst, has not diminished the creativity of Africans in the diaspora. Other catalysts include the protesters' African heritage, with a firm belief in God and fueled by their own aesthetic and soulful gifts. In that context, the slaves and freedom fighters want the experience of being treated as a child of God, a human being. This desire stands, as Black folk are Black in a world where some desire their extinction. They stand as believers who love God and appreciate themselves, but they live in a world where too great a sense of self-worth may "get you dead." In order to protect themselves, Black songsters signify so that those who need not know the ramifications of their messages will not know. In maintaining this partial camouflage, "Walk with Me, Lord" pushes one to ask: Lord, how long? Are you walking with us even if we continue to suffer? Will our quest for freedom be one of your miracles, like when you walked on the water? Are we walking the way we need to, the way we ought to? While the questions raged and the whips during antebellum times and the billy clubs during the 1960s cracked heads, the children, God's children, kept on walking, by faith.

> *We've come this far by faith,*
> *Leaning on the Lord;*
> *Trusting in His Holy Word,*
> *He's never failed me yet.*
> *Oh, can't turn around,*
> *We've come this far by faith*
>
> *Don't be discouraged*
> *With trouble in your life*
> *He'll bear your burdens*
> *And move all misery and strife,*
> *That's why we. . . .*[50]

Faith and Thought

Faith rests as a firm foundation undergirding "Walk with Me, Lord." God is the God who cares. Human beings are the created, not the Creator, but that difference does not cause a separation or distance between the two. "Walk with Me, Lord" understands that the wheels of justice sometimes turn slowly. Yet the hope remains for a theodicy that exposes and overcomes feigned superiority by all persons and all oppression, that requires faithful justice, and that, like a mud flower, does "not grow easily . . . is not all bitter . . . [occurs with] time/space to play . . . [may have] a spirit of whimsy . . . [and calls everyone to honor the collectiveness of] our remembering, our naming, our silences, and our speech."[51]

The possibility of such collective living is the work of justice and liberation. God, revealed in Jesus, is one who cares and who desires intimacy. Human beings also want, though on some level may fear, an intimacy that creates *agape* (Christlike love), understanding, support, tolerance when needed, and response that give both oppressed and oppressor an opportunity to change. "Walk with Me, Lord" makes explicit the relationship of intimacy and relates a historical model for how people can and ought to get along. The point is not that one human being ought to worship another individual, but to get human beings engaged in mutual respect and a sense of reciprocity within the larger community, to walk together.

Walking together says "No!" to violence, suffering, and subjugation and says "Yes!" to a system of justice based on the truest sense of honor and respect that can look fear in the eye and say, "I've been there; you do not have to do that." This kind of justice focuses on life as a vital, empowering experience of good, of God. Hamer sang "Walk with Me, Lord" to allow one to make a mistake, to atone, and to live out a transformed life. "Walk with Me, Lord" does not assume a dishonest, romantic, or casual reading of life. This Spiritual, however, roots life in the eternal life of God, here and now—a here and now of freedom that respects differences without having to agree with them. We are to see the differences in the past and recite them; see the differences in the present and acknowledge them; and envision the differences of the future and work now in the hope that we can live peaceably together. Living with those differences now, within and outside African-American communities, calls for an appreciation of Blackness that has many ways of being, acting, and knowing the Spirit in the world.

Knowing the Spirit, the self, and the world involves celebrating the place of our traditional African heritage, as this affects all who live on the planet. The culture and customs of Africa helped shaped these United States and helped mold this song. The song relies on the closeness of God and the communal response to keep it alive. Keeping the message of hope and freedom alive now emerges from "Walk with Me, Lord," particularly in the call to act "now, Lord," to be my friend or to make a way for me. Here the music and the text call for an immediacy not found in deferred or delayed eschatological imagery. The call to walk with and be with Jesus now outlines the call to freedom now and exposes the oppression and the angst of past and present. As the Spiritual affirms the presence of Jesus and the somebodyness of all God's children, including Black children, the song remains liturgical, in praise of the Creator and of a good creation. While the traditional version of "Walk with Me, Lord" reflects more on past events that lead to current dilemmas, the redacted version urgently looks at the present tediousness with the Lord of that good creation.

An awareness of the goodness of creation and of the goodness of the self, despite our Augustinian notions of fallen humanity and the daily evil we see, develops when singing and listening to "Walk with Me, Lord." As the music empowers and inspires, it becomes therapeutic, serving as a thermometer to name the fever of oppression, as a balm to take away the sting of evil, and as a preventative homeopathy, so that when power becomes shared, the formerly oppressed do not need to become oppressor and the former oppressor does not have to become victimized or fear-driven. Hamer's "Walk with Me, Lord" calls for a life where people are willing to deal with the issues (e.g., economics, politics, greed, desire, psychology, sociology, and religion) that perpetuate racism, sexism, and classism. In so doing, this Spiritual calls for a theodicy of inclusion, of community. Such a shared theodicy knows that when one person wins, somehow we all win, making greed and jealousy unnecessary; at the same time when one loses, everyone loses, making it necessary that we all care. Hamer cared, and helped found the Mississippi Freedom Democratic Party (MFDP) to expose the racist practices of the "regular" Democrats and to register as many voters as possible, to foster inclusion. Fervently she exclaimed that summer in Chicago, "If the Democratic Party [MFDP] is not seated now, . . . is this America? The land of the free and the home of the brave? Where . . . our lives [are] threatened daily?"[52] Womanists understand these threats and that to practice "we care" requires change in all social parameters, not just those parameters that deal with race. "We care" goes beyond caring about those with whom we have biological or extended family ties, those we are fond of, or those who can do something for us. "We care" means that I do not have to like you or your views to treat you with common decency. "We care" means that all the blame for the current crisis within the African-American community cannot be levied outside that community. "We care" means that we all must learn about and own up to the many walks taken in the past; that we must live and cooperate so that many can walk to the fullest in the present, without the arrogance of undue sacrifice, martyrdom, or paranoia that do not allow us to live next door to each other; and, that, having so lived, we will leave a hopeful legacy and planet for the glory of God and the well-being of future generations.

PART V

INFERENCE
Our Living Texts

12

Womanist, Transforming Musings

Can we have:
A witness?
A voice of hope?
A call to freedom?
The Spirituals say: "Yes!"
"We can rise, be made new,
Be made whole!"
Sing, sing these old songs:
Live, transform, love.

Spirituals recite history, exude life, and afford transformation. These songs tell a story of the past and the present; they are living African-American "sacred texts,"[1] chants of collective exorcism that become vital in performance, living texts within the participants and the audience, for the singing proclaims and embraces their common story. Spirituals transcend the boundaries of sacred and secular and offer an opportunity to use music to identify, expose, exorcize, reveal, celebrate, and transform these changes in behavior triggered by music that ultimately effects healing of racism and slavery. The story embraces the quest for freedom, equality, and justice of those who desire freedom today, those who died for freedom yesterday, and those yet unborn.

These liturgical songs of reformation bolstered the morale of the freedom-singing integrationists and disarmed hostile segregationists. They were a part of the ongoing praxis of how African Americans used the Spirituals to respond to the evils and sins of peonage and racism then, and which Womanists insist include classism and sexism today. Civil rights protesters knew alienation and powerlessness and thus committed themselves to the Movement, to becoming, to self-survival, and to self-determination.[2] Song was and remains a mode of overcoming and survival. By breaking the ice of fear, music was the most effective way to communicate with many who never had the opportunity to speak out before. In jails, some guards joined in singing freedom songs. Music sprang from the urgent need to provide courage and fortitude to those fighting a nonviolent battle for freedom across the South. The songs and the singing rang true to their desires, hopes, and dreams.[3] The literary texts of these songs were coded, yet they were simple phrases similar to the recurring themes in the Dies Irae, "day of judgment, day of wrath." The musical texts shaping the literary texts enhanced communication, depth, and adaptability. The redacted Spirituals used the thread of theodicy accentuated by the combined music and poetic texts throughout, as a leitmotif extolling a message of liberation. Music made a difference. Music, the activists' palette, stirred their creative imagination to paint melodic, rhythmic, harmonic scenarios of freedom.

These redacted songs helped humanize an impersonal and life-threatening environment.[4] Together, music and words in a sociocultural and political setting of protest became living texts; they were motion and event that created transcendence[5] and combated racism, "the chief profanity of the nation."[6] The redacted freedom songs were variations on a theme of life and freedom, as the singers used improvisatory hums and chants to "bear up," to support their singing, resembling a "liquefying of words."[7] The Spirituals exposed slavery as the pivotal fact of Black history and antislavery as the crucible of African-American rhetorical expression.[8] An exegesis of these Spirituals, then, moves us to the brink of discovery. These complex cultural artifacts hold a wealth of knowledge about the human struggles of being-in-the-world, including the political process that enhances self-knowledge and personal and communal well-being. Even the singing process becomes political, as various usages (or lack thereof) of power exist each time people sing a Spiritual or freedom song, as they champion justice.

As we sing with the true recognition of acknowledging the exposed evil, the power of this racist, sexist, classist evil over an individual can be exorcized, cut out, removed. The process of exorcism brings personal, social, and cultural knowledge, personal and communal well-being, and a time to celebrate new possibilities. Discovery and celebration are the beginnings of transformation and healing, of therapy and enhanced consciousness. Conversely, some Spirituals are dangerous, because, despite their enthusiasm for freedom, we can become so mesmerized by the embodied rituals and the cathartic spiritual and emotional experience that the power and transformative nature of the Spirituals are lost, notwithstanding the fact that slaves created these powerful songs as affirmation, inspiration, and exorcism. The call to social action, moral responsibility, and transformed status is hidden within the signifying of the singers. The Spirituals can effect healing for both the oppressed and the oppressor, if both want, and are willing to work, for change.

Wanting change and being conscious of aesthetic, spiritual power pressed slaves and freedom fighters toward using the Spirituals in their fight for freedom. Both the words and the music signify the import of freedom. The words read alone cannot and do not arouse the awakening, exorcizing, transforming process in an individual or community. The music which accompanies rituals and ceremonies, embodied in an African heritage within the Spirituals, passes on religious knowledge, strengthens communal feelings and solidarity, preserves history, and develops naturally from a worldview of traditional sacrality. The singers use the words and the musical impetus behind the words to dramatize the plight of the oppressed and the disenfranchised and to inspire change. In the mass meetings and with song leaders and ensemble groups, the desire for freedom fueled the musicking. The musicking event included physical, mental, and emotional energies orchestrated in a manner that would override the fear of physical death and failure. A singer or singers, gifted with melody, poetic sensibilities, and an ability to craft and lead an appealing, catchy tune, can adjust words when merging them with melody and rhythm by skillfully using pitch, inflection, tone, and the body, or visceralness. For African Americans, Spirituals demand freedom, call for change on earth, desire inclusion, affirm their dignity and humanity, and respond to their life experiences as songs of protest, adaptation, transcendence, communication, and documentation.[9] The traditional and redacted Spirituals of the 1960s are life-changing documents.

The traditional Spirituals addressed the larger issue of human sin and the suffering and pain that come from the evil of slavery. These songs accepted the reality of God and blamed White masters for the sins perpetuated through slavery. God was an ever-present help, parent, friend, and confidant. God touched the human heart, causing a Spiritual conversion which helped change human attitudes, social and cultural customs, and legal statutes. Salvation, then, meant the conversion and ultimate liberation of all aspects of human existence. Change involved an immanent divine presence as liberator of human sin, and empowered human beings operating out of divine grace. The redacted Spirituals protest modern unjust, racist systems—slavery without legal status.

The other concerns for human transformation imbedded within the Spirituals were contextual, for many of the churched activists were already "working out their soul's salvation" by "leaning and depending on Jesus." The redacted Spirituals also accepted the reality of God and blamed a Eurocentric society for the evils of racism. God was on their side and effected conversion of people and systems. The focus of the Movement using these songs was "freedom now!" Freedom meant the experience of equal access to all the constitutional rights and privileges granted an American citizen. Freedom meant the end of racism, Jim Crow, disenfranchisement, and segregation. In a word, integration embodied the thrust of this change. Ideally, integration would create an environment which would change attitudes, practices, and law. A new experience of mutuality between the races would make the United States a true melting pot and would put an end to racism. This belief, undergirded by the Movement rhetoric, filtered through the singing in an atmosphere sustained by a holistic sociocultural, religious, and musical communal experience. The music provided a way to reflect on past hypocrisy as well as present and future possibilities.

African Americans knew the hypocrisy of the American civil religion which subjugated Blacks and deferred their dream of freedom. The religious foundation of the Movement's leadership encouraged the freedom fighters to believe they could attain their dream. Black ministers stood at the center of the Movement, and Black churches were the meeting places. Black ministers' belief in the Movement and in the religious nature of their mission helped the activists stand despite racist violence and governmental lethargy. On a federal level, the Kennedy administration viewed the chaos raging in the South from the perspective of global image. President Kennedy did not object to the continuation of racial segregation. The cold war moved toward the Cuban missile crisis in 1962, and the struggle with Russia meant that dying Black children in the South would jeopardize the United States' geopolitical standing. Even after the passage of the 1964 civil rights bill in the Johnson administration, racist violence continued, and many Black activists began to see the limitations of reform. By 1965, rebellion had supplanted reform.[10]

During the dynamic period of the Movement, God was the key to finding solutions for the community. As the Movement continued, a larger battle concerned African-American economic equality with Whites. White America was ready to demand that Blacks be freed from brutality and degradation, but there was little commitment to moving Blacks out of poverty. While some strides were made during the 1960s, racial segregation remained in residential housing, and the struggle for socioeconomic equality remained.[11] Some situations changed; others remained the same: such was the sociocultural milieu of the singing Movement.

Toward the height of the Movement in 1964, the power base shifted from a singing SNCC rural southern base to a northern, middle-class, interracial base. Much internal tension in the Movement concerned the sexual tension created when northern White female SNCC students became active in the South.[12] White female civil rights victims aroused national attention, but Black martyrs did not make the evening news.[13] Despite legal gains, there were no basic social or economic gains for poor Blacks: "There are a thousand ways for a people who are weaker than the rest to be kept in their place."[14] Having a law on the books did not secure the means for advancement. This retrospective view of the Movement's social history chronicles the denouement of a Movement that held much promise. The singing stopped when the Black power movement superseded nonviolent direct protest. When the activist groups could not sing together any longer because "radical" youth were not tuned to Martin Luther King, Jr.'s theology or ideology, the dissonance of their silence became more audible to those who listened on.

The 1960s Movement music documents that turbulent, exciting era of storms, lightning, thunder, and rainbows. These freedom songs expressed the profoundly revolutionary cadences, the longings and dreams, and the radical goals of the Movement. The music, teeming with the poetic and full of spirit, focused on protest and civil disobedience, and embraced a playfulness and whimsicality, an openness to all those who wanted to be free.[15] The songs express the hopes and dreams of those who wish to dance the dance of freedom, including folk singers, college-trained singers, traditional singers, and rhythm-and-blues singers from all parts of the United States and from all professions, in harmony and disharmony, together for the larger purpose of effecting change. The singers helped change their world with song. They heightened the awareness about 1960s racism, which encouraged the activism of many who otherwise would not have participated. Song, in Black congregational style, drew people in. A leader began singing, those with courage let their voices fill the air, and the sound enveloped them.[16] People were different because of the transformed space around them. This possibility for transformation makes the Spirituals vital for theological and ethical discourse, specifically for the issue of theodicy, the move for justice.

For Bernice Johnson Reagon, singing and protesting in the Movement was a theological and ethical process: she experienced a conversion. Conversion experiences are enhanced by singing Spirituals, since these soulful utterances, which involve the bathos and pathos of human experiences, create a mystical environment. Mysticism, the ongoing revelation wherein persons directly experience the divine, involves the preparation of the soul and getting the soul's attention; illumination, as the spirit and the self come together and focus; and contemplation, where the divine meets, penetrates, and frees the individual.[17] Part of Reagon's conversion experience involved learning important religious/moral values which were critical in developing her own persona and in developing a commitment to the Black liberation struggle.

Black theology and the 1960s Civil Rights/Black Power Movement focused on Black men but denied the contributions and needs of Black women and their need for liberation. During the late 1960s, a male-consciousness motif pervaded Black society, due to the male revolt against postwar societal expectations. Despite Black and White male chauvinism, Black and White women remained a vital part of the Movement. Black theologians did not address sexism. Feminists did not address racism. Neither addressed the combination of race, sex, and class. Then Womanist theology came into being. Womanist theology has been the most significant recent advance in American Black theology.[18] Womanist theology champions Black women's struggle to be free and to endure. Because many Womanists see Christ as central for Black women, the concern about sexism means differentiating between Jesus' gender of maleness and him being the Christ.[19] Womanist theology deals with oppression in society and in the church— the mandate for silence and submission, respectively.[20] Sexism, racism, and classism cause violence and subjugate. African-American plays, movies, and novels of the 1970s stressed violence and male assertiveness, and Black women's weakness and passiveness, and celebrated Black men's sexual exploits and the role of the pimp.[21] This picture of Black life, coming upon the heels of the Movement, indicated what went on before and points to what occurs today. An in-depth exegesis of the Spirituals requires a Womanist reading, one that intentionally listens for the silenced voices and asks the reader to be conscious of the pathology of racism, classism, and sexism.

> Sister Justice and Mother Freedom cried;
> Daughter Equality shook her head
> at the disarray in the world;
> So much pain in people's hearts, souls, brains,
> Caused each one to bleed, slowly dying—
> the turbulence, the chaos, the evil rains,
> Out beyond the human eye.

A Womanist's idea of freedom concerns strength, courage, and commitment to intracommunal bonding. In contrast, most Black men tend to address intercommunal, conflictual, or confrontal situations. Both women and men sang the Spirituals in the 1960s. Based on their testimonies, however, Womanists singing freedom songs indicted oppression and creatively channeled their anger by working for the Movement despite the omissions of their contributions and lack of recognition by the popular press and Movement leadership. Black women saw freedom as the engagement of internal and external struggle. Womanist thought celebrates the courage and intellect and totality of Black women's experience that necessarily includes those oppressed by race, gender, and class. One could not extract a Womanist's experience of singing freedom songs from her social or political context. Mutual participation, reform and reordering, and the need for redistribution are ideas resonant with Womanist thought. Male exclusivity in Black theologies and in general scholarship warrants the development and utilization of Womanist theodicy. A Womanist Christian perspective has shaped my study as an expression of the truest sense of the freedom within the Spirituals. Womanist sensibilities afford a life of freedom and mutuality as an ethical, inclusive, eschatological life of immediacy wherein one encounters community as well as personal identity, the potential beauty and the despair in the human spirit.

Womanist theory challenges us to shift from pure individualism, apathy, blaming others, being victims, and bemoaning all our present social ills toward a place of having an outrageous joie de vivre for life, wholeness, and proactive possibility. Singing the Spirituals offers us a catalyst for that shift and provides excellent forums for opening people to the possibility of having many conversations with people who are different, who have diverse concerns and cultural experiences. Both liturgy and teaching are aspects of bringing about holistic salvation and liberation. The Black church, all churches, and all institutional religions need to see that liberation must span from the spirit to the mind and the body. People cannot hear about a God in their lives if stomachs growl and beds of concrete are harder than the sermons we preach. We must approach personal and communal ills, for no one is truly free if any remain oppressed, and we must recognize, name, unmask, engage, and exorcize the oppression.

Spirituals represent an uncompromising exorcizing of the oppression and a commitment to the liberation of African-American people and of all people. There are hundreds of Spirituals that can be used to teach the values of liberation, justice, hope, and new life. Parents, teachers, ministers, and mentors can use these Spirituals to empower all persons of all ages, from kindergarteners to senior citizens. Since we often forget speeches and written words but remember even childhood songs, what would happen if children at risk, before they join gangs, were introduced to empowerment, love, values, and self-worth through experiencing the Spirituals? What would happen if their parent(s) or guardian(s) and communities formed impromptu singing groups for singing these songs; and, in the process of singing, came to believe in the possibilities of change; and, in coming to believe, actually began to live the possibilities, to change? I offer this prolegomenon as a challenge for another use of the Spirituals in the 1990s: the practice of singing, understanding, interpreting, and *living* them toward creating a wholeness of all peoples.

Current domestic tensions and harassment of persons across the United States because of differences recall the antebellum conflicts, the abolitionist struggles, and the battles for freedom fought thirty years ago. The emotionalism generated by racist evil makes it appear that discrimination is acceptable, moral, and natural. Because the past stays in the present, prejudice and bias remain society's enemies. As long as difference can sanction the position of superiority, the "historical comfort of the illusion inspires the racial animus and makes it seem both necessary and proper."[22] Both the traditional and the redacted African-American Spirituals confront that animus.

These chants of collective exorcism address theodicy, dealing with issues from the presence and absence of freedom as power, and celebrating the ability to choose or not choose movement; to going from being oppressed to a transcendent essence in historical time, becoming an empowered self who can participate in a balanced relationship with God, self, and others—the key to the aim of theodicy as a theology of justice. The question of theodicy based on the Spirituals bypasses most of the philosophical and theological questions from the Augustinian and Irenaean mythological perspectives. The Spirituals do not explicitly set up abstract, nonhistorical dialogue but, rather embrace notions of relationship and responsibility. The Spirituals subscribe to an aesthetically perfected creation, to communal evil powers and a personal devil, and to the import of divine purpose related to human existence. The Spirituals do not ultimately blame God for evil, do not give assent to a *felix culpa*, where God allowed evil for some good reason, nor find logical limitations for God's omnipotence. These Spirituals presume God's existence, find plausible the unanswered-questions argument, and critique the relationship between God and humanity within society. God and human beings choose their own behavior. The choice to condone slavery or racism achieves legitimation through the propagation of myth and the practice of oppressive ritual. The Spirituals qualify the questions and provide a context for discerning how historically suffering persons dealt with evil.

Consequently, I use the term *theodicy* to discuss the nature and implications of God's justice in concert with the relationship between God and human beings (both oppressed and oppressor) in freedom and amid the societal evils of slavery and racism, and sexism and classism, in the context of justice. In the Spirituals, theodicy becomes the taskmaster for articulating acts and responsibilities, in the language of relationships, freedom, and justice, for the divine and humanity as they participate together in a racist society. Justice here refers to the Thomist notion of the necessary alignment of the world with God's will.

Thus, the redacted Spirituals of the 1960s Civil Rights Movement confront areas of conceptualization, application, hermeneutics, and human actualization within the larger American social and cultural setting. In the African-American setting, the sacred and the secular, together with politics and piety, are integral to daily life. That intimacy arises from a strong communal sense and a sense of being intimate with the divine. The role of a benevolent divinity in relationship with humanity in the presence of evil concerns the theodicy expressed in the Spirituals and classical theodicy, because the creators and thinkers behind both experiences are theists. The theodicy expressed in the redacted Spirituals shares some, but not all, of its concerns with classical theodicy.

The redacted Spirituals assert the presence of racist evil. Therefore, they do not give assent to the concept of nonbeing, which regards evil as illusory, or to the theory of dualism, where evil stands coequal with God. They are rooted in the logic of reality, but they do not question the analytical consistency of claims about God, humanity, and evil. The Spirituals do not ask "why"; their motive is not the task of fielding a rational, adequate justification as to why God allows evil to exist. The Spirituals do not attempt to show evil's cosmological purpose, to empower evil, to redefine the terms to eliminate the question, or to diminish God's power. The theodicy expressed in the Spirituals takes exception to many of the myths of the Augustinian "free-will" and Irenaean "soul-making" arguments.

Both the Spirituals and Augustine contend that evil occurs because of misused freedom. The Spirituals deal with the reality of a racist evil that embraces a practical philosophy and theology of evil. Like Irenaeus, the creators of the Spirituals claim that the relationship is an intimate fellowship. The mythic Fall of humankind (which was actually portrayed as an expulsion) is not central to these Spirituals. The Spirituals remember the past and hope for the future, but primarily they desire change in the present. They reflect St. Francis's and Reinhold Niebuhr's "Serenity Prayer":

> God grant me
>> the serenity to accept the things I cannot change;
>> the courage to change the things I can;
>> and the wisdom to know the difference.

In the Spirituals, salvation tends to be universal—imminent salvation as liberation for the oppressed and the oppressor. That experience of liberation embraces the freedom of God's sustaining grace and social freedom, the divinely inspired empowerment of individuality and democracy.[23] Freedom is an essential element to the theodicy expressed in the redacted Spirituals. The unfolding of freedom amid the vital experiences that birthed both the traditional and the redacted Spirituals emerges as applied theology, as praxis and process.

A theological exegesis of the Spirituals shows that people confronted the issues of God's nature and the problem of evil and suffering as they lived in bondage or within racism. Blacks from both periods relied on the presence of an immediate God; consequently, the Spirituals take God's existence as a given. God as liberator, parent, and friend is a composite of Lord, God, Christ, Jesus, and Moses. When divine names or imagery are not present, God's presence is implicit. Evil exists and exacts a devastating price in life-and-death concerns. Although the holistic nature of the Spirituals causes the recognition of diverse manifestations of sin and evil, the texts specifically define slavery and racism to be evil per se. Those members of White dominant culture who perpetrate bondage are responsible for racist evil and suffering. God is not. The redacted Spirituals or freedom songs identify the problem and call for a solution.

During the 1960s Civil Rights Movement, a solution meant freedom, equality, and justice for all, including reconciliation and salvation for the oppressed and the oppressor—mutuality and respect that would allow difference to coexist. This transformation included the equal access and full citizenship possible through integration. The oppressed did not seek vengeance but did seek the rights granted to all American citizens. People from all backgrounds participated in the Movement. African American and Euro-American, Jew and gentile began to protest, sing, and work together; people began to see clearly their similarities and differences, and became open to shared experiences. The power generated through the freedom songs helped change the social and political climate of the 1960s, as civil rights legislation became law and some racists' hearts began to change. The model of change reflected in the Spirituals showed both the problem and the process that led to a solution. Not everyone was changed, nor has racism disappeared, but the singing Movement made a difference.

In the Spirituals, the act of struggle for good in the midst of evil was a good, even if the outcome—the pain, the suffering, the desperation, and the feelings of hopelessness—were not good. The struggle for freedom does not guarantee that the victory of good over evil will be immediate and total, but evil will not succeed, because God is good. The good of the struggle and the good of the many successes, which included equal access to education, public accommodations, and constitutional privilege, demonstrate that the light and the good are not overcome by darkness and evil (Jn 1:5; 12:35, NIV). The shift from the practical to the theoretical involves the method and process of analysis, or hermeneutics.

The process of doing theology from praxis to theory concerns moving "from the bottom up." Similar to most liberation theologies, theodicy in the Spirituals places the oppressed at the center of the dialogue. Such a practical theology begins with describing the practice. Following critical analysis and reflection, we can suggest a theory about the context, the function, and the ramifications of an applied theology. Having discerned the essential elements of the theological experience further, the process then shifts to that of prescription. Theodicy was not superimposed upon the Spirituals by scholarship. The theodicy is present because the experience of right relationship with God and with the neighbor, and the need to deal with evil and suffering, is central to the sensibilities of the antebellum slaves and the 1960s protesters. Spirituals require that the scholar address divine and human justice within a given society. The Spirituals show how one can adapt a cultural expression to serve new purposes. Using the Spirituals as tools for theological dialogue also illuminates the possibility for scholars to use other cultural artifacts to find out the concerns and feelings of those persons whom the religious claim to serve. The study of movement through time is one function of studying history, and analyzing theodicy and the Spirituals becomes an adventure in time. Historical awareness allows us to use theoretical and practical categories to clarify concrete realities with integrity. Studying theodicy through these cultural artifacts reiterates the impact of social politics on theology, the need to use interdisciplinary scholarship in order to unpack the numerous issues central to the inner workings of the Spirituals, and the complexity of human language and human existence.

Slave bards and the 1960s freedom fighters used language and music in the form of the Spirituals as tools of theodicy. But the Spirituals continue to illumine historically institutionalized evil and continue to offer ways to cope with suffering. We must use them.

We must use Spirituals to effect freedom, now. Freedom stands for the liberation of all and the end to oppression, punitive school tracking systems, lynchings, church burnings, abuse, and the denial of personhood because of skin color, gender, age, or economic status. We must use Spirituals to curb addictive and criminal activities. We must use Spirituals to reclaim extended families in our neighbors, which were lost with the massive mobilization after the 1960s. The demand for freedom experienced as justice for all concerns the ability to exercise that freedom by living responsibly in right relationship with God and other human beings within a given society. The commitment to living with justice includes the notion that change is critical for both oppressed and oppressor.

An African-American philosophical historicist Womanist view says we can use the Spirituals to help create change, to reform. This reformation confronts the multidimensional problems of evil and suffering (oppression), or justice, to reflect a vision of theodicy that champions immediacy and inclusivity. Womanist vision searches for a way to champion the freedom, dignity, and justice of all people. A theodicy with such an immediate and inclusive bent champions a freedom shaped by ethical and social concerns.

As reformation songs, the Spirituals call for change in the faith and thought dictates of American civil religion, particularly in recognizing the instances of injustice. The belief system embodied in the Spirituals during the nineteenth-century antebellum and post–World War II eras called for an awakening of the American conscience toward equality and freedom for all. This call addresses the issues of God, society, relationships, and justice. The call for justice is the call for divine and human accountability for integrity in relationships. Part of this call for change is discerning who God was for the slaves, who God was for the 1960s activists, and whom God calls us to be today, which informs the nature of human accountability.

Are "we" willing to become accountable? Do "we" really believe "My country 'tis of thee, sweet land of liberty," or do "we" need to have that liberty available only to those who look like, think like, and feel like our own individual group designation? Do "we" believe the promises of the Constitution, or are we so greedy, so fearful, and have so bought into a sense of lack that the thought that there is enough to go around and that everyone can get a piece of the action so traumatizes us that we just cannot think about equality and justice? Do "we" have the capacity to envision the possibility of "we" as families, communities, states, and a nation working at creating a forum for justice and for respect in every area of our lives?

What are the limits posed by an African-American theodicy for the 1990s? The Spirituals are one way to envision a quest for self-affirmation, peace, and wholeness. How can theorists build on theodicy in the Spirituals? How can a theodicy develop that has value to both the scholar and the one who suffers? What questions must a contemporary theodicy ask, given the resurgence of blatant racism, sexual harassment, and persistent unemployability? When babies die from AIDS, what justification can be offered concerning innocent suffering? Does theodicy remain a valid area of theological discourse? Do we need to change the questions or look for different answers?

No one has ever wanted to be a slave. African Americans did not come to these shores as willing immigrants, bondservants, or convicted criminals. Using their God-consciousness, creative imagination, and sense of community, the slave bards responded to their bondage. Their response is the cultural artifact that history has titled the Spirituals. Racism, sexism, and classism are the 1960s and 1990s version of slavery. No one chooses to be a victim of these "isms." To what drumbeat do victims march? What songs do victims sing? What questions do old and new voices ask about theodicy and justice? What is the meaning of freedom and equality? Who are the singers of justice, freedom, and equality?

A Womanist justice reading sees the Spirituals as stories about God-talk, stories about human beings that unveil an oppressive racist, sexist, and classist society to identify, reveal, and then transform the collective possession and sins of slavery, racism, and all oppression by experiencing a collective exorcism of grace, divinely ordained and divinely and humanly enacted.

> Who sings the song,
> that helps us to belong to a society where
> Sisters Community, Truth, and Love make a trio,
> Sister Justice, Mother Freedom, Daughter Equality sing, too.
> A host of angelic choruses create no greater song
> than the song of this family
> whose song is an invitation
> to sing louder than hate, mistrust, and evil
> Toward resurrection day.
>
> "Is anybody listening?
> Can I get a witness?"

Notes

Preface: Genesis of a Pilgrimage

[1]Robert Jay Lifton, *The Nazi Doctors: Medical Killing and the Psychology of Genocide* (New York: Basic Books, 1986), 418-19.

[2]Michael W. Harris, *The Rise of Gospel Blues: The Music of Thomas Andrew Dorsey in the Urban Church* (New York: Oxford University Press, 1992), xx; and George W. Stroup, *The Promise of Narrative Theology: Recovering the Gospel in the Church* (Atlanta: John Knox Press, 1981), 20-21.

[3]Hannah Arendt, *The Human Condition* (Chicago: University of Chicago Press, 1958), 7-9, 184.

[4]Many texts have examined the Spirituals from a literary and anthropological perspective: *Slave Songs of the United States,* by William Francis Allen, Charles Pickard Ware, and Lucy McKim Garrison (New York: Peter Smith, 1867, 1951), is a collection of the Spirituals, with general sociohistorical and stylistic commentary. Thomas P. Fenner's *Religious Folk Songs of the Negro* (Hampton, VA: Hampton Institute Press, 1909) records those Spirituals popularized by the Hampton Institute. *The Books of American Negro Spirituals,* by James Weldon Johnson and J. Rosamond Johnson (New York: Harper & Row, 1926), is a collection of the music with a general introduction.

Miles Mark Fisher was one of the first scholars to show that the Spirituals were oral historical documents: "He was able to demonstrate that [the Spirituals] revealed the innermost thoughts of the slaves on religion, slavery, relations with their masters, aspirations for the future, and all the multitudinous problems faced by a people held in bondage . . . These revelations are typical of the many that dot Dr. Fisher's fine study. Startling as they are, they are dwarfed by another that emerges in his final chapters: the eagerness of the slaves for self improvement. For in all the history of migration, few peoples have shown an ability to adapt to a strange civilization so completely as the Negroes. This was manifest—*and reflected in their songs*—from the time they were first introduced to the mysteries of the Caucasian world." Ray Allen Billington, foreword to *Negro Slave Songs in the United States*, by Miles Mark Fisher (New York: Citadel Press, 1953, 1981), viii-ix.

The definitive work on the Spirituals, by John Lovell, Jr., *Black Song: The Forge and the Flame; The Story of How the Afro-American Spiritual Was Hammered Out* (New York: Macmillan, 1972), is a masterpiece and is integral to my work. Lovell surveys the sociohistorical, cultural, and religious experience of the slaves and also includes an international bibliography. James Cone's *The Spirituals and the Blues: An Interpretation* (New York: Seabury Press, 1972; Maryknoll, NY: Orbis Books, 1992) analyzes terminology, theological concepts, and cultural meaning. I use all these authors in my own work to support my analysis, but none of them specifically does detailed musical analysis on a song-by-song basis, and they especially do not relate the impact of the musical text on the literary text when discussing theodicy.

[5]Maulana Karenga, *Introduction to Black Studies* (Los Angeles: University of Sankore Press, 1982).

[6]Charles Small, *Music of the Common Tongue: Survival and Celebration in Afro-American Music* (London: John Calder, 1987), 20-22. Musicking is the present participle of "to music."

[7]David Darling, international performing cellist, recording artist, and composer, quoted in Ann Cushman, "Are You Creative?" *Utne Reader* 50 (March-April 1992): 57.

[8]Jon Michael Spencer, ed., "Preface," *The Theology of American Popular Music*, in *Black Sacred Music: A Journal of Theomusicology* 3 (Fall 1989); v. These issues are at stake in the discipline of theomusicology. Theomusicology, developed by Jon Michael Spencer, a scholar of music, theology, and culture, is a musicological method and discipline for theologizing about the sacred, the secular, and the profane. Spencer claims that theology proper is unequipped to critique the irreligious. Theomusicology incorporates methods borrowed from anthropology, sociology, psychology, and philosophy. Using music as the lens, this process includes sacred and nonsacred music functioning in church and community. By focusing the analysis on the context of music making, the connection between the message of theodicy and how music is an agent can be derived. Though he uses the language of theology, philosophy is the vehicle for theomusicological analysis, because Spencer has given extensive thought to the effect of music on the human psyche.

[9]Alice Walker, *In Search of Our Mothers' Gardens: Womanist Prose* (New York: Harcourt Brace Jovanovich, 1983), xi.

[10]James H. Cone, *For My People: Black Theology and the Black Church* (Maryknoll, NY: Orbis Books, 1984), 125, 128-29; and Deborah Gray White, *Ar'n't I a Woman: Female Slaves in the Plantation South* (New York: W. W. Norton, 1985), 14, 23.

[11]Cheryl Townsend Gilkes, "Mother to the Motherless, Father to the Fatherless: Power, Gender, and Community in an Afrocentric Biblical Tradition," *Semeia: An Experimental Journal for Biblical Criticism* 47 (1989): 57-85.

[12]Walker, *In Search*, xi.

1. Meaning and Knowing

[1]*African American* and *Afro-American* refer to those people who represent the merging of African and European cultural experience and genetic origins. I use the terms *African American* and *Black American* synonymously. The term *Negro* is not suitable for current writing but is used for the historical era when it was normative in literature and social parlance.

[2]Slave bards created Spirituals on American soil before the United States formally existed. The creators of the Spirituals had African religious and musical attitudes, and thus sang before and after slave traders stole Africans from their homeland. See John Lovell, Jr., *Black Song: The Forge and the Flame; The Story of How the Afro-American Spiritual Was Hammered Out* (New York: Macmillan, 1972), 16-17.

[3]Bernice Johnson Reagon, ed., *Voices of the Civil Rights Movement: Black*

American Freedom Songs, 1960-1966 (Washington, DC: Smithsonian Institution Program in Black Culture, 1980), phonodisc R023. There are sixteen redacted Spirituals on this disc. Earlier publications of original Spirituals and sound recordings were made by anthropologists such as Alan Lomax, with the Federal Works Progress Administration. Contemporary concert arrangements of Spirituals, various manuscripts of Spirituals, and personal experiences of performances of Spirituals are additional sources. See William Francis Allen, Charles Pickard Ware, and Lucy McKim Garrison, *Slave Songs of the United States* (New York: Peter Smith, 1867, 1951); Thomas P. Fenner, *Religious Folk Songs of the Negro* (Hampton, VA: Hampton Institute Press, 1909); James Weldon Johnson and J. Rosamond Johnson, *The Books of American Negro Spirituals* (New York: Harper & Row, 1926); and Bernice Johnson Reagon, *Wade in the Water Series*, vols. 1-2 (Washington, DC: Smithsonian/Folkways Recordings, 1994).

Other background materials are found in the Archive of Folk Songs, Library of Congress, Washington, DC; and the Works Progress Administration Records-Slave Stories, Barker Texas History Center, Austin TX. These archives contain manuscripts of Negro Spirituals and field recordings. A critical analysis of the antebellum Spirituals provides a dialogical context for describing and analyzing the expressions of theodicy found in the redacted African-American Spirituals from the Movement. My question of these sources is, "How did these songs function and comment on theodicy during slavery and the 1960s civil rights era?" That is, "How did the slaves and civil rights activists signify their experience both with the evils of institutionalized racism and with a just, good, and righteous God in the Spirituals?"

[4] Taylor Branch, *Parting the Waters: America in the King Years, 1954-1963* (New York: Simon & Schuster, 1988), 532.

[5] Henry Krehbiel, *Afro-American Folksongs: A Study in Racial and National Music* (Portland, ME: Longwood Press, 1913), 9, 14, 16, 30, 46; Anne Kenny, *The Negro Spiritual and Other Essays* (Cairo, IL: R. Schindler, 1943), 16; and Helen Kaufman, *From Jehovah to Jazz: Music in America from Psalmody to the Present Day* (Port Washington, NY: Kennikat Press, 1937), 30.

[6] Branch, *Parting the Waters,* 532.

[7] See L. M. Friedel, *The Bible and the Negro Spirituals* (Bay St. Louis, MS: St. Augustine Seminary, 1947); and Lovell, *Black Song,* 3-11.

[8] Mary Speers, "Negro Songs and Folk-lore," *Journal of American Folk-lore* (1910): 435; and Augustine T. Smythe et al., *The Carolina Low-Country* (New York: Macmillan, 1931), 197-201.

[9] Smythe, *The Carolina Low-Country,* 191; Wallace McKenzie, "E. A. McIlhenny's Black Spiritual Collection from Avery Island, Louisiana," *American Music* 8 (Spring 1990): 99, 101, 104, 109; Sarah Thrower, "The Spiritual of the Gullah Negro in South Carolina" (thesis, B.M., College of Music of Cincinnati, 1954), 7, 14, 20; Harry Oster, "Negro French Spirituals of Louisiana," *Journal of the International Folk Music Council* 14 (1962): 166; and Merrill Singer, " 'Now I Know What the Songs Mean!': Traditional Black Music in a Contemporary Black Sect," *Southern Quarterly* 23 (Spring 1985): 126-29, 135-39.

[10] See my discussion of the story of Emmett Till in Chapter 5.

[11] Kwame Anthony Appiah and Henry Louis Gates, Jr., "Editors' Introduction: Multiplying Identities," *Critical Inquiry* 18 (Summer 1992): 626, 627-29.

[12] Leonard Harris, ed., *The Philosophy of Alain Locke: Harlem Renaissance and Beyond* (Philadelphia: Temple University Press, 1989), 11, 12, 14, 15, 32, 40.

[13]Patricia Hill Collins, *Black Feminist Thought: Knowledge, Consciousness, and the Politics of Empowerment* (New York: Routledge, 1991).

[14]Ibid., 103-7, 206-19.

[15]Katie G. Cannon, *Black Womanist Ethics* (Atlanta: Scholars Press, 1988), 105-16, 125, 127, 143-44.

[16]K. Anthony Appiah, "Inventing an African Practice in Philosophy: Epistemological Issues," in *Surreptitious Speech: Présence Africaine and the Otherness, 1947-1987*, ed. V. Y. Mudimbe (Chicago: University of Chicago Press, 1992), 229, 231-37.

[17]Michael Hecht, Mary Jane Collier, and Sidney Ribeau, *African American Communication: Ethnic Identity and Cultural Interpretation* (Newbury Park, CA: Sage Publications, 1993), 14-28, 82.

[18]Charshee Lawrence-McIntyre, "The Double Meanings of the Spirituals," *Journal of Black Studies* 17 (June 1987): 382-84, 389, 398-99.

[19]Paul Laubenstein, "An Apocalyptic Reincarnation," *Journal of Biblical Literature* 51 (1932): 239.

[20]Anthony Appiah, "Thick Translation," *Callaloo* 16 (1993): 818; and Lawrence W. Levine, "Slave Songs and Slave Consciousness," in *American Negro Slavery: A Reader*, ed. Allen Weinstein and Frank Catell (New York: Oxford University Press, 1968, 1973), 160-61, 167, 170, 173.

2. Context: The Social and Historical Setting

[1]Nowhere in the Constitution is the term *slave* found; instead, the term *other person*, which excludes Native Americans, is used.

[2]Orlando Patterson, *Slavery and Social Death: A Comparative Study* (Cambridge: Harvard University Press, 1982), 1; and Lerone Bennett, *Before the Mayflower: A History of the Negro in America, 1619-1964*, rev. ed. (New York: Penguin Books, 1961, 1962, 1964), 30-34.

[3]Bennett, *Before the Mayflower,* 30, 36; and Paul Jacobs and Saul Landau, *To Serve the Devil,* vol. 1, *Natives and Slaves* (New York: Vintage Books), 89. The first Black slaves to come to United States territory actually arrived in South Carolina with Lucas Vásquez de Ayllón in 1526. They rebelled, the colony failed, and the whites sailed away, leaving the Blacks behind. See William Z. Foster, *The Negro People in American History* (New York: International Publishers, 1954), 37.

[4]Michael Paul Rogin, "The Sword Became a Flashing Vision: D. W. Griffith's *The Birth of a Nation*," in *Ronald Reagan, the Movie and Other Episodes in Political Demonology* (Berkeley: University of California Press, 1987), 197-98.

[5]See Spike Lee, *Jungle Fever* (New York, Forty Acres and a Mule Filmworks, Inc., 1991); and Spike Lee, *The Films of Spike Lee: Five for Five* (New York: Stewart, Tabori, Chang, 1991).

[6]"Representatives and direct Taxes shall be apportioned among the several States which may be included within this Union, according to the respective Numbers, which shall be determined by adding to the whole Number of free Persons [White males], including those bound to Service for a Term of Years, and excluding Indians not taxed, three fifths of all other Persons." U.S. Constitution, Art. I, sec. 2.

[7]George Frederickson, *The Arrogance of Race: Historical Perspectives on Slavery, Racism, and Social Inequality* (Middletown, CT: Wesleyan University Press, 1988), 7.

[8]"No other case was so monumentally wrong and error-ridden not only because it denied the essence of humanity to the black population but also because at least its worst features could so easily have been avoided." Jethro K. Lieberman, *Milestones! 200 Years of American Law* (St. Paul, MN: West Publishing, 1976), 135.

[9]Bennett, *Before the Mayflower*, 35.

[10]Ibid., 30-39, 47. For in-depth discussion on the processing of slaves and the difference between treatment by Protestants vs. Roman Catholic, and Spanish vs. French or English captors, see ibid., chapter 2. The entire volume bears thoughtful reading and reflection.

[11]Unlike the indentured servant class, the yoke of slavery was extended to the as yet unborn descendants of slaves. In addition, the child of a slave and a White was a slave. A child of an indentured person was normally exempt from the parents' contractual bondage. Children of mixed marriages became slaves. When Congress banned further slave imports from Africa in 1808, the breeding of slaves for the marketplace became a profitable and economically efficient endeavor: in 1790, 750,000 Blacks lived in the United States; the Black population increased to 1,378,000 in 1810, and to 4,442,000 in 1860. See Foster, *Negro People*, 38, 71.

[12]Winthrop Jordan, *White over Black: American Attitudes toward the Negro, 1550-1812* (Chapel Hill, NC: University of North Carolina Press, 1968), 80.

[13]Frederickson, *Arrogance*, 131-33, 193-205.

[14]Mary Frances Berry and John W. Blassingame, *Long Memory: The Black Experience in America* (New York: Oxford University Press, 1982), 4-7, 15.

[15]Frederickson, *Arrogance,* 48-72; Berry and Blassingame, *Long Memory*, 13.

[16]Frederickson, *Arrogance*, 209-15. Frederickson and other social psychologists and historians argue that White control and dominance created the idea of slave docility. Revolutionary America expected slaves, like all human beings, to crave liberty; pre–Civil War America, however, did not.

[17]For example, see Thomas Dixon Jr.'s pseudohistoric romances, which influenced his confidant, President Woodrow Wilson, to impose segregation upon an integrated federal civil service, as well as the translation of Dixon's novel *The Clansman: An Historical Romance of the Ku Klux Klan* (New York: Doubleday, 1905) into D. W. Griffith's film *Birth of a Nation* (127 minutes, 1915, videocassette).

[18]Frederickson, *Arrogance*, 214-15.

[19]Charles Small, *Music of the Common Tongue: Survival and Celebration in Afro-American Music* (London: John Calder, 1987), 31-32; John Blassingame, *The Slave Community: Plantation Life in the Ante-bellum South* (New York: Oxford University Press, 1979), 6; and ibid., 206-8.

[20]Blassingame, *Slave Community*, 223-30. Blassingame's work refutes Stanley Elkin's arguments for slave docility and the comparison between the cruelty of slavery and the World War II concentration camp. Blassingame's *The Slave Community* received mixed reviews, from praise to pointed criticism. For critiques of his work, see Al-Tony Gilmore, ed., *Revisiting Blassingame's* The Slave Community: *The Scholars Respond* (Westport, CT: Greenwood Press, 1978). Blassingame suggests that the slave's fear usually resulted from harsh treatment and led to acquiescence, not acceptance and desires for revenge; the slave gave us analytical tools for viewing God; and the Spirituals are songs of hope, sorrow, resignation, and rebellion. See Stanley M. Elkins, *Slavery: A Problem in American Insti-*

tutional and Intellectual Life (Chicago: Chicago University Press, 1976).

[21]Blassingame, *Slave Community*, 6, 47; John Earl Taylor, "The Sociological and Psychological Implications of the Texts of the Ante-bellum Negro Spirituals" (Ed.D. diss., University of Northern Colorado, 1971), 189, 192; and Albert Beckham, "The Psychology of Negro Spirituals," *Southern Workman* 60 (1931): 393. Beckham concluded that singers languishing in pity relayed their plight. Others told of experiencing pity but did something about it. Some Spirituals were either palliative or sorrow songs, whereas others celebrated hope and transformation.

[22]Vincent Harding, "Religion and Resistance among Ante-bellum Negroes, 1800-1860," in *The Making of Black America: Essays in Negro Life and History*, vol. 1, *The Origins of Black Americans*, ed. August Meier and Elliot Rudwick (New York: Athenaeum, 1969), 190; and Blassingame, *Slave Community*, 297. One slave couple murdered their children and took their own lives to avoid separation. Some parents became morose and indifferent or went insane.

[23]Stanley Campbell, interview by the author, Waco, TX, Summer 1988. Campbell has studied more than fifteen hundred accounts of fugitive slaves.

[24]Deborah Gray White, *Ar'n't I a Woman: Female Slaves in the Plantation South* (New York: W. W. Norton, 1985), 92.

[25]Ibid., 13, 15, 92, 105, 118, 142. Additional information on the behavior and life of enslaved children and their age-segregated world can be found in Eugene Genovese, *Roll, Jordan, Roll: The World the Slaves Made* (New York: Pantheon Books, 1974).

[26]Dena Epstein, *Sinful Tunes and Spirituals: Black Folk Music to the Civil War* (Urbana: University of Illinois Press, 1977), 63-76. The songs studied include celebrations for holidays, rites, and the work, field, and boat songs.

[27]John Lovell, Jr., "Social Implications of the Negro Spiritual," in *The Social Implications of Early Negro Music in the United States*, ed. Bernard Katz (New York: Arno Press and the *New York Times*, 1969), 128-29.

[28]See accounts of slave insurrections led by Nat Turner, Gabriel Prosser, and Denmark Vesey in the colonies, and by Toussaint L'Ouverture in Haiti and Jamaica, in Genovese, *Roll, Jordan, Roll*; David Brion Davis, *The Problem of Slavery in Western Culture* (Ithaca, NY: Cornell University Press, 1966), 62, 72, 222, 337-80; and E. N. Elliot, *Cotton Is King, and Pro-slavery Arguments: Comprising the Writings of Hammond, Harper, Christy, Stringfellow, Hodge, Bledsoe, and Cartwright, on This Important Subject* (Augusta, GA: Pritchard, Abbott & Loomis, 1860), 337.

[29]Cornel West, *Prophesy Deliverance! An Afro-American Revolutionary Christianity* (Philadelphia: Westminster Press, 1982), 47-65.

[30]Sydney Ahlstrom, *A Religious History of the American People* (New Haven: Yale University Press, 1972), 635.

[31]Genovese, *Roll, Jordan, Roll*, 71; and ibid., 644, 650, 652.

[32]John Fletcher, *Studies On Slavery, In Easy Lessons: Compiled Into Eight Studies, And Subdivided Into Short Lessons For The Convenience Of Readers* (Miami: Mnemosyne Publishing, 1852; repr. 1969), 53, 62, 178, 507.

[33]Bennett, *Before the Mayflower*, 62-63, 132; and William S. McFeely, *Frederick Douglass* (New York: W. W. Norton, 1991), 39, 107.

[34]Ann Wortham, *The Other Side of Racism: A Philosophical Study of Black Race Consciousness* (Columbus: Ohio State University Press, 1981), 53-58; and Jim Wallis, "America's Original Sin: The Legacy of White Racism," *Sojourners* (November 1987): 16-17.

[35]Joseph R. Washington, Jr., *Black Religion: The Negro and Christianity in the United States* (Boston: Beacon Press, 1964), 167; and Ahlstrom, *Religious History*, 699.

[36]John Lovell, Jr., *Black Song: The Forge and the Flame; The Story of How the Afro-American Spiritual Was Hammered Out* (New York: Macmillan, 1972), 31. Christianity was well established in North Africa as early as the fourth century A.D. Many writings by Africans were lost in the fire that destroyed the Alexandrian Library.

[37]Liberia was founded for the purpose of returning Blacks to Africa, and its capital, Monrovia, was named to honor American president James Monroe. See Foster, *Negro People*, 67, 91. The "polarizing pressure[s]" pitting established slavery against abolition were "the annexation of Texas (1845), the Mexican war, legislation for the vast territory won from Mexico, fugitive slave laws, the Kansas-Nebraska Act, 'Bleeding Kansas,' the assault on Senator Sumner, the Dred Scott decision, [and] the Lincoln-Douglas debates." Ahlstrom, *Religious History*, 656.

[38]Ahlstrom, *Religious History*, 655-56, 659-69.

[39]W. E. B. Du Bois, *The Souls of Black Folk* (Chicago: A. C. McClurg, 1903; repr., with an introduction by Henry Louis Gates, Jr., New York: Bantam Books, 1989), 134; Ahlstrom, *Religious History*, 711-12; and Catherine Albanese, *America: Religions and Religion* (Belmont, CA: Wadsworth Publishing, 1981), 120.

[40]William C. Turner, Jr., "The Musicality of Black Preaching: A Phenomenology," *Journal of Black Sacred Music* 2 (Spring 1988): 21.

[41]Joseph A. Johnson, Jr., *The Soul of the Black Preacher*, with an introduction by C. D. Coleman (n.p.: Pilgrim Press, 1970), vi-vii.

[42]Albanese, *America*, 119-22.

[43]Historically, doctrinal differences between African-American sects have always been ancillary to the unifying force engendered by a common ethnicity and a shared oppression.

[44]Ida Mukenge, *The Black Church in Urban America: A Case Study in Political Economy* (Lanham, MD: University Press of America, 1983), 1, 6.

[45]C. Eric Lincoln and Lawrence H. Mamiya, *The Black Church in the African American Experience* (Durham, NC, and London: Duke University Press, 1990), 50-60. The authors contend that three key interests for the Free African Society were racial solidarity, abolitionist activity, and education. See also Kristin E. Holmes, "Black Churchgoers Trace Their Heritage in Religion," *Austin American-Statesman*, 6 June 1992, D4; and Charles T. Davis and Henry Louis Gates, Jr., *The Slave's Narrative* (New York: Oxford University Press, 1985), 306, 308.

[46]Du Bois, *Souls of Black Folk*, 63.

[47]Bennett, *Before the Mayflower*, 71-78.

[48]Du Bois, *Souls of Black Folk*, 115-25.

[49]Eugene Genovese, *Rebellion to Revolution: Afro-American Slave Revolts in the Making of the Modern World* (Baton Rouge: Louisiana State University Press, 1979), 46.

[50]The parallel between this African religious tradition and the Roman Catholic tradition of saints interceding with God on behalf of living human beings is striking.

[51]Albanese, *America*, 114-16.

[52]For reflections on these four philosophies and roles in Black protest, see the following works: Louis R. Harlan, *Booker T. Washington: The Making of a*

Black Leader, 1856-1901 (New York: Oxford University Press, 1972); Louis R. Harlan, *Booker T. Washington: The Wizard of Tuskegee, 1901-1915* (New York: Oxford University Press, 1983); Elliot Rudwick, *W. E. B. Du Bois: A Study in Minority Group Leadership* (Philadelphia: University of Pennsylvania Press, 1960); Anna Julia Cooper, *A Voice from the South, by a Black Woman of the South* (Westport, CT: Greenwood Press, 1976, 1892); Ida Wells-Barnett, *A Red Record* (Chicago: Donohue & Henneberry, 1895); Edmund D. Cronon, *Black Moses: The Story of Marcus Garvey and the Universal Association* (Madison University of Wisconsin Press, 1955); William H. Harris, *Keeping the Faith: A. Philip Randolph, Milton P. Webster, and the Brotherhood of Sleeping Car Porters, 1925-37* (Urbana: University of Illinois Press, 1977); Theodore Cross, *The Black Power Imperative: Racial Inequality and the Politics of Nonviolence* (New York: Faulkner, 1987); and Leonard Broom and Norval Glenn, *Transformation of the Negro American* (New York: Harper & Row, 1965), 60. For example, President Roosevelt issued Executive Order 8802, which forbade discrimination by those holding government war contracts when Randolph, president of the Brotherhood of Sleeping Car Porters, threatened a march on Washington by African Americans to obtain better job possibilities.

[53]347 U.S. 483 (1954).

[54]Juan Williams et al., *Eyes on the Prize: America's Civil Rights Years, 1954-1965* (New York: Penguin Books, 1987), vi.

[55]George D. Kelsey, *Racism and the Christian Understanding of Man* (New York: Charles Scribner's Sons, 1965), 9, 19-35, 156-61.

[56]Ibid., 156-61.

[57]Frederickson, *Arrogance*, 221.

[58]Albert L. Truesdale, Jr., "A Tillichian Analysis of White Racism in the South" (Ph.D. diss., Emory University, 1976), 11, 117, 216. Truesdale uses the term *demonic* following Paul Tillich's thought. For Tillich, the demonic "is the form-destroying eruption of the creative basis of things. . . . There is a unity of the form-creating and form-destroying qualities of life in Being-itself. Everything that comes into being takes on a form. But in everything there is also the tendency to break out of a being's own form to realize infinity and make a prideful assertion." During the late 1920s, Tillich saw capitalism and nationalism as the major demonic movements. They both express "the vitality of creative life that produces helpful forms of existence. However, they both also contain the drive to destroy form and to deprive people of their essential humanity." See also John P. Newport, *Paul Tillich*, Makers of the Modern Theological Mind, ed. Bob E. Patterson (Waco, TX: Word Books, 1984), 225; and Paul Tillich, *The Interpretation of History* (New York: Charles Scribner's Sons, 1936), 77-122.

[59]Truesdale, "Tillichian Analysis," 151.

[60]Lee Gibbs and W. Taylor Stevenson, eds., *Myth and the Crisis of Historical Consciousness* (Missoula, MT: Scholars Press/American Academy of Religion, 1975), 3-5.

[61]Langdon Elsbree, *The Rituals of Life: Patterns in Narratives* (Port Washington, NY: Kennikat Press, 1982), 5-8.

[62]Dixon, *Clansman*; Griffith, *Birth of a Nation*. See Richard Herrnstein and Charles Murray, *The Bell Curve: Intelligence and Class Structure in American Life* (New York: Free Press, 1994); and Dinesh D'Souza, *The End of Racism* (New York: Free Press, 1995) as current racist mythology. *Time* magazine (2 October 1995) dubs D'Souza's book "The Bigot's Handbook," written by a wunderkind who bashes women, minorities, and gays: "It contains so much sophistry, half-baked

erudition and small-minded zealotry that even right-wingers who share many of D'Souza's ideas are outraged by its, well, political incorrectness" (87). D'Souza posits that rationalized discrimination is credible and that our notions about civil rights and racism are obsolete. D'Souza critiques African-American poverty, crime, and rage without looking at the counterevidence for progress, participation, and success.

[63]Louis N. Williams, *Black Psychology: Compelling Issues and Views*, 3d ed. (Washington, DC: University Press of America, 1981), 49-57.

[64]163 U.S. 537 (1896).

[65]Williams, *Black Psychology,* 73. See also D'Souza, *End of Racism.*

[66]Frederickson, *Arrogance*, 3-7, 17-25.

[67]Kenneth Clark, *Pathos of Power* (New York: Harper & Row, 1974), 70-82.

[68]Frederickson, *Arrogance*, 59-67, 121.

[69]Kelsey, *Racism*, 9-11, 19-33.

[70]Clark, *Pathos*, 157, 159, 162.

[71]Ibid., 166.

[72]The Compromise of 1877, or "The Redemption," dates the overthrow of the carpetbagger system. The "Redeemers" were the southern leaders who executed the overthrow. Though the term *Jim Crow* was used by writers in the 1890s, its origin as applied to African Americans is unknown. Thomas D. Rice wrote a dance and song named "Jim Crow" in 1832. The term was in use as an adjective by 1838. C. Vann Woodward, *The Strange Career of Jim Crow*, rev. ed. (New York: Oxford University Press, 1955, 1957), vii, 3-4, 7.

[73]Ibid., 26-52, 77-87.

[74]Wortham, *Other Side*, xviii-xix.

[75]Ibid., 130-37.

[76]Truesdale, "Tillichian Analysis," 73-77, 88.

[77]Woodward, *Strange Career*, xii, 14.

[78]Ibid., 51.

[79]Truesdale, "Tillichian Analysis," 89, 92, 95.

[80]Ibid., 98.

[81]Gibbs and Stevenson, *Myth and Crisis*, vii, 1-2; and Frederickson, *Arrogance*, 105.

[82]Truesdale, "Tillichian Analysis," 210; Wallis, "America's Original Sin," 16-17; and C. T. Vivian, "Racial Violence in the '80s," *Sojourners* (November 1987): 24.

[83]Anne Wortham, *Other Side*, ix.

[84]Ibid., ix-xi, xvi.

[85]Jean-Jacques Rousseau coined the phrase "civil religion" in Enlightenment France. Civil religion means religious nationalism, a religious system existing alongside churches, with a creed (theology or mythology), a code (ethic), and a culture (set of symbols and rituals) related to the political state or nation. Albanese, *America*, 284-85.

[86]George C. Bedell, Leo Sandon, Jr., and Charles T. Wellborn, in *Religion in America* (New York: Macmillan, 1982), 15-69, illustrate that every American president since Washington has made an overt statement about a special relationship between the nation and God when sworn into office. The tension between the separation of church and state versus the reclamation of Jewish and Christian beliefs as basic tenets of American civil religion remains. Scholars assess the value and function of this religiousness in diverse ways: as idolatry; as a solution to denominational conflicts by subscribing to the pluralism and inclu-

siveness of the First Amendment; and as coexistence.

[87]Ibid., 18, 30.

[88]Eric Lincoln, *Race, Religion, and the Continuing American Dilemma* (New York: Hill and Wang, 1984), xiv-xviii.

[89]Roger G. Betsworth, *The Radical Movement of the 1960's* (Metuchen, NJ: Scarecrow Press and the American Theological Library Association, 1980), 6. From a political perspective, the movement of American civil religion has involved three phases since the 1960s, from pacifism and resistance to more private activity: pacifism, protest, and reform (1960-1966); confrontation, radicalization, and resistance (1965-1970); and a decline from large-scale public to more private forms of sectarian action (1970-1980s). See Betsworth, 6-11, 20-21. The 1990s seem to be a combination of grassroots protest, disillusionment, and calls for reform in the public sector.

[90]Kelsey, *Racism*, 11; Lincoln, *Race, Religion*, xvii.

[91]Kelsey, *Racism*, 20-22.

[92]Ibid., 132; see also 124-31.

[93]Clark, *Pathos*, 32-33. The use of the term *god* here is apropos, using Paul Tillich's idea that the object of one's ultimate concern is that person's god.

[94]The U.S. Constitution declares that a slave is three-fifths of a person. See chapter 2, note 6.

[95]The usage here of the term *White man* is purposely race- and gender-specific.

[96]Williams et al., *Eyes,* vi-vii, 106-7.

[97]Renita Weems, "Reading Her Way through the Struggle: African American Women and the Bible," in *Stony the Road We Trod*, ed. Cain Hope Felder (Minneapolis: Fortress Press, 1991), 69.

[98]Molefi Asante, *The Afrocentric Idea* (Philadelphia: Temple University Press, 1987), 125. The movement toward sanity is a historical and a philosophical act.

[99]Taylor, "Implications," 189, 192; and Beckham, "Psychology," 393. Beckham claims that singers languishing in pity relayed their dire plight. Many others knew pity, but they did something about it. Some of the Spirituals were palliative, i.e., they mentally reduced the intense pain of slavery. Some were sorrow songs. Depending upon the text and performer, these categories are not mutually exclusive. Sometimes the emotional context overlapped.

[100]James Farmer, qtd. in Henry Hampton and Steve Fayer, *Voices of Freedom: An Oral History of the Civil Rights Movement from the 1950s through the 1980s* (New York: Bantam Books, 1990), 94-96; see also 38, 108.

3. Theodicy in White and Black

[1]Lerone Bennett, Jr., *Before the Mayflower: A History of the Negro in America 1619–1964*, rev. ed. (Baltimore: Penguin, 1964), 360, 373, 404.

[2]Children's Defense Fund, © 1997; these statistics and additional information found on the internet: http://www.childrensdefense.org/facts.html.

[3]Joseph A. Komonchak, Mary Collins, and Dermont Lane, eds., *The New Dictionary of Theology* (Wilmington, DE: Michael Glazier, 1987), s.v. "Problem of Evil," by T. W. Tilley; David Hume, *Dialogues Concerning Natural Religion*, ed. H. D. Aiken (New York: Harper, 1948), 66.

[4]Alan Richardson and Alan Bowden, ed., *The Westminster Dictionary of Christian Theology* (Philadelphia: Westminster Press, 1983), s.v. "The Problem of Evil,"

by John Hick.

[5]These thinkers include David Hume, Immanuel Kant, Georg Hegel, and Thomas Jefferson. See Henry Louis Gates, Jr., *Figures in Black: Words, Signs, and the "Racial Self"* (New York: Oxford University Press, 1987), 14-25.

[6]Michele Bowen-Spencer, "C. Eric Lincoln: Historiography" (Bowling Green, OH: Bowling Green University, 1991, photocopy), 5. The reality of this statement becomes apparent when one finds that little has been written on the question of Jesus and racism as a problem of evil.

[7]Komonchak, Collins, and Lane, "Problem of Evil," by Tilley; Kenneth Surin, *Theology and the Problem of Evil* (New York: Basil Blackwell, 1986), 2, 8; Mircea Eliade, *The Encyclopedia of Religion* (New York: Macmillan, 1987), s.v. "Theodicy," by Ronald M. Green; John Hick, *Evil and the God of Love*, rev. ed. (San Francisco: Harper & Row, 1977), viii.

[8]Hick, *Evil and the God*, 211.

[9]Irenaeus, *Against Heresies*, Ante-Nicene Library, vols. 4-5 (Grand Rapids: Eerdman, 1979), 3.20.1; 4.38.3; 5.6.1.

[10]Ibid., 4.38.3; 4.39.1.

[11]Hick, *Evil and the God*, 53-63, 170-92; *Augustine: Confessions and Enchiridion*, Library of Christian Classics, ed. Albert Outler (Philadelphia: Westminster Press, 1955), *Confessions*, bk. 7, chaps. 3-5, 12-16, *Enchiridion*, chaps. 3-5; and Augustine, *The City of God*, in *Basic Writings of Saint Augustine*, ed. Whitney J. Oates (Grand Rapids: Baker Book House, 1948), bk. 11, chaps. 16-18; bk. 12, chaps. 1-9.

[12]Hick, *Evil and the God*, 93-113. See also Thomas Aquinas, *Summa Theologica* (London: R. & T. Washbourne, 1912), 1.25.6; 1.47.1-2; 1.48.2, 5; 1.49.1-2.

[13]Hick, *Evil and the God*, 117-26. See also John Calvin, *Institutes of the Christian Religion*, 2 vols, ed. John T. McNeil (London: SCM Philadelphia: Westminster Press, 1961), 1.15.8; 2.1.5; 3.21.5; 3.23.1; 3, 6, 7. I use the term *omni-God* as a referent for an omnipotent, omniscient, and infinitely good and loving Creator.

[14]Hick, *Evil and the God*, 214-22; and Friedrich Schleiermacher, *The Christian Faith*, ed. H. R. Mackintosh and J. S. Stewart (Edinburgh: T & T Clark, 1928), 233-40, 270-74.

[15]Hick, *Evil and the God*, 224.

[16]Schleiermacher, *Christian Faith*, 327, 338; and Hick, *Evil and the God*, 227-34.

[17]Karl Barth, *Church Dogmatics*, ed. G. W. Bromiley and T. F. Torrance (Edinburgh: T & T Clark, 1956), 3:3.50.

[18]Hick, *Evil and the God*, 126-29.

[19]Ibid., 126-37. See also Barth, *Church Dogmatics*, 3:1.41.2, 42.3; 41.2, par. 42.3; IV/1, par. 59.

[20]Barth, *Church Dogmatics*, 3:3.304-5.

[21]Alvin Plantinga, "The Free Will Defense," in *Philosophy of Religion: Selected Readings*, ed. William L. Rowe and William J. Wainwright (New York: Harcourt Brace Jovanovich, 1973), 217-30.

[22]Alvin Plantinga, "God's Foreknowledge and Human Free Will Are Compatible," in *Philosophy of Religion: An Anthology*, ed. Louis Pojman (Belmont, CA: Wadsworth Publishing, 1987), 152, 228; Michael Beaty, "The Problem of Evil: The Unanswered Questions Argument," *Southwest Philosophical Review* 5 (January 1988): 58-59; and William J. Wainwright, *Philosophy of Religion* (Belmont, CA: Wadsworth Publishing, 1988), 79-82.

[23]Eleanor Stump, "The Problem of Evil," *Faith and Philosophy* 2 (1985): 392-93, 398-99, 415. Technically in Genesis 3, the source of the "Fall doctrine," Adam and

Eve did not fall, they were expelled from the garden.

[24]Ibid., 409, 411.

[25]Hick, *Evil and the God*, 245-56, 261.

[26]Ibid., 243-93; and Stephen Davis, *Encountering Evil: Live Options in Theodicy* (Atlanta: John Knox, 1981), 39-52.

[27]Hick, *Evil and the God*, 288-91, 334-35.

[28]G. Stanley Kane, "The Failure of Soul-Making Theodicy," *International Journal for Philosophy of Religion* 6 (1975): 2-15; John Roth, "Critique by John Roth," in Davis, *Encountering Evil*, 61-63; Frederick Sontag, "Critique by Frederick Sontag," in Davis, 55-58; Stephen Davis, "Critique by Stephen Davis," in Davis, 58-61; and David Griffin, "Critique by David Griffin," in Davis, 53-55.

[29]Surin, *Theology and the Problem*, 2-3, 6-7.

[30]Ibid., 8-10, 13, 15-18, 19. Gnostics were persons who championed a higher and secret knowledge of some humans as the key to salvation, and the coequal existence of good and evil, and denied the unity of Scripture and of God.

[31]Ibid., 24-27, 47-58.

[32]Plantinga, "Free Will Defense," 217-30; Richard Swinburne, *The Existence of God* (Oxford: Clarendon, 1979), 203-20; Richard Swinburne, "The Problem of Evil," in *Reason and Religion*, ed. Stuart C. Brown (London and Ithaca: Cornell University Press, 1977), 81-101; and Surin, *Theology And the Problem*, 70-85, 92-96. Surin doubts Hick's arguments regarding inevitable joy versus acquiring individual freedom, the degrees of evil, and divine justice.

[33]Surin, *Theology and the Problem*, 104-5.

[34]Dorothee Soelle, *Suffering* (London: Darton, Longman & Todd, 1975); Jürgen Moltmann, *The Crucified God*, trans. R. Z. Wilson and John Bowden (London: SCM, 1974); Peter Taylor Forsyth, *The Justification of God: Lectures for War-Time on a Christian Theodicy* (London: Duckworth, 1916), 32-62, 124-72; and ibid., 136-37.

[35]Surin, *Theology and the Problem*, 121-37, 142-45.

[36]Ibid., 149.

[37]From "Lift Every Voice and Sing," the Black National Anthem, by James Weldon Johnson and J. Rosamond Johnson, Edward B. Marks Music Corporation, 1927.

[38]Howard Thurman, *The Search for Common Ground: An Inquiry Into the Basis of Man's Experience of Community* (New York: Harper & Row, 1971); and Walter E. Fluker, *They Looked for a City: A Comparative Analysis of the Ideal of Community in the Thought of Howard Thurman and Martin Luther King, Jr.* (Lanham, MD: University Press of America, 1989), 3, 29.

[39]Thurman, *Search for Common Ground*, 4; Howard Thurman, "Community and the Will of God," Mendenhall Lectures, De Pauw University, February 1961, Thurman Papers, Mugar Memorial Library, Boston University; Howard Thurman, *Deep Is the Hunger* (New York: Harper & Brothers, 1951), 64; Howard Thurman, *The Creative Encounter* (New York: Harper & Row, 1954; repr., Richmond Publishers, 1972), 37-38, 53-54, 66.

[40]Howard Thurman, *Disciplines of the Spirit* (New York: Harper and Row, 1963; repr., Richmond, IN: Friends United Press, 1973), 66; Howard Thurman, "Freedom Under God," Second Century Convocation, Washington University, February 1955, Thurman Papers, Mugar Memorial Library, Boston University; Thurman, *Deep Is the Hunger*, 27; Howard Thurman, *With Head and Heart: The Autobiography of Howard Thurman* (New York: Harcourt Brace Jovanovich, 1979), 134, 268;

and Fluker, *They Looked For A City*, 49-52.

[41]Howard Thurman, *The Luminous Darkness: A Personal Interpretation of the Anatomy of Segregation and the Ground of Hope* (New York: Harper & Row, 1965), 5-12; Howard Thurman, "What Can I Believe In?" *Journal of Religion and Health* 12 (November 1972): 111-19; Howard Thurman, *The Inward Journey* (New York: Harper and Row, 1961), 105.

[42]Kenneth Smith and Ira Zepp, Jr., *Search for the Beloved Community: The Thinking of Martin Luther King, Jr.* (Valley Forge: Judson Press, 1974), 119-40; and Fluker, *They Looked For A City*, 81, 90-91, 107.

[43]Martin Luther King, Jr., *Where Do We Go From Here: Chaos or Community?* (Boston: Beacon, 1967), 97-98.

[44]Martin Luther King, Jr., *Strength to Love* (Philadelphia: Fortress Press, 1981), 110; and ibid., 171-72.

[45]Martin Luther King, Jr., "The Ethical Demands of Integration," in *A Testament of Hope: The Essential Writings of Martin Luther King, Jr.*, ed. James M. Washington (San Francisco: Harper & Row, 1986), 118.

[46]Martin Luther King, Jr., "Nonviolence: The Only Road to Freedom," in Washington, *Testament of Hope*, 54-61.

[47]Martin Luther King, Jr., "Suffering and Faith," in Washington, *Testament of Hope*, 41; King, *Strength to Love*, 45, 83, 87-90; King, *Where Do We Go*, 59-61; and Martin Luther King, Jr., "Love, Law, and Civil Disobedience," *New South* (December 1961): 6.

[48]King, *Where Do We Go*, 173-86; and *Strength to Love*, 40, 120.

[49]"Black theology" refers to theology derived from the Black experience and focuses on racism as the evil. In contrast, "Eurocentric (White) theology" is derived from a common Greek and Roman tradition and experience. One of the paradoxes presented by Eurocentric (White) theology is that one of its major Christian progenitors, Augustine, was of African (Black) ethnicity.

[50]Deane William Ferm, *Contemporary American Theologies: A Critical Survey*, rev. ed. (San Francisco: Harper & Row, 1981, 1990), 44; and James H. Cone, *Black Theology and Black Power* (San Francisco: Harper & Row, 1969, 1989), 1, 6-7.

[51]Cone, *Black Theology*, 13-29.

[52]Ibid., 34-61, 117; and James H. Cone, *The Spirituals and the Blues: An Interpretation* (New York: Seabury, 1972; Maryknoll, NY: Orbis Books, 1992), 5-7, 16-19.

[53]Willie Wright, "Theodicy: Black Suffering" (D.Min. professional project, School of Theology at Claremont, 1976), 6-10, 16. See also Joseph R. Washington, *The Politics of God* (Boston: Beacon, 1967), 155-73.

[54]William R. Jones, *Is God a White Racist?* (New York: Doubleday, 1973), 88.

[55]Wright, "Theodicy," 17.

[56]Ibid., 36. See also Major Jones, *Black Awareness: A Theology of Hope* (Nashville: Abingdon, 1971), 124-25.

[57]Major Jones, *Christian Ethics for Black Theology* (Nashville: Abingdon, 1974), 6; Wright, "Theodicy," 39, 40, 42, 44.

[58]See Samuel Beckett, *Waiting for Godot: A Tragicomedy in Two Acts*, ed. Harold Bloom (London: S. French, 1957); and Samuel Beckett, *Krapp's Last Tape*, ed. Harold Bloom (New York: Chelsea House, 1987).

[59]See Howard Thurman, *Deep River and the Negro Spirituals Speak of Life and Death* (Richmond, IN: Friends United Press, 1973); Washington, *Testament of Hope*; and Cone, *Spirituals and the Blues*.

[60]Alice Walker coined the term *Womanist* from *womanish*, used by Black moth-

ers to tell their daughters not to act too grown before their time. A Womanist is courageous, in charge, and loves and commits to the wholeness and survival of all people. Womanist scholars use this term as a forum to talk about the oppressions of sexism, racism, and classism experienced by poor Black women. See Alice Walker, *In Search of Our Mothers' Gardens: Womanist Prose* (San Francisco: Harcourt Brace Jovanovich, 1981).

[61]Kelly Delaine Brown Douglas, "Womanist Theology: What Is Its Relationship to Black Theology?" in *Black Theology: A Documentary History, Vol. II: 1980-1992,* ed. James Cone and Gayraud Wilmore (Maryknoll, NY: Orbis Books, 1993), 291-92.

[62]See James H. Cone, *Martin & Malcolm & America: A Dream or a Nightmare* (Maryknoll, NY: Orbis Books, 1991).

[63]Juan Williams et al., *Eyes on the Prize: America's Civil Rights Years, 1954-1965* (New York: Penguin, 1987), 74.

4. Story: R-e-v-o-l-u-t-i-o-n

[1]See Charles T. Davis and Henry Louis Gates, Jr., *The Slave's Narrative* (Oxford: Oxford University Press, 1985); Marion Wilson Starling, *The Slave Narrative: Its Place in American History,* 2d ed. (Washington, DC: Howard University Press, 1981; and George P. Rawick, *The American Slave: A Composite Autobiography,* 41 vols. (Westport, CT: Greenwood Publishing Company, 1972, 1978, 1979).

[2]See Len Holt, *The Summer That Didn't End* (New York: William Morrow, 1965); Anthony Lewis, *The Second American Revolution: A First Hand Account of the Struggle for Civil Rights* (London: Faber and Faber, 1966); Debbie Louis, *And We Are Not Saved: A History of the Movement as People* (Garden City: Doubleday, 1970); Anne Moody, *Coming of Age in Mississippi* (New York: Dial Press, 1968); Pat Watters, *Down to Now: Reflections on the Southern Civil Rights Movement* (New York: Random House, 1971); and Howard Zinn, *SNCC: The New Abolitionists* (Boston: Beacon Press, 1964).

[3]The initial success of *Brown v. Board of Education of Topeka* was tempered by the Supreme Court's decision to allow "orderly" integration of previously segregated school systems with "all deliberate speed."

[4]Stephen Crites, "The Narrative Quality of Experience," *Journal of the American Academy of Religion* 39 (September 1971): 305.

[5]John A. Burrison, ed., *Storytellers: Folktales and Legends from the South* (Athens: University of Georgia Press, 1989), 13-15.

[6]Crites, "Narrative Quality," 305.

[7]George W. Stroup, *The Promise of Narrative Theology: Recovering the Gospel in the Church* (Atlanta: John Knox Press, 1981), 72.

[8]In *Promise,* Stroup reviews literature that sees the necessary link between personal experience and religious symbols. He also reflects how certain master images, embedded within narratives as player, sufferer, and vandal, form the individual.

[9]Ibid., 86-97.

[10]Molefi Kete Asante, *The Afrocentric Idea* (Philadelphia: Temple University Press, 1987), 160-72.

[11]Dickson D. Bruce, Jr., *Black American Writing from the Nadir: The Evolution of a Literary Tradition, 1877-1915* (Baton Rouge: Louisiana University Press, 1989), 208, 226, 227; Dena Epstein, *Sinful Tunes and Spirituals: Black Folk Music to the*

Civil War (Urbana: University of Illinois Press, 1977), 63-76; and Charles Small, *Music of the Common Tongue: Survival and Celebration in Afro-American Music* (London: John Calder, 1987), 20.

[12]Stephen Kepnes, "Telling and Retelling: The Use of Narrative in Psychoanalysis and Religion," in *The Challenge of Psychology To Faith*, Concilium: Religion in the Eighties Series, ed. Stephen Kepnes and David Tracy (Edinburgh: T & T Clark, 1982), 28-32.

[13]Harold A. Jackson, Jr., "The New Hermeneutic and the Understanding of Spirituals," *Journal of the Interdenominational Theological Center* 3 (September 1976): 36-39.

[14]W. E. B. Du Bois, *The Souls of Black Folk,* with an introduction by Henry Louis Gates, Jr. (1903; repr., New York: Bantam Books, 1989), xxxi-xxxii, 43-48, 56-65.

[15]Paul Laurence Dunbar, "We Wear the Mask," in *Black Voices: An Anthology of Afro-American Literature*, ed. Abraham Chapman (New York: New American Library, 1968), 355.

[16]William M. Tuttle, Jr., *W. E. B. Du Bois* (Englewood Cliffs, NJ: Prentice Hall, 1973), 1.

[17]David M. Simms, "The Negro Spiritual: Origins and Themes," *Journal of Negro Education* 35 (Winter 1966): 37.

[18]Howard Thurman, *Deep River and The Negro Spiritual Speaks of Life and Death* (Richmond, IN: Friends United Press, 1975), 20.

[19]Although modern translations are "theological" and historically correct, no present-day translation matches the literary quality, cadences, and poetry of the King James Version. This version was the translation most available in colonial America.

[20]Albert Beckham, "The Psychology of Negro Spirituals," *Southern Workman* 60 (1931): 392.

[21]Walter Brueggemann, *The Message of the Psalms* (Minneapolis: Augsburg, 1984), 74-75.

[22]W. H. Bellinger, Jr., *The Psalms: Reading and Studying the Book of Praises* (Peabody, MA: Hendrickson, 1990), 73.

[23]Ibid., 16.

[24]Guy Carawan and Candie Carawan, *Sing for Freedom: The Story of the Civil Rights Movement Through Its Songs* (Bethlehem, PA: Sing Out Corporation, 1990), 18.

[25]Ibid., 27-29.

[26]Ibid., 86. Sam Block and Willie Peacock (of SNCC) redacted this spiritual.

[27]Fannie Lou Hamer led this redacted version of "Go Tell It."

[28]Members of the Albany Movement created this version from traditional song. They applied the term "Nervous Nelly" to a typical segregationist.

[29]Du Bois, *Souls*, 180-81.

[30]Willis H. King, "The Negro Spirituals and the Hebrew Psalms," *Methodist Review* 114 (May 1931): 318-26.

[31]Stephen Kepnes, "Telling and Retelling: The Use of Narrative in Psychoanalysis and Religion," in *The Challenge of Psychology to Faith*, Concilium Religion in the Eighties Series, ed. Stephen Kepnes and David Tracy (Edinburgh: T & T Clark, 1982), 27.

[32]Jackson, "New Hermeneutic," 40-47.

[33]Donald H. Matthews, "The Spiritual: An African-American Narrative

Hermeneutics" (Ph.D. diss., Temple University, 1992), 11-12.

[34]Ibid., 17, 19, 34-35.

[35]Ibid., 71.

[36]Ibid., 3. According to Arnold Rampersad, Du Bois relied on the work of nineteenth-century psychologist Oswald Kulpe and the thought of William James. The divided self is characterized "by the existence of a more or less complete separation of two aggregates of conscious process . . . often times of entirely opposite character." See Gates, "Introduction," in Du Bois, *Souls*, xix; see also Arnold Rampersad, *The Art and Imagination* (Cambridge: Harvard University Press, 1976).

[37]Deborah E. McDowell and Arnold Rampersad, eds., *Slavery and the Literary Imagination* (Baltimore: Johns Hopkins University Press, 1989), 117. Du Bois does not compare the "divided self" of the general populace and that lived by African Americans.

[38]August Meier, "The Paradox of W. E. B. Du Bois," in Tuttle, Jr., *Du Bois*, 145-46; Gates, "Introduction," in Du Bois, *Souls*, 2. Du Bois first experienced the veil as a boy, when one White girl, a new student, refused to exchange cards with Du Bois when she saw he was Black. Being rejected was his impetus for excellence. He "had thereafter no desire to tear down that veil, to creep through."

[39]Melvin Wade and Margaret Wade, "The Black Aesthetic in the Black Novel," *Journal of Black Studies* (June 1972): 391-408. Du Bois's seminal work has influenced the majority of African-American scholars doing sociocultural, historical, psychological, theological, and anthropological analyses.

[40]Even Du Bois showed evidence of ethnic self-hatred, insofar as he considered mulattos like himself to be superior to coal-black persons of African descent. One element of the famed dispute between him and Booker T. Washington was Du Bois's prejudice against darker-hued African Americans, such as Washington. One may speculate that a subconscious motive for the rejection of Supreme Court Justice Clarence Thomas by many of the liberal Black intelligentsia, was the visible evidence that Thomas is truly a *Black* African American.

[41]Tuttle, *Du Bois*, 11.

[42]Du Bois quoted in ibid., 2.

[43]Du Bois, *Souls*, xvii.

[44]Ibid., 186-87. Erik Erickson, in *Identity: Youth and Crisis* (New York, W. W. Norton, 1968), unites the divided self in the conversion experience. One overcomes the twoness through spiritual unity. Persons are redefined as children of God as a religious, transformed self. Time as event is the totality of past, present, and future. Frederick Douglass and McNeal Turner talk about the twoness, the divided self, in their respective biographies.

[45]Meier, "Paradox," 159.

[46]Gates, "Introduction," xx.

[47]Asante, *Afrocentric*, 124. Du Bois had a Germanic notion of race as a unit of cultural advancement in world-historical development. Asante argues that this concept of race is contrary to the idea that culture, not a biological idea of race, shapes human advancement.

[48]Matthews, "The Spiritual," 1-6.

[49]Ibid., 4.

[50]An immediate analogy is the dilemma posed by the theories of quantum mechanics in modern physics. A light photon is defined as both a particle (*quanta*) and a wave at the same instant. Similarly, one may determine either the position

or acceleration of a particle, but not both simultaneously. Measuring one aspect destroys the possibility of measuring the other.

[51]Carl F. Keppler, *The Literature of the Second Self* (Tucson: University of Arizona Press, 1972), ix-3, 209. This simultaneity is striking when stated mathematically: 1 + 1 = 2 [base 10]; 1 + 1 = 10 [base 2]. Both answers express the same algebraic sum: 2 [base 10] is the same as 10 [base 2])!

[52]The naming, unmasking, and engaging the powers follows the thought of Walter Wink. This process includes that of identification and ends with an exorcism or expelling of the evil. See Walter Wink, *Naming the Powers: The Language of Power in the New Testament*, vol. 1 of, *The Powers* (Minneapolis: Fortress, 1984); and *Unmasking the Powers: The Invisible Forces That Determine Human Existence*, vol. 2 of *The Powers* (Minneapolis: Fortress, 1986).

[53]Consider the impact of Greek thought that presses for cause and effect; the preference for a concentric or centrifugal model; the cultural disposition toward opposites; the impact of non-Euclidean geometry, where many parallel lines meet at none, one, or many points; or the thrust of chaos theory, which concludes that a well-ordered universe degenerates into logical confusion. The Greek hypothesis claims that disorder eventually becomes ordered.

[54]Ralph Ellison, *The Invisible Man* (New York: New American Library, 1952), 7-8.

[55]Du Bois, *Souls*, 175.

[56]Asante, *Afrocentric*, 4-6.

[57]Bernice Johnson Reagon, ed., *Voices of the Civil Rights Movement: Black American Freedom Songs, 1960-66* (Washington, DC: The Smithsonian Institution Program in Black Culture, 1980), phonodisc R023, 4.

[58]New Testament scholar and theologian Walter Wink developed the concepts of naming, unmasking, and engaging "the powers" in his three volume work on evil as relates to church and society. See his *Naming the Powers: The Language of Power in the New Testament* (Minneapolis: Fortress Press, 1984); *Unmasking the Powers: The Invisible Forces That Determine Human Existence* (Minneapolis: Augsburg Fortress, 1986); *Engaging the Powers; Discernment and Resistance in a World of Domination* (Minneapolis: Augsburg Fortress, 1992).

5. Creative Spirit

[1]See Manfred Clynes, "The Communication of Emotion: Theory of Sentics," in *Emotion, Theory, Research, and Experience*, ed. R. Plutchhik and H. Kellerman (New York: Academic Press), 271-300; and Manfred Clynes, "The Living Quality of Music," in *Music, Mind, and Brain*, ed. Manfred Clynes (New York: Plenum Press, 1982), 47-82.

[2]Bernice Johnson Reagon, "Program Notes," *Voices of the Civil Rights Movement, 1960-1966* (Washington, DC: Smithsonian Institution, Program in Black American Culture, 1980), 6.

[3]My use of "hearers' response" relates to a definition of modern reader response theory which concentrates on what readers do and how they do it. See Robert Davis and Ronald Schleifer, *Contemporary Literary Criticism: Literary and Cultural Studies*, 2d ed. (New York: Longman, 1989), 67-73.

[4]Norman Harris, *Connecting Times: The Sixties in Afro-American Fiction* (Jackson: University Press of Mississippi, 1988), 5, 10-12.

[5]Olly Wilson, "Black Music as an Art Form," *Black Music Journal* (1983): 21; see also 7, 9.

[6]James Standifer, "Musical Behaviors of Black People in American Society," *Black Music Research Journal* (1980): 57.

[7]John Lovell, Jr., *Black Song: The Forge and the Flame; the Story of How the Afro-American Spiritual Was Hammered Out* (New York: Macmillan, 1972), 637.

[8]Houston Baker, Jr., *Blues, Ideology, and Afro-American Literature: A Vernacular Theory* (Chicago: University of Chicago Press, 1984), 110-11. This approach or hermeneutic involves an imagination that taps into the use of tropes or figures of speech that include irony, satire, and overstatement.

[9]Michel Foucault, *The Archaeology of Knowledge* (New York: Harper & Row, 1972), 56; see also 131. Discourse occurs in modes (e.g., economics, history, music).

[10]Ibid., 79-87; and Baker, *Blues*, 17-19.

[11]Vincent Harding, *Hope and History: Why We Must Share the Story of the Movement* (Maryknoll, NY: Orbis Books, 1990), 1-10.

[12]Baker, *Blues*, 22.

[13]Ibid., 25, 27, 100.

[14]Ibid., 77-78, 80-95.

[15]Ibid., 60; Henry Louis Gates, Jr., *Figures in Black: Words, Signs, and the "Racial" Self* (New York: Oxford University Press, 1987), xxxi; and Henry Louis Gates, Jr., *The Signifying Monkey: A Theory of Afro-American Literary Criticism* (New York: Oxford University Press, 1988), xxiii, 45, 50-51.

[16]Guy Carawan and Candie Carawan, *Sing for Freedom: The Story of the Civil Rights Movement through Its Songs* (Bethlehem, PA: Sing Out, 1990), 18, 70-71.

[17]Gates, *Signifying Monkey*, xxiv.

[18]Lovell, *Black Song*, 287-88.

[19]Gates, *Signifying Monkey*, 50-52, 58-67.

[20]Ibid., 73, 75, 80, 86, 88.

[21]Robert Escarpit, *L'humour* (Paris: n.p., 1960), 38; qtd. in Gerard Bessiere, "Humour—A Theological Attitude?" in *Theology of Joy*, Concilium Religion in the Seventies Series, ed. Johann Metz and Jean-Pierre Jossua (New York: Herder and Herder, 1974), 83-84.

[22]Bessiere, "Humour," 84-86. Humor, split in two during the eighteenth century, has a visceral part (sense of humor) and an intellectual part (the aesthetic or conscious humor).

[23]Ibid., 87. Bessiere notes that without the demands for relationship with the divine and for conversion, irony would simply be mental eccentricity.

[24]Miles Mark Fisher, *Negro Slave Songs in the United States* (1953; repr., with a foreword by Ray Allen Billington, New York: Citadel Press, 1981), ix.

[25]Bessiere, "Humour," 88-89; and Harvey Potthoff, "Humor and Religious Faith," in *Summary of Proceedings, 34th Annual Conference, American Theological Library Association* (n.p.: 1980), 75-79.

[26]Potthoff, "Humor," 75-79.

[27]See Juan Williams et al., *Eyes on the Prize: America's Civil Rights Years, 1954-1965* (New York: Penguin Books, 1987), vi-vii.

[28]Ibid., 7-25.

[29]Bernice Johnson Reagon, interview by author, tape recording, Washington, DC, November 1991.

[30]Bessiere, "Humour," 92-93.

[31]Harding, *Hope and History*, 127, 134-35.

[32]Ibid., 136.

[33]Robbie Lieberman, *"My Song Is My Weapon": People's Songs, American Communism, And The Politics Of Culture, 1930-1950* (Chicago: University Of Illinois Press, 1989), xv, 115. See also Peter Tamony, "Hootenanny," *John Edwards Memorial Foundation Quarterly* 16 (Summer 1980): 95-98; and Pete Seeger, *Incompleat Folksinger*, ed. Jo Metcalf Schwartz (New York: Simon and Schuster, 1972), 326-28.

[34]Raymond Williams, *Marxism and Literature* (Oxford: Oxford University Press, 1977), 123-24; qtd. in Lieberman, *"My Song,"* xviii.

[35]Lieberman, *"My Song,"* xvi, xix.

[36]Ibid., 91, 110-112.

[37]Darlene Clark Hine, ed., *Black Women in America: An Historical Encyclopedia* (Brooklyn, NY: Carlson Publishing, 1993); and Septima Clark with Blythe, *Echo in My Soul,* (New York: E. P. Dutton), 186, 206-17.

[38]Lieberman, *"My Song,"* 45-46; 63-81.

[39]Ibid., 91, 110-12.

[40]Ibid., 91, 146.

[41]Russell Ames, "Protest and Irony in Negro Folk Song," *Science and Society* 14 (Summer 1950): 207-12; and Wayne McLaughlin, "Symbolism and Mysticism in the Spirituals," *Phylon* 24 (1963): 70.

[42]Christa Dixon, *Negro Spirituals: From Bible to Folk Song* (Philadelphia: Fortress Press, 1976), x.

[43]Bernice Johnson Reagon, untitled article on the Spirituals, Archives, National Museum of American History, Program in Black Culture, n.d., 1.

[44]Robert Mendl, *The Divine Quest in Music* (London: Salisbury Square, 1957), 158.

[45]Natalie Curtis Burlin, "How Negro Folksongs are 'Born,' " *Current Opinion* 66 (March 1919): 166.

[46]Ibid.

[47]Robert Sherman, "Sing a Song of Freedom," *Saturday Review* (September 28, 1963): 65-67, 81.

[48]Bernice Johnson Reagon, "Ella's Song," *Sweet Honey in the Rock: We All . . . Everyone of Us,* cassette FF 90317, Flying Fish, 1983.

[49]Gerard Behague, ed., *Performance Practice: Ethnomusicological Perspectives* (Westport, CT: Greenwood Press, 1984), 3-8.

[50]Gerard Behague, interview by author, September 21, 1992, Austin, TX.

[51] Willi Apel, *Harvard Dictionary of Music*, 2nd ed. (Cambridge, MA: Belknap Press, 1969) s.v., "Rhythm"; Joseph Mussulman, *The Uses of Music: An Introduction to Music in Contemporary American Life* (Englewood Cliffs, NJ: Prentice-Hall, 1974), 40; Leonard B. Meyers, *Emotion and Meaning in Music* (Chicago: University of Chicago Press, 1956), 103; and Harold M. Best, *Music Through the Eyes of Faith,* Christian College Coalition Series (San Francisco: HarperCollins, 1993), 11-12. Tilford Brooks, in *America's Black Musical Heritage* (Englewood Cliffs, NJ: Prentice-Hall, 1984, 1993), contends that while African-American music is similar to African music regarding polyrhythmic complexity, the approach to cross rhythms for African-American music is divisive and for African music it is additive. With the additive principle, music builds from a small, constant time unit that is never forsaken—even with the entrances of other voices or instruments with different basic time units. The differentiation between divisive and addi-

tive rhythmic approaches locates African-American music closer to the European additive tradition.

[52]Meyers, *Emotion and Meaning*, 102-3.

[53]Mussulman, *Uses of Music*, 47-48, 55.

[54]Brooks, *America's Black Musical Heritage*, 19-20. Heterophony is a product of improvisation wherein each instrument or voice often performs simultaneous rhythmic and melodic variations.

[55]Apel, *Harvard Dictionary*, s.v. "Antiphonal singing."

[56]Brooks, *American Black Musical Heritage*, 16-17. A tempered scale refers to a system of tuning. Equal temperament allows a musician to begin on any pitch knowing the intervals will be in tune, and to freely move from key to key within one basic pitch system. This tuning system works only for fixed pitched instruments (harp, organ, piano) and fretted instruments; see Mussulman, *Uses of Music*, 22.

[57]Brooks, *American Black Musical Heritage*, 17.

[58]Meyers, *Emotion and Meaning*, 199-202.

[59]Mussulman, *Uses of Music*, 33.

[60]Ibid., 38-39; and Willi Apel, s.v. "Texture," in *Harvard Dictionary of Music*, 2d ed.

[61]Helen L. Bonny and Louis M. Savary, *Music and Your Mind: Listening with a New Consciousness* (Barrytown, NY: Station Hill Press, 1973, 1990), 17, 19, 30, 37.

[62]Frank Burch Brown, *Religious Aesthetics: A Theological Study of Making and Meaning* (London: Macmillan, 1990), 101.

[63]Ibid., 101-12. Where Frank Burch Brown talks about art as being religious, I regard music synonymously. His view of art serves as an umbrella to include the activity of music.

[64]Deryck Cooke, *The Language of Music* (London: Oxford University Press, 1959), x-xi; and Christopher Ballantine, *Music and Its Social Meanings* (New York: Gordon and Breach Science Publishers, 1984), x, xi, xvi.

[65]Kathleen Higgins, *The Music of Our Lives* (Philadelphia: Temple University Press, 1991), 17, 101, 123, 128.

[66]Cooke, *Language of Music*, 34-37.

[67]Peter Kivy, *The Fine Art of Repetition: Essays in the Philosophy of Music* (Cambridge: Cambridge University Press, 1993), 17, 21, 26-28.

[68]Ibid., 129, 147-49, 252.

[69]Arthur Schnabel, *Music and the Line of Most Resistance* (Ann Arbor: University Microfilms,1962), 8.

[70]Mendl, *Divine Quest*, 158.

[71]Best, *Music through the Eyes of Faith*, 6.

[72]Ibid., 7, 9, 13, 28-29, 42-44, 113, 120.

[73]Alan Lomax, "Folk Song Style," *American Anthropologist* 61 (1959): 927-54; repr. in *Music as Culture*, ed. Kay Kaufman Shelemay (New York: Garland Publishing, 1990), 61-82; and Steven Feld, "Sound Structure as Social Structure," *Ethnomusicology* 25 (1981): 383-409; repr. in Shelemay, 301-3.

[74]Jon Michael Spencer, ed., "Preface to *The Theology of American Popular Music*," *Black Sacred Music: A Journal of Theomusicology* 3 (Fall 1989): v.

[75]Andrew Greeley, *God in Popular Culture* (Chicago: Thomas More Press, 1988), 13-14, 16, 87.

[76]Ernst Bloch, *Essays on the Philosophy of Music*, trans. Peter Palmer (Cambridge: Cambridge University Press, 1985), 227; qtd. in Spencer, "Preface," vi.

[77]Spencer, "Preface," ix. These three phases of theomusicology, then, include, respectively, the descriptive, the normative, and the predictive.

[78]Jon Michael Spencer, *Theological Music: Introduction to Theomusicology* (New York: Greenwood Press, 1991), xi.

[79]Ibid., 116.

[80]Molefi Kete Asante, *The Afrocentric Idea* (Philadelphia: Temple University Press, 1987), 160; Robert Schmidt, "Hearing, Calling and Naming: Aspects of Nommo in Toni Morrison's *Beloved*" (Bowling Green, OH: Bowling Green University, n.d.), photocopy; and Janheinz Jahn, *Muntu: The New African Culture* (New York: Grove Press, 1961), 121-57.

[81]Catherine Albanese, *America: Religions and Religion* (Belmont, CA: Wadsworth Publishing, 1981), 120-21.

[82]Roy Lester Clark, "A Fantasy Theme Analysis of Negro Spirituals" (Ph.D. diss., Southern Illinois University at Carbondale, 1979), 4, 48, 86, 101-5, 145.

[83]Marcia Herndon and Norma McLeod, *Music as Culture* (Darby, PA: Norwood Editions, 1982), 12-23; Feld, "Sound Structure," 299; C. Marcel-Du Bois, "L'ethnomusicologie, as vocation et as situation," *Revue de l'enseignement superieur* 3 (1965), 38; and Stanley Sadie, ed., *The New Grove Dictionary of Music and Musicians*, 6th ed. (New York: St. Martin's Press, 1980), s.v. "Ethnomusicology," by Barbara Krader. The term *ethnomusicology* first occurs in this edition.

[84]Timothy Rice, "Toward the Remodeling of Ethnomusicology," in *Ethnomusicological Theory and Method*, ed. Kay Kaufman Shelemay (New York: Garland Publishing, 1990), 329; Bonnie Wade, "Prolegomenon to the Study of Song Texts," in Shelemay, 207; and Sadie, s.v. "Ethnomusicology," by Krader.

[85]Sadie, "Ethnomusicology," by Krader; and Lomax, "Folk Song Style," 59, 61.

[86]Spencer, *Theological Music*, 6.

[87]Ibid., 116.

[88]James W. Button, *Blacks and Social Change: Impact of the Civil Rights Movement in Southern Communities* (Princeton: Princeton University Press, 1989), 77, 162. Button analyzes and documents changes caused by the impact of the Civil Rights Movement within southern communities from the 1950s to the mid-1980s.

[89]Standifer, "Musical Behaviors," 61; see also 54-55.

[90]Richard M. Dalbiume, "The 'Forgotten Years' of the Negro Revolution," *Journal of American History* 55 (June 1968): 90-99.

[91]See Alan Durant, "Improvisation in the Political Economy of Music," in *Music and Politics of Culture*, ed. Christopher Norris (New York: St. Martin's Press, 1989), 255; and Jon Michael Spencer, *Protest and Praise: Sacred Music of Black Religion* (Minneapolis: Fortress, 1990), 93, 97.

[92]Samuel Floyd, "Black American Music and Aesthetic Communication," *Black Music Research Journal* 1 (1980): 4, 7, 10, 11; and Hall Johnson, "Notes on the Negro Spiritual," in *Readings in Black American Music*, ed. Eileen Southern (New York: W. W. Norton, 1971), 269.

[93]See Reagon, "Program Notes."

[94]Frederick Hall definitively traced many Spiritual tunes to Africa. He cited the peculiar use of pentatonic (five-tone), hexatonic (six-tone) and heptatonic (seven-tone) scales, lowered thirds, raised sixths, and lowered sevenths (scale degrees). Hall found a perpetual rhythmic motion and recognized that rhythms served the feeling rather than an accurately measured accent. The rhythms and the scales reinforced the text. See Lovell, *Black Song*, 65.

[95]Ibid., 126.

[96]Wilson, "Black Music," 3.

[97]Johnson, "Notes," 271.

[98]Ibid.

[99]Lovell, *Black Song*, 420; and Wendell Phillips Whalum, "Black Hymnody," *Review and Expositor* 70 (Summer 1973): 352.

[100]Carl Seashore, *Psychology of Music* (1938; repr. New York: Dover, 1967), 9-10.

[101]Peter Kivy, *Sound and Semblance: Reflections on Musical Representation* (Princeton, NJ: Princeton University Press, 1984), 12, 17; and ibid., 14.

[102]Kivy, *Sound and Semblance*, 93, 157, 165, 167. Although Kivy does not specifically analyze Spirituals, his theories are apropos to this genre.

[103]Ibid., 133; see also 59, 63.

[104]See Reagon, "Program Notes," 9, 15.

[105]Kivy, *Sound and Semblance*, 194-95.

[106]Durant, "Improvisation," 252-54.

[107]Peter Kivy, *Sound Sentiment: An Essay on the Musical Emotions* (Philadelphia: Temple University Press, 1989), 97, 105.

[108]Ibid., 99, 103, 108, 111.

[109]Gordon C. Bruner II, "Music, Mood, and Marketing," *Journal of Marketing* 54 (October 1990): 94.

[110]Seashore, *Psychology,* 346-59.

[111]Reagon, "Program Notes," 6.

[112]Kivy, *Sound Sentiment*, 256, 258.

[113]Guy Carawan and Candie Carawan, "'Freedom in the Air': An Overview of the Songs of the Civil Rights Movement," *Black Music Research Bulletin* 12 (Spring 1990): 1.

[114]Ibid., 2. See pages 88ff. for a discussion of the Highlander School.

[115]Bernice Johnson Reagon, "Let the Church Sing 'Freedom,'" *Black Music Research Journal* (1987): 105.

[116]Ibid., 109-11.

[117]Ibid., 106.

[118]Spencer, *Protest and Praise*, 84-85.

[119]Reagon, "Let the Church," 107-8, 116. Cordell Reagon, Bernice Johnson, Rutha Harris, and Chuck Neblett were the SNCC freedom singers. They traveled throughout the country to raise money and to tell the Movement's story.

[120]Carawan and Carawan, "Freedom in the Air," 3.

[121]Roy Palmer, *The Sound of History: Songs and Social Comment* (Oxford: Oxford University Press, 1988), vii.

[122]Bernice Johnson Reagon, "The Lined Hymn as a Song of Freedom," *Black Music Research Bulletin* 12 (Spring 1990): 6-7.

6. Faith and Thought

[1]James Cone, *The Spirituals and the Blues: An Interpretation* (New York: Seabury Press, 1972; Maryknoll, NY: Orbis Books, 1992), 73.

[2]James H. Cone, "Black Spirituals: A Theological Interpretation," in *Music and the Experience of God*, Concilium Religion in the Eighties, ed. Mary Collins, David Power, and Mellonee Burnim (Edinburgh: T & T Clark, 1989), 48-49.

[3]Dominique Zahan, *The Religion, Spirituality, and Thought of Traditional Africa* (Chicago: University of Chicago Press, 1979), 9, also 4-5; and John S. Mbiti,

African Religions and Philosophy (New York: Praeger, 1969), 1-3.

[4]Leonard Barnett, "African Religion in the Americas: The Islands in Between," in *African Religions: A Symposium*, ed. Newell S. Booth, Jr. (New York: NOK Publishers, 1977), 185.

[5]Newell S. Booth, Jr., "The View from Kasongo Niembo," in Booth, *African Religions*, 59; and Zahan, *Religion, Spirituality*, 14-15.

[6]Richard C. Onwuanibe, "The Human Person and Immortality in Ibo (African) Metaphysics," in *African Philosophy: An Introduction*, ed. Richard A. Wright, 3rd ed. (Lanham, MD: University Press of America, 1984), 184; and Benjamine Ewuku Oguah, "African and Western Philosophy: A Comparative Study," in Wright, *African Philosophy*, 219.

[7]Janheninz Jahn, *Muntu: The New African Culture* (New York: Grove Press, 1961), 100-106. I am indebted to Valerie Dixon, Womanist ethicist at Temple University, for introducing me to the concept of *muntu*.

[8]Mbiti, *African Religions*, 29, 35.

[9]Zahan, *Religion, Spirituality*, 14-17, 125, 156-57; and ibid., 15-16.

[10]Mbiti, *African Religions*, 207.

[11]Ibid., 204-6.

[12]Roman Catholic theology, for example, insists that infants who die without baptism go to *limbo*, a kind of hell.

[13]The family (i.e, the living, the dead, and the unborn) achieved full existence. Dena Epstein, *Sinful Tunes and Spirituals: Black Folk Music to the Civil War* (Urbana: University of Illinois Press, 1977), 63-76. Songs included songs for celebrations for holidays and rites, and the work, field, and boat songs.

[14]Cone, *Spirituals and Blues*, 40.

[15]John Lovell, Jr., *Black Song: The Forge and the Flame; The Story of How the Afro-American Spiritual Was Hammered Out* (New York: Macmillan, 1972), 386-87. The slaves' communal sense was stronger than any sense of individualism. Unlike the radical and more conservative thinkers of the 1960s Movement, unity exceeded division: "If the slaves or their song-makers had been divided on details, their progress to freedom would have been ever so slow, or even nonexistent. They might never, by their heroic moves, have inspired an Abolition movement and a war to set them free."

[16]Howard Thurman, *Deep River and The Negro Spiritual Speaks of Life and Death* (Richmond, IN: Friends United Press, 1975), 77-95; and Wayne McLaughlin, "Symbolism and Mysticism in the Spirituals," *Phylon* 24 (1963): 69-77. Introducing the word *Hallelujah* signals a call to praise, the contact between the singer and God's luminous reality. *Hallelujah* symbolizes the mystic moment of unity, the highs and lows of life. H. H. Proctor, "The Theology of the Songs of the Southern Slave," *Southern Workman* 36 (1907): 586-87; and Christa Dixon, *Negro Spirituals: From Bible to Folk Song* (Philadelphia: Fortress Press, 1976), 3-5.

[17]Wendy Farley, *Tragic Vision and Divine Compassion: A Contemporary Theodicy* (Louisville, KY: Westminster/John Knox Press, 1990), 117.

[18]Mircea Eliade, *The Sacred and the Profane* (New York: Harper, 1959), 12.

[19]Newell S. Booth, Jr., "An Approach to African Religion," in Booth, *African Religions*, 5.

[20]Ibid., 5-9.

[21]Ibid., 38, 48, 66.

[22]Cornel West, "The Historicist Turn in Philosophy of Religion," in *Knowing Religiously*, ed. Leroy S. Rouner (Notre Dame, IN: University of Notre Dame Press, 1985), 44.

[23]Ibid., 44-49.

[24]John Blassingame, *The Slave Community: Plantation Life in the Antebellum South* (New York: Oxford University Press, 1979), 145; and Lovell, *Black Song*, 230-35, 550-51. In writing on Spirituals and Jewish thought, Lovell cites Paul Laubenstein's "An Apocalyptic Reincarnation," in the *Journal of Biblical Literature*, 1932, which notes that Spirituals composers used only certain parts of the Bible. Laubenstein says that the African consciousness supported the slaves' use of history, narrative, and apocalyptic themes.

[25]Alexander Di Lella, "An Existential Interpretation of Job," *Biblical Theology Bulletin* 15 (April 1985): 49, 54; and Walter Brueggemann, "Theodicy in a Social Dimension," *Journal for the Study of the Old Testament* 33 (1985): 4-5. One must also recognize that an exploration of the meaning of suffering is also an attempt to reduce God to human understanding, since humans by definition cannot possess divine understanding. Gustavo Gutiérrez, *On Job: God-Talk and the Suffering of the Innocent* (Maryknoll, NY: Orbis Books, 1987), 88-91.

[26]Cone, *Spirituals and Blues*, 61-62.

[27]Cain Hope Felder, "Race, Racism, and the Biblical Narratives," in *Stony the Road We Trod: African-American Biblical Interpretation*, ed. Cain Hope Felder (Minneapolis: Fortress Press, 1991), 127-45; and Cornel West, *Prophesy Deliverance! An Afro-American Revolutionary Christianity* (Philadelphia: Westminster, 1982), 53.

[28]West, *Prophesy Deliverance!*, 53-61. See also Richard Herrnstein and Charles Murray, *The Bell Curve: Intelligence and Class Structure in American Life* (New York: Free Press, 1994).

[29]West, "Historicist Turn," 48-49.

[30]Traditional theories of atonement include Origen's ransom theory, where Jesus' death on the cross paid the price for human sin; Abelard's moral theory, where the cross brings humanity repentance and shows God's love and the pain and suffering toward that love because of the pain of human sin; and Calvin's substitution theory, where Jesus offers himself as a substitute who undergoes the penalty for human sin.

[31]Delores S. Williams, *Sisters in the Wilderness: The Challenge of Womanist God-Talk* (Maryknoll, NY: Orbis Books, 1993), x, 2, 4-6, 60-61, 109, 161-67.

[32]See Ex 29:36-37; 30:10; 32:30; and Lv 1:3-9; 4:13-21; 4:30-35. In Leviticus, the writer claims that the people, forgiven and restored, are to live in God's holy presence and to avoid things which harm their health and well-being and which separate them from God and from their place as a holy people called to render divine services to the world. Burnt offerings, sacrifices of well-being, and sin offerings involved killing an animal, which substituted and therefore made an atonement for the sin(s) of the worshipping person. Sacrifices helped restore the balance and make Israel's people (individually or collectively) at-one with God.

[33]Jeremiah A. Wright, Jr., "Music as Cultural Expression in Black Church Theology and Worship," *Journal of Black Sacred Music* 3 (Spring 1989): 5; see also 1-4.

[34]Cone, *Spirituals and Blues*, 47, 54, 57; James Cone, *A Black Theology of Liberation* (Philadelphia: Lippincott, 1970), 21; Proctor, "Theology," 587; and Thurman, *Deep River*, 21.

[35]Some of the Spirituals talk of the "Spirit movin'." This refers either to the human animus or to the divinity in general. It may also refer to the Third Person

of the Trinity. See David Simms, "The Negro Spirituals: Origins and Themes," *Journal of Negro Education* 35 (Winter 1966): 39; McLaughlin, "Symbolism," 75; and Proctor, "Theology," 588-89.

[36]Jon Michael Spencer, *Protest and Praise: Sacred Music of Black Religion* (Minneapolis: Fortress, 1990), 32.

[37]That absence is unusual, given the social environment and the adaptation by the Spirituals of biblical texts. Proctor, "Theology," 655-56; and C. J. Ryder, "The Theology of the Plantation Songs," *American Missionary* (1892): 15. Although many Louisiana Blacks had Catholic masters, Ryder never heard nor found any praises sung to the Virgin anywhere in the plantation melodies, despite the prominence of Mariology in the Roman Catholic tradition elsewhere. In a 1990 compact disc of fourteen Spirituals, four of the songs celebrate Mary but do not idolize her. *Black Christmas: Spirituals in the African-American Tradition*, compact disc CD 1011, ESSAY Recordings, 1990.

[38]Karen Lebacqz, *Justice in an Unjust World* (Minneapolis: Augsburg, 1987), 17.

[39]Ibid., 70-86, 90-91, 103-12.

[40]Ibid., 101; see also 99-102.

[41]Ibid., 100.

[42] On the ancient communal meal, see Dennis E. Smith and Hal E. Taussig, *Many Tables: The Eucharist in the New Testament and Liturgy Today* (London: SCM Press, 1990), 22, 31-35, 43, 69, 81.

[43]Cone, "Black Spirituals," 49, 50; and Jürgen Moltmann, *Theology of Hope* (New York: Harper & Row, 1967), 329.

[44]Cone, "Black Spirituals," 46-47.

[45]Nicholas C. Cooper-Lewter and Henry H. Mitchell, *Soul Theology: The Heart of American Black Culture* (San Francisco: Harper & Row, 1986), viii-11; 29-42, 95-111.

[46]McLaughlin, "Symbolism," 72-73. The query about "time" seems contradictory. McLaughlin talks about an immediate and a traditional future eschatology. McLaughlin claims that clock-time (past, present, and future) is an illusion and that true time is eternal time. Perhaps true time for slaves occurred when they knew the time of heaven, of fulfillment in God's time—an immediate and future interpretation.

[47]Martin Buber, *I and Thou*, trans. Walter Kaufmann (New York: Charles Scribner's Sons, 1970), 48-51.

[48]Herbert O. Edwards, "Black Theology and Liberation Theology," in *Black Theology: A Documentary History, 1966-1979*, ed. Gayraud Wilmore and James Cone (Maryknoll, NY: Orbis Books, 1979), 526.

[49]"Liberation Movements: A Critical Assessment and a Reaffirmation"; A Position Paper of the African Methodist Episcopal Church, 40th Session of the General Conference of the African Methodist Episcopal Church, June 16-27, 1976, Atlanta, in Wilmore and Cone, *Black Theology*, 291.

[50]Desmond M. Tutu, "Black Theology/African Theology—Soul Mates or Antagonists?" in Wilmore and Cone, *Black Theology*, 486; Paul Holmes, "About Black Theology," in Wilmore and Cone, *Black Theology*, 197; and Cone, *Spirituals and Blues*, 62.

[51]Clifton H. Johnson, ed., *God Struck Me Dead: Religious Conversion Experiences and Autobiographies of Ex-Slaves* (Philadelphia: Pilgrim Press, 1969), vii.

[52]Ibid., vii-xiii, 13, 111, 115. The consistency in slaves' testimonies tend to

bear out the validity of these testimonies as the slaves' best recollections, as opposed to interpretative impressions of what really happened.

[53]Walter Wink, *Naming the Powers: The Language of Power in the New Testament*, vol. 1 of *The Powers* (Philadelphia: Fortress Press, 1984), 4.

[54]Ibid.

[55]Karen Lebacqz, *Six Theories of Justice: Perspectives from Philosophical and Theological Ethics* (Minneapolis: Augsburg, 1986), 9.

[56]Jim Wallis, "America's Original Sin: The Legacy of White Racism," *Sojourners* (November 1987): 15.

[57]George Kelsey, *Racism and the Christian Understanding of Man* (New York: Charles Scribner's Sons, 1965), 23-33.

[58]Ibid.; and Calvin S. Morris, "We, the White People: A History of Oppression," *Sojourners* (November 1987): 20. While any sin perpetrated against God can be idolatry, the significance of calling racism idolatry is to point out the impact of racism: it is not just a human system but a divine infraction of the two prime commandments for Christians—"Love the Lord your God with all your heart" and "Love your neighbor as yourself" (see Mt 22:37-40).

[59]Among those of a lower economic status, regardless of race, who fight for survival on a day-to-day battleground, a disproportionate number tend to engage in *and are apprehended for* crime and are more prone to disease. Since African Americans as a group are lower on the economic scale than are those of Eurocentric ancestry, ignorance attributes these undesirable social characteristics to ethnicity rather than social position.

[60]C. T. Vivian, "Racial Violence in the '80s," *Sojourners* (November 1987): 23-24.

[61]Lebacqz, *Six Theories*, 9-10.

[62]Richard Rorty, *Contingency, Irony, and Solidarity* (Cambridge: Cambridge University Press, 1989), xiii-xvi.

[63]Farley, *Tragic Vision*, 79, 90, 93, 107, 111, 112, 114.

[64]Alasdair MacIntyre, *After Virtue: A Study in Moral Virtue*, 2d ed. (Notre Dame, IN: University of Notre Dame Press, 1984), 229-63.

[65]Jeffrey Stout, *Ethics after Babel: The Languages of Morals and Their Discontents* (Boston: Beacon Press, 1988), 220-42.

[66]Guy Carawan and Candie Carawan, *Sing for Freedom: The Story of the Civil Rights Movement through Its Songs* (Bethlehem, PA: Sing Out, 1990), 71, 73, 86.

[67]Wink, *Naming the Powers*, 5. The work of New Testament theologian and pacifist Walter Wink informs my using the terms *naming, unmasking,* and *engaging* the powers. *Naming the Powers* and *Unmasking the Powers* are the first two volumes of his work *The Powers*. His book *Engaging the Powers* addresses practical issues of meaning and of confronting the powers.

[68]Buber, *I and Thou*, 56, 62-63, 68, 75; and Stephen M. Panko, *Martin Buber,* Makers of the Modern Theological Mind (Waco, TX: Word Books, 1976), 24, 47-48, 150.

[69]Buber, *I and Thou*, 84-89, 95-97, 100-101; Panko, *Martin Buber*, 52, 61, 150; and Molefi Kete Asante, *Afrocentricity* (Trenton, NJ: Africa World Press, 1989), 15.

[70]Lebacqz, *Justice,* 62-66, 70-75, 122-35.

[71]Ibid., 7-50, 77-79, 158.

[72]Carawan and Carawan, *Sing for Freedom*, 62, 15; and James H. Evans Jr., "African-American Christianity and the Postmodern Condition," *Journal of American Academy of Religion* 58 (Summer 1990): 208.

[73]Cone, *Spirituals and Blues*, 62-64. Cone states that for the slaves, God is the ultimate answer to the question of faith. They hold to God's righteousness and God's vindication of the oppressed. Suffering and evil are givens in life; but slaves can withstand either, as long as they remain in community.

[74]Ibid.

[75]Bill Moyers, "Facing Evil with Bill Moyers," *The World of Ideas*, Public Affairs Television, March 28, 1988.

[76]William R. Jones, *Is God a White Racist? A Preamble to Black Theology*, C. Eric Lincoln Series on Black Religion (Garden City, NY: Anchor Press/Doubleday, 1973), vii-25, 185-97. One approach Jones eliminates is quietism, a system of religious mysticism which teaches that perfection and spiritual peace are attained by annihilation of the will and passive absorption in contemplation of God and divine things. Jones says that another way to talk about a quietistic theodicy is Marx's opiate. He argues that eschatological theodicy is not acceptable, because it presupposes divine intrinsic benevolence, where a difficult present will be replaced by a future bliss. Such a theodicy involves an unresolved mystery.

[77]Major J. Jones, *The Color of God* (Macon, GA: Mercer Press, 1987), 65-67.

[78]Keith Crim et al., *The Interpreter's Dictionary of the Bible,* supplement (Nashville: Abingdon, 1962), s.v. "Vengeance," by J. E. Lindsey, Jr.

[79]Sharon L. Moore, "Walter Wink on 'The Powers '" (Waco, TX: Baylor University, Fall 1989), photocopy, 15-20. See also Wink, *Unmasking the Powers: The Invisible Forces That Determine Human Existence*, vol. 2 of *The Powers* (Philadelphia: Fortress Press, 1986), 9-68.

[80]Cone, *Spirituals and Blues*, 80.

[81]Thomas Webber, *Deep like the Rivers: Education in the Slave Quarter Community, 1831-1865* (New York: W. W. Norton, 1978), 140-45. The slave-free duality is an example of how attitudes were projected back on the slaves by White society. This statement does not deny that there were African Americans who owned slaves; their group, however, was the exception.

[82]See the discussion on Black slave life and the Black church in chapter 2, "Context: The Social and Historical Setting."

[83]Vincent Harding, "Religion and Resistance Among Ante-bellum Negroes, 1800-1860," in *The Making of Black America: Essays in Negro Life and History*, vol. 1 *The Origins of Black Americans*, ed. August Meier and Elliot Rudwick (New York: Athenaeum, 1969), 181. Reflecting recent scholarship, Harding argues that the invisible institution of antebellum days became the visible and chief institution of freed Blacks. After the Civil War and the gradual breakdown of the customary, partially integrated but paternalistic ecclesiastical system of the Old South by 1865, the Black church became the chief agency of social control.

[84]Cheryl Townsend Gilkes, "Mother to the Motherless, Father to the Fatherless: Power, Gender, and Community in Afrocentric Biblical Tradition," *Semeia: An Experimental Journal for Biblical Criticism* 47 (1989): 58-61, 65; and Vincent Wimbush, "Historical/Cultural Criticism as Liberation: A Proposal for an African-American Biblical Hermeneutic," *Semeia: An Experimental Journal for Biblical Criticism* 47 (1989): 45.

[85]Katie Geneva Cannon, "Slave Ideology and Biblical Interpretation," *Semeia: An Experimental Journal for Biblical Criticism* 47 (1989): 11-16.

[86]Asante, *Afrocentricity*, 31-33.

7. Womanist Thought

[1]Alice Walker, *In Search of Our Mothers' Gardens: Womanist Prose* (New York: Harcourt Brace Jovanovich, 1967, 1983), xi; and Jacquelyn Grant, *White Women's Christ and Black Women's Jesus: Feminist Christology and Womanist Response* (Atlanta: Scholars Press, 1989), 200-202.

[2]Grant, *White Women's Christ*, 205.

[3]That behavior may involve (1) conversion, changing ourselves; (2) missionary work, convincing others their view is wrong; (3) accommodation, incorporating some of their view so it is no longer threatening; or (4) destruction, annihilating the person who is different. The best way to understand war is, for example, not politically, economically, or rationally, but to note that all wars are fought over ideology and deal with the conflict that we have with people who are different from us, as we need to deny the right of the other to exist. Sheldon Solomon, "The Thought of Ernest Becker," lecture presented by the Ernest Becker Foundation, University of Washington at Seattle, April 28, 1994; see also Ernest Becker, *Escape from Evil* (New York: Free Press, 1975).

[4]James H. Cone, *For My People: Black Theology and the Black Church* (Maryknoll, NY: Orbis Books, 1984), 125, 128-29.

[5]Ibid.; and Deborah Gray White, *Ar'n't I a Woman: Female Slaves in the Plantation South* (New York: W. W. Norton, 1985), 14, 23.

[6]Kelly Delaine Brown, "God Is as Christ Does: Toward a Womanist Theology," *Journal of Religious Thought* 46 (Summer-Fall 1989): 11.

[7]Womanist theologians, like other groups, do not agree on all issues. Cheryl Sanders argues that Christianity forms the center of ethical and theological identity, that the term *Womanist* overemphasizes secularity and lesbian love over heterosexual love, and that it does not focus on Christianity enough. However, most Womanists, myself included, affirm a strong biblical and christological heritage. See Ferm, *Contemporary American Theologies: A Critical Survey*, rev. ed. (San Francisco: Harper & Row, 1981, 1990), 58.

[8]Cheryl Townsend Gilkes, "Mother to the Motherless, Father to the Fatherless: Power, Gender, and Community in an Afrocentric Biblical Tradition," *Semeia: An Experimental Journal for Biblical Criticism* 47 (1989): 57-85.

[9]Kelly Brown Douglas, "To Reflect the Image of God," in *Living the Intersection: Womanism and Afrocentrism in Theology*, ed. Cheryl J. Sanders (Minneapolis: Fortress Press, 1995), 76-77.

[10]M. Shawn Copeland, " 'Wading through Many Sorrows' ": Toward a Theology of Suffering in Womanist Perspective," in *A Troubling in My Soul: Womanist Perspectives on Evil and Suffering*, ed. Emilie Townes (Maryknoll, NY: Orbis Books, 1993), 109-29.

[11]Katie Geneva Cannon, " 'The Wounds of Jesus' ": Justification of Goodness in the Face of Manifold Evil," in Townes, *Troubling in My Soul*, 222-31.

[12]Grant, *White Women's Christ*, 212-22; and Jacquelyn Grant, "The Sin of Servanthood: And the Deliverance of Discipleship," in Townes, *Troubling in My Soul*, 199-210.

[13]Grant, "Sin of Servanthood," 210-16.

[14]Delores Williams, *Sisters in the Wilderness: The Challenge of Womanist God-Talk* (Maryknoll, NY: Orbis Books, 1993), 2-6, 15-33, 60-62, 84-107. See also Genesis, chapters 16 and 21. The experience of motherhood also involves the institutionalization of mammy; the reinstitutionalization of denominational "mothers"

of the church; the shift of authority from Black women to a Black male patriarchal authority; the literary concretization of that shift in blues songs and postbellum Black male protest thought; the patriarchal, androcentric African-American denominational liturgy and the male religious leaders who exploit Black female constituency; the celebration of Black female spirituality by Black female postbellum writers; the role of Black women as catalysts for social change; and the impact of structures of domination on the lives of African-American mothers and nurturers.

[15]Delores S. Williams, "A Womanist Perspective on Sin," in Townes, *Troubling in My Soul*, 137-47.

[16]Williams, *Sisters in the Wilderness*, 164-67.

[17]Ibid., 108-9, 113, 117. The wilderness is the place where God meets Black women in times of trouble, impending death, or destruction; where God cares and gives the believer personal direction, which helps her make a way out of no way in a religious wilderness experience of transformation. Wilderness has a different connotation for the dominant White American culture. Early pioneers envisioned the wilderness as a hostile place that required conquering, not living in. The wilderness was a remote, strange place of solitude and freedom in European romanticism.

[18]Paula Giddings, *When and Where I Enter: The Impact of Black Women on Race and Sex in America* (New York: Bantam Books, 1984), 314; Brown, "God Is as Christ Does," 10-13, 16; and Grant, *White Women's Christ,* 219.

[19]Douglas, "To Reflect the Image of God," 67-77.

[20]Kelly Brown Douglas, *The Black Christ* (Maryknoll, NY: Orbis Books, 1994), 116-17.

[21]Grant, *White Women's Christ,* 220-22.

[22]Patricia Hunter, "Woman's Power—Woman's Passion: And God Said, 'That's Good,' " in Townes, *Troubling in My Soul*, 189-98.

[23]Cheryl Townsend Gilkes, "The 'Loves' and 'Troubles' of African-American Women's Bodies: The Womanist Challenge to Cultural Humiliation and Community Ambivalence," in Townes, *Troubling in My Soul*, 233-42.

[24]Sweet Honey in the Rock, "No Mirrors in Nana's House," *Still on the Journey*, compact disc 9 42536-2, EarthBeat!, 1993.

[25]Conversation with author, Spring, 1994, Atlanta, Georgia.

[26]Rosita deAnn Mathews, "Using Power from the Periphery: An Alternative Theological Model for Survival in Systems," in Townes, *Troubling in My Soul*, 93-104.

[27]Delores Williams, "Womanist Theology: Black Women's Voices," in *Weaving the Visions: New Patterns in Feminist Spirituality*, ed, Judith Plaskow and Carol P. Christ (San Francisco: HarperCollins, 1989), 183-85.

[28]See Abraham Maslow, *Motivation and Personality*, 2d ed. (New York: Harper & Row, 1970).

[29]Alice Walker, "A Day with Alice Walker," the second annual Auburn Lecture at Union Theological Seminary, New York, NY, April 25, 1995.

[30]Ibid.

[31]Katie G. Cannon, *Black Womanist Ethics* (Atlanta: Scholars Press, 1988), 6-7.

[32]Ibid., 6-7, 13-14, 68.

[33]Evelyn Parker, "Twenty Seeds of Hope: Religious-Moral Values in African-American Adolescents in Chicago Land" (Ph.D. diss., Garrett-Evangelical Theological Seminary/Northwestern University, in process).

[34]Ibid., 28, 48.

[35]Cannon, *Black Womanist Ethics*, 2-3.

[36]Ibid., 125-43.

[37]Katie G. Cannon, "Hitting a Straight Lick with a Crooked Stick: The Womanist Dilemma in the Development of a Black Liberation Ethic," in *Sisters Struggling in the Spirit: A Women of Color Theological Anthology*, ed. Nantawan Boonprasat Lewis, Lydia Hernandez, Helen Locklear, and Robina Marie Winbush (Louisville, KY: Women's Ministries Program Area, National Ministries Division, and Christian Faith and Life Program Area Congregational Ministries Division, Presbyterian Church (U.S.A.), 1994), 93-98.

[38]Marcia Y. Riggs, *Awake, Arise, and Act: A Womanist Call for Black Liberation* (Cleveland, OH: Pilgrim Press, 1994), ix-xi.

[39]Ibid., 16, 21-26, 29, 67-69, 71-75, 79, 83, 93-97. In the social, economic, political, religious, and ethical work of Black club women, they acknowledged diversity, moved to work for the uplift of all, and provided practical opportunities toward these goals. For example, along with conferences to focus on these issues, Black club women developed schools to train women, boycotted oppressive markets, analyzed and worked on Black labor concerns, and worked for reform in many areas, including segregated public accommodations, lynching, criminal justice, care for the aged, childhood education, and the health and protection of women from brutality and abuse.

[40]Audre Lorde, "The Uses of Anger: Women Responding to Racism," in *Sister Outsider* (Trumansburg, NY: Crossing Press, 1984), 128-30.

[41]Emilie Townes, "Living in the New Jerusalem: The Rhetoric and Movement of Liberation in the House of Evil," in Townes, *Troubling in My Soul*, 73-86.

[42]Ibid., 86-91; and Emilie Townes, *In a Blaze of Glory: Womanist Spirituality as Social Witness* (Nashville: Abingdon, 1995), 11, 48, 58, 60, 64-67, 71, 77, 81-84, 87, 109, 115, 117-19, 130-36, 143-44.

[43]Renita Weems, "Reading Her Way through the Struggle: African American Women and the Bible," in *Stony the Road We Trod*, ed. Cain Hope Felder (Nashville: Abingdon, 1991), 57-77.

[44]Clarice Martin, "Biblical Theodicy and Black Women's Spiritual Autobiography: 'The Miry Bog, the Desolate Pit, a New Song in My Mouth,'" in Townes, *Troubling in My Soul*, 13-28.

[45]Cheryl J. Sanders, "Black Women in Biblical Perspective: Resistance, Affirmation, and Empowerment," in Sanders, *Living the Intersection*, 130.

[46]Toinette Eugene, "Moral Values and Black Womanists," in *Black Theology: A Documentary History, Vol. II: 1980-1992*, ed. James Cone and Gayraud Wilmore (Maryknoll, NY: Orbis Books, 1993), 310.

[47]Cherríe Moraga and Gloria Anzaldúa, eds., *This Bridge Called My Back: Writings by Radical Women of Color* (New York: Kitchen Table: Women of Color Press, 1981, 1983), 96, 98, 116.

[48]bell hooks, *Ain't I a Woman: Black Women and Feminism* (Boston: South End Press, 1981), 9, 49, 55, 91, 121, 156-57, 183-93.

[49]Delores S. Williams, "Womanist Theology: Black Women's Voices," in Cone and Wilmore, *Black Theology*, 269-70.

[50]Howard Thurman, *Deep River and The Negro Spiritual Speaks of Life and Death* (Richmond, IN: Friends United Press, 1975), 5-6.

[51]Cone, *For My People*, 128-29.

[52]Ferm, *Contemporary American Theologies*, 57.

[53]Ruth El Saffar, "Unbinding the Doubles: Reflections on Love and Culture in the Work of Rene Girard," *Denver Quarterly* 18 (Winter 1984): 19. See also China Galland, *Longing for Darkness, Tara and the Black Madonna* (New York: Viking/Penguin, 1990-91), repr. forthcoming Penguin Arkana, Winter, 1998, and her forthcoming work, *Fierce Compassion*, Riverhead Books/Putnam, Spring, 1998.

8. Womanist Musings

[1]See the work of authors Alice Walker, the late Audre Lorde, Toni Morrison; Katie Cannon in Womanist ethics; Jacqueline Grant and Delores Williams in Womanist theology; and Cheryl Gilkes in Womanist sociology of religion.

[2]Anthony Pinn, *Why God? Suffering and Evil in Black Theology* (New York: Continuum, 1995), 19.

[3]Kesho Yvonne Scott, *The Habit of Surviving* (New York: Ballantine Books, 1991), 3-10.

[4]Bernice Johnson Reagon, interview by author, tape recording, Washington, DC, November 19, 1991.

[5]Darlene Clark Hine, Elsa Barkley Brown, and Rosalyn Terborg-Penn, *Black Women in America: An Historical Encyclopedia* (Bloomington: Indiana University Press, 1993), 1174-76.

[6]Ibid., 1113-14.

[7]Ibid., 1176-80; and Jessie Carney Smith, ed., *Epic Lives: One Hundred Black Women Who Made a Difference* (Detroit, MI: Visible Ink, 1993), 529-37.

[8]Hine, Brown, and Terborg-Penn, *Black Women in America*, 532-36.

[9]Ibid., 363-67.

[10]Ibid., 982-84.

[11]Ibid., 80-82.

[12]Ibid., 33-34.

[13]Ibid., 1157-59.

[14]Ibid., 201-6.

[15]Ibid., 690-93.

[16]Ibid., 825-26.

[17]Ibid., 552-55.

[18]Ibid., 236-38.

[19]Ibid., 110-12.

[20]Ibid., 377-79.

[21]Ibid., 175-76.

[22]Ibid., 1242-46; and Smith, *Epic Lives,* 579-86.

[23]Hine, Brown, and Terborg-Penn, *Black Women in America*, 248-52.

[24]Ibid., 70-74.

[25]Ibid., 907-9.

[26]Ibid., 518-19.

[27]Ibid., 94-96.

[28]Ibid., 822-24.

[29]Ibid., 138-39.

[30]Ibid., 886-87.

[31]Ibid., 658-59.

[32]Ibid., 105-6.

[33]Ibid., 275-81.

[34]Ibid., 113-26.

[35]Ibid., 260-61.
[36]Ibid., 513.
[37]Ibid., 505-7.
[38]Ibid., 36-38.
[39]Ibid., 525-27.
[40]Ibid., 1003-5.
[41]Ibid., 487-90.
[42]Ibid., 29-33.
[43]Ibid., 620-23.
[44]Ibid., 901.
[45]Ibid., 941-43.

[46]Ibid., 881. See also Kathleen Battle and Jessye Norman, *Spirituals in Concert*, Deutsche Grammophone 429 790-2, 1991; Jessye Norman, *Spirituals*, with Dalton Baldwin and the Ambrosian Singers, Philips 416 462-2, 1978; Jessye Norman, *Amazing Grace*, Philips 432 546-2, 1991.

[47]Hine, Brown, and Terborg-Penn, *Black Women in America*, 97; see also Battle and Norman, *Spirituals in Concert*.

[48]Hine, Brown, and Terborg-Penn, *Black Women in America*, 556-57. See also Barbara Hendricks, *Negro Spirituals*, EMI 7470262, 1983; *Great American Spirituals*, vol. 9, Angel CD 7 664669, 2 1992; and *Great American Spirituals*, Musical Heritage Society CD 513725Z, 1994.

[49]Smith, *Epic Lives*, 434-39.

[50]Ibid., 1134.

[51]Bernice Johnson Reagon and Sweet Honey in the Rock, *We Who Believe in Freedom: Sweet Honey in the Rock . . . Still on the Journey* (New York: Anchor/Doubleday, 1993), 21.

[52]Sweet Honey in the Rock, "A Priority," *In This Land*, Redway, CA: EarthBeat, CA 9 42522-2, 1992.

[53]Hine, Brown, and Terborg-Penn, *Black Women in America,* 156-57.

[54]Title from Marcia Riggs, *Awake, Arise, and Act: A Womanist Call for Black Liberation* (Cleveland, OH: Pilgrim Press, 1994).

[55]Ibid., 635-36.

[56]Ibid., 147-48; and Helen Walker-Hill, *Music by Black Women Composers: A Bibliography of Available Scores,* CBMR Monographs, no. 5 (Chicago: Center for Black Music Research, Columbia College, 1995), 271.

[57]Hine, Brown, and Terborg-Penn, *Black Women in America*, 814; and Walker-Hill, *Music by Black Women Composers*, 56-57, 91-93.

[58]Shirelle Phelps, ed., *Who's Who in Black America, 1994-95*, 8th ed. (Detroit, MI: Gale Research, 1994), 451-52; and Walker-Hill, *Music by Black Women Composers*, 50, 81-82.

[59]Hine, Brown, and Terborg-Penn, *Black Women in America,* 773; Phelps, ed., *Who's Who in Black America,* 1004; and Walker-Hill, *Music by Black Women Composers*, 89-91.

[60]See Walker-Hill, *Music by Black Women Composers,* 51-54, 57-58, 80, 84-85, 94-99, 100.

[61]Elizabeth Cady Stanton, Susan Anthony, and Matilda Joslyn Gage, eds., *The History of Woman Suffrage*, vol. 1 (Rochester, NY: n.p., 1881), 115-17; and Eleanor Flexner, *Century of Struggle: The Women's Rights Movement in the United States* (Cambridge, MA, and London: Belknap Press/Harvard University Press, 1959, 1975, 1979), 91.

[62]Paula Giddings, *When and Where I Enter: The Impact of Black Women on Race and Sex in America* (New York: Bantam Books, 1984), 57, 65, 73, 85-89, 94, 102, 108, 113-17, 130, 135-44.

9. Mass Meeting

[1]Bernice Johnson Reagon, "Program Notes," *Voices of the Civil Rights Movement, 1960-1966* (Washington, DC: Smithsonian Institution, Program in Black American Culture, 1980), 11-12; and Bernice Reagon, "Songs of the Civil Rights Movement, 1955-1965: A Study of Cultural History" (Ph.D. diss., Howard University, 1975), 100.

[2]Reagon, "Program Notes," 2, 15.

[3]Robert Sherman, "Sing A Song of Freedom," *Saturday Review* (September 28, 1963)): 66-67; and Bernice Johnson Reagon, "Untitled, 23. Reagon notes, Archives, Smithsonian Institution, Program in Black American Culture. Reagon notes that during the 1930s, Reverend John Hancock of the Southern Tenant Farmers Union in Arkansas altered the text thus:

> *Oh freedom, Oh freedom,*
> *Oh freedom, after 'while*
> *And before I'll be a slave,*
> *I'll be buried in my grave*
> *Take my place with those who loved and fought before.*

[4]*Songs of Zion*, 12 United Methodist Church Supplemental Worship Resources (Nashville: Abingdon, 1981, 1982), 102.

[5]Guy Carawan and Candie Carawan, *Sing for Freedom: The Story of the Civil Rights Movement through Its Songs* (Bethlehem, PA: Sing Out, 1990), 74-75. Ross Barnett was the governor of Alabama; Laurie Pritchett was the police chief in Albany, Georgia.

[6]Juan Williams, *Eyes on the Prize: America's Civil Rights Years, 1954-1965* (New York: Penguin Books, 1988), 218. See also 219-28; and Henry Hampton and Steve Fayer, *Voices of Freedom: An Oral History of the Civil Rights Movement from the 1950s through the 1980s* (New York: Bantam Books, 1990), 123-76.

[7]Williams, *Eyes*, 213; and Hampton and Fayer, *Voices*, 144-45, 182-83.

[8]George C. Bruner, III "Music, Mood, and Marketing," *Journal of Marketing* (October 1990), 95.

[9]Qtd. in Hampton and Fayer, *Voices*, 143-44, 145-46.

[10]Carawan and Carawan, *Sing for Freedom*, 32-36.

[11]Bernice Johnson Reagon, "In Our Hands: Thoughts on Black Music," *Sing Out!* 24 (January-February 1976): 1.

[12]Kathleen Higgins, *The Music of Our Lives* (Philadelphia: Temple University Press, 1991), 129, 137.

[13]Ibid., 130-31. Higgins's comment about musical encounter applies to the encounter of singing "Oh, Freedom."

[14]See James Cone, *Martin & Malcolm & America: A Dream or a Nightmare* (Maryknoll, NY: Orbis Books, 1991).

[15]Higgins, *Music*, 129.

[16]Ibid., 7.

[17]Pat Watters, *Down to Now: Reflections on the Southern Civil Rights Movement*

(New York: Pantheon Books, 1971), 175-77.

[18]Ibid., 13.

[19]Ibid., 12, 13, 177-80.

[20]Ibid., 178-79, 184.

[21]Reagon, "In Our Hands," 1.

[22]Bernice Johnson Reagon, speaking in *The Songs Are Free, with Bernice Johnson Reagon and Bill Moyers*, Public Affairs Television, (February 6, 1991).

[23]"In Egypt Land," *Time* (December 30, 1946): 60.

[24]William L. Dawson, "Interpretation of the Religious Folk-Songs of the American Negro," *Etude* 73 (March 1955): 61.

[25]Edward Avery McIlhenny, *Befo' De War Spirituals* (Boston: Christopher Publishing House, 1933), 21.

[26]"Texture" refers to the dynamics and elements which color and define the human voice.

[27]Eileen Southern, *The Music of Black Americans: A History*, 2d ed. (New York: W. W. Norton, 1983), 200.

[28]"Introductions through Song II," James Bevel, respondent. "Voices of the Civil Rights Movement: A National Working Conference on Civil Rights Movement Culture," cosponsored by the Smithsonian Institution and Howard University, auspices of the Program In Black American Culture, Smithsonian Institution, January 30-February 3, 1980. VCRM videotape no. 3.

[29]Reagon, *Songs Are Free*.

[30]See Katie Cannon, *Womanist Ethics* (Atlanta: Scholars Press, 1990).

[31]Waldo B. Phillips, "Negro Spirituals in Retrospect," *Negro History Bulletin* 22 (February 1952): 51; and Leroy Moore, "The Spiritual: Soul of Black Religion," *Church History* 40 (1971): 79, 80.

[32]Moore, "Spiritual," 79.

[33]William H. McClendon, "Black Music: Sound and Feeling for Black Liberation," *Black Scholar* 7 (January-February 1976): 21. McClendon appreciates the creative, intimate, tasteful exuberance of Black music, but he ascribes a sense of "accommodation rather than liberation" to the labels of gospel, Spiritual, church, jazz, and blues. Spirituals enabled slaves both to endure and to fight against oppression; thus, to say they kept Blacks enslaved is not pure fact, as it is part of the philosophical-theological dialectic. The Spirituals are inclusive of deliverance prayers but have also been used to communicate with humanity.

[34]Ibid., 23.

[35]Theo Eldridge Phillips, "White Racism in Black Church Music," *Negro History Bulletin* 36 (1973): 20.

[36]Bernice Johnson Reagon, "Songs That Moved the Movement," *Perspectives* (Summer 1983): 28.

[37]Ibid.

[38]Manning Marable, *Race, Reform, and Rebellion: The Second Reconstruction in Black America, 1945-1990*, 2d ed. (Jackson: University Press of Mississippi, 1991), 229.

[39]Sharon Anderson, "Bernice Johnson Reagon," *The Other Side's Faces of Faith: A Collection of Our Favorite Interviews* (1990): 11.

[40]Bernice Johnson Reagon, interview by author, tape recording, Washington, DC, November, 19 1991.

[41]Marable, *Race, Reform*, 71.

[42]Ibid., 73.

[43]Reagon, "In Our Hands," 1.

[44]John Lovell, Jr., *Black Song: The Forge and the Flame; The Story of How the Afro-American Spiritual Was Hammered Out* (New York: Macmillan, 1972), 505; see also 115, 384.

[45]Reagon, interview by author.

[46]Marable, *Race, Reform*, 42, 44, 50-55, 61, 62-69, 71-74.

[47]Andrea Canaan, "Brownness," in *This Bridge Called My Back: Writings by Radical Women of Color*, ed. Cherríe Moraga and Gloria Anzaldúa (New York: Kitchen Table: Women of Color Press, 1981, 1983), 232-33.

[48]Many older African Americans' prayers of thanksgiving included thanking God that their bed was not a cooling board and their bedclothes not their winding sheet. After death, bodies were prepared and "laid out," or placed on a board, as the body temperature cooled in preparation for burial. The winding sheet was a bed sheet that was wrapped around the body until the body was placed in clothes for burial.

[49]Wyatt Tee Walker, *"Somebody's Calling My Name": Black Sacred Music and Social Change* (Valley Forge, PA: Judson Press, 1979), 56-59.

[50]Audre Lorde, "The Master's Tools Will Never Dismantle the Master's House," in Moraga and Anzaldúa, *This Bridge*, 99.

[51]Waldo Phillips, "Negro Spirituals," 51; and "Voices of the Civil Rights Movement Conference," VCRM videotape no. 1.

[52]"Voices of the Civil Rights Movement Conference," VCRM videotape no. 2.

[53]Reagon, interview by author.

[54]Ibid.

[55]Williams, *Eyes*, 241-42.

[56]Ibid., 49.

[57]Rhoda Lois Blumberg, *Civil Rights: The 1960s Freedom Struggle* (Boston: Twayne Publishers, 1984), 88-89.

[58]Reagon, interview by author.

[59]Cannon, *Womanist Ethics*, 18-19.

[60]Ibid., 19.

[61]Reagon, *Songs Are Free*.

[62]Ibid.

[63]Cain Hope Felder, *Troubling Biblical Waters: Race, Class, and Family* (Maryknoll, NY: Orbis Books, 1989), 104. See also Jeremiah 34, a call to free the slaves and to review the Jubilee experience.

[64]Ibid., 105.

[65]James H. Cone, *The Spirituals and the Blues* (New York: Seabury Press, 1972; Orbis Books, 1991), 30.

[66]Walter Brueggemann, *The Message of the Psalms: A Theological Commentary* (Minneapolis: Augsburg, 1984), 78-80.

[67]Ibid., 81.

[68]"The Greek verb usually translated 'overcome' can also mean 'comprehend,' a suggestive double meaning." See James L. Mays, gen. ed., *Harper's Bible Commentary* (San Francisco: Harper & Row, 1988), 1047.

[69]Stephen Breck Reid, *Experience and Tradition: A Primer in Black Biblical Hermeneutics* (Nashville: Abingdon, 1990), 15-17.

[70]Cheryl Townsend Gilkes, "Mother to the Motherless, Father to the Fatherless: Power, Gender, and Community in Afrocentric Biblical Tradition," *Semeia: An Experimental Journal for Biblical Criticism* 47 (1989): 58-61, 64-65.

[71]Joseph R. Washington, Jr., *Black Religion: The Negro and Christianity in the United States* (Boston: Beacon Press, 1964), 42.

[72]Jon Michael Spencer, *Protest and Praise: Sacred Music of Black Religion* (Minneapolis: Augsburg Fortress Press, 1990), 9, 11-12.

[73]Jon Michael Spencer, *Theological Music: Introduction to Theomusicology* (New York: Greenwood Press, 1991), 77.

[74]Rosario Morales, "The Other Heritage," in Moraga and Anzaldúa, *This Bridge*, 93.

[75]Arthur C. Jones, *Wade in the Water: The Wisdom of the Spirituals* (Maryknoll, NY: Orbis Books, 1993), 86-87.

[76]Williams, *Eyes*, 252-53.

[77]Clayborne Carson, David J. Garrow, Gerald Gill, Vincent Harding, and Darlene Clark Hine, eds., *The Eyes on the Prize Civil Rights Reader: Documents, Speeches, and Firsthand Accounts from the Black Freedom Struggle, 1954-1990* (New York: Penguin, 1991), 204-5.

[78]Ibid., 208-11; and Hampton and Fayer, *Voices*, 210-15.

[79]Lovell, *Black Song*, 535.

[80]In 1996, George Wallace publicly admitted that his 1960s racist ploys were wrong.

[81]Henry Hampton, *Eyes on the Prize: America's Civil Rights Years, 1954-1965; Vol. 4, No Easy Walk (1961-1963)*, produced and directed by James De Vinney and Callie Crossley, 60 min., Blackside, 1987, videocassette.

[82]Reagon, "Program Notes," 12.

[83]Ibid., 6, 12.

[84]Nicolas Slonimsky, *Lectionary of Music* (New York: McGraw-Hill, 1989), 50.

[85]Anthony Storr, *Music and the Mind* (New York: Free Press, 1992), 32-33.

[86]Bernice Johnson Reagon quoted in Hampton and Fayer, *Voices*, 108.

[87]Lovell, *Black Song*, 286-88.

[88]Ibid., 167.

[89]Ibid., 168.

[90]Robert E. Hood, *Begrimed and Black: Christian Traditions on Blacks and Blackness* (Minneapolis: Fortress, 1994), 2-4. Blackness becomes problematic in ancient India from 3000 to 2000 B.C.E., in China with the Zhou (1027-256 B.C.E.), and in Japan's Nara period (710-793 C.E.). For an exploration of the complexities involved in discerning the different meanings of Blackness, see Hood's work in toto.

[91]Ibid., 181-87.

[92]Christa Dixon, *Negro Spirituals: From Bible to Folk Song* (Philadelphia: Fortress Press, 1976), 55-60.

[93]Williams, *Eyes*, 228-29; and Hampton and Fayer, *Voices*, 177.

[94]Hampton and Fayer, *Voices*, 189-205; and Carson et al., *Eyes on the Prize Reader*, 177-78. Both the White Mississippi delegation and the mixed MFDP wanted to be seated and brought their concerns to the credentials committee, the group that would determine who could represent Mississippi on the convention floor. President Johnson ordered Hubert Humphrey to stop the Mississippi situation. The MFDP knew that if ten percent of the credentials committee delegates would say the MFDP had a valid case, the situation would be brought before the entire convention. President Johnson sent over a Black congressman to befriend the MFDP members, and they reluctantly gave him a list of their supporters. All those supporters received a call and were told that they stood

to lose a lot. The supporters acquiesced. No one could think of a solution that would please everyone. The offer to the MFDP was two delegates-at-large and a promise never to seat an all-White delegation again. All the liberals and many civil rights leaders began to crumble. Only the MFDP refused. The MFDP did not, could not compromise, because they represented Black Mississippians who had laid their lives on the line; because of the great risk they had already taken, it did not make sense to them to accept what they knew amounted to nothing. At the next Democratic Convention, in 1968, the MFDP challenged the all-White delegation and won.

[95]Reagon, interview by author.

[96]Hampton and Fayer, *Voices*, 148-49.

[97]Jones, *Wade in the Water*, 61.

[98]Hampton and Fayer, *Voices*, 116, 122.

[99]Carawan and Carawan, *Sing For Freedom*, 205.

[100]Vincent Harding, *Hope and History: Why We Must Share the Story of the Movement* (Maryknoll, NY: Orbis Books, 1990), 4, 82.

[101]Trudier Harris, *Exorcising Blackness: Historical and Literary Lynching and Burning Rituals* (Bloomington: Indiana University Press, 1984), x-xi.

[102]Anthony Pinn, *Why God? Suffering and Evil in Black Theology* (New York: Continuum, 1995), 29-30.

[103]See Peter J. Parish, "Slavery, Capitalism, and Religion," in *On Moral Business: Classical and Contemporary Resources for Ethics in Economic Life*, ed. Max Stackhouse, Denis P. McCann, Shirley Roels, and Preston Williams (Grand Rapids, MI: William B. Eerdmans, 1995), 312-22.

10. Ensembles

[1]Bernice Johnson Reagon, "Program Notes," *Voices of the Civil Rights Movement, 1960-1966* (Washington, DC: Smithsonian Institution, Program in Black Culture, 1980), 17-19.

[2]Ibid., 18.

[3]*Songs of Zion*, United Methodist Church Supplemental Worship Resources 12 (Nashville: Abingdon, 1981, 1982), 35. This supplemental volume lists "I Shall Not Be Moved" as a hymn; this work was traditionally a Spiritual. Traditionally, the hymn is considered a religious song which has been formally referenced for use in worship services, usually exalting God's character, whereas the Spiritual is a spontaneous form of religious music suitable for secular as well as worship settings. This version also retains the original first-person singular.

[4]Guy Carawan and Candie Carawan, *Sing for Freedom: The Story of the Civil Rights Movement through Its Song* (Bethlehem, PA: Sing Out, 1990), 25.

[5]Juan Williams, *Eyes on the Prize: America's Civil Rights Years, 1954-1965* (New York: Penguin Books, 1987), 163-65.

[6]Ibid., 167; and Henry Hampton and Steve Fayer, *Voices of Freedom: An Oral History of the Civil Rights Movement from the 1950s through the 1980s* (New York: Bantam Books, 1990), 113.

[7]Robert Shelton, "Singing for Freedom: Music in the Integration Movement," *Sing Out* 12 (December-January 1962-1963): 6.

[8]Qtd. in Williams, *Eyes*, 177.

[9]Charles Sherrod quoting Chief Pritchett in Hampton and Fayer, *Voices of Freedom*, 106, 107.

[10]Ibid., 114; see also 102.

[11]"Introductions through Song I and II," Rutha Harris and Cordell Reagon, Respondents. "Voices of the Civil Rights Movement: A National Working Conference on Civil Rights Movement Culture," January 30-February 3, 1980, Archives Center, National Museum of American History, Smithsonian Institution, Washington, DC.

[12]Charles Sherrod, qtd. in Hampton and Fayer, *Voices of Freedom*, 114; see also 109-10. Sherrod, a SNCC organizer, reflected on his experience of protest in Albany. Fifteen years after he first arrived in Albany, Charles Sherrod was elected to the city commission of Albany, Georgia, in 1976.

[13]Joseph de Rivera, ed., *Conceptual Encounter: A Method for the Exploration of Human Experience* (Washington, DC: University Press of America, 1981), 109.

[14]George L. Cummings, "The Slave Narratives as a Source of Black Theological Discourse: 'The Spirit and Eschatology,' " in *Cut Loose Your Stammering Tongue: Black Theology in the Slave Narratives*, ed. Dwight N. Hopkins and George Cummings (Maryknoll, NY: Orbis Books, 1991), 61.

[15]Ibid., 60.

[16]Reagon, "Program Notes," 17. There were three groups of SNCC ensembles. The original SNCC Freedom Singers made their first national tour in 1963. Freedom Singers (II) were followed by a third group, Freedom Voices.

[17]Bernice Johnson Reagon, "Let the Church Sing 'Freedom,' " *Black Music Research Journal* 7 (1987): 107.

[18]This rhyme ditty is common to national African-American oral history tradition.

[19]Reagon quoted in Hampton and Fayer, *Voices of Freedom*, 108.

[20]Bernice Johnson Reagon, "Songs That Moved the Movement," *Perspectives* (Summer 1983): 27-35.

[21]Shelton, "Singing for Freedom," 5. Here Shelton cites SNCC Field Secretary Charles Jones. Shelton went to Albany and wrote several articles on the music he heard.

[22]Quiet qualifies Black women's invisible dignity, together with their silent courage that has enabled them to craft ethical boundaries on their own terms as they have overcome and often destroyed the negations set out by larger society. See Katie Cannon, *Black Womanist Ethics* (Atlanta: Scholars Press, 1988), 17, 45-78, 125.

[23]Williams, *Eyes,* 177.

[24]Bernice Johnson Reagon, interview by author, tape recording, Washington, DC, November 19, 1991.

[25]J. H. Kwabena Nketia, "Musical Interaction in Ritual Events," *Music and the Experience of God: Concilium 202* (April 1989): 112.

[26]There are numerous related readings. For example, see Jb 14:9; Ps 52:8; 92:12-14; Is 44:4; Jer 14:1-6; Ez 17:6; 19:10; 47:12.

[27]Julie W. Rust, "Wisdom in the Psalms" (Waco, TX: Baylor University, 1990, photocopy), 1, 3.

[28]Patrick D. Miller, Jr., *Interpreting the Psalms* (Philadelphia: Fortress Press, 1986), 82-85.

[29]Rust, "Wisdom," 24-25.

[30]Dwight N. Hopkins, "Slave Theology," in Hopkins and Cummings, *Cut Loose,* 4.

[31]Ibid., 2, 17.

[32]Lucius Outlaw, "Language and the Transformation of Consciousness: Foundations for a Hermeneutic of Black Culture" (Ph.D. diss., Boston College, 1972), 2-6.

[33]James Turner, "The Sociology of Black Nationalism," *Black Scholar* 1 (December 1969): 18.

[34]Hopkins and Cummings, *Cut Loose*, 36-43.

[35]Williams, *Eyes,* 164; and Hampton and Fayer, *Voices of Freedom*, 98.

[36]Williams, *Eyes*, 178.

[37]Ibid., 179.

[38]Eric Blom, ed., *Grove's Dictionary of Music and Musicians*, 5th ed. (New York: St. Martin's Press, 1954), s.v. "Aesthetics," by Robert Donington.

[39]Bernice Johnson Reagon, "Songs of the Civil Rights Movement, 1955-1965: A Study in Cultural History" (Ph.D. diss., Howard University, 1975), 131.

[40]Mary Milligan, "The Text of Experience: Biblical Interpretation in a Basic Christian Community in Brazil" (paper presented to the sixth annual Casassa Conference, "Text and Experience: Toward a Cultural Exegesis of the Bible," Loyola Marymount University, Los Angeles, March 19-21, 1992).

[41]Rivera, ed., *Conceptual Encounter*, 21.

[42]Reagon, "Songs That Moved," 32; and Reagon, "Program Notes," 16-17.

[43]Reagon, "Songs That Moved," 32.

[44]John Lovell, Jr., *Black Song: The Forge and the Flame: The Story of How the Afro-American Spiritual Was Hammered Out* (New York: Macmillan, 1972), 342.

[45]Reagon, "Let the Church Sing," 110.

[46]Deryck Cooke, *The Language of Music* (London: Oxford University Press, 1959), 190, 194, 225.

[47]Reagon, "Program Notes," 16.

[48]John Beaulieu, *Music and Sound in the Healing Arts: A Healing Approach* (Barrytown, NY: Station Hill Press, 1987), 17, 76, 127.

[49]John F. Szwed, "Afro-American Musical Adaptation," in *Afro-American Anthropology: Contemporary Perspectives* (New York: Free Press, 1970), 224.

[50]Beaulieu, *Music and Sound*, 84-85.

[51]Maya Angelou, "Our Grandmothers," in *I Shall Not Be Moved* (New York: Random House, 1990), 33-37.

[52]Hopkins and Cummings, *Cut Loose*, 60; see also 64-65.

[53]Rhoda Lois Blumberg, *Civil Rights: The 1960s Freedom Struggle* (Boston: G. K. Hall, 1984), 2.

[54]Bernice Johnson Reagon, qtd. in Hampton and Fayer, *Voices of Freedom*, 107-8.

[55]Nicholas Cooper-Lewter and Henry Mitchell, *Soul Theology: The Heart of American Black Culture* (Nashville: Abingdon, 1986), 147; see also 140-46.

[56]Williams, *Eyes*, 164-65.

[57]Lovell, *Black Song*, 286.

[58]Ibid.

[59]Marie Hadley Robinson, "The Negro Spiritual: An Examination of the Texts, and Their Relationship to Musical Performance Practice" (Ph.D. diss., Florida State University, 1973), 19, 33, 38, 39.

[60]Ibid., 142-47.

[61]Bernice Johnson Reagon, "Program Notes," 17.

[62]Ibid., 19; Jerry Silverman, *Songs of Protest and Civil Rights* (New York: Chelsea Publications, 1992), 56.

[63]Ibid., 56-57; Carawan and Carawan, *Sing for Freedom*, 62.

[64]Vincent Harding, *Hope and History: Why We Must Share the Story of the Movement* (Maryknoll, NY: Orbis Books), 78-79.

[65]Ibid., 79.

[66]Reagon, interview by author.

[67]"Economic Justice: Stewardship of Creation in Human Community," adopted by the Tenth Biennial Convention of the Lutheran Church in America, Seattle, Washington, June 24-July 2, 1980, in *On Moral Business: Classical and Contemporary Resources for Ethics in Economic Life*, ed. Max Stackhouse, Denis McCann, Shirley Roels, and Preston Williams (Grand Rapids: William B. Eerdmans, 1995), 431-32.

[68]Diana L. Hayes, *And Still We Rise: An Introduction to Black Liberation Theology* (New York: Paulist Press, 1996), 140-41.

[69]Reagon, "Program Notes," 17.

[70]Clayborne Carson, David J. Garrow, Gerald Gill, Vincent Harding, and Darlene Clark Hine, eds., *The Eyes On the Prize Civil Rights Reader: Documents, Speeches, and Firsthand Accounts from the Black Freedom Struggle, 1954-1990* (New York: Penguin, 1991), 108-9.

[71]Karen Lebacqz, *Justice in an Unjust World* (Minneapolis: Augsburg, 1987), 158.

[72]Emilie Townes, "Keeping a Clean House Will Not Keep a Man at Home: An Unctuous Womanist Rhetoric of Justice," in *New Visions for the Americas: Religious Engagement and Social Transformation*, ed. David Batstone (Minneapolis: Fortress Press, 1993), 127-43.

11. Song Leaders

[1]Bernice Johnson Reagon, "Program Notes," *Voices of the Civil Rights Movement, 1960-1966* (Washington, DC: Smithsonian Institution, Program in Black American Culture, 1980), 20.

[2]Ibid., 3, 20.

[3]*Songs of Zion*, United Methodist Church Supplemental Worship Resources 12 (Nashville: Abingdon, 1981, 1982), 144.

[4]Leon Litwatck, *Been in the Storm So Long: The Aftermath of Slavery* (New York: Random House, 1979), i.

[5]Ibid.

[6]Bernice Johnson Reagon and Sweet Honey in the Rock, *We Who Believe in Freedom: Sweet Honey in the Rock . . . Still on the Journey* (New York: Anchor Books, 1993), 134-36; 145-50; and Dick Cluster, *They Should Have Served That Cup of Coffee: Seven Radicals Remember the '60s; The Borning Struggle: The Civil Rights Movement."* (n.p., n.d.), 16-18, 28-30.

[7]Paul Fritz Laubenstein, "Race Values in Aframerican Music," *Music Quarterly* 16 (July 1930): 401.

[8]Juan Williams, *Eyes on the Prize: America's Civil Rights Years, 1954-1965* (New York: Penguin Books, 1987), 228-29.

[9]Ibid., 232-35.

[10]Ibid., 241-44.

[11]Ibid., 244, 247.

[12]Vincent Harding, *Hope and History: Why We Must Share the Story of the Movement* (Maryknoll, NY: Orbis Books, 1990), 18-19. In 1992, Bernice Johnson Reagon

continued to travel across the world singing freedom songs in solo appearances and with the all-women a cappella group she founded, Sweet Honey in the Rock. Reagon, ethnographer and musicologist, is a curator of the Smithsonian Institution, National Museum of American History, and a recipient of a prestigious MacArthur fellowship.

[13]Bernice Johnson Reagon, speaking in *The Songs Are Free, with Bernice Johnson Reagon and Bill Moyers*, Public Affairs Television, February 6, 1991.

[14]Fernando F. Segovia, "The Text as Other: The Eruption of Contextualization" (paper presented to the sixth annual Casassa Conference, "Text and Experience: Toward a Cultural Exegesis of the Bible," Loyola Marymount University, Los Angeles, March 19-21, 1992).

[15]Ibid.

[16]Sharon Anderson, "Bernice Johnson Reagon," *The Other Side's Faces of Faith: A Collection of Our Favorite Interviews* (1990): 8-12.

[17]Ntozake Shange, *for colored girls who have considered suicide/when the rainbow is enuf: a choreopoem* (New York: Macmillan, 1975, 1976, 1977).

[18]"Friends of Mind: A Lively Conversation between bell hooks and Cornel West on Race, Culture and Faith," *Other Side* (March-April 1992): 20. bell hooks uses lowercase letters in writing her name.

[19]Anderson, "Bernice Johnson Reagon," 9-10.

[20]Guy Carawan and Candie Carawan, *Sing For Freedom: The Story of the Civil Rights Movement through Its Songs* (Bethlehem: PA: Sing Out, 1990), 5-6; and Daniel J. Gonczy, "The Folk Music Movement of the 1960s: Its Rise and Fall," *Popular Music and Society* 10 (1985): 19. Pete and Toshi Seeger helped to book the SNCC Freedom Singers and other song-leading social activists, like Joan Baez and Bob Dylan, on college campuses throughout the country.

[21]Gonczy, "Folk Music Movement," 25.

[22]Many singing movements were active in Mississippi, Alabama, and Georgia.

[23]Carawan and Carawan, *Sing for Freedom*, 6.

[24]Ibid., 111. The words "keep your eyes on the prize" replaced the traditional "keep your hand on the plow." Alice Wine, one of the first products of the voter education schools of Johns Island, South Carolina, created this redacted version in 1956. The song was particularly significant for the sit-in participants and freedom riders who spent many days "bound in jail."

[25]Dorothy Sterling, ed., *We Are Your Sisters: Black Women in the Nineteenth Century* (New York: W. W. Norton, 1984), 214.

[26]Peter J. Welding, "Sing a Song of Segregation," *Saturday Review* 44 (April 29, 1961): 42.

[27]Carawan and Carawan, *Sing for Freedom*, 237.

[28]Ibid., 236-37.

[29]Alain Locke, "Spirituals," in *Seventy-Five Years of Freedom: Commemoration of the 75th Anniversary of the Proclamation of the Thirteenth Amendment to the Constitution of the United States* (Washington, DC: U.S. Library of Congress, 1940), 7-8.

[30]Helen L. Bonny and Louis M. Savary, *Music and Your Mind: Listening with a New Consciousness* (Barrytown, NY: Station Hill Press, 1973, 1990), 37; and Carawan and Carawan, *Sing for Freedom*, 4, 6. The music acted as a catalyst in gathering people to come together and have folk festivals.

[31]Donald Byrd, "The Meaning of Black Music," *Black Scholar* 3 (Summer 1972): 30-31.

[32]William H. McClendon, "Black Music: Sound And Feeling for Black Liberation," *Black Scholar* 7 (January-February 1976): 22-23.

[33]Vivian Collier Douglas, "Music as a Cultural Force in the Development of the Negro Race," *Negro History Bulletin* 13-15 (February 1952): 87.

[34]Waldo B. Phillips, "Negro Spirituals In Retrospect," *Negro History Bulletin* 22 (February 1952): 51; and Leroy Moore, "The Spiritual: Soul of Black Religion," *Church History* 40 (1971): 80.

[35]Charles Albert Tindley, "Stand by Me," in *Songs of Zion*, 41-42.

[36]Marvin V. Curtis, "How to Survive in Your Native Land: A Look at the History of African-American Music in America," *Western Journal of Black Studies* 12 (1988): 109.

[37]Manly P. Hall, *The Therapeutic Value of Music, Including the Philosophy of Music* (Los Angeles: Philosophical Research Society, 1982), 39-40.

[38]Ibid., 41.

[39]Bernice Johnson Reagon, "Songs That Moved the Movement," *Perspectives* (Summer 1983): 35.

[40]John E. Taylor, "Something on My Mind: A Cultural and Historical Interpretation of Spiritual Texts," *Ethnomusicology* 19 (September 1975): 396.

[41]Bernice Johnson Reagon, interview with author, tape recording, Washington DC, November 19, 1991.

[42]Reagon and Sweet Honey in the Rock, *We Who Believe in Freedom*, 152-62.

[43]Ibid., 163-67; Cluster, *They Should Have Served*, 20-22, 28-30; Smith, ed., Notable Black Women, 926-928; and Jessie Carney Smith, ed., *Epic Lives: One Hundred Black Women Who Made a Difference* (Detroit: Visible Ink, 1993), 438-39.

[44]Fannie Lou Hamer, "Sick and Tired of Being Sick and Tired," *Katallagete* 1 (Fall 1968): 19; Danny Collum, "Fannie Lou Hamer: Prophet of Hope for the Sick and Tired," *Sojourners* 11 (December 1982): 4, 11-13; Mamie E. Locke, "Is This America? Fannie Lou Hamer and the Mississippi Freedom Democratic Party," in Vicki L. Crawford, Jacqueline Anne Rouse, and Barbara Woods, *Women in the Civil Rights Movement: Trailblazers & Torchbearers 1941-1965* (Bloomington: Indiana University Press, 1993) 27-29.

[45]Locke, "Is This America?" 32-33.

[46]Fannie Lou Hamer, "It's in Your Hands," in *Black Women in White America: A Documentary History*, ed. Gerda Lerner (New York: Vintage, 1972), 613.

[47]For the full context of the story of Jesus walking on water, see Mt 14:22-36; Mk 6:45-52; and Jn 6:16-21. In John, the story represents one of the seven signs (miracles) that point out who Jesus is.

[48]Charles Converse and Joseph Scriven, "What a Friend We Have in Jesus," in *The Hymnal of the Christian Methodist Episcopal Church* (CME) (Memphis: CME Publishing House, 1987), 340. The other two verses are as follows:

> *Have we trials and temptations?*
> *Is there trouble anywhere?*
> *We should never be discouraged*
> *Take it to the Lord in prayer.*
> *Can we find a friend so faithful*
> *Who will all our sorrow share?*
> *Jesus knows our ev'ry weakness*
> *Take it to the Lord in prayer.*

Are we weak and heavy laden,
Cumbered with a load of care?
We should never be discouraged
Take it to the Lord in prayer.
Do thy friends despise, forsake thee?
Take it to the Lord in prayer;
In His arms He'll take and shield thee
Thou wilt find a solace there.

[49]Ibid., 356; see also *Songs of Zion*, 46. This compilation of hymns, Spirituals, African-American liberation songs, gospel songs and other service music resulted from a consultation on the Black church in Atlanta, Georgia, in 1973 that recommended the United Methodist Church develop a songbook from the Black religious tradition.

[50]Albert A. Goodson, "We've Come This Far by Faith," arr. Thurston G. Frazier, in *Hymnal of the C. M. E. Church,* 222.

[51]The Mud Flower Collective, *God's Fierce Whimsy: Christian Feminism and Theological Education* (Cleveland, OH: Pilgrim Press, 1985), xi.

[52]Williams, *Eyes*, 241.

12. Womanist, Transforming Musings

[1]Howard Wiley, a Ph.D. candidate at Union Theological Seminary in New York City, applied the term "our sacred texts" to the Spirituals. Wiley shared his idea in a conversation about his project, which examines the history of interpretation of the Spirituals.

[2]Marvin D. Wyne, Kinnard P. White, and Richard H. Coop, *The Black Self* (Englewood Cliffs, NJ: Prentice-Hall, 1974), 50, 56, 85.

[3]Robert Shelton, "Singing for Freedom: Music in the Integration Movement," *Sing Out* 12 (December-January 1962-63): 4, 5, 6, 12, 17.

[4]David King Dunaway, "Music and Politics in the United States," *Folk Music Journal* 5 (1987): 289; and Joseph Mussulman, *The Uses of Music: An Introduction to Music in Contemporary American Life* (Englewood Cliffs, NJ: Prentice-Hall, 1974), 94-97.

[5]John Beaulieu, *Music and Sound in the Healing Arts: A Healing Approach* (Barrytown, NY: Station Hill Press, 1987), 76.

[6]Arthur Lee Smith and Stephen Robb, eds., *The Voice of Black Rhetoric: Selections* (Boston: Allyn and Bacon, 1971), 9.

[7]Lindsay Patterson, ed., *The Afro-American in Music and Art*, International Library of Afro-American Life and History (Cornwells Heights, PA: Publisher's Agency, 1976), s.v. "Spirituals and Neo-Spirituals," by Zora Neale Hurston.

[8]Smith and Robb, *Voice of Black Rhetoric*, 1-8.

[9]Charshee C. Lawrence-McIntyre, "The Double Meanings in the Spirituals," *Journal of Black Studies* 17 (June 1987): 380-85.

[10]Ibid., 65-85.

[11]Debbie Louis, *And We Are Not Saved: A History of the Movement as People* (New York: Doubleday, 1970), 247; and James W. Button, *Blacks and Social Change: Impact of the Civil Rights Movement in Southern Communities* (Princeton: Princeton University Press, 1989), 175, 203-5.

[12]Paula Giddings, *When and Where I Enter: The Impact of Black Women on*

Race and Sex in America (New York: Bantam Books, 1984), 296.

[13]Ibid. The tension caused by bringing primarily northern White middle- and upper-middle-class students into the southern Movement was intensified by the presence of White female students, which led to sometimes emotional, sexual attention—given the reality of a number of interracial liaisons.

[14]Ibid., 297.

[15]Alice Walker, "Silver Writes," in "The Silver Writer's Movement," *Perspective* (Summer 1982): 22-23.

[16]Bernice Johnson Reagon, interview by author, tape recording, Washington, DC, November 19, 1991. While other studies have commented on the function of music as a political force, this study documents multiple sources about the social and political function of the Spirituals from an interdisciplinary perspective.

[17]Carl Marbury, "Hebrews and Spirituals: Soulful Expressions of Freedom," in *God and Human Freedom: A Festschrift in Honor of Howard Thurman*, ed. Henry James Young (Richmond, IN: Friends United Press, 1983), 76-77, 92.

[18]Deane William Ferm, *Contemporary American Theologies: A Critical Survey*, rev. ed. (San Francisco: Harper & Row, 1981, 1990), 57.

[19]Giddings, *When and Where*, 314; and Kelly D. Brown, "God Is as Christ Does," *Journal of Religious Thought* 46 (Summer-Fall 1989): 10-13, 16.

[20]See Ferm, *Contemporary American Theologies*, 58.

[21]James H. Cone, *For My People: Black Theology and the Black Church* (Maryknoll, NY: Orbis Books, 1984), 128-29.

[22]Bruce Wright, *Black Robes, White Justice* (New York: Carol Publishing Group, 1987),133; see also 22, 26, 29.

[23]Cornel West, *Prophesy Deliverance! An Afro-American Revolutionary Christianity* (Philadelphia: Westminster Press, 1982), 18.

Bibliography

Books

Ahlstrom, Sidney. *A Religious History of the American People.* New Haven: Yale University Press, 1972.

Albanese, Catherine. *America: Religions and Religion.* Belmont, CA: Wadsworth Publishing, 1981.

Allen, William Francis, Charles Pickard Ware, and Lucy McKim Garrison. *Slave Songs of the United States.* New York: Peter Smith, 1867, 1951.

Ames, Russell. *The Story of American Folk Songs.* New York: Grosset and Dunlap, 1955.

Apel, Willi. *Harvard Dictionary of Music.* Cambridge, MA: Belknap Press, 1969.

Aquinas, Thomas. *Summa Theologica.* London: R. & T. Washbourne, Ltd., 1912.

Arendt, Hannah. *The Human Condition.* Chicago: University of Chicago Press, 1958.

Asante, Molefi Kete. *The Afrocentric Idea.* Philadelphia: Temple University Press, 1987.

————. *Afrocentricity.* Trenton, NJ: Africa World Press, Inc., 1989.

Ashraf, Mary. *Political Verse and Song.* Berlin: Seven Seas Press, 1975.

Augustine, Bishop of Hippo. *The City of God.* In *Basic Writings of Saint Augustine.* Ed. Whitney J. Oates. Grand Rapids: Baker Book House, 1948.

Baker, Jr., Houston. *Blues, Ideology, and Afro-American Literature: A Vernacular Theory.* Chicago: University of Chicago Press, 1984.

Barnett, Ida Wells. *A Red Record.* Chicago: Donohue & Henneberry, 1895.

Barth, Karl. *Church Dogmatics.* Ed. G. W. Bromiley and T. F. Torrance. Vol. III/3. Edinburgh: T & T Clark, 1956.

Beaulieu, John. *Music and Sound in the Healing Arts: A Healing Approach.* Barrytown, NY: Station Hill Press, 1987.

Becker, Ernest. *Escape from Evil.* New York: Free Press, 1975.

Bedell, George C., Leo Sandon, Jr., and Charles T. Wellborn. *Religion in America.* New York: Macmillan, 1982.

Behague, Gerard, ed. *Performance Practice: Ethnomusicological Perspectives.* Westport, CT: Greenwood Press, 1984.

Bellinger, Jr., W. H. *The Psalms: Reading and Studying the Book of Praises.* Peabody, MA: Hendrickson, 1990.

Bennett, Lerone. *Before the Mayflower: A History of the Negro in America 1619-1964.* rev. New York: Penguin Books, 1961, 1962, 1964.

Berry, Mary F., and John W. Blassingame. *Long Memory: The Black Experience in America.* New York: Oxford University Press, 1982.

Best, Harold M. *Music Through the Eyes of Faith;* Christian College Coalition Series. San Francisco: HarperCollins, 1993.

Betsworth, Roger G. *The Radical Movement of the 1960's*. Metuchen, NJ: Scarecrow Press and The American Theological Library Association, 1980.

Blassingame, John. *The Slave Community: Plantation Life in the Antebellum South*. New York: Oxford University Press, 1979.

Blauner, Robert. *Racial Oppression in America*. New York: Harper & Row, 1972.

Bloch, Ernst. *Essays on the Philosophy of Music*. Trans. Peter Palmer. Cambridge: Cambridge University Press, 1985.

Blom, Eric, ed. *Grove's Dictionary of Music and Musicians*. 5th ed. New York: St. Martin's Press, Inc., 1954. S.v. "Aesthetics," by Robert Donington.

Blumberg, Rhoda Lois. *Civil Rights: The 1960s Freedom Struggle*. Boston: Twayne Publishers, 1984.

Bonny, Helen L., and Louis M. Savary. *Music & Your Mind: Listening with a New Consciousness*. Barrytown, NY: Station Hill Press, 1973, 1990.

Branch, Taylor. *Parting the Waters: America in the King Years 1954-1963*. New York: Simon & Schuster, 1988.

Brooks, Tilford. *America's Black Musical Heritage*. Englewood Cliffs, NJ: Prentice-Hall, Inc., 1984, 1993.

Broom, Leonard, and Norval Glenn. *Transformation of the Negro American*. New York: Harper & Row, 1965.

Brown, Frank Burch. *Religious Aesthetics: A Theological Study of Making and Meaning*. London: Macmillan, 1990.

Bruce, Jr., Dickson D. *Black American Writing from the Nadir: The Evolution of a Literary Tradition, 1877-1915*. Baton Rouge: Louisiana University Press, 1989.

Brueggemann, Walter. *The Message of the Psalms*. Minneapolis: Augsburg, 1984.

Buber, Martin. *I and Thou*. Trans. Walter Kaufmann. New York: Charles Scribner's Sons, 1970.

Burlin, Natalie Curtis. *Negro Folk Songs*. New York: G. Schirmer, 1918.

Burrison, John A., ed. *Storytellers: Folktales & Legends from the South*. Athens, GA: University of Georgia Press, 1989.

Butcher, Margaret Just. *The Negro in American Culture*. New York: Alfred A. Knopf, 1956.

Button, James W. *Blacks and Social Change: Impact of the Civil Rights Movement in Southern Communities*. Princeton: Princeton University Press, 1989.

Calvin, John. *The Institutes of the Christian Religion*. Ed. John T. McNeil. 2 Vols. London: SCM, and Philadelphia: Westminster Press, 1961.

Cannon, Katie G. *Black Womanist Ethics*. Atlanta, GA: Scholars Press, 1988.

Carawan, Guy, and Candie Carawan. *Sing for Freedom: The Story of the Civil Rights Movement through Its Songs*. Bethlehem, PA: Sing Out, 1990.

Carr, Ian. *Miles Davis: A Biography*. New York: William Morrow, 1982.

Carson, Clayborn, David J. Garrow, Gerald Gill, Vincent Harding, Darlene Clark Hine, eds. *The Eyes on the Prize Civil Rights Reader: Documents, Speeches, and Firsthand Accounts from the Black Freedom Struggle, 1954-1990*. New York: Penguin, 1991.

Clark, Kenneth. *Pathos of Power*. New York: Harper & Row, 1974.

Collins, Patricia Hill. *Black Feminist Thought: Knowledge, Consciousness, and the Politics of Empowerment*. New York: Routledge, 1991.

Cone, James H. *A Black Theology of Liberation*. Philadelphia: Lippincott, 1970; Maryknoll, NY: Orbis Books, 1990.

———. *Black Theology and Black Power*. San Francisco: Harper & Row, 1969,

1989; Maryknoll, NY: Orbis Books, 1997.

————. *For My People: Black Theology and the Black Church*. Maryknoll, NY: Orbis Books, 1984.

————. *Martin & Malcolm & America: A Dream or a Nightmare*. Maryknoll, NY: Orbis Books, 1991.

————. *The Spirituals and the Blues: An Interpretation*. New York: Seabury Press, 1972; Maryknoll, NY: Orbis Books, 1992.

Cooke, Deryck. *The Language of Music*. London: Oxford University Press, 1959.

Cooper, Anna Julia. *A Voice from the South, by a Black Woman of the South*. Westport, CT: Greenwood Press, 1976, 1892.

Cooper-Lewter, Nicholas C., and Henry H. Mitchell. *Soul Theology: The Heart of American Black Culture*. San Francisco: Harper & Row, 1986.

Crim, Keith, ed. *The Interpreter's Dictionary of the Bible, Supplement*. Nashville: Abingdon, 1962. S.v. "Vengeance," by J. E. Lindsey, Jr.

Cronon, Edmund D. *Black Moses: The Story of Marcus Garvey and the Universal Association*. Madison, WI: University of Wisconsin Press, 1955.

Cross, Theodore. *The Black Power Imperative: Racial Inequality and the Politics of Nonviolence*. New York: Faulkner, 1987.

Davis, Charles T., and Henry Louis Gates, Jr. *The Slave's Narrative*. New York: Oxford University Press, 1985.

Davis, David Brion. *The Problem of Slavery in Western Culture*. Ithaca, NY: Cornell University Press, 1966.

Davis, Robert, and Ronald Schleifer. *Contemporary Literary Criticism: Literary and Cultural Studies*. 2d ed. New York: Longman, 1989.

Davis, Stephen. *Encountering Evil: Live Options in Theodicy*. Atlanta: John Knox, 1981.

de Rivera, Joseph, ed. *Conceptual Encounter: A Method for the Exploration of Human Experience*. Washington, DC: University Press of America, 1981.

Dett, Nathaniel. *Religious Folk-Songs of the Negro*. Hampton, VA: Hampton Institute Press, 1927.

Dixon, Christa. *Negro Spirituals: From Bible to Folk Song*. Philadelphia: Fortress Press, 1976.

Dixon, Jr., Thomas. *The Clansman: An Historical Romance of the Ku Klux Klan*. New York: Doubleday, 1905.

DjeDje, Jacqueline Cogdell. *American Black Spiritual and Gospel Songs from Southeast Georgia: A Comparative Study*. Los Angeles: Center for Afro-American Studies; University of California, 1978.

Douglas, Kelly Brown. *The Black Christ*. Maryknoll, NY: Orbis Books, 1994.

D'Souza, Dinesh. *The End of Racism*. New York: Free Press, 1995.

Du Bois, W. E. B. *The Souls of Black Folk*. With an Introduction by Henry Louis Gates, Jr. New York: Bantam Books, 1989; reprint, Chicago: A.C. McClurg, 1903.

Dumochel, Paul, ed. *Violence and Truth: On the Work of Rene Girard*. London: Athlone Press, 1988.

Eliade, Mircea. *The Encyclopedia of Religion*. New York: Macmillan, 1987. S.v. "Theodicy," by Ronald M. Green.

————. *The Sacred and the Profane*. New York: Harper, 1959.

Elliot, E. N. *Cotton Is King, and Pro-slavery Arguments: Comprising the Writings of Hammond, Harper, Christy, Stringfellow, Hodge, Bledsoe, and Cartwright, on This Important Subject*. Augusta, GA: Pritchard, Abbott & Loomis, 1860.

Ellison, Ralph. *The Invisible Man*. New York: New American Library, 1952.

Elsbree, Langdon. *The Rituals of Life: Patterns in Narratives.* Port Washington, NY: Kennikat Press, 1982.

Epstein, Dena. *Sinful Tunes and Spirituals: Black Folk Music to the Civil War.* Urbana, IL: University of Illinois Press, 1977.

Erickson, Erik. *Identity: Youth and Crisis.* New York: W. W. Norton, 1968.

Farley, Wendy. *Tragic Vision and Divine Compassion: A Contemporary Theodicy.* Louisville, KY: Westminster/John Knox Press, 1990.

Felder, Cain Hope, ed. *Stony the Road We Trod: African American Biblical Interpretation.* Minneapolis: Fortress, 1991.

————. *Troubling Biblical Waters: Race, Class, and Family.* Maryknoll, NY: Orbis Books, 1989.

Fenner, Thomas P. *Religious Folk Songs of the Negro.* Hampton, VA: Hampton Institute Press, 1909.

Ferm, Deane William. *Contemporary American Theologies: A Critical Survey,* rev. ed. San Francisco: Harper & Row, 1981, 1990.

Fisher, Miles Mark. *Negro Slave Songs in the United States.* Foreword by Ray Allen Billington. New York: Citadel Press, 1953, 1981.

Fletcher, John. *Studies On Slavery, In Easy Lessons: Compiled Into Eight Studies, And Subdivided Into Short Lessons For The Convenience Of Readers.* Miami: Mnemosyne Publishing Co., 1852, repr. 1969.

Flexner, Eleanor. *Century of Struggle: The Women's Rights Movement in the United States.* Cambridge, MA and London: Belknap Press/Harvard University Press, 1959, 1975, 1979.

Fluker, Walter E. *They Looked for a City: A Comparative Analysis of the Ideal of Community in the Thought of Howard Thurman and Martin Luther King, Jr.* Lanham, MD: University Press of America, 1989.

Forsyth, Peter Taylor. *The Justification of God: Lectures for War-Time on a Christian Theodicy.* London: Duckworth, 1916.

Foster, William Z. *The Negro People in American History.* New York: International Publishers, 1954.

Foucault, Michel. *The Archaeology of Knowledge.* New York: Harper & Row, 1972.

Franklin, John Hope. *From Slavery to Freedom.* New York: Alfred A. Knopf, 1956.

Frederickson, George. *The Arrogance of Race: Historical Perspectives on Slavery, Racism, and Social Inequality.* Middletown, CT: Wesleyan University Press, 1988.

Friedel, L. M. *The Bible and the Negro Spirituals.* Bay St. Louis, MS: St. Augustine Seminary, 1947.

Gates, Jr., Henry Louis. *Figures in Black: Words, Signs, and the "Racial Self."* New York: Oxford University Press, 1987.

————. *The Signifying Monkey: A Theory of Afro-American Literary Criticism.* New York: Oxford University Press, 1988.

Genovese, Eugene. *Rebellion to Revolution: Afro-American Slave Revolts in the Making of the Modern World.* Baton Rouge, LA: Louisiana State University Press, 1979.

————. *Roll, Jordan, Roll: The World the Slaves Made.* New York: Vintage Books, 1972, 1974.

Gibbs, Lee, and W. Taylor Stevenson, eds. *Myth and the Crisis of Historical Consciousness.* Missoula, MT: Scholars Press/American Academy of Religion, 1975.

Giddings, Paula. *When and Where I Enter: The Impact of Black Women on Race and Sex in America*. New York: Bantam Books, 1984.

Gilmore, Al-Tony, ed. *Revisiting Blassingame's The Slave Community: The Scholars Respond*. Westport, CT: Greenwood Press, 1978.

Girard, René. *The Scapegoat*. Trans. Yvonne Freccero. Baltimore: Johns Hopkins University Press, 1986.

———. *To Double Business Bound: Essays on Literature, Mimesis, and Anthropology*. Baltimore: Johns Hopkins University Press, 1978.

Gleick, James. *Chaos: Making a New Science*. New York: Viking, 1987.

Grant, Jacquelyn. *White Women's Christ and Black Women's Jesus: Feminist Christology and Womanist Response*. Atlanta: Scholar's Press, 1989.

Greeley, Andrew. *God in Popular Culture*. Chicago: Thomas More Press, 1988.

Grissom, Mary Allen. *The Negro Sings a New Heaven*. Chapel Hill, NC: University of North Carolina Press, 1930.

Gutiérrez, Gustavo. *On Job: God-Talk and the Suffering of the Innocent*. Maryknoll, NY: Orbis Books, 1987.

Hall, Manly P. *The Therapeutic Value of Music Including the Philosophy of Music*. Los Angeles: Philosophical Research Society, Inc., 1982.

Hampton, Henry, and Steve Fayer. *Voices of Freedom: An Oral History of the Civil Rights Movement from the 1950s through the 1980s*. New York: Bantam Books, 1990.

Harding, Vincent. *Hope and History: Why We Must Share the Story of the Movement*. Maryknoll, NY: Orbis Books, 1990.

Harlan, Louis R. *Booker T. Washington: The Making of a Black Leader, 1856-1901*. New York: Oxford University Press, 1972.

———. *Booker T. Washington: The Wizard of Tuskegee, 1901-1915*. New York: Oxford University Press, 1983.

Harris, Leonard, ed. *The Philosophy of Alain Locke; Harlem Renaissance and Beyond*. Philadelphia: Temple University Press, 1989.

Harris, Michael W. *The Rise of Gospel Blues: The Music of Thomas Andrew Dorsey in the Urban Church*. New York: Oxford University Press, 1992.

Harris, Norman. *Connecting Times: The Sixties in Afro-American Fiction*. Jackson, MS: University Press of Mississippi, 1988.

Harris, Trudier. *Exorcising Blackness: Historical and Literary Lynching and Burning Rituals*. Bloomington: Indiana University Press, 1984.

Harris, William H. *Keeping the Faith: A. Philip Randolph, Milton P. Webster, and the Brotherhood of Sleeping Car Porters, 1925-37*. Urbana: University of Illinois Press, 1977.

Hayes, Diana L. *And Still We Rise: An Introduction to Black Liberation Theology*. New York: Paulist Press, 1996.

Hecht, Michael, Mary Jane Collier, Sidney Ribeau. *African American Communication: Ethnic Identity and Cultural Interpretation*. Newbury Park, CA: Sage Publications, 1993.

Held, David. *Introduction to Critical Theory: Horkheimer to Habermas*. Berkeley and Los Angeles: University of California Press, 1980.

Herndon, Marcia, and Norma McLeod. *Music as Culture*. Darby, PA: Norwood Editions, 1982.

Herrnstein, Richard and Charles Murray. *The Bell Curve: Intelligence and Class Structure in American Life*. New York: Free Press, 1994.

Hick, John. *Evil and the God of Love.* Rev. San Francisco: Harper & Row, 1977.

Higgins, Kathleen. *The Music of Our Lives.* Philadelphia: Temple University Press, 1991.

Hine, Darlene Clark, Elsa Barkley Brown, Rosalyn Terborg-Penn. *Black Women in America: An Historical Encyclopedia,* 2 Vols. Bloomington, IN: Indiana University Press, 1993.

Holt, Len. *The Summer That Didn't End.* New York: William Morrow, 1965.

Hood, Robert E. *Begrimed and Black: Christian Traditions on Blacks and Blackness.* Minneapolis: Fortress, 1994.

hooks, bell. *Ain't I A Woman: Black Women and Feminism.* Boston: South End Press, 1981.

Horkheimer, Max, and Theodor W. Adorno. *Dialectic of Enlightenment.* New York: Continuum, 1991.

Hume, David. *Dialogues Concerning Natural Religion.* Ed. H.D. Aiken. New York: Harper, 1948.

Irenaeus. *Against Heresies.* Ante-Nicene Library, Vols. 4, 5. Grand Rapids: Eerdmans, 1979.

Jacobs, Paul, and Saul Landau. *To Serve the Devil,* Vol. 1, *Natives and Slaves.* New York: Vintage Books.

Jahn, Janheninz. *Muntu: The New African Culture.* New York: Grove Press, 1961.

Johnson, Clifton H., ed. *God Struck Me Dead: Religious Conversion Experiences and Autobiographies of Ex-Slaves.* Philadelphia: Pilgrim Press, 1969.

Johnson, James Weldon, and J. Rosamond Johnson. *The Books of American Negro Spirituals.* New York: Harper & Row, 1926.

Johnson, Jr., Joseph A. *The Soul of the Black Preacher.* With an Introduction by C. D. Coleman. N.p.: Pilgrim Press, 1970.

Jones, Arthur C. *Wade in the Water: The Wisdom of the Spirituals.* Maryknoll, NY: Orbis Books, 1993.

Jones, Major. *Black Awareness: A Theology of Hope.* Nashville: Abingdon Press, 1971.

————. *Christian Ethics for Black Theology.* Nashville: Abingdon Press, 1974.

————. *The Color of God.* Macon, GA: Mercer Press, 1987.

Jones, William R. *Is God a White Racist? A Preamble to Black Theology.* C. Eric Lincoln Series on Black Religion. Garden City, NY: Anchor Press/Doubleday, 1973.

Jordan, Winthrop. *White Over Black: American Attitudes toward the Negro, 1550-1812.* Chapel Hill, NC: University of North Carolina Press, 1968.

Karenga, Maulana. *Introduction to Black Studies.* Los Angeles: University of Sankore Press, 1982.

Kaufman, Helen. *From Jehovah to Jazz: Music in America from Psalmody to the Present Day.* Port Washington, NY: Kennikat Press, 1937.

Kelsey, George D. *Racism and the Christian Understanding of Man.* New York: Charles Scribner's Sons, 1965.

Kenny, Anne. *The Negro Spiritual and Other Essays.* Cairo, IL: R. Schindler, 1943.

Keppler, Carl F. *The Literature of the Second Self.* Tucson, AZ: University of Arizona Press, 1972.

King, Jr., Martin Luther. *Strength to Love.* Philadelphia: Fortress Press, 1981.

————. *Where Do We Go From Here: Chaos or Community?* Boston: Beacon Press, 1967.

Kivy, Peter. *Sound and Semblance: Reflections on Musical Representation.* Princeton, NJ: Princeton University Press, 1984.

───. *Sound Sentiment: An Essay on the Musical Emotions.* Philadelphia: Temple University, 1989.

Komonchak, Joseph A., Mary Collins, and Dermont Lane, eds. *The New Dictionary of Theology.* Wilmington, DE: Michael Glazier, 1987. S.v. "Problem of Evil," by T. W. Tilley.

Krehbiel, Henry. *Afro-American Folksongs: A Study in Racial and National Music.* Portland, ME: Longwood Press, 1913.

Lebacqz, Karen. *Justice in an Unjust World.* Minneapolis: Fortress Press, 1987.

───. *Six Theories of Justice: Perspectives from Philosophical and Theological Ethics.* Minneapolis: Fortress Press, 1986.

Lee, Spike. *The Films of Spike Lee: Five for Five.* New York: Stewart, Tabori, Chang, 1991.

Lewis, Anthony. *The Second American Revolution: A First Hand Account of the Struggle for Civil Rights.* London: Faber and Faber, 1966.

Lieberman, Jethro K. *Milestones! 200 Years of American Law.* St. Paul, MN: West Publishing, 1976.

Lieberman, Robbie. *"My Song Is My Weapon": People's Songs, American Communism, and the Politics of Culture 1930-1950.* Chicago: University of Illinois Press, 1989.

Lifton, Robert Jay. *The Nazi Doctors: Medical Killing and the Psychology of Genocide.* New York: Basic Books, 1986.

Lincoln, C. Eric and Lawrence H. Mamiya. *The Black Church in the African American Experience.* Durham and London: Duke University Press, 1990.

Lincoln, C. Eric. *Race, Religion, and the Continuing American Dilemma.* New York: Hill and Wang, 1984.

Litwatck, Leon. *Been in the Storm So Long: The Aftermath of Slavery.* New York: Random House, 1979.

Locke, Alain, ed. *The New Negro.* New York: A and C Boni, 1925.

Lomax, Alan, and Sidney Robertson Cowell. *American Folk Song and Folk Lore: A Regional Bibliography.* Washington, DC: P.E.A. Service Center, 1942.

Lomax, John Avery, and Alan Lomax, comps. *American Ballads and Folk Songs.* New York: Macmillan Company, 1934.

Louis, Debbie. *And We Are Not Saved: A History of the Movement as People.* Garden City, NY: Doubleday, 1970.

Lovell, Jr., John. *Black Song: The Forge and the Flame; The Story of How the Afro-American Spiritual Was Hammered Out.* New York: Macmillan, 1972.

MacIntyre, Alasdair. *After Virtue: A Study in Moral Virtue,* 2d ed. Notre Dame, IN: University of Notre Dame Press, 1984.

Macmillan, Terry. *Breaking Ice: An Anthology of Contemporary African-American Fiction.* New York: Penguin Books, 1990.

Marable, Manning. *Race, Reform, and Rebellion: The Second Reconstruction in Black America, 1945-1990.* 2d ed. Jackson, MS: University Press of Mississippi, 1991.

Maslow, Abraham. *Motivation and Personality,* 2d ed. NY: Harper & Row, 1970.

Mbiti, John S. *African Religions and Philosophy.* New York: Praeger, 1969.

McDowell, Deborah E., and Arnold Rampersad, eds. *Slavery and the Literary Imagination.* Baltimore: Johns Hopkins University Press, 1989.

McFeely, William S. *Frederick Douglass.* New York: W. W. Norton, 1991.

McIlhenny, Edward Avery. *Befo' De War Spirituals.* Boston: Christopher Publishing House, 1933.

Meier, August. "The Paradox of W. E. B. Du Bois." In *W. E. B. Du Bois,* William M. Tuttle, Jr., ed., 141-61. Englewood Cliffs, NJ: Prentice Hall, 1973.

Mendl, Robert. *The Divine Quest in Music.* London: Salisbury Square, 1957.

Miller, Jr., Patrick D. *Interpreting the Psalms.* Philadelphia: Fortress Press, 1986.

Moltmann, Jürgen. *The Crucified God.* Trans. R. A. Wilson and John Bowden. London: SCM, 1974.

————. *Theology of Hope.* New York: Harper & Row, 1967.

Moody, Anne. *Coming of Age in Mississippi.* New York: Dial Press, 1968.

Moraga, Cherríe, and Gloria Anzaldúa, eds. *This Bridge Called My Back: Writings by Radical Women of Color.* New York: Kitchen Table: Women of Color Press, 1981, 1983.

Mosala, Itumeleng J. *Biblical Hermeneutics and Black Theology in South Africa.* Grand Rapids: Eerdmans, 1989.

Mukenge, Ida. *The Black Church in Urban America: A Case Study in Political Economy.* Lanham, MD: University Press of America, 1983.

Newport, John P. *Paul Tillich.* Makers of the Modern Theological Mind,. Ed. Bob E. Patterson. Waco, TX: Word Books, 1984.

Oden, Thomas C. *The Word of Life. Systematic Theology.* Vol. 1. San Francisco: Harper & Row, 1989.

Odum, Howard W., and Guy B. Johnson. *The Negro and His Songs.* Chapel Hill, NC: University of North Carolina Press, 1925.

Outler, Albert, ed. *Augustine: Confessions and Enchiridion.* The Library of Christian Classics. Philadelphia: Westminster Press, 1955.

Palmer, Roy. *The Sound of History: Songs and Social Comment.* Oxford: Oxford University Press, 1988.

Panikkar, Raimun. *Myth, Faith and Hermeneutics: Cross-Cultural Studies.* New York: Paulist Press, 1979.

Panko, Stephen M. *Martin Buber.* Makers of the Modern Theological Mind. Ed. Bob E. Patterson. Waco, TX: Word Books, 1976.

Patterson, Orlando. *Slavery and Social Death: A Comparative Study.* Cambridge, MA: Harvard University Press, 1982.

Phelps, Shirelle, ed. *Who's Who in Black America,* 1994-95, 8th ed. Detroit, MI: Gale Research Inc., 1994.

Pinn, Anthony. *Why God? Suffering and Evil in Black Theology.* New York: Continuum, 1995.

Pojman, Louis, ed. *Philosophy of Religion: An Anthology.* Belmont, CA: Wadsworth Publishing, 1987.

Rampersad, Arnold. *The Art and Imagination.* Cambridge: Harvard University Press, 1976.

Rawick, George P. *The American Slave: A Composite Autobiography.* 41 vols. Westport, CT: Greenwood Publishing Company, 1972, 1978, 1979.

Reagon, Bernice Johnson and Sweet Honey in the Rock. *We Who Believe in Freedom: Sweet Honey in the Rock . . . Still on the Journey.* New York: Anchor/ Doubleday, 1993.

Reid, Stephen Breck. *Experience and Tradition: A Primer in Black Biblical Hermeneutics.* Nashville: Abingdon, 1990.

Richardson, Alan and Alan Bowden, eds. *The Westminster Dictionary of Christian*

Theology. Philadelphia: Westminster Press, 1983. S.v. "Predestination," by Michael Langford.

———. *The Westminster Dictionary of Christian Theology*. Philadelphia: Westminster Press, 1983. S.v. "The Problem of Evil," by John Hick.

Riggs, Marcia Y. *Awake, Arise, & Act: A Womanist Call for Black Liberation*. Cleveland, OH: Pilgrim Press, 1994.

Rorty, Richard. *Contingency, Irony, and Solidarity*. Cambridge: Cambridge University Press, 1989.

Rudwick, Elliot. *W. E. B. Du Bois: A Study in Minority Group Leadership*. Philadelphia: University of Pennsylvania Press, 1960.

Sadie, Stanley, ed. *The New Grove Dictionary of Music and Musicians*. London: Macmillan Publishers, Ltd., 1980. S.v. "Ethnomusicology," by Barbara Krader.

Schleiermacher, Friedrich. *The Christian Faith*. Ed. H. R. Mackintosh and J. S. Stewart. Edinburgh: T & T Clark, 1928.

Schnabel, Arthur. *Music and the Line of Most Resistance*. Ann Arbor: University Microfilms, Inc., 1962.

Scott, Kesho Yvonne. *The Habit of Surviving*. New York: Ballantine Books, 1991.

Seashore, Carl. *Psychology of Music*. N.p.: 1938; repr. New York: Dover, 1967.

Seeger, Pete. *Incompleat Folksinger*. Ed. Jo Metcalf Schwartz. New York: Simon and Schuster, 1972.

Slonimsky, Nicolas. *Lectionary of Music*. New York: McGraw-Hill, 1989.

Small, Charles. *Music of the Common Tongue: Survival and Celebration in Afro-American Music*. London: John Calder, 1987.

Smith, Arthur Lee, and Stephen Robb, eds. *The Voice of Black Rhetoric: Selections*. Boston: Allyn and Bacon, Inc., 1971.

Smith, Dennis E., and Hal E. Taussig. *Many Tables: The Eucharist in the New Testament and Liturgy Today*. London: SCM Press, 1990.

Smith, Jessie Carney, ed. *Epic Lives: One Hundred Black Women Who Made a Difference*. Detroit, MI: Visible Ink, 1993.

Smith, Kenneth, and Ira Zepp, Jr. *Search for the Beloved Community: The Thinking of Martin Luther King, Jr.* Valley Forge, PA: Judson Press, 1974.

Smythe, Augustine T., et al. *The Carolina Low-Country*. New York: The Macmillan Company, 1931.

Soelle, Dorothee. *Suffering*. London: Darton, Longman & Todd, 1975.

Southern, Eileen. *The Music of Black Americans: A History*, 2d ed. New York: W. W. Norton, 1983.

Spariosu, Mihai, ed. *Mimesis in Contemporary Theory: An Interdisciplinary Approach; The Literary and Philosophical Debate*. Philadelphia: John Benhamins Publishing, 1984.

Spencer, Jon Michael. *Protest & Praise: Sacred Music of Black Religion*. Minneapolis: Fortress Press, 1990.

———. *Theological Music: Introduction to Theomusicology*. New York: Greenwood Press, 1991.

Stanton, Elizabeth Cady, Susan Anthony, and Matilda Joslyn Gage, eds. *The History of Woman Suffrage*. Vol. 1. Rochester, NY: n.p., 1881.

Starling, Marion Wilson. *The Slave Narrative: Its Place in American History*. 2d ed. Washington, DC: Howard University Press, 1981.

Stepto, Robert B. *From Behind the Veil: A Study of Afro-American Narrative*. Chicago: University of Illinois Press, 1979.

Sterling, Dorothy, ed. *We Are Your Sisters: Black Women in the Nineteenth Cen-

tury. New York: W. W. Norton, 1984.

Storr, Anthony. *Music and the Mind.* New York: Free Press, 1992.

Stout, Jeffrey. *Ethics after Babel: The Languages of Morals and Their Discontents.* Boston: Beacon Press, 1988.

Stroup, George W. *The Promise of Narrative Theology: Recovering the Gospel in the Church.* Atlanta: John Knox Press, 1981.

Surin, Kenneth. *Theology and the Problem of Evil.* New York: Basil Blackwell, 1986.

Swinburne, Richard. *The Existence of God.* Oxford: Clarendon, 1979.

Thoreau, Henry David. *Walden.* Time Reading Program Special Edition. New York: Time Incorporated, 1962.

Thurman, Howard. *The Creative Encounter.* New York: Harper and Row, 1954; Richmond Publishers, 1972.

———. *Deep Is the Hunger.* New York: Harper and Brothers, 1951.

———. *Deep River and the Negro Spiritual Speaks of Life and Death.* Richmond, IN: Friends United Press, 1975.

———. *Disciplines of the Spirit.* New York: Harper and Row, 1963; Richmond, IN: Friends United Press, 1973.

———. *The Inward Journey.* New York: Harper and Row, 1961.

———. *The Luminous Darkness: A Personal Interpretation of the Anatomy of Segregation and the Ground of Hope.* New York: Harper and Row, 1965.

———. *The Search for Common Ground: An Inquiry into the Basis of Man's Experience of Community.* New York: Harper and Row, 1971.

———. *With Head and Heart: The Autobiography of Howard Thurman.* New York: Harcourt Brace Jovanovich, 1979.

Tillich, Paul. *The Interpretation of History.* New York: Charles Scribner's Sons, 1936.

Townes, Emilie. *In a Blaze of Glory: Womanist Spirituality as Social Witness.* Nashville, TN: Abingdon, 1995.

———. ed. *A Troubling in My Soul: Womanist Perspectives on Evil and Suffering.* Maryknoll, NY: Orbis Books, 1993.

Tuttle, Jr., William M., ed. *W. E. B. Du Bois.* Englewood Cliffs, NJ: Prentice Hall, 1973.

Wainwright, William J. *Philosophy of Religion.* Belmont, CA: Wadsworth Publishing, 1988.

Walker, Alice. *In Search of Our Mothers' Gardens: Womanist Prose.* New York: Harcourt Brace Jovanich, 1967,1983.

Walker, Wyatt Tee. *"Somebody's Calling My Name": Black Sacred Music and Social Change.* Valley Forge, PA: Judson Press, 1979.

Walker-Hill, Helen. *Music by Black Women Composers: A Bibliography of Available Scores;* CBMR Monographs, No. 5. Chicago: Center for Black Music Research, Columbia College, 1995.

Washington, Jr., Joseph R. *Black Religion: The Negro and Christianity in the United States.* Boston: Beacon Press, 1964.

———. *The Politics of God.* Boston: Beacon Press, 1967.

Watters, Pat. *Down to Now: Reflections on the Southern Civil Rights Movement.* New York: Random House, 1971.

Webber, Thomas. *Deep Like the Rivers: Education in the Slave Quarter Community, 1831-1865.* New York: W. W. Norton, 1978.

West, Cornel. *Prophesy Deliverance! An Afro-American Revolutionary Christian-*

ity. Philadelphia: Westminster Press, 1982.

———. *Prophetic Fragments.* Grand Rapids: Eerdmans, 1988.

White, Deborah Gray. *Ar'n't I a Woman: Female Slaves in the Plantation South.* New York: W. W. Norton, 1985.

Williams, Delores. *Sisters in the Wilderness: The Challenge of Womanist God-Talk.* Maryknoll, NY: Orbis Books, 1993

Williams, Juan, with the "Eyes on the Prize" Production Team. *Eyes on the Prize: America's Civil Rights Years, 1954-1965.* New York: Penguin Books, 1987.

Williams, Louis N. *Black Psychology: Compelling Issues and Views,* 3d ed. Washington, DC: University Press of America, 1981.

Williams, Raymond. *Marxism and Literature.* Oxford: Oxford University Press, 1977.

Wink, Walter. *Naming the Powers: The Language of Power in the New Testament.* Minneapolis: Fortress Press, 1984.

———. *Unmasking the Powers: The Invisible Forces That Determine Human Existence.* Minneapolis: Fortress Press, 1986.

———. *Engaging the Powers: Discernment and Resistance in a World of Domination.* Minneapolis: Fortress Press, 1992.

Woodson, Carter G. *The History of the Negro Church.* Washington, DC: The Associated Publishers, 1921.

Woodward, C. Vann. *The Strange Career of Jim Crow.* Rev. New York: Oxford University Press, 1957, 1955.

Work, Frederick J., ed. *Folk Songs of the American Negro.* Nashville, TN: Fisk University Press, 1907.

Work, John W. *American Negro Songs and Spirituals.* New York: Crown Publishers, 1940.

Wortham, Anne. *The Other Side of Racism: A Philosophical Study of Black Race Consciousness.* Columbus, OH: Ohio State University Press, 1981.

Wright, Bruce. *Black Robes, White Justice.* New York: Carol Publishing Group, 1987.

Wyne, Marvin D., Kinnard P. White, and Richard H. Coop. *The Black Self.* Englewood Cliffs, NJ: Prentice-Hall, 1974.

Zahan, Dominique. *The Religion, Spirituality, and Thought of Traditional Africa.* Chicago: The University of Chicago Press, 1979.

Zinn, Howard. *SNCC: The New Abolitionists.* Boston: Beacon Press, 1964.

Articles

"Friends of Mind: A lively conversation between bell hooks and Cornel West on race, culture and faith." *The Other Side* (March-April 1992): 14-21.

"In Egypt Land." *Time* (December 30, 1946): 59-60, 62, 64.

Ames, Russell. "Protest and Irony in Negro Folk Song." *Science and Society* 14 (Summer, 1950): 193-213.

Anderson, Sharon. "Bernice Johnson Reagon." *The Other Side's Faces of Faith: A Collection of Our Favorite Interviews* (1990): 8-12.

Appiah, K. Anthony. "Inventing an African Practice in Philosophy: Epistemological Issues." In *Surreptitious Speech: Présence Africaine and the Otherness 1947-1987,* 227-237. Ed. V. Y. Mudimbe. Chicago: University of Chicago Press, 1992.

———. "Thick Translation." *Callaloo* 16 (1993): 818.

——— and Henry Louis Gates, Jr. "Editor's Introduction: Multiplying Identities."

cal Inquiry 18 (Summer 1992): 625-629.

Barnett, Leonard. "African Religion in the Americas: The Islands in Between." In *African Religions: A Symposium.* Ed. Newell S. Booth, Jr., 183-216. New York: NOK Publishers, 1977.

Beaty, Michael. "The Problem of Evil: The Unanswered Questions Argument." *Southwest Philosophical Review* 5 (January 1988): 57-63.

Beckham, Albert. "The Psychology of Negro Spirituals." *The Southern Workman* 60 (1931): 391-94.

Berry, Mary F., and John W. Blassingame. "Africa, Slavery and the Roots of Contemporary Black Culture." In *Chant of Saints: A Gathering of Afro-American Literature, Art, and Scholarship.* Ed. Michael S. Harper and Robert Stepto, 241-56. Urbana, IL: University of Illinois Press, 1979.

Bessiere, Gerard. "Humour—A Theological Attitude?" In *Theology of Joy. Concilium: Religion in the Seventies Series.* Ed. Johann Metz and Jean-Pierre Jossua, 81-95. New York: Herder and Herder, 1974.

Booth, Jr., Newell S. "The View from Kasongo Niembo." *African Religions: A Symposium.* Ed. Newell S. Booth, Jr., 31-68. New York: NOK Publishers, 1977.

Brodwin, Stanley. "The Veil Transcended: Form and Meaning in W. E. B. Du Bois' *The Souls of Black Folk." Journal of Black Studies* (March 1972): 306-14.

Brown, Kelly Delaine. "God Is as Christ Does: Toward a Womanist Theology." *Journal of Religious Thought* 46 (Summer-Fall, 1989): 7-16.

Brueggemann, Walter. "Theodicy in a Social Dimension." *Journal for the Study of the Old Testament* 33 (1985): 3-25.

Bruner, II, Gordon C. "Music, Mood, and Marketing." *Journal of Marketing* 54 (October 1990): 94.

Bultmann, Rudolf. "Is Exegesis Without Presuppositions Possible?" In *Existence and Faith: Shorter Writings of Rudolf Bultmann.* New York: Meridian Books, 1960.

Burlin, Natalie Curtis. "How Negro Folksongs Are 'Born.' " *Current Opinion* 66 (March 1919): 164-66.

Byrd, Donald. "The Meaning of Black Music." *The Black Scholar* 3 (Summer, 1972): 28-31.

Canaan, Andrea. "Brownness." In *This Bridge Called My Back: Writings by Radical Women of Color.* Ed. Moraga, Cherríe and Gloria Anzaldúa, 232-33. New York: Kitchen Table: Women of Color Press, 1981, 1983.

Cannon, Katie Geneva. "The Wounds of Jesus": Justification of Goodness in the Face of Manifold Evil." In *A Troubling in My Soul: Womanist Perspectives on Evil and Suffering,* 219-31. Ed. Emilie Townes. Maryknoll, NY: Orbis Books, 1993.

Cannon, Katie Geneva. "Slave Ideology and Biblical Interpretation." *Semeia: An Experimental Journal for Biblical Criticism* 47 (1989): 9-23.

———. "Hitting a Straight Lick with a Crooked Stick: The Womanist Dilemma in the Development of a Black Liberation Ethic." In *Sisters Struggling in the Spirit: A Women of Color Theological Anthology,* 93-103. Nantawan Boonprasat Lewis, Lydia Hernandez, Helen Locklear, Robina Marie Winbush, eds. Louisville, KY: Women's Ministries Program Area, National Ministries Division, and Christian Faith and Life Program Area Congregational Ministries Division, Presbyterian Church (U.S.A.), 1994.

Carawan, Guy, and Candie Carawan. "'Freedom in the Air': An Overview of the

Songs of the Civil Rights Movement." *Black Music Research Bulletin* 12 (Spring 1990): 1-3.

Clynes, Manfred. "The Communication of Emotion: Theory of Sentics." In *Emotion: Theory, Research, and Experience*. Ed. R. Plutchhik and H. Kellerman, 271-300. New York: Academic Press, 1989.

Collum, Danny. "Fannie Lou Hamer: Prophet of Hope for the Sick and Tired." *Sojourners* 11 (December 1982): 3-21.

————. "The Living Quality of Music." In *Music, Mind, and Brain*. New York: Plenum Press, 1982.

Cone, James H. "Black Spirituals: A Theological Interpretation." In *Music and the Experience of God, Concilium: Religion in the Eighties*. Ed. Mary Collins, David Power, and Mellonee Burnim, 41-51. Edinburgh: T & T Clark, 1989.

Copeland, M. Shawn. " 'Wading through Many Sorrows': Toward a Theology of Suffering in Womanist Perspective." In *A Troubling in My Soul: Womanist Perspectives on Evil and Suffering*, 109-29. Ed. Emilie Townes. Maryknoll, NY: Orbis Books, 1993.

Crites, Stephen. "The Narrative Quality of Experience." *Journal of the American Academy of Religion* 39 (September 1971): 291-311.

Cummings, George L. "The Slave Narratives as a Source of Black Theological Discourse: The Spirit and Eschatology." In *Cut Loose Your Stammering Tongue: Black Theology in the Slave Narratives*. Ed. Dwight N. Hopkins and George Cummings, 46-66. Maryknoll, NY: Orbis Books, 1991.

Curry, George E. "The Death That Won't Die: Memories of Emmett Till 40 Years Later." *Emerge* 6 (July/August 1995): 24-32

Curtis, Marvin V. "How to Survive in Your Native Land: A Look at the History of African-American Music in America." *The Western Journal of Black Studies* 12 (1988): 101-11.

Cushman, Ann. "Are You Creative?" *Utne Reader* 50 (March-April, 1992): 52-60.

Dalbiume, Richard M. "The 'Forgotten Years' of the Negro Revolution." *Journal of American History* 55 (June 1968): 90-106.

Darling, David. International performing cellist, recording artist, and composer, quoted in Ann Cushman, "Are You Creative?" *Utne Reader* 50 (March-April, 1992): 52-60.

Davis, Stephen. "Critique by Stephen Davis." In *Encountering Evil: Live Options in Theodicy*. Ed. Stephen Davis, 58-61. Atlanta: John Knox, 1981.

Dawson, William L. "Interpretation of the Religious Folk-Songs of the American Negro." *Etude* 73 (March 1955): 11, 58, 61.

Denisoff, R. Serge. "Songs of Persuasion and Their Entrepreneurs." In *Sing a Song of Social Significance*. Bowling Green, OH: Bowling Green University Press, 1972.

Di Lella, Alexander. "An Existential Interpretation of Job." *Biblical Theology Bulletin* 15 (April 1985): 49-55.

Douglas, Kelly Brown. "Womanist Theology: What Is Its Relationship to Black Theology?" In *Black Theology: A Documentary History, Vol. II: 1980-1992*, 290-99. Ed. James Cone and Gayraud Wilmore. Maryknoll, NY: Orbis Books, 1993.

————. "To Reflect the Image of God." In *Living the Intersection: Womanism and Afrocentrism in Theology*, 76-77. Ed. Cheryl J. Sanders. Minneapolis: Fortress Press, 1995.

Douglas, Vivian Collier. "Music as a Cultural Force in the Development of the

Negro Race." *Negro History Bulletin* 13-15 (February 1952): 87.

Dunaway, David King. "Music and Politics in the United States." *Folk Music Journal* 5 (1987): 268-93.

Durant, Alan. "Improvisation in the Political Economy of Music." In *Music and Politics of Culture*. Ed. Christopher Norris, 252-82. New York: St. Martin's Press, 1989.

Edwards, Herbert O. "Black Theology and Liberation Theology." In *Black Theology: A Documentary History, 1966-1979*. Ed. Gayraud Wilmore and James Cone, 516-530. Maryknoll, NY: Orbis Books, 1979.

El Saffar, Ruth. "Unbinding the Doubles: Reflections on Love and Culture in the Work of René Girard." *Denver Quarterly* 18 (Winter, 1984): 6-22.

Escarpit, Robert. *L'humour*. Paris: n.p., 1960. Quoted in Gerard Bessiere. "Humour—A Theological Attitude?" *Concilium: Theology of Joy* (1974): 81-88.

Eugene, Toinette. "Moral Values and Black Womanists." In *Black Theology: A Documentary History, Vol. II: 1980-1992*. Ed. James Cone and Gayraud Wilmore. Maryknoll NY: Orbis Books, 1993.

Evans, Jr., James H. "African-American Christianity and the Postmodern Condition." *Journal of American Academy of Religion* 58 (Summer, 1990): 207-22.

Feld, Steven. "Sound Structure as Social Structure." In *Ethnomusicological Theory and Method*. Ed. Kay Kaufman Shelemay, 299-315. New York: Garland Publishing, 1990.

Feld, Steven. "Sound Structure as Social Structure." In *Music as Culture*. Ed. Kay Kaufman Shelemay, 299-325. New York: Garland Publishing, 1990; repr. *Ethnomusicology* 25 (1981): 383-409.

Felder, Cain Hope. "Race, Racism, and the Biblical Narratives." In *Stony the Road We Trod: African American Biblical Interpretation*. Ed. Cain Hope Felder, 127-45. Minneapolis: Fortress Press, 1991.

Floyd, Samuel. "Black American Music and Aesthetic Communication." *Black Music Research Journal* 1 (1980): 1-17.

Gilkes, Cheryl Townsend. "The 'Loves' and 'Troubles' of African-American Women's Bodies: The Womanist Challenge to Cultural Humiliation and Community Ambivalence." In *A Troubling in My Soul: Womanist Perspectives on Evil and Suffering*, 232-49. Ed. Emilie Townes. Maryknoll, NY: Orbis Books, 1993.

———. "Mother to the Motherless, Father to the Fatherless: Power, Gender, and Community in Afrocentric Biblical Tradition." *Semeia: An Experimental Journal for Biblical Criticism* 47 (1989): 57-85.

Gonczy, Daniel J. "The Folk Music Movement of the 1960s: Its Rise and Fall." *Popular Music and Society* 10 (1985): 15-31.

Griffin, David. "Critique by David Griffin." In *Encountering Evil: Live Options in Theodicy*. Ed. Stephen Davis, 53-55. Atlanta: John Knox, 1981.

Hamer, Fannie Lou. "Sick and tired of being sick and tired." *Katallagete* 1 (Fall 1968): 19-26.

Harding, Vincent. "Religion and Resistance Among Ante-bellum Negroes, 1800-1860." In *The Making of Black America: Essays in Negro Life and History*, vol. 1 of *The Origins of Black Americans*. Ed. August Meier and Elliot Rudwick, 179-97. New York: Athenaeum, 1969.

———. "W. E. B. Du Bois and the Black Messianic Vision." In *Black Titan: W. E. B. Du Bois, An Anthology by the Editors of Freedom Ways*. Ed. John Henrik Clarke,

Esther Jackson, Ernest Kaiser, J. H. O'Dell, 52-68. Boston: Beacon Press, 1970.

Hasker, William. "Suffering, Soul-making, and Salvation." Huntington, IN: Huntington College, n.d. Draft, photocopied.

Holmer, Paul. "About Black Theology." In *Black Theology: A Documentary History, 1966-1979*. Ed. Gayraud Wilmore and James Cone, 183-92. Maryknoll, NY: Orbis Books, 1979.

Holmes, Kristin E. "Black Churchgoers Trace Their Heritage in Religion." *Austin American-Statesman*, 6 June 1992, D4.

Hopkins, Dwight N. "Slave Theology." In *Cut Loose Your Stammering Tongue: Black Theology in the Slave Narratives*. Ed. Dwight N. Hopkins and George Cummings, 1-45. Maryknoll, NY: Orbis Books, 1991.

Hunter, Patricia. "Woman's Power—Woman's Passion: And God Said, "That's Good." In *A Troubling in My Soul: Womanist Perspectives on Evil and Suffering*, 189-98. Ed. Emilie Townes. Maryknoll, NY: Orbis Books, 1993.

Jackson, Jr., Harold A. "The New Hermeneutic and the Understanding of Spirituals." *Journal of the Interdenominational Theological Center* 3 (September, 1976): 36-48.

Johnson, Hall. "Notes on the Negro Spiritual." In *Readings in Black American Music*. Ed. Eileen Southern, 268-75. New York: W. W. Norton, 1971.

Kane, G. Stanley. "The Failure of Soul-Making Theodicy." *International Journal for Philosophy of Religion* 6 (1975): 1-22.

Kepnes, Stephen. "Telling and Retelling: The Use of Narrative in Psychoanalysis and Religion." In *The Challenge of Psychology to Faith. Concilium: Religion in the Eighties Series*. Ed. Stephen Kepnes and David Tracy, 27-33. Edinburgh: T & T Clark, 1982.

Keppler, Carl F. *The Literature of the Second Self*. Tucson, AZ: The University of Arizona Press, 1972.

King, Jr., Martin L. "The Ethical Demands of Integration." In *A Testament of Hope: The Essential Writings of Martin Luther King, Jr.* Ed. James M. Washington, 117-25. San Francisco: Harper and Row, 1986.

————. "Love, Law, and Civil Disobedience." *New South* (December 1961): 3-11.

————. "Nonviolence: The Only Road to Freedom." In *A Testament of Hope: The Essential Writings of Martin Luther King, Jr.* Ed. James M. Washington, 54-61. San Francisco: Harper and Row, 1986.

————. "Suffering and Faith." In *A Testament of Hope: The Essential Writings of Martin Luther King, Jr.* Ed. James M. Washington, 41-42. San Francisco: Harper and Row, 1986.

King, Willis H. "The Negro Spirituals and the Hebrew Psalms." *The Methodist Review* 114 (May 1931): 318-26.

Kirk-Duggan, Cheryl. "Afro-American Spirituals: Exorcising Evil through Song." In *Womanist Perspectives on Evil and Suffering*. Ed. Emilie Townes. Maryknoll, NY: Orbis Books, 1993.

Kofman, Sara. "The Narcissistic Woman: Freud and Girard." *Diacritics*, 10 (Fall, 1980): 36-45.

Laubenstein, Paul Fritz. "Race Values in Aframerican Music." *The Music Quarterly* 16 (July 1930): 378-403.

Lawrence-McIntyre, Charshee. "The Double Meanings of the Spirituals," *Journal of Black Studies* 17 (June 1987): 379-401

Levine, Lawrence W. "Slave Songs and Slave Consciousness." In *American Negro Slavery: A Reader*, 808-819. Ed. Allen Weinstein and Frank Catell. New York:

Oxford University Press, 1968, 1973.

Locke, Mamie E. "Is This America? Fannie Lou Hamer and the Mississippi Freedom Democratic Party." In *Women in the Civil Rights Movement: Trailblazers and Torchbearers, 1941-1965*, 27-37. Ed. Vicki L. Crawford, Jacqueline Rouse, Barbara Woods. Bloomington, IN: Indiana University Press, 1990, 1993.

Lomax, Alan. "Folk Song Style." In *Music as Culture*. Ed. Kay Kaufman Shelemay, 61-82. New York: Garland Publishing, 1990; repr., *American Anthropologist* 61 (1959): 927-54.

Lorde, Audre. "The Master's Tools Will Never Dismantle the Master's House." In *This Bridge Called My Back: Writings by Radical Women of Color*. Ed. Cherríe Moraga and Gloria Anzaldúa, 98-106. New York: Kitchen Table: Women of Color Press, 1981, 1983.

———. "The Uses of Anger: Women Responding to Racism." In *Sister Outsider: Essays and Speeches*. Trumansburg, NY: The Crossing Press, 1984.

Lovell, Jr., John. "Social Implications of the Negro Spiritual." In *The Social Implications of Early Negro Music in the United States*. Ed. Bernard Katz, 127-37. New York: Arno Press and The New York Times, 1969.

Mack, Burton. "Introduction: Religion and Ritual." In *Violent Origins: Walter Burkert, René Girard, and Jonathan Z. Smith on Ritual Killing and Cultural Transformation*. Ed. Robert Hammerton-Kelly, 1-70. Stanford, CA: Stanford University Press, 1987.

Marbury, Carl. "Hebrews and Spirituals: Soulful Expressions of Freedom." In *God and Human Freedom: A Festschrift in Honor of Howard Thurman*. Ed. Henry James Young, 74-95. Richmond, IN: Friends United Press, 1983.

Marcel-DuBois, C. "L'ethnomusicologie, as vocation et as situation," *Revue de l'enseignement superieur* 3 (1965). In *The New Grove Dictionary of Music and Musicians*, Vol. 6. Ed. Stanley Sadie. New York: St. Martin's Press, 1980. S.v. "Ethnomusicology," by Barbara Krader.

Martin, Clarice. "Biblical Theodicy and Black Women's Spiritual Autobiography: 'The Miry Bog, the Desolate Pit, a New Song in My Mouth.'" In *A Troubling in My Soul: Womanist Perspectives on Evil and Suffering*, 13-36. Ed. Emilie Townes. Maryknoll, NY: Orbis Books, 1993.

Mathews, Rosita deAnn. "Using Power from the Periphery: An Alternative Theological Model for Survival in Systems." In *A Troubling in My Soul: Womanist Perspectives on Evil and Suffering*, 92-106. Ed. Emilie Townes. Maryknoll, NY: Orbis Books, 1993.

Matthews, Donald H. "The African American Spiritual Implications for Black Theology and Ethics." Arlington, VA: Society for Christian Ethics, Spring 1990. Photocopied.

McClendon, William H. "Black Music: Sound and Feeling for Black Liberation." *Black Scholar* 7 (January-February 1976): 20-25.

McKenzie, Wallace. "E. A. McIlhenny's Black Spiritual Collection from Avery Island, Louisiana." *American Music* 8 (Spring 1990): 95-109.

McLaughlin, Wayne. "Symbolism and Mysticism in the Spirituals." *Phylon* 24 (1963): 69-77.

Moi, Toril. "The Missing Mother: The Oedipal Rivalries of René Girard." *Diacritics* 12 (Summer, 1982): 21-31.

Moore, Leroy. "The Spiritual: Soul of Black Religion." *Church History* 40 (1971): 79-83.

Morales, Rosario. "The Other Heritage." In *This Bridge Called My Back: Writings by Radical Women of Color.* Ed. Cherríe Moraga and Gloria Anzaldúa, 107-8. New York: Kitchen Table: Women of Color Press, 1981, 1983.

Morris, Calvin S. "We, the White People: A History of Oppression." *Sojourners* (November 1987): 19-21.

Nketia, J. H. Kwabena. "Musical Interaction in Ritual Events." In *Music and the Experience of God. Concilium: Religion in the Eighties.* Ed. Mary Collins, David Power and Mellonee Burnim, 111-24. Edinburgh: T & T Clark, 1989.

Oguah, Benjamine Ewuku. "African and Western Philosophy: A Comparative Study." In *African Philosophy: An Introduction.* Ed. Richard A. Wright, 213-25. Lanham, MD: University Press of America, 1984.

Onwuanibe, Richard C. "The Human Person and Immortality in Ibo (African) Metaphysics." In *African Philosophy: An Introduction.* Ed. Richard A. Wright, 183-97. 3rd ed. Lanham, MD: University Press of America, 1984.

Oster, Harry. "Negro French Spirituals of Louisiana." *Journal of the International Folk Music Council* 14 (1962): 166-67.

Paris, Peter J. "Slavery, Capitalism, and Religion," 312-22. In *On Moral Business: Classical and Contemporary Resources for Ethics in Economic Life.* Ed. Max Stackhouse, Dennis P. McCann, Shirley Roels, and Preston Williams. Grand Rapids, MI: Eerdmans, 1995.

Patterson, Lindsay, ed. *The Afro-American in Music and Art.* International Library of Afro-American Life and History. Cornwells Heights, PA: The Publisher's Agency, 1976. S.v. "Spirituals and Neo-Spirituals," by Zora Neale Hurston.

Phillips, Theo Eldridge. "White Racism in Black Church Music." *The Negro History Bulletin* 36 (1973): 17-20.

Phillips, Waldo B. "Negro Spirituals in Retrospect." *The Negro History Bulletin* 22 (February, 1952): 51-52.

Plantinga, Alvin. "The Free Will Defense." In *Philosophy of Religion: Selected Readings.* Ed. William L. Rowe and William J. Wainwright, 217-30. New York: Harcourt Brace Jovanovich, 1973.

———. "God's Foreknowledge and Human Free Will Are Compatible." In *Philosophy of Religion: An Anthology.* Ed. Louis Pojman, 228-31. Belmont, CA: Wadsworth Publishing, 1987.

Potthoff, Harvey. "Humor and Religious Faith." In *Summary of Proceedings 34th Annual Conference,* 74-80. N.p.: American Theological Library Association. June 16-20, 1980.

Proctor, H. H. "Let the Church Sing 'Freedom.' " *Black Music Research Journal* (1987): 105-18.

Reagon, Bernice Johnson. "In Our Hands: Thoughts on Black Music." *Sing Out!* 24 (January-February, 1976): 1-2, 5.

———. "The Lined Hymn as a Song of Freedom." *Black Music Research Bulletin* 12 (Spring 1990): 4-7.

———. "Songs That Moved the Movement." *Perspectives* (Summer, 1983): 27-35.

———. "The Theology of the Songs of the Southern Slave." *Southern Workman* 36 (1907): 584-92; 652-56/2.

———. "Untitled Article on the Spirituals," Archives, National Museum of American History; Program in Black Culture, n.d., 1.

Rice, Timothy. "Toward the Remodeling of Ethnomusicology." In *Ethnomusicological Theory and Method.* Ed. Kay Kaufman Shelemay, 329-46. New York: Garland Publishing, 1990.

Rogin, Michael Paul. "The Sword Became a Flashing Vision: D. W. Griffith's *The*

Birth of a Nation." In *Ronald Reagan, the Movie and Other Episodes in Political Demonology.* Berkeley: University of California Press, 1987.

Roth, John. "Critique by John Roth." In *Encountering Evil: Live Options in Theodicy.* Ed. Stephen Davis, 61-63. Atlanta: John Knox, 1981.

Ryder, C. J. "The Theology of the Plantation Songs." *American Missionary* (1892): 9-16.

Sanders, Cheryl J. "Black Women in Biblical Perspective: Resistance, Affirmation, and Empowerment." In *Living the Intersection: Womanism and Afrocentrism in Theology.* Ed. Cheryl J. Sanders. Minneapolis: Fortress Press, 1995.

Schmidt, Robert. "Hearing, Calling and Naming: Aspects of Nommo in Toni Morrison's *Beloved."* Bowling Green, OH: Bowling Green University, n.d. Photocopied.

Shelton, Robert. "Singing for Freedom: Music in the Integration Movement." *Sing Out!* 12 (December-January, 1962-1963): 4-7, 12-14, 16-17.

Sherman, Robert. "Sing a Song of Freedom." *Saturday Review* (September 28, 1963): 65-67, 81.

Simms, David M. "The Negro Spiritual: Origins and Themes." *Journal of Negro Education* 35 (Winter 1966): 35-41.

Singer, Merrill. " 'Now I Know What the Songs Mean!': Traditional Black Music in a Contemporary Black Sect." *The Southern Quarterly* XXIII (Spring 1985): 125-40.

Smith, Theophus H. "King and the Nonviolent Religion of Black America." In *Curing Violence: Religion and the Thought of René Girard.* Ed. Theophus H. Smith and Mark Wallace. Polebridge Press, 1993.

Sontag, Frederick. "Critique by Frederick Sontag." In *Encountering Evil: Live Options in Theodicy.* Ed. Stephen Davis, 55-58. Atlanta: John Knox, 1981.

Speers, Mary. "Negro Songs and Folk-lore." *Journal of American Folk-lore* (1910): 435-39.

Spencer, Jon Michael, ed. "Preface." *The Theology of American Popular Music; Black Sacred Music: A Journal of Theomusicology Journal,* 3 (Fall 1989): v-xi.

Standifer, James. "Musical Behaviors of Black People in American Society." *Black Music Research Journal* (1980): 51-62.

Stump, Eleanor. "The Problem of Evil." *Faith and Philosophy* 2 (1985): 392-424.

Swinburne, Richard. "The Problem of Evil." In *Reason and Religion.* Ed. Stuart C. Brown, 81-101. London and Ithaca: Cornell University, 1977.

Szwed, John F. "Afro-American Musical Adaptation." In *Afro-American Anthropology: Contemporary Perspectives,* 19-27. New York: Free Press, 1970.

Tamony, Peter. "Hootenanny." *John Edwards Memorial Foundation Quarterly* 16 (Summer 1980): 95-98.

Taylor, John E. "Something on My Mind: A Cultural and Historical Interpretation of Spiritual Texts." *Ethnomusicology* 19 (September 1975): 387-99.

Thurman, Howard. "What Can I Believe In?" *Journal of Religion and Health* 12 (November 1972): 111-19.

Townes, Emilie M. "Voices of the Spirit: Womanist Methodologies in the Theological Disciplines." *The Womanist* 1 (Summer 1994): 1-2

———. "Keeping a Clean House Will Not Keep a Man at Home: An Unctuous Womanist Rhetoric of Justice." In *New Visions for the Americas: Religious Engagement and Social Transformation,* 127-44. Ed. David Batstone, Minneapolis: Fortress Press, 1993.

———. "Living in the New Jerusalem: The Rhetoric and Movement of Liberation in the House of Evil." In *A Troubling in My Soul: Womanist Perspectives on Evil and Suffering*, 73-86. Ed. Emilie Townes. Maryknoll, NY: Orbis Books, 1993.

Turner, James. "The Sociology of Black Nationalism." *The Black Scholar* 1 (December 1969): 18-27.

Turner, Jr., William C. "The Musicality of Black Preaching: A Phenomenology." *Journal of Black Sacred Music* 2 (Spring 1988): 21-29.

Tutu, Desmond M. "Black Theology/African Theology—Soul Mates or Antagonists." In *Black Theology: A Documentary History, 1966-1979*. Ed. Gayraud Wilmore and James Cone, 483-91. Maryknoll, NY: Orbis Books, 1979.

Vivian, C.T. "Racial Violence in the '80s." *Sojourners* (November 1987): 24.

Wade, Bonnie. "Prolegomenon to the Study of Song Texts." In *Ethnomusicological Theory and Method*. Ed. Kay Kaufman Shelemay, 205-20. New York: Garland Publishing, 1990.

Wade, Melvin and Margaret Wade. "The Black Aesthetic in the Black Novel." *Journal of Black Studies* (June 1972): 391-408.

Walker, Alice. "Silver Writes." In "The Silver Writer's Movement." *Perspective* (Summer, 1982): 22-31.

Wallis, Jim. "America's Original Sin: The Legacy of White Racism." *Sojourners* (November 1987): 15-17.

Weems, Renita. "Reading Her Way through the Struggle: African American Women and the Bible." In *Stony the Road We Trod*. Ed. Cain Hope Felder, 57-77. Minneapolis: Fortress Press, 1991.

Welding, Peter J. "Sing a Song of Segregation." *Saturday Review* 44 (April 29, 1961): 42.

West, Cornel. "The Historicist Turn in Philosophy of Religion." In *Knowing Religiously*. Ed. Leroy S. Rouner, 36-51. Notre Dame, IN: University of Notre Dame Press, 1985.

Whalum, Wendell Phillips. "Black Hymnody." *Review and Expositor* 70 (Summer, 1973): 341-55.

Whedbee, William. "The Comedy of Job." *Semeia* 7 (1977): 1-30.

Williams, Delores S. "A Womanist Perspective on Sin." In *A Troubling in My Soul: Womanist Perspectives on Evil and Suffering*, 130-49. Ed. Emilie Townes. Maryknoll, NY: Orbis Books, 1993.

————. "Womanist Theology: Black Women's Voices." In *Weaving the Visions: New Patterns in Feminist Spirituality*, 183-85. Ed. Judith Plaskow and Carol P. Christ. San Francisco: HarperCollins, 1989.

Wilson, Olly. "Black Music as an Art Form." *Black Music Journal* (1983): 1-22.

Wimbush, Vincent. "Historical/Cultural Criticism as Liberation: A Proposal for an African American Biblical Hermeneutic." *Semeia: An Experimental Journal for Biblical Criticism* 47 (1989): 43-56.

Wright, Jr., Jeremiah A. "Music as Cultural Expression in Black Church Theology and Worship." *Journal of Black Sacred Music* 3 (Spring 1989): 1-5.

Other Sources

"Introductions through Song II and I," Rutha Harris and Cordell Reagon, Respondents. "Voices of the Civil Rights Movement: A National Working Conference on Civil Rights Movement Culture, January 30-February 3, 1980"; Archives Center, The National Museum of American History; The Smithsonian Institution, Washington, DC.

"Introductions through Song II," James Bevel, Respondent. "Voices of the Civil Rights Movement: A National Working Conference on Civil Rights Movement Culture"; January 30-February 3, 1980. Co-sponsored by the Smithsonian Institution and Howard University. Auspices of Program in Black American Culture, Smithsonian Institution. Bernice Johnson Reagon, director. VCRM, Video Tape No. 3.

"Liberation Movements: A Critical Assessment and a Reaffirmation." A Position Paper of the African Methodist Episcopal Church, 40th Session of the General Conference of the African Methodist Episcopal Church, in Atlanta, June 16-27, 1976. In *Black Theology: A Documentary History, 1966-1979.* Ed. Gayraud Wilmore and James Cone, 288-95. Maryknoll, NY: Orbis Books, 1979.

"Lift Every Voice and Sing," the Black National Anthem, by James Weldon Johnson and J. Rosamond Johnson. Edward B. Marks Music Corporation, 1927.

Angelou, Maya. "Our Grandmothers." In *I Shall Not Be Moved.* New York: Random House, 1990.

Barker, Kenneth, ed. *The New International Bible.* Grand Rapids: Zondervan Corporation, 1985.

Beckett, Samuel. *Krapps Last Tape.* Ed. Harold Bloom. New York: Chelsea House Publishers, 1987.

———. *Waiting for Godot: A Tragicomedy in Two Acts.* Ed. Harold Bloom. London: S. French, 1957.

Behague, Gerard, Professor of Music, Ethnomusicologist. Interview by author, 21 September, 1992, Austin. The University of Texas at Austin, Austin.

Bowen-Spencer, Michele. "C. Eric Lincoln: Historiography." Bowling Green, Ohio: Bowling Green University, September 2, 1991. Photocopied.

Campbell, Stanley, Professor of History, Baylor University, Waco, TX. Interview by Author, Summer 1988, Waco, TX.

Dickens, Charles. *David Copperfield.* Ed. Nina Burgis. Oxford: Clarendon Press, 1981.

Dunbar, Paul Laurence. "We Wear the Mask." In *Black Voices: An Anthology of Afro-American Literature.* Ed. Abraham Chapman, 355. New York: New American Library, 1968.

Goodson, Albert A. Arr. by Thurston G. Frazier. "We've Come This Far by Faith." Manna Music, Inc., 1963.

Griffith, D.W. *The Birth of a Nation.* 1914. Filmstrip. Based on Thomas Dixon's *The Clansmen.* Premiered, Clune's Auditorium, Los Angeles, 1915.

Hampton, Henry. *Eyes on the Prize: America's Civil Rights Years 1954-1965,* Videocassette (6 Part Series); *Eyes on the Prize: America at the Racial Crossroads, 1965-1985,* Videocassette (Eight part continuation). Boston: Blackside, Inc.

Lee, Spike. "*Jungle Fever.*" New York: Forty Acres and a Mule Filmworks, Inc., 1991.

Locke, Alain. "Spirituals." In *75 Years of Freedom: Commemoration of the 75th Anniversary of the Proclamation of the 13th Amendment to the Constitution of the United States.* Washington, DC: The U.S. Library of Congress, 1940.

Marriott, Michael. "Afrocentrism in Schools Stirs Educational Controversy." *Austin American-Statesman,* Sunday, August 11, 1991, sec A, 10.

Milligan, Mary. "The Text of Experience: Biblical Interpretation in a Basic Christian Community in Brazil." The Sixth Annual Casassa Conference, "Text and Experience: Toward A Cultural Exegesis of the Bible." Loyola Marymount University, Los Angeles, March 19-21, 1992.

Moore, Sharon L. "Walter Wink on 'The Powers.' " Waco, TX: Baylor University, Fall 1989. Photocopied.

Moses, Jonathan M. "Michael Jackson's Classical Sampling May Be Dangerous." *The Wall Street Journal*, 27 April 1992, B98.

Moyers, Bill. "Facing Evil with Bill Moyers." *The World of Ideas*. Public Affairs Television, Inc., March 28 1988.

Reagon, Bernice Johnson. "Program Notes." *Voices of the Civil Rights Movement 1960-1966*. Washington, DC: Smithsonian Institution, Program in Black American Culture, 1980.

———. Interview by author, 19 November 1991, Washington DC Tape recording. The Smithsonian Institution, Program in African American Culture, The National Museum of American History; Washington, DC .

Ruffins, Fath, Chief Historian, "Collection of Advertising History," Archives Center. Interview by author, 9 September 1991. Washington, DC: The National Museum of American History, Washington, DC.

Rust, Julie W. "Wisdom in the Psalms." Waco, TX: Baylor University, 1990. Photocopied.

Segovia, Fernando F. "The Text as Other: The Eruption of Contextualization." The Sixth Annual Casassa Conference, "Text and Experience: Toward a Cultural Exegesis of the Bible." Loyola Marymount University, Los Angeles, March 19-21, 1992.

Shakespeare, William. *The Tragedy of Macbeth*. Ed. Louis B. Wright and Virginia LaMar. New York: Washington Square Press, 1959.

Shange, Ntozake. *for colored girls who have considered suicide/when the rainbow is enuf: a choreopoem*. New York: Macmillan Publishing, 1975, 1976, 1977.

Songs of Zion. United Methodist Church. Supplemental Worship Resources 12. Nashville: Abingdon, 1981, 1982.

The Auburn Lecture: A Day with Alice Walker, the second annual Auburn Lecture at Union Theological Seminary, April 25, 1995.

The Hymnal of the Christian Methodist Episcopal Church. Memphis: The CME Publishing House, 1987.

Thurman, Howard. "Community and the Will of God." Mendenhall Lectures, Depauw University, February 1961, Thurman Papers, Boston University.

———. "Freedom Under God." Second Century Convocation, Washington University, February 1955, Thurman Papers, Special Collections, Mugar Memorial Library, Boston University.

Tindley, Charles Albert. "Stand by Me." In *Songs of Zion*. Supplemental worship resources: 12, United Methodist Church. Nashville: Abingdon, 1981, 1982, 41-42.

Theses and Dissertations

Clark, Roy Lester. "A Fantasy Theme Analysis of Negro Spirituals." Ph.D. diss., Southern Illinois University at Carbondale, 1979.

Kirk-Duggan, Cheryl. "Justice, Freedom, Equality: A New Song." Waco, TX: Baylor University, 1992.

———. "Theodicy and the Redacted African American Spirituals of the 1960s Civil Rights Movement." Ph.D. diss., Baylor University, 1992.

Marks, Morton Allen. "Performance Rules and Ritual Structures in Afro-American Music." Ph.D. diss., University of California, Berkeley, 1972.

Matthews, Donald H. "The Spiritual: An African American Narrative Hermeneutics." Ph.D. diss., Temple University, 1992.

Outlaw, Lucius T. "Language and the Transformation of Consciousness: Foundations for a Hermeneutic of Black Culture." Ph.D. diss., Boston College, 1972.

Parker, Evelyn. "Twenty Seeds of Hope: Religious-Moral Values in African-American Adolescents in Chicago Land." Ph.D. diss., Garrett-Evangelical Theological Seminary/Northwestern University, 1997.

Raichelson, Richard M. "Black Religious Folksong: A Study in Generic and Social Change." Ph.D. diss., Howard University, 1975.

Reagon, Bernice Johnson. "Songs of the Civil Rights Movement, 1955-1965: A Study in Cultural History." Ph.D. diss., Howard University, 1975.

Robinson, Marie Hadley. "The Negro Spiritual: An Examination of the Texts, and Their Relationship to Musical Performance Practice." Ph.D. diss., Florida State University, 1973.

Taylor, John Earl. "The Sociological and Psychological Implications of the Texts of the Ante-bellum Negro Spirituals." Ed.D. diss., University of Northern Colorado, 1971.

Thrower, Sarah. "The Spiritual of the Gullah Negro in South Carolina." Thesis, B.M., College of Music of Cincinnati, 1954.

Truesdale, Jr., Albert L. "A Tillichian Analysis of White Racism in the South." Ph.D. diss., Emory University, 1976.

Williams, Robert Carroll. "A Study of Religious Language: Analysis/Interpretation of Selected Afro-American Spirituals with Reference to Black Religious Philosophy." Ph.D. diss, Columbia University, 1975.

Wright, Willie. "Theodicy: Black Suffering." D.Min, professional project. School of Theology at Claremont, 1976.

A Selective Discography

Acappella Spirituals: The Series. CD EK 57113. Word, Incorporated, 1993.

Anderson, Marian, *Marian Anderson at Constitution Hall, Washington, DC, Farewell Recital*. Phonodisc, RCA Victor. LSC-2781, 1965.

——. *He's Got the Whole World in His Hands: Spirituals*. CD09026-61960-2. BMG Music, 1994.

——. *Marian Anderson*. CD 9318. Pavilion Records LTD, 1988.

Battle, Kathleen, and Jessye Norman. *Spirituals in Concert*. CD 429 790-2, Deutsche Grammophone, 1991.

Been in the Storm So Long: Spirituals, Folk Tales and Children's Games from John's Island, South Carolina. CD SF 40031. Smithsonian Folkways, 1990.

Black Christmas: Spirituals in the African-American Tradition. CD 1011. ESS.A.Y Recordings, 1990.

Caesar, Shirley. *Throw Out the Lifeline*. CD HBD-3802. HOB Records, 1983.

Great American Spirituals: Kathleen Battle, Barbara Hendricks, Florence Quivar. CD 513725Z. Musical Heritage Society, 1994.

Great Ladies of Gospel. CD HBD-3801. HOB Records, 1993.

Hendricks, Barbara. *Negro Spirituals*. CD 7470262. EMI, 1983.

Jubilation! Great Gospel Performances. Vol. One: *Black Gospel*. CD R2 70288. Rhino Records Inc., 1992.

My Lord What A Mornin': Spirituals in Arrangements by Hall Johnson, Roland Hayes, and H.T. Burleigh. CD MHS 512250K. Musical Heritage Society, 1988.

Norman, Jessye. *Amazing Grace.* CD 432 546-2. Philips, 1991.

Norman, Jessye with Dalton Baldwin and the Ambrosian Singers. *Spirituals.* CD 416 462-2 Philips, 1978; CD 512935L. Musical Heritage Society, 1986.

Parker, Alice, Conductor and the Musicians of Melodious Accord. *Spiritual Songs.* CD MHS 512412K. Musical Heritage Society, 1989.

Pickens, Jo Ann. *My Heritage: American Melodies/Negro Spirituals.* CD 3-1447-2. Koch-Schwann, 1003.

Quivar, Florence with the Harlem Boys' Choir. *Ride on King Jesus.* CD 7 49885 2. EMI Records, 1990.

Reagon, Bernice Johnson, ed. *African American Gospels: The Concert Tradition.* Wade in the Water Series. Vol. 3. CD SF 40074, Smithsonian/Folkways Recordings of the National Public Radio, 1994.

————. *African American Spirituals: The Concert Tradition.* Wade in the Water Series. Vol. 1. CD SF 40072, Smithsonian/Folkways Recordings & National Public Radio, 1994.

————. *Voices of the Civil Rights Movement: Black American Freedom Songs 1960-1966.* Phonodiscs R023. Washington, DC: The Smithsonian Institution Program in Black Culture, 1980.

————. "Ella's Song." *Sweet Honey in the Rock, We All . . . Everyone of Us.* Cassette FF 90317. Flying Fish, 1983.

Robeson, Paul. *Green Pastures.* CD AJA 5047R. Academy Sound and Vision LTD, 1987.

————. *Paul Robeson: Great Voices of the Century.* CD Moir 415. Memoir Records, 1992.

————. *Spirituals/Folksongs/Hymns; The Song of the Volga Boatmen.* Pearl Gemm CD 9382. Pavilion Records LTD., 1989.

Sounds of the South: Negro Church Music/White Spirituals. CD 7 S2496-2. Atlantic, 1993.

Swados, Elizabeth. *Bible Women.* CD 7313835714-2. Swados Enterprises, 1995.

Sweet Honey in the Rock. "A Priority." From *In This Land.* CD CA 9 42522-2. EarthBeat, 1992.

————. *All for Freedom.* CD 9 42505-2. Music for Little People, 1992.

The Great Gospel Men: 27 Classic Performances by the Greatest Gospel Men. CD LC 5762 6005. Shanachie, 1993.

The Great Gospel Women: 31 Classic Performances by the Greatest Gospel Women. CD LC 5762 6004. Shanachie, 1993.

The Great Gospel Women: 33 Classic Performances by the Greatest Gospel Women, Vol. 2. CD LC 5762 6017. Shanachie, 1993.

Verity Records Presents: A Tribute to Mrs. Rosa Parks. CD 01241-43013-2. Zomba Recording Corporation, 1995.

Watch and Pray: Spirituals and Art Songs by African-American Women Composers. CD 3-7247-2 H1. Koch International Classics, 1994.

6496

6059